The Diaspora Story

Overleaf *Jewish immigrants arriving in New York*

The Diaspora Story

The Epic of the Jewish People among the Nations

Joan Comay

in association with Beth Hatefutsoth –
The Nahum Goldmann Museum
of the Jewish Diaspora, Tel Aviv

Steimatzky's Agency Ltd.
Jerusalem Tel Aviv Haifa

First published in Great Britain by
George Weidenfeld and Nicolson Ltd
91 Clapham High Street, London SW4

Published in Israel by
Steimatzky's Agency Limited 1981
Reprinted 1982

Editing and picture research
by Miranda Ferguson
Designed by Graham Keen
Filmset by Keyspools Ltd, Golborne, Lancs
Printed in Hong Kong
Colour separations by Newsele Litho Ltd

Contents

*(This book is based on the Museum of the
Jewish Diaspora, Tel Aviv, and the
illustrations are drawn from it.)*

Introduction

The term 'Diaspora' comes from a Greek word meaning dispersion. It is used here to denote the world-wide dispersion of the Jewish people outside its ancestral homeland, the Land of Israel.

The Diaspora has lasted for over twenty-five centuries. For most of that time the political independence of the Jewish people was crushed; the central sanctuary of its faith, the Temple of Jerusalem, lay in ruins; and its homeland was a minor province of one imperial power after another. Diaspora was then called Exile (in Hebrew, *Golah* or *Galut*). The stubborn refusal of this little people to disappear, from repression or assimilation, remains one of the startling enigmas of human history.

The first period of the Galut was the Babylonian captivity, starting just before the Hebrew kingdom of Judah was destroyed in 586 BC.

In the 2nd century BC another Jewish Commonwealth arose, after the Maccabean Revolt. It was wiped out by the Romans in AD 70, after four years of war. Jewish independence would not arise again until the State of Israel was proclaimed in 1948. For nearly nineteen centuries before that, the Jews were a minority everywhere, subject to the whims of rulers and the attitudes of the populace. At times they were the hapless victims of intolerance and greed and suffered segregation, economic restrictions, crippling taxes, pogroms and pillage, forced baptism, blood-libel charges, expulsion or death at the stake. At other times they enjoyed periods of relative calm, and they poured their gifts into the surrounding society.

As with other living species, the Jew survived largely through his ability to adapt to his environment. That environment was neither uniform nor static. It changed in different localities and in different periods. Always, Jews strove to reconcile their two worlds. They clung to their own faith and traditions, while in varying degrees adopting the customs, language, dress and occupations of the countries in which they lived.

Migration was in itself a factor of survival. Persecuted in one country, or pushed out of it, Jews found refuge elsewhere. As Diaspora centres declined, others arose. The Jews expelled from Spain at the end of the 15th century AD settled in North Africa, Italy, or the Ottoman Empire. Jews fleeing the persecution of mediaeval Germany were welcomed into Poland-Lithuania. The misery of Jewish life in the 19th-century Russian Pale of Settlement propelled a mass exodus westward. These people went mainly to the United States. Migration

A replica from the relief on the Arch of Titus. The holy vessels from the destroyed temple in Jerusalem are carried in triumphal procession.

constantly widened the frontiers of the Diaspora.

In the last 2,000 years there have been two major streams of Jewish dispersion, with some intermingling between them. The more southerly route remained within the Near East – the Mediterranean area. It comprised the successive centres of Jewish life in Babylonia, North Africa, Spain, and the Ottoman Empire. That part of the Jewish world lay generally in the lands of Islam. It became known as Sephardi, from the Hebrew word for Spanish. The more northerly route was the European one – the Byzantine empire, Franco-Germany, Eastern Europe and the New World. This was the part of Jewry known as Ashkenazi, from the Hebrew word for German. Its involvement was with Christianity.

With the Nazi rise to power in our time, the Jews that came under Hitler's sway found themselves with nowhere to go. The gates of

Western countries had been all but closed, and the gates of the Jewish Homeland forcibly barred. Most of the Jewish people ended up in the gas chamber.

After Israel became an independent state in 1948, the surviving Displaced Persons in European camps and the endangered communities in Arab countries streamed back to the land from which their forefathers had started. For them, the wheel of migration had come full circle.

It is unlikely that the Jews as a people would long have survived the disaster of AD 70, unless the instruments of its survival had been forged beforehand in a unique spiritual and cultural heritage. It was as if the nation had instinctively trained itself for exile.

The most important instrument of survival was the Book that the wandering Jew carried in his knapsack. To call the Old Testament a Book is in a sense misleading. It is a sacred anthology of ancient Hebrew literature compiled and edited over a period of more than a thousand years. The works in it include religious writings, historical narratives, laws, legends and folk tales, prophecies, proverbs and poetry. Its central theme is the Covenant between God and the Hebrew people, and everything that happens to the people, for good or bad, is related to that theme. Embedded in the Old Testament is the unique Hebrew creed of monotheism, the Mosaic legal system, and the promise of a Messianic Return to Zion.

After the fall of Jerusalem in AD 70, it was a wise and logical reaction for the sages gathered at Yavneh on the coast to complete the canon of the Writings (the third part of the Old Testament) and thus give the Hebrew Bible its final and enduring shape.

The Oral Law was the body of commentary, rulings and opinions that the religious leaders had been already evolving for centuries before AD 70. It was meant to interpret and expand the biblical Written Law, and apply it to the detailed needs of daily life. At the beginning of the 3rd century AD the Oral Law was given a systematic codification in the Mishnah, later to be broadened into the Jerusalem Talmud (4th century AD) and the more comprehensive Babylonian Talmud (5th-6th century AD). Judaism had consciously become a portable faith and way of life that could function without a State, a Temple or a fixed abode. Its adjustment to changing conditions would continue throughout Diaspora history.

In addition to the Bible and the Oral Law there were other basic institutions that had already been tested during centuries of Diaspora life before the disaster of AD 70, and would help to preserve the identity and cohesion of Jewry after it. They included the tightly-knit family, the autonomous community, the synagogue, the religious education system and the belief in a Messianic Return. Through the vicissitudes of the next nineteen centuries, all these factors would form the survival kit for a dispersed and battered people.

Part One

The Inner World
of the Diaspora

*A grandmother and granddaughter in Eastern Europe
before the Second World War.*

Contemporary Jewish Faces

These faces are some of a group of nearly 200 camera portraits gathered by Cornell Capa, an internationally-known photographer. The assortment provides a random sample of Jewish faces of both sexes, all ages and many countries. The overwhelming impression they make is that there is no standard Jewish physical type.

## Chapter One

Faces

The great diversity of Jewish facial characteristics is confirmed by modern scientific surveys. For the anthropologist a key indicator is the cephalic index, the ratio between the length and breadth of the skull. The range of the measurements for Jews is just about as wide as that for the human race as a whole. There are also great variations in different communities regarding the blood type and the colour of the eyes and hair. For instance, up to twenty per cent of Eastern European Jews have blue eyes, compared to less than two per cent of Iraqi Jews.

The wide physical differences between Jews result from three processes that have operated over thousands of years: intermarriage with neighbouring peoples; conversions of non-Jews to the Jewish faith; and environmental factors. As a result, different physical types have evolved in different localities. A Georgian Jew tends to look like other Georgians; a Yemenite Jew tends to look like other Yemenites; but Georgian and Yemenite Jews do not resemble each other.

Throughout later Diaspora history the rate of intermarriage varied. It increased where conditions were relaxed and Jews mingled freely with the general population. It virtually ceased where Jews were persecuted, restricted and segregated. To this day, the Halachic (Jewish Law) definition of a Jew is one whose mother is Jewish or one who has converted to Judaism. The ethnic origin of the mother is the determining factor, and the father need not be Jewish at all.

The Jews have been so widely dispersed for so long that environmental factors, like climate and diet, have also contributed to the diversity of types. Like their neighbours, Jews from tropical and semi-tropical countries are dark-skinned, while their brethren from colder European countries are pale-skinned. Against the historical background of these various processes, it is not surprising that the Jewish people should have such a remarkable variety of faces.

Jewish Faces in Art

See colour pages 17, 18 and 19

Jews portrayed in ancient synagogue wall-paintings, mediaeval manuscripts, church frescoes, and 17th- to 19th-century oil paintings. There are no common facial characteristics.

The artist is not a cameraman. In depicting people, he is influenced by his own personal style and the artistic conventions of his time. He may also be subject to prevailing prejudices, as embodied in group stereotypes.

Anti-Semitic Caricatures

The Jew became the classic victim in Europe of the group-stereotype portrait. Until about the 11th century, Jews were depicted in much the same style as non-Jews. In the Dark Age of persecution that ensued, Jews were forced to wear special hats or badges to distinguish them from Christians. At the same time they were depicted in art as sinister creatures with crooked figures and facial expressions of cunning and greed. There is a direct line of descent from these mediaeval drawings to the vicious Nazi caricatures of *Der Stuermer* and other modern anti-Semitic literature.

Left A mediaeval caricature of Joseph (Joselman) of Rosheim (c.1478–1554), the greatest of the Jewish shtadlanim *in Germany in the Middle Ages. Right A cartoon from a Polish brochure of the 1930s, 'In the grip of communism'. The Jew leads Death to his harvest in Poland.*

Wzor okladki do broszury „W szponach komunizmu".

Below *Uncle Sam becomes the modern Moses, parting the waters of intolerance and oppression to welcome European Jews to America. From* Puck, *30 November 1881.*

Chapter Two

The Traditional Jewish Home

The main channel for transmitting Jewish traditions from generation to generation was the home. Being a Jew was first and foremost a family affair.

In the early biblical period (the Patriarchs and the Judges) the social unit was the extended family or family clan, called the *mishpachah*. The head of the family had complete authority over its members – mayl? three or four generations of them – and over all family property. Within the extended family group were small sub-units, each made up of parents and their children, and known as a *bet av* ('father's house'). The members of the extended family were responsible for each other's protection and welfare. If one of them was murdered, his kinsmen were duty-bound to avenge him. Each Israelite tribe was a loose combination of such family clans. The heads of the important families were the elders of the tribe.

In the course of time the authority of the family heads and tribal leaders waned as centralized institutions were established: the monarchy, the Temple priesthood, and regular courts to punish wrongdoers and settle disputes. The emphasis shifted to the small family, the 'bet av', as the basic unit of society.

The conditions and needs of the Diaspora strengthened the role of the restricted family as the bastion of traditional values and customs. Ties of sentiment and loyalty continued to exist with a wide circle of blood relatives or relatives by marriage. But the focus of Jewish family law and custom was based on the tight system of relationships between husband and wife and between parent and child. However, even in modern times the wider family unit, the 'clan', remained strong among the communities in Moslem lands.

The Jewish attitude to marriage was always a very positive one. Ideals of celibacy and monasticism which developed in Christianity remained alien to Judaism. In Jewish thought, marriage was the only road to personal fulfilment, and procreation was a sacred duty. The Talmud states: 'He who has no wife lives without joy, without blessing and without goodness.' Another down-to-earth Talmudic saying points out that, were it not for the sexual urge, no man would build a house, marry a wife or beget children.

The relationship between husband and wife required by Judaism

(continued on page 21)

Mezuzah

Two similar passages in the *Book of Deuteronomy* prescribe ways for keeping God's word constantly in men's minds:

'*Hear, O Israel: The Lord our God is one Lord; and you shall love the Lord your God with all your heart, and with all your soul, and with all your might. And these words which I command you this day shall be upon your heart; and you shall teach them diligently to your children, and shall talk of them when you sit in your house, and when you walk by the way, and when you lie down, and when you rise. And you shall bind them as a sign upon your hand, and they shall be as frontlets between your eyes. And you shall write them on the doorposts of your house and on your gates.'* (Deut. 6:4–9)

From ancient times the last-mentioned requirement has been fulfilled by inserting a coiled square of parchment, inscribed with these two biblical passages, into a case that is fixed in slanting position to the upper part of the right-hand doorpost. The affixed object is called a *mezuzah*, a Hebrew word that originally referred to the doorpost itself. The word *Shaddai* is written on the back of the parchment so that it is visible through a small aperture in the case. Shaddai is one of the names for the Almighty; the word is also formed by the initial letters of a Hebrew phrase meaning 'guardian of the doors of Israel'.

On passing through the door a pious Jew will kiss the mezuzah or touch it and then kiss his fingers. This is a mark of respect, not a commandment.

Strictly speaking, the mezuzah is required only on the entrance door to a house and on the doors of rooms that are used for living purposes. It has become customary, however, to affix a mezuzah also at the entrances of synagogues and other Jewish public buildings. After the Six-Day War in 1967, a mezuzah was placed on each of the gates leading into the recaptured Old City of Jerusalem.

The mezuzah became a favourite object of Jewish ceremonial art and occurs in many decorative styles from different periods.

Interior of the Jewish home

Such rooms varied in different places and periods, but certain traditional objects remained as constant features of them. In this picture there can be seen the Sabbath candles and *kiddush* sanctification cup, the *chanukkiah* and the *mizrach*.

The chanukkiah is a candelabrum used in a Jewish home for the celebration of the Feast of Chanukkah (Dedication) that occurs about the time of Christmas.

In 164 BC, the leader of the Maccabean Revolt, Judah the Maccabee,

A table set for the Sabbath meal in 18th-century Poland

recaptured Jerusalem, restored the defiled Temple and re-dedicated it. According to the accepted Jewish legend, only a small jar of undefiled holy oil was found, sufficient to light the great candelabrum for one night; but by a miracle the oil replenished itself and lasted for eight days. Therefore it was laid down that the event would be commemorated each year by the Feast of Chanukkah, sometimes called the Feast of Lights, which would also last for eight days.

In celebrating the festival, one candle on the chanukkiah is lit the first night and an additional one on each succeeding night until all eight have been lit. A ninth candle, popularly known as a *shammash* (beadle) is used to light the others.

The chanukkiah was originally a round or star-shaped oil lamp with the requisite number of wicks. From the late Middle Ages onwards the oil was replaced by candles. The chan-ukkiah varies greatly in appearance in different times and places, and can be made of silver, metal, pottery or stone.

The Hebrew word *mizrach* means 'east'. It is applied in Western countries to a wall-plaque which is hung on the eastern wall of a living-room or synagogue, so that Jews can face towards Jerusalem when praying. (Naturally, communities living to the east, north or south of the Holy Land would face Jerusalem from those directions.)

The plaque usually has the word 'mizrach' in the centre, surrounded by biblical verses and pictures of holy places, animals, birds, fruit, flowers, or other decorative motifs. The painting may be done on parchment or metal, or it may consist of tinted paper cut-outs between sheets of glass, a popular form of Jewish folk-art in Eastern Europe.

Faces in Art

Previous page '*A Jewess from Morocco*', a detail from a painting by Alfred Dehondencq, 19th century.

Left '*Rabbi Jacob Sasportas*' of Amsterdam, a detail from a painting by I. Luttichuys, 1671.

Right '*A Jewess*', a detail of the oil painting by Maurycy Gottlieb, c.1878.

Moses, from the 3rd-century synagogue murals of Dura Europos.

'*Personification of Autumn*'. *A replica of the mosaic from the 4th-century synagogue of Hammath-Tiberias.*

Jews from France. A replica of part of a 15th-century cavalry, from Carcassonne.

Süsskind of Trimberg', a detail from the Minnesänger manuscript, Germany, 14th century.

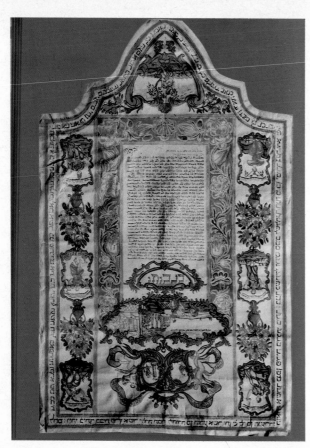

Left *The Ketubbah. An illuminated 'ketubbah' from Rome, 1771.*

Below *The Circumcision Ceremony. A model of a circumcision ceremony in Algeria, 19th century.*

was summarized by the great 12th-century scholar, Maimonides:

Thus the sages lay down that a man shall honour his wife more than his own self and shall love her as he loves himself, and shall constantly seek to benefit her according to his means; that he shall not unduly impose his authority on her and shall speak gently with her; that he shall be neither sad nor irritable. Similarly they lay down that a wife shall honour her husband exceedingly and shall accept his authority and abide by his wishes in all her activities ...

Jewish tradition always stressed that the primary purpose of marriage was to produce and rear children. In the first chapter of *Genesis* the Lord commanded Adam and Eve to 'be fruitful and multiply'. The greatest misfortune that could befall a wife was to be barren, as illustrated by the Old Testament stories of Abraham's wife Sarah, Isaac's wife Rebecca, Jacob's wife Rachel, and Hannah the mother of the prophet Samuel. By Talmudic law (Halachah), a wife who remains childless for ten years can be divorced by her husband on that ground alone.

The wife was legally subordinate to her husband, but extensive protection was given by the Halachah to her person, her property rights and her claims on her husband for cohabitation, maintenance, medical care, and to make provision for her after his death. The husband's obligation to maintain his wife was, however, conditional on her obligation to perform her household duties.

Although subject to her husband's authority, the Jewish wife and mother enjoyed a position of honour and respect, and had a strong influence on family affairs. In the Old Testament, the matriarchs Sarah, Rebecca, Leah and Rachel are treated with deference by their male kinfolk. At the end of the *Book of Proverbs* there is a wonderful acrostic poem lauding the good wife who is 'far more precious than jewels'. The passage describes her manifold activities and says of her:

She looks well to the ways of her household,
and does not eat the bread of idleness.
Her children rise up and call her blessed;
her husband also, and he praises her: ...
(Prov. 31:27, 28)

Throughout the Diaspora centuries, in conditions of poverty, persecution and migration, the main burden fell on the woman to keep the home and family intact. She was responsible for maintaining the intricate dietary laws and for infusing the home with the luminous spirit of the Sabbath and the festivals. Frequently she shared with her husband the task of bread-winner, especially when he devoted himself to learning.

The memory of the old-fashioned 'Yiddishe mama' has at times been the butt of contemporary Jewish humorists. But she was usually the mainstay of the family in the vanished *shtetl* (small town) of Eastern Europe, or in the desperate immigrant struggle of London's

Whitechapel or New York's Lower East Side.

In traditional Jewish society, the primary role of the woman lay in the home. The synagogue and the study house were a masculine domain. The lay leaders of the community and its religious officials – the rabbi, the cantor, the beadle, the ritual slaughterer, the mohel (circumciser) – were all males as a matter of course, as were both the teachers and the pupils in the talmudic seminaries. Only men were counted for the *minyan*, the prayer quorum of ten. In the synagogue, women were segregated in a gallery or separate section, usually behind a screen.

That was the traditional pattern not only in Judaism, but in early Christianity and Islam as well. It is only today that the pattern is beginning to change under the pressure of the modern movement towards equality of the sexes. Orthodox Jews are naturally more determined to maintain tradition than are the Conservative and Reform movements in the United States and their counterparts elsewhere.

The fifth of the Ten Commandments concerns the duty of children to honour their parents. By Jewish law a grown son is obliged to support his needy parents. On the other hand, the law is remarkably

The Sabbath Meal

The Sabbath starts on Friday evening and ends on Saturday evening. The poorest of families stints itself during the week to have something extra on the Friday night Sabbath table. The food is prepared before the eve of the Sabbath, and the house cleaned.

Shortly before the Sabbath starts, the wife lights the two candles with a special benediction. This custom is not mentioned in the Bible or Talmud and dates back to about the 8th century in Babylonia, during the Gaonic period. In rabbinical writings the Sabbath candles symbolized the duty of a wife and mother to ensure peace and warmth in the house.

The father blesses the children before the meal. In front of his place at table stands a kiddush cup of wine and two *challot* (twisted or plaited loaves of white bread made especially

progressive in protecting minors, even to the extent of curbing the authority of the father. A father cannot arbitrarily dispose of a child's property. By marriage-contract husband and wife can renounce or alter the property relations between them, but not to the detriment of their future children. A father is under a legal obligation to teach his son the Torah and a trade or profession; to ensure a good marriage for a daughter; and to provide for unmarried daughters in his will. If there was a divorce, a rabbinical court would decide the custody of a young child according to the interests of the child rather than the claim of the respective parents. As a general rule, illegitimate children have the same status and rights as legitimate ones, and suffer no legal disabilities.

The Jews were unique in the ancient world in hallowing one day a week as a complete rest from toil. The day also served as spiritual refreshment for the individual Jew and an affirmation of the family spirit. The practice is related to the story of the Creation in the *Book of Genesis*:

> *So God blessed the seventh day and hallowed it, because on it God rested from all his work which he had done in creation.*

(Gen. 2:3)

The Hebrew word for 'rested' in this passage is *shavat*, the origin of the name for the Sabbath. Sabbath observance is the second of the Ten Commandments, immediately after the primary injunction to worship a single God. That fact underlines the high degree of sanctity given to the Sabbath from biblical times.

What exactly *is* the work that is forbidden on the Sabbath? This question has exercised the minds of Jewish scholars through the generations, and produced an intricate set of rulings and definitions. For instance, in mediaeval times the limit for walking was set at 2,000 cubits (about half a mile) beyond the walls of a town. A whole array of fresh problems have arisen in a modern technological society. The day of rest applied to the animals on which one rode and Orthodox Jews have extended this to all mechanical transport. They also hold that pressing a switch to set machinery in motion is prohibited on the Sabbath, and automatic devices have been introduced to operate electric lighting and elevators on that day.

Any act involving *pikuach nefesh* (the saving of life) is permitted even if it means breaking the Sabbath laws. It is related in the *Book of Maccabees* that a group of ultra-Orthodox zealots who had joined in the revolt were attacked on the Sabbath, and most of them were killed because they would not take up arms to defend themselves on that day. When the survivors joined the Maccabees, the priest Mattathias, who led the Revolt at the beginning, rejected that rigid interpretation of the Law. From the Talmudic period onward the rabbis applied the principle of *pikuach nefesh* to a wide range of cases.

The Sabbath acquired added significance in the Diaspora, as a means of preserving the spirit of Jewish life under adverse conditions.

for the Sabbath) covered by an embroidered cloth. He holds up the cup of wine and recites the prayer for the sanctification of the Sabbath. Another prayer is made over the challot and small pieces are broken from it for everybody at the table.

At the end of the Sabbath comes the ceremony of *havdalah* (separation), marking the transition to the beginning of the working week. Again, a blessing is pronounced over the goblet of wine. A ritual object used in this ceremony is the spice-box or *hadas*. It is made, as a rule, of silver filigree and often takes the form of a tower decorated with the shapes of animals, fish, fruit, or flowers.

Down the ages, the Sabbath has been an interlude when the hardships and dangers of the week are transcended, and each Jewish home seems touched by the divine spirit, the *Shechinah*.

The terms *kosher* and *kashrut* are derived from a Hebrew root that means 'fit' or 'proper'. In the post-biblical period they came into use for food that can be eaten in accordance with the Jewish dietary laws.

The distinction between clean and unclean animals is based on the rules in the biblical books of *Leviticus* and *Deuteronomy*. Animals must have cloven hooves and chew the cud. This double requirement excludes, for instance, pigs (who do not chew the cud) and rabbits (who do not have cloven hooves). Fish must have both fins and scales; shellfish and eels are, therefore, excluded. Twenty-four species of birds, practically all kinds of birds of prey or scavengers, are listed as unclean. Even a creature from a clean species is barred if it has died from natural causes or injuries. Methods of ritual slaughter are designed to drain the blood, which was held to contain the life-force.

An elaborate set of rules evolved after the biblical period to keep meat and milk separate in the cooking, serving and consuming of food. Certain types of food, such as fish, eggs, fruit and vegetables, are classified as *parva* – that is, they can be eaten with either meat or milk.

Every housewife in a traditional Jewish home becomes expert in the rules of kashrut. In cases of doubt, it is the rabbi who gives the ruling.

The family ties and the Jewish atmosphere of the home were strengthened by the strict observance of the dietary laws; by the use of certain traditional objects; by the festive ceremonial meals on the Sabbath and the Passover; and by the shared joys and sorrows of family events – circumcisions, bar-mitzvahs, weddings and the mourning for the dead.

Chapter Three

Family Events
Brit Milah (Circumcision)

Circumcision has been practised since prehistoric times in different parts of the world. It was a common religious rite among the peoples of the ancient Middle East. As a rule, the rite was associated with initiation ceremonies of boys at the age of puberty. Only the Jewish faith requires it at the age of eight days.

According to the biblical account, the origin of the custom goes back to the time of Abraham, to whom God said:

You shall be circumcised in the flesh of your foreskins, and it shall be a sign of the covenant between me and you. He that is eight days old among you shall be circumcised; every male throughout your generations, whether born in your house, or bought with your money from any foreigner who is not of your offspring. . . .
Any uncircumcised male who is not circumcised in the flesh of his foreskin shall be cut off from his people; he has broken my covenant.

(Gen. 17:11, 12, 14)

(That passage explains the Hebrew name *brit milah*, which means 'the covenant of circumcision'.)

After God's commandment Abraham circumcised himself (at the age of ninety-nine) together with his son Ishmael and all the males in his household, including slaves. When his wife Sarah gave birth to Isaac the following year, he became the first child to be circumcised on the eighth day.

The custom seems to have lapsed during the forty years the Israelites wandered in the desert after the Exodus from Egypt. When he crossed the river Jordan into the Promised Land, one of Joshua's first acts was to have all the males circumcised with flint knives, thereby renewing the Covenant.

In the 2nd century BC, a ban on circumcision was one of the anti-Jewish measures of the Seleucid (Syrian) ruler Antiochus Epiphanes that precipitated the Maccabean Revolt. A similar ban by the Roman Emperor Hadrian in the 2nd century AD helped to provoke the Bar Kochba Revolt. These two historical episodes indicated that Jews were willing to fight to the death to defend a religious practice that

The Circumcision Ceremony

See colour page 20

This model shows a *mohel* (circumciser) about to perform the operation of the *brit milah*. The infant rests on a pillow placed on the knees of the *sandak* (godfather), an honour usually given to a grandfather or to a senior male member of the family. The sandak is seated in the 'chair of Elijah'. Blessings are said over a goblet of wine, and it is customary to place a few drops in the baby's mouth. He is then given his Hebrew name. The ceremony is followed by a festive meal or refreshments.

By Jewish law, the operation can be performed by any person, including a woman. (Zipporah, the Midianite wife of Moses, circumcised their infant son in the desert.) In practice it is done by a mohel, who is a religious official trained and licensed for the purpose by the rabbinical authorities. The mohel uses a special circumcision knife and a lyre-shaped shield is slipped over the foreskin.

Brit Milah

Right The model shows an infant's older sister sewing and embroidering the swaddling cloth.

One special custom that grew up in mediaeval German communities concerned the linen cloth placed under the infant during the circumcision. It was afterwards cut into four strips that were joined together into a long band. This was then richly embroidered with the name and birth-date of the child and presented to the synagogue when he visited it for the first time. It would later be used as a binding for the Torah scroll at the boy's bar-mitzvah.

symbolized their sacred and individual tie with God.

When the Christian sect was still newborn, a debate took place in its Council of Apostles and Elders in Jerusalem as to whether Gentile converts had to be circumcised. The majority view supported a waiver of the rite in such cases. That decision was a significant step in the turning away of the sect from Judaism.

The Church never actually forbade circumcision for Christians, but it became in practice a mark distinguishing Jews from Gentiles. That was not the case in Moslem lands, for Islam has retained circumcision rites for boys at the age of puberty.

Bar-mitzvah

The Hebrew term *bar-mitzvah* means 'son of the commandment'. It has come to be applied both to the boy and to the ceremony.

The age of thirteen is a turning-point in a Jewish boy's life. From then on he is regarded as having assumed the status and obligations of an adult. This concept crystallized in the post-biblical period, and was clearly established from about the 2nd century AD.

A formal bar-mitzvah ceremony at the age of thirteen became the custom many centuries later, and is not recorded before the 15th century AD. It was adopted by most but not all Diaspora communities – for instance, it was unknown in the Yemen, where the boy becomes a 'man' on the decision of the Rabbi and the community heads.

(continued on page 28)

Bar-mitzvah

This model depicts a bar-mitzvah boy appearing in synagogue in contemporary United States, flanked by his father and the Cantor.

On the Sabbath after his thirteenth birthday a boy is called up to the reading of the Torah, in the synagogue. He chants the portion of the Torah reading for that day, and the corresponding portion from the Prophetic Books. He then receives the blessing of the Rabbi, whose address to the congregation stresses the significance of the occasion. At the festive meal that follows, the bar-mitzvah boy is expected to make a speech, which among strictly Orthodox Jews takes the form of a Talmudic discourse on a chosen topic.

After his bar-mitzvah the youth is obliged to carry out the religious duties of an observant Jew, and is counted as one of the ten males eligible to form a minyan, the minimum quorum for communal prayers.

Tefillin *left*
From the date of his bar-mitzvah an observant Jew will regularly lay phylacteries (*tefillin*) with his morning prayers, except on the Sabbath and Holy Days. That practice is based on four similar passages in *Exodus* and *Deuteronomy* which require the words of the Law to be 'as a mark on your hand or frontlets between your eyes' *Ex. 13:16*. The four scriptural passages are inscribed on parchment and inserted into each of two small black leather boxes. The boxes are then tied on with black leather straps, one to the forehead and the other to the left arm above the elbow. In the latter case the strap is wound seven

The notion of marking a Jewish girl's twelfth birthday with a *bat-mitzvah* ('daughter of the commandment') ceremony is of very recent origin. It started in France and Italy in the 19th century and spread to other Western communities. Compared to the *bar-mitzvah*, the emphasis here is more on the family and social aspects than on the assumption of religious responsibilities.

Marriage

The importance Judaism attaches to marriage goes back to the story of Adam and Eve in the Book of Genesis:

It is not good that the man should be alone; I will make him a helper fit for him ...: Therefore a man leaves his father and his mother and cleaves to his wife, and they become one flesh.

(Gen. 2:18, 24)

The sanctity of the Jewish marriage tie is borne out by the Hebrew word for betrothal, *kiddushin*, which means 'consecration'. At the same time, marriage is not regarded as an indissoluble sacrament as in the Catholic Church, and divorce can be obtained on various grounds.

Though there was no formal prohibition against a man having more than one wife, polygamy became uncommon in post-biblical times. Of the hundreds of Talmudic sages recorded over several centuries, there may have been only one with more than a single wife. In the Jewish communities of mediaeval Europe a ban on polygamy became accepted. It was attributed to Rabbi Gershom of Mainz in Germany (960–1028), the leading Jewish scholar of his time. There was no similar restraint regarding Jews in Moslem lands, although in practice polygamy was the exception. After the State of Israel was established in 1948, a few immigrants from Arab countries came to it with more than one wife. Legislation in Israel has banned polygamy for Jewish citizens.

Orthodox Jews regard early marriage as desirable, with eighteen as a

(continued on page 30)

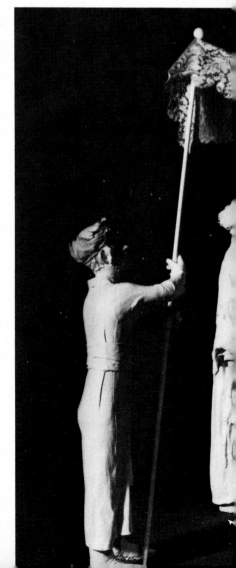

times around the arm between the elbow and the wrist – by custom in a clock-wise direction by Sephardim, and anti-clockwise by Ashkenazim.

A Jewish Wedding

Below *A wedding ceremony in 19th-century Galicia, Poland.*

A Jewish marriage takes place under a decorative canopy (*chuppah*) held up by four poles, the pole-holders being male members of the family or close friends. The chuppah is a symbolic representation of the bridegroom's tent or house, to which the bride was originally brought. The bridegroom, therefore, waits under the canopy for

the bride to be brought in. In some oriental communities there is no canopy. Instead the groom places a prayer-shawl over the bride.

The bride is covered by a veil and stands to the right of the groom. They are flanked by relatives. A group of musicians is often at hand to play the traditional wedding tunes.

Under the canopy the officiating rabbi blesses the couple over a goblet of wine from which the groom and bride then sip. The groom places a ring on the bride's finger and declares: 'By this ring you are hereby betrothed to me according to the law of Moses and Israel.' The *ketubbah*, marriage-contract, is then read out by

the rabbi. That concludes the first or betrothal stage of the ceremony (*kiddushin* or *erusin*). The next stage is the marriage proper (*nissu'in*). Seven marriage benedictions are recited and the groom breaks a glass by stamping his foot on it, as a sign of mourning for the destruction of Jerusalem.

In early centuries the period of betrothal could last up to a year, during which time the parties were subject to certain legal rights and obligations. From about the 12th century it became the general custom to join the two stages in one ceremony.

Some local marriage customs are meant to ward off evil spirits. Thus it

was an Ashkenazi practice to lead the bride seven times round the bridegroom under the canopy, forming a magic circle against bad influences. The breaking of the glass by the groom may also have originated as a device to frighten off demons. In certain Oriental communities, the womenfolk gather the night before at the bride's home and paint her hands with red henna to protect her against evil. In some localities butter and honey were smeared on the doorposts of the groom's house to ensure good fortune.

Local fertility customs have included eating a ceremonial dish of fish, throwing rice, wheat, nuts or confetti over the couple; and having the bride hold a borrowed infant in her arms before the wedding.

The Betrothal Ring

Left *A replica of a betrothal ring from 19th-century Germany surmounted by the model of a house.*

The ring is a token payment for the bride, and her acceptance of it signifies her agreement to the symbolic transaction. Originally a coin could be used for the purpose, and this custom has survived in a few Oriental communities.

The Ketubbah (Marriage Contract)

See colour page 20

The *ketubbah* or marriage contract sets out the obligations the husband assumes towards his wife. It is usually written on parchment in the ancient Aramaic language, with a decorative border painted round the text. A summary is sometimes read out by the rabbi in the language of the country where the wedding is taking place.

suitable age for a young man. In theory the Halachah permits marriage for girls from the age of puberty, but that is not the case in contemporary practice. Israel legislation has fixed a minimum age of seventeen for girls of all creeds. All other civilized countries also have a legal minimum age.

Bereavement

Jewish mourning customs when there is a death in the family go back to ancient times. Various biblical passages refer to rending the garments, wearing sackcloth, fasting, refraining from washing or arranging the hair, sitting or lying down, or partaking of bread and wine as a reaffirmation of life. In the Talmudic period such customs were adapted into a pattern that has remained essentially unchanged to the present. It seeks to ensure both respect for the dead and the easing the grief of the mourners – as the Talmud puts it, 'the dignity of the departed' together with 'the dignity of the living'.

The main requirement is a mourning period of seven days, in which the members of the immediate family *sit Shivah* at home. They refrain from normal personal or business activities and spend each day seated

A funeral procession in Fez, Morocco.

on the floor or on low stools. Relatives and friends come to visit them, and on departing recite the blessing: 'May the Lord comfort you among the other mourners for Zion and Jerusalem.' The men have a tear in their clothes as a token 'rending of garments', wear felt slippers instead of leather shoes, and refrain from shaving. A candle burns continuously, and mirrors are covered or turned to the wall. A *minyan* (the prayer quorum of ten males) gathers for the morning, afternoon and evening services. A close male relative will say the Kaddish, the prayer recited by the mourners. The *Shivah* fulfils the need for the family to come together to express its solidarity when it suffers a loss, and for the community to give a bereaved family its support.

A modified form of mourning is kept up for the *Shloshim*, the rest of the thirty days from the funeral, while certain restrictions last a whole year. Every year thereafter on the anniversary of the death by the Jewish calendar, there is a *yahrzeit*, memorial prayers for the departed, with male survivors saying Kaddish.

The wearing of black mourning clothes or black armbands is frowned upon, since these are regarded as Gentile customs.

## Chapter Four

Autonomy

Throughout Diaspora history until modern times, Jews lived in separate communities that exercised autonomy in their internal affairs and kept in close contact with each other. The communities served as the framework for preserving the Jewish faith and way of life. They also provided mutual protection against hostility and attack.

The structure of different communities, and the way of life maintained within them, were by no means uniform. Each community was influenced by the culture, economy, and attitudes of the local society that surrounded it. Despite these variables, the essential features of the Jewish community remained fairly constant down the ages. It occupied segregated quarters (whether voluntary or forced); it had its own internal administration and taxation system; and its network of institutions provided for a wide range of group-needs: religious, educational, legal and social welfare.

As a rule, Jewish autonomy did not run counter to the general pattern in the host countries. An Imperial domain such as the Roman, the Ottoman or the Austro-Hungarian was a mosaic of different peoples and creeds. The rulers had no incentive to interfere in the internal life of subject communities, as long as they were politically docile and paid their taxes. It was actually convenient for rulers to have their Jewish subjects living in organized communities. Their leaders could be the official spokesmen in dealings with the authorities, and could commit communities to collective lump sums in taxes.

After the French Revolution, and the 19th century emancipation of Jews that followed in the Western World, the Jewish community as an autonomous unit, a 'state within a state', declined in importance. As individuals, Jews became citizens of liberal democratic states, with religious freedom, civic rights and equality before the law guaranteed by constitution. In some of these countries, church and state were separated, and the national life had a secular framework. It appeared as if freedom and assimilation might erode the innate strength of the Jewish community where persecution had failed to do so.

But developments in the latter part of the century demonstrated that emancipation was not in itself an answer to the Jewish question. The newly-won freedom of the Jews in Western society provoked a backlash of ugly anti-semitism, with the Dreyfus Affair in France as its most dramatic expression. Even where anti-semitism was not overt,

Autonomy: Mediaeval Spain

Right *The Seal of the mediaeval Jewish community of Seville.*

In general, the Jewish communities in mediaeval Spain were led by their most prominent members – the gifted men who attained high office at the courts of the Moslem and Christian rulers. The outstanding example was Hisdai ibn-Shaprut in the 10th century. He served the Moorish caliphs at Cordoba while protecting his fellow-Jews and promoting their scholarship. Another was Samuel ha-Nagid, who was the chief minister to the Moslem court at Granada in the 11th century, and the acknowledged leader of Spanish Jewry. In Christian Spain, too, the kings tended to appoint Jewish royal counsellors and top officials who at the same time were accepted as the heads of their communities.

The rule of the Spanish-Jewish grandees over their communities caused social tension and discontent among the middle-class and poorer elements, who demanded a greater voice in communal affairs. The class factor is illustrated by the Barcelona Jewish Council set up by royal decree in 1327. The decree divided the community into three 'classes', each of them delegating ten members to the council.

political, economic and social barriers continued to exist. Jews migrating from Eastern Europe flooded into the static Western communities. Against a background of European national movements, the modern Zionist Movement organized itself for a return to the homeland. All these factors, both positive and negative, once more strengthened the sense of identity and peoplehood in the Jewish Diaspora. In Western lands the Jewish communities grew stronger and more organized.

After the First World War the international law concept of minority rights was promoted as a restriction on national sovereignty. At the Versailles Peace Conference in 1919 the Committee of Jewish Delegations spearheaded the campaign for the special minority provisions that were written into the peace treaties with the defeated powers of Austria, Hungary, Bulgaria and Turkey and the successor states of Poland, Czechoslovakia, Rumania, Yugoslavia and Greece. The ethnic, religious, national, cultural and linguistic minorities in these countries (including, of course, the Jewish communities) were guaranteed group rights under international supervision to be exercised through the League of Nations.

These minorities clauses and treaties had, before 1914, been given an ideological basis by the great Russian-Jewish historian Simon

(continued on page 41)

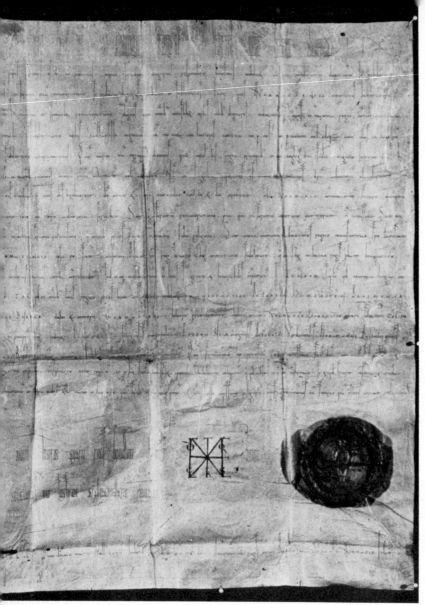

German region would congregate at the great annual trade fairs held in one or other city. From time to time advantage was taken of these gatherings to convene a synod of rabbis and communal leaders, in order to discuss common problems of Jewish life. The conclusions would serve as guidance for local communities. Such synods took place in France, the Rhineland and Italy.

Christian Europe in the Middle Ages was not a monolithic society. It had a corporate structure made up of various contending power-centres: the kings and princes, the great landowning nobles with their serfs and private armies, the Church and monastic Orders, the burgeoning mercantile cities with their privileges gained by royal charter, and the craft guilds. Although the Jews stood outside this feudal framework, they were in a sense another autonomous corporate entity that performed limited but valuable economic functions.

In the absence of an official regional leadership recourse was often had to a *shtadlan* (a person who intercedes). The shtadlan was an individual Jew who had the requisite position, language and connections to deal with the authorities on behalf of his fellow-Jews. He might plead for relief from ruinous taxes and protection from mob violence, anti-Jewish laws, the 'blood-libel' and other fabricated offences against Jews. This one-man lobby was an important device at a time when Jews were at the mercy of rulers and hostile clergy. In Czarist Russia, and other countries with autocratic regimes in Eastern Europe, the shtadlan remained a feature of Jewish communal life until the 19th century.

A letter dated 1074 from the Emperor Heinrich IV to the Jews of the German city of Worms, granting them communal rights and the privileges of freedom of trade.

Autonomy: Ashkenaz (Mediaeval Franco-Germany)

In mediaeval Ashkenaz (Franco-Germany) the autonomous *Kehillah* (local community) emerged as the basis for organized Jewish life. As a rule, all the Jews residing in a particular centre formed a single community under one communal board.

This local unity was disrupted in certain countries in the 16th century, with the influx of Jewish refugees from Spain and Portugal. In Holland and Italy the newcomers tended to set up separate Sephardi congregations, parallel with the existing Ashkenazi ones. (The literal meanings of the Hebrew words Sephardi and Ashkenazi are 'Spanish' and 'German'.)

Jews from all over the Franco-

The Council of the Four Lands meet in Lublin, Poland.

Autonomy: Mediaeval Poland–Lithuania

By the 15th century, Jews migrating eastward from Germany had settled in different parts of Poland, and in the Grand Duchy of Lithuania that came under the Polish crown. They were made welcome and given communal rights by Polish rulers eager to gain their financial and trading skills and their international ties. A regular countrywide institution developed, known as the Council of the Four Lands (Great Poland, Little Poland, Galicia and Volhynia). The Council consisted of thirty delegates – six rabbis and twenty-four lay leaders. It met in two annual sessions, at the spring fair in Lublin and the autumn fair at Jaroslav in Galicia. Its functions included the division among the communities of the annual collective tax imposed on Polish Jewry by the authorities; a special fund to protect Jewish interests; the promotion of Jewish education and welfare; and guidelines regarding business ethics and undue competition. The Council set up a high court of justice that sat at the same time.

While these councils played an essential co-ordinating role, the basic unit of Jewish life in Eastern Europe remained the self-contained local community (Kehillah), with its network of institutions under the democratic control of all its members.

A Rabbi in Salonika.

Above *Bet Din (the Rabbinical Court)* and below *Ritual Slaughter. Details from the 'Sefer ha-Turim', a legal code by Rabbi Jacob ben-Asher appearing in Mantua, Italy, 15th century.*

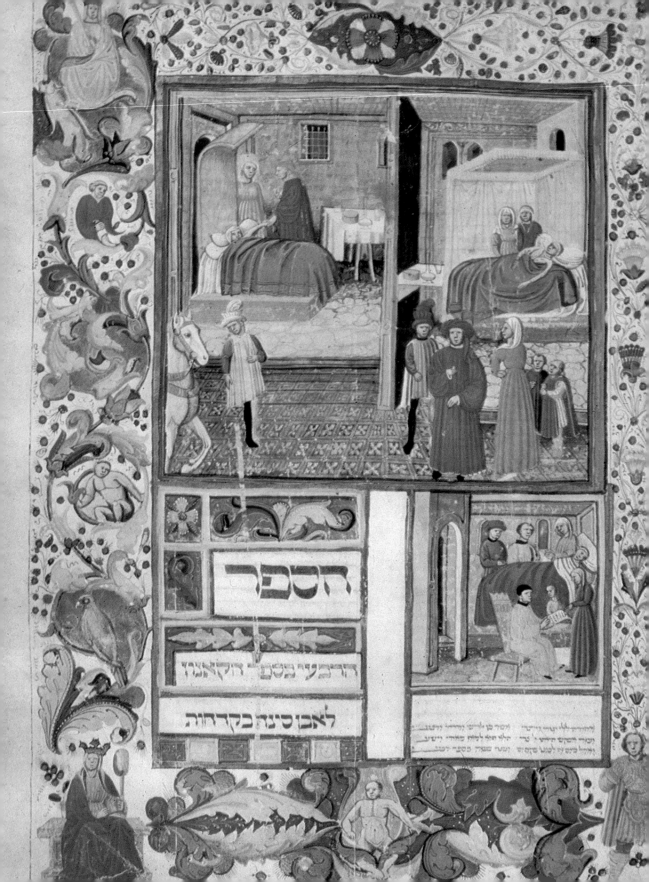

Above *Painted ceiling, Chodorov. A reconstruction of the wooden ceiling of a synagogue.*

Left *Bikkur Cholim (tending the sick). An illuminated page from the Hebrew translation of the Canon of Medicine of Avicenna, the renowned 11th-century Islamic philosopher and physician.*

Below *Dura Europos. A reconstruction of the wall-paintings in the synagogue on the Euphrates river in Syria.*

Left *A double page from a replica of the Birds Head Haggadah,* AD *1300, one of the oldest Ashkenazi illuminated manuscripts of the Haggadah that survives.*

Below *'Days of Awe' (High Holy Days). A representation taken from a painting by Maurycy Gottlieb.*

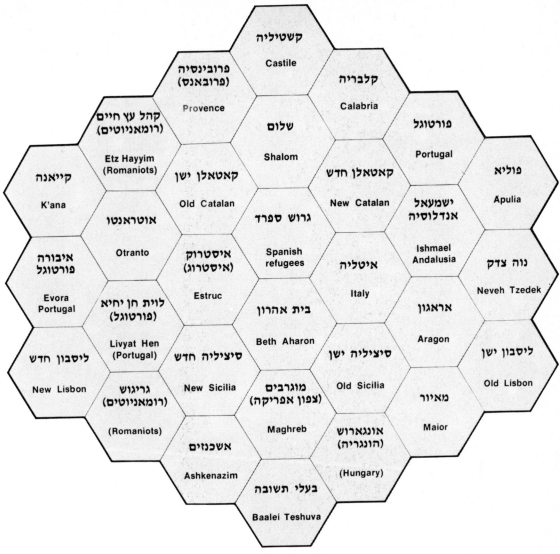

קשטיליה
Castile

פרובינסיה
(פרובאנס)
Provence

קלבריה
Calabria

קהל עץ חיים
(רומאניוטים)
Etz Hayyim
(Romaniots)

שלום
Shalom

פורטוגל
Portugal

קייאנה
K'ana

קאטאלן ישן
Old Catalan

קאטאלן חדש
New Catalan

ישמעאל
אנדלוסיה
Ishmael
Andalusia

פוליא
Apulia

אוטראנטו
Otranto

גרוש ספרד
Spanish
refugees

איבורה
פורטוגל
Evora
Portugal

איסטרוק
(איסטרוג)
Estruc

איטליה
Italy

נוה צדק
Neveh Tzedek

לוית חן יחיא
(פורטוגל)
Livyat Hen
(Portugal)

בית אהרון
Beth Aharon

אראגון
Aragon

ליסבון חדש
New Lisbon

סיציליה חדש
New Sicilia

סיציליה ישן
Old Sicilia

ליסבון ישן
Old Lisbon

גריגוש
(רומאניוטים)
(Romaniots)

מוגרבים
(צפון אפריקה)
Maghreb

מאיור
Maior

אשכנזים
Ashkenazim

אונגארוש
(הונגריה)
(Hungary)

בעלי תשובה
Baalei Teshuva

Dubnow, who developed the concept of Galut Nationalism, also called Autonomism. Dubnow maintained that the existing European Jewish communities in the Diaspora had become a permanent national entity, with Yiddish as the cornerstone of its national culture. However, the minorities treaties were poorly implemented between the two World Wars, and faded away with the demise of the League of Nations.

In the Western world Jews are free citizens of the countries where they live, but remain strongly organized in communities, on the basis of voluntary affiliation. The outstanding example is the United States, where an organized Jewry with millions of members fits comfortably into a highly pluralistic society. On the local level, communities continue to be centred on their synagogues and Reform temples with a network of ancillary institutions: community centres, parochial

Autonomy: The Salonika Community

This is a diagram of the congregations that made up the Salonika Jewish Community in the 17th century. As the names indicate, these congregations are formed according to the places of origin of their members, and thus roughly correspond to the *landsmanshaften* (country-of-origin associations) set up by European immigrants to the United States and elsewhere.

schools, youth organizations, charitable and fund-raising agencies, social and recreation facilities. On the national level there are a large number of Jewish bodies but no single organization that speaks for American Jewry as a whole.

In Britain, France and other Western countries, the pattern of voluntary organizations is similar. In each of these countries there is a single representative body on the national level, such as the Board of Deputies of British Jews.

After the Bolshevik revolution of 1917, the huge Jewish community in Soviet Russia was virtually cut off from the rest of the Jewish world. Soviet policy towards the Jewish minority was self-contradictory. The anti-Jewish restrictions of the Czarist era were abolished. The Jews were officially recognized as one of the many different nationalities within the Soviet Union. Since each of the others had a territorial base, an Autonomous Jewish Region was set up in Birobidjan, in the Far Eastern region of the Soviet Union. This experiment proved a dismal failure. Less than one per cent of Soviet Jews live there, and those that do constitute a small minority of the local population. At the same time the distinctive features of Jewish group identity – religion, language, culture, ties with Jewish communities elsewhere, Zionist sentiments – were discouraged and suppressed by the Soviet authorities. In these conditions, Jewish communal life virtually ceased in Russia and declined in the Baltic States of Lithuania, Latvia, Esthonia and other territories annexed by the Soviet Union at the beginning of the Second World War.

Autonomy: The Ottoman Empire

In the Ottoman Empire, what was called the 'millet system' gave non-Moslem religious groups the right to organize their communal lives, practise their own faiths and apply their religious laws in their own courts in matters of personal status. The overall structure of the Ottoman Jewish community was fragmented. In Constantinople, the capital, the pattern resembled that in Salonika. There were about forty congregations established according to localities of origin, each with its own synagogue, officials and institutions, but with little co-ordination between them. Only as late as 1865 was a law adopted that set up central organs representing all the Jews of the Ottoman Empire. A Chief Rabbi (*Haham Bashi*) was to be appointed by the Sultan, with extensive powers. In addition there was to be a General Council of eighty members, with two committees, one rabbinical and one secular.

Chapter Five

Communal Institutions

The internal structure of local communities has varied. In some areas communal leadership has been exercised by an aristocracy of scholars, notables and influential families. That has been the general pattern in the Moslem world. In the Western world, from the Middle Ages, the system of a community administration was a mixture of democracy and oligarchy. Sometimes decisions were taken by a majority vote, sometimes by lot, sometimes by a few individuals. The assembly elects a communal board (*kahal*) presided over by the elected president of the community (*parnass*). The other important honorary officer is the treasurer (*gabbai*) who is also the senior warden for charitable funds. The board administers the affairs of the community and appoints its officials.

The central institution of a community has always been the synagogue. Its primary function is worship, but the building and its courtyard have also served as a meeting place and as a venue for bar-mitzvahs and weddings. Other institutions, like the law court (*bet din*), the study house (*bet midrash*) and the ritual bath-house (*mikveh*), have usually been clustered round it. Next to the synagogue, the essential communal property is the burial ground, for Jews have to be buried in consecrated soil.

The most important community official is the rabbi. In Judaism there is no clerical hierarchy, as, for instance, in the Catholic Church. Each rabbi is responsible only to God's law and to the community that engaged him. The practise of formally ordaining a rabbi goes back to mediaeval Germany. Among other officials are the cantor (*chazzan*) who leads the prayers in synagogues; the beadle (*shamash*) and the ritual slaughterer (*shochet*).

In traditional Jewish society elementary education took place in a *cheder* (schoolroom) where boys from three to thirteen were taught religious subjects by rote. After his bar-mitzvah a boy would move to a *yeshivah* (Talmudic academy) until he was seventeen or eighteen. The closed system of religious education started breaking down from the beginning of the 19th century, with the demand for more general secular studies. Until modern times the education of Jewish girls was virtually confined to reading and reciting the prayers; more serious study was regarded as a male preserve.

(continued on page 45)

The Shulhof Complex

The Shulhof was an imposing example of the traditional role of the synagogue as the focal point of community activities. There were some twenty small synagogues and other institutions round the courtyard, as well as the main synagogue. The complex was founded in 1572, and twenty years later the street passing the main entrance gates was officially named the 'Street of the Jews'.

On the left-hand side of the model is the academy bearing the name of the Vilna Gaon, Rabbi Elijah ben-Solomon Zalman (1720–97), the most renowned Jewish scholar of his day.

On the right-hand side of the model are the Great Synagogue and a Jewish public library.

Bet Din

See colour page 37

The *Bet Din* is usually presided over by the community rabbi aided by two or more *dayanim* (judges of a rabbinical court). In larger centres of population the Bet Din might have city-wide or regional jurisdiction, serving a group of communities.

The general pattern of Jewish autonomy in Diaspora lands included the administration of Jewish law through an internal court system. The extent of the jurisdiction permitted to these courts varied. Everywhere they dealt with ritual matters, as well as with questions of family and personal status, including marriage, divorce, guardianship and inheritance. Usually the Bet Din could also hear civil cases where both parties were Jews. As a rule it could not try criminal cases, though in mediaeval Spain that was one of the privileges granted by the kings.

Charity has always been regarded as a supreme virtue, which would gain merit in the world to come. The Hebrew word for charity, *tzedakah*, means righteousness, which stresses that it was a religious duty for the well-off to take care of the needy. In the local community the mechanism for relief services was the charity fund (*kuppah*) to which each member of the congregation contributed according to his means. It was administered by three elected charity wardens. The fund provided money, food and clothing to the indigent, dowries for poor brides, burial of paupers and ransom money for captives. The remarkable record of modern Jewish philanthropy is in the direct tradition of *tzedakah*.

Among the charitable features of the community were the duty to visit and help the sick (*bikkur cholim*) and the maintenance of a poorhouse-infirmary (*hekdesh*) and a soup kitchen (*tamchui*). As a rule the hekdesh was used for transients, since families within the

Left *A reconstructed model of part of the Shulhof synagogue complex in Vilna, Lithuania, destroyed by the Nazis in the Second World War.*

Below *Bikkur Cholim (tending the sick). A detail from the Canon of Medicine of Avicenna.*

Bikkur Cholim

See colour page 38 and detail right

A special act of piety in a Jewish community was *bikkur cholim* (visiting the sick). The visitors were required to attend to the wants of the invalid and the disabled, to cheer them up, and to pray for their recovery. The sages gave detailed guidance how to avoid untimely, protracted or depressing visits. A special point was made of fulfilling this duty in cases where the sick person was poor, for 'many go to a rich man to pay him honour'.

Ritual Slaughter

See colour page 37 and detail right

One of the basic services rendered by the community has been to ensure a regular supply of kosher meat. From early times communities have arranged for the ritual slaughter (*shechitah*) of animals and birds under the supervision of the rabbinical authorities. The fees paid for this service have been a major source of revenue for the community.

By Jewish law, any adult sufficiently versed in the dietary laws can perform the ritual act. But from the Middle Ages, it has always been done by a professional *shochet* (slaughterer) who has been licensed after passing an examination. In small communities this task was often combined with other paid communal offices, such as cantor or teacher.

The ritual method makes the death of the animal as instantaneous and painless as possible. The essence of the method is the slitting of the throat in a single stroke with an extremely sharp knife. The carcase is drained of blood, which by Jewish belief contains the life-force and should not be consumed. In modern times the method has been questioned by animal welfare bodies but the weight of scientific and medical opinion has endorsed it, and it is expressly legalized in the United States, Britain and elsewhere.

Distorted accounts of Jewish ritual slaughter have featured in antisemitic literature, and it was banned by the Nazis in all the territories they occupied.

Ritual Slaughter, a detail from the 'Sefer ha-Turim'.

community would generally look after members who needed help.

A characteristic of Jewish communal life was the *chevrah*, a society under the general control of the community board, and often subsidized from community funds. These societies served various charitable and social purposes. The most influential was the *Chevrah Kaddisha* (burial society) that attended to funerals and cemeteries. *Bikkur Cholim* societies also operated as voluntary sick funds.

With its elaborate system of religious, educational and charitable agencies, the Jewish community functioned as a social welfare state in miniature.

## Chapter Six

The Synagogue

The form of public worship embodied in the synagogue was, like monotheism itself, a unique Jewish concept in the ancient world. It was in due course taken over and adapted by the two later monotheistic faiths, Christianity and Islam.

The roots of the synagogue lie in the Babylonian captivity after the destruction of the kingdom of Judah and the First Temple, in 586 BC. As the Jewish exiles settled down on the alien soil of Babylonia, they clung to their Mosaic creed and sacred Books, and developed local meeting-places for prayer and study. After the disaster that had uprooted them, they had to be reassured that God had not abandoned them. The answer came through the great prophet of the Exile, Ezekiel. 'Thus says the Lord God: Though I removed them far off among the nations, and though I scattered them among the countries, yet I have been a sanctuary to them for a while in the countries where they have gone.' (*Ezek. 11:16*) In a later age the Talmudic sages interpreted this passage to mean that the Divine Presence had remained with the exiles in the houses of worship that formed the early synagogues.

Certainly the synagogue was a well-established institution, both in the Land of Israel and in the Diaspora, long before the destruction of the Second Temple in AD 70. The New Testament mentions those synagogues where Jesus preached and those elsewhere in the Roman Empire where St Paul preached. From inscriptions and archaeological remains, it is estimated that hundreds of synagogues co-existed with the Second Temple. The synagogue, however, was not a small local replica of the Temple. There were profound differences between the two institutions.

The mystic act of sacrifice could only be carried out at the central sanctuary, the Temple. The rituals there, including the sacrifices and benedictions, were performed by a hereditary caste of priests. Psalms of thanksgiving and praise to the Lord were sung to musical instruments by professional choirs of Levites. The services took place outside the Temple, with the worshippers gathered in the courtyard. Only the priests had access to the sanctuary itself, and only the High Priest had access to the Holy of Holies, once a year on the Day of Atonement. The building was not only a house of worship – it was also God's dwelling-place.

In the case of a synagogue, the congregation assembled inside the building. (The Greek work 'synagogue' and the Hebrew equivalent *bet knesset* have the meaning of 'a meeting-house'.) There were no sacrifices, and in fact sacrifices ceased altogether to be a feature of Jewish worship when the Temple went out of existence. The synagogue service rested on collective prayers and Scripture readings. A quorum (minyan) of ten or more males over the age of thirteen constituted a congregation for public worship at any place, and any person able to do so could conduct the service, without the need for a priest.

These three elements of the service – the order of prayers, Scripture readings and the sermon – were already regular features of the synagogue by the time the Second Temple was destroyed and the synagogue became the major institution of Jewish life everywhere. Since the Temple priesthood no longer existed, authority in religious matters lay informally with the learned sages and scholars whom their pupils called by the title *rabbi*, meaning 'my teacher'. They had no official standing in the congregations; it was at a much later stage that communities appointed paid rabbis.

The synagogue did retain or adapt certain Temple customs. The times and names of the daily services corresponded to those of the daily Temple sacrifices: morning (*shacharit*) and afternoon (*minchah*). To these were added the evening service (*ma'ariv*) and an additional service (*mussaf*). The priestly blessing from the Temple was repeated in the synagogue by members of the congregation who were descendants of the priestly families (*Cohanim*). Men and women were separated in the synagogue, as they had been at the Temple, where

Sardis, Turkey, *above.*

Originally built as a secular basilica, this edifice became a synagogue from the late 2nd century AD. The model has been constructed on the basis of archaeological excavations.

Prague, Czechoslovakia, *right.*

The 'Altneuschul' is the oldest synagogue in Europe still in use. It was built in the 13th–14th centuries, and influenced by the Gothic church architecture of the period. Although restrictions were imposed by the authorities at that time on the height of synagogues, the Altneuschul dominates the surrounding houses, as it is located in the heart of the old Jewish quarter of Prague.

(continued on page 51)

Kai-Feng Fu, China, *above.*

A community of Chinese Jews was at Kai-Feng-Fu, capital of the Honan province of Central China. It was established at the beginning of the 12th century by Jews from Persia or India, engaged in the production of cotton fabrics. The synagogue was built in 1163, and after being destroyed by flood, was rebuilt in 1653, through the efforts of a Jewish mandarin. The community fell into decay and had assimilated by the 19th century. The first report about them to reach Europe came from an Italian Jesuit missionary in the 18th century.

Dura-Europos

See colour page 39

The synagogue of Dura-Europos, on the Euphrates River in Syria, was built in AD 245. It was excavated in 1932 and moved to the National Museum in Damascus.

The four inside walls of the synagogue were entirely covered by coloured frescoes, in a style that is a fusion of Hellenist and Persian art. The murals include scenes from the *Pentateuch*, the *Prophets* and the *Book of Esther*. The subjects of some of the paintings have not been definitely identified. Certain ones may be derived from legends that have been lost.

Zabludov, Poland, *above right.*

This model of a 17th-century wooden synagogue represents the type of synagogue building common in the small towns of Eastern Europe in the 17th and 18th centuries. Over a hundred of them still existed in Poland, Lithuania and the Ukraine at the outbreak of the Second World War. All of them were destroyed by the Nazis during the War.

there was a special Women's Court. The eternal light (*Ner Tamid*) before the Ark in the synagogue represented the great menorah in the Temple. A degree of the holiness attached to the Temple precincts was transferred to the synagogue building.

By the period of the Mishnah (2nd–3rd century AD), the basic order of prayers in the synagogue liturgy had already become fixed. In the course of time variations developed in different Jewish centres, mainly by the addition of liturgical poems (*piyyutim*) for the Sabbath, festivals and High Holy Days. Thus there were differences between the Palestinian and Babylonian rites (*minhagim*) that eventually evolved into the Ashkenazi and Sephardi variants in the liturgy.

In its external aspect, the synagogue has had no special Jewish style, and its architecture has been influenced by that prevailing in different countries and periods of Diaspora life. Jewish law and tradition are much concerned with the interior functions of the synagogue, but have had little to say about its outward appearance.

In Christian Europe synagogues were apt to be targets of hostility or mob violence, so the tendency was to place them in the heart of the Jewish quarter or ghetto and to make them outwardly plain and inconspicuous, even where the interior was lavishly decorated. One restriction imposed by the Church was that a synagogue had to be lower than any churches in the vicinity; as a result, it became customary for the ground floor to be sunk below street level, so as to afford more height inside.

Early synagogues, to about the 8th century AD, generally conformed to the rectangular design of the Roman basilica. That was the case both in the Land of Israel and in the Diaspora.

In mediaeval Europe synagogues were built in the successive styles of Romanesque and Gothic, and later, Renaissance and Baroque. However, in Spain the synagogues were strongly influenced by Moorish architecture, with its courtyards and colonnades. After the Expulsion from Spain, the new synagogues built by the Spanish and Portuguese congregations in Holland and Britain were modelled on the Protestant churches in those countries.

The wooden synagogues that appeared all over Poland in the 17th and early 18th century developed a distinctive character. The painted ceilings in some of these synagogues were an expression of an authentic Jewish folk-art.

In 17th-century Eastern Europe some synagogues were of the fortress type, designed to withstand attack from raiding bands of Cossacks and Tartars.

The Chassidic movement that sprang up in Eastern Europe in the 18th century had a modest and austere attitude towards the synagogue. It was usually a small room known as a *shtiebl*, furnished with tables and benches rather than pews. The services were informal and full of fervour.

In 19th-century Western Europe and America, Jewish emancipation and growing wealth produced a great number of large synagogues in an eclectic mixture of styles – Egyptian, Moorish, Renaissance or neo-classical – and many of them with exuberant ornamentation. Particularly noticeable was a revival of the Moorish idiom of mediaeval Spain, reflected in fanciful domes.

Contemporary synagogue architecture, particularly in the United States, shows a complete break with the past. The stress is on the functional aspect of modern architecture with its new technology, its use of concrete and glass, and its austere appearance. Wealthy American congregations, especially of the Reform trend, engage the leading architects of the day to design their great new temples – including Erich Mendelsohn, Percival Goodman, Louis Cahn and Frank Lloyd Wright. In general these buildings provide for multiple community functions: halls for social occasions, classrooms, and recreation and sport facilities. The sanctuary within such a complex can be expanded for the High Holy Days by opening the partition dividing it from the large social hall.

The interior design of every synagogue down the ages has had two focal points: the Ark and the *bimah*.

The Ark is the cabinet containing the parchment Scrolls of the Law, the most sacred objects in the synagogue. (The Ashkenazi name for it is *Aron Kodesh* and the Sephardi one is *Heichal*.) It is always placed on the wall facing in the direction of Jerusalem, which in the Western world would be the East wall. From the late Middle Ages the Ark was usually built into the wall and was of elaborate design, with an embroidered or velvet curtain hanging in front of it. A representation of the twin tablets of the Law is often set as a decorative motif above the Ark. The congregation stands facing the Ark when it is opened for

Fez, Morocco, *above right.*

The Danan synagogue was built in the mid-17th century and renovated in its present form at the end of the 19th century. A distinctive feature is the Arks. The platform, set in the western wall, is surmounted by a crown, and on it stands the Chair of Elijah used for circumcision ceremonies.

Cochin, India, *below right.*

Model of the Paradesi ('foreigners') synagogue of the 'White Jews' of Cochin – so-called because they originated from Syria, Spain, Holland and Germany and had fairer skins than the native Cochinis who were called 'Black Jews'. The synagogue was built in 1568 and enlarged in 1761. The present structure shows European influence.

Painted Ceiling, Chodorov

See colour page 39

A reconstructed segment on a reduced scale of the painted ceiling of the synagogue in Chodorov, near Lvov in Poland. Dating from 1651, this was the oldest wooden synagogue in Europe.

In the centre is a double-headed eagle enclosed in a circle and surrounded by smaller circles containing the signs of the Zodiac. The rest of the ceiling is filled with animals, birds, plants and biblical and Talmudic verses.

This type of painted ceiling was found in a number of the Polish synagogues that were destroyed during the Nazi occupation.

The Tallit

The *tallit* was originally a mantle or gown of wool or linen worn by men as an outer garment. In the Dispersion it evolved into a prayer-shawl worn in the synagogue over the shoulders (sometimes over the head) during the morning service, and all day on the Day of Atonement.

There are two main types of tallit. The ordinary one is of white wool, linen or cotton, with blue or black horizontal stripes at either end. The type worn by rabbis, cantors and important members of the congregation is of cream-coloured wool with black stripes. Round the edge that rests on the neck an extra strip is sewn called the *atarah* (diadem), decorated with silver or gold thread.

At the four corners of the tallit are tassels (*tsitsiot*) made of threads inserted through holes and tied together with knots. This fringe fulfills the biblical commandment in the Books of *Numbers* and *Deuteronomy* to make tassels on the corners of garments, as a reminder to observe religious duties. A tallit is carried to synagogue in a decorated bag.

An Orthodox Jew also wears under his outer garment a rectangle of white cloth with a similar fringe hanging from the corners, in such a way that it is visible. This garment is known as a 'small tallit' (*tallit katan*).

the Scrolls to be taken out and brought to the bimah for reading and when they are returned, or when certain prayers are recited.

The bimah is a raised platform used primarily for reading the Torah Scrolls that are unrolled on a table or desk. In Sephardi communities it is known as a *tevah*, the Hebrew word for a box. Traditionally the bimah is in the centre of the synagogue. In one type of early mediaeval synagogue, the vaulted ceiling was supported by two columns, with the bimah between them in the centre. Later, in the 17th century, there evolved in Central and Eastern Europe a design with the bimah between four central pillars, thereby stressing its importance. This tradition was so strong that some later wooden synagogues retained four wooden posts round the bimah though they were not required structurally to support the roof span.

Italian synagogues of the 16th and 17th centuries departed from the centrality of the bimah by placing it at the end of the synagogue opposite the Ark, thus creating a bi-polar design. The 18th-century Reform Movement went the opposite way. The bimah was linked to the Ark with a platform in front of it facing the congregation seated in rows. This break with tradition was strongly attacked by the Orthodox authorities, who went as far as to declare the arrangement a violation of the Halachah, the religious law. Nevertheless this has become the regular design in Reform and Conservative synagogues. Orthodox synagogues usually have a reading desk apart from the bimah and in front of the Ark, for the use of the cantor and for the rabbi's sermon.

The bimah has had different shapes – square, round, curved or octagonal. It usually has a low railing round it. In mediaeval Spain the bimah was a wooden platform raised high above the ground on columns.

The traditional place for women in a synagogue is in an upper gallery. Where the architectural design did not allow for a gallery, the women would sit on the same level as the men but separated from them by a lattice division (*mechitzah*) or in an adjoining chamber. In Reform temples the segregation between the sexes has been abolished. In Conservative synagogues men and women either sit together or sit on opposite sides of an aisle with no screen between them.

Under the Nazi regime the destruction of synagogues was carried out as a deliberate and planned operation. In the Kristalnacht (Crystal night) of 1938, 280 of them were demolished in a single night in Germany alone. As the Nazi occupation spread across Europe, thousands of synagogues were burnt down by special squads, and in some recorded cases the congregations were locked inside and burnt alive. Altogether, 33,914 European Jewish communities with their synagogues were wiped out by the Nazis.

Chapter Seven

Festivals

Traditional Jewish life has always been regulated by the Hebrew calendar. It is based on the lunar cycle and is adjusted to the solar year by the device of the leap year – except that the lunar year adds a month and not merely a day. There are seven such leap years in each nineteen-year period, so that a Hebrew date and its corresponding secular date will coincide once every nineteen years. For example, the State of Israel was proclaimed on 15 May 1948, which was the fifth day of the Hebrew month of Iyar. Since Israel Independence Day is celebrated according to the Hebrew date, it again occurred on 15 May in 1967, and will do so next time after a further nineteen years, in 1986.

The Christian calendar is reckoned from the putative year when Jesus was circumcised; the Jewish calendar from the putative year of the Creation. The year AD 1980 corresponds to the Jewish year 5740.

For traditional Jewry the pivotal dates of the year have always been the festivals that punctuate the Jewish calendar. The most ancient of the festivals are those that are laid down in the Torah (Pentateuch). They fall into two groups. The first is the New Year (*Rosh ha-Shanah*) that ushers in ten days of penitence culminating in the Day of Atonement (*Yom Kippur*). This is the most solemn religious interlude in the year, known traditionally as the 'Days of Awe' and called in the Western world by the term High Holy Days.

The second group are the three 'pilgrim festivals', Passover (*Pesach*) in the Spring, the Feast of Weeks (*Shavuot*) in the early summer, and the Feast of Booths (*Succot*) in the autumn. (Succot is followed immediately by the festive day of *Simchat Torah*, the Rejoicing of the Law.) On these occasions the farming population used to bring their offerings to the Temple in Jerusalem and mingle with crowds of pilgrims from the Diaspora communities. These three festivals originate in the agricultural cycle of the year in the Land of Israel.

In whatever climate Jews find themselves – even in the southern hemisphere where the seasons are reversed – Pesach, Shavuot and Succot are celebrated at times and with rites that are directly related to farm life in the ancient homeland. Each of these festivals has also acquired an historical context related to the great national and religious experience of the Exodus.

In the Diaspora a 'Second Day' is added in the observance of the

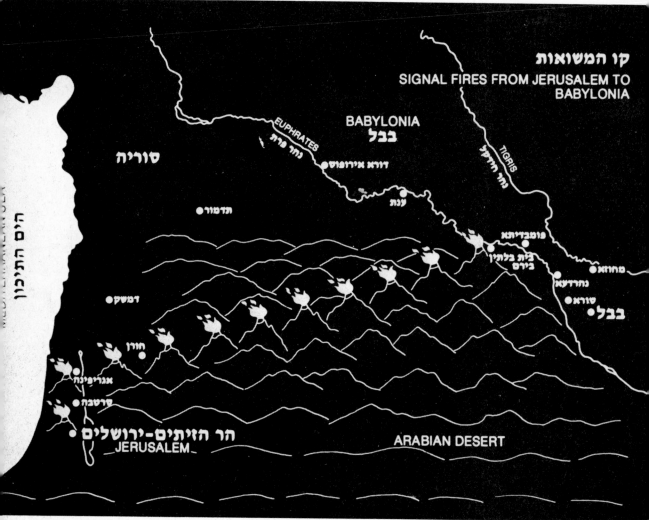

קו המשואות
SIGNAL FIRES FROM JERUSALEM TO BABYLONIA

BABYLONIA
בבל

EUPHRATES נהר פרת

TIGRIS נהר חדקל

סוריה

דורא אירופוס

ענת

תדמור

פומבדיתא
בית בלתין בירם

מחוזא
נהרדעא

דמשק

סורא

בבל

חזור

אגריפינה

ערבה

הר הזיתים-ירושלים
JERUSALEM

ARABIAN DESERT

Signalling the New Month

The map shows a chain of bonfires on high points stretching from the Mount of Olives in Jerusalem across the desert to Babylonia. When two witnesses reported to the religious leaders in Jerusalem that they had sighted the new moon, this indicated the start of the lunar month. That fact was communicated to Diaspora communities by the speediest means possible, so that their calendar could be kept in line with that in the Land of Israel. The line of beacons was used to 'telegraph' that signal to Babylonia.

biblical festivals – except for Yom Kippur, since a two-day fast would be too onerous; and for the New Year, which came to be celebrated for two days in the Land of Israel as well. In the case of Passover, the *Seder* is repeated on the second evening in the Diaspora.

The reason for the extra Diaspora day is to ensure that at least one of them will be the correct one. In ancient times, it was the Sanhedrin in Jerusalem who determined the opening day of each Hebrew month by reporting the time of the new moon, and passing the word to the Diaspora communities. Communications were uncertain, and increasing one day to two reduced the risk of getting the date wrong.

Other festivals are of later origin, and are 'minor' in the sense that they do not have the same degree of sanctity as the Torah festivals. *Purim*, in early spring (March) is connected with an episode at the Persian court, related in the *Book of Esther*. The Feast of Dedication (*Chanukkah*) occurs about the same time as Christmas and is post-

56

(continued on page 59)

Passover (Pesach)

This model depicts a family sitting down to the Passover meal (*Seder*) in 15th-century Spain.

Passover (*Pesach*) is the most festive and important family occasion of the Jewish year. It originated in ancient times as the Spring festival in the Land of Israel, marking the end of the rainy season and the beginning of the grain harvest. During the Temple period Pesach was one of the three great pilgrimage festivals, when farmers brought their offerings to the Temple, and Jerusalem was crowded with thousands of pilgrims from the Diaspora communities.

Passover commemorates a central event in the biblical story, the Exodus from Egypt and God's deliverance of the Children of Israel from bondage:

'And when your children say to you, 'What do you mean by this service?' you shall say, 'It is the sacrifice of the Lord's passover, for he passed over the houses of the people of Israel in Egypt, when he slew the Egyptians but spared our houses.
(Ex. 12:26,27)

In Israel the festival lasts seven days, with the ceremonial family meal (*Seder*) on the first evening. The first and last days are holidays while those in between, though festive, are days when work is permitted. In the Diaspora there are eight days of Passover, with the Seder repeated on the second evening as well.

Before the start of the festival, every scrap of leaven (*chametz*) must be collected and destroyed – bread, pastry, and any foodstuffs such as porridge or beer made from grain. The Ashkenazim, but not the Sephardim, include rice in the ban. Cooking utensils, dishes and cutlery must be cleansed by boiling or heating, though many households keep duplicate sets just for Passover use. From then until the end of the Passover, *matzah* (unleavened bread) is eaten instead of bread, in accordance with the passage in the *Book of Exodus*: 'And they baked unleavened cakes of the dough which they had brought out of Egypt . . . because they were thrust out of Egypt and could not tarry . . .' (*Ex. 12:39*)

On the festive Seder table are a number of items that have a symbolic use during the evening. Three cakes of matzot are placed one above the other, and covered by an ornamental cloth. On a special Seder dish, usually painted with quotations and scenes from the Haggadah, the following are set out in a prescribed order:

a shank bone of lamb, to recall the paschal lamb sacrificed by each family at the Temple of Jerusalem.

a roasted egg symbolizing the burnt offering at the Temple (it may have been an ancient Spring fertility symbol).

a dish of salt water symbolizing the Israelite tears.

lettuce, parsley or celery (*karpas*) dipped into the salt water and eaten.

bitter herbs (*maror*), usually horse-radish, symbolizes the bitter lot of the Israelites under the yoke of the Egyptians.

charoset, a sweet paste made from grated apples, almonds and wine as a symbol of the mortar used by the Israelites when laying bricks during their Egyptian bondage.

The Seder evening is devoted to the reading of the Haggadah. The reading is interrupted for the meal and resumed afterwards. Woven through the Haggadah are a series of ritual acts: partaking of the karpas, bitter herbs, and charoset, drinking four cups of wine (two before the meal and two after), the various blessings, and the washing of the hands. At the outset the middle one of the three cakes of matzot is broken into two and one piece, called the *afikoman*, is hidden by the head of the family, to be ransomed with a gift when the children find it.

A full cup of wine called 'Elijah's cup' stands on the table. As the Prophet Elijah will herald the coming of the Messiah, it symbolizes the hopes for a final redemption. To-wards the end of the service the front door is opened to indicate that all Jews are awaiting the arrival of Elijah.

The Haggadah's theme, the Exodus from Egypt, must have had ominous overtones for a 15th-century Spanish-Jewish family such as that depicted in the model. The Golden Age of the Jews in Spain was over, and the clouds of persecution were gath-ering over their heads. Already some of their number had accepted formal baptism as New Christians, while continuing to practise the Jewish faith in secret. Towards the end of that century, in 1492, all the Jews would be expelled from Spain.

'Days of Awe' (High Holy Days)

See colour page 40

Jews at prayer on the Day of Atone-ment – representation taken from a painting by Maurycy Gottlieb, dated 1878. Gottlieb (1856–79) was an outstanding Polish-Jewish artist who died at the age of twenty-three. Many of his paintings are on Jewish themes. His younger brother Leopold (1883–1934), also a painter, became a well-known member of the Paris school.

The 'Days of Awe' (or High Holy Days) are the most solemn period of the Jewish religious year. The New Year (*Rosh ha-Shanah*) is the begin-ning of ten days of penitence that reach their climax on the Day of Atonement.

Unlike the other holidays, the High Holy Days are neither agricul-tural in origin nor do they com-memorate any significant episode in the national history. They concern the individual Jew and his relation-ship with God and his fellow men.

According to Jewish belief, the New Year ushers in the period of ten days when the conduct of each person during the preceding year will be judged by God, and it will be decreed who shall be inscribed in the 'Book of Life' and who in the 'Book of Death'. The key rite in the synagogue service on Rosh ha-Shanah is the blowing of the ram's horn (*Shofar*), in a fixed series of notes.

The rituals of the High Holy Days give central importance to the con-cept of repentance. God is not only just but merciful, and the remorseful sinner can gain divine forgiveness and a suspended sentence. That is why the first ten days of the New Year must be set aside as a period of penitence, and the Day of Atone-ment, when the verdict is 'signed', devoted entirely to prayer and fast-ing. The spirit of this, the holiest day of the year, is reflected in the passage in *Leviticus* that '. . . on this day shall atonement be made for you, to cleanse you; from all your sins you shall be clean before the Lord. It is a sabbath of solemn rest to you, and you shall afflict yourselves; . . .' (*Lev. 16:30–31*)

A confession covering a long list of sins is recited ten times during the day's service, which is concluded with the blowing of the Shofar.

The most celebrated prayer in the Yom Kippur liturgy is the *Kol Nidre* ('all vows') sung to an ancient melody on the eve of the Holy day. It is a formula in Aramaic for the annul-ment of all personal vows and oaths made unwittingly and not affecting other persons. The tradition goes back to about the 9th century AD.

Pesach: The Haggadah

See colour page 40

The *Haggadah* has been the most popular and the most profusely il-lustrated Jewish religious work in Diaspora history. The Birds Head Haggadah is one of a number of beautiful illuminated versions that have survived from the Middle Ages. One of the earliest and most sumptu-ous Sephardi ones is the 14th-century Golden Haggadah, now in the British Museum. Haggadot started to be printed in the 15th century. Since then there have been thousands of different examples, many of them illustrated with quaint woodcuts.

The Haggadah is a collection of benedictions, biblical and talmudic references, commentaries, stories and folk songs. Its central theme is an account of the Exodus and a discus-sion of its meaning. The recital is introduced by a young child asking four set questions that concern the difference between that particular night and all other nights. The expla-nations that follow expand on the Haggadah injunction that 'in every generation each Jew should regard himself as though he personally went forth from Egypt'.

biblical. It commemorates the deliverance of the Temple during the Maccabean Revolt in the 2nd century BC. Various memorial days were added in the course of time. The ninth day of the month of Av (*Tish'a be'Av*) was accepted as the day of mourning and fast for the destruction of the First Temple in 586 BC and the Second Temple in AD 70. In the present generation, Holocaust Day was established in 1951 by the Israel Parliament (*Knesset*) as a national day of remembrance for victims of the Nazis. It coincided with the date of the Warsaw Ghetto uprising in 1943. It is suitably marked by Diaspora communities.

Israel's Independence Day in May is also celebrated throughout the Jewish world.

Pesach Seder Plate

Above *A replica of a German Seder plate of engraved pewter c.1800, with a scene of a group celebrating the Passover.*

The Seder plate has taken a variety of forms. Some European Ashkenazi communities have used a three-tiered stand for the three cakes of matzot. The Sephardim as a rule have a large platter or flat basket with the matzot in the centre and the other items around it.

Pesach: The 'Four Sons'

Above *A replica of a gilded silver wine goblet for Pesach from 17th-century Germany. It is decorated with the figures of the 'Four Sons' from the Haggadah.*

The Haggadah interprets four passages from the Bible as the reaction of four sons attending the Passover ceremony: one wise, one foolish, one simple and one who does not know enough to ask any questions.

Shavu'ot

Above right *Moses on Mount Sinai holding the Tablets of the Law. A miniature from the Sarajevo Haggadah, Spain, 14th century.*

Shavu'ot, the Feast of Weeks, is one of the three 'pilgrimage festivals', the other two being Passover and Succot (the Feast of Booths). In ancient Israel, it was an agricultural festival in early summer, marking the end of the barley harvest and the beginning of the wheat harvest. Its name is derived from the passage in *Leviticus* stating that seven weeks must be counted from the second day after Passover, and on the following day an offering of new grain must be brought to the Temple. The festival is also known in the Bible as 'the Harvest Feast' and as 'the Festival of the First Fruits'.

Shavu'ot commemorates the date on which the Law was given to Moses on Mount Sinai, and Orthodox Jews often spend the whole night of the festival reading and discussing scriptural and other passages.

On this festival it is customary to read the *Book of Ruth* in the synagogue. The setting for that idyllic story is harvest time in the Judean hills.

Succot

Right *A blessing over the four species at the Western Wall.*

The festival of *Succot* (Booths or Tabernacles) occurs in the autumn and lasts for seven days. Like the other two biblical pilgrimage festivals, Passover and the Feast of Weeks, Succot has a double dimen-

Simchat Torah in the Great Synagogue, Moscow, in the 1960s.

sion: the first is the agricultural aspect, denoting the season of the autumn harvest (it is also called 'the feast of harvest' in the *Book of Exodus*). The second significance is historical, recalling the sojourn of the Children of Israel in the desert after the Exodus. The two distinctive customs of Succot are the booths and the Four Species.

The booths are constructed adjacent to the house, on a porch or in a yard. They are roofed with branches, and decorated inside with fruit and gay curtains or wall hangings. The members of the family eat their meals in the booth during the week of the festival, thereby identifying themselves with the nomadic life of their ancestors in the wilderness, and also with their former ancestors in ancient Israel who erected booths in the fields at harvest time to provide shade while guarding the crops.

The 'four species' carried in procession in synagogue are a citron (*etrog*), and a palm branch bound with twigs of myrtle and willow (called the *lulav*).

Throughout every teeming ghetto and shtetl, Succot with the booths and plant species would bring alive the nostalgic folk-memory of the rural life in the homeland.

Simchat Torah

Simchat Torah (the Rejoicing of the Law) is celebrated in Eretz Israel on the eighth day from the beginning of Succot, and on the ninth day in the Diaspora.

The Torah (*Pentateuch*) is read in its entirety in the synagogue services during the course of one year. On Simchat Torah the cycle is completed and re-started, when one worshipper reads the last portion of *Deuteronomy* and another the first portion of *Genesis*.

It is a joyful occasion. All the Torah Scrolls are taken out of the Ark and carried seven times in procession

Lighting the Chanukkah lights in the synagogue. A drawing by Wilhelm Thielmann, Germany, 1898.

round the synagogue to the loud singing of prayers. By tradition, the children get gifts of candy, nuts and raisins.

Discouraged from giving public expression to their Jewish identity, many Russian Jews nevertheless do so by congregating inside and outside synagogues on special occasions such as Simchat Torah. Tens of thousands gather in Moscow, marking the revival of Jewish sentiment in the Soviet Union.

Chanukkah

Chanukkah (Dedication) is the late-comer among important Jewish festivals, and came into existence in the post-biblical period. It is both national and religious in essence, marking the successful revolt of the Maccabees in the 2nd century BC, and their re-dedication of the Temple in Jerusalem. According to legend, a miracle occurred when the sacred lamp that had only enough purified oil for one day went on burning for eight. It is, therefore, also called the Feast of Lights, and its emblem is the eight-branched candelabrum (*chanukkiah*). In every Jewish home a candle is lit the first evening and an additional candle is lit each evening thereafter for the eight days of the festival.

Chanukkah occurs in late December, usually about the time of Christmas. It is a time for parties and gifts for the children.

Actors in a Purim *play. A woodcut from the 'Sefer ha-Minhagim' ('Book of Customs'), Italy, 1400.*

Purim

The early spring festival of *Purim* is the merriest event in the Jewish calendar of festivals. By tradition it has a carnival atmosphere, with folk-dancing, the children decked out in fancy-dress, the performance of Purim plays and the consumption of triangular buns stuffed with poppy seed, called 'Haman's ears'.

The background for the celebration is set out in the biblical *Scroll of Esther*, which is read out in synagogue on the festival. The Diaspora episode it describes is supposed to have taken place in Persia during the reign of the monarch Xerxes I (486–65 BC), who is called Ahasuerus in Hebrew. The massacre planned by his wicked chief minister Haman was foiled by the beautiful Queen Esther and her sagacious relative Mordecai. The word 'purim' refers to the lots cast by Haman to pick a propitious day for the evil deed.

It is strange that the Scroll of Esther should have been among the works included in the Writings, the last group of books in the Old Testament. It has no religious aspect, and God is not even mentioned in it. It was probably written about the 2nd century BC by an unknown author, and it is questionable whether the events described in it actually took place – at any rate, there is no corroboration of them in Persian records. Yet the story has had a strong hold on Jewish sentiment down the centuries. It stands for a rare victory against the evil forces arrayed against the Jewish people. Hitler was in direct descent from Haman, with a long line of persecutors in between. In the bloody context of Jewish history, a pogrom that did *not* take place is indeed a cause for celebration.

Chapter Eight

The World of the Talmud

The ancient Hebrews drew no clear distinction between legal, moral and religious precepts. All laws came from God and were sacred, whether they dealt with forms of worship, family relations, property, criminal offences or any other aspect of daily life. God's commandments appear in all the Books of the Torah (Pentateuch). Together, these biblical precepts formed the Written Law or Mosaic Code.

After the text of the Torah took its final form, its legal provisions continued to be discussed, interpreted and adjusted to changing conditions and needs by succeeding generations of Jewish sages and scholars. Not only did moral and social ideas alter and external circumstances change, but in the Mosaic Code itself there were gaps to be filled and obscurities to be clarified. For instance, very little was laid down concerning so basic and complicated a subject as marriage and divorce.

The continuous process of interpretation of the Written Law produced a vast body of rulings and opinions known as the Oral Law. However, the terms 'Written' and 'Oral' are somewhat misleading. The Torah itself was derived from centuries of oral traditions that began to be written down about the 10th century BC, several centuries after Moses received the Ten Commandments on Mount Sinai. On the other hand, the Oral Law was in due course compiled in written form, in the *Mishnah* and then in the expanded Talmud.

A modern secular analogy for the relationship between Written and Oral Law is that between statutes passed by parliament and the case law that comes into being as the courts interpret and apply the statutes.

The Oral Law came to be accepted as having virtually equal validity with the Written Law. Both are regarded as having divine authority, and by tradition the origin of both is attributed to Moses the great Lawgiver. There is one essential difference between the two. The provisions of the Written Law are fixed and immutable in the Scriptures. Yet by its very nature, the Oral Law can never be given final form. Its development is an open-ended process that has gone on for 2,000 years and will go on as long as the Jewish people remains a living entity.

The development of the Oral Law was well advanced before AD 70. By the reign of the Hasmonean ruler John Hyrcanus I (134–104 BC),

(continued on page 68)

Ten Topics from the Talmud

1   *A man is responsible for damage caused by his property. One of the four main categories of damages is that caused by a goring ox.*

2   *A bill of divorce is handed over. Detailed discussions in the Talmud are devoted to the form of marriage and divorce documents, their legal formulation, the method of handing them over, and how they are witnessed.*

3   *Two men have found a garment and both claim it. The Talmud deals with ways to establish ownership of goods in case of such disputes.*

4   *'A Sabbath of Sabbaths Holy to the Lord.' The synagogue prayer for Sabbath eve was instituted in Babylonia. The existence of synagogues outside the towns made it necessary to lay down special regulations for attending the services without violating the Sabbath.*

5 In the picture, an emissary of the rabbinical court comes to Rabbi Huna and asks him to judge a case. Since he gets no payment the rabbi agrees, provided arrangements are made for someone to pick his fruit while he is away. Many outstanding rabbis were engaged in agriculture.

6 Babylonian Jews, especially the more distinguished, brought their dead to the Land of Israel for burial. The seven days of mourning began when the body left the city.

7 Sabbath desecration. The Jewish inhabitants of a village in Babylonia went out on the Sabbath to collect fish which had been washed up into a field from a flooded pond. The sages excommunicated them.

8 Purification is an important subject in the Talmud. The ritual bath is a basic requirement.

9 The Talmud says that a scholar who brings his produce to the market has a right to offer it for sale first. The question is, who is a scholar? One rabbi brought his figs by boat to sell, but a local scholar examined his erudition and failed him. The figs were a dead loss.

10 A man who owns property along the river is not allowed to cultivate it right up to the bank but he must leave a path for people to walk along, or for the use of animals pulling boats along the towpath.

two conflicting trends and parties existed in Eretz Israel: the Sadducees and the Pharisees. The Sadducees represented an Establishment that included the palace, the Temple priesthood and an affluent upper class. It was natural for this privileged group to be conservative in its outlook. The Sadducees took their religious stand on the diligent performance of Temple rituals and sacrifices, and on the literal adherence to the Mosaic Code as set out in the Old Testament.

The Pharisees were a party that appealed to the artisans, the petty traders and the peasant farmers. They wanted the Law to be expounded directly to the people, as Ezra the Scribe had started doing when he came to Jerusalem from Babylon several centuries earlier. They asserted that this could be done by any scholar who was learned in the Law, outside the ranks of the Temple priesthood. The Pharisees interpreted the Scriptures in a flexible manner, and adjusted them to changing ideas. The liberal attitude of Hillel, the leading Pharisee sage in the 1st century BC, is illustrated by an oft-quoted remark. When a Gentile convert challenged him to expound the basic tenets of Judaism while standing on one foot, he answered: 'What is hateful to you, do not unto your neighbour; this is the entire Torah, all the rest is commentary.'

According to the Pharisees, the Oral Law had equal validity with the Written Law, and both originated with Moses. During the reign of Herod the Great (37–4 BC) the Pharisaic movement had produced two great schools of law, headed, respectively, by Hillel and Shammai, the leaders of the *Sanhedrin* (Supreme Religious Council). It is related that when Shammai was asked by a puzzled Gentile, 'How many Torahs do you have?', he replied, 'Two – one written and one oral.'

After the fall of Jerusalem in AD 70, the bulk of the Palestinian Jewish community (*Yishuv* in Hebrew) remained intact in the rest of the country, under Roman rule. With the monarchy and the Temple priesthood swept away, the leadership of the community passed exclusively to an aristocracy of learning – the sages and teachers who expounded and applied the Torah. One of the eminent rabbis, Yochanan ben-Zakkai, had gained permission from Titus, the Roman commander, to leave the doomed city of Jerusalem and start an academy at the small town of Yavneh in the coastal plain (near present-day Rehovot). Legend has it that he was carried out of the city in a coffin borne by two of his disciples. Other scholars gathered around Rabbi Yochanan. The Sanhedrin, which had been the highest council in the State, was reconstituted with the leading Yavneh sages as its members. Rabbi Gamaliel, a respected scholar who was a direct descendant of the great Hillel, succeeded Yochanan ben-Zakkai and became President (*Nasi*) of the Sanhedrin. The office was to remain an hereditary one for the next few centuries. The Nasi was accepted by the Roman authorities as the Patriarch or official head of Palestinian Jewry, and he was accepted by the Diaspora Jewish communities as their spiritual leader.

A major measure of consolidation taken at Yavneh, about AD 90, was to finalize the canon of the Old Testament. It consisted of twenty-four books, grouped into three sections: *The Torah* or *Five Books of Moses* (*Pentateuch*); *The Prophets* (including the historical *Books of Joshua*, *Samuel* and *Kings*); and *The Writings*. This Canon was to remain fixed throughout the ages. It may be said that at Yavneh the Jewish religious heritage was preserved after the great disaster.

Jewish national sentiment continued to smoulder in Palestine and burst into flames again with the Bar Kochba Revolt of AD 132. At first it was successful. The Roman garrisons were driven out of southern Judea, Jerusalem was recaptured, and new coins were struck to mark the liberation. But within three years the emperor Hadrian had brutally crushed the insurrection. The southern half of the country was left devastated and almost denuded of its population. Jerusalem was barred to Jews and on its ruins Hadrian built a Roman garrison town called Aelia Capitolina. The embers of national resistance had been stamped out. The Jews from now on were a minority in their own land.

Akiba was the foremost Jewish sage in the early part of the 2nd century AD, with his school located at Bnai Brak. He devoted himself to the arduous task of bringing order into the Oral Law, sorting it out according to subjects and relating it to the biblical text. Akiba supported the Bar Kochba Revolt, and when it was crushed he was arrested and tortured to death by the Roman authorities.

Akiba's outstanding pupil **Rabbi Meir** established his own school at Tiberias, and continued the collation of the Oral Law.

Judah ha-Nasi was the most erudite Jewish teacher of the late 2nd and early 3rd centuries AD, and head of the rabbinical court. His prestige was such that in the later Talmudic literature he is referred to simply as 'Rabbi'. As *Nasi* (Patriarch), he was the official leader of Palestinian Jewry. At that time the centre of Jewish life in the country had shifted to the Galilee, in the wake of the Bar Kochba tragedy.

Judah's historic achievement was the editing of the Mishnah. He organized a panel of the most eminent Jewish scholars to work with him on the systematic codification of the Oral Law. The project took over half a century.

The Aramaic word *Tannaim* (teachers) was applied to the five generations of Palestinian scholars between the deaths of Hillel and Shammai (AD 10 and AD 30 respectively) and the completion of the Mishnah. Some 140 individual Tannaim can be listed from various sources. The key figures among them were Rabbis Jochanan ben-Zakkai, Akiba, Meir and Judah ha-Nasi.

In compiling the Mishnah, the teachings of the Tannaim were collated, and on disputed points the opinions were quoted of the Hillel and Shammai schools and of other leading authorities. The work already done by Akiba and Meir provided a point of departure. The Code was completed about AD 210, but it is uncertain whether it was reduced to writing at that time or at a later date.

The Mishnah was divided into six Orders; each Order was sub-divided into tractates dealing with specific topics (63 in all) and each tractate into chapters. The six Orders were:

1 'Seeds' (*Zera'im*) – laws relating to agriculture;
2 'Seasons' (*Mo'ed*) – laws relating to the Sabbath and Jewish festivals;
3 'Women' (*Nashim*) – laws relating to marriage, divorce and kindred family topics;
4 'Damages' (*Nezikin*) – laws relating to civil claims and criminal offences;
5 'Holy things' (*Kodashim*) – laws relating to Temple sacrifices and rituals. (Though the Temple was destroyed, it was felt necessary to preserve its regulations for the future.)
6 'Purities' (*Tohorot*) – laws concerning ritual purity and impurity.

Amora is an Aramaic word meaning a spokesman or an interpreter. The primary function of an amora was to repeat in a loud, clear voice

The Spread of the Talmud

Above *One of four rabbinical scholars, captured by Moslem pirates at sea, being ransomed by the leaders of the Jewish community of Kairouan, North Africa (modern Tunisia).*

The story of the Four Captives was current in mediaeval Spain and was preserved in the important work *Sefer ha-Kabbalah* (the 'Book of Tradition'), written by the Spanish-Jewish philosopher, physician and astronomer Abraham ibn-Daud (1110–80). According to this account, four rabbis from Babylonia set sail from Bari in southern Italy on a mission to raise funds for charity. When they were captured and sold into slavery, they were redeemed by the Jewish communities in Kairouan, Alexandria and Cordoba in Spain, and were instrumental in establishing new Talmudic academies in these cities.

Although the story is of doubtful authenticity, it can be seen as a parable for the decline in the paramount authority of the Babylonian academies in the Jewish world, and the rise of new centres of learning in North Africa and Spain, based on the Babylonian Talmud.

The Karaite Movement

See colour page 105

This diorama shows the Sabbath being observed without lights, one of the practices of the Karaite sect of Judaism that sprang up in the 8th century AD.

It is accepted that the founder of the Karaite movement was Anan ben-David. It is said that he was aggrieved at having been passed over in the succession to the hereditary post of exilarch, the titular head of the Babylonian community. Whether that was so or not, Anan came out against the pre-eminence of Talmudic scholarship, and in favour of a return to the biblical source of authority. His followers called themselves *Karaites* ('Scripturalists') as opposed to the Rabbanites, who clung to the Oral Law expounded by the rabbis.

Karaism became a popular movement in revolt against the complexities of the Talmud and the intellectual sophistication of the scholars. As usually happens with a breakaway movement, it attracted to itself elements of social protest among the under-privileged. Developing its own literature, it spread rapidly from Babylonia through the rest of the Islamic world, including Palestine, Egypt and Spain.

Karaism might well have become the dominant ideology of Jewish religious life, except for one single but very powerful opponent. He was Saadyah ben-Joseph (AD 882–942), a brilliant Egyptian-born scholar who was appointed head of the academy of Sura and therefore one of the two Geonim of Babylonia – the other being the head of the academy of Pumbedita. As the foremost Jewish

the words of a rabbi teaching a large class, or to repeat a Hebrew lesson in Aramaic, a Semitic language akin to Hebrew, that was the colloquial daily tongue of the Jews in that era. The term came to be used in a wider sense, for the scholars who interpreted and expounded the law during the three centuries between the Mishnah and the conclusion of the Talmud. This work went on in two centres, the Palestinian and the Babylonian, with a constant interchange of scholars and opinions between them.

From Talmudic quotations and references, over two thousand Amoraim can be identified by name. The titles they were given differed in the two centres. The Palestinian scholars were called *rabbi* (my teacher), with some of the most distinguished given the more ceremonious form of *rabban*. The Babylonian sages were given the title of *rav* or *mar*, both meaning 'master' (*Mar* has survived in modern Hebrew as the equivalent of 'Mr'.)

By Jewish tradition, religious teaching and study were an unpaid profession. Those teachers who were unable to support themselves by other work, such as traders or artisans, were helped by donations from the well-to-do or by scholarship funds available to the academies.

The Hebrew word *Talmud* means 'teaching' and is used for each of the two great compilations of the Oral Law, the Palestinian (or Jerusalem) Talmud and the Babylonian Talmud.

The two centuries of expounding the Mishnah that produced the Jerusalem Talmud was carried out mainly in the Palestinian academies of Sepphoris and Tiberias in the Galilee, and Caesarea and Lydda on the coastal plain. By about AD 400 this scholarly impetus petered out as the Palestinian community declined under Roman rule. The Jerusalem Talmud has survived only in an incomplete form and came to be overshadowed by the much larger and more comprehensive Babylonian Talmud.

From the 3rd century, the centre of Jewish scholarship moved eastwards from Palestine to Babylonia (Mesopotamia). The two pioneers of the new centre were Abba the Tall (simply known as Rav) and Mar Samuel. **Rav** was sent from Babylon to Palestine to study under Judah ha-Nasi and was his most brilliant pupil. On returning to his adopted land, he founded a new school at Sura. It soon became the most popular one in the country, and was to last for 800 years. Rav's contemporary, **Mar Samuel**, a noted scholar, physician and astronomer, headed the academy at Nehardea, the principal Jewish settlement in Babylonia at that time. After the city was sacked by an invading force in the 3rd century, another school founded at Pumbedita came to rival Sura in importance. A modern historian has termed these two academies 'the Oxford and Cambridge of Babylonian Jewry'.

The main compiler of the Babylonian Talmud was **Rav Ashi**, head of the Sura academy in the 4th century. During his fifty-two years in this post he sifted and arranged the bulk of the commentary that had grown up round the Mishnah. The vast accumulation of material was

(continued on page 74)

intellect of his time, Saadyah Gaon launched a powerful counter-attack on the Karaite movement. At the same time, his own positive achievements undermined the validity of their protests. He championed traditional Judaism, gave it a philosophical basis in his book *Beliefs and Opinions*, compiled a prayer book, founded the scientific study of Hebrew, translated the whole of the Old Testament into colloquial Arabic, and gave a fresh emphasis to biblical study.

With so formidable a champion of the scholastic establishment, the growth of the Karaite movement was arrested. From then on it declined steadily in numbers and influence. Before the Second World War, there were about 10,000 members of the sect in Russia, mostly in the Crimea, and 2,000 elsewhere, mostly in Egypt.

The Burning of the Talmud

See colour pages 108 and 109

This diorama shows cartloads of Talmudic literature being collected in 1242 in the square in front of the Notre Dame Cathedral, Paris, before being fed into a nearby bonfire. Twenty-four cartloads were destroyed on that occasion.

The attack on the Talmud was one aspect of the persecution of the Jews in mediaeval Europe. It figures in the public disputations that took place during this period between Christian churchmen and Jewish rabbis. These unequal contests, designed to 'prove' the error of Judaism, were usually promoted by the Dominican Order that served the Church as a heresy-hunting agency. The witnesses for the church were as a rule Jewish apostates, eager to vindicate their change of faith. One such apostate was Nicholas Donin, who had become a Dominican monk. In AD 1239, he submitted to Pope Gregory a formal denunciation of the Talmud as containing blasphemous and immoral material, with a list of thirty-five alleged examples. The Pope decreed that all copies of the Talmud should be seized, pending a public investigation. The kings of England

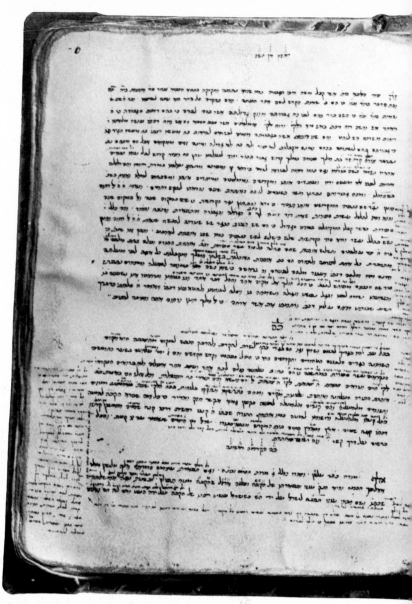

A representation of the ten Sefirot (divine emanations) from the 'Sefer ha-Zohar' ('The Book of Splendour'), Italy, 1400.

and Spain ignored the decree, but in France it was carried out by the pious King Louis IX (afterwards canonized as St Louis). At his order, Jewish institutions in Paris were raided on a Sabbath and a large number of copies of the Talmud and other sacred books were impounded.

The public 'case' took place before a panel of bishops and Dominican friars, in the presence of the Queen Mother. The case against the Talmud was presented by Donin. Appearing for the defence were four eminent Jewish scholars, whose refutation of the charges fell on deaf ears. What is more, the scholars were obliged to speak in Latin, a tongue less familiar

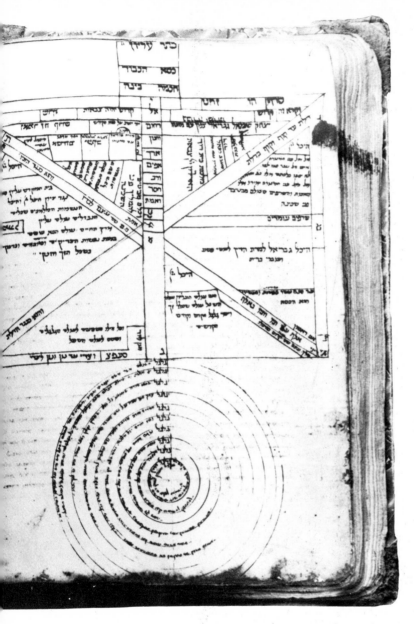

example followed elsewhere in Italy.

In 1757 hundreds of volumes of the Talmud were burnt in Poland by order of the ecclesiastical authorities, after the fierce controversies that broke out between the rabbis and the Frankists, a mystical sect founded by the pseudo-messiah Jacob Frank (1726–91). When the sect was excommunicated by the rabbinical authorities it gained the protection of the local bishop by renouncing the Talmud and accepting the concept of the Holy Trinity.

The Kabbalah

Left *The ten Sefirot.*

The ordinary meaning of the Hebrew word Kabbalah is tradition. In the religious context it denotes the mystical trend that has existed in the Jewish faith since antiquity. The subject matter included the attributes of God, the mysteries of Creation, the future Messianic redemption, the hidden meanings in biblical verses and the powers latent in certain combinations of letters and numbers.

Kabbalah was the preoccupation of small coteries of scholars, whose mystical frame of mind was usually attained by fasting and intense meditation. As a branch of Jewish lore, it came to a climax in the appearance in 13th-century Spain of the *Zohar* or *Book of Splendour*. This was said to have been written by a 2nd-century Jewish sage. The *Zohar* was the basis for all later Kabbalistic documents. Translated into Latin, it also had an influence on some mediaeval Christian churchmen.

After the expulsion of the Jews from Spain at the end of the 15th century, the leading Kabbalists settled in Safad in the Galilee, one of the four Jewish holy cities in Palestine. The most important personality among them was Isaac Luria, later known by his acronym *Ha' Ari* ('the Lion'). His teachings, written down by his disciples, gave Kabbalah a widespread impact on the Jewish world. They were eagerly studied by the Baal Shem Tov and were absorbed into the beliefs of the Chassidic movement.

to them than to the Christian clergy. The verdict was a foregone conclusion: the rigged court condemned the Talmud and ordered all copies to be destroyed by fire. The order was carried out in Paris two years later, in 1242. Talmud burning then spread to other parts of France.

A similar step was taken in Italy three centuries later. The Renaissance popes had been tolerant towards the Jews, until the Catholic Counter-Reformation brought about a revival of mediaeval anti-Jewish bigotry. In the middle of the 16th century, Pope Paul IV banned the use of the Talmud and ordered copies to be burnt. A vast pile of Talmudic and rabbinical works was destroyed in Rome on 9 September 1553 – an reduced to writing by the end of the 5th century. The final editing of the text was carried out during the next half-century by a succession of scholars known as the *Saboraim* (Reasoners).

The Babylonian Talmud is a gigantic work, running to some $2\frac{1}{2}$ million words on nearly 6,000 folio pages. An English translation, the Soncino Talmud, has been published in thirty-five volumes.

In the Talmud each short extract from the Mishnah was followed by the rabbinical discussion on it, known as the *Gemara*, an Aramaic word meaning 'completion'. All printed editions of the Talmud since the 16th century have added, on either side of the text, further explanatory notes from later commentaries, chiefly Rashi, the 11th-century French scholar and his pupils.

The lay-out and pagination of each page of the Talmud was standardized in the first printed edition, made by a non-Jewish printer, Daniel Bomberg of Venice, in AD 1520–3.

While the Mishnah itself is straightforward and concise, the Gemara commentary is not easy to read. The contents of the Talmud were not originally devised as a written document. It is really a synopsis of the verbal discussions that went on in the academies for several centuries. That fact accounts for the discursive style, the frequent digressions from one topic to another, the detours into byways of anecdote and homily, and the raising of points that to a modern mind may seem trivial and irrelevant. The language is not Hebrew but colloquial Aramaic.

There are actually two different categories of material. Woven into the Halachah, the exposition of religious law, is the Aggadah – a miscellany of non-legal elements: legends about biblical figures, sayings and reminiscences of the Talmudic sages, moral instruction, philosophical discourse, parables and prayers. Roughly a quarter of the total text of the Babylonian Talmud consists of Aggadic material.

What emerges strongly in the Talmud is the interplay between critical intellects trained to dialectic methods of a specialized kind, probing and testing all possible answers to Halachic problems. The Talmud has aptly been compared to an ocean – somewhat formless, full of cross-currents, and so vast that few men can swim across it in their life's span.

Because of its bulk, its discursive style, and its method of reflecting diverse opinions on a single issue, the Talmud was not a convenient source of guidance. The post-Talmudic centuries saw a continuing stream of rulings on specific problems and learned treatises on individual tractates. In the mediaeval period there were several important efforts to clarify the general body of the Halachah. Outstanding among them were the works of Rashi, Maimonides and Joseph Caro.

Rashi (1040–1105) – the initials in Hebrew for Rav Solomon ben-Isaac – compiled a set of concise and lucid notes on the Talmud that have remained the accepted key for later studies. Rashi had no sons of his own, but his learned sons-in-law and grandsons, as well as his

The Opponents of Chassidim

Above At the main gate of the Shulhof, the synagogue complex in Vilna, two Chassidim seek an audience with the Vilna Gaon but are turned away by one of his aides.

Rabbi Elijah ben-Solomon Zalman, the Vilna Gaon (1720–97) was the Talmudic genius of his age. He led the fight against the Chassidic movement, and the world of traditional Jewish scholarship rallied behind him. The anti-Chassidic groups were known as the *Mitnagdim* ('Opponents').

The Chassidim were accused of rejecting the values and traditions of Talmudic study, of adopting superstitious practices, and of building up around their 'tzaddikim' a personality cult that almost amounted to idolatry. Feeling against the new sect ran so high that in 1772, and again in 1781, the established leadership issued a ban against it. The edict read: 'They must leave our communities with their wives and children . . . and they should not be given a night's lodging; their ritual slaughter is forbidden; it is forbidden to do business with them, to inter-marry with them, or to assist at their burial.'

pupils and his pupils' pupils, added important supplements known as *Tosephot* (additions), to his commentary. Later editions of the Talmud incorporated Rashi's notes and sometimes passages from the Tosephot, alongside the Talmudic text.

The **Rambam** (the initials stand for Rabbi Moses ben-Maimon) who lived in 12th-century Egypt, was the commanding figure of the mediaeval Jewish world. He is commonly known by the Greek form of his name, Maimonides. Among his major works was the *Mishneh Torah*, a detailed, clear and systematic exposition of the Halachic law. He produced it, as he wrote to a friend, 'to save himself in his advanced age the trouble of consulting the Talmud on every occasion.'

In 16th-century Safad in the Galilee, the scholar and mystic **Joseph Caro** produced the *Shulchan Aruch* (the Arranged Table) as a practical manual of Talmudic Law. It remained the accepted guide for daily Jewish life. The domination of Jewish life by the Oral Law, as compiled in the Talmud, did not go unchallenged. The strong hold of rabbinic learning was twice shaken by movements of dissent – the Karaite schism in the 8th century, and Chassidism in the 18th century.

From early times, the evolution of Judaism was marked by two contending trends. There were the rabbis and teachers who developed the Oral Law as a living, organic and flexible tradition, derived from Holy Writ but adapting it to changing needs. Against that was a more fundamentalist approach that thought the Scriptures must be taken literally and not be subject to interpretation. In the latter part of the Second Temple period, before the destruction in AD 70, this difference was already reflected in the conflict between the Pharisees and the Sadducees. It came to the surface again nearly a thousand years later in Babylonia, with the Karaite movement that sprang up in the 8th century. It spread rapidly and caused a major upheaval in Jewish life at the time. But the movement faded out again, and left little permanent impact.

The mainstream of Jewish religious life once again faced a major challenge in the Chassidic revivalist movement that originated in 18th-century Ukraine. Its founder was Israel ben-Eliezer (AD 1700–60). He was not a learned man, and earned a modest living as a digger of lime. But he seems to have been one of the natural holy men that have arisen from time to time in different faiths and have strongly affected their course. He was given to solitary communion in the countryside, to visions and revelations, and to an intense absorption in the esoteric doctrines of the Kabbalah, the Jewish mysticism that had spread from its centre at Safad in the Galilee. Among simple Jews in Eliezer's native province of Podolia, his reputation spread as a faith-healer of the sick and the afflicted. As a result of the miraculous powers attributed to him, he became known as the **Baal Shem Tov** (the 'Good Wonder Worker'). The facts of his life are little known and are obscured by the legends that afterwards clustered round his memory.

The background to the rise of Chassidism was a period of upheaval and bloodshed in the life of Eastern European Jewry, with the Chmelnicki massacres of 1648 as its grim highlight. During the century that followed conditions remained disturbed in the area, with the Jews subjected to local pogroms, blood-libel accusations and other harassments. A steady stream of refugees moved into Western Europe and the Ottoman empire.

The mood of despair among the Jews aroused the Messianic longings that are embedded in Jewish tradition, and accounted for the extraordinary episode of the false messiah Shabbetai Zevi (AD 1626–76). The belief swept through Jewry that the long-awaited redemption and the Return to the Holy Land were at hand. The hopes collapsed with Shabbetai Zevi's conversion to Islam.

These troubled events left the Jewish masses in Eastern Europe groping for a brand of faith more emotionally satisfying than the sophisticated Talmudic scholarship. The movement that sprang up

The Chassidic Way of Life

See previous page

As a doctrinal system, Chassidism held that the whole universe was a manifestation or 'garment' of God, and the separate existence of living things was an illusion. Through piety and fervent prayer any Jew, however lowly, could attain a state of exultation in which he could experience personal communion with God. In order to do so he had to try to eliminate his own ego. Since everything that existed partook of the divine essence there was no room in life for melancholy or despair. A Jew had to feel joy and a 'burning enthusiasm', expressed not only in prayer but in group singing and dancing.

The Chassidic pattern of life was dominated by the special role of the *tzaddik* ('righteous one'), the religious leader of the group. He was regarded as having a mystical relationship with God, and as able to use the power this gave him in order to bring his disciples closer to their Creator. The tzaddik was venerated by his disciples and had absolute authority over them, even in their personal and business affairs. They maintained him and his court, where they attended on him at the Sabbath meal and came on pilgrimage from afar on the High Holy Days.

from the personality and teaching of the Baal Shem Tov spread rapidly through the communities in the region. Its progress was accelerated by the missionary zeal of the Baal Shem Tov's disciple and successor Dov Baer, the *Maggid* ('the Great Preacher'). The adherents called themselves Chassidim ('the pious ones').

The movement was bitterly fought by the traditional leadership, the so-called *Mitnagdim* ('Opponents'). They rallied behind the great Vilna Gaon, the leading Talmudic scholar of the age. The struggle raged for a generation, up to the Napoleonic Wars, but then gradually died down as the two camps moved into middle ground. The Chassidic movement regained respect for systematic study of the Bible and injected new life into the study of the Talmud. For its part, the rational world of rabbinical law regained some of the emotional elements that lie at the subconscious roots of all religion. Chassidism became part of the Orthodox establishment, while retaining its distinctive ways and beliefs. It was the first dissident movement, since the fall of Jerusalem in AD 70, to win acceptance in the mainstream of Jewish religious life.

Chassidism never evolved into a single cohesive movement with a central leadership. It was divided into a number of local centres, each a self-contained community under its own independent Tzaddik. In some cases these acquired a family dynasty of leaders descended from their original spiritual heads.

In the 20th century the Russian revolution and the Nazi Holocaust eliminated all the Chassidic centres in Europe, just as they eliminated so much else in Jewish life. Some of the survivors of the Chassidic sects re-established themselves in the United States and other Western countries as well as in the State of Israel. For instance, the Williamsburg district of New York is the seat of various Chassidic sects of which the largest is the Satmar dynasty ruled by the Teitelbaum dynasty. Like traditional Chassidic groups elsewhere, they resist the inroads of modern secular life and cling to the traditional and now vanished ways of Eastern European Jewry.

The literature produced by the Chassidic movement has consisted mainly of anthologies of stories and sayings about the Baal Shem Tov and the later masters. A well-known 20th-century collection is the *Tales of the Chassidim* compiled by the celebrated philosopher Martin Buber. The basic tenets of Chassidism had a strong impact on Buber's semi-mystical doctrine of a direct encounter, an 'I-Thou' relationship, between Man and God.

## Chapter Nine

Jewish Religious Culture

A gifted nation leaves its own distinctive mark on human culture. The roots of Western civilization go back to two small peoples in the ancient Mediterranean world – the Greeks and the Hebrews. The Greeks were brilliant innovators in philosophy, the natural sciences, democratic institutions, drama, architecture, sculpture and athletics. The Hebrews excelled in none of these fields. Their special genius lay in religious thought and its literary expression. They originated the concept of a single and universal God, and in the course of its development transmitted it to two daughter faiths, Christianity and Islam. They evolved the Mosaic Code, embodying ethical and social values far ahead of their age, with the Ten Commandments as its focus. The sublime message of the Hebrew prophets still reverberates down the corridors of time. And, in the Old Testament, the ancient Hebrews produced a thousand-year anthology of sacred literature that has been without parallel in the story of man.

For millennia after the biblical period, the Jews remained the People of the Book. As a dispersed nation they clung to their unique God-centered culture, with the written and spoken word as its medium. The stream of religious discourse and writings flowed on from century to century. In its course it shaped the contours of the Diaspora way of life.

Religious learning was the most revered activity open to Jews, and it engaged the best minds of each generation. Indeed, study of the sacred books ranked with prayer as a way to serve God. Moses, through whom God transmitted the Torah to his people, is customarily referred to as Moshe Rabbenu – that is, Moses our Teacher. The central cultural achievement of the Diaspora was the immense accumulation of law, morality and story in the Babylonian Talmud, and the layer upon layer of commentary that derived from it.

There were times of despair when the intricate logic of the Halachah and the discipline of the study-house seemed somehow arid and unsatisfactory. Jews then turned for emotional nourishment to the mysticism of the Kabbalah, to the wild hopes raised by false messiahs, or to the fervour of the Chassidic movement with its holy Tzaddikim and its ecstatic group dances and tunes. But the powerful intellectual thrust of Jewish culture always reasserted itself. In modern times, it

The Torah Scribe

The Torah Scribe belongs to an honourable profession that goes back to biblical times. He spends his life writing Scrolls of the Law, also the inscriptions used in *tefillin* (phylacteries) and in the mezuzot affixed to doorposts.

Meticulous rules are laid down for the scribe. He writes with a feather quill held in an upright position, in indelible ink, and along straight lines on specially prepared parchment. Since he is engaged in setting down God's word, he must be a strictly observant Jew and is expected to approach his task in a reverent spirit and must purify himself by immersion in a ritual bath – a *mikveh*.

The oldest extant edition of the Old Testament in Hebrew is that of the Masoretic (traditional) text written in Tiberias in the 10th century AD. This shows the care and devotion the scribes have traditionally brought to bear on their work.

has projected itself outwards into a wealth of secular books, plays and newspapers, subconsciously inspired by the traditional reverence for the Word.

In every Diaspora community, high priority was given to the education of boys. Elementary education took place in a *cheder*. The ordinary meaning of this Hebrew word is 'room', but in this context it was a schoolroom attached to a synagogue or a room in the home of the teacher. In either case, the *melamed* (teacher) was paid by the parents and not by the community.

The children in a cheder were roughly divided into three age groups: 3–5, 6–7, 8–13. No secular subjects were taught in the traditional cheder. The three 'classes' would concentrate on learning to read the prayers, then the Bible with the help of Rashi's commentary, and finally elements of Talmud. The teaching method concentrated on memory and repetition. After their bar-mitzvah, some boys would move to an academy or yeshivah, where they would plunge into more advanced Talmudic study until they were seventeen or eighteen years old. The sons of poor families were taught in a free elementary school which was maintained out of the community funds; if it was necessary, provision was made for the pupils' food and clothing as well.

From the beginning of the Enlightenment movement (Haskalah)

The Yeshivah

Right *Rav Ashi (AD 352–427), head of the famous Talmudic academy of Sura in Babylonia, giving a public lecture during what was called the* kallah *month.*

In a Palestinian or Babylonian academy of that period, the main lecture was given daily by the head of the school. If he appeared before a large class, one of his assistants would repeat his words in a loud voice (a kind of public address system) or simultaneously translate them from Hebrew into Aramaic, the spoken language of the time. The students were encouraged to ask questions, to express their own opinions or even to argue with their teachers. The pedagogic aim was to develop their critical faculties and enable them to apply their knowledge to practical problems.

A unique practice in Babylonia was the kallah months. Twice a year scholars would assemble from all over the country at one of the main academies for a month-long seminar on a prescribed chapter of the Mishnah. At the public lectures the first seven rows in the hall were reserved for the most respected scholars.

During the fifty-six years Rav Ashi headed the Sura Academy, he was responsible for arranging and editing the vast accumulation of material that formed the Babylonian Talmud.

towards the end of the 18th century, the closed system of Jewish religious schools started to break down and the demand grew for a more general secular education. Today, in a modern community, Jewish day-schools prepare their pupils for the general examinations of the country, while at the same time giving them a grounding in Hebrew and in Jewish subjects. Those Jewish children who attend general schools can get some Jewish knowledge in Sunday schools and other part-time educational institutions run by the community. In all but the most extreme Orthodox circles, practically as much educational attention is given today to girls as to boys.

For over 2,000 years religious learning has been concentrated in a type of regular academy known as a *yeshivah*, from the Hebrew word for 'sitting'.

Before the destruction of AD 70, there were noted schools of religious law in Jerusalem. The central one was attached to the Temple. It had jurisdiction to settle disputed questions by a majority vote of its members, to appoint local judges and to examine the credentials of priests. The most eminent sages had their own schools, including Hillel, Shammai, Jochanan ben-Zakkai and Gamaliel – with whom St Paul studied as a youth.

After the destruction of Jerusalem and the Temple the academies became of vital importance as instruments for preserving and developing the distinctive laws and traditions of Judaism. Starting with that founded by Jochanan ben-Zakkai at Yavneh, some ten schools sprang up during the next two generations on the coastal plain and in the Galilee. They prepared the ground for the classic codification of the Oral Law in the Mishnah, completed at the beginning of the 3rd century. As Palestinian scholarship declined after that, the Babylonian academies became the new centres of learning. By the 4th century those at Sura and Pumbedita held a commanding position in the Jewish world.

From the 11th century onwards, as the dominant role of the Babylonian community receded, academies were established in the new Diaspora centres emerging to the west – in the Islamic lands of Egypt, North Africa and Moorish Spain, and the Christian lands of Northern Spain, Italy, France and Germany. Some of these schools attracted students from far and wide because of the fame of the scholars that headed them.

As European Jews migrated eastward into Poland and Lithuania, they carried the torch of learning with them. During the next four centuries, yeshivot flourished in many large Jewish communities in Eastern Europe.

The expulsion from Spain dispersed great Spanish-Jewish scholars through the Mediterranean lands. Talmudic academies flourished in the Ottoman Empire, particularly in Constantinople, Salonika, and Safad in the Galilee.

From the Middle Ages, yeshivot served as professional schools for the training of rabbis and other religious officials, but their basic function remained learning for learning's sake. Students ranged from young boys of bar-mitzvah age to elderly men with a lifelong commitment to study. Yeshivah students who went on to earn their living in secular occupations would continue to read and discuss the sacred books in their spare time. It was said that 'the yeshivah has an entrance but no exit.' In the mediaeval world it was only among the Jews that the ordinary man was not an illiterate.

It is hard to exaggerate the prestige that Jews attached to traditional learning. In the Jewish scale of values, the learned man had a status superior to that of the man of property. A merchant was proud to have his daughter marry a poor but promising student, and was willing to support his son-in-law so that he could go on studying. Private households of even modest means would gladly share their food with needy students, under a rotation system called in Yiddish *essen-tag* ('eating-days').

The Eastern European yeshivot, especially in Poland, evolved a

The **Cheder.** *A singing lesson at a school in the Warsaw Ghetto, May 1940. Even under Holocaust conditions, with the doomed Jews herded together inside Nazi-built walls, they stubbornly persisted with the education of their children.*

method of Talmudic argument called *pilpul* from the Hebrew for 'pepper'. It involved an intricate chain of logic in order to link apparently unrelated or contradictory passages in the Torah or the Talmud. Pilpulistic skill became much admired, though some eminent scholars, including the great Vilna Gaon, dismissed it as a hair-splitting exercise that did not bring real understanding of the texts. However, the method of pilpul undoubtedly helped to develop the remarkable keenness and subtlety of the Jewish intellect.

From the late 18th century onwards, the closed world of the yeshivah was threatened by the Haskalah (Enlightenment) movement. The object of Haskalah was to inject a knowledge of Western secular culture into Jewish life. In spite of opposition by the Orthodox leadership, Haskalah did stimulate change in some types of yeshivot. Their curriculum was broadened to cover general Jewish studies, Hebrew as a modern language and secular subjects like science and mathematics. Ultra-Orthodox yeshivot concentrated only on Talmudic studies.

The yeshivot in Soviet Russia were closed down after the Revolution. Those in Poland, Lithuania and elsewhere in Europe were wiped out during the Nazi occupation. Since then, however, there has been a rapid spread of yeshivot in the United States and some Western countries, and in the State of Israel. Some of these were founded by the displaced remnants of famous Eastern European academies. Different types of contemporary yeshivot evolved, ranging from high-school level to the *kolel* – an adult group engaged in advanced religious study. As an institution, the yeshivah thus continues to survive and even prosper in the markedly secular Jewish world of today.

In periods of repression Jewish cultural and intellectual life turned inwards, and entrenched itself behind the fortress walls of tradition. But there were more relaxed periods when particular Diaspora communities participated freely in the society and culture of their environment. In such cases Jewish intellectuals faced the problem of

(continued on page 85)

Right: Woman preparing for the Sabbath, *an oil painting by Reuben Rubin, 1920. See also colour pages 106 and 107.*

Modern Ideological Pluralism

The twenty-two Jews appearing in this composite picture (in roughly chronological order), have all lived in the modern era, from the beginning of the 18th century. They personify some of the religious and political trends that reflect the ideological pluralism of Jewish life during that period.

Israel Baal Shem Tov (1700–60). Founder in Poland of the Chassidic revivalist movement.

Elijah Ben-Solomon Zalman, the Vilna Gaon (1720–97). The greatest Talmudic sage of his time, and the main opponent of Chassidism.

Hayyim Joseph David Azulai (1724–1806). Renowned Kabbalist and bibliographer from Hebron.

Moses Mendelssohn (1729–86). Brilliant German-Jewish philosopher and writer and leading spokesman for Jewish emancipation and the Haskalah (Enlightenment).

Shalom Sharabi (1720–77). Yemenite rabbi in Jerusalem revered as miracle-worker and exponent of Kabbalism (mystical doctrines).

Leopold Zunz (1794–1886). German-Jewish scholar and pioneer of modern scientific Jewish studies.

Samson Raphael Hirsch (1808–88). Frankfurt rabbi and leader of German neo-Orthodoxy, who combined strict adherence to traditional Judaism with European culture.

Judah Alkalai (1798–1878). Sephardi rabbi in Serbia who promoted the idea of Jewish colonization in Palestine and paved the way for religious acceptance of Zionism.

Ahad Ha'am (Asher Ginsberg) (1856–1927). Hebrew writer and Zionist from Odessa, whose *Cultural Zionism* called for renewal of the inner creative forces of the Jewish people through the national centre in Palestine.

Abraham Isaac Kook (1865–1935). Important religious thinker and Ashkenazi Chief Rabbi of Palestine, who sought understanding between religious and secular elements in Jewry.

Simon Dubnow (1860–1941). Leading Russian-Jewish historian of his time, who advocated national and cultural autonomy for Jewish minorities in the Diaspora.

Vladimir Medem (1879–1923). Russian-Jewish socialist and the leading figure in the Bund, a Jewish workers' party in Eastern Europe, that combined socialist doctrines with a claim for cultural Jewish autonomy in Eastern European countries.

Theodore Herzl (1860–1904). The founder of the World Zionist Organization, launched at the First Zionist Congress in 1897, and the father of political Zionism.

Dov Ber Borochow (1881–1917). Russian Zionist and socialist who helped found the Poale Zion, the first Zionist workers' party.

Aharon David Gordon (1856–1922). Russian Zionist philosopher whose teaching and personal example promoted the ideals of Jewish labour and cultivation of the soil in Palestine.

84

Martin Buber (1878–1965). Religious philosopher. In his books, religious faith was presented as a dialogue between man and God, and biblical history as a dialogue between the people of Israel and God.

Chaim Weizmann (1874–1952). Zionist leader and first President of Israel. A research chemist, his pragmatic attitude to Zionist ideology called for a synthesis between political activity, cultural revival and practical colonization.

Joseph Dov Soloveitchik (1903–). Talmudist and philosopher, professor of Talmud and Jewish philosophy at Yeshiva University, New York, and the leading exponent today of enlightened Orthodox Judaism.

Vladimir (Ze'ev) Jabotinsky (1880–1940). Russian-Jewish Zionist leader, orator and writer, and founder of the militant Revisionist Party in opposition to the official leadership of the Movement.

Berl Katzenelson (1887–1944). A leader and ideologist of the Jewish Labour movement in Israel.

David Ben-Gurion (1886–1973). Coming to Palestine as a young Zionist pioneer, he helped found the Israel Labour Party and the Histadrut (Labour Federation). He was the central figure in Israel's struggle for independence and became its first Prime Minister.

Menachem Mendel Shneersohn (1902–). The present head of the family dynasty that rules over the Lubavitcher Chassidic sect that has its headquarters in New York.

bridging two worlds, of absorbing outside culture without losing their own. In the nature of things such a synthesis was never stable for an indefinite period.

A situation of this kind existed in ancient Alexandria, where the Jewish community tried to maintain its own faith and identity in a Hellenist (Greek) environment. The cultural dualism is reflected in the writings of the community's foremost intellectual, Philo (20 BC – AD 40). A devout Jew, he read the Old Testament in Greek translation, and his philosophical ideas sought to combine Jewish monotheism with Greek rationalism.

Another remarkable chapter in cultural synthesis was the Jewish-Arab relationship from the 10th century onwards. The most famous work of Spanish-born Maimonides, his *Guide of the Perplexed*, was written in Egypt in Judeo-Arabic, and its exposition of Judaism was influenced by the Arab philosophers. At the same time, Moorish Spain was one of the most creative and flourishing periods in the history of Jewish religious culture in spite of the Jewish involvement with Arab culture.

In the modern era the hold of the traditional religious culture and way of life has weakened, and ideological trends have developed in many directions. There were those who saw the solution to the Jewish problem in the disappearance of the Jewish people, either through assimilation or in the classless and atheist society of the Marxist dream. But even those who remained within the Jewish frame of reference and had a common desire to preserve the Jewish identity in a changing world, differed sharply about the answers. There were diverse currents in Judaism, diverse approaches to Zionism, and abortive attempts to gain a national and cultural minority status in the Diaspora.

From the beginning of the 18th century to the present there has been a greater ferment of ideas in Jewish life than ever before. The most striking fact about the modern Jewish age has been its ideological and cultural pluralism.

In traditional Jewish life, art was not pursued for art's sake. The visual arts served as the handmaiden of the faith. Their chief outlets were in synagogue architecture and decoration; the diversity in style of ceremonial objects (Torah scrolls, kiddush cups, Chanukkah lamps, Passover dishes, havdalah spice boxes, prayerbook covers and betrothal rings); and the illumination and adornment of books and manuscripts (religious commentaries, Passover haggadot, marriage-contracts and the like). In modern life there have been notable Jewish artists, but strictly speaking their works can be categorized as Jewish art only when they depict Jewish subjects.

## Chapter Ten

Jewish Languages

The letter *Aleph*, the first letter of the Hebrew alphabet, symbolizes Jewish literacy, and the continuity of the Hebrew language from biblical times to the present. It is remarkable that an Israeli schoolboy of today can read and understand the Dead Sea Scrolls written 2,000 years ago. Jews also used the Hebrew alphabet for other languages they absorbed in the Diaspora. Hebrew throughout Diaspora history has remained the sacred tongue (*leshon ha-kodesh*) for prayer and literature.

Aramaic was a Semitic language closely akin to Hebrew and used the same alphabet. From about the 6th century BC onwards, it served in the Middle East as a lingua franca for diplomatic and commercial intercourse between the countries of the region. Its use by the Palestinian and Mesopotamian Jews as their daily tongue accounts for the fact that the Talmud is mostly written in Aramaic, while some of the familiar Jewish prayers (notably the Kaddish, the mourner's prayer) have survived only in that language. Aramaic fell into disuse by the time of the Arab Conquest in the 7th century AD.

In general, Diaspora communities adopted the languages of the countries where they were settled. That was so, for instance, with the Greek-speaking Jews in ancient Egypt, a country of Hellenist (Greek) culture after its conquest by Alexander the Great.

In later centuries 'Jewish' versions evolved of a number of local languages. These versions had two characteristics in common: they were written in Hebrew script; and they had an infusion of Hebrew-Aramaic elements transposed from the religious literature – the Bible, the Talmud, and the prayer-book. In the lands conquered by the Arabs, from Mesopotamia to Spain, the language of the Jewish communities was Ladino. In mediaeval Europe there were Jewish versions of Spanish, Portuguese, French, Italian, German, Greek and a number of other local languages. Only two of these survived on a substantial scale in modern times: Ladino and Yiddish (Judeo-German).

Yiddish has been by far the most important and widespread Jewish language to emerge in the Diaspora. It evolved in early mediaeval Germany as an amalgam of local German dialects, mixed with Hebrew-Aramaic and elements of the Romance languages. As the

'Aleph'. On the letter are the ten commandments.

Yiddish Writers

See illustrations overleaf

Yiddish literature began in the 16th century. In its early phase it consisted mainly of collections of tales based on the narrative books of the Bible or on Talmudic fables and popular folk-tales, and written in the form of verse epics. In the latter half of the 19th century, under the influence of the Haskalah (Enlightenment) movement in Eastern Europe, a modern secular literature emerged at the same time in Yiddish and Hebrew. The leading Yiddish authors of the period wrote in both languages.

The first modern master of Yiddish was **Mendele Mocher Seforim** (1835–1917). The name means Mendele the Bookseller, and was a pseudonym for S.J. Abramowitz. His fiction depicted Russian-Jewish life with a mixture of satire and sentiment. He also collaborated in translating the Torah into Yiddish.

Shalom Aleichem ('Peace upon you'), the standard greeting in Hebrew) was the pen-name of Shalom Rabinowitz (1859–1916), the most popular Jewish writer of all time. His stories and sketches created a galaxy of characters, like Tevye the dairyman in the modern musical *Fiddler on the Roof* who is based on the central character in a lengthy series of stories. Tevye exemplified the wry humour, hardship and resilience of the Jews in the Russian Pale of Settlement. Like Dickens, whom Shalom Aleichem greatly admired, his works came out in instalments over many years, and he travelled around giving public recitals from them, including two journeys to the United States.

The third of the classic Yiddish writers was **Isaac Leib Peretz** (1852–1915), known for his short stories and plays. Peretz popularized the mystical tales that emerged from the Chassidic movement.

A Yiddish writer of the next generation was **Shalom Asch** (1880–1957) who achieved international standing as a novelist in the wider European tradition. His historical trilogy on the life and period of Jesus made him a

Jews migrated eastward into Poland and Lithuania, the Yiddish they carried with them gathered Slavic elements and moved further away from its German origins. Regional dialects developed, particularly in the pronunciation of certain vowel sounds. By their Yiddish speech a Lithuanian Jew in the north could easily be distinguished from a Polish Jew in the centre, and both of them from a Rumanian Jew in the south.

In the 19th century the Yiddish-speaking Jews of Eastern Europe expanded rapidly in numbers, and from 1880 onwards a great wave of them moved into Western Europe and onwards to the New World beyond the seas: the United States and Canada, Latin America, South Africa and Australia. On the eve of the Second World War there were an estimated eleven million Jews who spoke Yiddish or had a Yiddish-speaking background. They constituted two-thirds of all the Jews in the world at that time.

Yiddish is a highly expressive tongue. It became saturated with the intellectual subtlety, the sardonic wit, the faith and fortitude, the poverty and insecurity, the love of stories, the humour, sentiment and pathos that marked the life of the Jewish masses in Eastern Europe. These traits were mirrored in the works of the great Yiddish writers.

Modern Hebrew literature started with the Haskalah movement in Prussia towards the end of the 18th century. The movement aimed at breaking down the ghetto isolation of the Yiddish-speaking Jewish community, and drawing it into the mainstream of European culture. It was felt that Yiddish was not intellectually respectable and Hebrew could serve as a transition stage for Jews who did not yet know German. The German Haskalah lasted for half a century, roughly from 1780 to 1830. It faded out as the emerging Jewish middle class became increasingly assimilated into German life.

Meanwhile the Haskalah movement had spread to Polish Galicia, then a part of the Austro-Hungarian empire with a dense Jewish population. Between 1820 and 1860 a network of Hebrew schools developed. There was also the beginning of scientific Hebrew studies under the leadership of the scholar and philosopher Nachman Krochmal (1785–1840). His major work was the *Guide of the Perplexed of the Time*, a title that deliberately echoed Maimonides'.

The Lithuanian city of Vilna was the major centre for the early Russian Haskalah up to about 1880. After that the focus of Hebrew letters in Russia shifted to the Ukrainian port-city of Odessa.

The modern revival of spoken Hebrew was stimulated by the rise of the Zionist movement. The aim of making the biblical tongue the national language of the restored Jewish homeland had a strong historical and emotional appeal. But at first the concept seemed unrealistic. There was opposition from several Jewish quarters. Religious Jews objected to using the sacred tongue for secular purposes. The champions of Yiddish claimed that it had become the *mamme loshen* (mother-tongue) of the majority of Jews, and should be preserved as such. The sceptics maintained that an ancient

(continued on page 90)

A portrait of Shalom Rabinowitz, whose pen-name was 'Shalom Aleichem'.

controversial figure in the Jewish press.

In the first decades after the Russian Revolution, a new generation of Yiddish writers, poets and playwrights arose in the Soviet Union; and so did an active Yiddish theatre. But Yiddish culture was suppressed during the Stalinist purges, and some of the Jewish writers were liquidated. The Soviet drive against the so-called 'cosmopolitan' tendencies of Jewish intellectuals was savagely renewed in the last years of Stalin's life, culminating in the execution on 12 August 1952 of the leading Jewish writers. Yiddish literature in the Soviet Union never fully recovered.

Yiddish writing continued to flourish in Poland between the two

The Khaliastre ('The Gang'). Left to right Mendl Elkin, Peretz Hirschbein, Uri Zvi Greenberg, Peretz Markish, Melech Ravitch and Israel Joshua Singer in Warsaw, 1922.

89

World Wars, only to be wiped out in the Holocaust, together with so much else.

Meanwhile the United States, and especially New York, had become a major Yiddish centre. But Yiddish culture declined there as the children of the immigrants became Americanized, moved up the social and economic ladder and often dispersed into middle class urban suburbs.

On receiving the Nobel Prize for Literature in 1978, the Yiddish novelist **Isaac Bashevis Singer** (1904–   ), *right*, who emigrated to America from Poland, sadly suggested that the award was a last tribute to a dying language and culture.

Isaac Bashevis Singer, the Nobel prize winner.

language not spoken for 2,000 years was unsuited to the complexities of modern life.

Fresh impetus was given to the Hebrew-speaking movement by the early Zionist pioneers who arrived in Palestine from Russia and Poland in the decade before the First World War. A major breakthrough was achieved in 1922, when the new British Mandatory Administration made Hebrew together with English and Arabic the official languages of the country.

Today, in the State of Israel, Hebrew is the firmly established medium for all aspects of the nation's life: the educational system from kindergarten to university, politics, business, public services, the armed forces, the press and media, science and technology, recreation and sport. The language is also being learnt to an increasing extent by Jews elsewhere, as a living link with Israel. Hebrew is the only case of an ancient tongue that has successfully been revived in the modern age.

In the last half-century a Hebrew literature of great range and vitality has emerged in Eretz Israel. For the most part its themes have been insular, reflecting Israeli life before and after independent statehood – the hardships and dreams of the early pioneers on the land; immigrant absorption; the Jewish-Arab conflict; war experiences; and the self-critical mood of a younger Israeli generation.

The Yiddish Theatre

The father of the modern Yiddish theatre was **Abraham Goldfaden**. He founded his own touring company in Rumania and Russia and wrote, directed and acted in a large number of Yiddish plays and operettas. Yiddish theatre companies sprang up all over Eastern Europe. Prominent among them were the Vilna Troupe, the Moscow Yiddish Theatre and, after the Second World War, the Jewish State Theatre in Poland, headed by **Ida Kaminska**.

Nowhere did the Yiddish theatre flourish more than among the dense concentration of immigrant Jews on the Lower East Side of New York. At one time about twenty Yiddish companies were performing in New York City. The most prolific playwright was **Jacob Gordin**, whose 100 plays included such popular favourites as *Mirele Efros* and *The Yiddish King Lear*. The repertoires of these theatres contained original plays by Gordin and others, works adapted from the great Yiddish story-writers, and after the First World War, translations into Yiddish of plays by Shakespeare, Molière, Shaw and Brecht. The outstanding actor at that time was **Maurice Schwartz**, whose full-blooded renderings of Shylock or King Lear delighted his audiences. The lively New York Yiddish theatre has long vanished together with its immigrant audience, who had flocked to the performances.

Abraham Goldfaden (1840–1908), father of the Yiddish theatre.

Left *Maurice Schwartz (1890–1960) was the most celebrated actor on the New York Yiddish stage. He is shown here as Rab Melech in a 1933 production of I. J. Singer's play* Yoshe Kalb.

Right *Ida Kaminska (1899–1980) as Mother Courage in the play of that name by Berthold Brecht, in the Jewish State Theatre, 1957. She was the head of the Jewish State Theatre of Poland.*

Below The Dybbuk *by S. An-Ski, performed by the Habimah in Hebrew in Moscow.*

The Modern Hebrew Language

The struggle to revive Hebrew as a modern colloquial tongue was led by **Eliezer Ben-Yehuda** (1850–1922). He arrived in Palestine from Lithuania, via Paris, in 1881, and devoted his life to this objective with single-minded zeal. For years his home was the only one where nothing but Hebrew was spoken, and his children were the first in modern times to be reared in that language. He ran a weekly Hebrew newspaper, set up a Hebrew Language Council and worked on a monumental dictionary that ultimately filled seventeen volumes.

The main problem facing Ben-Yehuda and his successors was to fill out the vocabulary. Hebrew, it is true, had not remained static since biblical times. The religious laws that were developed in the Mishnah and in later rabbinical commentaries and rulings, had stretched the language to meet the comprehensive needs of Jewish family and community life. In mediaeval Spain, Jewish intellectuals had used Hebrew in such secular fields as poetry, philosophy, medicine and mathematics, and a range of Arabic literature had been translated into Hebrew. Nevertheless the lexicon was woefully inadequate for modern life. Ben-Yehuda complained that he and his family 'felt every moment a lack of words without which living speech cannot take place'.

In evolving present-day Hebrew thousands of new words have been coined, old words have acquired new meanings, and technological terms have been absorbed from international usage (such as 'telephone' and 'autobus').

Eliezer Ben-Yehuda, the father of modern Hebrew, c.1912.

Ladino

Above *A Ladino text*, Il Regimiento della Vida *by Moses Almosnino, Salonika, 1564.*

After the Expulsion from Spain at the end of the 15th century, Ladino (Judeo-Spanish) was carried by Jewish refugees eastward into the Balkans and Turkey. At the beginning of the 20th century there were about 250,000 Jews speaking Ladino in the eastern Mediterranean area.

An extensive Ladino literature developed. The Bible and several other ethical books were given a Ladino translation. Original writing included poetry and works of mysticism. The best-known work is *Me-Am Lo'ez* (*From a People of Strange Language*, Psalm 114:1), a religious encyclopaedia begun by the 18th-century writer Jacob Culi (*c.*1685–1732). In the 19th century secular Ladino writing included novels, drama and an active press. With the virtual extinction of many of these communities during the Second World War, and the absorption of their remnants into Israel, Ladino is today fading out as a living language.

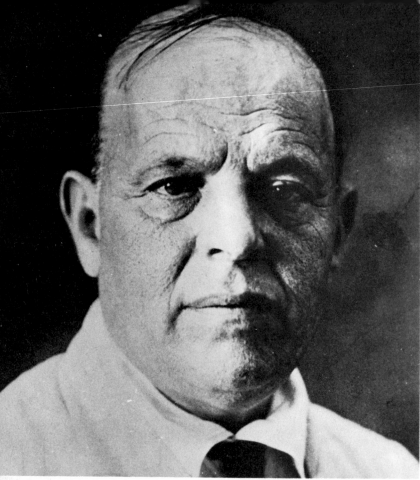

Chaim Nahman Bialik (1873–1934).

Modern Hebrew Writers

In the second half of the 19th century the dominant figures in the Vilna school of Hebrew letters was the poet **Judah Leib Gordon** (1831–92). At home in both European culture and traditional Jewish learning, he evolved a precise and realistic Hebrew style. Among his many translations were the Pentateuch from Hebrew into Russian and the poems of Byron into Hebrew. Gordon summed up his Haskalah anti-isolationist philosophy in the saying, 'Live as a Jew at home and a man in the street'.

Lithuania also produced the first Hebrew novelist, **Abraham Mapu** (1808–67). His two most popular works were historical romances with biblical settings – Judah under King Hezekiah and Samaria under King Ahab.

Towards the end of the century the focus of Hebrew writing shifted to Odessa in the Ukraine. The mentor of this literary circle was the great Yiddish writer **Mendele Mocher Seforim**. From 1886 onwards he switched from Yiddish to Hebrew, which he wrote in a simple and colloquial-sounding style, although it had not yet become a spoken language in his time. He produced a three-volume national history in Hebrew, grappling with the lack of an adequate scientific vocabulary.

In the generation after Mendele two major Hebrew writers came to the fore in Odessa: the essayist Asher Ginsberg (1856–1927) who wrote under the name of **Ahad Ha'am** ('One of the People'), and the poet **Chaim Nachman Bialik**.

Ahad Ha'am was the father of the modern Hebrew essay, to which he brought an analytic mind and a lucid style. He expounded the concept of Judaism as a nation-society with an organic system of ideas, laws, and mores. The spiritual genius of the nation would be revived through the return to the ancestral soil, but Ahad Ha'am was sceptical of Herzl's hopes for a political charter for Palestine and mass migration to it. Ahad Ha'am's *Cultural Zionism* had a potent influence over the movement's intellectuals.

Bialik was the greatest Jewish poet of modern times, and the outstanding literary figure in the Hebrew national renaissance. In his hands Hebrew was a pliable modern instrument that yet

Shmuel Yosef Agnon (1888–1970), receiving the Nobel Prize for Literature in Stockholm in 1966. On the left King Gustav VI of Sweden is seen applauding. (Nellie Sachs can be seen in the centre of the picture.)

echoed the idioms and rhythms of the Bible. The themes of his poems were wrath at the persecution of the Russian Jews; the hope of Zionist redemption; the tension between traditional Judaism and the secular modern world; and a lyrical nostalgia for the countryside of his childhood. Bialik also excelled as an essayist, a writer of short stories, a literary editor and a lecturer. In 1924 he settled in Palestine, where he became president of the Hebrew Language Academy and head of the Hebrew Writers Association.

The poet **Saul Tchernichowsky**

(1875–1943), a younger contemporary of Bialik in Odessa, was the most 'European' of the Hebrew national writers. He mastered a number of modern and classical languages and translated into Hebrew works of Homer, Sophocles, Shakespeare, Molière and Goethe. Traditional Jewish circles were offended by Tchernichowsky's agnostic tendencies and his somewhat pagan attitude to life and nature. However, the brilliance of his poetry and his ardent Zionist commitment gained him a wide following. Like Bialik, he settled in Palestine in later life.

The one modern Israeli writer to gain international recognition was **S.Y. Agnon**, who in 1966 shared the Nobel Prize for Literature with the poet Nellie Sachs, a Jewish refugee from Nazi Germany. Agnon came to Palestine from Galicia at the age of nineteen. His novels straddle two worlds – the Eastern European *shtetl* ('small town') and the Israel scene, especially in Jerusalem. His style is highly individualistic, blending biblical and Talmudic elements with modern Hebrew, and filled with echoes of the folklore, Chassidic tales and symbols of the Jewish past.

GAZETA
DE AMSTERDAM
De Lunes 12. de Setiembre. 1672.

The Jewish Press

In modern times the Jewish press has been a basic ingredient of Diaspora cultural activity. It has mirrored every event of contemporary Jewish history, and expressed every ideological, social and literary trend in the Jewish world. The Jew read his daily newspaper with the same avid concentration that his forefathers gave to a page of the Talmud.

The first two Jewish papers in any language appeared in 17th-century Amsterdam. They were the *Gazeta de Amsterdam* (1672) in Ladino, and the *Dienstagishe Kurant* (1686) in the Western European dialect of Yiddish. The first journals in Hebrew appeared in Prussia (1858) and Odessa (1860). The first Yiddish periodical was published in Odessa in 1861.

From that time on a wide-ranging press developed in Yiddish, Hebrew and Ladino. In addition, hundreds of Jewish papers have been printed in the local languages of the Diaspora countries. The London *Jewish Chronicle*, a weekly in English, goes back to 1841, making it the oldest Jewish paper still in existence.

In the 1970's it was estimated that 629 Jewish dailies and periodicals (weeklies, monthlies and quarterlies) were appearing in Diaspora communities.

An American Jewish press developed from about 1840. At first it appeared in German and English, but with the mass immigration of Eastern European Jews after 1880, Yiddish became the dominant language. There were some small periodicals in Hebrew, and in the early 20th century also in Ladino, introduced by immigrants from the Balkan countries.

The Yiddish daily press in New York reached hundreds of thousands of readers. The two major dailies were the *Jewish Daily Forward* and the *Jewish Morning Journal*. They vied fiercely with each other for circulation, advertising and talent, and provided their readers with a lively mixture of news, politics, fiction and magazine features. During the First World War, the subscriptions to all the New York Yiddish dailies rose to the staggering figure of half a million. In the post-war years there was a steady decline, since the US immigration law of 1924 cut the flow of Yiddish-speaking immigrants, and a new American-born generation moved over to the English-language general press.

Top left *Ghetto Politicians, a painting by Lazar Krestin, 1904.*

Top right *The* Gazeta de Amsterdam, *12 September 1672.*

Above *The first issue of* Olam Katan, *an illustrated children's weekly published in Warsaw and Vienna, 1901.*

100TH BIRTHDAY NUMBER

The Jewish Chronicle

THE ORGAN OF BRITISH JEWRY    ספר זכרון   INCORPORATING THE "JEWISH WORLD"

One Hundred and First Year   Established November 1841

No. 3,788.
REGD. AS A NEWSPAPER   **Friday, November 14, 1941 — Marcheshvan 24, 5702**   Price : 4d.

CENTENARY OF THE JEWISH CHRONICLE

Messages from State and Religious Leaders

From THE PRIME MINISTER

(The Right Hon. Winston S. Churchill)

On the occasion of the centenary of THE JEWISH CHRONICLE, a landmark in the history of British Jewry, I send a message of good cheer to Jewish people in this and other lands. None has suffered more cruelly than the Jew the unspeakable evils wrought on the bodies and spirits of men by Hitler and his vile regime. The Jew bore the brunt of the Nazis' first onslaught upon the citadels of freedom and human dignity. He has borne and continued to bear a burden that might have seemed to be beyond endurance. He has not allowed it to break his spirit; he has never lost the will to resist. Assuredly in the day of victory the Jew's sufferings and his part in the struggle will not be forgotten. Once again, at the appointed time, he will see vindicated those principles of righteousness which it was the glory of his fathers to proclaim to the world. Once again it will be shown that, though the mills of God grind slowly, yet they grind exceeding small.

Winston S. Churchill

From THE CHIEF RABBI :

This is the first time that a Jewish religious journal anywhere has lived to celebrate its centenary. Jewry would, in gladness, have taken note of such a landmark in our latter-day history, but for the appalling contrast between Israel's position and outlook in 1841 and the heart-breaking situation that confronts us a hundred years after.

THE JEWISH CHRONICLE was founded one year after the Jews of the Old and the New World had united, under the leadership of Sir Moses Montefiore, for their successful protest against the Damascus Blood Libel. This moral triumph was followed within a generation by the removal of every Jewish disability in England, and Jewish entranchisement in the Central Empires and

been hurled into the abyss of defamation and misery, and are facing annihilation.

All the changes in the fortunes of the Jew, his hopes and fears, during these eventful decades are faithfully mirrored in the columns of THE JEWISH CHRONICLE. It has from the very first been a wise defender of Jewry against dangers from without, and a fearless mentor of failings within, Pan-Jewish in its cultural consciousness, it has opposed every form of spiritual self-obliteration or revolution in religion; but given its utmost support to all movements that stood for Jewish life and the deepening of Jewish self-respect. It has aimed to be the voice both of our Unknown Warriors and of the architects of Israel's future; and that noble aim has been crowned with a gratifying measure of success.

"Each age is a dream that is dying, or one that is

From THE ARCHBISHOP OF CANTERBURY:

I congratulate THE JEWISH CHRONICLE on having reached its centenary year. That it should have been issued regularly for these 100 years is a striking proof of the security which British Jewry have had in this country, in contrast with the cruel treatment to which their brethren in other lands have been subjected, especially in recent years. In this country we regard them as in every sense our fellow-citizens. In the present struggle the Jewish people have given abundant proof of their wholehearted association with the British Commonwealth and its Allies. I have always admired the remarkable generosity with which British Jewry have done their utmost to alleviate the lot of their brethren who, in other lands, have been so cruelly

The message of encouragement from Winston Churchill on the first page of the centenary number of the Jewish Chronicle, *14 November 1941.*

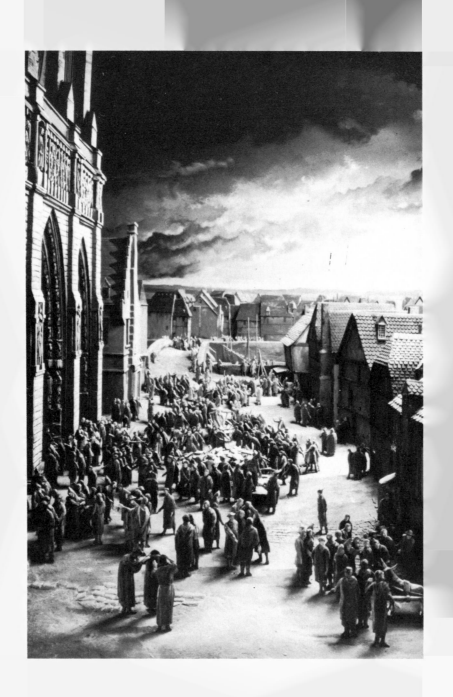

Part Two

Jews Among the
Nations

*The burning of the Talmud. A diorama of the
square before Notre Dame, 1242. See pages 72 and 73.*

## Chapter Eleven

The Ancient Middle East

The Biblical Period

After King Solomon's death in 922 BC, the United Monarchy split into two. The southern kingdom, Judah, contained the tribe of that name and the tribe of Simeon in the Negev, already absorbed into Judah. The rest of the twelve Israelite tribes seceded and established the northern kingdom of Israel. (In theory Israel included ten tribes; actually, they were nine plus a part of Benjamin, the other part of Benjamin being incorporated into Judah.)

The kingdom of Israel lasted for just two centuries. In 722 BC it was overrun by an Assyrian army and its capital, Samaria, was sacked. All but the lowliest of the citizens were carried away into captivity in Assyria, at that time the dominant Near Eastern power. They were resettled in Mesopotamia – according to the Bible, in 'Halah, and on the Habor, the river of Gozan, and in the cities of the Medes' (*2 Kings 17:6*). From that time they disappeared from history. But the belief persisted among Jews that their brethren of the Lost Ten Tribes had survived and would one day return home. That faith was echoed in the visions of great Hebrew prophets like Isaiah and Ezekiel.

The legend kept recurring in the Diaspora after the end of the Second Temple. The 12th-century Jewish traveller Benjamin of Tudela recorded reports that the Lost Ten Tribes were living in Persia and in Arabia. In 1650 the celebrated Amsterdam rabbi Manasseh Ben-Israel published his book *The Hope of Israel*, which discussed the supposed discovery of the Tribes in South America.

From the 19th century, nations in different parts of the world have been 'identified' as the descendants of the Lost Ten Tribes, on ingenious but flimsy grounds. These include the British, the North American Indians and the Japanese.

One of the Jewish sages, the redoubtable Rabbi Akiba in the 2nd century AD had had the courage to state bluntly that 'The ten tribes shall not return again'. That must be regarded as the verdict of history.

The Assyrian liquidation of the kingdom of Israel in 722 BC did not produce an opening chapter in the history of the Jewish Diaspora. The first experiment in Diaspora life came with the Babylonian Exile. In 598 BC, the troops of Nebuchadnezzar besieged and took Jerusalem

The Biblical Period: Assyria and the Hebrew Kingdoms

These Jewish captives are being presented to the Assyrian monarch Sennacherib (reigned 705–681 BC). The detail is from the wall-relief in the excavated royal palace at Nineveh, the Assyrian capital.

Sennacherib's father, Sargon II, had captured Samaria and destroyed the northern Hebrew kingdom of Israel in 722 BC. He carried away a large number of captives who gave rise to the legends of the Lost Ten Tribes.

Under Sennacherib the Assyrian empire continued to expand southward into Egypt. In 701 BC he led a victorious army in a sweep down the coastal plain of Syria and Palestine and defeated an Egyptian force that tried to stem his advance. According to the account of this campaign among the palace records at Nineveh, he captured 66 cities in the southern Hebrew kingdom of Judah, took 200,150 Jewish prisoners of war and exacted from King Hezekiah a heavy tribute in gold and silver.

Assyria lay along the Upper Tigris river in the north-eastern part of Mesopotamia. Obsessed with war and conquest, they were a ruthless 'herrenvolk' that built up the strongest military machine seen in the world until then and dominated the Near East for centuries. Their empire finally collapsed with the fall of Nineveh in 612 BC.

It was Assyrian policy to uproot the populations of the territories they conquered by interchanging them. Thus, Sargon deported some of the Hebrews from the vanquished kingdom of Israel to the north-western part of his empire, and transferred the peoples of that territory to what had been Israel. The newcomers merged with the remaining Israelite inhabitants, and the mixture became known to later history as the Samaritans, who practised their own form of Judaism. A small number of them still exist.

and plundered the Temple. The young king of Judah, Jehoiachin, the leading citizens and most of the merchants and artisans were taken off as captives. The king's uncle, Zedekiah, was installed as a puppet ruler in his stead. Eleven years later he led a revolt, but was quickly crushed and cruelly punished, by Nebuchadnezzar who now, in 586 BC put an end to the southern Hebrew kingdom, Judah. He sacked Jerusalem, destroyed the Temple – known as the First (Solomon's) Temple – and sent into Babylonian captivity the bulk of the survivors. The Bible states that the Babylonian commander 'left some of the poorest in the land to be vine-dressers and ploughmen.' *2 Kings 25:12*

Groups of refugees, including the prophet Jeremiah, found their way to Egypt. The Bible does not state where they settled. It is known that a Jewish settlement already existed in the garrison town on the island of Elephantine (Yeb), on the Nile in Upper Egypt.

It is remarkable that the small Judean people, crushed and largely uprooted, did not at this point fade out of history, as their brethren in the northern Hebrew kingdom had done. The disaster was not only political and physical; it was also religious. For four centuries the nation had been taught to put its faith in Divine protection. Since God had made a promise to King David ensuring that his dynasty would occupy the throne forever, how could the kingdom go under? Since God's Presence was in the Holy of Holies, how could the Temple be destroyed? It now appeared as if God had turned against His Chosen People. The *Book of Lamentations* is filled with a sense of bitter betrayal:

> *The Lord has become like an enemy,*
> * he has destroyed Israel; ...*
> *the Lord has brought to an end in Zion*
> * appointed feast and sabbath,*
> *and in his fierce indignation has spurned*
> * king and priest.*
> *The Lord has scorned his altar,*
> * disowned his sanctuary;*
>
> Lam. 2:5,6,7

The agony of exile cried out in the words of Psalm 137:

> *By the waters of Babylon,*
> * there we sat down and wept,*
> * when we remembered Zion. ...*
> *How shall we sing the Lord's song*
> * in a foreign land?*
>
> Psalm 137:1,4

The Babylonian Exile

This copy of a cuneiform tablet is from the archive of Murashu's Sons, a prominent Jewish banking and commercial family in the Babylonian city of Nippur in the 5th century BC.

Above *The Karaite movement. A diorama of the Karaite Sabbath in darkness.* Below *The Jewish Revolt of AD 115–17. The Great Synagogue goes up in flames during the suppression of the revolt.*

Right '*At the Gates of Jerusalem*', part of a triptych by Mordechai Ardon, 1967.

Left '*Jew in Bright Red*' by Marc Chagall, 1914–15.

Below '*Fire in Water*' sculpture by Ya'acov Agam, 1969–71.

Left *The Burning of the Talmud. A diorama of the square before Notre Dame.*

Overleaf *Battles for Jerusalem. Jerusalem was conquered by three successive invaders: Persian (AD 614), Byzantine (AD 629) and Arab (AD 638).*

Jewish occupations in Egypt. This mural depicts the Egyptians harvesting, tending their animals and weaving.

But in time they settled down in their new home. Writing from Jerusalem to the first group of deportees, the prophet Jeremiah gave them some pragmatic advice:

> *Build houses and live in them; plant gardens and eat their produce. Take wives and have sons and daughters. ... But seek the welfare of the city where I have sent you into exile, and pray to the Lord on its behalf, for in its welfare you will find your welfare.*
>
> Jer. 29:5–7

Little is known about the life of the exiles for the next sixty years. They maintained their group identity, clung to their distinctive faith, language and traditions, developed organized communities, and presumably resumed their occupations as farmers, artisans and merchants. Instead of the elaborate sacrificial rituals of the Jerusalem Temple, now lying in ruins, they came together in regular meeting-places for prayer and study, thus creating the prototype of the synagogue. According to the Old Testament, the captive king of Judah, Jehoiachin was released on the accession to the Babylonian throne of Evil-Merodach in 561 BC; and in the records of the excavated royal palace in Babylon it is mentioned that Jehoiachin, his family and other Judean captives were maintained from the king's own stores.

The survival of Judaism in the Babylonian captivity was helped by two earlier developments that were to be of the greatest importance in

The Elephantine Community

This island in the River Nile, near Aswan in Upper Egypt, was known in Greek as Elephantine and in Aramaic as Yeb. In ancient times the island was important as a military outpost guarding the southern frontier of Egypt against raids from Nubia (modern Sudan), further to the south. Even before the destruction of Jerusalem by the Babylonians in 587 BC, the army garrison of Elephantine included units of Jewish mercenaries. They lived here with their families, and were later joined by Jewish civilian settlers. The small community prospered, partly from the trade in ivory from Nubia. A temple was built for 'Yahu' and sacrifices were made. The settlement continued under Persian occupation, from 525 BC onwards.

Light has been shed on the life of this isolated community by the discovery at the beginning of the 20th century of a collection of documents by them in Aramaic, known as the Elephantine Papyri. Some of them deal with such legal matters as marriage, divorce, inheritance and transfers of immovable property. One document quotes a decree in 419 BC from the Persian monarch Darius II to the local Persian governor providing for the observance of the Passover (including the use of unleavened bread) by the Jewish trooops stationed in Elephantine. It is unclear why an internal Jewish festival should have required royal authority. One explanation may be that pressure was being exerted by the priesthood of the Egyptian god Khnub, to whom Elephantine was sacred. At all events, in 411 BC the Jewish temple there was destroyed, apparently at the instigation of the Egyptian priests. A later papyrus refers to an appeal from the Jewish community to the Persian governor of Judea, Bigvai, for assistance in reconstructing their temple.

After the Persian occupation ended at the end of the 4th century BC, Elephantine declined as an inhabited town. However, the Ptolemaic rulers of Egypt during the 3rd century BC seem to have revived the use of a Jewish force brought from Judea to guard the southern frontier of Egypt.

later Diaspora history – indeed, in the spiritual history of mankind. One was the emergence of a written Torah; the other was the Hebrew prophetic movement.

The process of compiling the Torah from oral traditions started in the kingdom of Judah in the 10th century BC and in the kingdom of Israel in the 9th to 8th centuries BC. The *Book of the Law* discovered in the Temple during the reign of the good king Josiah (640–609 BC) was probably an early version of *Deuteronomy*. The Babylonian conquerors had carried away with them as booty the sacred gold and silver vessels from the Temple. The Judean captives carried away with them even more precious baggage: their Scriptures.

During the Exile the biblical works were further edited and expanded by the Hebrew priests. About a century and a half later Ezra the Scribe came from Babylon on a mission to Jerusalem, bearing with him 'the book of the Law of Moses which the Lord had given to Israel'. (*Neh. 8:1*) He assembled the whole community in the public square and read the sacred scroll out to them.

Even before the Exile the great Hebrew prophets had warned their people that God's covenant with them could not be taken for granted: unless the nation purged itself of moral corruption, it would be brought to judgment. But they also held out hope for the future. The disaster, when it came, would not end the national destiny. The first of the classical prophets, Amos, ends his message on this note of rebirth:

I will restore the fortunes of my people Israel
and they shall rebuild the ruined cities and inhabit them.
Amos 9:14

Isaiah speaks of the remnant that will return to Zion, and of the Messianic kingdom to come. Jeremiah even predicted that the Return would take place after seventy years of exile. Two of the greatest prophets emerged in the Babylonian captivity, and reaffirmed the message of hope. One was Ezekiel, whose visions created for his fellow-exiles a detailed blueprint for the restored kingdom and the rebuilt Temple. His powerful symbol for the resurrection was the valley of dry bones brought to life again. The identity of the other sublime exilic prophet is unknown, and he is simply called the Second Isaiah, or Deutero-Isaiah. To him is attributed the latter part of the *Book of Isaiah*, opening with the words:

Comfort, comfort my people,
says your God.
Speak tenderly to Jerusalem,
and cry to her
that her warfare is ended,
that her iniquity is pardoned,
that she has received from the
Lord's hand.
Double for all her sins.
Isa. 40:1–2

In 539 BC the Persian ruler Cyrus the Great took Babylon. In the following year he issued his famous Edict, permitting the return of the Jews to their homeland, and the rebuilding of the Temple in Jerusalem. Only a minority went back. The rest preferred to remain in what had become an established Diaspora community, and to support the first 'Zionist' venture with funds.

The Hellenist-Roman World

In the last three centuries before AD 70 the Babylonian community remained quietly under Persian rule, on the fringe of recorded Jewish history. During this period Jews spread throughout the Hellenist-Roman Mediterranean world.

By the beginning of the Christian era a chain of Jewish communities stretched through the Near East and Southern Europe and along sections of the North African coast. Jewish trading posts sprang up in the wake of the Roman legions as far as Spain and Gaul.

The New Testament accounts of the missionary journeys of St Paul in the middle of the 1st century AD throw some light on the Jewish dispersion at that time. He was born into a Diaspora Jewish community, that of Tarsus in Asia Minor, and given the name Saul. His father, a devout Pharisee, sent the youth to study Torah with the renowned Rabbi Gamaliel in Jerusalem. After his mystic experience on the road to Damascus, he tried to persuade his fellow-Jews that the advent of Jesus was the fulfilment of the Messianic prophesies in the Old Testament. Among the synagogues in which he preached during the decade from AD 48 were those in Damascus, Cyprus, Tarsus, Antioch and Ephesus in Asia Minor; Thessalonica and Beroea in Macedonia; and Athens and Corinth in Greece. When Saul, now called Paul, was arrested and taken to Rome, there was already an established Jewish community there.

How large was the total Jewish population at the beginning of the Christian era? There are no reliable statistics, and any estimate can at best be very tentative. Scholars generally agree, however, that the number was relatively large, more than five million; that the majority lived in the Diaspora communities outside Palestine; and that the Jews were at least ten per cent of the general population in the Mediterranean-Middle East world. One noted modern authority, in the *Encyclopaedia Judaica*, suggests that the total was at least eight million, including about two and a half million in Eretz Israel, and over a million in each of four other areas: Egypt, Syria, Mesopotamia (Babylonia) and Asia Minor. Writing in the first century BC, the famous Greek geographer Strabo commented:'It is not easy to find a region in the whole world where this people has not been accepted, and where it has not assumed a leading position.' That was an exaggerated view, but it does indicate that the Jewish presence was generally felt in the ancient world by the first century AD.

Wherever Jews lived they maintained their ties with the homeland. Eretz Israel was the national and spiritual centre of their people even

A Document from Elephantine

A photostat of one of the papyri in Aramaic found at Elephantine. This document is a contract of sale of a house to Hananiah ben-Azariah, in the year 437 BC.

through it had come into the orbit of imperial Rome. Diaspora Jews travelled the long overland caravan routes or risked storms and pirates at sea to congregate in Jerusalem for the great pilgrimage festivals. Each community sent its annual tribute for the upkeep of the Temple, based on a voluntary tax of a half-shekel per person. Bright young men came to study Torah in the academies. By correspondence or special emissaries, authoritative rulings were requested on knotty problems of Jewish Law. Whether near or distant, communities were dependent on Jerusalem for determining the beginning of the Jewish calendar months. It was in the Palestinian centre, too, that major trends in religious life were taking shape that would profoundly affect the Diaspora future – particularly the crystallization of the biblical text, the evolution of the Oral Law – and the beginning of the Christian sect.

The disaster of AD 70 left the Diaspora like the circumference of a wheel with its hub smashed. It is at this point that 'Dispersion' once more became 'Exile', as it had been with the Babylonian captivity over six centuries earlier.

Alexandria: (1st–2nd centuries AD)

When Egypt was occupied by the Romans in 30 BC, it had a Jewish population estimated at one million. The Jews had entered every sphere of life. There was an affluent and cultured middle class of merchants, bankers, scholars, officials and army officers. The bulk of the community formed a working class of peasant farmers, skilled artisans, soldiers, seamen, port-workers and peddlers. *See colour page 112.*

For 300 years before the Roman advent, Egypt had been ruled by the Greek Ptolemaic dynasty, founded by one of the generals of Alexander the Great. Alexandria had become not only the leading port in the Mediterranean but also the major centre of Hellenic (Greek) culture. Of the Jewish inhabitants of Egypt at that time, a majority lived in Alexandria. They occupied two of its five wards, and were prominent in its business and artistic life. They were organized as an autonomous entity under an ethnarch (the head of a separate ethnic community) with a council of elders and a network of institutions.

The Jews of Alexandria adhered faithfully to their own religion and identity. Their neighbourhood synagogues were the centres of communal life. They sent their offerings to the Temple in Jerusalem and many of them went there on pilgrimage. At the same time, they were strongly influenced by Hellenism. They spoke Greek, had Greek names and wore Greek dress. The Hebrew Bible was translated into Greek for their use – the Septuagint version.

Relations between the Jewish and Greek communities in Alexandria were anything but harmonious. One reason for this was competition among the merchants, sharpened by the business slump that followed the Roman occupation. Another issue concerned civil rights. The Roman authorities had confirmed the existing rights of the

Jewish Literature in Alexandria

The Jewish intellectuals and writers of ancient Alexandria produced a body of literature that sought to bridge two cultures. They wanted to familiarize their fellow-Jews in Alexandria, as well as their Greek neighbours, with the Old Testament and Jewish history; to extol the basic values of Judaism; and to show that these values were not in conflict with the ideas of classical Greek philosophy. Some of their writings are among the Apocrypha, the additional works included in the Septuagint but not in the Hebrew Bible. One of these works is the *Wisdom of Solomon*; another is *Ecclesiasticus* or the *Wisdom of Ben Sirach* (the latter actually a Greek translation from a Hebrew original). Both of them praise the Hebrew concept of Wisdom as the guide to a good life, and uphold the validity of Jewish traditions as compared with pagan beliefs. Another Apocryphal work in Greek, the *Second Book of Maccabees*, is a summary of a fervently nationalist and pious account of the Maccabean Revolt in the 2nd century BC.

An interesting survival from that period is a fragmentary verse-play by Ezekiel, an Alexandrian Jew described as 'a writer of tragedies'. In form and style it is a typical Greek play, but its theme is biblical – the Exodus from Egypt.

In the Hellenist-Jewish literature of the period one can sense the urge of a minority group to explain and justify its different religion and outlook to the dominant majority. That is apparent in the works of the philosopher Philo Judaeus (20 BC–AD 45), the outstanding Jewish intellectual to emerge in Alexandria. He came from a wealthy and assimilated family, and his education was mainly Hellenist. In his writings the Alexandrian synthesis between Jewish beliefs and Greek learning found its most articulate expression. Philo's complex philosophic system contained both Hebrew and Greek elements. It maintained that God's concern with human affairs was remote and indirect, that man had a dual nature (body and soul), and that the Scriptures were to be understood in their allegorical rather than their literal meaning. Such abstract concepts were more akin to Greek than to Hebrew modes of thought; Judaism has always been more concerned with moral conduct than with formal intellectual systems. Philo had virtually no impact on the subsequent development of rabbinic Judaism. But he was to have an influence on the new Christian creed founded by two of his Jewish contemporaries, Jesus of Nazareth and Saul of Tarsus (St Paul).

A model of a seated Jew engaged in discussion with an Alexandrian Hellenist, whose son is listening.

Jewish community to practise its own religion and to regulate its own internal affairs. But the privilege of citizenship, which also carried with it certain tax exemptions, was restricted to the Greeks, who fiercely opposed the Jewish claim to equal status. The animosity of the Greeks was increased because under the Romans they were not the ruling establishment, as they had been under the Ptolemaic dynasty.

These mingled resentments bred the kind of ugly anti-semitism that would later become chronic in Europe. In 1st-century Alexandria the crude anti-Jewish smears were made intellectually respectable when repeated by scholars. One of them was Chaeremon, an historian and priest who was invited to Rome as a tutor to the young Nero. His version of the Exodus was that the Jews were descended from a band of lepers expelled from Egypt, and had remained an unclean race. The most scurrilous writer of the time was Apion, a demagogue who roused

(continued on page 120)

In the port of Alexandria, the leaders of the Jewish community await the return of the delegation led by Philo Judaeus to Rome, in AD 40.

The Delegation to Rome

In AD 38 the inter-communal tension in Alexandria burst out in Greek mob violence against the Jews. A number of them were killed or injured, and the community was penned up in one quarter of the city. Their homes and businesses were plundered, their synagogues were polluted and statues of the emperor were set up in them. Flaccus, the Roman prefect in Egypt, did nothing to protect the Jews. Among other things, he would not order the offending statues to be removed from Jewish places of worship. The deranged Caligula had

mounted the imperial throne in Rome the previous year and was demanding that his subjects worship him as a god. (His order to install a golden statue of himself in the Jerusalem Temple would have provoked an insurrection if his representatives in the field had not stalled off its implementation.)

A delegation of Alexandrian Jews headed by Philo travelled to Rome to plead with the emperor, but they were repulsed with derision. Soon afterwards, Caligula was assassinated. The Jews of Alexandria armed themselves and counter-attacked the Greek quarters. The disturbances were suppressed by Roman troops.

The new emperor, Claudius, tried to damp down the conflict by a compromise decree. He restored to the Jews all the rights that had been taken from them during the riots; but he appeased the Greeks by rejecting the Jewish claim to citizenship. The relations between the Alexandrian Jews and their Roman masters remained brittle.

The Jewish Revolt of AD 115–17

See colour page 105

The Great Synagogue was the largest and most splendid in the ancient diaspora, and symbolized the size and wealth of the Alexandrian community. A colourful description appears in the Talmud, attributed to Judah ha-Nasi (late 2nd century AD):

He who has not seen the double stoa of Alexandria in Egypt has never seen the glory of Israel. It was said that it was like a huge basilica, one stoa within another, and it sometimes held twice the number of people that went forth into Egypt. There were in it seventy-one cathedras of gold, corresponding to the seventy-one elders of the Great Sanhedrin, not one of them containing less than twenty-one talents of gold, and a wooden platform in the middle upon which the attendant of the synagogue stood with a flag in his hand. When the time came to answer Amen he waved his flag and all the congregation duly responded. They moreover did not occupy their seats indiscriminately, but goldsmiths sat separately, silversmiths separately, blacksmiths separately, metalworkers separately and weavers separately, so that when a poor man entered the place he recognized the members of his craft and on applying to that quarter obtained a livelihood for himself and the members of his family.

(The waving of the flag as a signal for the responses was required because the cantor's voice could not be clearly heard by everyone in the huge hall.)

After the Jewish War in Judea had ended in the national calamity of AD 70, feelings of bitterness continued to simmer in the Diaspora communities against their Roman masters. In Alexandria the disaffection was fed by zealot refugees from Judea, and by the Messianic expectations running through the Jewish world at the time. Revolt flared up in AD 115. The Roman emperor Trajan had launched a large-scale campaign on the Eastern frontier against the rival Parthian power. The Roman army temporarily occupied Mesopotamia, and brutally suppressed local Jewish elements that had taken up arms against them. The Jews of Alexandria rebelled, but were ruthlessly put down. The burning of the Great Synagogue in Alexandria marked the end of an era in that city.

The uprising spread to other Jewish communities – the rural towns and villages of Upper Egypt; Cyrene, Egypt's neighbour westward along the African coast; and the island of Cyprus. At one stage a force of Jewish militia from Cyrene actually penetrated into Egypt. It took two years of bloody and destructive fighting over a wide area before the Roman legions put out the flames of Jewish revolt.

the Greek rabble in Alexandria against the Jews. One of his allegations was that Jewish religious rites called for the human sacrifice of non-Jews – the first appearance of the blood-libel that would recur for the next eighteen centuries. Towards the end of that century the Jewish historian Flavius Josephus, in a book written in Rome and entitled *Against Apion*, set himself the task of refuting the anti-semitic propaganda.

In AD 66 the revolt against Rome in Judea produced anti-Roman disturbances among the Jews in Alexandria. The prefect of Egypt at the time was Tiberius Julius Alexander, the Jewish philosopher Philo's able and ambitious nephew, who had joined the Roman military service as a young man and turned away from his Jewish background. He had served a term as procurator of Judea, and in the Jewish War would become chief-of-staff to Titus. At the outset of the war he used the Roman garrison in Alexandria to smash the resistance of the community into which he had been born. Josephus later wrote that 50,000 Jews were killed in these troubles, but that figure may have been exaggerated.

The AD 115–17 revolt of the Jews in the Roman Empire left the Egyptian community decimated, and its economic life in ruins. The once proud and prosperous Jewry of Alexandria would fade from the Jewish scene for centuries to come.

Babylonia (2nd–7th centuries AD)

At the time of the destruction of Jerusalem in AD 70, the Babylonian Jews had lived for 200 years under Parthian rule. The homeland of the Parthians was the mountainous region south-east of the Caspian Sea (now in northern Iran). Noted for their martial skill as horsemen and archers, they had swept through Persia and Mesopotamia and established a new empire. When Rome moved into the Near East during the 1st century BC, and occupied Palestine and Syria, its further expansion eastward was blocked by the Parthians. The Jews found themselves on both sides of the imperial power-struggle, but the Babylonian community maintained its close links with the Land of Israel.

In AD 226 Parthian rule was ended by a new Persian dynasty, that of the Sassanids. The autonomy of the Jewish community in Babylonia remained intact, under its Exilarch, known in Jewish records by the Aramaic title of 'Resh Galuta', which means Head of the Exile. Numbering at least a million, the community ran its own internal affairs and was free to develop its religious and cultural traditions. By the 4th century it had taken over from the declining Palestinian community the spiritual leadership of the Jewish world.

The economic base of the Babylonian community was a wide one, and there were no legal limits imposed on its range of occupations. There was an upper stratum of merchants and property-owners; a medium stratum of Jewish artisans in every skilled craft; while Jewish peasant farmers laboured in the humid heat along the irrigation canals

(continued on page 122)

Jewish Occupations in Babylonia

Left A rural scene in Babylonia in the style of Dura-Europos. Jews are seen in various agricultural occupations.

The majority of the Jews in Babylonia were cultivators of the soil. From time immemorial Mesopotamia had been a river civilization based on watering the flat plain through a network of canals from the Tigris and Euphrates rivers. Since the intricate irrigation system required centralized control, there was no room for small, independent farm holdings. The land belonged legally to the State, and in practice was controlled by absentee landlords. The peasants, Jewish and non-Jewish alike, were tenant farmers, share-croppers or day labourers, kept on a subsistence level by the burden of taxes exacted from them by the landlords and the government.

Urban occupations had a stronger base. Much of the trade was in Jewish hands, and some of the merchants became affluent from the export of wool, flax, grain and wine, the import of metals and gems and the passing trade in silk from China. Jewish artisans worked in many crafts, and in some of them had a reputation extending far beyond the borders of the country. They were weavers and dyers of cloth, sailors, fishermen and boat-builders, blacksmiths, carpenters and porters.

The marked disparity in living standards between the rich and the poor, especially between the urban merchants and property owners and the rural cultivators, caused resentment and social tension in the Babylonian Jewish community.

The Exilarch

See colour page 177
For over a thousand years, from the 2nd to the 13th centuries AD, the Exilarch was the official head of the Babylonian community. It was a hereditary office, with its incumbents claiming descent from King David. The Exilarchs lived in princely style, wore the ornamental sash of a high official and had an honoured position at the courts of the rulers. Their functions included the collection of taxes from the Jews, the appointment of judges to Jewish courts and the appointment of market inspectors. In religious matters, however, authority lay with leading scholars, and later was concentrated in the heads of the two major academies of learning at Sura and Pumbedita.

The Sassanid Period

The neo-Persian dynasty of the Sassanids ruled over Babylonia from AD 226 to the conquest of the country by the Arab followers of Mohammed in AD 642. On the whole, the attitude of the regime to its Jewish subjects was benign, and it did not interfere in the internal affairs of the community. But at the outset of the Sassanid period the Babylonian Jews encountered religious intolerance for the first time. The new regime had revived the fire-worshipping Persian creed of Zoroastrianism that dated back to the 6th century BC. It now became the state religion, and its zealous 'magi' (priests) tried to force other faiths to conform.

One particularly sensitive issue concerned the disposal of the dead. The Zoroastrian custom was to expose corpses where they would be consumed by vultures and wild animals. (This is still done by the Parsees in India, a surviving Zoroastrian sect.) The Jewish community was shaken by incidents of bodies being exhumed in the cemeteries and synagogues being desecrated, and by the banning of some Jewish rituals.

The position improved with the second Sassanid ruler, the tolerant Shapur I. He had a great esteem for Mar Samuel, the leading Jewish scholar in Babylon at that time. The Talmud gives a resume of the discussions between the two men. As a result, religious coercion was stopped. An understanding was also reached in the legal sphere. While maintaining its internal jurisdiction in religious and family matters, the

King Chosroes I of Persia (559–531 BC), seated on his throne.

and carted their produce to the weekly markets in the towns and cities.

The Babylonian community adjusted to its non-Jewish environment in a manner that differed from that of the Alexandrian Jews. The latter had tried to achieve a synthesis between their Jewish heritage and the dominant Hellenist culture. The Babylonian Jews felt no similar need to reconcile their Judaism with Persian culture. All their intellectual and spiritual energies were funnelled into the task of developing and enriching the Jewish legacy they had received from the Land of Israel. The mainstream of the Oral Law, of Talmudic and rabbinic Judaism, passed through Babylonia and from there spread throughout the Jewish world. That process was facilitated by the Arab conquest, one of the turning-points of human history.

community agreed to abide by the laws of the state on such general subjects as land tenure and taxation. Mar Samuel summed this up by stating that 'the law of the land is law', a dictum that was to be of fundamental importance in the future relations between Diaspora communities and their host countries.

The king may also have been influenced by factors other than friendship for Samuel and benevolence towards his Jewish subjects. He had embarked on a military campaign against the Roman border provinces to the west, and needed both the financial support of his own Jews and the goodwill (at least tacit) of their fellow-Jews living under Roman rule in Galilee and elsewhere.

The community did not again experience religious persecution until the 5th century AD. In circumstances of political disorder and economic decline at that time, the Jews were cast in the familiar role of scapegoat. The Exilarch and other leading Jews were executed. A good part of the local community in the city of Isfahan was wiped out on the allegation that they had killed two priests. Many Jewish children were forcibly converted to the Zoroastrian faith. The climate of insecurity induced by these events reinforced the urge to reduce to writing three centuries of learned discussion in the academies, in order to preserve the record for the future. That decision gave birth to the Babylonian Talmud.

Important Events

The Biblical Period

BC

722	Destruction of Samaria and the end of the Hebrew Kingdom of Israel. Origin of the legend of the Lost Ten Tribes.
598	Beginning of the Babylonian captivity.
587	Destruction of Jerusalem and the First Temple and the end of the Hebrew Kingdom of Judah.
538	The Edict of Cyrus and the beginning of the Return.
520–15	Temple rebuilt.
458(?)	Mission of Ezra to Jerusalem.
445	Walls of Jerusalem reconstructed under Nehemiah.

The Hellenist-Roman Period

334–1	Conquests of Alexander the Great.
167	Beginning of Maccabean Revolt.
19	Herod the Great rebuilds Temple.

AD

48–58	Missionary journeys of St Paul.
66–70	Five-year war in Judea.
70	Titus sacks Jerusalem and destroys Temple. End of Second Jewish Commonwealth.
c.210	Completion of Mishnah.
c.390	Jerusalem Talmud completed.

Alexandria (*1st century* BC–*2nd century* AD)

BC

30	Roman occupation of Egypt.

AD

38	Anti-Jewish riots in Alexandria.
40	Philo Judaeus heads delegation to Rome.
66	Romans crush Jewish disorders.
115–17	Jewish Revolt in Egypt, Cyrene and Cyprus.

Babylonia (*2nd–6th centuries* AD)

226	End of Parthian rule. Beginning of Sassanid (neo-Persian) rule.
c.500	Babylonian Talmud completed.
589	Beginning of Gaonate period.

## Chapter Twelve

In the Shadow of the Cross

Byzantium: 4th–15th centuries AD

From the middle of the 2nd century AD Jewish life in the pagan Roman empire had become relatively secure and peaceful. The Edict of 212 AD, that extended Roman citizenship to all free inhabitants of the empire, applied to the Jews as well. Their religion was officially recognized and they were not required to make sacrifices to the Roman gods. There was no interference with the internal autonomy of the Jewish communities, including the right to settle disputes between Jews. Jewish citizens were exempt from military service. There were no occupational restrictions on them, whether as tillers of the soil, traders or artisans. They could live and work anywhere – except in Jerusalem, which was still closed to Jews. The only financial imposition on them was the *fiscus judaicus*, the head tax all Jews had to pay to the imperial treasury.

This tolerable situation started changing for the worse during the reign (306–37) of the emperor Constantine the Great. By his time Christianity was a pervasive force throughout the Roman world. He sought Christian support in his long power-struggle to become sole ruler of the Empire. In AD 313 he issued the Edict of Milan, extending freedom of worship to all Roman citizens. For the Jews, the decree confirmed the existing status quo. For the Christians, it marked a sudden change from official repression to official recognition. Due to imperial patronage, Christianity soon became the dominant faith in the Empire.

In little more than three centuries an obscure Jewish sect in Judea had expanded to become a major power. That turning point in history boded ill for the Jewish citizens of the Roman Empire – for Christianity, the daughter religion of Judaism, had set in a mould of hostility to its parent.

The early Church Fathers had given this hostility a doctrinal framework: the advent of Jesus Christ was regarded as a direct fulfilment of the messianic prophecies in the Old Testament (a thesis argued by St Paul in his Epistle to the Hebrews, where Jesus is called a High Priest and 'the mediator of a new Covenant'); after their rejection of Jesus, the Jews had ceased to be God's Chosen People, while the

Medallions with the heads of Constantine the Great (top) *and Julian the Apostate* (below).

The Byzantine Emperors and the Jews

See colour page 177

In the reign of Constantine the Great (AD 306–37) Christianity became the official religion of the Roman Empire (though the Emperor was only baptized on his deathbed).

(continued on page 126)

In AD 325 the Church Council of Nicaea was convened by Constantine to deal with the deep doctrinal schism in Christianity. Among other matters the Council called for the 'seclusion and humiliation' of the Jews. This was followed by a number of anti-Jewish imperial edicts by Constantine and his successors. The death penalty would be incurred by Christians who converted to Judaism, and by Jews who obstructed the conversion of other Jews to Christianity. Intermarriage was proscribed. Jews could not hold public office. They were not allowed to own Christian slaves, and later even pagan slaves – a serious economic blow, since slave-labour was the only available manpower for agriculture or industry.

There was a brief respite for the Jews during the reign of the emperor Julian the Apostate (361–3), who tried to turn the wheel back from Christianity to the old pagan gods. He was well disposed to the Jews, even promising to restore them to Jerusalem and to rebuild the Temple. After his death official policy relapsed into religious intolerance.

In 529 Emperor Justinian began to publish his famous legal Code, the *Corpus Juris Civiles*. In the chapters devoted to the status of the Jews, it amplified the provisions in the earlier Code of the emperor Theodosius II (408–50).

Certain specific topics were also dealt with in *Novellae* (Imperial Directives) issued by Justinian.

Justinian's Code fixed the legal status of the Jews in Byzantine society for the next seven centuries. Of special import was his *Novella 146* of the year 553. For the first time a Christian ruler had interfered in the internal religious practices of his Jewish subjects. The *Novella* forbade the Jewish practice of reading the Sacred Books in synagogue exclusively in the original Hebrew text, and it insisted that translations in other languages, such as Greek and Latin, be used. The Mishnah and other rabbinic interpretations of the Old Testament were banned, on the ground that they had no divine authority but were purely the handiwork of man and were responsible for spreading error. This *Novella* anticipated by many centuries the Talmud burnings of mediaeval Europe. The effect of Justinian's legislation was to make the Jews 'second-class citizens', with their religion tolerated but their lives severely restricted.

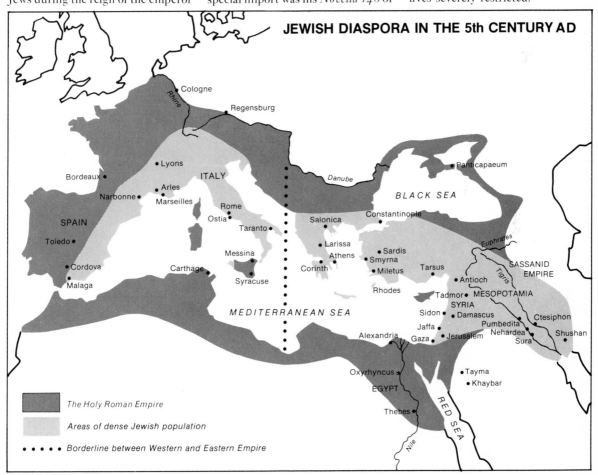

JEWISH DIASPORA IN THE 5th CENTURY AD

Cologne
Regensburg
Rhine
Lyons
Bordeaux
ITALY
Danube
Panticapaeum
Arles
Narbonne
Marseilles
BLACK SEA
Rome
Constantinople
SPAIN
Ostia
Salonica
Taranto
Toledo
Larissa
Athens
Sardis
Euphrates
Messina
Smyrna
Tarsus
SASSANID
Corinth
Miletus
EMPIRE
Cordova
Carthage
Antioch
MESOPOTAMIA
Malaga
Syracuse
Rhodes
Tadmor
SYRIA
Tigris
MEDITERRANEAN SEA
Sidon
Damascus
Ctesiphon
Jaffa
Pumbedita
Nehardea
Shushan
Alexandria
Gaza
Jerusalem
Sura

Oxyrhyncus
Tayma
Khaybar
EGYPT
RED SEA
Thebes
Nile

The Holy Roman Empire

Areas of dense Jewish population

• • • • • Borderline between Western and Eastern Empire

Church had become 'Israel according to the spirit'; the Jews had been kept in existence only to serve as living witnesses to the truth of the new faith; they should suffer punishment and humiliation to make them admit their error and embrace Christianity.

The Christian charge against the Jews was not just that they had rejected Jesus, but that they were collectively responsible for his death. The Gospels were written long after the events they described, at a time when the Jewish Revolt of AD 66–70 had been crushed by the military power of Rome. While there are discrepancies in the four Gospels, their writers had a common urge to shift the blame for the Crucifixion from the Roman authorities to the Jewish religious leaders. The stigma of 'Christ-killers' was cast on all Jews in subsequent ages; it would not be modified by the Church until 1965, at the Second Vatican Council convened by Pope John XXIII.

In AD 330 the emperor Constantine established his new capital in the town of Byzantine on the Bosphorus and renamed it Constantinople after himself. Sixty-five years later the Roman empire permanently split into two. During the 5th century the Western

(continued on page 128)

126

Separating the Two Faiths

Above *The Christian preacher John Chrysostom, which means 'Golden-mouthed' (AD 345–407), eventually became the Bishop of Constantinople. Here he is shown appearing near the synagogue at Antioch in Syria and railing against 'Jewish Christians' who still attended synagogue services, brought their disputes to Jewish courts or consulted Jewish doctors.*

The early Church was concerned about the fact that the dividing line between the old religion and the new remained blurred. There were still many Jewish Christians – Jews who were influenced by the tenets of the new creed but had not cut themselves off from their synagogues and their ancestral traditions. Moreover, there

The Late Byzantine Empire

The *Chronicle of Ahimaaz* – Ahimaaz was the son of Paltiel – was compiled in 1054 in the southern Italian town of Oria. The work sets out the author's family history from the 9th century, covering different communities in Italy and North Africa. It shows that the active religious, cultural and economic activities of the Jews in southern Italy continued uninterrupted under Byzantine rule.

The actual conditions of Jewish life in the Byzantine Empire were less oppressive than official decrees might suggest, and the Jews adjusted themselves to discrimination with all their ingrained resilience. Established communities maintained their synagogues, institutions and culture in Constantinople; on the islands of Cyprus and Rhodes; at Bari, Oria, Brindisi and Otranto in the 'heel' of Italy; at Salonika and Corinth in Greece; and at Izmir (Smyrna) and other places along the coast of Asia Minor. Regular contact was maintained with Eretz Israel.

Many of the Jews were traders, some of them prosperous. Others were engaged in the distinctive Jewish crafts of cloth dyeing, silk weaving and tanning. In certain areas Jewish peasants still tilled the soil. Soon after the Byzantine empire ended in the 15th century and was replaced by the Ottoman Empire, the Jewish population in that area was solid enough to absorb a wave of refugees from Spain and Portugal.

Massacre in Jerusalem

See colour pages 110 and 111

Not all later Byzantine emperors respected even the limited status given the Jews in Justinian's Code. The emperor Heraclius (610–41) tried to forbid the practice of Judaism and to force baptism on the Jews. In 614 the Jews in the Holy Land assisted an invading Persian force to capture Jerusalem. When Heraclius regained the city fifteen years later, he had its Jewish inhabitants massacred or expelled in revenge. Within less than a decade Byzantium lost the Holy Land again, this time to the emergent power of Islam.

In addition to the Holy Land, the

Rabbi Shephatiah sails to Constantinople and enters into a disputation with Basil, who recognizes Shephatiah's superior wisdom but does not cancel his edicts. From the Chronicle of Ahimaaz.

were a number of Roman proselytes to Judaism, a trend that could only increase as the paganism of the Roman world waned. Church leaders campaigned vigorously against what they called 'the Jewish temptation'.

From the beginning of the 4th century a series of Church Councils adopted measures designed to separate Christianity more sharply from Judaism. The weekly Sabbath day (a Jewish custom unknown in the pagan world) was shifted for Christians from Saturday to Sunday. The date of Easter would no longer be tied to that of the Passover. Intermarriage was forbidden; so was conversion to Judaism, and even sitting down to table with Jews. Some of the Church's anti-Jewish pronouncements found their way into the legal codes of the Byzantine emperors.

Empire disintegrated under the blows of invading barbarian hordes – such as the Germanic tribes of the Goths and the Vandals, and the Huns who had come surging out of Central Asia. The Eastern Empire was to last almost a thousand years longer, until the Ottoman Turks took Constantinople in 1453. It became known as the Byzantine Empire, from the original name of its capital. Its territory expanded and contracted from time to time, but the Byzantine heart-land remained the area now covered by Greece, Bulgaria and Turkey.

Byzantine Empire lost Syria, Egypt, North Africa and Sicily to the conquering Arab armies. The majority of the Jewish people was now under Moslem rule. Official attitudes stiffened against the Jewish communities left within the confines of the shrunken empire. Thus an imperial Council in 692 prohibited mixed bathing of Jews and Christians and the employment of Jewish physicians by Christians. Decrees ordering forced baptism were issued by the emperors Leo III in 721, Basil I in 873, and Romanus I in 943, but they were not seriously enforced in practice.

Christian Spain

The Christian Visigoth kingdom of Spain lasted from the 5th century to the Moorish (Moslem Arab and Berber) invasion of AD 711. The Moslems occupied the whole Iberian Peninsula (Spain and Portugal) except for a small Christian enclave in the north-east corner of the country. The next eight centuries witnessed a fluctuating struggle between the Crescent and the Cross for the mastery of Spain. Gradually the Christian kingdom led by Castile expanded southward, and Moslem-held territory shrank. In 1492 Granada, the last Moorish foothold in Spain, surrendered to the forces of Ferdinand and Isabella, and the Christian 'Reconquista' was completed.

In the course of the 'Reconquista' the majority of Jews in Spain passed from Moslem to Christian rule, where they came under the direct protection of the Catholic kings, on the model of the rest of mediaeval Europe.

Jewish life in Christian Spain flourished until the 14th century, continuing the Golden Age that had started in Moslem Spain. The Jews then came under increasing pressure; the community did not recover from the disastrous persecutions of 1391. Many Jews were killed, others fled, and there were large-scale conversions, bringing into existence a substantial community of 'Conversos', also called New Christians and Marranos. The final blow came with the expulsion decree of 1492, immediately after the fall of Granada.

With the Expulsion, twelve centuries of Jewish life in Spain came to an end. That experience, under Roman, Visigoth, Moslem and Catholic regimes, cannot be reduced to one single pattern. Interludes of freedom and glittering achievement alternated with repression and tragedy, and the double life of the Marranos formed a strange thread in the story. (See page 134.)

Under Visigoth Rule
As early as the 3rd century AD there was a substantial Jewish community in what was then the Spanish province of the Roman Empire. The Jews were mostly located in the south

Below *A Jewish tombstone of the girl Meliosa from Tortosa in northern Spain, inscribed in Hebrew, Latin and Greek. Its date is probably between the 4th and 6th centuries AD.*

in the Cordoba area. They were traders, craftsmen and tillers of the soil, cultivating their own vineyards and olive groves. As Roman citizens, they were free of legal restrictions.

With the break-up of the Western Roman Empire in the 5th century, Spain became a kingdom ruled by the Visigoths, one of the Germanic tribes that had dismembered the empire. The Visigoth kings were at first sympathetic to their Jewish subjects, and treated them on the same footing as the other former Roman citizens of the country. But the official attitude changed for the worse towards the end of the 6th century, and the Byzantine measures regarding the Jews were applied under pressure from the Church. From time to time a fanatical ruler would present the Jews with a blunt choice between conversion and exile. When that happened thousands of them left Spain to take refuge elsewhere. A number of others went through a formal rite of baptism, while remaining Jews in private.

At the beginning of the 8th century the Visigoth rulers were already fearful of the wave of Arab conquest that had swallowed up North Africa. The Jews were suspect as potential collaborators with the Moslem enemy.

Those Jews who did not manage to escape were declared slaves and handed over to Christian masters. Their property was confiscated and their children from the age of seven were taken away to be brought up as Christians. It is hardly surprising that the Moorish invasion in 711 should have been welcomed by the Jews.

A Synagogue Wall from Toledo

See below

This is part of the eastern wall of the Toledo synagogue built in 1357 by Don Samuel ha-Levi Abulafia. The wall decorations contain foliate designs and biblical quotations in stylized Hebrew lettering. The inscriptions seen in the picture are from the Psalms. After the Expulsion of 1492, the synagogue became a church named El Transito. In the 19th century the building was renovated and declared a national monument. In 1964 it was turned into a historical museum for the Jews of Spain.

Before the persecutions of 1391 the Toledo community was one of the largest and most flourishing in Spain, with a number of fine synagogues and

a reputation for Jewish scholarship. The Abulafias were one of the city's leading families. Don Samuel's house was later occupied for a while by the painter El Greco.

The Reconquista and the Jews

See map overleaf

For nearly eight centuries after the Moorish invasion of AD 711, Spain remained a battlefield between the opposing forces of the Cross and the Crescent. The Christian reconquest of the country (known in the history books by the Spanish name 'Reconquista') started in the north with the establishment of the kingdoms of Castile, Navarre and Aragon. Slowly the area under Christian control expanded southward, until in 1085 a Castilian army scored a resounding victory with the capture of Toledo, the former Visigoth capital. A Moslem counter-offensive halted the Christian advance, but it was resumed a half-century later.

In the early phase of the Reconquista, the Christian rulers in northern Spain reverted to the anti-Jewish laws of the late Visigoth kingdom. But as more of the country

came under their control, they found the Jews a valuable asset. They helped to revive trade in the newly-occupied territories, took over abandoned Moslem estates and served as a source of tax revenue and loans. No hindrance was imposed on Jewish worship and communal autonomy. As each town was regained, its Jewish quarter was left unharmed, and was given better treatment than the local Moslems received. An influx of Jews from Moslem Spain and elsewhere was officially encouraged. Members of wealthy and aristocratic Jewish families were appointed to offices at the Christian courts. Prominent rabbis enjoyed wide respect and influence even outside the Jewish fold,

such as Moses ben-Nachman (Nachmanides) of Catalonia (1194–1270), known from his initials as Ramban; Solomon ben-Abraham Adret of Barcelona in Aragon (1235–1310) known from his initials as Rashba; and the Abulafia family in Toledo. Jewish intellectual and cultural life continued to flourish. To this period belonged the greatest of mediaeval Jewish poets, Judah ha-Levi (1074–1141); also the wandering scholar and poet Abraham ibn-Ezra (1092–1167). It is mistaken to regard the Golden Age of Jewish civilization in Spain as related only to the Moorish regime, it extended also to Christian Spain.

The Jewish position deteriorates *See right*

From the 13th century onwards the situation of the Jews in Spain deteriorated, and the climate of bigotry and persecution in France and Germany permeated south of the Pyrenees in the wake of the Crusades. In 1391 there was a bloody outbreak of mob violence against the Jewish quarter in Seville. It sparked off a wave of massacres that spread across Castile and into neighbouring Navarre and Aragon. Measures taken by the authorities to check the disturbances were belated and ineffective. Tens of thousands of Jews were murdered; Jewish quarters were

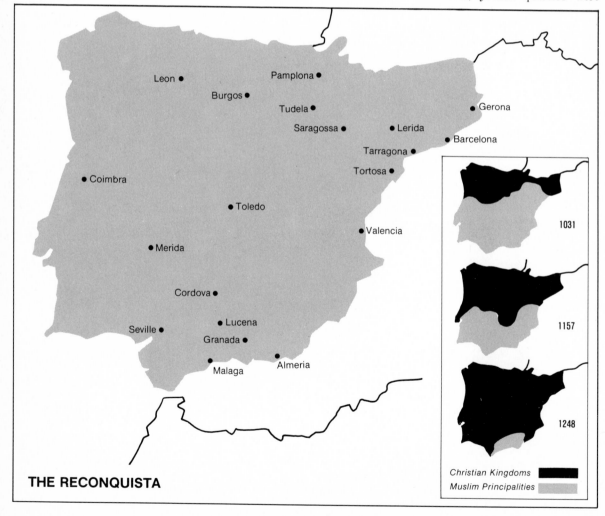

THE RECONQUISTA

Christian Kingdoms
Muslim Principalities

The fanatical Dominican friar Vicente Ferrer (1350–1419) bursting into a synagogue in Toledo.

pilfaged, and synagogues destroyed. There were wholesale baptisms, including in some cases entire small congregations. The face of Spanish Jewry had been brutally altered in that one year, and a large community of 'Conversos', or 'New Christians', had come into existence.

At the beginning of the 15th century, Friar Vicente Ferrer was the arch-enemy of the Spanish Jews. In 1411, with royal backing, he embarked on a crusade from synagogue to synagogue, first in Castile and then elsewhere in the country. Everywhere he denounced Judaism and demanded conversion. He met with some success, especially in small country communities, since Spanish Jewry was still weakened by the violent outbreaks of 1391.

The Jewish role in navigation

See map overleaf

Jewish scholars introduced into Christian Spain the fruits of Arab-Jewish co-operation in Moorish Spain in philosophy, medicine, and science. This contribution was of special importance in the fields of cartography and astronomy, at a time when Spanish and Portuguese navigators were setting out on epoch-making voyages of exploration that would lead to the discovery of America and the opening of the sea-route to India round Africa.

The world map was executed in 1375–7 by the Majorcan Jewish cartographer Abraham Cresques and his son Judah for Pedro IV, King of Aragon.

The map was regarded as so important that in 1381 a copy was sent as a gift to Charles VI of France. Pedro IV granted father and son royal protection, generous revenues and exemption from wearing the Jewish badge. After Abraham's death in 1387, Judah continued to serve as the royal cartographer in Aragon. In the massacres in Spain in 1391, he converted to Christianity and changed his name. He was later employed as map-maker by the famous Portuguese sea explorer, Prince Henry the Navigator.

One of the greatest astronomers of the period was Abraham ben-Samuel Zacuto (1452–c.1515) of Salamanca. He taught astrology and astronomy at the University of Salamanca, and wrote a major astronomical textbook (1473–8). The work was apparently written in Hebrew, but survived only in Spanish translation. He invented an accurate copper astrolabe, and produced greatly improved astronomical tables and maritime charts, which were used by Christopher Columbus to cross the Atlantic and by Vasco da Gama to reach India round Africa.

The Disputations

In mediaeval Europe of the 13th to 15th centuries the Church authorities from time to time arranged public Christian-Jewish 'disputations' in order to demonstrate the validity of Christianity as opposed to the 'errors' of Judaism. As a rule, the Church spokesman was a Jewish apostate familiar with Jewish religious writings.

In Spain there were two notable Disputations, one in Barcelona, Aragon in 1263, and the other at Tortosa, Catalonia, in 1413–14.

The Barcelona Disputation took place in the palace in the presence of the king, James I, and his court, as well as leaders of the Dominican and Franciscan Orders. The side of the church was represented by a French-

A detail from the Catalan Nautical Atlas *by Abraham and Judah Cresques.*

born Jewish convert to Christianity. He had taken the name of Pablo Christiani, joined the Dominican Order and was sent to Aragon to proselytize the Jews. The defender of the Jewish side was the leading Jewish scholar of his time, Rabbi Moses ben-Nachman, usually known as Nachmanides. Christiani undertook to prove from the Talmud itself that the Messiah foretold by the Prophets had already come, in the person of Jesus.

Having obtained the right to speak freely, without fear of punishment, Nachmanides made a remarkably frank reply. The Prophets had foretold that the coming of the Messiah would usher in an era of universal peace, yet the Christian world had

Nachmanides in a Disputation before James I, king of Aragon.

never ceased to engage in warfare and extol martial virtues. How difficult it would be for the king and his knights if war was no longer permitted! Clearly, therefore, the messianic age had not yet come. As for the dogma of the divinity of Christ, the Son of God born of a woman and killed by man, reason could not agree to it, nature opposed it, and the Prophets never said such a thing. Such beliefs could not convince any Jew.

The king had great esteem for Nachmanides, and had on occasion consulted him on matters concerning the Jewish community. At the end of the Disputation the king commended him on the eloquence of his argu-ments and made him a gift of 300 dinars in appreciation. When the angry Dominicans had him summoned to trial for attacks on Chris-tianity, Nachmanides invoked the king's promise that he could speak openly without retribution, and was saved by royal intervention. The Dominicans then obtained a letter from Pope Clement IV demanding that the king punish the blasphemous Jew. Realizing he was now in grave danger, Nachmanides escaped from Spain and settled in the Land of Israel.

The Tortosa Disputation lasted for nearly two years and took up sixty-nine sessions. Again, the Church side was represented by an apostate, the former Talmudic scholar Solomon ha-Levi, who had adopted the name of Pablo de Santa Maria, taken Holy Orders and become Bishop of Burgos. The proceedings were con-ducted in Latin. Only one of the twenty-two-member Jewish dele-gation of rabbis and scholars was familiar with Latin, and he therefore served as the main spokesman. Among the issues debated were the nature of the messianic prophecies and the alleged immoral and anti-Christian elements in the Talmud. This time, without a royal umpire, the verdict was in favour of the Christian side.

The Marranos

During the 15th century the attention of the Church and the public in Spain was focused less on the Jews than on the Conversos or New Christians. While the Jews were regarded as infidels, adherents of another religion, those of the Conversos whose acceptance of Christianity was less than whole-hearted were regarded as heretics, which was much worse in the eyes of the Church. After the mass conversion of 1391, a small number of the New Christians joined the ranks of the Jew-baiters with self-justifying ardour. The majority of the Conversos outwardly adhered to Catholicism but secretly continued to practise the Jewish faith. It was the Old Christians who scornfully called the New Christians 'Marranos' (swine).

For several generations the Marranos prospered. A number of them became affluent, rose to prominent positions in public service, the professions and academic life and intermarried with established Spanish families. There are few old families in modern Spain or Latin America today that do not have a Marrano ancestor. But the very success of the Marranos inevitably provoked a backlash of envy and dislike.

Queen Isabella, an extremely devout Catholic, was persuaded that heresy had to be stamped out among the New Christians. For this purpose, the Inquisition was introduced and the Queen's own confessor, the fanatical Tomas de Torquemada, was appointed Inquisitor-General. As an instrument for dealing with heretics the Inquisition had already existed in Western Europe for 250 years, under

A Marrano family secretly observing the Sabbath in a cellar.

the direct control of the Popes. The newly-launched Spanish Inquisition operated as an independent agency, with a ferocity unequalled elsewhere. Good Christians were required to inform on Marrano neighbours who showed the slightest sign of a Jewish 'taint', such as giving biblical names to their children, washing their hands before meals or prayers, wearing clean garments on Saturdays or the dates of Jewish festivals, and eating unleavened bread during the Passover period.

The Spanish Inquisition started in 1478, and it is estimated that during the following seven years about 700 Marranos were burnt alive at the stake, and over 5,000 more punished after they had confessed under torture and recanted the 'sin' of clinging in private to the faith of their ancestors.

The Inquisition continued for centuries, and extended to the Spanish colonies in the New World. Many Marranos fled, reverted to Judaism and joined Sephardic (Spanish) communities that had grown up in other countries; others, probably the majority, eventually accepted Christianity and lost any Jewish identification. In Belmonte, Portugal, there is still a small Christian group that retains some crypto-Jewish customs of Marrano origin. A few families came to Israel from the island of Majorca, claiming to be Jews of Marrano descent, but they went back again.

A modern secular mind is repelled by the belief that souls should be saved by tearing bodies to pieces on the rack or burning them alive. Yet mediaeval men would have found it equally hard to grasp that in 20th-century totalitarian states racial or political purity should be sought by means of gas-chambers and Gulag archipelagoes.

The Expulsion

In 1468 Isabella, heir to the throne of Castile, was married to Ferdinand, the crown prince of Aragon. They became co-rulers of Castile in 1474 and of a joint kingdom when Castile and Aragon were joined five years later. At first the royal pair showed no special hostility towards their Jewish subjects. In fact, professing Jews held important offices at the court. One of them, Don Abraham Seneor, was the Chief Rabbi of Castile and at the same time the tax commissioner for the whole of the joint kingdom. Another, Don Isaac Abrabanel, was a member of an illustrious Jewish family and a leading biblical commentator. Born in Lisbon, he had been the treasurer to the king of Portugal until 1484, when he moved to Castile and took service with Ferdinand and Isabella. He acted as tax farmer under Abraham Seneor for a good part of Castile, and as the promoter of huge loans for the Crown, to finance the campaign against the remaining Moslem state of Granada in the south.

The Expulsion edict signed by Ferdinand and Isabella.

To the head of the Spanish Inquisition, Torquemada, and to his associates, it was intolerable that they should be busy sniffing out surviving traces of Judaism among the Marranos while Jews could go on practising their religion openly. An historic opportunity to drive home that point came with the surrender of Moslem Granada in 1492, thereby bringing the whole of Spain under Christian rule. Ferdinand and Isabella were prevailed upon to celebrate the occasion with a decree expelling all Jews from Spain. The decree was signed in the magnificent Moorish palace of the Alhambra in Granada on 31 March 1492, and was to be carried out within four months. On the return of the king and queen to Toledo, Abraham Seneor and Isaac Abrabanel gained an audience with them and pleaded in vain for the decree to be annulled. Their appeal was directed less to compassion than to greed; Abrabanel offered to arrange for the cancellation of the royal loans he had raised, and to place further sums at the disposal of the treasury. It is related that Torquemada burst into the chamber with his eyes blazing, flung down a crucifix and cried out, 'Judas sold his Master for thirty pieces of silver; you would sell Him again.'

During the next few months over 100,000 Jews streamed out of Spain, leaving behind nearly all their property and possessions. On 31 July, exactly four months after the signing of the decree, the last person professing to be a Jew left Spanish soil.

The largest contingent of the *emigrés* crossed the border into Portugal, where the Jews had on the whole led a more sheltered existence. This haven was theirs for only another five years. The young Portuguese king, Manoel the Fortunate, wanted to keep the Jews in his realm. At the same time, he wanted to marry the daughter of Ferdinand and Isabella, and the match was made conditional on his ridding Portugal of infidels, whether Jewish or Moslem. He too signed an expulsion order, then did everything possible to thwart it by forcing Christianity on his Jewish subjects. First the children were seized and baptized.

Abraham Seneor and Isaac Abrabanel appearing before the Spanish rulers Ferdinand and Isabella in 1492. The inquisitor Torquemada is on the left.

tized. Then, before the parents could embark, they were declared royal slaves and put willy-nilly through a hurried token baptism.

These Portuguese New Christians remained Jews in all but name for nearly fifty years, until the Inquisition was permitted into Portugal as well. Some of the Marranos then left the country; the rest were absorbed into the Portuguese people.

Most of the Jewish refugees from Spain and Portugal scattered through the Moslem lands in North Africa, the Balkans and the Near East, including Palestine. Other groups settled in Italy and France. In these countries of refuge, whether Moslem or Christian, they were drawn into the Sephardic (Spanish) congregations established by earlier emigrés. In the next two centuries or so these communities were augmented by Marranos who escaped from the continuing harassment of the Inquisition and reverted to Judaism.

Organized Jewish life had come to an end in the Iberian Peninsula, but a widespread Sephardi Diaspora had come into existence elsewhere.

slowly through the Provence region of southern France, noting the centres of Jewish scholarship that had developed in the communities of Narbonne, Montpellier, Arles, Avignon, and elsewhere. He took ship to Genoa and travelled down Italy from Pisa to Rome, where among other matters he gave a fine tourist-guide description of the antiquities.

Sailing from southern Italy, he went through Corfu and Greece to Constantinople, where he stayed for a while, studying life there in some depth. He continued by boat through the Aegean Sea to Rhodes and Cyprus. Landing at Antioch in Syria, he went to Aleppo, Damascus and Baghdad, where he described the Caliph's court and wrote down the extraordinary story of the false messiah, David Alroy. In Palestine, then under Crusader rule, he visited all the main towns and holy places. He returned to Spain via Egypt, Sicily and France.

The information in his book about Persia, India, Ceylon and China obviously relies on travellers' tales from other sources, and is coloured by fancy. Where Benjamin bases himself on his own observations he is sober, clear and factual. Of particular interest is his account of specialized Jewish crafts in certain locations, like the cloth-dyers of Brindisi in southern Italy, the silk-weavers in Greece, the tanners in Constantinople and the glass-workers of Aleppo and Tyre. However, his stories about the fearsome Jewish brigand tribes of central Arabia and the Yemen must be treated with reserve, as it is unlikely that he penetrated the Arabian Peninsula.

Since it is the most important and detailed account of the Mediterranean and Middle East region at that period, Benjamin's book has been translated into nearly all European languages and is a valuable source for students of Jewish and general mediaeval history.

Benjamin of Tudela

See colour pages 178 and 179

Benjamin ben-Judah, from the town of Tudela in northern Spain, was the great 12th-century roving reporter of Jewish life in the Mediterranean – Near East region. His journeys may well have taken up to eight years (the exact duration is uncertain) and ended about 1173. He must have kept detailed journals from which he composed his *Book of Travels* (*Sefer ha-Massa'ot*). It first appeared in Constantinople in 1543, and from a somewhat different manuscript in Ferrara, Italy, in 1556.

Nothing is known about Benjamin's personal background, not even his occupation or the reason for the lengthy travels he undertook. From evidence in his book, it is surmised that he may have been a merchant, possibly in precious stones. Although he depicted conditions and places of general interest in the countries he visited, his primary concern was with their Jewish communities. He investigated and described them in detail – their size, their occupations, their way of life, their scholars and communal leaders and the way they were treated.

From Spain, Benjamin travelled

Ashkenaz

Ashkenaz is a Hebrew word commonly used for Germany. The Jews who settled in the Rhineland and northern France spread across France and Germany, and later migrated into Eastern Europe, were known as Ashkenazim.

The history of the Ashkenazi Jews started with the Jewish traders who followed the Roman legions into Gaul, and settled in the new towns that grew out of the military camps along the Rhine valley. In AD 800 Charlemagne founded the Carolingian Empire that covered Western and Central Europe and lasted almost two centuries. Jews were encouraged to come into the empire and its successor states, in order to derive advantage from them as traders. In that period the Jews participated in the international commerce between Europe, the Mediterranean and the East. Living in both the Christian and Moslem worlds, Jewish merchants could act as a bridge between them.

In 1000 there were a number of established Jewish communities along the river valleys that formed the main trade routes: at Cologne, Mainz, Worms and Speyer in the Rhine Basin, at Augsburg and Regensburg on the Danube, at Prague in the east, at Paris and Troyes on the Seine, and at Avignon, Arles, Narbonne and other centres in Provence round the lower course of the Rhone. After 1066 French Jews reached England with William the Conqueror.

Up to the end of the 11th century, Jewish life in the Ashkenaz region was relatively unharassed, except for spasmodic local incidents. Reactionary churchmen continued to press for enforcement of the anti-Jewish laws enacted in the Byzantine empire and endorsed by Church Councils. But rulers found it expedient to ignore this ecclesiastical pressure. There does not seem to have been widespread hostility to Jews among the general populace; in fact, some prelates complained bitterly about this co-existence between Jew and Gentile. One of the most vocal of these was Agobard, the Archbishop of Lyons (814–40), whose anti-semitic pamphlets castigated the Jews as 'sons of darkness'. Matters had reached a stage, he wrote, 'where ignorant Christians claim that the Jews preach better than our priests ... some Christians even celebrate the Sabbath with the Jews and violate the holy repose of Sunday ... Men of the people, peasants, allow themselves to be plunged into such a sea of errors that they regard the Jews as the only people of God, and consider that they combine the observance of a pure religion and a truer faith than ours.'

Agobard and his equally virulent successor Bishop Amulo failed to convince the emperors to repress the Jews. Moreover, there still lingered in the Church the less fanatical school of thought enunciated in the 7th century by the revered Pope Gregory I, and before that by the most learned of the early Church Fathers, St Augustine. Yet the attacks of men like Agobard sank into the popular mind, and would bear evil fruit in the Middle Ages.

During this period Jewish scholarship flourished in the area.

Ecclesia and Synagoga

These two graceful effigies of queens appear at the side entrance of Strasbourg Cathedral in Alsace, completed in 1230. One represents Ecclesia (the Church), a crown on her head. The other, Synagoga, is blindfolded, dejected of mien, without a crown and holding a broken staff.

Such figures, denoting the triumph of Christianity and the defeat of Judaism, were frequently

The First Crusade. In the massacres of 1096, the communities of Mainz, Speyer, Worms, Cologne and others were destroyed.

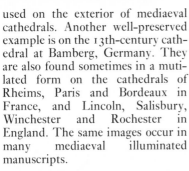

used on the exterior of mediaeval cathedrals. Another well-preserved example is on the 13th-century cathedral at Bamberg, Germany. They are also found sometimes in a mutilated form on the cathedrals of Rheims, Paris and Bordeaux in France, and Lincoln, Salisbury, Winchester and Rochester in England. The same images occur in many mediaeval illuminated manuscripts.

Important academies developed in some of the cities, while renowned scholars like Rabbi Gershom of Mainz and Rabbi Shlomo ben-Isaac of Troyes (Rashi) had an influence throughout the European region and beyond it. Ashkenaz had become a new and major centre of Jewish learning.

The era of relative tolerance came to an end for the Jews of Europe at the end of the 11th century. From then on they were plunged into an inferno of mediaeval persecution. The turning-point was the First Crusade (1095–9). An emotional reaction had been provoked in Europe by stories from returning pilgrims that the Holy Land and the sites in it sacred to Christianity were being defiled by the Moslem Arabs, who had taken the country four centuries earlier from Christian Byzantium. On 26 November 1095, in a sermon to the Church Council in Clermont, France, Pope Urban II called on Christendom to recover the Holy Land from the infidel. The princes and knights who responded to this call were called Crusaders, from the ceremony of 'taking the cross'.

The movement quickly spread through Europe. It was fuelled by

(continued on page 141)

The Jews in England: 11th –12th centuries AD

The mass suicide of the York Jews in the royal castle, known as Clifford's Tower, took place on 16 March 1190. It was the worst incident in the outbreak of anti-Jewish disorders in a number of English towns that spring. The background was the religious fervour aroused by the Third Crusade, of which Richard I (the Lionheart) of England was a leading figure.

In September of the previous year Richard had been crowned in Westminster Hall, London. The excited crowd outside ran amok, killed a number of Jews and looted their homes. Order was quickly restored, but after the departure of Richard and his troops for the Holy Land, the disturbances flared up again in the provincial centres.

In York the Jews took refuge in the castle. They were led by the head of the community, Josce, and their rabbi, Yomtov ben-Isaac, a well-known scholar and liturgical poet who had come from France to York a decade earlier. The castle was cut off and besieged by the mob. When the situation of the Jews had become hopeless, and they suspected that the warden was about to hand them over, they decided to take their own lives. Each man killed the members of his family and then himself. Finally the rabbi ended Josce's life and took his own.

When Richard fell captive to the Saracen foe, his ransom money was to a large extent exacted from the English Jews. On his return to England, the king was angry at the anti-Jewish attacks that had occurred in his absence. As elsewhere in Western Europe, the Jews belonged to the king and were under his direct protection. Moreover their money-lending transactions (the only occupation still permitted to them) provided substantial tax revenues for the Royal Exchequer. During the disturbances many of those who had received Jewish loans had simply burnt the bonds and refused to pay. In order to preserve for the future the royal stake

Clifford's tower in York.

in such dealings, Richard instituted a system whereby an official registry of Jewish loans was kept in each one of the larger English towns. In Whitehall an 'Exchequer of the Jews' was established to oversee this process in twenty-six different towns and collect the king's share of the interest. Richard also created the office of Jewish Archpresbyter, held by a succession of leading Jews. The Archpresbyter served as liaison between the palace and the Jewish community in England.

The Jews were latecomers to England, arriving shortly after 1066 from France with the Norman Conquest and provided financial services to William the Conqueror and his barons. They retained links with French Jewry, and for a generation or two continued to speak French among themselves. By the middle of the 12th century there were about

4,000 Jews in England. The largest community was in London, which at that time had the only consecrated Jewish burial-ground in the country. Smaller communities existed in several provincial towns, including Lincoln, Winchester, York, Oxford, Norwich and Bristol. A few of the Jews prospered. One of them, Aaron of Lincoln (1125–86) became very wealthy, and was considered one of the richest men in England. When he died, his estate was confiscated by the Royal Treasury, and a special department, called the Exchequer of Aaron, was set up to collect his outstanding loans. The huge loans owing to him by the king were simply cancelled. All the bullion and other treasure seized from Aaron's estate was despatched by ship to France to finance a military campaign there, but the ship sank in a storm in the English channel.

mixed motives: religious zeal, greed for land and booty, the opening up of lucrative trade routes and the lure of adventure. For the Jewish community that lay in its path (especially in the Rhineland), the Crusade was a bloody disaster. Undisciplined bands of peasants fell upon the defenceless Jewish communities, murdering and looting, as did the camp followers who accompanied or preceded the main body of the Crusaders. There were smaller contingents of knights who also saw the Jews as fair game. Many of the Jewish communities were wiped out before the first Crusader had left Europe. The climax came in the Holy Land in July 1099, when the Crusader army led by Godfrey of Bouillon captured Jerusalem and slaughtered all the Moslem and Jewish inhabitants of the city.

In the next two centuries there were eight more Crusades (not including the tragic Children's Crusade). Their object was to support the Latin kingdom of Jerusalem and the adjacent Crusader principalities, that were battling to survive against the Moslem counter-offensive. The final Crusade was not long before the fall in 1291 of Acre, the last Crusader stronghold in Palestine.

The brutal treatment of the Jews in the mediaeval period was not caused only by the religious bigotry worked up by the Crusades, but the anti-Jewish excesses must also be seen in the context of the general conditions. Western Europe was still a barbarous and insecure region. The nobility was a military caste, prizing above all the skills and the code of honour of the fighting man. The bulk of the population lived in ignorance, squalor and superstition. All calamities – whether pestilence, famine or the outbreaks of fire that ravaged the towns – were attributed to malignant forces. The region was torn by religious

Trade between a Jew, wearing the pointed hat, and a Christian peasant. From the Dresden Sachsenspiegel, Germany, 1220.

wars that devastated whole countries. The Jew, the only non-Christian minority in a Christian world, was the natural scapegoat for the ills and tensions of mediaeval society. He stood outside the feudal structure of that society, composed as it was of the land-owning aristocracy, the Church, the peasants, and the burgeoning cities.

The vulnerability of the Jews increased as their economic base shrank. They had long been cut off from the soil and were concentrated in the towns. As urban traders and artisans, they were now largely squeezed out with the rise of tightly-organized merchant and craft guilds from which Jews were excluded. In international trade, the Crusades opened up lucrative business opportunities for such powerful Christian interests as the Italian port-republics of Venice, Genoa and Amalfi.

The one occupation left open to Jews, because it was forbidden to Christians, was money-lending. It was despised, unpopular, degrading and often hazardous. But for some while it was essential. By the mediaeval period, Church doctrine had crystallized against 'usury', which meant the lending of money at any interest, large or small. The Third Lateran Council, which met in Rome in 1179, formally banned money-lending for Christians and ruled that anyone violating the ban would be denied a Christian burial.

Jewish doctrine on the subject was derived from the *Book of Deuteronomy*, which laid down that: 'To a foreigner you may lend upon interest, but to your brother you shall not lend upon interest.' *Deut. 23:20*. This was interpreted to mean that a Jew was permitted to make a loan to a non-Jew and charge interest on it. For the Jews in mediaeval Europe that rabbinical ruling became the key to sheer survival. As they were pushed out of regular trading, their capital was diverted into what was in effect the earliest banking and financial services for Christian Europe. Everyone needed money: the kings and barons for their perpetual wars, the landowners to tide them over poor harvests, the Church and the monastic orders to build their splendid churches and abbeys, the city merchants to finance their business ventures, the squires to buy their way out of military service (by the custom known as 'scutage'), and the artisans to purchase the tools of their trade. The Jew was the source of loan capital for all these purposes. Interest rates were very high, but so were the risks. When the Jewish money-lender was murdered or driven out, the loan went to the king.

The king had a double financial interest in his Jewish subjects. They raised money directly for his needs, and they also paid him taxes on the loans they made to others. The Jews were a valuable asset to the rulers, and their legal status became that of *servi camerae regis* (Latin for 'servants of the king's chamber').

The principle was clearly stated in 12th-century England in the *Laws of Edward the Confessor*. The relevant provision reads: 'All Jews, wherever in the realm they are, must be under the king's liege protection and guardianship, nor can any of them put himself under

The citizens of Tournai burying their dead during the Black Death. From a Belgian manuscript, 14th century.

The Black Death

The Black Death was an epidemic of bubonic plague that started in Constantinople in 1344 and spread all over Europe and Asia, decimating the population. It may have been carried by returning Crusaders and pilgrims to Western Europe, where it raged for the two years, 1348–50. By the time it burnt itself out an estimated one-third of the inhabitants of the region had died a horrible death.

In 1894 medical science established that the source of the disease lay in bacteria transmitted by the fleas carried by rats. Five centuries earlier, in mediaeval Europe, no rational explanation was available. A person would mysteriously start to shake with fever and then rant in delirium; suppurating sores would break out from the lymph glands; the blood would turn blackish (hence the name Black Death); and within a few days the person would be dead.

The Church declared the plague a scourge of God, and called on sinners to repent while there was yet time. The populace sought the cause in some malignant human design. The

(continued on page 144)

story spread like wildfire that the Jews had poisoned the wells. Some said the Jews had plotted with the Moslem enemy to destroy Christianity. Some credence was added to this story by the fact that the Jews seemed to have greater resistance to the ravages of the plague. It was useless to point out that they lived in segregated quarters and maintained a higher standard of hygiene than their neighbours.

Throughout the Ashkenaz region there were spontaneous outbreaks of violence. The mobs overran Jewish quarters, murdering the inhabitants and destroying their homes. A special bull issued by Pope Clement VI discounted the charge and called for the attacks on the Jews to cease, but in the prevailing atmosphere it had little effect.

The frenzied attacks were also fed by a material factor. Loans obtained from Jewish money-lenders were usually wiped out when they were killed. In Germany alone the disturbances occurred in some 350 localities, 60 of the larger Jewish communities and 150 of the smaller ones were completely liquidated. It was by far the worst series of massacres suffered by the Jews in mediaeval Europe.

Jews being burned at the stake. A woodcut from Schedel's Weltchronik, *1495.*

the protection of any powerful person without the king's license, because the Jews themselves and all their chattels are the king's. If, therefore, anyone detain them or their money, the king may claim them, if he so desire and if he is able, as his own.' That status cut both ways. The Jews were given royal protection where their royal master was able and willing to extend it; but they were also at the mercy of royal greed. There were kings who ruined 'their' Jews by exorbitant taxes and levies, or imprisoned and expelled them in order to confiscate their assets and wipe out their debts to them.

In the later mediaeval period the Jews lost their exclusive function even as money-lenders. Christian rivals moved into this field by adopting various legal devices and fictions to get round the anti-usury laws. Thus, the capital amount of the loan might be inflated in the bond, or interest disguised as a penalty for non-payment on due date. In particular, there were the thriving groups of French money-lenders known as 'Lombards' or 'Cahorsins' – the forerunners of later banking-houses.

The Middle Ages left embedded in the European mind an image of the Jew as a rapacious usurer. It was a Shylock-image without the redeeming touches of humanity and pathos Shakespeare gave to his stage character.

In general, Jewish life in mediaeval Europe from the 12th to the 15th centuries was a picture of unspeakable persecution. Tens of thousands of Jews were massacred, tortured, burnt alive at the stake or driven to suicide. In place after place the fury of religious fanaticism and mob violence was unleashed on them. They were accused of ritual murder, of drinking Christian blood, of venting their spleen on the consecrated Host, of poisoning the wells. They were forced to wear badges as a visual symbol of their inferior status. One country or city after another expelled them, after robbing them of their possessions.

Nevertheless some Jewish life survived in the Ashkenaz region after centuries of this ordeal because all the Jews in it were not under attack at one and the same time. When fleeing from one place they could generally find refuge elsewhere. Sometimes those who had expelled them realized how useful they were and tried to lure them back. In a number of cases rulers, nobles, bishops or city authorities sheltered them from mob violence. What was remarkable was not that Jews survived, but that they emerged with their belief in God intact and their spirit unbroken. At any time they could have ended their sufferings by accepting baptism, and coming under the protective umbrella of the Church. Yet few took this escape route. Many found the strength to endure by means of a social and spiritual withdrawal and an intensified attachment to their own faith. From this inner source they gained a stoical acceptance of suffering and death. It was an attitude summed up in the phrase *Kiddush ha-Shem* – 'Sanctification of the Name' (of God).

The concept of Kiddush ha-Shem goes back to ancient times. In general, it stands for conduct in a Jew that demonstrates his staunch adherence to his ancestral religion and values. The opposing concept is *Chilul ha-Shem* ('Desecration of the Name') – that is, unworthy or impious conduct. In mediaeval Europe Kiddush ha-Shem acquired a special and poignant dimension, it denoted martyrdom in the name of God. Death under these circumstances, even death by one's own hand, was touched by holiness. It could be faced with a calm, sometimes with an ecstasy, that baffled the tormentors and executioners of the mediaeval Jews.

In the 16th century a movement of religious dissent sprang up in Germany that became known as the Reformation. It would permanently divide the Christians of the Western world into two camps, Catholics and Protestants. The Jewish communities in Western Europe, shrunken and impoverished by the mediaeval persecutions and expulsions, were at first hopeful that the Reformation would usher in for them a new era of tolerance. Its leader, Martin Luther (1483–1546), and other important figures in it appeared sympathetic. They took a renewed interest in the Old Testament and turned to the rabbis to teach them Hebrew. Luther himself translated the Old Testament into German. Some Protestant groups even started leaning towards Jewish practices, like the Anabaptists in Moravia and other Sabbatarian sects.

The title page of Martin Luther's pamphlet Concerning the Jews and their Lies, *Wittenburg, 1543.*

Why should the Jews convert, Luther asked, when the Christians treated them like dogs? His great hope was that they would find it easier to embrace Christianity in its Protestant form. When that failed to happen, he was bitterly disappointed, and in his last years turned violently anti-Jewish. In his treatise *Of the Jews and their Lies* (1543), he repeated the well-worn calumnies of the blood-libel and the poisoning of wells, and advocated that the synagogues and schools of the Jews be burnt down, their sacred books confiscated, their assets taken from them and their livelihood as money-lenders forbidden. As a result of this incitement two German Protestant states, Saxony and Hesse, did in fact expel the Jews.

A more humane Protestant attitude to the Jews found an eloquent spokesman in a respected German Christian scholar, Johannes Reuchlin. He mastered Hebrew, and published the first Christian textbook on the Hebrew language in 1506. Reuchlin also studied the Kabbalah (Jewish mysticism) and the biblical commentaries of Rashi and other Jewish scholars. When the emperor Maximilian set up an ecclesiastical commission in 1510 to study whether the Talmud should be destroyed, Reuchlin was the only Christian academic who had the courage to appear before it and defend the Jews. He denounced the charges against them and their sacred writings as wholly false. For a while Reuchlin himself came under attack as a 'Jew-lover', and a pro-Jewish pamphlet he had written was condemned.

While there were these conflicting trends among Protestants, the Jews on the whole were no better off as a result of the Reformation. In some respects they suffered more. Thrown onto the defensive, the Catholic Church regarded the Jews as sympathetic to the Reform-

Jews extracting blood from Simon of Trent, the subject of the Italian blood libel of 1475. A German woodcut, 15th century.

ation. The Counter-Reformation swept away the humanist attitude towards the Jews shown by some of the Renaissance Popes, and revived all the harsh anti-Jewish ordinances of the mediaeval period.

It was only in the 17th century that the Jews began to enjoy tolerance in two Protestant countries, Holland and England. Both of them were mercantile and seafaring powers with rising prosperity and the beginnings of overseas empires. In them, the Jews driven out of Spain and elsewhere could find new homes and opportunities.

The Blood-Libel

In the evil image of the Jew shaped by mediaeval Europe, one ingredient was the grotesque 'blood-libel' – the charge that Jews killed Christians to use their flesh or blood for ritual purposes.

That myth occurs in the anti-semitic writings of Apion, an Alexandrian Greek of the 1st century AD. According to him, the Jews would annually kidnap a Greek, fatten him in the Jerusalem Temple, then sacrifice him and eat his flesh. But it was not only the adherents of Judaism who faced such an allegation. Ironically, the early Christian sect suffered from it too. The 2nd-century Church Father, Tertullian, wrote that, 'We [the Christians] are said to be the most criminal of men on the score of our sacramental baby-killing and the baby-eating that goes with it...' He complained that the Roman authorities arrested and tortured Christians to wring out of them 'confessions' concerning the number of babies they had tasted.

The first blood-libel case in the Middle Ages was at Norwich, England, in the year 1144. The body of a skinner's apprentice called William was found in a wood on Easter Saturday. A rumour spread that the youth had been taken into a Jewish home during the Passover and had been crucified in mock imitation of the death of Jesus. The Jews in the town took refuge in the castle from an angry mob and were protected by the sheriff. The body of the 'boy martyr' was buried in Norwich Cathedral and miracles were attributed to it.

A Jewish apostate named Brother Theobald later offered 'evidence' of the alleged ritual murder. He claimed that an assembly of Jewish leaders met each year at Narbonne in France and decided on the next place for a human sacrifice. This story contained two sinister elements that would figure prominently in later antisemitic literature, with tragic consequences for the Jews. One was the claim that Jews were required by their religion to kill Christian boys at Passover; the other was that an international assembly of Jews met secretly to plot the overthrow of the Christian world – a foretaste of the notorious *Protocols of the Elders of Zion*.

There were another seven blood-libel cases in English towns before the expulsion of the Jews from England in 1290. The most famous of these occurred at Lincoln in 1255. The body of an eight-year-old boy was found in the cesspool of a house in the Jewish quarter. The owner of the house, a Jew named Copin, was arrested and tortured until he 'confessed' that the child had been murdered for Passover ritual purposes. King Henry III sentenced him to death, and he was publicly hanged. Ninety other members of the Lincoln community were rounded up and thrown into the Tower of London, and eighteen of them were executed.

In the 12th and 13th centuries scores of blood-libel cases erupted all over Western Europe, generally at the time of the Jewish Passover and the Christian Easter. While the emphasis was on the crucifixion theme, the stories developed a further feature, namely, a ritual drinking of the victim's blood – hence the term 'blood-libel'. In Eastern Europe, where the blood-libel spread in the late Middle Ages, it acquired yet another twist – that Christian blood was used in the baking of matzot, the unleavened bread eaten during the Passover.

Enlightened Christian leaders tried to counteract the charges. One of them was the Holy Roman Emperor, Frederick II (reigned 1220–50). In 1235, thirty-four Jews in the small German town of Fulda in Hesse were burnt to death on a blood-libel charge. The emperor sought the opinion of Church leaders whether there was any basis to such charges, and received inconclusive answers. He then convened a synod of learned Jewish converts to Christianity who, he presumed, would know the true facts. They advised him that 'there is not to be found, either in the Old or the New Testament, evidence that the Jews are desirous of human blood. On the contrary, they avoid contamination with any kind of blood.' The emperor published their finding that blood libel charges were 'cruel and unnatural'.

A few years later, in 1247, Pope Innocent IV also condemned the blood-libel. But neither emperor nor Pope could eradicate a belief that would remain rooted in popular myth-ology right up to the 20th century. In some areas local Church authorities were themselves responsible for perpetuating the myth. For instance, in 1475 the whole of the small Jewish community in Trent, northern Italy, was put to death on the allegation that it had murdered a boy, called Simon, for religious purposes. The relics of this 'boy martyr' were preserved in the cathedral, where there was an annual ceremony in his memory, and in 1582 he was officially beatified. Only in 1965 did the Church reopen the case and annul the beatification.

In the 18th century the blood-libel had become so prevalent in Poland that the Council of the Four Lands, the representative body of Polish Jewry, sent an emissary to Rome with a request that the Holy See investigate the whole subject. The task was entrusted to Cardinal Ganganelli, later Pope Clement XIV. In 1759 he produced a lengthy report calling the charges a calumny against Judaism and asking that measures be taken to protect the Jews of Poland.

In spite of such authoritative declarations, there were a number of blood-libel cases from the 18th to the 20th century, mainly in Czarist Russia, but also in Germany and in the Ottoman empire. Two of these cases in particular attracted worldwide attention. One was the Damascus libel case of 1840; it drew the personal intervention of the most influential Jewish leaders in the West, Sir Moses Montefiore of England and Adolphe Cremieux of France. Another was the Beilis case in Kiev, Ukraine, in 1911. The 'evidence' was deliberately fabricated by the Russian authorities as part of their effort to divert popular discontent into anti-Jewish channels. The case roused a storm of protest inside and outside Russia. Beilis was acquitted for lack of proof.

The blood-libel charge featured prominently in the Nazi propaganda drive against the Jews. Dr Goebbels discovered that in the 20th century, 800 years after the Norwich case, the malevolent story that Jews were ritual murderers of Christians could still be used as a potent weapon against them.

The Desecration of the Host

This German broadsheet, printed about 1480, depicts in twelve scenes the alleged desecration of the Host by Jews in the town of Passau, Bavaria, in 1478.

According to the account, a Christian steals consecrated wafers from a church and sells them for one gulden to local Jews, identified in the pictures by the circular badges on their clothes. The Jews take the wafers to the synagogue and stab one of them, drawing blood. Some of the wafers are sent to the communities of Prague and Salzburg and the Jews try to burn the rest in an oven. Angels and doves fly out of the oven, while the face of a child appears on the wafers. The Jews who take part in this act of desecration are tortured and two of them beheaded. The rest of the Jews are hanged. The synagogue is converted into a church.

Charges of desecrating the Host, like the blood-libel charges, were widespread in mediaeval Europe and added to the picture of the Jew as a sinister enemy of the Christian faith.

In 1215 the Fourth Lateran Council officially endorsed the Doctrine of Transubstantiation, whereby the wine and the bread wafers (called the Host) used in the sacrament of the Eucharist during Mass are miraculously transformed into the actual substance of Christ's body. The story gained credence that Jews obtained consecrated wafers, pierced them to make them bleed, thereby reenacting for their own satisfaction the Passion of Christ. In many places this alleged act of desecration resulted in Jews being persecuted and put to death, as was the case in Passau.

A prophet, depicted as a contemporary Jew, wearing a badge in the shape of the Tablets of the Law. From an English manuscript of 1275.

'The Badge of Shame'

Jews were first obliged to wear a distinctive item of apparel in the Islamic countries. This rule applied to all non-Moslem communities, Christians as well as Jews. Yellow was often used for Jews and blue for Christians. The same practice was enforced for the Jews in Christian Europe during the Middle Ages.

A distinctive mark for Jews was made compulsory for the whole Christian world by the Fourth Lateran Council in 1215. The specific reason given by the Council was that Christians might inadvertently fall into grievous sin by having sexual intercourse with Jews. The Council's decree did not specify what kind of mark should be used. It took different forms in different countries. In Germany, in the 13th and 14th centuries, Jews were depicted wearing yellow, pointed, 'Jewish hats'. In the 15th century a yellow patch sewn onto the outer garment became the rule. By the laws of England, the badge was a patch of yellow cloth in the form of the tablets of the Law, worn on the left side of the breast. In France a round disk was worn on the breast and sometimes also on the back. It was yellow in some localities, and in others half red and half white. The royal treasury in France gained revenue from these badges, since the Jews had to buy them from the tax collectors. In Spain the Jewish badge was a circular red patch. In Italy the round badge was usually yellow, but red in the Venetian republic. The distinguishing mark laid down in the Papal dominions was a yellow hat for Jews and a yellow kerchief for Jewesses.

The so-called 'badge of shame' for Jews gradually fell out of use between the 16th century and the beginning of the Emancipation in the 18th century. It was not formally abolished until the French Revolution, first in France and then in other European countries occupied by the French armies.

The Jewish badge in the form of a yellow six-pointed star, the Shield of David, was revived by the Nazis in the Second World War throughout Nazi-occupied Europe.

The Expulsions

See illustration overleaf

From the 12th to the 15th centuries the Jews were expelled at one time or another from most of the countries of Western Europe. The causes were partly religious bigotry, partly the avarice of rulers eager to replenish their treasuries by the seizing of Jewish property.

At first the Jews were banished from a number of individual towns. In this way the rising guilds of Christian merchants and craftsmen were able to rid themselves of Jewish competitors. Since these were local measures, the Jewish communities concerned were able to move elsewhere in the area though stripped of their possessions. In most cases, some of them came back after an interval, and their organized communities slowly revived.

The first national expulsion order

The expulsion of the Jews from France in 1182. A miniature from Grandes Chroniques de France, *1321.*

was that signed by King Philip Augustus of France in 1182. It was only partially implemented, because powerful and independent barons ignored it in their own domains. Sixteen years later it was repealed, and the Jews were invited back.

The Jews of England were expelled in 1290. On mounting the throne in 1272, Edward the Confessor found that the situation of the Jews in the kingdom had gravely deteriorated. They had been impoverished by the crushing exactions of previous rulers, and their occupation of money-lending was no longer an important source of revenue for the crown. Popular feeling had been inflamed against them by charges of blood-libel and desecration of the Host, culminating in the classic case of Hugh of Lincoln in 1255. The Jews had been banished on local initiative from a number of provincial towns, such as Newcastle, Leicester, Derby and Windsor. There were increasing incidents of mob attacks on Jewish quarters. King Edward felt that the problem of the Jews could be settled, together with the religious problem of

usury, if they were permitted to enter other occupations such as trade, handicrafts and the leasing of farms. He instituted an economic programme to this effect, but it proved ineffectual. The king thereupon decided to get rid of the Jews altogether, and signed the expulsion order of 1290. About 5,000 Jews were shipped out of England, after being stripped of their property. They made their way as refugees to France and Germany. There would not be another person professing to be a Jew in England for 400 years – until the time of Oliver Cromwell.

In the 14th century there were fresh expulsion orders in France. The one in 1306 was actuated by purely mercenary motives: the desire of King Philip the Fair to take over the property and outstanding loans of the Jews. The order was reversed nine years later by Louis X, and the Jews were allowed to return, initially for a period of twelve years. Another expulsion order was signed in 1322, and repealed only in 1359. In 1394, the Jews were again banned from France, by the deranged Charles VI. Most of

them found refuge in Italy, Spain and the kingdom of Provence.

In Germany, where the worst persecutions and massacres of the Jews took place in the mediaeval period, there was no general expulsion order against them. The authority of the Holy Roman Emperor had waned, and political power was distributed among a great number of small autonomous units: principalities and duchies, bishoprics and certain towns. This fragmentation meant that the Jews could no longer rely on the protection of the emperor, to whom they in theory belonged. On the positive side, they could not be the victims of a single decree banishing them from the whole of Germany, as had happened in England and France, and later in Spain and Portugal.

Though sadly depleted by persecution and constantly uprooted in one locality or another, the Jewish community of Germany had a continuous existence on German soil. At the end of the mediaeval period, local communities of any size were left only in two German cities, Worms and Frankfurt.

The last and most permanent of the general expulsions in the Middle Ages was that from Spain in 1492. In Portugal in 1497, though Manoel II ordered the Jews expelled, he changed his mind and had them converted. In both cases a community of Marranos remained behind. Many of them would also leave to escape the pressure of the Inquisition, revert to Judaism and join the Sephardic congregations in other lands.

Renaissance Italy

Italy, like Germany, did not become a single united country until the late 19th century. From the 10th to the 13th century the northern part of the Italian peninsula was part of the Holy Roman Empire, and nominally under the rule of the German emperor. But his authority was weak south of the Alps and was contested by the popes. In effect, Italy was a mosaic of small and virtually independent political units. In the south there were two feudal kingdoms, those of Naples and Sicily. Apart from being the spiritual head of the Church, the Pope was also a temporal ruler over the Papal States in the centre of the country, including Rome.

Among nearly a score of other separate entities in Italy were half-a-dozen duchies, like Milan and Savoy, and a number of rising city-states. Some of these cities were ruled by hereditary dynasties, others were republics. The most prominent of the latter were Venice, Genoa and Florence. Indeed, the merchant port-cities of Venice and Genoa developed into Mediterranean powers in their own right, with colonial possessions, fleets and ambassadors.

These duchies and cities had chronic feuds with each other that spilt

Italian Jews and Renaissance culture

During the Renaissance, Italian Jews were drawn into the mainstream of general and artistic intellectual life, while continuing to contribute to Jewish scholarship. As elsewhere, they were noted for their medical skill, and many Jewish physicians served at the courts of the Popes and at the courts of local rulers. They were writers, poets and translators. The latter vocation was especially import-ant since erudite Jews in Sicily and southern Italy were familiar with Arabic literature and could translate philosophical and scientific works from that language into Italian and Latin, the European language of scholarship. Like the Spanish Jews, therefore, they helped to introduce ancient Greek writings, especially those of Aristotle, into mediaeval Europe through the works of Arab scholars.

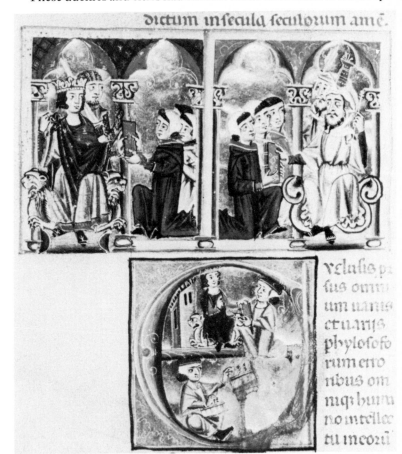

Faraj ben-Solomon (bottom drawing) *translating the Arabic medical encyclopaedia* Al Harvi *into the Latin* Liber coninens, *and presenting it to the King of Naples. From a 13th-century Sicilian manuscript.*

over into recurrent local wars. The fighting was conducted by hired mercenaries called *condottiere*, and did not seriously disrupt normal life and business.

In such a fragmented Italy, policy towards the Jews was not uniform. They were better off in some places and times, and worse off in others. But on the whole the attitude towards them by Popes, nobles and city authorities was more enlightened and tolerant than that which prevailed in the Ashkenaz region. Anti-Jewish attacks were sporadic and localized, without the scale and ferocity of the persecutions in Germany. Until the late Middle Ages the Jews were able to find their own distinctive place in both the economic and cultural life of mediaeval Italy. They were mainly concentrated in the southern parts of the country and the island of Sicily.

These communities were well-established and flourishing from the 9th century, and evolved their own considerable centres of Jewish learning. In the centre and north of the country the largest and oldest community was that in Rome, dating back to at least the 2nd century BC. Other organized communities developed in Florence, Mantua, Ferrara, Venice, Padua and Ancona. The northern communities were augmented from the 14th century by an influx of refugees from Germany.

Economic activity was less restricted for the Jews in Italy than in

The opening page of Madrigaletti *by Salomon de Rossi (1570–1629), the greatest Jewish composer of his time, who introduced many innovations into Jewish liturgical music.*

Jews were active in the performing arts – in music, dance and the theatre, where they appeared as playwrights, actors and directors.

Some of the leading Renaissance Christian intellectuals developed an interest in Hebrew, Jewish learning and the Kabbalah, and received tuition from rabbis.

Franco-Germany. There was a relatively small and well-to-do class of money-lenders, but the Jews were by no means confined to that occupation. Nor were Gentile interests dependent for loans just on the Jews, since a class of Italian Christian money-lenders and bankers arose in the mediaeval period. (That was the basis for the fortune of the celebrated Medici family in Florence.) The growing prosperity of the Italian states and cities derived mainly from commerce. The Italian merchants served as the middlemen in the trade route between Europe and the East through the Mediterranean, and the Italian ports flourished from the *entrepôt* trade that was stimulated by the Crusades. In the general conditions of prosperity and economic growth, there was no strong incentive to oust Jewish traders or skilled craftsmen. A notable example was the spinning and weaving of silk in southern Italy, an industry that was mainly Jewish. Inevitably some Christian guilds did try to restrict Jewish competitors.

The Christian Hebraist, Giovanni Pico della Mirandola and his Jewish teacher (the bearded figure). A detail from a fresco by Cosimo Rosselli, Florence, 15th century.

Servi camarae regis. *The Jews of Rome receive a charter of privileges from Emperor Heinrich VII in 1312. From* Codex Baldvini, *the Rhine, early 14th century.*

In the 14th century there started in Italy that epoch of cultural flowering known as the Renaissance (the French word for rebirth). It was marked by intellectual freedom, brilliant innovations in literature, art and architecture, and a liberation from the dead hand of feudal Europe. It had a permanent impact on Western civilization as we know it. For the Italian Jews the Renaissance brought about one of the periods of cultural synthesis between traditional Jewish scholarship and a surrounding culture of a high level. That had happened in ancient Alexandria and in the Golden Age in Spain.

At the end of the 15th century the Jewish community in southern Italy fell victim to the expulsion of the Jews from Spain. After periods of Moslem Arab and then Norman rule, the kingdom of Sicily had become a dependency of the Spanish kingdom of Aragon. The expulsion order signed by Ferdinand and Isabella in 1492, therefore, applied to the Jews on the island as well. The total community, numbering nearly 40,000 souls, was expelled, and their homes and businesses confiscated. Most of them moved into the neighbouring kingdom of Naples, while others found refuge in North Africa and the

Servi camerae regis

From the 10th century to the latter part of the 13th century, Italy belonged to the Holy Roman Empire, and the Italian Jews, like the German Jews, had the legal status of *servi camerae regis*, that is, they were 'servants of the royal chamber' and nominally under the protection of the German emperor. In practice his rule was distant and ineffectual. It was said that his realm was neither Holy nor Roman nor an Empire.

Ottoman empire, chiefly in Constantinople and Salonika. The expulsion decree also applied to the smaller Jewish community on the island of Sardinia, another Spanish possession.

In addition to Sicilian Jews, thousands of Spanish Jews and Marranos found refuge in the kingdom of Naples; a few years later that kingdom also came under Spanish rule. In 1515 the majority of its Jews were expelled, leaving 200 affluent families who were allowed to remain on payment of a large annual subsidy to the crown. In 1541 what remained of the community was finally banished. There would be no Jewish life in Naples for the next three centuries, until it was revived on a small scale by Baron Karl von Rothschild, a member of the banking family.

In the middle of the 16th century the mild air breathed by the Jews in Renaissance Italy gave way to the bleak winds of the Counter-Reformation. A warning blast came with the edict in 1553, and the public burning of copies of the Talmud and other Jewish religious works in a square in Rome. The last case of this kind had been in France three centuries earlier. This time, as before, the 'evidence' for the condemnation of the Talmud was provided by a Jewish apostate. The occurrence was instigated by the powerful and fanatical Cardinal Caraffa. Two years later he was elected Pope, and took the name of Paul IV. He promptly issued a papal bull launching a programme of anti-Jewish measures that had previously been enforced in other countries. The ghetto institution, existing until then only in Venice, now became general in Italian cities. The Jewish badge was introduced; the Jewish merchants were to be confined to dealing in rags and second-hand clothing; Jewish physicians would not be permitted to treat Christian patients.

These and other harsh provisions were only partially implemented by the rulers of many of the Italian petty states, some of whom resisted papal pressure. But in general the era of tolerance had ended for the Italian Jews, and the benevolence towards them of the Renaissance popes was replaced by hostility from the Holy See.

In the Renaissance period the Italian Jewish communities were augmented in size and their culture and economic activities enriched by the immigration of Spanish Jews. This movement started with the anti-Jewish riots in Spain in 1391. It became a large-scale influx with the expulsions from Spain in 1492 and the exodus from Portugal in 1497. Where they settled in sufficient numbers in any locality, they set up their own Sephardic congregations.

With the establishment of the Inquisition in Spain and Portugal at the end of the 15th century, there was also a steady stream of Marrano refugees from those two countries. Those of them who had been secret Jews reverted openly to Judaism in Italy. Others retained the Christian faith, and formed distinctive Marrano communities. In the earlier part of the 16th century the Marranos were well received, and even encouraged to settle, by local rulers eager to utilize their trading and financial skills. But their position remained insecure. The normal

(continued on page 159)

The Ghetto

In 1509 a group of Jewish immigrants from Germany sought permission to live in Venice, which had been closed to Jews for a number of years. They were allotted a small island among the city's canals, and were obliged to live there enclosed by a high wall. The island was less than two acres in extent, and reached by three bridges. The quarter was known as Ghetto Nuovo, Italian for the New (iron) Foundry, built there for the making of cannon. Later, an adjacent area, the 'Ghetto Vecchio' (Old Foundry) was added to accommodate a group of Turkish Jews.

From then on, the word 'ghetto' was adopted for all the urban quarters where Jews were segregated. In contemporary usage the term has been extended to cover an urban district inhabited by any ethnic minority group – for instance, Negro Harlem or Spanish (that is, Puerto Rican) Harlem in New York.

From the beginning of the Diaspora it was customary for Jews to cluster in separate quarters in the towns in which they lived. They did so for mutual protection against attack, and in order to maintain organized communal life around their synagogues. In mediaeval Europe such quarters were called Jewry in England, Juiverie in France, Judengasse in Germany, Juidecca in Italy and Juderia in Spain (except where the Arabic word Aljama survived from Moorish Spain). The same system prevailed in the Islamic countries. In Morocco it was known as the Mellah, and elsewhere by various Arabic equivalents of the term 'Jewish Quarter'.

What was new about the Venetian ghetto was that the segregation had been made compulsory. That symbolized a hardening anti-Jewish attitude in Italy from the beginning of the 16th century. In 1555 the precedent of Venice was followed in Rome. By papal order the ancient Jewish com-

Campo del Ghetto Nuovo – a view of the New Ghetto in Venice – a contemporary photograph.

munity was concentrated in a swampy area on the left bank of the river Tiber, and a wall built around it to isolate it from the rest of the city. It remained the most rigid and restricted of all Italian ghettoes.

In the latter half of the 16th century the rulers of other Italian states followed suit, under pressure from the Church. The institution of the ghetto was one aspect of a general anti-Jewish drive also marked by the forced wearing of Jewish badges, restrictions on Jewish occupations and the enforced attendance of Jews at church sermons that aimed to convert them.

The compulsory ghetto also spread to German cities and states. As the

Piazzetta del Pancotto (Bread Square) in the Rome Ghetto, 1886.

Jews had by then already been expelled from England, Spain and Portugal, and to a large extent from France, the ghetto institution was not relevant to those countries.

Since the ghettoes were not increased in area as the Jewish communities expanded, they became overcrowded and unhealthy, with the houses rendered unsafe by the additional storeys added to them. As a general rule the gates were locked at night and were in the charge of Christian gatekeepers. It was only at the end of the 18th century, shortly after the French Revolution, that European ghettoes were abolished. Wherever the French Revolutionary armies advanced, notably in Italy, they knocked down the ghetto gates and gave their occupants freedom. After the defeat of Napoleon the ghetto was reinstated in Rome by the Pope. The restriction was lifted only in 1870 when the recently-unified kingdom of Italy annexed the Papal States, and the ghetto was demolished in 1885.

The name and concept of the Jewish ghetto acquired a new and tragic dimension during the Nazi Holocaust. The Jews in Nazi-occupied Europe were rounded up and herded together in ghettoes enclosed by walls. From there they were ultimately transported to the death camps. In some cases, like that of the Warsaw ghetto, Jews organized a brave but hopeless resistance.

The Soncino printing family

The Soncinos were a famous family of Hebrew printers in the 15th–16th centuries. They took their family name from the small town of Soncino in Lombardy, northern Italy, where they came to settle from Germany in 1454. Their printer's mark was probably taken from the municipal crest of the town. The printing activities of the family covered six generations, and spread to a number of Italian cities, as well as to Salonika, Constantinople and Cairo. They published more than 130 Hebrew books and about the same number in Italian and Latin. The most important Hebrew work was a complete Bible with over 400 illustrations.

For some years at the end of the 15th century theirs was the only Hebrew press in the world. In the early 16th century their main rival was the Christian printer Daniel Bomberg in Venice, who specialized in high-quality Hebrew books. He was the first to produce a complete printed edition of the Talmud.

Printing from movable type was adopted by Jews within a generation after it began with Johann Gutenberg in Mainz, Germany, in the year 1454. At first Hebrew printing encountered some rabbinic reservations, since the scribes who copied the Torah and other religious documents by hand were regarded as being engaged in a sacred task. The rapid proliferation of printed Hebrew books had a revolutionary impact on the religious and cultural life of Jewish communities everywhere. Copies of the Bible, the Talmud, prayer books, grammars and dictionaries were now for the first time plentiful and relatively cheap. Printing was accepted as a means to realize the prediction of the prophet Isaiah that 'the earth shall be full of the knowledge of the Lord' (*Isa. 11:9*).

The printer's mark used by Gershon Soncino between 1533 and 1552, in Rimini, Salonika and Constantinople.

The Norsa family

The Norsas (or Nurzis) were a wealthy and distinguished family of bankers and rabbinical scholars who settled in Mantua in the 15th century. At that time the Gonzaga dynasty that ruled the duchy of Mantua encouraged Jewish bankers and merchants to settle in their domain. The community prospered and became a centre of Jewish music and theatre. In the 16th century it suffered attack and persecution in the hostile atmosphere of the Counter-Reformation. The Norsa family home was seized and demolished by order of the Duke, and the Church of Santa Maria built on the site, to commemorate the victory of Mantua over a French army.

Four members of the Norsa family wearing Jewish badges, a detail from an anonymous oil-painting Madonna della
Vittoria, *Mantua, 15th century.*

local resentments against competitive immigrants was compounded in
their case by their Jewish descent and by the pressure exerted on Italy
by the Spanish Inquisition. In the atmosphere of the Counter-
Reformation that pressure was reinforced by the papal authorities in
Italy. Marranos who had remained Christians were thus also caught
up in the reactionary drive against the Jews.

A glaring example was Ancona, a port under papal rule on the east
coast of Italy. A group of Portuguese Marranos was invited by the
Pope to settle there, in order to develop its port and the trade with the
Ottoman empire. They were given a guarantee of immunity from the
attentions of the Inquisition. Pope Paul IV rescinded that immunity.
Twenty-five of the town's Marranos, including one woman, were
burnt at the stake as heretics, and a similar number were condemned to
be galley-slaves. The Jewish leaders of Constantinople and Salonika
tried to organize a punitive boycott of Ancona.

A flourishing Marrano community grew up in Ferrara under the protection of its rulers. In 1581 the Duke of Ferrara yielded to the pressure of the Pope. Many of the Marranos were imprisoned, and three of them were taken to Rome where they died at the stake. Some of the stronger and more independent Italian rulers resisted the Church and prevented the Inquisition from molesting their Marrano communities. That happened in Venice, and the Grand Duchy of Tuscany, whose ruler granted a special charter in 1593 to the Marranos willing to settle in Leghorn. A similar charter was granted to the Marranos by the Duke of Savoy in 1572. His object was to use them for the development of Nice as a major Mediterranean port. But he came under the combined pressure of the Holy See and the king of Spain, and in the following year he cancelled the charter and signed a decree expelling the Marranos.

From the 16th century onwards Italy was a cockpit for the imperial rivalries of Spain, France and Austria. Compared to their position during the Renaissance period, the Italian Jews sank into obscurity. They remained confined to their ghettoes until they were liberated by the invading French forces after the French Revolution of 1789.

17th-century Amsterdam

The Jewish community in Amsterdam in the 17th century provided one of the shining pages in the Diaspora story. Its context was the rapid rise at that time of the small Dutch nation.

In 1578 the seven northern provinces of the Low Countries, all of whom had become Calvinist Protestant, banded together in a union and shortly after declared their independence of Spanish rule. That independence was not finally recognized until 1648, by the Peace of Westphalia that ended the Thirty Years War. By then the wealth and power of the United Provinces (Holland) was expanding at a rate that turned it into a major European power. Dutch ships sailed the seven seas; Dutch merchants dealt with every continent; and Dutch trading posts in the New World and the Far East were turning into colonial possessions, the nucleus of a sprawling empire. The emergence of a prosperous middle-class was accompanied by a cultural golden age in

The Marranos in Holland

A Hebrew historical work, She'erit Israel (The Remnant of Israel), published in Amsterdam in 1741, gives an interesting account of the arrival of the first group of Marranos in Holland. The story is illustrated by this series of five pictures. The accompanying captions are based on She'erit Israel and other sources.

A Safe Refuge. In 1604 two ships arrived from Spain carrying – apart from valuable merchandise – ten Marranos with their wives and children. After enduring violent storms,

(continued on page 165)

they landed at Emden in Friesland.

A Hebrew store sign. They found a place to stay in Emden and went out to view the town. They saw a Hebrew sign: 'The world is founded on truth and peace' and nearby a man carrying a goose. They were delighted to find Jews there.

Secret consultation. The next day, two of them went to the home of Rabbi Moses Uri Halevi and his son Rabbi Aaron and, in strict privacy, revealed they were of Jewish origin and that all the males wished to be circumcised. Then they went on to

Amsterdam, and soon Rabbi Moses and Rabbi Aaron came and circumcised them. There was great rejoicing and the rabbis arranged a special room in their home to serve as a synagogue and they prayed there in fear and trepidation.

Permission is granted. Shortly afterwards, they were reported to the city councillors and Rabbi Moses and Rabbi Aaron were imprisoned. The judge asked whether they had permission to make a new faith. Rabbi Moses answered: 'We have an old faith – the faith of our ancestors. May God be praised for freeing your land

from the yoke of Spain. As a result of that, these people have come here and they will advance the commerce of the country. Moreover, their brothers in Spain will also come, and the city will benefit.' And the judges gave them every freedom.

More Marranos Return to Judaism. Immediately they wrote letters to all their relatives and loved ones about the rights and liberties they had received in Amsterdam. Within a short while many more Marrano families had gathered and over 2,500 males were circumcised.

The central square of the Jewish quarter in Amsterdam with the Great Portuguese Synagogue on the left, and the Great Ashkenazi Synagogue on the right. An engraving by Adolf van der Laan, c.1710.

The Great Portuguese Synagogue *See above*

The Great Portuguese Synagogue in Amsterdam was dedicated in 1675. The splendid building is in an elegant but restrained style that has been described as Protestant Baroque. In the 17th century it was a visible symbol of the wealth, piety and good taste of the Sephardi community in the city. The synagogue still stands today as originally built. Its high barrel-vaulted ceiling is supported by a double row of massive Ionic columns. It is lit by the glow of hundreds of candles in four great central candelabra and a number of smaller ones.

The 'bimah' and warden's pew are carved from Jacaranda wood originally imported from Brazil. The edifice includes offices, schoolrooms and a fine library.

The synagogue became a prototype for Sephardi houses of worship built elsewhere in Western Europe. One example is the Bevis Marks synagogue in London, completed in 1701 for the Spanish and Portuguese congregation. Its Quaker architect adapted the plan from the Amsterdam one.

Jewish occupations in Amsterdam *See right*

The prosperity of the Amsterdam Jewish community – like that of Holland as a whole – was based mainly on international commerce. Jewish merchants were involved in the lucrative trade with the Ottoman Empire, Italy and Spain, the Far East, via the sea-route round the Cape of Good Hope opened by the Portuguese navigators; and the colonies in the New World, where some of the Dutch Jews began to settle. Jews were substantial shareholders in the two great chartered corporations, the Dutch East India Company and the

As was the case elsewhere in the Diaspora, Jews were outstanding in the medical profession. Eminent Marrano physicians from Spain and Portugal reached Amsterdam as refugees. One of them was Joseph Bueno (who died in 1641), who was also a distinguished Hebrew-Spanish scholar, translator and poet. In 1625 he was called in to attend the Prince of Orange on his death-bed. He was a close friend of Rembrandt and was the model for Rembrandt's painting *The Jewish Doctor*. The most renowned Jewish physician of the time was Abraham Zacuto (1575–1642) who was born in Lisbon into an illustrious Marrano family. At the age of fifty he moved to Amsterdam, openly returned to Judaism, had himself circumcised and shed his Portuguese name – Manuel Alvares de Tavara. In addition to his huge clinical practice, he wrote a number of influential medical treatises that were collected and published in two volumes after his death.

Amsterdam was a major centre for both general and Hebrew printing and book publishing. The first Hebrew press in the country was set up in 1626 by the noted Sephardi rabbi, Manasseh Ben-Israel. He adapted to Hebrew printing the Dutch style of type, format, composition and decoration. The Amsterdam model became dominant for Hebrew printing all over Europe. The most successful of the Amsterdam Sephardi printers and publishers was Joseph Athias (died 1698), succeeded by his son. The best-known Athias publication was the 1661 Hebrew Bible. Athias said he printed more than a million Bibles in English for export to England and Scotland.

Diamond polishing. An engraving from Luiken's Het Menselyk Bedryf.

Dutch West India Company, that were laying the foundations for Holland's overseas empire.

Jewish bankers and stockbrokers played an active part in Amsterdam financial circles and were prominent in the Stock Exchange. In 1688, when William III of Orange sailed from Holland to gain the throne of England for his English wife Mary and himself, the expedition was financed to the extent of two million gulden by the richest Dutch-Jewish banker of the 17th century, Isaac (Lopes) Suasso.

In addition to commerce and finance, the Dutch Jews helped to develop the tobacco, silk, diamond, printing and optics industries. Diamond-cutting and polishing became a very Jewish craft.

MEDICUS. ÆTATIS SUÆ. LVIIII Anno 1634 DOCTOR ZACUTUS LUSITANUS

Zacuti faciem proclive est sculpere, mentem
Quod memoret Coelum? quod vel Agalma ferat?
Quod nequeunt oculi, monstret doctrina Zacuti,
Et memorandi acies praedicet ingenium.

Nicolaus Fontanus MED.

S. Saveri fc

The physician Abraham Zacuto (Zacutus Lusitanus). An etching by S. Savari, 1634, Amsterdam.

literature, architecture, and above all, art. It was the period of Rembrandt, Franz Hals, Vermeer and the new landscape school of Ruysdael and others. Amsterdam replaced Catholic Antwerp as the major port and commercial centre in the North Sea region. The city was marked by a high intellectual and cultural level, solid bourgeois comfort and religious tolerance. Jewish life flourished in this atmosphere as it had not done in Europe for centuries.

The Amsterdam Jewish community began with a small group of Spanish and Portuguese Marranos who settled there about 1590. Marrano colonies already existed before then in a number of other European cities, among them Bordeaux, Hamburg, Antwerp, London. All these Marranos still outwardly professed the Catholic faith, but they openly reverted to Judaism in Amsterdam long before that became possible in other countries.

On throwing off the Spanish yoke, Holland had opened its gates to refugees from religious persecution elsewhere. These included Protestants from the Spanish Netherlands, and Huguenots, a Protestant minority suffering discrimination in France. This Dutch policy combined a humane attitude with shrewd commonsense, for the newcomers brought with them skills and business acumen that helped to build up the material wealth of Holland.

Some of the Marrano immigrant families in Amsterdam had been Christian for over a century, without breaking their ties with their Jewish past. Once they found themselves free of religious pressure in their new home, they changed their Spanish or Portuguese names to Hebrew ones, the males had themselves circumcised, and they sought instruction in religious observance and Hebrew. By 1620 there were three small Sephardi congregations in Amsterdam. (Although the word Sephardi means Spanish, the Sephardim in Holland were generally known as 'Portuguese'.) By a supreme touch of paradox, the Calvinist clergy and city fathers were, for a while suspicious of these newcomers with their strange rituals, thinking that they might really be a fifth column of Spanish Catholics pretending to be Jews while celebrating the Mass in secret. But they soon came to be accepted as genuine Jews and to be regarded with tolerance and respect.

The willingness of the Dutch to accept Jewish refugees was not limited to the Marranos. From 1620 there was a steady stream of Jews fleeing the persecution in Germany. After the Chmielnicki massacres in Poland in 1648, there was an influx of destitute Jewish immigrants from that country. The German and Polish Jews were Ashkenazi who did not merge with the Sephardi community but set up their own congregations. By the late 17th century the Ashkenazim were the majority of Amsterdam Jewry, though the upper class of wealth and culture remained Sephardi.

The Amsterdam Jews were fortunate in that they could participate freely in Dutch life. While maintaining their own traditions without any hindrance, the community supported fine Jewish schools and academies, and produced Hebrew scholars, teachers, writers and

(continued on page 167)

Rembrandt and Amsterdam Jews

The great Dutch painter Rembrandt van Ryn (1606–69) lived in Amsterdam next to the Jewish Quarter, and took a keen interest in its life. Two eminent members of the Sephardi congregation were his friends – the Rabbi Manasseh Ben-Israel and the physician Ephraim Bueno. He may also have known Spinoza, but that is uncertain.

Apart from Jewish portrait commissions, Rembrandt liked to make ink-and-chalk drawings of bearded old Jews in their long coats. Some of these may have served as models for figures in the artist's many paintings of Old Testament scenes. Perhaps the atmosphere and types in the Jewish community were a welcome change for him from the staid Dutch burghers whose individual and group portraits provided him with a living.

Above Ashkenazi Jews in the Synagogue, *an etching by Rembrandt, Holland, 1648.*

Left *Dr Ephraim Bueno, a detail from a painting by Rembrandt, Holland, 17th century.*

poets. Amsterdam provided rabbis, teachers and religious books for other Sephardi communities in Western Europe. It had particularly close relations with the Marrano communities in Hamburg and in London. In 1626 that remarkable rabbi, Manasseh Ben-Israel, founded a Hebrew printing press in the city. In 1672 a newspaper appeared in Ladino, the *Gazeta de Amsterdam*. It was the first Jewish newspaper in the world. In 1686–7 the Ashkenazi community followed suit with the *Dienstagish Kurant*, the first Yiddish newspaper to appear. Apart from Jewish culture, Jewish scholars and poets wrote extensively in the Spanish and Portuguese languages.

In later centuries the Amsterdam community remained one of the largest and most important in Europe, but it suffered economic decline. However, relations between Jew and Gentile remained good throughout. Unlike Jews in so many other lands in Diaspora history, the Dutch Jews never had to endure the swing of the pendulum from tolerance to repression.

A portrait of Baruch Spinoza, Holland.

Spinoza

The philosopher Baruch (Benedict) de Spinoza (1632–77) was by far the most important intellectual figure to emerge from the Amsterdam Jewish community. His father was a Portuguese Marrano who settled in Amsterdam, resumed the Jewish faith and became a prosperous and respected member of the Sephardi congregation. The young Baruch received a thorough Jewish education, including an excellent knowledge of Hebrew – in fact he compiled a new manual of Hebrew grammar.

The young Spinoza's studies ranged far beyond Jewish scholarship. He mastered the Dutch, Portuguese, Spanish and Latin languages, and was schooled in the scientific and philosophical works of Galileo, Kepler and Descartes. He became interested in the science of optics and took up the skilled profession of lens-making.

Spinoza's powerful and rational intellect focussed on the fundamental problems of religion and biblical interpretation – the most challenging but dangerous field of philosophical enquiry open to a man of his time. The core of the metaphysical and ethical system he evolved was the concept of a universal God, immanent in all creation. (He was later called 'a God-intoxicated man'.) Yet he regarded conventional religion, whether Jewish or Christian, as the product of men's minds; the Scriptures as a human document, not divine revelation; and the existence of an immortal soul apart from the body as an unproved thesis. He therefore helped to usher in the rationalist outlook of 18th-century Europe and the Higher Criticism of Bible scholarship in the 19th century. It is hardly surprising however, that his heterodox views should have provoked the anger and dismay of the Amsterdam rabbis. In 1656, at the age of twenty-four, he was formally excommunicated, and remained an outcast from the Jewish community for the rest of his life. He died in poverty at the age of forty-four. He had been consumptive from childhood, and this condition must have been aggravated by the fine dust from the lenses he ground and polished in order to eke out a modest livelihood.

In retrospect, the leaders of the Sephardi community have been criticized as narrow-minded and rigid for having banished their most gifted son. Yet with their Marrano background it was natural for them to stress the orthodox observance of Judaism, and to reject ideas that would undermine the traditions to which they had returned after so much suffering. Moreover, they must have been afraid to antagonize their Calvinist hosts. It must be remembered that the Jews were an immigrant group without full civic status, which they gained only at the beginning of the 19th century.

Spinoza retired to a village near Leiden and devoted himself to philosophical writings. He lived very simply, refused the offer of friends to give him an annuity and later rejected the chair of philosophy at the University at Heidelberg. His major works were *Philosophical Principles of Descartes* (1663), the *Treatise on Religious and Political Philosophy* (1670) and, above all, the *Ethics* (1677) which contains his doctrine of human happiness and freedom and his description of the right way of life.

His books remained neglected until interest in them was aroused by two great minds at the end of the 18th century, Lessing and Goethe. Since then Spinoza has been studied and admired by philosophers of every shade of thought.

The Return to England

See colour page 182

After the Jews were expelled from England in 1290, no English Jewish community came into existence for nearly 400 years. Before the end of the 16th century a small group of Spanish and Portuguese Marranos had settled in London, and some others were among the merchants of Bristol. Outwardly they were Catholics. One of them, Roderigo Lopes, was physician to Queen Elizabeth 1, who had him hanged in 1594 on a charge of being connected with the plot of the hapless Earl of Essex.

The reappearance of open Jewish observance was brought about mainly by the Messianic zeal of one man, Manasseh Ben-Israel, a Sephardi scholar from Amsterdam. The historical context was the Puritan victory in the English Civil War and the appointment of Oliver Cromwell in 1653 as the Lord Protector of Britain.

Manasseh Ben-Israel (1604–67) came from a Portuguese Marrano family in Madeira. Soon after his birth, his father settled in Amsterdam, became openly Jewish, took the name of Joseph Ben-Israel and renamed his two sons Manasseh and Ephraim, after the sons of the Biblical Joseph. Manasseh was an accom-

Manasseh Ben-Israel, an etching by Rembrandt, Holland, 1636

plished scholar and linguist, writing theological works in Hebrew, Spanish and Latin. In 1650 he published *The Hope of Israel* in Latin and Spanish. In it he referred to the supposed discovery of the Lost Ten Tribes in South America. The advent of the millennium (he argued) and with it the redemption of the Jewish people would occur only when the Dispersion had reached all the corners of the earth. The only place left for the completion of this process was England. (Its name in French, 'Angleterre', could be taken to mean 'corner of the earth'.)

The Latin edition was dedicated to the English Parliament and an English translation aroused much interest. Manasseh followed this up by personal contacts and correspondence with a number of influential Englishmen, and then by a 'Humble Address' to the Lord Protector. Cromwell's response was sympathetic. The proposal appealed to him for both religious and economic reasons. Holland was England's chief trading rival. It was generally recognized that the Jews were making a significant contribution to Dutch commercial success, and Cromwell hoped to draw some of the Dutch Jews to England. He put the issue to the Council of State and invited Manasseh Ben-Israel to London to appear personally before the Council.

In London Manasseh encouraged some of the local Marranos to come out into the open as Jews. Together with six of them he signed a petition addressed to the Lord Protector, dated 24 March 1655. The petition boldly described its signatories as 'Hebrews at present residing in this city of London'. It made two requests: permission to conduct Jewish prayer meetings in private homes, and the right to acquire a burial ground outside the city.

Cromwell found the Council of State divided on the question of readmitting the Jews to England. He thereupon convened a Whitehall Conference in December 1655, made up of public figures, clergymen and lawyers. Manasseh Ben-Israel attended the conference at the head of a Jewish delegation. The constitutional experts advised that the expulsion decree of 1290 had been issued under royal prerogative; it did not have the status of a law, the repeal of which would require an act of parliament. However, strong reservations were expressed in the conference – partly from clerical quarters, partly from business interests that were loth to let in Jewish competitors. The opponents stirred up public agitation, and anti-Jewish pamphlets were widely distributed. When Cromwell found that the conference was likely to insist on onerous conditions and restrictions on the return, he disbanded it.

It was assumed that Cromwell would now feel free to issue his own decree, by virtue of his powers as Lord Protector. But he refrained from doing so, no doubt because the subject had become too controversial. He did, however, give an affirmative reply to the petition of March 1655, thereby enabling the Marranos who were already residing in London to have services in their homes and a burial ground.

Manasseh Ben-Israel stayed on in London for a further year. During this time he published another book, *Vindication of the Jews*, refuting the anti-Jewish pamphlets in circulation. He returned to Amsterdam in the belief that his mission had failed. As a conciliatory gesture, Cromwell granted him an annuity of £100.

To this day the expulsion decree of Edward the Confessor has not been cancelled, nor has there been any formal enactment permitting Jews to return to England and live there; but the question was resolved in the pragmatic English fashion. After Cromwell had assented to the request in the petition of the Marranos, organized Jewish life in Britain was simply allowed to develop again of its own accord.

Important Events

Byzantium (from the 4th century AD)

306–33	Reign of Constantine the Great. Christianity becomes State religion.
313	Edict of Milan – first step towards establishing dominance of Christianity.
325	Church Council of Nicaea calls for 'seclusion and humiliation' of Jews.
330	Constantinople established as new capital.
395	Roman Empire split – separate Byzantine (Eastern) Empire.
361–3	Emperor Julian the Apostate sympathetic to Jews.
529	Code of Justinian – Jews allowed to practise their religion but subject to many disabilities.

Christian Spain

694   Jewish religion outlawed in Visigoth kingdom of
          Spain.
711   Moorish invasion
1085   Christian capture of Toledo marks turning-point
          in 'Reconquista'.
1165–73(?) Travels of Benjamin of Tudela.
1263   Nachmanides appears in Barcelona Disputation.
1391   Outbreaks of mob violence against Spanish Jews.
1413–14   Tortosa Disputation.
1478   Start of Spanish Inquisition.
1492   Expulsion Decree of Ferdinand and Isabella.
1497   Forced baptism of Jews in Portugal.

Ashkenaz

c.800   Beginning of Jewish settlement in Franco-
          Germany.
1066   Jews reach England with William the Conqueror.
1096   First Crusade. Massacre of Rhineland Jews.
1144   Norwich blood-libel.
1190   Massacre of York Jews.
1236   Frederick II introduces *servi camerae* concept.
1242   Burning of Talmud in Paris.
1290   Jews expelled from England.
1306   First expulsion from France.
1348–50   Black Death massacres.
1394   Second expulsion from France.
1517   Martin Luther launches Reformation.

Renaissance Italy

1492   Expulsion of Jews from Sicily.
1516   Ghetto initiated in Venice.
1541   Expulsion of Jews from kingdom of Naples.
1553   Burning of Talmud.
1555   Pope Paul IV orders compulsory ghettos.
1797–99   French revolutionary army abolishes ghettos.

17th-century Amsterdam

1590   First Marrano group arrives.
1620   Jewish refugees from Germany.
1656   Spinoza excommunicated.

The Return to England

1655   Manasseh Ben-Israel heads delegation to London.
1656   Cromwell receives Jewish petition.

## Chapter Thirteen

The Lands of Islam

The Covenant of Omar

The Prophet Mohammed fled from Mecca in AD 622, established himself at Medina, gained control of the Arabian peninsula and sent his armies marching northwards on their campaign of conquest. Though the local Jewish tribes had helped him in his earlier struggles, they later denied their support and refused to accept the new religion he had founded. It was then, in the first fervour of the new faith, that Mohammed turned against them, destroyed them, and thus eliminated Jewish life in most of Arabia.

As the victorious Arabs swept through the Near East and North Africa, it became impractical to put to the sword those segments of the conquered population that did not embrace Islam. Under the Caliph Omar and his successors a more rational policy evolved for regulating the status of non-Moslem communities. The position of the Jewish minority in the new areas under Moslem rule had much in common with that under Byzantine rule. One essential difference was that Islam was not impregnated like Christianity with a strong religious bias against Judaism and Jews. Ironically, another difference was that the status of the Christians under Islam was equated with that of the Jews. Both were 'peoples of the book' with a guaranteed but inferior status as *dhimmi* – that is, protected non-Moslems. As a rule they enjoyed religious freedom, communal autonomy, protection of life and property, exemption from military service and the right to administer justice in civil and family matters where only members of their own communities were involved. On the other hand, a number of restrictions were imposed on them in accordance with the injunction in the Koran that non-Moslems should be clearly separated from the faithful. They had to pay a special poll tax; they were not allowed to erect new places of worship; they could not have Moslem employees or slaves; they were not eligible for official posts; they were forbidden to accept Moslem converts, or to prevent the conversion of their own people to Islam; they could not build their homes higher than those of their Moslem neighbours; they were not permitted to ride on horses or mules; and they could not bear arms. They also had to wear distinctive items of dress, that could take the form of special hats, mantles, sashes

The Arab Empire
See illustration right

After Mohammed's death in AD 632, his first successor (Caliph) was his father-in-law and closest disciple Abu Bakr (Caliph 632–4), who brought the whole of the Arabian peninsula under Moslem rule.

Omar, the second Caliph (634–44) was the great Arab empire-builder. His generals conquered the whole Persian empire and wrested Palestine, Syria and Egypt from Byzantium.

In the ninety years of the Ummayad dynasty (661–730), with its capital in Damascus, the empire expanded dramatically. To the East it was extended as far as India. To the West it took North Africa from the Byzantine Empire and Spain from the Visigoth kingdom. By 750, when another dynasty of Arab Caliphs, the Abbasids, came into power, the Moslem Empire stretched in a great arc from Spain along North Africa and through the Near East to Central Asia.

In 762 the Abbasids established their capital at Baghdad on the Tigris river, in Mesopotamia. It remained the centre of the Moslem world for five centuries, until Abbasid rule was swept away in 1258 by the hordes of Mongol horsemen invading from the steppes of Asia.

The Caliph Omar takes Jerusalem
See colour pages 110 and 111

In AD 638 Jerusalem surrendered to a Moslem army, and Byzantine rule

Muslim horsemen riding to battle. From the Magamat *of Al-Harini, Baghdad 1237.*

over the Holy Land came to an end. The Caliph Omar entered the city on foot, as a mark of respect. The Christian population was left unharmed and permitted to maintain their holy places and practise their religion. Omar annulled the Christian ban on Jews residing in Jerusalem, and allowed them to return to it for the first time in centuries. The ban was reimposed on Jews, and extended to Moslems as well, when the Crusader assault in 1099 regained the Holy City for Christianity.

Saadiah Gaon
See colour page 182

Saadiah ben-Joseph (882–942), the most illustrious Jewish scholar of his day, was the head of the Talmudic

or badges. As a rule the colour yellow was specified for Jews and blue for Christians.

These rights and disabilities concerning Christians and Jews were collated in the so-called Covenant of Omar, which remained the basic Islamic directive on the subject until modern times. As the name suggests, the Covenant is by tradition attributed to Omar, the second Caliph. He is remembered in Jewish history as a humane and friendly ruler. It is unlikely that Omar was the author of the long list of discriminations against non-Moslems set out in the Covenant. They were probably introduced at different times by various later Caliphs.

The Covenant of Omar was not uniformly carried out in practice. In some places restrictions were modified or ignored for economic reasons or through the personal influence on the rulers of Jewish financiers, advisers or physicians. On the other hand, there were fanatical regimes that trampled on the rights and protection promised to the Jews by the Covenant.

Under Moslem rule, far-reaching changes occurred in Jewish

academy of Sura in Babylonia. As such, he was one of the two Geonim (spiritual leaders) of the community, the other being the head of the academy of Pumbedita.

The official head of the Babylonian community was the hereditary exilarch or *Resh Galuta* ('Prince of the Exile'), who lived in regal style and enjoyed a position of honour at the Caliph's court.

In 930 Saadiah Gaon attacked the incumbent exilarch, David ben-Zakkai, on the grounds that he failed to observe the Halachah (religious law) properly, exploited his office for personal gain and followed an extravagant life-style. The fierce controversy between the two went on for years and virtually tore the Babylonian community apart. Eventually, in 937, a reconciliation was brought about between the two, and given formal public expression in a ceremony before the Caliph. In the picture the Exilarch is seated at the Caliph's left, as a mark of honour, and Saadiah Gaon, in white robes, is standing in front of the throne.

Even before the Moslem conquest in the 7th century the Babylonian community had become the leading centre of Jewish learning, and had produced the monumental Babylonian Talmud. After the conquest the community attained unquestioned primacy among Diaspora Jewry. Apart from its scholarly pre-eminence, it was now situated at the centre of an Arab empire that extended as far as Spain and included the bulk of the Jewish people. The Exilarch was regarded as the unofficial king of all the Jews.

The Babylonian Talmud was generally accepted elsewhere as the basis for religious observance and daily life. The Responsa (rulings) of the Geonim were treated as binding in matters of faith (except by the Karaite sect after the 8th century). As the power of the Abbasid caliphate in Baghdad declined, in the 11th and 12th centuries, so did the dominance of the Babylonian centre in Jewish life. Other centres in the Arab Diaspora rose to spiritual autonomy in Egypt, North Africa and Spain.

economic life. As in Christian lands, Jews were squeezed out of agriculture by onerous taxes and by the restrictions on using slave labour. There was a movement away from rural areas into the growing Arab cities. The overwhelming majority of Jews became townspeople, traders and artisans inhabiting crowded Jewish quarters. Such urban communities developed in a number of Arab cities. The most important was Baghdad in Iraq. Others were Basra, also in Iraq; Fostat (old Cairo) and Alexandria in Egypt; Kairouan and Fez in North Africa; Cordoba and Toledo in Moslem Spain. As merchants, Jews had the great advantage gained by their international ties with their fellow-Jews along the trade routes, both through the sprawling Arab empire and in Christian Europe.

On the social and cultural level, there was a steady adaptation to Arab life. Jews spoke Arabic as their daily tongue, wore Arab dress and Arabized their names. Jewish scholars started absorbing and then contributing to Arabic literature, philosophy and medicine. This intellectual co-operation reached its zenith in the Golden Age in Moorish Spain.

Moorish Spain

In AD 711 the Arab commander Tarik led his Moorish army from North Africa across the Straits of Gibraltar into Spain. (The name Gibraltar is derived from the Arabic Jebel-al-Tarik – the Mount of Tarik.) The Moors were a mixed force of Arabs and Berbers, the indigenous North African tribes that had been conquered by the Arabs and converted to Islam. Tarik swept through the Visigoth kingdom without serious resistance and occupied the whole of the Iberian peninsula up to the Pyrenees, except for a Christian enclave that held out in the rugged terrain of north-east Spain. The new Moslem regime evolved into an Ummayad Caliphate independent of Baghdad, with its capital in Cordoba.

Moorish Spain became the most cultured and enlightened country in Europe. Under its auspices Spanish Jewry rapidly revived. Its numbers were swelled by Conversos who reverted to Judaism, by exiles returning from North Africa, and by new settlers from other parts of the Moslem empire. Though they bore a heavy tax burden, the Jews shared in the rising level of prosperity and spread into a wide range of occupations. *See colour pages 250 and 251.*

Contact was resumed with the Geonim and academies in Babylonia, and local schools of learning started attracting scholars from elsewhere, notably that at Lucena, south of Cordoba, headed by the eminent scholar Isaac Alfasi. By the 10th century, a cultural renaissance was under way that would make Spain a major centre of Jewish scholarship, as the pre-eminence of Babylonian Jewry declined. During the next two centuries the Spanish Jews were to demonstrate a remarkable capacity to develop their own religious and spiritual heritage while at the same time taking a conspicuous part in the Arab life and culture of the country. This era was ushered in by the

(continued on page 176)

Hisdai ibn-Shaprut

See colour page 183

This mural, painted in the style of mediaeval Spanish illuminated manuscripts, shows scenes from the career of the Jewish leader Hisdai ibn-Shaprut (915–75) from Cordoba in Spain. He is shown conducting political negotiations with the envoys of the German Emperor; entertaining a gathering of scholars, poets and friends in his garden; receiving an epistle from the king of the Khazars; and as a judge and champion of his own people.

Hisdai grew up in Cordoba, the capital of the Caliphate in Spain, where his father was a wealthy and learned member of the Jewish community. Hisdai became an eminent physician and the chief diplomatic adviser to the Caliph. As such he received and dealt with the envoys from the emperor of Byzantium in 944 and the emperor of Germany in 953. In 958, as a Jew serving a Moslem ruler, he performed the remarkable political feat of mediating between the warring Christian kings of Leon and Navarre, and bringing them to Cordoba to negotiate and sign a peace treaty. While he was visiting Navarre on this mission, the Queen invoked his medical skills to cure her corpulent grandson of his weight problem – which he did successfully.

Hisdai used his prestige and influence to help his fellow-Jews in other lands. Two letters have recently come to light in which he addressed himself to the Byzantine emperor and empress, pleading for greater religious freedom to be given to the Jews in their domain. Inside the Spanish community Hisdai promoted the cause of Jewish learning. He sponsored a Talmudic academy in Cordoba, and he invited the noted Hebrew grammarian Menachem ben-Saruk from Tortosa in Christian Spain to come to Cordoba as his secretary. While occupying this position ben-Saruk published a famous Hebrew dictionary.

Hisdai heard stories of a Jewish kingdom of the Khazars on the shores of the Caspian Sea, ruled by a king

A model of Joseph, king of the Khazars, dictating to his scribe a letter addressed to Hisdai ibn Shaprut of Cordoba, in Spain.

called Joseph. When he questioned the envoys of the Byzantine emperor, they gave some confirmation to the story. Hisdai thereupon wrote Joseph a letter '...to ascertain...whether there indeed exists a place where the dispersed of Israel have retained a remnant of royal power, and where the Gentiles do not govern and oppress them.' He explained in the letter that the existence of such a kingdom would be of great importance as the absence of Jewish independence anywhere was regarded as evidence that the Jews were no longer the chosen people of God. The letter was carried by Jewish merchants via Hungary and Russia. Years later Hisdai received a reply from Joseph confirming the fact of his Jewish kingdom. The authenticity of these two letters has been the subject of much scholarly controversy.

The Khazar Kingdom

See above

Joseph was a 10th-century king of the Khazars, a nomadic people of Turkish stock in the region of the Volga River, the Caucasus and the Black Sea. There was a persistent legend that Khazaria, which existed as a separate state from AD 740, was ruled by a Jewish king. Certainly the country had a large Jewish population, for the 10th-century Arab writer Mukaddasi says of Khazaria, 'sheep, honey and Jews exist in large quantities in that land'. According to the Arab historian al-Masudi, writing around 943, the Khazar king became a Jew between 786 and 809.

When word reached Hisdai ibn-Shaprut in Cordoba, Spain, that there was a Jewish king in Khazaria and that his name was Joseph, Hisdai determined to write to him to find out if it was true. Joseph's reply, which reached Cordoba in 955, recounts that his ancestor Bulan converted to Judaism around AD 740 with 4,000 of his nobles; and that Bulan's successor, Obadiah, invited to the country 'Jewish sages from all places who explained to him the Torah'. Synagogues and schools were founded throughout the country, although Christianity and Islam were still widespread.

In all probability only the king and his nobles converted to Judaism. The country's supreme court was a model commanding figure of Hisdai ibn-Shaprut, leading physician and counsellor to the Caliphate.

Early in the 11th century the Caliphate that had ruled over Moorish Spain collapsed, and was succeeded by a score or so of petty principalities, each under its own Arab or Berber ruler. The local Jewish communities were not seriously affected by this fragmentation, and continued to enjoy freedom and opportunities for advancement. Many of the minor Moslem kings relied heavily on Jewish political and financial advisers, emissaries, tax officials and physicians. In their internal affairs Jewish communities were dominated by an *élite* of courtiers, and there was a growing demand for a more democratic, elected structure of communal leadership. The outstanding Jewish personality of the time was Samuel ha-Nagid, the Vizier (chief minister) and military commander of the Berber kingdom of Granada from 1030 to 1056.

With the fragmentation of Moorish Spain the Christian Reconquista gained momentum. In 1085 the army of Castile won a notable victory in the capture of Toledo, that had been the old Visigoth capital before the Arab invasion.

The alarmed Moslem rulers appealed for help to their brethren in North Africa. That region was dominated at the time by the fanatical Berber sect of the Almoravids. They swept into Spain and defeated a Christian army in 1086, thereby halting the Reconquista for the next half-century. At first these extremist newcomers were hostile to the Jews, but in time they became attuned to the easy-going atmosphere of Andalusia and took up the benign attitude of the Ummayad Caliphate towards the Jews.

In 1146 renewed Christian pressure was countered by a fresh eruption of Berber tribesmen, this time belonging to the even more fanatical Moslem sect of the Almohads from the Atlas mountain area of Morocco. (This was one of the periodic upsurges of fundamentalist fervour that have occurred throughout the history of Islam, the most recent being that headed by the Ayatollah Khomeini in Iran.) The Almohad dynasty ruled Moslem Spain for the next century. It felt no indulgence for Jewish life and proceeded to eliminate it as far as possible. The practice of Judaism was banned; the synagogues and Talmudic academies were closed down; and the Jews were ordered to become Moslems. A great number of Jews streamed across the line into what had become, by a strange reversal, the relative security of Christian Spain. The Jews were discovering that in the Moslem-Christian struggle for the mastery of Spain, there was a shifting balance of tolerance as well as territory.

of religious tolerance. It comprised seven judges, two of whom were Jews, two Christians, two Moslems and one pagan. Joseph was nevertheless a resolute if rough defender of his faith. When he heard that Byzantine Jews had been forced to accept baptism, he exacted revenge from the Christians living in his country.

In Joseph's reply to Hisdai's letter he refers to raids which began around 913 on the kingdom of Khazaria from Russia along the Volga River. These attacks intensified in 965, and the kingdom did not survive for long after that, although there is some doubt about the date of its disappearance.

There is considerable difference of scholarly opinion concerning the authenticity of the Khazar Correspondence, as the exchange of letters between Joseph and Hisdai is called. Joseph's reply exists in two versions, one long, one short, and the existence of these texts has been known since the 16th century. From the style of the Hebrew in which they are written, it is evident that these letters could not possibly have been 16th-century forgeries. Moreover, there is a marked difference in style between the Hebrew of Hisdai's letter and that of Joseph's, and the language of the latter strongly suggests that it was composed in a non-Arabic-speaking environment. A number of scholars agree that these two texts were probably composed in the 11th century on the basis of an original letter written by the Khazarian king and no longer extant.

Samuel ha-Nagid

See colour pages 180 and 181

The brilliant and many-sided career of Samuel ibn-Nagrela marks the highest achievement of a Jew in Moorish Spain. He was born in Cordoba and received an all-round education not only in Jewish studies but also in Arabic and the Koran. Fleeing from Cordoba when it was occupied by fanatical Berber troops in 1013, he reached Granada in the south, and entered the service of its Berber ruler. According to the 12th-century Jewish historian Abraham

Above *The Exilarch in Babylonia and his court. A lawsuit is being heard at the gate of his residence.*

Right *The Byzantine Emperors and the Jews. The Emperior Justinian I (AD 527–565) seated on his throne.*

Benjamin de Tudela

We know of the journey made by Benjamin bar Jona (1), a merchant of Tudela in Spain, because he wrote an account of it.

(2). Rome. 'Rabbi Jechiel, who is the grandson of Rabbi Nathan, has the entry of the Pope's palace, for he is the steward of his house and all he hath.'

(3). Thebes. '2,000 Jews. They are the most skilful artificers in silk and purple cloth through all Greece.'

(4). Constantinople. 'No Jews live in the city, for they have been placed behind an inlet of the sea.'

(5). Jerusalem. When he reached Eretz Israel, he found Jerusalem still in the hands of the Christians.

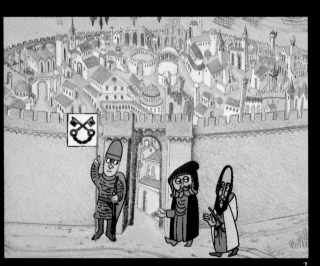

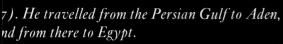

6). Baghdad. 'Over all the Jews of Babylon is
Daniel the son of Hisdai, who is styled our
Lord, the head of the captivity of all Israel.
He possesses a book of pedigrees going back as
far as David, King of Israel.)'

7). He travelled from the Persian Gulf to Aden,
and from there to Egypt.

8). And, his journey ended, Benjamin bar
Jona sat down to write the full account of his
journey as we have it today.

Samuel ha-Nagid (AD 993–1055), vizier of the Moslem Berber kingdom of Granada in Spain, composing a farewell poem to his son Jehoseph on the eve of battle.

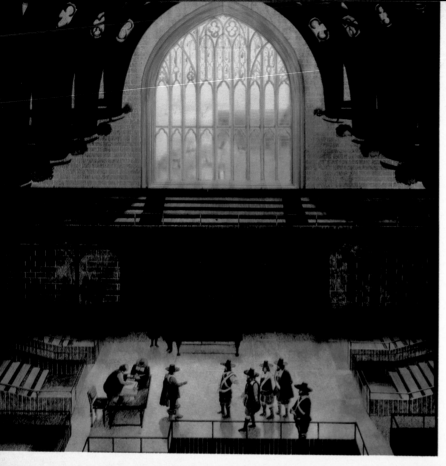

Left *The Return to England. A scene in Whitehall, London, during the negotiations for the return of the Jews to England.*

Right *Hisdai ibn-Shaprut. A mural painted in the style of mediaeval Spanish illuminated manuscripts.*

Overleaf *The Cairo Genizah. A diorama showing men gaining access by ladder to the Cairo Genizah.*

Below right *Kairouan. A diorama of a betrothal ceremony.*

Below *Saadiah Gaon and the Exilarch at the palace of the Caliph in Baghdad.*

ibn-Daud, Samuel had opened a spice-shop in Malaga, where he was asked by a maid-servant to write some letters for her master, an official at the court. The latter was so impressed by Samuel's elegant Arabic style that he obtained an appointment for him on the royal staff. His rise was meteoric. He became Vizier to the kingdom, and dominated its domestic, foreign and military affairs for nearly thirty years until his death. The Jews of Spain conferred on him the title of Nagid (Governor), to indicate their acceptance of him as their national leader.

For nearly the whole of his period of office, Samuel was involved in the military campaigns of Granada against the rival Moslem kingdom of Seville. The Jewish world took great pride in his victories, while the Islamic world became accustomed to the spectacle of a Moslem army being led into battle by a devout Jew.

His military experiences figured prominently in the large body of poetry he left. The epic battle poems among them are unique in Jewish literature. With all the manifold burdens of politics and war, this remarkably versatile man remained actively engaged in Jewish scholarship, and carried on a correspondence on legal and religious problems with eminent scholars in Babylonia and elsewhere. He endowed Talmudic academies in Spain and scholarships for poor students and carried out works of philanthropy among the Jews throughout the Moslem world, even including the supply of olive oil to the synagogues in Jerusalem. It is apparent from his poetry that in spite of his dazzling personal success he regarded Jewish life in exile as one of suffering and longed for the return of his people to Zion.

Samuel's awareness of the uncertainties of Jewish Diaspora life was tragically confirmed. He died on a military campaign in 1056, and his son Jehoseph succeeded him as head of the Granada Jewish community. Eleven years later, in 1066, there were Moslem riots against the Jews in which Jehoseph was murdered, together with some 1,500 local Jews.

Egypt and the Maghreb

Egypt

The Arab conquest of Egypt in AD 640 found there a relatively small and undistinguished Jewish community that had not recovered its vigour since the crushing of the great Alexandrian community in the 2nd century AD. Under Moslem rule the community concentrated mainly in the new city of Fostat (not far from the site of the later capital, Cairo), and became to a great extent Arabized in its language and mode of living. Little was known about Egyptian Jewish life during the ensuing centuries until it was illuminated by the documents found in the Cairo *Genizah* at the end of the 19th century.

The prestige of Cairo in the Jewish world was raised by the great Maimonides, who lived and worked there from 1165 to his death in 1204. The office of the Nagid, the head of Egyptian Jewry, was made a hereditary one occupied by the descendants of Maimonides.

In the 19th century the community grew and prospered as Western influence permeated Egypt. Wealthy and influential families emerged, such as the Cattauis and the Mosseris. Many of the Egyptian Jews had British, French, Italian or other foreign nationality and under the Capitulation treaties were protected persons enjoying certain privileges and immunities.

By the Second World War the community numbered 90,000 and was on the whole prosperous and well-established. But its position was undermined by the growth of Egyptian nationalism accompanied by pan-Arab, anti-Western and anti-Zionist feelings. With the proclamation of Israel's independence in 1948, and the Arab-Israel war that followed, the Egyptian authorities turned on the local Jews. Some of them were imprisoned, and some emigrated. By 1955, the number had dropped to 30,000.

After the Sinai campaign of 1956 the Nasser regime revenged itself for its defeat by putting 3,000 Jews in detention camps, expelling a number of others and taking over many Jewish businesses. The new Exodus from Egypt continued until the whole community had gone except for a few hundred elderly people. That ended the history of a community that went back to the 6th century BC.

The Maghreb

The Arab word *Maghreb* means 'west', and was applied to the adjoining North African states of Tunisia, Algeria and Morocco. Jewish settlements sprang up along this coast in ancient times, while Rome and Carthage vied for mastery of the western Mediterranean. When the area was conquered by the Arabs in the 7th century its Christian inhabitants were for the most part either eliminated or converted, but the Jewish communities were left intact and remained autonomous in their own internal affairs. During this period the leading centre of Jewish scholarship in the west was in Kairouan.

(continued on page 188)

Maimonides

'I dwell in Fostat and the Sultan resides in Cairo. These two places are two sabbath days journey from each other. My duties to the Sultan are very heavy. I am obliged to visit him daily early in the morning.'

'I am now getting hungry but I find the antechambers filled with people – Gentiles and Jews, important persons and common people, judges and bailiffs, friend and foe – a mixed multitude awaiting my return. I dismount from my animal, wash my hands, and request them to be patient until I have eaten a quick meal. I then go to attend to them, writing directions and prescriptions for their ailments. Patients come and go until night.'

'I have to lie down from sheer tiredness and when night falls I am so exhausted I can hardly speak.'

'When the Sultan, or one of his sons, or one of his concubines, is indisposed, I do not leave Cairo. Most of the day I am in the palace. If any of the royal officials fall sick, I have also to attend them.'

'As a consequence none of my fellow-Jews can get to speak with me or have a private interview except on the Sabbath. Then most of the congregation come to me after prayers. I instruct them as to what is to be done during the week. We stay together a little until noon when they leave. Some return and read with me again after the afternoon service until the evening prayer. This is how I spend my days.'

The above excerpts are from a letter in Judeo-Arabic written by Maimonides to his translator Samuel ibn-Tibbon. Ibn-Tibbon, a scholar and physician, translated Maimonides's *Guide of the Perplexed* and other of his works from Arabic into Hebrew under the author's guidance. (Four generations of the remarkable Tibbon family produced a large body of Hebrew translations and commentaries and played an important part in the development of the Hebrew language in the mediaeval period.)

Maimonides is the Greek form of the name of Moses ben-Maimon (1135–1204). In Hebrew writing he is generally known by the abbreviation *Rambam*. He was the intellectual giant of mediaeval Jewry and one of the most influential Jewish scholars and philosophers of all time. As a boy, he received an intensive education in Jewish and Arabic studies in his native city of Cordoba in Spain. When he was thirteen, his family fled from the persecution of the fanatical Moslem regime of the Almohads. After some years in Morocco and a short sojourn in Crusader Palestine, they settled in old Cairo. In due course Maimonides became the leader of the Egyptian community. He devoted himself to two parallel careers – medicine and Talmudic scholarship – with dazzling achievements in both.

As the excerpts from his letter to ibn-Tibbon show, he served as court physician to the Sultan of Egypt, while at the same time his medical reputation and skills drew a throng of patients, both Moslems and Jews, to his home. He produced a dozen treatises in Arabic on medical topics as varied as the art of healing, the therapeutic use of drugs, poisons, asthma, haemorrhoids and sexual hygiene. Some of these works were translated into Latin and used in European schools of medicine for centuries.

Maimonides's attitude to the physician's vocation strikes a relevant note today. He valued the human relationship between doctor and patient as much as professional skill,

and wrote: 'Medical practice is no knitting and weaving and the labour of hands, but it must be inspired with soul, filled with understanding and equipped with the gift of keen observation.'

It is astonishing that with all the demands upon his time and energy of his medical work and communal leadership, Maimonides should have been a major figure in the history of Jewish learning. While still a teenager he had published commentaries on the Hebrew calendar, the 613 precepts of Judaism and the technical terminology of logic. His monumental work was the Mishneh Torah, a codification of the whole of the Talmud, on which he spent the ten years from 1170 to 1180. Making use of both the Jerusalem and the Babylonian Talmuds and the commentaries of the Babylonian, Spanish and Franco-German scholars, he systematically clarified all the traditional doctrines. The Mishneh Torah was accepted as a standard work in the centuries to come.

As Maimonides's fame spread he was more and more consulted by Jewish communities all over the Moslem Diaspora, as far afield as Yemen in Arabia. In giving them guidance, he insisted on a rational approach to the problems of Jewish life and disapproved of the Messianic expectations that swept through the Jewish world. 'Let no one think', he wrote firmly, 'that in the days of the Messiah any of the laws of the world will be abolished or any innovation of nature will be introduced. The world will follow its normal course.'

Maimonides's epoch-making work of philosophy was the *Guide of the Perplexed*, produced in Arabic in 1190 when he was fifty-five years old. It set out to reconcile the tenets of Judaism with the logic and reason of Aristotle as transmuted through the leading Moslem philosophers. The work was widely-read and respected by Moslem scholars, and in Latin translation by Christian theologians. But the Hebrew translation stirred up fierce controversy in Jewish circles. It was bitterly attacked and even banned by Orthodox rabbis and

scholars, especially in the Franco-German region, on the ground that Maimonides's stress on reason as a source of religious belief would undermine the foundations of faith. The work was stoutly defended by other scholars (including its translator Samuel ibn-Tibbon) who formed the camp of the 'rationalists'. Only a century later was the study of philosophical works permitted by rabbinical authority, and even then it was confined to men over the age of twenty-five. In a later age Maimonides came to be accepted without reservation as one of the pillars of rabbinic Judaism, and revered as 'the second Moses'.

The Cairo Genizah

See colour page 184

Genizah is the Hebrew word for a hidden place used by synagogues from ancient times to store sacred writings and vessels that were no longer in use but could not be destroyed because they were regarded as holy. Such places have been found in the walls, foundations or attics of old synagogues in various countries. As a rule the documents have mouldered away in the course of time. A dramatic exception has been the Genizah found in the attic of the Ezra synagogue in Cairo, built in 882 on the site of a disused Coptic Church bought by the Jewish community. The attic is located at the end of the women's gallery, but it has no doors or windows, and can be entered only through an opening that is reached by ladder. The vast hoard of written material, accumulated over many centuries, was preserved in darkness in the dry desert air of Cairo, just as the Dead Sea Scrolls were preserved in Judean caves under similar conditions. Entry into the Genizah was discouraged because of the local superstition that any disturbance of its contents would bring ill-fortune to the congregation. Nevertheless, from time to time pages or fragments were stolen and sold to Western visitors. The first case on record was in 1763. It was only in 1896 that material was

The Jewish population suffered under the repressive Almohad regime in the 12th and 13th centuries. The communities were revitalized by the influx of Spanish Jews after the 1391 pogroms in Christian Spain and the Expulsion of 1492. The Sephardi newcomers soon dominated Jewish business and intellectual life in the Maghreb. They developed the type of communal leadership that had been the custom in Spain – through wealthy and important families.

In the 16th century the Ottoman empire expanded to take in the whole of North Africa – except Morocco, which remained independent under its own sultan. But the Ottoman overlord was remote and lax, and in practice the Bey of Algiers and the Bey of Tunis were rulers in their own right. In the 17th and 18th centuries all three Maghreb countries, together with Tripolitania (later part of Libya) were known as the Barbary Coast – that is, the coast of the Berbers. They were the indigenous tribes who had been conquered by the Arabs but remained the majority of the inhabitants. The chief source of revenue for these countries was piracy, preying on the Mediterranean sea-lanes with rich rewards in booty, slaves, and ransom for captives. The Jews were frequent travellers through these waters on business, family or religious affairs. The communities were constantly called upon to find ransom money for captured Jews – a *mitzvah*, religious duty. It was not until the beginning of the 19th century that the navies of the Western powers were able to suppress the Barbary corsair industry and secure the Mediterranean route.

With the local Moslem regimes in the Maghreb weakened and the Ottoman empire disintegrating, the power vacuum was filled by France. In 1830 French forces occupied Algeria and made it a province of Metropolitan France. French citizenship was conferred on all the Algerian Jews under the so-called Crémieux Decree of 1870 (Adolphe Crémieux was at the time the Minister of Justice in Paris and also the leader of French Jewry). Tunisia was made a French protectorate in 1881. The kingdom of Morocco came under French administration in 1912.

The Maghreb Jewish communities felt increasingly insecure in the face of rising Arab nationalism. They welcomed French control and their educated classes eagerly imbibed the French language and culture. The Moslem population resented the Jewish identification with their French masters. In Algeria there were a number of anti-Jewish outbreaks in the last two decades of the 19th century. In the Algerian Revolt that started in 1954, the Jews found themselves caught in the middle, and their emigration increased. After Algerian independence was conceded by General de Gaulle there was a general exodus of the Jewish population, mainly to France, which they were entitled to enter as citizens. Conditions in Morocco and Tunisia were less tense and hostile for the Jewish community, but here too emigration was stimulated by a feeling of insecurity. After Israel was established in 1948 the bulk of the Jewish population of Morocco and Tunisia settled there.

removed on a large scale and examined. This came about by chance.

Two Scottish ladies on a visit to Egypt were offered some old pages of Hebrew writing and bought them as a souvenir. On their return they showed the fragments to the renowned Jewish scholar, Dr Solomon Schechter, at Cambridge University (later President of the Jewish Theological Seminary in New York). To his amazement, he found himself looking at a portion of a manuscript copy in Hebrew of the Apocryphal work *Ecclesiasticus* or *The Wisdom of Ben Sirach*. Originally written in Hebrew in the 2nd century BC, it was known till then only in a Greek translation. The document was traced to the Genizah. With the support of Cambridge University and the consent of the synagogue, Schechter spent some months in Cairo extracting and crating documents for study at Cambridge. They comprised about 100,000 manuscript pages. A similar quantity was later removed by other scholars and acquired by large libraries around the world. The task of deciphering and analyzing this great mass of old documents has not yet been completed.

Among the finds of special historical and literary value are most of the Ben-Sirach Hebrew manuscript; portions of the Greek translation of the Hebrew Bible made in the 2nd century AD by Aquila (a Roman scholar who converted to Christianity and then to Judaism, and studied under the great Rabbi Akiba); many old liturgical poems ('piyyutim') previously unknown, composed in Eretz Israel, Babylonia and Spain; and a great number of letters and papers relating to important individuals. The oldest dated document is from 750 AD.

The Genizah material has thrown light on Jewish life in Egypt and Palestine during the period between the Arab Conquest in the 7th century and the Crusaders in the 12th century. Much valuable information has also been gleaned about the Karaite movement.

Kairouan

See colour page 183

The betrothal ceremony of the daughter of Nissim, the rabbi of Kairouan in North Africa, to Jehoseph, son of Samuel ha-Nagid, the chief minister in the Moslem kingdom of Granada in Spain and the acknowledged leader of Spanish Jewry in the 11th century. The union cemented the close ties that existed between Kairouan, an important centre of Jewish commerce and learning in what is today Tunisia, and the Jewish community of Spain. In 1056 Jehoseph succeeded his father as Nagid or head of Granada Jewry, but eleven years later he was killed in anti-Jewish riots. The following year Kairouan was destroyed by Bedouin tribes.

The Ottoman Empire

In the 11th century, nomadic Turkish tribes that had embraced Islam started moving into the Middle East and overran portions of the Byzantine and Arab empires. One of these tribes was the Ottoman Turks, so called after their leader Othman. In the 13th century they occupied an area of Asia Minor south of the Bosphorus and established a state ruled by a sultan. The small Jewish community in this area had been there from Roman times and were known as Romaniots. They were treated much better by the Turks than they had been by their previous Byzantine masters. They were permitted to practise their religion, carry on trade and own property without restriction. On the other hand, they were required to pay a poll-tax that the community leaders were responsible for collecting.

In the 15th and 16th centuries the Ottoman domain expanded by conquest in every direction to form a huge empire. The crucial event was the fall of Constantinople in 1453 – the death-knell of the Byzantine empire. The Ottoman empire reached its zenith under its greatest sultan, Suleiman the Magnificent (1520–66). It then extended into the Balkans and Eastern Europe, including Hungary and Rumania; over the whole Arab Middle East; and along North Africa from Egypt to Algeria.

The Holy Land was now under Turkish rule, as well as a great proportion of Diaspora Jewry – probably more than a million in number. In practice the Empire was loosely organized, and in most countries the local rulers were free to carry out their own domestic policies, while acknowledging Turkish suzerainty. That explains the variations in the treatment of the Jewish communities in different regions of the empire.

In Palestine the Ottoman regime came as a relief from Mamluk repression. The Jewish community increased by immigration and its conditions improved. Safad in the Galilee became of particular importance for its scholarship. Suleiman rebuilt the walls that still surround the Old City of Jerusalem.

In the heartland of the empire (roughly corresponding to modern Turkey) the major Jewish centres were in Constantinople, Salonika, Adrianople and Smyrna (Izmir). The Jews of this region enjoyed economic prosperity and a high level of culture, and developed important Talmudic academies. The first printing press in the Ottoman empire was a Hebrew one in Constantinople. The Islamic restrictions under the Covenant of Omar were not strictly observed, though Jews were required to wear yellow headgear to distinguish them from the Moslems, who wore green. There was little social or cultural integration with the Turkish majority, and no 'Judeo-Turkish' language evolved on the analogy of Judeo-Arabic, Ladino (Judeo-Spanish) or Yiddish (Judeo-German).

Eager to increase the beneficial economic activities of their Jewish subjects, the Ottoman rulers encouraged the immigration of Jews from Christian lands where they were oppressed or had been expelled. In the mediaeval period there was a steady settlement of Jewish refugees from Germany, France, Hungary and elsewhere. The most significant influx occurred after the 1492 expulsions from Spain and the exodus from Portugal in 1497. The Ottoman Sultan at the time, Bayazid II, is reported to have remarked that the Spanish king, Ferdinand (who together with his queen Isabella had signed the expulsion decree), could not be very intelligent since he was impoverishing his country and enriching that of the Sultan. A score of Sephardi (Spanish) congregations sprang up in mainland Turkey, while small numbers of the Spanish and Portuguese immigrants settled in Safad and Jerusalem, and in Egypt. Some of them were Marranos who reverted to Judaism.

Jewish medical skill (especially that of the Spanish Jews) was so highly regarded that it was customary for the Sultans to have Jewish physicians. As a mark of distinction they were allowed to wear tall red hats instead of the yellow headgear of their fellow-Jews. It was also common for Jews to hold high public office in the financial services, as directors of customs, tax officials and advisers.

The most influential Jewish figure in the history of the Ottoman empire was Don Joseph Nasi (1524–79), a Portuguese Marrano who settled in Constantinople at the age of thirty and returned to Judaism. He rose to be the diplomatic counsellor and friend of the powerful Sultan Selim II, who made him Duke of Naxos and the Cyclades.

The status of the non-Moslem religious communities was governed by the 'millet system'. Each creed had internal autonomy in the religious, administrative, legal, educational and taxation spheres. The religious leaders were the official heads of the respective millets and were responsible for them to the authorities.

Before the 19th century there was no centralized leadership for all of Turkish Jewry. Jewish communities were organized according to their places of origin. By the end of the 16th century there were over forty such congregations in Constantinople alone. In the 17th and 18th centuries the communal separation started breaking down. The original Jewish settlers, the Ashkenazim and the Sephardim, mingled and intermarried.

In the 19th century the structure of the millets was re-organized and given a detailed legislative framework. The official regulations were approved for the Greeks in 1862, the Armenians in 1863 and the Jews in 1865.

Internal and external trade in Turkey was concentrated mainly in the hands of these three non-Moslem minorities. On the whole the Jews were favoured by the authorities, since the Christian communities were regarded as sympathetic to the European Christian powers, of whose intentions the Ottoman rulers were always suspicious.

The Ottoman empire was at the time a land of opportunity for commerce. It was spread over three continents and lay astride the

(continued on page 192)

Donna Gracia Mendes

Donna Gracia Mendes (1510–69) was the aunt of the famous Don Joseph Nasi and the outstanding Jewess of her day. She is seen here holding a meeting in her Constantinople home in the year 1556, to discuss a possible Jewish boycott against the Italian port of Ancona, where twenty-five Portuguese Marranos have been burnt at the stake as heretics.

It was natural for Donna Gracia to react strongly to this grim event. She had been born into a distinguished Marrano family in Lisbon, and had grown up with the Spanish name of Beatrice de Luna. She married Francisco Mendes, also a Marrano, a wealthy banker and dealer in gems.

A meeting in Donna Gracia's home in Constantinople.

When her husband died, she left Portugal with her family, including her young nephew who later became Don Joseph Nasi, and settled in Antwerp, where her husband's brother and partner was running the branch of the family business. From this base she organized the flights and helped the resettlement of Marrano families fleeing from the Inquisition in Portugal. Moving to Venice in 1545, she carried on with this task until she was denounced by her own sister as a secret Jew, and flung into prison. Her nephew obtained her release through diplomatic intervention.

Undaunted, Donna Gracia went to Ferrara in Italy where she openly professed Judaism and renounced her Spanish name. The Ferrara Spanish Bible published in 1553 was dedicated to her. In that year she finally settled in Constantinople, where she was joined by her nephew and took him into partnership in her business enterprises. She was associated with him in the lease from the Ottoman authorities in 1558 of the ruined town of Tiberias and its surrounding land on the Sea of Galilee, for the purpose of settling Jews in the Holy Land. Don Joseph Nasi had the tumbledown walls restored, took initial steps to introduce wool and silk industries, and wrote to Marrano refugee groups in Italy, inviting them to settle in Tiberias; but apparently nothing came of this project.

In Constantinople Donna Gracia became a patron of Jewish religious life, promoting the establishment of new synagogues and yeshivas there and in Salonika. She was so renowned in the Jewish community by this time that everyone referred to her simply as 'La Senora' or, in Hebrew, *Ha-Geveret*. One of the Constantinople synagogues bore this name in her honour.

Ottoman Jewish Types. Three pictures of 16th-century Ottoman Jews from the book of travels by N. Nikolai, Les Quatre Premiers Livres des navigations et pérégrinations orientales, *Lyons 1568: a rich Jewess from Adrianople; a Jewish physician; a Jewish cloth merchant from Constantinople.*

main international trade routes. As merchants the Jews had certain advantages. They had widespread contacts in Christian Europe, and the immigrants had brought in with them the main European languages – German, French, Spanish and Italian. In addition, Jewish merchants and shippers were long established in the principal Moslem ports and cities in the Empire outside Turkey, including Alexandria, Cairo, Damascus, Baghdad and Basra on the Persian Gulf.

The Ottoman Jews developed certain types of industry. The most important was the weaving and dyeing of woollen cloth and the manufacture of the finished garments. The major centre for this textile industry was Salonika. The community there even paid part of its taxes in kind by the supply of blue uniforms to the Ottoman army. Jews were predominant in the leather trade, especially in the tanning of hides and skins. They were also expert wine-makers and traditional craftsmen in gold and silver jewellery. The Spanish Jews brought with them an expertise in the manufacture of fire-arms that contributed to Ottoman military strength.

As a rule Jewish commerce, industry and finance were conducted as tight family businesses. When branches were opened in different centres, members of the family were usually sent to run them.

The 'Capitulations' were the treaty concessions made in favour of

foreign nationals living in the Ottoman empire. They included a variety of privileges, legal immunities and tax exemptions. The first such treaty was signed with the republic of Venice in 1521, followed in due course by all the European powers. Large numbers of Christian and Jewish residents managed to acquire or buy 'berats' (certificates of nationality) from foreign consuls, and thus became protected persons of the European states concerned. As the Ottoman empire weakened, the Capitulations became a wedge for European intervention in internal Ottoman affairs.

From the late 17th century onwards the Ottoman empire declined. Its borders were steadily pushed back by the wars with Russia and by successful rebellions in vassal states. Internal decay set in. The rulers and pashas lived in indolence and extravagance. The civil service and provincial governors became corrupt, with bribery an accepted practice of government. The armed forces were disaffected, and some Sultans were dependent on the 'janissaries', the Turkish conscript militia. The maximum taxes were squeezed from subject peoples.

The position of the Jews deteriorated in the context of the general decline. The religious tolerance for non-Moslems, that had been such a redeeming feature of the earlier Ottoman regime, started to be less evident. There were no longer Jews with positions of influence at the

(continued on page 196)

Salonika

Salonika (or Thessalonike, the official name) is a large port-city in Macedonia, the north-eastern province of Greece. Its early importance lay in its location at the head of the Aegean Sea and on the Via Egnatia, the main highway from Rome to Asia.

Founded in 315 BC by the king of Macedon, it passed through many hands: Roman, Byzantine, Crusader, Greek, Venetian, Ottoman (from 1430) and again Greek (from 1912).

One constant factor in the history of the city was its Jewish community, which went back over twenty centuries. St Paul preached in its synagogue on three consecutive Sabbaths in the year AD 50 during his second missionary journey, and later wrote to Jewish and pagan converts to Christianity in his two Epistles to the Thessalonians (i.e. Salonikans).

From the beginning of the Turkish occupation, the old Romaniot Jewish community was swelled by refugees from elsewhere. The first immigrant group came from Bavaria in 1470. Since these German Jews had little in common with their local brethren, they set up a separate Ashkenazi community. In the 15th and 16th centuries there was a stream of newcomers who had been expelled from Spain, France, Italy and Portugal. They set up their own Sephardi synagogues and congregations. These were named after their places of origin. By the middle of the 17th

Salonika Jews being deported to the Nazi death camps in March 1943.

century there were about 30,000 Jews, organized in thirty congregations. They united in 1680 and set up a joint council of three rabbis elected for life, and seven lay leaders.

The Jewish population inhabited three different quarters – the original one at the port, next to the city wall; the more elegant quarter of the *Francos* (Europeans); and the quarter of the Greek Jews.

In the 16th and 17th centuries Salonika was an important centre of Talmudic learning, and attracted a number of prominent rabbis and

scholars. It was also renowned for the study of the Kabbalah. The most dramatic event in the life of the community during this period was the arrival in the town of the false messiah Shabbetai Zevi. At first he was welcomed, but when he proclaimed himself as the Messiah, the local rabbis took a collective decision to expel him. After his death Salonika was the religious centre for a group of his followers who copied his example by converting to Islam. They were called *Doenmeh*, from the Turkish word for 'apostates'. It was the upheaval caused by the Shabbetai Zevi affair that induced the different congregations in the town to unite.

The Salonika community pursued a remarkable variety of occupations. The well-to-do merchant class was engaged in the export trade in grain, textiles, cotton, wool and silk. The major industry lay in the weaving and dyeing of woollen cloth and the manufacture of woollen garments. Jews had their own guilds of skilled craftsmen, such as the goldsmiths, silversmiths and jewellers. At the port the stevedores and porters were largely Jewish. There were also Jewish workers in the gold and silver mines further inland, and in tobacco growing. Since about half the population of Salonika was Jewish from about the 17th century, the port and most of the business area were closed on the Sabbath and on Jewish festivals.

In 1900 the Jewish community numbered 80,000. It was already declining owing to the general stagnation in the Ottoman Empire. There was a steady stream of emigration, especially of younger people, to Palestine, the United States and Western Europe. By the outbreak of the Second World War the Jews constituted only a fifth of the city's population.

On 9 April 1941, the first German panzer columns rolled into Salonika. In the opening phase of the Nazi occupation Jewish adult males were sent to forced labour camps, where many of them died of malaria and malnutrition. Jewish businesses and

property were confiscated; the Nuremberg race laws were applied; the contents of Jewish libraries and the ritual objects from synagogues were crated and sent to Germany. The centuries-old cemetery, with its graves, was turned into a quarry, and the tombstones used for building stones, and for lining army latrines.

By the beginning of 1943, the 'final solution' stage of the Holocaust programme got under way in Nazi-occupied Europe. Between 14 March and 7 August, 43,880 of the Salonika Jews were transported in nineteen train convoys to the death-camps of Auschwitz and Birkenau. A small number managed to escape to the countryside and to Athens, and survived. When the war was over a remnant returned to find their homes occupied, their property looted, and all but two out of nineteen synagogues destroyed. They started to pick up their lives in the ruins of what had been a sturdy and creative community for over 2,000 years.

Sublime Porte, as the Sultan's court was called. Jewish economic and intellectual activity failed to maintain the levels that had been reached in the previous century. The community was shaken by the meteoric rise in the 17th century of the false messiah Shabbetai Zevi from Smyrna, and the shattering anti-climax when he saved himself by converting to Islam.

Blood-libel charges crept in from Christian Europe and reached a dramatic high point in the notorious Damascus Affair of 1840. A number of leading Syrian Jews were imprisoned and tortured (two of them to death) on charges of having murdered two missing persons and used their blood for ritual purposes on the Passover. The prisoners were released through the efforts of a delegation of Western Jewish leaders headed by Sir Moses Montefiore of England and including Adolphe Crémieux of France. The delegation obtained from the Sultan a decree making the blood-libel a punishable offence. Though blood-libel charges recurred after that in a number of places in the Ottoman empire, their consequences were usually averted through European Jewish intervention and judicious bribery.

It was in this, the 19th century, that a shrunken and bankrupt Ottoman empire was called 'the sick man of Europe'. The statesmen of the leading Western powers (including Disraeli in England) were much concerned with the Eastern Question, which in essence meant propping up the Ottoman empire in order to preserve the European status quo and to block the southward expansion of Czarist Russia. Unable to repay its huge debt to Western countries, the Empire became financially dependent on its creditors; it had to permit the duty-free import of European goods and the taking over of public utilities by European capital. The result was a further erosion in the local economy, and therefore in the situation of the Jewish community.

By the Young Turk Revolution of 1908 the despotic Sultan Abdul Hamid II was overthrown and a republic proclaimed. Six years later the First World War broke out. It led to the defeat and dissolution of the Ottoman empire and the emergence of the present-day Turkish Republic, shorn of imperial possessions.

Yemen

Yemen occupies the south-western corner of the Arabian Peninsula, at the entrance to the Red Sea. It is a poor and primitive land, with the coastal strip barren and humid and the interior a high plateau cut up by mountain ranges. The beginnings of Jewish settlement here are shrouded in legend. One romantic but unlikely version is that the first Jewish sojourners arrived after the famous visit of the Queen of Sheba to King Solomon, in the 10th century BC (the country of Sheba or Saba was in the Red Sea area). The Yemenite Jews believe that their community began after the destruction of Solomon's Temple at the beginning of the 6th century BC, and that their sufferings were God's punishment for their failure to join the Return in the days of Ezra and

The Jews of San'a

See above *A street in San'a c. 1900. In the background is Jebel Nuqum, a mountain 7,790 feet high and seven miles east of San'a.*

The earliest Jewish settlement in this area was on its slope, where the remains of two ancient synagogues still exist. A Jewish quarter was later established next to the city gate, on the site of the present bazaar of the coppersmiths. The San'a community remained the centre of Jewish life in Yemen.

In 1678 the Imam exiled the whole community, together with most of the Jews in other parts of Yemen, to Mawza in the desolate coastal region. Many of them died of hunger and disease. A year or so later they were allowed to return, but not to their

(continued on page 199)

previous homes. Instead, they were assigned to another Jewish quarter (*Qa al-Yhud*) outside the city wall.

Disaster again struck the community in 1905, when the Imam revolted against Ottoman rule, and conducted a prolonged siege of San'a. It was reported that only 150 Jews were left alive when the city fell. One traveller wrote: 'During the siege entire families died stolidly in the street, or turning their faces to the wall in their own house, for it was little use begging when bread was sold at thirty shillings per pound.'

In 1948 there were an estimated 6,000 Jews in San'a. They were permitted to leave for Israel on payment to the Imam of a large ransom.

Maimonides's letter to Yemen

The letter arose out of a major crisis in the history of the Yemenite Jewish community. About 1160, the Imam (ruler) of Yemen launched a religious persecution of the Jews, giving them a choice between conversion to Islam or death. Some of them did convert. The rest clutched desperately at the words of a pseudo-messiah who told them that these tribulations were sent by God to mark the advent of the Messianic Age.

The head of Yemenite Jewry, Rabbi Jacob ben-Nathanel al-Fayyummi, turned for help to Maimonides in Old Cairo. The great scholar and communal leader used his behind-the-scenes influence, as the personal physician to the Egyptian sultan, to alleviate the burdens on his brethren in Yemen. His reply to Rabbi Jacob was designed to strengthen their faith and hope. It was deliberately written in simple terms, and he requested that it be distributed to every local community in Yemen. In his letter Maimonides told them to reject the pseudo-messiah.

The letter had a powerful impact on the Yemenite Jews, who stood firm until the crisis passed. They showed their gratitude by introducing into the Kaddish, the prayer recited by mourners, which is a plea for 'the life of our teacher Moses ben-Maimon' (Maimonides). This unique tribute had until then been reserved only for the Exilarch in Babylonia, who was regarded as the representative of all the Jews in Islamic lands.

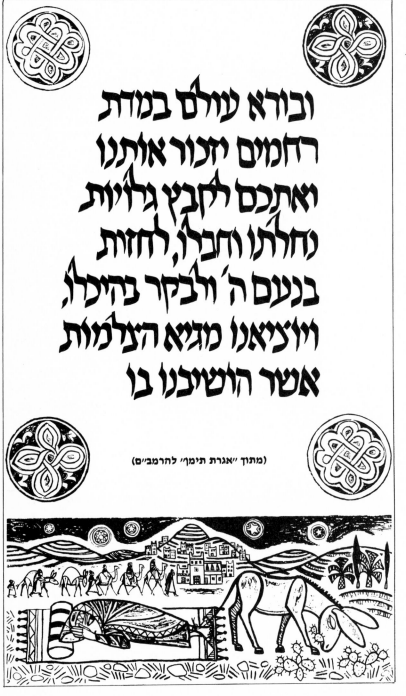

וּבוֹרֵא עוֹלָם בְּמִדַּת
רַחֲמִים יִזְכּוֹר אוֹתָנוּ
וְאֶתְכֶם לְקַבֵּץ גָּלֻיּוֹת
נַחֲלָתוֹ וְחֶבְלוֹ, לַחֲזוֹת
בְּנֹעַם ה' וּלְבַקֵּר בְּהֵיכָלוֹ,
וְיוֹצִיאֵנוּ מִגִּיא הַצַּלְמָוֶת
אֲשֶׁר הוֹשִׁיבָנוּ בּוֹ

(מתוך "אגרת תימן" להרמב"ם)

Messianism in Yemen

There is a Yemenite Jewish folk-tale about a devout woman who lived alone. At night she slept tied to a rope with its end fastened to the leg of a donkey standing at her door. She relied on the donkey to awaken her when he heard the approaching footsteps of the Messiah.

The naive story illustrates how deep-rooted in the consciousness of the Yemenite Jews was the belief in the Messianic advent that would redeem them from their hard life and degrading status, and lead them back to the Promised Land. That fervent hope explains why the Yemenite community was even more vulnerable to Messianic movements than Jews in other countries.

The appearance of the pseudo-messiah Shabbetai Zevi in the late 17th century, which caused an upheaval throughout the Jewish world, swept the Yemenite community into a state of ecstasy. They paid dearly for their expectations in bloody persecution by the Imam of Yemen.

In the second half of the 19th century at least three pseudo-messiahs appeared in Yemen. The most serious of them was Judah ben-Shalom of San'a, who called himself by the Arab name of Shukr Kuhail. In a dream he was called upon by the prophet Elijah to be the Redeemer. During 1862–4 he travelled through the villages and gained a large following from among both Jews and Moslems. The Imam had him murdered, but his followers believed he would return. Three years later they accepted for a while an impostor who proclaimed himself the resurrected Shukr. He even took Shukr's widow to himself and had a son by her.

Another pseudo-messiah, Joseph ben-Abdallah, appeared in Yemen in 1893, and gained wide influence until he was exposed as a confidence man, out to make money from Jewish hopes. By that time the migration of Yemenite Jews to Eretz Israel was already on the increase. The promised Return had in fact begun, and would be completed by 1950.

Nehemiah. Another possibility is that among the earliest settlers there may have been soldiers from the Judean contingent attached by Herod the Great to the Roman expedition that came to conquer South Arabia in 25 BC. Jewish traders may also have taken root in Yemen at that time. What seems certain is that by the 3rd century AD a community of some thousands of Jews had already been living in Yemen for a long time. They sent the bodies of some of the leaders by camel caravan all the way to the catacomb of Beit She'arim in the valley of Jezreel for burial.

The country was then called the kingdom of Himyar. Some of its rulers and a number of its tribesmen were converted to Judaism. According to Arab traditions, one such Jewish ruler was Ab Karib As'ad (AD 385–420). The last king of Himyar, Dhu Nuwas, was also a convert to Judaism, and took the name of Joseph. At that time there was increasing pressure on Himyar from Abyssinia across the Red Sea. The Abyssinians had adopted Christianity and been drawn into the orbit of the Byzantine empire. With Byzantine support they invaded Yemen in 525 AD. Its Jewish king was killed and the kingdom of Himyar came to an end.

After its conquest by the Moslems in the 7th century, the country went into a decline. The Jews were granted freedom to practise their religion, but were subjected to degrading restrictions and at times persecuted. They lived in segregated quarters in the towns, or were scattered in small groups among the mountain villages. They were not allowed to ride a camel or a horse, and had to dismount even from a donkey when a Moslem passed. The men were forbidden to wear coloured robes, or to carry the mediaeval weapons of the area, flintlock guns and ornamental daggers. Ironically, these weapons were brought to the Jews for repair and adornment, for they were considered the best craftsmen in Yemen. They excelled as goldsmiths and silver-smiths, jewellers, basket-weavers, potters, carpenters, blacksmiths, gunsmiths and saddlers. The embroidered garments made by the Yemenite Jewish women were unique.

These craftsmen earned a humble living, as did the petty traders and peddlers. With few exceptions, the Yemenite Jews were in-credibly poor and ill-nourished, and were kept down to a subsistence level by the poll taxes collected for the Imam (the ruler) and the protection money paid to local Arab notables who were their 'patrons'.

During century after century of existence under these wretched conditions the Yemenite Jews never faltered in their faith, or gave up their hope of an ultimate return to Zion. Every boy was educated in a religious elementary school, where he studied the sacred books. Since there was seldom more than one book to a class, the pupils could read it just as well upside-down or sideways as right-side-up. Amidst surroundings of squalor they kept their homes and persons clean and hygienic, in strict accordance with the religious precepts. Their love of beauty was expressed in their delicate handiwork and in poetry, songs and folk-dances. Somehow their culture remained closer in spirit to

Jews of Yemen, South Arabia, being taken to Israel in 'Operation Magic Carpet', 1950.

Yemenite immigrants in 1950

When the news reached the Jews in Yemen that the State of Israel had come into existence, thousands of them started making their way to Aden, the British-held port on the Red Sea. They arrived exhausted, hungry and carrying their sick, after weeks of trekking by foot or on donkeys for hundreds of miles across mountains and desert. Their possessions had been stripped from them by hostile tribes, but they clung fiercely to their holy Scrolls of the Law.

The British authorities in Aden collected them in an abandoned military camp, where they were fed and cared for by Jewish welfare agencies. Since Egypt had blockaded the normal sea route through the Suez Canal, the Israel Government and the Jewish Agency decided to fly these refugees to Israel by an air shuttle service, using stripped-down American Skymasters. Each plane was loaded with more than the normal complement of passengers, which was possible since the average weight of the adults was only 86 lbs and their possessions were meagre. They had never seen a plane before, and simply

that of their biblical ancestors than that of more sophisticated communities elsewhere.

While they lived in a backwater, out of the mainstream of Jewish life, contact was maintained with the centres of learning and commerce in Babylonia, Egypt and North Africa. Some mediaeval correspondence survives with the capital of Yemen, San'a, where its largest Jewish community lived.

The lot of the Jews, the only non-Moslem community in Yemen, became more precarious when the country was annexed to the Ottoman Empire in the 16th century. There were recurrent attempts by the native population, who belonged to the dissident Zaydi sect of Islam, to throw off the shaky Turkish rule. As usual in such conflicts, the Jews were distrusted by both sides and suffered from both.

One point of contact with this remote community was through the port of Aden, where Jewish merchants were engaged in the transit trade between the Near East and India. The route acquired world importance with the opening of the Suez Canal in 1869. The Western presence greatly increased in the strategic Red Sea area, and Yemen (including its Jews) were drawn into closer touch with the outside world. At that time there were about 80,000 Jews in Yemen, most of them living in the rural villages.

When the Yemenite Jews heard of the Zionist settlement that started in Palestine in the 1880s, they were convinced that this was the beginning of God's redemption, and began to make their way in increasing numbers to the Holy Land.

When Yemen became independent in 1911, all the anti-Jewish measures from the past were enforced with greater severity. The worst blow was an ordinance of 1925 requiring Jewish orphans to be brought up as Moslems. As many of them as possible were adopted into Jewish families or smuggled out of the country.

These events further stimulated the urge to leave the country for Eretz Israel. By 1948, when the State of Israel was proclaimed, some 18,000 Yemenite Jews had already settled there. In 1949–50 almost the whole of the remaining community was evacuated from Aden to Israel by an airlift, in what was known as 'Operation Magic Carpet'.

The Yemenites were in certain respects unlike any other immigrant group. They had emerged into the modern world from conditions more primitive than those prevailing in any other Diaspora community. They had never known beds, chairs or toilets, electric light or piped water, a railway, a bus or an aeroplane. Yet by common consent, these hardworking pious people of slender build are one of the most appealing of Jewish communities. Their artistic traditions in the dance, jewellery and embroidery have made a distinctive contribution to Israeli culture.

related their journey to the biblical promise that the Lord would bring them to Israel 'on eagles' wings' (*Exod. 19:4*).

By the end of the airborne operation in September 1950, nearly 49,000 Yemenite Jews had been brought to Israel in 430 flights. Operation Magic Carpet had transported to the homeland the whole of a Diaspora community whose beginnings were shrouded in the mists of antiquity.

Important Events

The Covenant of Omar

624–8	Mohammed destroys Jewish tribes in Arabia.
638	Caliph Omar takes Jerusalem.
762	Beginning of events leading to Karaite schism.
930	Dispute between Saadiah Gaon and Exilarch.
1099	Jerusalem captured by Crusaders.

Moorish Spain

711	Moorish conquest of Spain.
955	Supposed letter from Joseph king of the Khazars to Hisdai ibn Shaprut.
1026(?)	Samuel ha-Nagid, vizier of Granada, appointed Nagid.
1146	Start of fanatical Almohad rule.

Egypt and the Maghreb
Egypt

640	Arab Conquest.
1165	Maimonides settles in Cairo.
1896	Schechter recovers material from Cairo Genizah
From 1948	Exodus of Egyptian community.

Maghreb

1830	French occupation of Algeria.
1881	Tunisia made French protectorate.
1912	Morocco under French administration.
1950–62	Most Maghreb Jews emigrate.

Ottoman Empire

1453	Constantinople captured by Ottoman Turks.
From 1492	Influx of Spanish and Portuguese refugees.
1562	Lease of Tiberias to Don Joseph Nasi.
1840	Damascus blood-libel case.

Yemen

c. 1172	Maimonides letter to Yemen.
1678	Jews exiled to coast.
1949–50	Operation Magic Carpet – airlift to Israel.

## Chapter Fourteen

Eastern European Jewry

Poland – Lithuania: 15th–18th centuries

Eastern European Jewry started as an offshoot from the communities of mediaeval Germany and other countries of the Balkans.

In the early 13th century the towns of Poland were devastated by the incursions of the Mongols and Tartars, Central Asian peoples that had conquered Russia. The country was left with a backward and stagnant economy, based on landowning nobles and their serfs. The Polish princes became eager to create a new urban middle class that would revive both trade and skilled crafts. For this purpose they gave inducements to Germans to repopulate Polish towns. Among the new settlers were a number of Jews escaping persecution in Germany and seeking a more secure life in Eastern Europe. They were promised protection and economic opportunities by the Polish rulers.

The basic document determining their status was the Charter of Privileges granted to them in 1264 by Prince Boleslav the Pious of Kalisz. After Poland became a united country in the 14th century its outstanding sovereign, Casimir the Great, reconfirmed and amplified the Charter of Boleslav. The Polish Jews were therefore under royal protection, on the analogy of the *servi camerae regis* ('servants of the royal chamber') in the German empire. In 1388 a similar charter was granted by the Grand Duke of Lithuania to the Jews settling in his country (later united with Poland). The Lithuanian charter expressly granted the Jews full economic equality with Christians.

However, life for the Jewish immigrants in Poland was far from tranquil. There were sporadic outbreaks of violence against them. The Polish clergy was hostile, and pressed for repeal of the privileges granted to Jews in royal charters. Some of the nobles too were infected by anti-semitism. In the towns the Christian merchants and craftsmen, organized into exclusive guilds on the German model, resented Jewish competition and in a number of cases succeeded in expelling or excluding Jews. Blood-libel charges cropped up in several places. Nevertheless, the Jews were on the whole much better off in Poland-Lithuania than they were in mediaeval Western Europe, where the

(continued on page 205)

Jewish Occupations in Poland–Lithuania

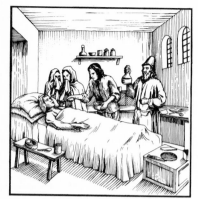

The original Jewish immigrants from Germany into Poland were mainly money-lenders. They were welcomed by the Polish princes for the financial services they could render in reviving the towns. With the growth in numbers of the Jewish community, its occupations became diversified. A large number moved into all branches of trade, particularly in horses and cattle, cloth, dyes, liquor and spices. Through their links with their brethren in the Ottoman empire, Polish Jewish merchants played an important part in the overland transit trade between the Eastern Mediterranean and Western Europe. Jews served as collectors of taxes and customs dues. They obtained concessions for working salt-mines and forests. They were involved in agricultural life as the stewards or lessees of large estates by the 'arenda' system. In this capacity they helped to open up and settle tracts of undeveloped land in Eastern Poland, which included the western district of the Ukraine and White Russia. They were engaged in a wide range of crafts and service occupations, as doctors and chemists, goldsmiths, tailors, shoemakers, furriers, weavers, butchers and soapmakers. The poorest class of Jews were the peddlers.

Six illustrations in the style of 16th-century woodcuts, showing some Jewish occupations of that period: a physician, a silversmith, a tailor, a shoemaker, a furrier, and a weaver.

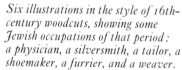

A model of a Jewish innkeeper being threatened by a village crowd.

appalling tale of repression, massacres, and expulsions was unfolding itself. Thus a steady stream of migration continued into Eastern Europe. By the end of the 15th century there were about sixty organized Jewish communities in Poland-Lithuania, containing a total of up to 30,000 souls. By the middle of the 17th century, the figure had risen to half a million.

The contacts of the Jews with non-Jews were confined to what was required for earning a living. Apart from that, the Jews lived an intense and inward-looking life of their own. With an unprecedented degree of self-government, they formed self-contained communities regulated by the Halachah. There was little integration with Polish society or culture. Among themselves the Jews continued to speak only Yiddish. Their intellectual life focused on Jewish religious learning and study. Numerous yeshivot sprang up and some of them gained a fame for their scholarship. In brief, Polish Jewry was a world within a world. By the 16th century it was a main centre of Ashkenazi life and culture. In spite of the pressures in the cities from Christian businessmen, the economic base of Polish Jewry was relatively broad and secure, and

The Arenda System

A Jewish tax-collector was a familiar feature of Polish village life. It tended to be an unpopular and sometimes dangerous occupation.

The Polish term 'arenda' covered leases and concessions of various kinds: landed property, mills, salt mines, timber forests, inns, tax-farming, collection of customs and the minting of the coinage. Some of these rights were derived from royal prerogatives. In the 15th and 16th centuries Jews obtained such concessions on a large scale in Eastern Poland, which was still 'an open frontier' for economic development. The lands leased to Jews might include villages and small towns. In Western Poland the nobles demanded these profitable concessions

A 17th-century painted jug with the head of a Jewish 'arenda' and a mocking inscription below it.

Above Bogdan Chmielnicki, the leader of the Cossacks.

was expanding eastward. The general picture was that of a vital and buoyant society.

That picture changed drastically for the worse from 1648, a watershed year in the history of Polish Jewry. A great part of the community was overrun and destroyed in the massacres that accompanied the Cossack revolt against Polish rule led by Bogdan Chmielnicki. Thirty years of war followed between Poland and its neighbours, with invasions by Swedish, Russian, and Tartar armies. From then on the kingdom of Poland started disintegrating, until it was partitioned among neighbouring powers towards the end of the 18th century. During this period the Jewish community became poorer, and subject to greater intolerance and restriction. Internally, it was shaken by the aftermath of the Shabbetai Zevi messianic movement, and the bitter conflict provoked by the rise of Chassidism.

(continued on page 209)

of the Crown for themselves and exerted strong pressure against their grant to Jews. At the same time, Jewish lessees, agents and managers were extensively used by nobles to run their agricultural estates

The 'agricultural arenda' in the countryside became an important aspect of the Jewish occupational structure in Poland. The Council of the Four Lands, the representative body of Polish Jewry, laid down regulations to obviate unfair competition between Jews in this field. The attitude of Jewish estate managers towards the peasants was often more humane than that of the landowning Polish nobility. Nevertheless, the Jews became the natural target for the resentment of the downtrodden serfs.

The Chmielnicki Massacres

In 1648 the Cossack leader Chmielnicki headed an uprising in the Ukraine against Polish rule. The Jews, identified with the Polish regime and blamed for economic difficulties, became the main victims of the violence. Bands of Cossack horsemen devastated and looted hundreds of communities and butchered tens of thousands of defenceless Jews. These occurrences sent a shock of horror through the Jewish world. In later Russian history, the Cossack on his horse would remain for Jews a savage and recurrent symbol of the pogrom.

Cracow and Kasimierz

Cracow was an important trading centre on the Vistula river and the capital of the Polish kingdom until 1609.

By 1350 there was an organized community of German Jews in Cracow with a synagogue and a cemetery. It encountered fierce hostility from the Christian townspeople, many of them also settlers from Germany. The reasons were resentment at Jewish competition reinforced by a religious bigotry that was fanned by the clergy. Throughout the 15th century the community was harassed by periodic outbreaks of violence, commercial restrictions and money extortion. In 1495 the king ordered all the Cracow Jews to move into nearby Kasimierz, where they were permitted to live and work unhindered. It had been founded as a separate town in the 14th century. Increased by refugees from Bohemia-Moravia, Germany, Italy, Spain and Portugal, Kasimierz became predominantly Jewish. Some of the Jews living there continued to own shops and property in Cracow, in the face of every effort to prevent them from doing so.

Below *Cracow and the adjacent town of Kazimierz. A 15th-century engraving.*

A street scene in the Jewish quarter of Lublin, Poland. The wall-poster in the street refers to a ban on the followers of the false messiah, Shabbetai Zevi.

The Jews of Lublin

Lublin was one of a number of Polish cities that in the early period of Jewish migration from Germany obtained from the Crown the privilege *de non tolerandis Judaeis* – that is, the right to ban Jews. In the 14th century a community nevertheless started on a site outside the city wall called 'Jewish Sands', placed at its disposal by the sympathetic Polish king, Casimir the Great. Later a Jewish quarter developed inside the city in the vicinity of the castle, by royal permission. This was a typical example of the way Polish kings encouraged Jewish settlement while the Christian city burghers resisted it.

Lublin was the venue of a great annual spring fair, where the Council of the Four Lands, the representative body of Polish Jewry, met regularly. In the 18th century the local community became a centre of the Chassidic movement and produced one of its leading 'Tzaddikim', Jacob Isaac, 'the Seer of Lublin'.

'Private Townships'

Above right A drawing of the town of Rzeszow, 1762.

The town of Rzeszow in south-east Poland was located on the estates belonging to the Lubomirsky princes. In 1657 they issued a charter of privileges to the Jews to induce more of them to settle in the town. In due course a thriving Jewish community developed that formed seventy-five per cent of the inhabitants. It became well known for its cloth, the work of its goldsmiths and its engraved seals. Some of the latter were supplied to the imperial courts in Moscow and Stockholm.

Rzeszow was one of hundreds of 'private townships' belonging to Polish noblemen, as distinct from the 'royal townships' – the older Polish cities established under charter from the Crown. For the most part, these newer towns were situated in the territories in eastern and south-eastern Poland and eastern Lithuania that were opened up to development

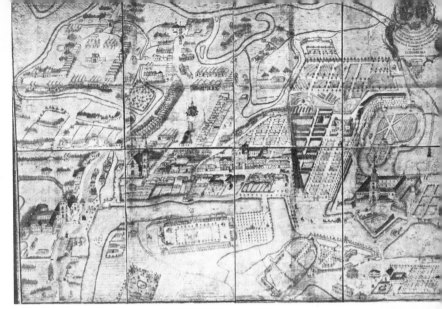

in the 16th–17th century. Large tracts of land had been acquired by aristocratic Polish families. They offered favourable conditions to Jews to settle in the local towns, in order to promote commerce and industry. Many Jews were attracted by the fresh opportunities proffered to them, and the relief from the pressures of Gentile merchants and craftsmen in the older cities. A number of these 'private townships' became predominantly Jewish, and in some cases wholly so. They also served as centres for Jews scattered in villages in the surrounding countryside as innkeepers, estate agents and other occupations under the arenda system.

Settlement in these private townships brought about a general shift of the Jewish population from Western to Eastern Poland.

In 1662 a proposal put before the Sejm (the Polish parliament) to expel the Jews from the country was defeated by nobles who had an interest in protecting the Jewish population living on their estates.

The Czars and the Jews

When Czarist Russia swallowed up most of Poland towards the end of the 18th century, she took over a million Polish Jews. It was for her an unwelcome acquisition. Since the days of Ivan the Terrible in the 15th century, Russia had firmly hung out a 'No Jew Wanted' sign. Requests from Polish-Jewish merchants for permission to come in, even for a temporary sojourn, were rejected. When Catherine the Great (ruled 1762–96) mounted the throne of Russia, she demonstrated her urge to westernize the country by issuing an imperial decree permitting foreigners to travel or live there. But the document expressly added the phrase 'except for Jews'. Now, after the dismemberment of Poland, the Czars found themselves ruling over the largest Jewish minority of any country in the world. It was the same Catherine, otherwise proud of her enlightened image, who in 1795 decreed the confinement of the Jews to the Pale of Settlement – that is, to the annexed Polish territories – and debarred them from moving into the rest of Russia.

Throughout the 19th and early 20th century the Jews of Russia were caught up in the wider struggle between liberalism and reaction. There were interludes when Catherine and her successors seemed willing to accept reforms and to bring their backward semi-Oriental realm into the modern age. But such tendencies were invariably crushed by an alignment of reactionary forces. The autocratic Czarist regime feared the revolutionary ideas spread by Napoleon's armies and they used the apparatus of a police state to resist change. The main pillar of the status quo was the Russian Orthodox Church, with its vast congregation of ignorant and superstitious serfs and its Byzantine legacy of anti-Jewish doctrines. The 19th century also saw the emergence of an emotional Slav nationalism that invoked an idealized Russian folk-past and spurned the liberal and democratic concepts in Western Europe.

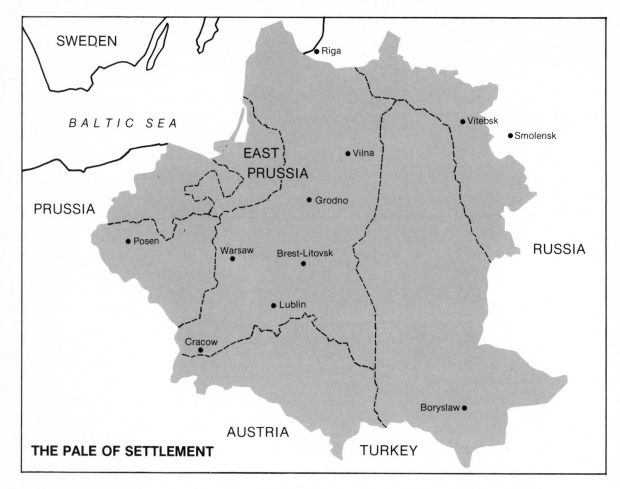

THE PALE OF SETTLEMENT

This was the background to the erratic Jewish policy of the Czars. The overall objective was to break down the separate identity of the Jews and 'amalgamate' them with the rest of the Russian population. This aim was sought at times by relaxing restrictions on the Jews, but more often by harsh coercion. Both approaches were self-defeating. Czarist 'Liberalism' stopped far short of real emancipation; while Czarist repression simply reinforced the barriers between Jews and Russians.

These conflicting trends could impinge on policy in the same reign, as was the case with Catherine's grandson Alexander I (ruled 1801–25). The young and handsome Czar had been given a progressive education at the insistence of his grandmother, and at the beginning was filled with reforming zeal. One of his first projects was to alleviate the hardships of the Jews, and to help them integrate into Russian life. A committee set up to study the problem raised Jewish hopes by proposing relief from certain disabilities. But in 1804 Alexander dashed these hopes with a statute that became known as the Constitution of the Jews. It had some well-meaning features. Russian

The Pale of Settlement

The Pale of Settlement, to which the Russian Jews were confined, covered the Polish territories annexed by Russia in the partitions of 1772, 1793 and 1795. ('Pale' is the accepted English equivalent for the Russian term 'Cheta'. It is an old English word for an enclosed area, and in the late mediaeval period was used to denote the districts of Ireland and of France that came under the jurisdiction of England.)

The Pale of Settlement was 386,000 square miles (a million square kilometres) in extent. So vast was the land mass of the Russian empire that the Pale represented only four per cent of its area. It stretched from the Baltic Sea to the Black Sea, through Lithuania, White Russia, the

Ukraine and Bessarabia.

At the Congress of Vienna in 1815, after the Napoleonic wars, the Duchy of Warsaw was made a small semi-independent Polish kingdom under the suzerainty of the Russian Czars. Not long afterwards this so-called 'Congress Poland' was absorbed into Russia, adding 200,000 Jews to those already in the Pale. Poland would not re-emerge as an independent country until 1918, at the end of the First World War.

The Russian census of 1897 provides an interesting statistical analysis of Jewish life in the Pale of Settlement at the end of the 19th century. In spite of the large-scale emigration from 1882 onwards, there were nearly five million Jews in the Pale, forming eleven per cent of its general population. Among the other national groups were Poles, Russians, Lithuanians, Ukrainians, Moldavians (in Bessarabia) and Germans. Since some eighty per cent of the Jews lived in towns, they formed more than one-third of the urban population of the Pale, and were the majority in many of the smaller towns.

In the second half of the 19th century a certain number of Jews received permits to reside outside the Pale. They included wealthy bankers and business magnates; students admitted to universities under the *numerus clausus* (the tiny percentage of places allotted to Jews); medical personnel; certain categories of skilled craftsmen who were in short supply; and Jewish army conscripts who had completed their twenty-five years of military service. Between 300,000 and 400,000 Jews lived in Russian cities outside the Pale, many of them illegally. As part of the sweeping anti-Jewish measures initiated by the May Laws of 1882, some 200,000 of these Jews were rounded up and deported back to the Pale. In 1891 the total Jewish community of Moscow was expelled in a single night. This was followed by the expulsion of the Jews from Leningrad and several other cities.

The Pale of Settlement was abolished in the Russian Revolution of 1917.

universities and schools would be open to Jews. They would be encouraged to enter productive occupations, especially as farmers in the territories in South Russia recently gained from Turkey. As against that, they were to be driven out of the villages and rural areas and concentrated in the towns – allegedly in the interests of the peasants.

The programme produced little change in practice. The Jews showed no desire to become peasants in distant areas, or to send their children to Russian schools where they would be brain-washed by the Orthodox Church. In resisting expulsion from the villages, they found allies in the Christian estate-owners and squires for whom the Jews provided essential economic services. But the shock of Napoleon's 1812 invasion of Russia, and especially the burning of Moscow, wiped away any liberal impulses in Alexander's unstable mind. He became reactionary and intensely religious, and his attitude to the Jews hardened. At the end of his reign they were suffering greater restrictions than they had at its beginning.

Alexander was succeeded by his brother Nicholas I (ruled 1825–55). He had imbibed none of the ambivalent liberal leanings of Catherine or Alexander I. A rigid military martinet, he sought to force the diverse elements in his realm into one disciplined Russian people, and to stamp out national and religious separation. The brutal way he crushed national uprisings in Poland and Hungary earned him the title of 'the policeman of Europe'.

Nicholas enacted scores of repressive laws against the Jews. They were expelled from the western border areas of the Pale, as they were considered an unreliable security factor. Restrictions were imposed on their domicile and their movements inside the Pale. They were not allowed to keep Christian servants. The use of Yiddish was forbidden for public purposes. Censorship was imposed on Jewish books and papers, including religious literature. Thousands of Jews were transported as colonists to Siberia, where most of them died in the bleak conditions.

No imposition on the Jews was as feared and hated as the special form of military conscription applied to them. For other national groups the draft was for a period of twenty-five years, from the age of eighteen. Jewish boys, however, were seized at the age of twelve and sent for a preliminary six years to 'cantonments', where they were forced to be baptized, and where as a rule they suffered starvation and ill-treatment. Few of these 'cantonists' or 'Nicholas-soldiers' were ever seen again by their families. Jewish parents were willing to do anything to save their children from the recruitment – hiding them in the woods, changing their names, or even maiming them. One abominable aspect of this system was that the responsibility for handing over the boys was placed on the 'kahals', the Jewish community councils, who hired Jews for this invidious task. They were known by the Yiddish word 'chappers' ('snatchers').

By 1840 it was clear to the regime that its repressive anti-Jewish

(continued on page 213)

The Shtetl

The Kremierniec Jewish community is first mentioned in 1438 in a charter granted by the Grand Duke of Lithuania. The Russian census of 1897 showed that the community at that time numbered 6,539 and formed thirty-seven per cent of the population of the town. With the Nazi occupation in June 1941, all Jews with academic degrees were rounded up and shot, the synagogue was burnt down, and a ghetto was imposed. In August 1942, 1,500 able-bodied Jews were despatched to a slave labour camp, where they later met their death. The rest of the community was murdered. They were brought to the edge of trenches dug outside the town and shot.

Shtetl is the diminutive form of *Shtot*, the Yiddish word for a town. It stands for the smaller Jewish communities that grew up in Poland-Lithuania from about the 16th century, and continued to exist in the Russian Pale of Settlement after the partition of Poland. The shtetl had no fixed size. It could hold anything from a few score to a few thousand families. But there was a distinction, however ill-defined, between the shtetl communities and the large urban ghettoes in cities like Warsaw, Odessa, Lodz, Vilna, Kishinev, Minsk or Bialystok.

Whatever their size, the shtetl communities shared a roughly similar religious, social, cultural and economic pattern. In Czarist times they suffered hardship and insecurity. The overwhelming majority of shtetl dwellers were desperately poor, eking out a bare living as peddlers, stall-holders in the market, tailors and cobblers. The market-place was the centre of the daily struggle, and the arena of contact with the Gentile world.

With all that, the atmosphere within the community was warm and intimate, and not without gaiety on Sabbaths and festivals. The shtetl strongholds were the synagogue, the study-house and above all the home. The authority of the rabbi was paramount. The two fundamental values of shtetl life were 'Yiddishkeit' ('Jewishness') and 'menshlichkeit' ('human decency').

In the 19th century the winds of change started to blow through the traditional fabric of shtetl life. The Haskalah movement introduced modern European culture. The liberal, socialist and revolutionary movements in Russia drew in many Jewish intellectuals. The Zionist movement quickened Jewish national sentiment. To a younger generation the shtetl seemed a cramped and arid prison from which they sought to escape through these new movements, or by migration to the United States and elsewhere in the Western world.

Long after the shtetl had been swept away by the Russian Revolution and the Holocaust, there was a revived nostalgic interest in its way of life, expressed in the novels of S.Y. Agnon, Isaac Bashevis Singer and others; in the pictures of Chagall; and in the re-reading of the Yiddish writers Sholem Aleichem and Mendele Mocher Seforim.

Right *Market day in the shtetl of Kremierniec, 1925. This town, one of the oldest settlements in eastern Poland, fell within the Russian Pale of Settlement.*

policy had wholly failed to 'Russianize' the Jews. The highly intelligent Minister of Education, Count Uvarov, gained the Czar's endorsement for a different and more sophisticated approach. Jewish stubbornness, it was argued, was rooted in their faith and their traditional Talmudic way of life. This could be broken down only if the young generation was given a secular education and exposed to the Russian language and culture. Experience showed that the Jews would not voluntarily send their children to Russian state schools (a survey at the time showed that out of 80,000 pupils in these schools, 48 were

Jews). The solution was to promote a secular school network *within* the Jewish community and under Jewish direction. As the overall director of the plan, Uvarov selected Dr Max Lilienthal, a brilliant twenty-five-year-old German rabbi and educator who had established secular schools in the community of Riga in Latvia. Lilienthal accepted the appointment in the sincere belief that the road had at last been opened to Jewish emancipation in Russia.

The adherents of the Haskalah (the Enlightenment movement) in Russia as well as the emancipated Jews in Western countries, hailed the plan as an important step forward. It took Lilienthal, with Uvarov's personal backing, three years to overcome the distrust of the local Jewish leaders in the Pale, who found it hard to believe that any good could come from a proposal put forward by a reactionary anti-Jewish regime. The new school system was launched in 1844.

The suspicion that there were ulterior motives behind the Uvarov plan was soon confirmed. An exchange of confidential memoranda between Uvarov and the Czar leaked out. It showed that the real intention was to phase out the Jewish content of the school curriculum and to pave the way for eventual conversion. By then Lilienthal had become disillusioned with the whole project and emigrated to the United States, where he became a Reform rabbi. In an article that appeared in a German-Jewish journal he wrote that 'only when the Jews will bow down to the Greek cross will the Czar be satisfied . . .' Uvarov's educational reforms soon faded away.

With Czar Alexander II (ruled 1855–81) there was again a shift towards liberal reform in general, accompanied by a more benevolent attitude to the Jews. The cantonist recruitment system for Jews was abolished; educated Jews were given greater freedom of movement and employment outside the Pale of Settlement. The Czar won the esteem of the Jewish community for his good deeds and intentions, but there was no basic change in the Jewish situation.

In 1881 Alexander II was assassinated by a bomb planted by the Nihilists, an underground revolutionary group. He was succeeded by his son Alexander III (ruled 1881–94). Once more there was an abrupt swing back to a reactionary anti-Jewish policy. Alexander III was a stern old-fashioned Russian nationalist, opposed to reform of any kind and determined to undo the liberal influences introduced by his father. His prescription for Russia contained three ingredients: an unquestioned autocracy, the Russian Orthodox faith and Slavophile patriotism.

Alexander believed that Jewish intellectuals were stirring up revolutionary ferment and he decided to be ruthless with the Jews. The first year of his reign saw the beginning of a series of ugly pogroms in the Pale of Settlement, instigated by agents of the Russian secret police. The official reports stated that the cause of the disturbances was Jewish exploitation of the local inhabitants, and called for economic curbs on the Jews. In 1882 the Czar signed a set of 'temporary regulations' called the May Laws, from the month in

Jews in Russian Left-wing Movements

Socialist doctrines had a strong appeal for the poor and repressed Jewish masses in Eastern Europe. Their aspirations for a free and progressive society found expression in three different directions: Communism, the Bund, and Zionist Socialism.

Jewish intellectuals who threw themselves into the Communist underground did so as individuals, breaking their ties with organized Jewish community life. They believed that anti-semitism was a by-product of capitalism, and would automatically disappear in the classless society of the future.

There were Jews among the leaders of the Russian Revolution of 1917. Outstanding among them was Leon Trotsky, a brilliant orator and writer who organized and led the Red Army in the revolutionary war, and was next in importance to Lenin. In the power-struggle after Lenin's death, Trotsky was ousted and driven into exile by Stalin, who later arranged for him to be murdered.

The Bund, a Jewish workers' party, was part of the general socialist movement in Eastern Europe, but differed sharply from the Communists in one vital respect. The Bund insisted on the distinctive identity of the Jews and their right to retain their national and Yiddish cultural autonomy in Eastern European states.

A third group was the Poale Zion (Zionist Socialist Party). It was an integral part of the Jewish national movement that sought to rebuild the ancient homeland in Palestine. It envisaged that homeland as a labour commonwealth, embodying socialist ideals of equality and co-operation.

The Jewish influence in the Communist parties behind the Iron Curtain was virtually eliminated in the Stalinist period. The Bund faded out with the Holocaust. Only the Zionist Socialists achieved some practical fulfilment of their socialist philosophy, in the State of Israel.

Leon Trotsky (1879–1940), revolutionary leader and founder of the Red Army. A contemporary drawing, 1919.

which they were promulgated. Jewish residence was to be restricted to the towns, as was Jewish ownership or lease of property. Jews already living in the villages were allowed to remain, but they were later stopped from moving their residence from one village to another. These provisions caused in effect a drastic contraction of the Pale of Settlement. They dealt a heavy economic blow to an already impoverished Jewish community. They also led to local expulsions, police harassment, and further overcrowding in the Jewish quarters of the towns.

The pogroms and May Laws were a major cause of the massive westward migration of Jews from the Pale of Settlement. In talking to a Jewish deputation, the Czar's chief adviser bluntly expressed the solution of the Jewish problem in Russia desired by the regime: 'One-third will die out, one-third will leave the country, and one-third will be completely dissolved in the surrounding population.' On 9 August 1890, the English satirical weekly *Punch* published a famous political cartoon. It showed Alexander III drawing a sword marked 'persecution', with his jackboot on a bound and prostrate Jew. Behind him loomed the shade of the Egyptian Pharaoh at the time of the Exodus, saying: 'Forbear! That weapon always wounds the hand that wields it.'

Alexander III was succeeded by his son Nicholas II (ruled 1894–1917), the last of the Russian Czars. He was a weak man, who had inherited much of the reactionary and anti-Jewish outlook of his father. His regime tried to make of the Jews a scapegoat for the seething discontent in the country and the underground revolutionary movement it produced. The wave of pogroms that started in Kishinev in 1903 (once more stirred up by the secret police) caused a storm of international protest. During the ensuing years the authorities connived at physical attacks on the Jews by the notorious 'Black Hundreds', armed bands organized by an anti-semitic right-wing society. In 1905 there appeared for the first time a pamphlet known as *The Protocols of the Elders of Zion*, disseminated by the authorities to 'prove' that the leaders of international Jewry were engaged in a conspiracy to conquer the Christian world. Although exposed as a crude forgery, the *Protocols* have continued to circulate elsewhere in the world, including the Arab countries. In 1911 the Czar's police even stooped to reviving the mediaeval blood-libel in the Beilis trial, which again drew international protest. With the Russian Revolution of 1917, Nicholas III was deposed and later murdered together with his family. The whole Czarist edifice, with its anti-Jewish laws and decrees, came tumbling down.

Important Events

Poland-Lithuania

1264	Charter of Bolislav the Pious.
1334	Casimir III extends the Charter.
1388	Charter of Grand Duke of Lithuania.
1648	Chmielnicki massacres.

The Czars and the Jews

1772, 1793, 1795	Partitions of Poland create the Pale of Settlement.
1804	Alexander I's Constitution of the Jews.
1827	'Cantonist' military service introduced for Jews.
1881–2	Widespread pogroms. May Laws. Beginning of mass emigration westward.
1903	Kishinev pogroms.
1913	Beilis blood-libel trial.
1917	Russian Revolution. Pale of Settlement abolished.

Chapter Fifteen

The Age of Emancipation

The rationalist philosophers in the 18th-century Western world evolved the explosive doctrine of Natural Rights, that would in due course lead to the emancipation of all repressed and exploited groups – slaves, working-men, women, children, coloured races, religious minorities and subject peoples. In this process the Jews too would be emancipated. Some of them were psychologically prepared for it by the Haskalah launched in 18th-century Germany by the philosopher, Moses Mendelssohn.

In the last quarter of the 18th century the concept of inherent human rights was enshrined in two epoch-making revolutionary documents. In 1776 the American Declaration of Independence declared: 'We hold these truths to be self-evident, that all men are created equal, that they are endowed by their Creator with certain inalienable rights, that among these are Life, Liberty and the Pursuit of Happiness ...' These bold principles were echoed in the Declaration of the Rights of Man that formed a preamble to the French Constitution of 1791. In the same year the French National Assembly granted the Jews equal citizenship, a status they had last enjoyed in the Roman empire about 1,500 years earlier. Wherever the revolutionary armies went, – Italy, Holland, Germany – the walls of feudal anti-Jewish discrimination came tumbling down.

In 1815 the statesmen of Europe met at the Congress of Vienna to reconstruct the map of the Continent after the Napoleonic upheaval. The goal was the establishment of a stable political order. The mood was conservative, even reactionary; the majority of the participants were concerned with containing the forces of change unleashed by the French Revolution. In France and Holland the Jews kept their new-won freedom. In other European countries anti-Jewish disabilities were partly restored in the backlash of reaction. This relapse was most evident in Italy. The Papal States went so far as to reimpose the ghetto in Rome and elsewhere, as well as the Jewish badge of shame.

In the next half-century the issue of Jewish emancipation was involved in the European struggle for liberalism and parliamentary democracy. The pressure came from the urban middle class that had grown out of the Industrial Revolution. Progress was uneven, with royalist, clerical and landowning elements fighting a rearguard action.

Moses Mendelssohn. From a painting by D. Rode.

Moses Mendelssohn

Moses Mendelssohn (1729–86) was the key figure in the 18th-century movement known as the Haskalah (Enlightenment). It aimed at drawing German Jews out of their ghetto isolation and into the mainstream of European culture and society. His own remarkable career bridged these two worlds and exemplified the first steps toward Jewish emancipation in Germany.

He was the son of a struggling Torah scribe in the ghetto of Dessau in Germany. At the age of fourteen he followed on foot to Berlin the erudite rabbi who had been his teacher. A hunchback (because of rickets in his childhood) and without means, he nevertheless rose to be a favourite of Berlin intellectual society. Moses became fluent in German, Hebrew, Latin, Greek, English, French and Italian, and achieved renown as a rationalist philosopher, a literary critic and a master of German style. Mendelssohn's mentor and close friend, the Christian poet and dramatist Gotthold Lessing, modelled on him the hero of the play *Nathan the Wise* (1779) with its message of respect and tolerance for the Jews.

It was surprising that a man devoted to the 18th-century cult of Reason, and accepted in German intellectual society, should choose to remain so attached to Judaism. Yet in controversies with Christian theologians Mendelssohn stoutly asserted his Jewishness. He also used his prestige on behalf of oppressed Jewish communities, and in support of the demand to grant the German Jew civic rights. In his book *Jerusalem* (1783) and other works, Mendelssohn presented his own view of Judaism as a non-dogmatic and humane faith which could be reconciled with the fashionable rationalist philosophy of the time.

One of Mendelssohn's most important undertakings, with a team of assistants, was a translation of the Old Testament into German written in Hebrew characters. It was meant to wean Jews away from Yiddish (also written in Hebrew characters) to the

In England the only real barrier left for Jews to overcome in this period was representation in parliament. In 1847 Lionel Rothschild, the head of the English family, was elected to the House of Commons by the City of London. He could not be seated because new members had to take an oath 'on the true faith of a Christian'. It took eleven years and five re-elections before a change in the rules allowed him to take an oath without reference to Christianity, and with his head covered. Yet prejudice died hard. In 1869 Gladstone, then Prime Minister, proposed to Queen Victoria that Lionel Rothschild be elevated to the House of Lords. The Queen refused, stating that she could not bring herself to make a Jew a peer. But sixteen years later the Queen granted a peerage to Lionel's son and successor Nathaniel, who became the first Lord Rothschild.

By the 1880s the emancipation of the Jews in Europe was an accomplished fact, except in Czarist Russia and Roumania. Russia remained feudal and despotic and kept its Jews in poverty and

 (continued on page 224)

German language; and to lay stress on the Bible rather than the Talmud as the foundation of the Jewish faith.

Mendelssohn undoubtedly helped to break down the ghetto walls and open wider cultural horizons for the Jews. On the other hand his stress on the German language and culture paved the way for the complete assimilation of many German Jews in the 19th century.

The French Revolution
See colour page 252

In 1791 the Declaration of the Rights of Man was adopted by the revolutionary National Assembly in Paris. It guaranteed to everyone the rights to liberty, property, security, resistance to oppression and freedom of speech and the press. The Declaration had a decisive effect on the European liberal movement during the 19th century.

In September 1791 full rights of citizenship were granted to the French Jews – though not without opposition, and two years after equality was extended to other non-Catholics. French Jews responded with fervour. They joined the army and the National Guard in thousands, and contributed lavishly to the cost of the military campaigns. In the next decade they made important strides towards integration into French life, entering professions previously closed to them, gaining public offices and in many cases sending their children to public schools.

As the French armies marched into neighbouring countries they carried with them the potent slogan of 'Liberté, Égalité, Fraternité'. They abolished the system of restrictions that had confined and degraded the Jews for centuries. The army battering-rams that knocked down ghetto gates were the symbol of the new order.

Though the French Jews had gained civil equality as individuals, the relations between the Jewish community and the State remained to be clarified. In 1806 the Emperor Napoleon convened an Assembly of 112 Jewish notables in Paris. It elected as president Abraham Fur-tado, a wealthy and cultured Bordeaux Jew of Marrano descent. The Emperor's representative confronted the delegates with a set of twelve questions covering a variety of topics: Jewish marriage and divorce, inter-marriage with Christians, the judicial and administrative powers of the organized community and the Jewish attitude to usury. The key question was: did Jews regard France as their country and were they willing to obey its laws and defend it? When the answers were handed in, Napoleon made a breathtaking announcement. He would convene a Sanhedrin modelled on the supreme Jewish body of that name in ancient Israel, which had remained dormant for 1,400 years.

The revived Sanhedrin was composed of the traditional number of seventy-one members, the majority of them rabbis, with the respected Rabbi Sinzheim of Strasbourg as its chairman. (Strasbourg was the main centre of Alsace-Lorraine, where three-quarters of the French Jews lived at that time.) The Sanhedrin gave its religious endorsement to the answers elicited from the Assembly of Notables, and was then adjourned. Soon after, Judaism was given the status of an officially-recognized faith in France.

In the enthusiasm engendered among the Jews by the dramatic Sanhedrin gesture, Napoleon was able to bring about certain reforms that they might otherwise have resisted. The French Jewish community lost its corporate autonomy, and was reorganized in a manner that made it virtually state-controlled. Much of the jurisdiction of Jewish rabbinical courts was transferred to the secular French courts. Crippling limitations were imposed on Jewish (but not Christian) money-lending, and on Jewish domicile in certain areas. These latter measures met some of the complaints made to Napoleon against the Jews by the Gentile population of Alsace.

With all that, the convening of the Assembly of Notables and the Sanhedrin highlighted the equal civic status accorded to the Jews in the wake of the French Revolution. Napoleon was hailed by Jews everywhere as the Great Liberator.

The results of these two gatherings had a marked impact on the way emancipated Jews in the Western world would define their own identity for some time to come. The French Jews had pledged their exclusive allegiance to the nation, and agreed to regard themselves purely as a religious group. In effect, they had renounced the concept of a separate Jewish people or nation. Only in the 20th century would it become generally accepted that Jews could be loyal citizens of their countries and at the same time feel identified with the Jewish people and its revived National Home.

Crossroads

With the transition from mediaeval to modern times, the path to civic equality opened for European Jews. Each Jew had to redefine the nature of his relationship to the Jewish people and to the country in which he lived. He faced crucial dilemmas at every stage.

I

I The French Revolution

After the French Revolution this French Jew is confronted with the thesis that emancipation gives him equal rights as an individual but denies him the right to be part of a wider Jewish nation. In accepting emancipation, should he

   A abandon his Jewish heritage? or
   B preserve it?

The outcome:

Choice A: He will throw himself fervently into the struggle for democratic rights, as a revolutionary rather than as a Jew. He believes that his loyalty to the cause will bring him and his children equal opportunities with all other Frenchmen. He will regard the Jewish community as an antiquated relic, and support the abolition of its autonomous status and privileges. His children will be sent to secular state schools and get the same education as non-Jewish children.

Choice B: He will dissociate himself from the ultra-Orthodox and seek a middle way between assimilation and traditional Judaism. In the synagogue on the Sabbath he will pronounce a prayer for the welfare of the new France. He will find an educational framework for his children that will teach them both French patriotism and Jewish values. Among Frenchmen he will be a Frenchman, at home he will be an observant Jew. Most French Jews will take this path.

2 Liberalism

After the defeat of Napoleon and the Congress of Vienna in 1815, there is a period of reaction against liberalism among European rulers. But by the middle of the century the process of emancipation for the Jews of Western Europe is breaking down the remaining barriers. This Viennese Jewish banker is embarrassed by traditional Judaism, which he feels is an obstacle to his social and economic advancement. His choice lies between

   A Total assimilation; and
   B Reform Judaism.

2

The outcome:

Choice A: He decides to embrace Christianity, in the belief that this is the way to escape the fate of a humiliated people. He sees baptism as the key to acceptance into European civilization.

Choice B: He refuses to abandon his faith but decides that acceptance in modern society requires the adjustment of religious law and customs to the needs of the times. He chooses Reform Judaism.

3

3 Reaction in Russia

The upsurge of modern nationalism in Europe has given rise to a fresh wave of anti-semitism towards the end of the 19th century. The world of this Jewish intellectual living in Odessa in 1883 has been shaken by a fresh outbreak of pogroms in 1881 and the anti-Jewish May Laws that follow. The impotence or indifference of his non-Jewish Russian liberal friends has undermined his confidence in the possibility of a Jewish future in Russia. He decides to emigrate. He must choose between

   A America; or
   B Palestine

The outcome:

Choice A: In New York he suffers hunger and toil in the sweatshops. But he also helps to build up the Jewish workers' movement and a lively Yiddish culture in the New World.

Choice B: He decides that the only solution is to be free in his own homeland. He sets out for a pioneering life in the land of Israel – but few join him there.

4 Radicalism

The year is 1920, in the wake of the First World War. Revolution and civil war sweep through Eastern Europe. The Jewish masses are impoverished and insecure. This young working-class Jewish mother in Vilna, Lithuania, deeply worried about the future of her children, joins a radical movement, together with many of her fellow-Jews. She, like them, is faced with the dilemma of choosing between

A The path of world revolution; and

B The path of Jewish socialism.

The outcome:

Choice A: She joins the underground Communist Party, in the belief that world revolution and a classless society will solve the Jewish problem as well. Fleeing the local police, she finds refuge in Soviet Russia. In one of the Stalinist purges she may be arrested and sent to a labour camp.

Choice B: She regards Zionists as mere dreamers and detests religious orthodoxy, but she wants the Jews to retain their Jewish identity and Yiddish culture in a socialist society. She therefore joins the Bund. The end of the Second World War finds her surviving as a destitute refugee,

4

searching the world for a new home. The Bund has vanished and the Yiddish culture has faded.

5

5 Crisis of Democracy

This is a 'German citizen of the Mosaic Faith.' In 1930 his hometown of Breslau is already a Nazi stronghold. He can still emigrate but refuses to believe that Hitler can come to power in Germany. He recognizes that Nazism must be fought, but should he

A Retain his faith in the democratic process? or

B Become a militant activist?

The outcome:

Choice A: Each time he goes to the polling booth to cast his vote, the Social Democrats assure him that the progressive forces in Germany will defend the constitution and withstand the Nazi challenge. He is therefore shocked when Hitler wins the election in 1933 and becomes Chancellor of Germany. He still pins his hopes on the intervention of the great democracies, but that will come too late for him.

Choice B: In his youth he was active in a left-wing socialist youth movement. He regards anti-semitism as a class problem and the Jewish question as marginal to the class struggle. In January 1933 he sees 25,000 Nazi

torch-bearers triumphantly parade through Berlin. The great working-class parties collapse. His socialist comrades are thrown into concentration camps. He escapes to Italy and joins a Zionist pioneering group.

6 Post-War Survivors

This Auschwitz survivor is one of the tragic remnants that has known at first hand how millions of helpless Jews were abandoned to their fate by the nations of the world. His faith in humanity and progress has been shattered. He is torn between

A Concern for his personal rehabilitation; or

B The struggle for Jewish national survival.

6

The outcome:

Choice A: He seeks a refuge as far from Europe as possible. He reaches San Francisco where he returns to his old occupation. He feels isolated and stays away from Jewish communal affairs – until his sense of identification is restored on the day the State of Israel is established in 1948.

Choice B: He joins in organizing groups of DPs (Displaced Persons) in the camps and leads them illegally across borders and seas, in an effort to burst open the closed gates of Eretz Israel. He and his fellow survivors from the concentration camps and the Jewish partisan bands are on their way to help build the Jewish homeland.

Heinrich Heine (1797–1856), poet and writer, Germany.

Above *Felix Mendelssohn-Bartholdy (1809–47), composer, Germany.*

Below *Benjamin Disraeli (1804–81), statesman, England.*

Some Famous Jews in Modern Western Europe

In the modern age, the Jewish contribution to general European culture has been phenomenal. The Emancipation produced an outburst of creative achievement in every field – in politics, in banking, finance, commerce and industry, in literature, art, music, theatre, film, publishing and the press, in medicine and law, and in the socialist and labour movements. Three German-speaking Jews – Karl Marx, Sigmund Freud and Albert Einstein – have each had a profound influence on the modern world.

The Nobel Prize, initiated in 1901, has been the world's most prestigious award for outstanding achievement in the fields of physics, chemistry, physiology, medicine, peace and literature – to which economics was added in 1969. It is a striking fact that about a fifth of the total number of Nobel Laureates have been Jews.

Sigmund Freud (1856–1939), founder of psychoanalysis, Austria.

Top *Sarah Bernhardt (1844–1923), actress, France.*

Above *Artur Rubenstein (1886–   ), pianist, Poland and America.*

Six Jews have been the elected prime ministers of major Western governments: Benjamin Disraeli in Britain, Léon Blum, Pierre Mendes-France and René Mayer in France, Luigi Luzzatti in Italy, and Bruno Kreisky in Austria.

Camille Pissarro (1830–1903), painter, France.

Zweig, Franz Kafka, André Maurois, Lion Feuchtwanger, Eugène Ionesco, and the Nobel Laureate poetess, Nelly Sachs.

Art
The painters Camille Pissarro, Amedeo Modigliani, Max Liebermann, Jules Pascin, Chaim Soutine, Marc Chagall and Leon Bakst; and the sculptors Jacob Epstein and Jacques Lipchitz.

Music
The composers Felix Mendelssohn, Giacomo Meyerbeer, Jacques Offenbach, Gustav Mahler and Darius Milhaud; the conductors Serge Koussevitsky, Otto Klemperer, Bruno Walter; the violinists Joseph Joachim, Mischa Elman, Jascha Heifetz, Bronislaw Huberman, Isaac Stern, Yehudi Menuhin; and the pianists Vladimir Horovitz, Artur Rubinstein and Artur Schnabel.

Theatre
Rachel, Sarah Bernhardt, Max Reinhardt and Marcel Marceau.

Jewish pioneers in other fields have included Henri Bergson in philosophy, Alfred Adler in psychiatry, Paul Ehrlich in medical research, Emile Durkheim in sociology and Claude Levi-Strauss in anthropology.

Top Franz Kafka (1883–1924), writer, Czechoslovakia.

Above Jacob Epstein (1880–1959), sculptor, America and England.

A selected list of other names will indicate the extensive Jewish role in the intellectual and artistic life of Europe:

Literature
Heinrich Heine, Franz Werfel, Marcel Proust, Arnold and Stefan

Above Marc Chagall (1887–   ), painter, Russia and France.

Below Albert Einstein (1879–1955), physicist, Germany and America.

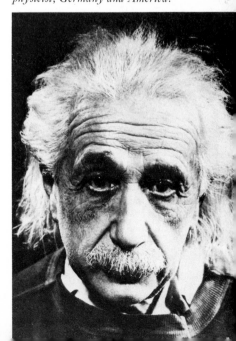

oppression, penned up in the Pale of Settlement. Their emancipation would come about only with the Russian Revolution of 1917. In Western and Central Europe, the Jews had as a rule attained full citizenship, religious freedom and access to all occupations. They assumed, rashly, that Jew-hatred was a hang-over from mediaeval religious bigotry and would disappear in the modern world.

But already dark forces were gathering for a virulent new onslaught on the emancipated Jew. Revived anti-semitism was a dangerous beast that in the 20th century would devour the Jews of Europe.

In France a warning note was sounded with the success of a violently anti-Jewish book, *La France Juive* (1886) by Edouard Drumont. It was a best-seller, and serialized in the right-wing press. It helped to pave the way for the extraordinary Dreyfus Affair that projected the Jewish question into the centre of French political, intellectual and social life for a number of years.

But it was Germany that became the home of modern anti-semitism as it had been in the Middle Ages. (The term 'anti-semitism' was first coined in 1879 by a rabid German anti-Jewish pamphleteer.) Conservative and Catholic circles in Germany had by no means reconciled themselves to the egalitarian spirit of the age, nor to the rising power of the middle class. They resented rich, Germanized Jews and tried to prevent their social acceptance. This attitude was reinforced by the pan-German nationalism that emerged after the unification of Germany in 1870.

The anti-semitism of the old privileged classes in Central Europe was curiously paralleled in the lower middle classes. This stratum of society contained the struggling and frustrated mass of small shopkeepers, white-collar workers, petty officials and school teachers, who felt themselves above the working class but were unable to rise on the economic and social ladder. The depression of the middle 1870s hit this group particularly hard. A new political faction, the Christian Social Workers Party, promised them welfare benefits and pointed to the Jewish capitalists as the source of their woes. Another body called the National Anti-Semitic League presented to the German Chancellor, Bismarck, a petition demanding that the Jews be disfranchised. It had a quarter of a million signatures.

In Austria the Christian Social leader was the formidable Karl Lueger, repeatedly elected as Mayor of Vienna on an anti-semitic platform. An ill-educated and complex-ridden youth who listened avidly to Lueger was called Adolf Hitler. His father was a petty customs clerk and his mother a domestic servant. His mind became filled with fantasies of Germanic grandeur and a pathological hatred for Communists and Jews.

The late 19th century produced a whole pseudo-scientific literature on the theme that the Germans were the descendants of a mythical Aryan or Nordic super-race, with flaxen hair and blue eyes. Their tribal ancestors out of the Teutonic forests were glorified in the thunderous operas of Richard Wagner, and in a distorted interpre-

(continued on page 230)

Ferdinand Lasalle (1825–64).

Karl Marx (1818–83).

Rosa Luxemburg (1871–1919)'

Jews in Western European Socialism

In 19th-century Europe it was natural that a number of Jews should be drawn into socialist and revolutionary movements. They lived under reactionary regimes, and antisemitism was rife in their countries. Although some Jewish radicals (including Karl Marx) spurned their Jewish roots, they were heirs to the profound concern for social justice that has pervaded Judaism from biblical times.

Marx's monumental work *Das Kapital* laid the theoretical foundations for socialism and communism. It was probably the most influential political-economic treatise to be published in the modern age.

Ferdinand Lassalle was for a while associated with Marx, but rejected his concept of a revolutionary class struggle and sought the attainment of a socialist society by democratic means. He became the father of the German Social Democratic movement. Another Jew, Victor Adler, founded the Austrian Social Democratic Party, headed in recent years by Chancellor Bruno Kreisky, also a Jew.

Rosa Luxemburg, a small crippled Polish Jewess, was a fiery leader of left-wing socialism in Germany and the founder of the German Communist Party in 1918 at the end of the First World War. She was arrested and murdered shortly afterwards by German army officers.

Maier Amschel Rothschild

(Gründer des Welthauses)

The House of Rothschild

See left and colour page 252

The Industrial Revolution propelled the Western World into an era of economic growth, population expansion and rising standards of life without parallel in human history. There was an unquenchable thirst for loan capital to finance the new industrial cities, railway construction, steamships, housing projects and mechanical equipment for the armies. It was the heyday for Jewish financial and merchant-banking houses that operated on an undreamt-of international scale. They included the Péreire Brothers and Baron Maurice de Hirsch in Paris, Lazard Brothers of Paris and New York, the Hambros of Copenhagen and London, the Goldsmid family in England – and above all the House of Rothschild. It has for nearly two centuries been a financial dynasty without precedent. In the remotest 'shtetl' of the Russian Pale of Settlement the name Rothschild stood for unimaginable wealth, a life-style of oriental splendour, benefactions on a vast scale – and with it a stubborn Jewishness. In the demonology of the anti-semites, the Rothschilds stood for a sinister 'Jew-power', manipulating thrones, currency systems and the press. Throughout it all the family went its own exotic and cohesive way. In point of fact, no Diaspora Jews have ever wielded more real power than the Rothschilds did in the 19th century.

The story starts in the 18th-century Frankfurt ghetto, where a Jewish community of some 3,000 souls lived together in crowded quarters. Here **Mayer Amschel Rothschild** was born in one of the meaner houses. Formerly the family had been in a better house, marked above the front door with a red shield – in German, *rothschild* – and that name stuck.

The young Mayer Amschel began to prosper, selling old coins to local nobles and cashing drafts for the princes of Hesse-Cassel. He married

Left *Mayer Amschel Rothschild (1744–1812), banker, Germany.*

and in due course had twenty children, of whom ten survived – five sons and five daughters. In his will he enjoined his sons always to work together and trust each other. Later, when they became barons, their crests contained a cluster of five arrows held together by a fist. Their family solidarity was their most important asset, after the brothers had settled as bankers in different countries. The eldest, **Amschel**, remained in Frankfurt, **Nathan** went to London, **James** (Jacob) to Paris, **Salomon** to Vienna and **Karl** to Naples.

The services the brothers rendered to the rulers in these countries were quite extraordinary. In Frankfurt, Amschel became the most powerful banker in Germany and the treasurer to the German Federation. Throughout, he remained a pious Jew, wearing traditional ghetto garb and keeping strict kashrut. In Italy Karl was the financial mainstay of the Bourbon dynasty, restored to the throne of Naples. In Austria, Salomon's state loans and financing of railway construction made his the wealthiest private family in the country. At the request of the powerful Chancellor, Prince Metternich, he was able to perform a signal and delicate personal service for the Emperor Francis I.

The Emperor's daughter, Marie Louise, was married to Napoleon, then languishing in exile on the island of St Helena. She consoled herself with an affair that produced two illegitimate offspring. Salomon devised a round-about method whereby the Emperor could provide for these bastard grandchildren without the connection being traced to him. As a reward Metternich obtained from the Emperor a grant of the hereditary title of Baron, not just for Salomon but also for his four brothers. In France, James adroitly kept the regimes that succeeded each other after Napoleon as his banking clients. Nathan, in London, managed on behalf of the British Government to transfer huge amounts of funds and gold bullion to finance Wellington's Peninsular campaign in Spain. The transfers actually took place through the enemy country, France! Since the Rothschilds's means of communication with their agents were more rapid than those of any government, Nathan was the first man in England to get news of Napoleon's defeat at Waterloo in 1815. He informed the government before repairing to the Stock Exchange to buy up government bonds.

During the forty-year reign of Nathan's son **Lionel** as head of the English family, the bank was involved in many historic loans to the government. They included those connected with the emancipation of the slaves, the Irish famine of 1847, the Crimean War of 1854 and the dramatic off-the-cuff loan to the Disraeli government in 1875 to buy the Suez Canal shares from the Khedive of Egypt. Lionel was the first professing Jew to be seated in the House of Commons, and his son Nathaniel the first Jewish peer.

Baron Edmond de Rothschild (1845–1934), of the French branch of the family, played a unique role in the early Zionist settlement in Palestine. He provided the financial and technical assistance without which the struggling pioneer colonies could hardly have survived.

The German Rothschild bank was dissolved in 1901, since there were no male heirs in that branch of the family. The Italian bank was wound up after the unification of Italy in 1860. When Hitler's troops occupied Austria in 1938 the head of the Viennese branch, Baron Louis, was imprisoned and released against the surrender of all his assets to the Germans. He emigrated to the United States. Only the English and French branches of the House of Rothschild remain intact today.

Mayer Amschel and his Five Sons

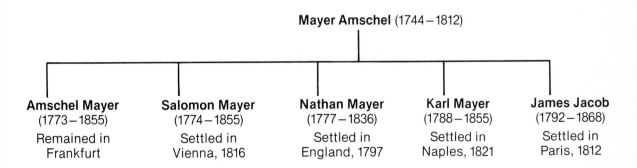

Mayer Amschel (1744–1812)

Amschel Mayer	Salomon Mayer	Nathan Mayer	Karl Mayer	James Jacob
(1773–1855)	(1774–1855)	(1777–1836)	(1788–1855)	(1792–1868)
Remained in Frankfurt	Settled in Vienna, 1816	Settled in England, 1797	Settled in Naples, 1821	Settled in Paris, 1812

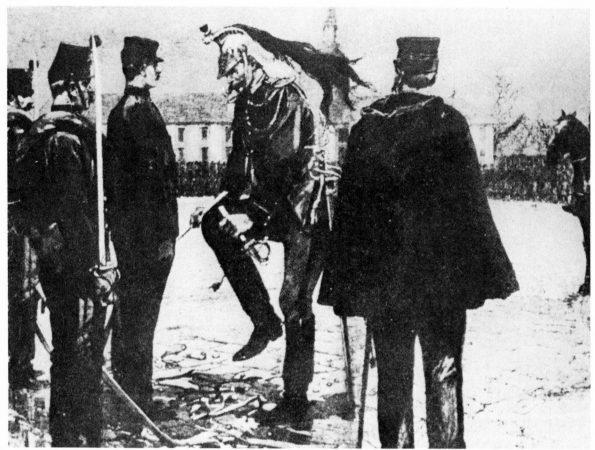

Alfred Dreyfus being stripped of his rank. The cover picture of Petit Journal Illustré, *5 January 1895.*

The Dreyfus Affair

Alfred Dreyfus (1859–1935) was the son of an assimilated middle-class Jewish family in Alsace. He took up the army as a career, and was posted as a captain to the General Staff in Paris. Earnest, serious, hardworking and withdrawn, of medium height and wearing pince-nez, he was a wholly unremarkable man. Yet he was suddenly propelled into world attention as the central figure in a drama that would obsess France for many years.

In 1894, the French counter-intelligence discovered that defence secrets were being passed on to Germany through its military attaché in Paris. Dreyfus was arrested, charged with treason and condemned *in camera* by a military tribunal. The evidence against him was flimsy, but the judges had been shown a secret file produced by the counter-espionage bureau of the army. It transpired later that the document in the file incriminating Dreyfus had been forged by an officer in the bureau. Dreyfus was publicly stripped of his rank and sentenced to life imprisonment. He was shipped to Devil's Island, a rocky islet off the coast of French Guiana, South America, where he was kept in chains under guard. To all intents and purposes the case was closed, and the prisoner was left to rot in isolation for the rest of his life.

However, his brother and a few other individuals in Paris continued to agitate for his release, insisting that there had been a miscarriage of justice. One of them was Bernard Lazare, a Jew and a distinguished man of letters who, in 1896, almost two years after the trial, published and distributed a pamphlet called *The Truth about the Dreyfus Affair*. Evidence came to light that the real culprit was another officer, Major Esterhazy, who was in the pay of the Germans. Important public figures took up the cause of 'revision' – the re-opening of the trial. They included the vice-president of the Senate, the leader of the Socialist party, the most formidable debater in the French parliament, Clemenceau, and the two famous writers Anatole France and Emile Zola.

At the beginning of 1898, the French government was obliged to put Esterhazy on trial; but he was acquitted, as a result of heavy army pressure behind the scenes. The next day Zola published, in Clemenceau's newspaper, a powerful indictment of the political and military establishment, under the banner headline *J'accuse*. In it he named the men whom he charged with an act of injustice and a subsequent cover-up, challenging them to sue him for libel. A case was brought against Zola and he was fined and condemned to a year in prison but escaped to England.

By now, however, the Dreyfus Affair had become a *cause célèbre* in the world press. In France it was the subject of the most bitter and divisive controversy that had rent the nation since the Revolution a century earlier. The honour and prestige of the army was now committed to the proposition that Dreyfus was guilty. Behind the army was ranged a powerful alignment of forces: right-wing conservatives, the Church, the upper classes and almost the entire press. Those political figures and intellectuals who fought for justice were reviled and attacked in the name of patriotism. It was an atmosphere in which families were split apart and old friends cut each other dead in the street.

The ugliest and most frightening aspect of the Affair was the anti-semitism it brought to the surface. Its spokesman was Edouard-Adolphe Drumont, author of a widely-read anti-Jewish book *La France Juive* (1886), and founder of the National Anti-Semitic League. The opponents of revision became infected with the belief that behind the Jew Dreyfus was a mysterious and powerful syndicate, organized by international Jewish finance to destroy France. This alleged syndicate, it was said, was in league with the Germans, the Freemasons, the atheists and every other enemy of the established order.

These fantasies dredged up from the Dark Ages were personified in the popular press by the stereotype of a fat, hooked-nose Jewish money-lender. After a century of emancipation, anti-semitism was once more politically and socially a potent force in France, as it was in Germany and Russia.

A French cartoon of Alfred Dreyfus, 1894.

In 1898 an independent examination established that the document incriminating Dreyfus had been forged by a Major Henry. He was arrested and committed suicide in his cell. A re-trial before a new military court could no longer be refused and it received world coverage. All in the court were shocked when Dreyfus appeared. Only forty years of age, he seemed an old man, bent and shrunken, with prematurely white hair. The most poignant irony was that he had been totally cut off from the world for nearly five years and was the only person present who was ignorant of the developments in the Dreyfus Affair during that time.

Once more the judges were presented with the uncompromising view that a verdict for Dreyfus was a verdict against the French army. The military court was unable to stand up to such pressure. It took the easy way out by reaffirming Dreyfus's guilt but recommended that his sentence be shortened. Soon after he was given a presidential pardon. It was only in 1906, when a Leftist government came into power, that the original conviction was set aside. Dreyfus was reinstated in the army with a higher rank and awarded the Order of the Legion of Honour.

The first Dreyfus trial in 1894 was covered by a Viennese Jewish press correspondent, Dr Theodor Herzl. Later, he witnessed the military ceremony in which Dreyfus was degraded, and heard the crowd screaming 'Death to the Jew!' Herzl wrote sadly: 'Where? In France. In republican, modern, civilized France, a hundred years after the Declaration of the Rights of Man.' The experience crystallized the distress that Herzl had felt for a long time over the Jewish question, and his disillusionment with assimilation as an answer. In 1897 he convened the first Zionist Congress in Basle. The Dreyfus Affair had been part of the backcloth to the emergence of the modern Zionist Movement.

tation of the superman motif in the works of Germany's most influential philosopher, Nietzche. The corollary of these intoxicating theories was that the Jews were an inferior race that threatened to contaminate the purity of German blood and morals. There was thus nothing very original about Nazi doctrines. They only had to await the proper historical moment before they could be translated into power. That situation came after the First World War. Germany had suffered a crushing defeat. Added to this humiliation were the punitive terms of the Treaty of Versailles. The German economy was in ruins. Hitler and his National Socialist Party, making full use of the anti-semitic weapon, appealed above all to the 'little men' of the submerged lower middle class. They found an emotional outlet in the parades and heady rhetoric of the Nazis, and their sons became the swastika-wearing thugs of the Nazi storm-troopers.

When Hitler came to power in 1933, anti-semitism was converted from a personal obsession and a propaganda weapon into the policy of a great State. It was systematically used to manipulate the mass psyche of the German people, to provide them with an age-old scapegoat, to make them submissive to totalitarian rule and to prepare them for the war to come.

The Nuremberg Laws of 1935 were a systematic programme for the economic, cultural and social elimination of the Jews from the general life of Germany. Many of its details were familiar from mediaeval times, but the basis had shifted. The only criterion now was genetic. A Jew could no longer escape by becoming a Christian. Nor did it matter whether his occupation was that of a peddlar or a professor; if he had had a Jewish grandparent, it was enough. The Western democracies failed to intervene. In this appeasement period, it was convenient to regard the persecution of the German Jews as an internal matter of the German Reich.

In the first two years of the Second World War many millions of Jews were trapped in Nazi-occupied Europe, which stretched from the English Channel to the heart of Russia. They were rounded up and transported to concentration camps, walled into ghettoes or used as slave labour in the German war industries. In the Spring of 1941 Hitler gave his approval for the 'Final Solution of the Jewish Question' – that is, the physical liquidation of the Jews. From the summer of 1941 trained mobile units were used for this mass murder. On 20 January 1942, a meeting was held at Wannsee, a suburb of Berlin, to adopt a detailed programme for the gigantic project. This was later to include the installation of specially designed gas-chambers in a number of concentration camps. The implementation was entrusted to the SS, the security apparatus headed by Himmler. In the midst of all the war pressures upon him, Hitler gave his personal attention to the extermination of Europe's Jews. In country after country the horror of genocide unfolded itself.

As the advancing Allied armies liberated one death camp after another in the last phase of the war, they found in them the pitiful

The Memorial Column in the Museum of the Jewish Diaspora, Tel Aviv, a reminder of Jewish martyrdom through the ages.

living skeletons of those inmates who still survived. By the time Hitler lay dead in a Berlin bunker, beneath the rubble of his Third Reich, the 'final solution' had accounted for the slaughter of six million Jews – one out of every three Jews on earth. The Holocaust was by far the greatest disaster in Jewish history.

Important Events

1776	American Declaration of Independence proclaims that 'all men are created equal'.
1783	Moses Mendelssohn's *Jerusalem* published.
1789	French Declaration of The Rights of Man.
1791	French Jews granted equal citizenship.
1807	Paris Sanhedrin convened.
1815	Congress of Vienna stimulates reaction.
1847	Lionel Rothschild elected to House of Commons.
1886	Drumont's *La France Juive* published.
1894	Dreyfus condemned. Start of Dreyfus Affair.
1933	Hitler comes to power.
1935	Nuremberg Laws.
1938	'Kristallnacht.' Economic ruin of German Jews.
1939–45	The Second World War. The destruction of European Jewry.

Chapter Sixteen

The New World

The United States of America

History seems to have its own peculiar sense of irony. In 1492 Ferdinand and Isabella signed the decree expelling all the Jews from Spain. Four days after the last professing Jew left the country, Christopher Columbus set sail from there under the patronage of the same monarchs. The New World he was about to discover would in time contain the largest and freest Jewish community the Diaspora has ever known.

To add another artistic touch to the story, the first member of the expedition to set foot in the New World was its only Jew, Columbus's interpreter Luis de Torres, who had hurriedly been baptized just before sailing. Whether Columbus himself was of Marrano extraction remains uncertain. It is remarkable that his account of the voyage begins with a reference to the Expulsion Decree.

During more than a century of English colonial rule, the small number of Jews in the American colonies had freedom of worship and trading. By the outbreak of the American Revolution in 1776 they numbered about 2500, organized in communities along the Atlantic regions such as New York, Newport, Philadelphia, Charleston, Savannah and Montreal. Practically all of them were engaged in trade. Most were small shopkeepers, but some were occupied in shipping, import-export, and the fur trade. In dress and language they were the same as other settlers, and intermarriage was not uncommon.

During the American Revolution the majority of the Jews threw in their lot with the rebels. They fought as officers, soldiers and militiamen, and one of them, Haym Solomon, had a key role in financing the American forces. In spite of the equality for all guaranteed in the Declaration of Independence, it took some time before the American Jews gained full civic rights, a matter under the jurisdiction of the individual States. By 1820 the Jews enjoyed citizenship in several of the thirteen original States. Disabilities remained concerning the requirement to take a Christian oath for public office. These were overcome by the middle of the 19th century.

In the Civil War (1861–5) an estimated 7,000 Jews fought on the side of the North and 3,000 on the side of the South. In 1862, General

NIEUW AMSTERDAM,
Op 't Eylandt Manhattans.

e Kerck . C. de wintmolen . D. dese Vlagge wort opgehaelt als daer Schepen in de haven komen . E. 't gevangen huys . F. de M.r Generaels huy
303,   304,   305,   306,   307,   308,

Above *A view of Manhattan Island, c.1664.*
Right *A model of the Touro synagogue in Newport, R.I.*

Grant's Order No. 11 called for the expulsion of Jewish cotton traders from the border areas, but it was revoked personally by President Lincoln.

From about 1840 there was an increasing influx of Jews from Germany, driven by political reaction and economic difficulties in that country. By 1881 the American Jewish community numbered some 300,000. The bulk of these Jews belonged to Reform congregations modified from the German model. They spread inland from the Eastern seaboard into the cities growing up along the Great Lakes and the Ohio and Mississippi rivers, and into Northern California after the Gold Rush of 1849. Reform Temples proliferated in the pleasant new residential areas of these cities.

From 1881 onwards this comfortable semi-assimilated American Jewry was confronted (somewhat to its dismay) by an avalanche of poor Yiddish-speaking Orthodox 'Ostjuden' (Eastern European Jews) streaming out of the Russian Pale of Settlement. Life was hard for this immigrant generation, but their children entered the mainstream of American life. They gained an education in the public schools, entered wider business, professional and academic fields, and moved out of the ghettoes. The difference between the 'uptown' and the 'downtown' Jews disappeared, and the American Jewish community became more cohesive.

The energy and talent released by the integration of the American Jews produced remarkable results. They have played a part in the public, economic, intellectual and artistic life of the country that is comparable to that of the Jewish communities in the Golden Age of mediaeval Spain or in modern pre-Hitler Germany.

As a community, American Jewry can be said to have come of age at the time of the First World War. A quarter of a million Jews served in the US Armed Forces. By that time the Jewish community of the

(continued on page 239)

Arrival at New Amsterdam

In the summer of 1654, a ragged band of twenty-three Jewish refugees – four men, two women and seventeen children – arrived at New Amsterdam, the settlement on Manhattan Island established by the Dutch West India Company. They were ending a journey that had begun some five months earlier in Recife, north-eastern Brazil. That area had been taken by the Dutch from Portugal in 1633, and some Dutch Jews, formerly Portuguese Marranos, had settled there. They fled when Portugal re-captured the area twenty-one years later. (Portugal and its possessions were barred to Jews, and Marranos who professed Christianity were subject to the Inquisition.)

Peter Stuyvesant, the autocratic governor of New Amsterdam, was unwilling to absorb these destitute newcomers but he was over-ruled by the Company. The party remained, but subject to restrictions. These were removed in 1664 when an English fleet took the settlement and renamed it New York.

The Touro Synagogue

The town of Newport, in the State of Rhode Island, was founded in 1639. Its Jewish community started in 1677, when a number of Jews arrived

. H. de Kaeck I Compagnies Pachuys K
309   310

from the island of Barbados in the West Indies. They started to trade, and bought a plot of ground for a cemetery.

Not long afterwards the community disbanded, and was not revived until the middle of the 18th century. A congregation was organized; a Cantor, Isaac Touro, came from Amsterdam, and in 1763 the congregation, then about twenty families, dedicated a handsome small synagogue, designed by the Colonial architect Peter Harrison.

Within a decade, the town had a flourishing community of about 200 Jews. Its leading (and wealthiest) member was Aaron Lopez. He had arrived as a young Portuguese Mar-

rano, openly embraced Judaism, had himself circumcised and remarried his wife in a Jewish ceremony.

In the American War of Independence the trade of Newport was ruined, and its Jewish congregation began to dwindle. It was already a dying community when President George Washington received an address of welcome from it on a visit to the town. By 1822 there were no Jews left in Newport. The synagogue building was preserved from funds bequeathed for the purpose by the son of Isaac Touro. It has since been declared a national historic site, as the oldest extant synagogue in North America.

The Newport community was not re-established until the 1880s.

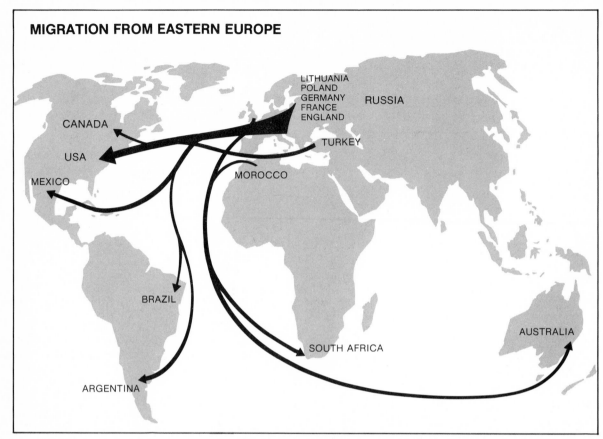

MIGRATION FROM EASTERN EUROPE

The German-Jewish Immigrants

Thousands of the German-Jewish immigrants in the 19th century started their new lives as peddlers, foot-slogging with packs on their backs through the rural areas and the Indian territories. Moving up the ladder meant the acquisition of a horse and buggy and then a store or trading-post.

The prosperity of the post-Civil War years established the Jewish community as a solid middle class, with an elite of German-Jewish banking and merchant families of wealth and importance, who distinguished themselves as philanthropists and patrons of the arts.

The banker Joseph Seligman handled the placing of US government securities in Europe during the Civil War, and later declined an offer from President Grant to appoint him Secretary of the Treasury. Jacob Schiff headed the investment house of Kuhn, Loeb and Company that financed much of the railroad construction. Through his great wealth, philanthropy and devotion to Jewish affairs, he was regarded as the most influential Jew in the United States at the turn of the century. His position in the bank and the community later devolved on his son-in-law, Felix Warburg. Julius Rosenwald developed the huge mail order business of Sears, Roebuck that distributed forty million copies annually of its famous catalogue. Levi Strauss started making blue denim pants, 'Levis', for the gold-miners in California, and made them the basis of a multi-million-dollar industry. Adam Gimbel and the Strauss family built up retailing empires and pioneered the department store. These men and others like them had one biographical fact in common: they had all come to the United States as penniless young Jewish immigrants from Germany.

Migration from Eastern Europe

In the forty-odd years from 1880 onwards, four million Jews moved westward out of the Russian Pale of Settlement and the adjacent areas of Rumania and Hungary. Nearly three million of them would reach what they hopefully called the 'Golden Land' of the United States. The rest would augment the declining Jewry of Western Europe and Britain, and expand the small communities of the New World in Latin America (especially the Argentine) and in the British Empire (Canada, South Africa, Australia). This was by far the most massive population shift in Jewish history. It transformed the shape and character of the Diaspora.

To the 'Golden Land'

From 1880 the Jews of Eastern Europe moved away in increasing numbers from abject poverty, overcrowding and persecution. Across the Atlantic the vast half-empty United States was experiencing the most rapid economic growth in the world. With an insatiable demand for immigrant labour, it had opened its gates to the surplus population of Europe. The Russian Jews joined a great flood of transatlantic immigrants – Irish, Swedes, Germans, Italians, Poles, Slavs, and many others. In the sixty years before the First World War the United States took in thirty million immigrants. (The Italians alone accounted for some eight million.)

The gigantic Statue of Liberty, erected in New York Harbour in 1882, carried the words of the

Below Before leaving port at Liverpool, the ship's doctor (in the bowler hat) examines Russian Jews embarking for the United States, 1891.

American Jewish poet Emma Lazarus:

Give me your tired, your poor
Your huddled masses yearning to breathe free
The wretched refuse of your teeming shore
Send these, the homeless, tempest-tossed to me
I lift my lamp beside the golden door

The mass movement was made possible by the revolutionary developments in transportation in the industrial age. One of the points of exit for the Jews from the Pale of Settlement was the town of Brody, on the Austrian side of the border. From there they could travel by train and ship to New York in about two weeks. Shipping companies found it profitable to cram these cut-rate passengers into the steerage holds of their transatlantic liners. About two-thirds of the Jewish migrants were carried on German liners from Hamburg and Bremen, and the rest by British Cunard liners from Liverpool.

The Gateway

See colour pages 270 and 271

During the first decade after 1880, the immigrants arriving in New York were cleared at Castle Garden, at the southern tip of Manhattan. In 1890 an important US Supreme Court judgment transferred responsibility for immigration from State to Federal Authorities. A new immigrant centre was opened on Ellis Island, used until then for harbour defence. For millions of immigrants thereafter, Ellis Island was the gateway to America and their first exposure to bureaucracy in the New World. They spent days or even weeks on the Island being questioned by immigration officers, undergoing medical examinations and filling in forms. Local Jewish organizations, especially the Hebrew Immigrant Aid Society (HIAS), helped the bewildered newcomers to cope with the red tape, trace relatives and find a place to live. Between a third and a half of them arrived penniless, having spent all they had on their tickets.

237

Lower East Side, New York

See colour pages 270 and 271

The Jewish immigrants arriving in the United States found the reality much bleaker than the dream. Other immigrant groups were drawn from the peasant communities of Europe, and a proportion of them could be settled on the land. But the Jews of Eastern Europe had been divorced from the soil for centuries. The old-established American Jewish community could help them but not absorb them, owing to their sheer numbers and the wide gap in culture and religious practice. They concentrated in specific slum quarters of the major cities – mostly in New York's Lower East Side and on a smaller scale in similar districts of Boston, Philadelphia, Chicago and elsewhere. They now 'breathed free', as the inscription on the Statue of Liberty had promised them – but in conditions of overcrowding and poverty little better than those they had left behind in the Old Country.

At one stage 350,000 Jews were huddled together in a square mile of teeming, dilapidated tenement houses on the Lower East Side. Some of them eked out a living as petty traders in the Jewish quarters, mostly with street-stalls and barrows. Their main occupation was in the sweat-shops. There was an expanding market for cheap ready-to-wear clothing. Parts of garments were cut and sewn in thousands of little work-shops, each with a handful of employees. The conditions were appalling. The rooms were crowded and dirty, with no proper ventilation, light or heating in winter. In the busy periods men, women and young girls worked sixteen hours a day for low wages.

However poor, these Eastern European immigrants were restless, ar-

Above *A sweatshop in Ludlow Street, 1890.*
Left *Market day in the Jewish quarter of New York, by J. Durkin. Derived from photographs of Jewish pedlars, 1891.*

United States was rapidly growing in size, influence and wealth. Its leadership moved out of an American parochial framework into the wider international concerns of the Jewish people. Louis Brandeis, Stephen Wise and others worked hard to gain endorsement from President Wilson for the Balfour Declaration of 1917 that promised a Jewish National Home in Palestine. At the Paris Peace Conference of 1919 Louis Marshall led a strong American Jewish delegation that fought for guarantees of minority rights for the Jewish communities in the new successor states in Europe. The American Joint Distribution Committee was set up as a relief agency for the Jews of Eastern Europe, victims of civil war, revolutions and pogroms sweeping through that region. Prominent American Jews like Marshall and Felix Warburg, though non-Zionist, nevertheless agreed to support Jewish immigration and economic development in Palestine, through Dr Weizmann's Jewish Agency created in 1929. There was growing Zionist sentiment in America, and some leading personalities came to settle in Palestine – including Henrietta Szold, the founder of Hadassah (the American Women's Zionist Organization), and Rabbi Judah Magnes, who became the first President of the Hebrew University of Jerusalem.

Three different trends developed in the contemporary religious practice of the American Jews: Modern Orthodoxy; Reform Judaism and Conservative Judaism. *Modern Orthodoxy*: For the majority of the Jews in the modern period the Talmud waned as the framework of a separate Jewish way of life. The ghetto and the shtetl were gone for good. Jews became citizens of the countries in which they lived and

ticulate and with a strong intellectual tradition. They created their own self-contained society. Yiddish was the language of the home and the street. The whole neighbourhood closed down on the Sabbath and Jewish festivals. According to their places of origin they belonged to *landsmanshaften* ('home-town associations'), that served as social clubs and mutual benefit societies. There was a flourishing Yiddish theatre and press. A vigorous struggle against sweatshop and factory conditions produced progressive labour unions.

The Day of Atonement Service in a New York synagogue. From Frank Leslie's Popular Monthly, *August 1877.*

Jews in American Public Life

The Jews have been one of the most politically conscious and active groups in the United States. Hundreds have held public office as Cabinet members, Senators, Congressmen, State Governors and Mayors of major cities. As President Roosevelt's Secretary of the Treasury (1934–45), Henry Morgenthau Jr helped bring the United States out of the Depression, and had a major share in the country's economic mobilization during the Second World War.

The highest public position held by an American Jew was that of Henry Kissinger as Secretary of

Henry Kissinger (b.1923), Secretary of State.

State. He became a world figure through his negotiation of the Vietnam peace (for which he was awarded the Nobel Peace Prize) and his 'shuttle diplomacy' in the Israel-Arab conflict.

The United States Supreme Court Justices Benjamin Cardozo, Louis Brandeis, Felix Frankfurter, Arthur Goldberg and Abe Fortas all belonged to the liberal wing of the Court. Cardozo and Brandeis in particular had a marked impact on contemporary American jurisprudence.

largely adapted themselves to the life-style of their neighbours. Traditional Judaism in the western world had been thrown onto the defensive by the Emancipation, the general secular temper of the age and the rise of the Reform movement.

The term 'Orthodox' came into use at the beginning of the 19th century. It embraced all those Jews who continued to accept that the Old Testament was the revealed will of God, and that the Halachah was the divinely-inspired guide for Jewish life. Yet that common premise could not in itself make of Orthodoxy a monolithic camp. It faced its own dilemmas, with different groups finding different answers to them.

The ultra-Orthodox wing, including certain Chassidic sects, have resisted change. They have tried to preserve a traditional Eastern

Louis Dembitz Brandeis (1856–1941), Supreme Court Justice.

Jews have played an important part in the American Labour movement. The grim conditions in the sweat-shops, the socialist ideals the Eastern European Jews brought with them, the age-old Jewish demand for social justice that went back to the Hebrew Prophets – all these produced progressive Jewish labour unions in the garment industry that were models of their kind. One was the International Ladies Garment Workers' Union, led by David Dubinsky. Another was the Chicago-based Amalgamated Clothing Workers of America – its leader, Sidney Hillman, was Roosevelt's chief adviser on labour affairs during the Second World War. Samuel Gompers, the architect of the American Federation of Labour, promoted a worker-employer co-operation that was attacked by more militant unionists but became the cornerstone of American labour relations.

European way of life. Yiddish remains their spoken tongue. The men wear beards and earlocks (*pevot*), and a garb that dates back to 16th-century Poland, while their married women shave their heads and use a wig (*sheitel*). The sexes are kept segregated in public places.

Such rigid traditionalism is today confined to relatively small enclaves. While striving to maintain traditional observance, the bulk of Orthodox Jews resemble Jews of other trends, as well as their non-Jewish fellow-citizens, in dress, language, occupations, leisure activities and political affiliations. A modern, educated Jew who is also an Orthodox Jew has to reconcile his faith with the culture and society in which he lives, and to accept the need for change. Even within the Orthodox fold, there is no consensus on the degree of change which is permissible. It is a far cry from the Yeshiva University in the Bronx to the Lubavitcher Yeshivah a few miles away in Brooklyn, yet both are expressions of Orthodox Judaism. Proposals to recreate an authoritative central body, as the Sanhedrin was in ancient Judea, have proved abortive.

One Orthodox faction became part of the modern Zionist Movement and called itself the Mizrachi Party. More fundamentalist factions, like Agudat Israel, rejected Zionism. They contended the Return to the Homeland depended on the coming of the Messiah in God's good time. However, when the State of Israel came in to existence in 1948 it was accepted as a fact by most of Orthodox Jewry including Agudat Israel, but still not by a few extremist groups like the Satmar Sect in New York or the Naturei Carta Sect in Jerusalem.

The European Emancipation from the end of the 18th century brought in its wake a large-scale drift away from traditional Judaism. The Reform movement started in Germany in the early 19th century. Its initial aim was to make the synagogue service more attractive to modern minds, as an antidote to assimilation. The liturgy was shortened, and most of it translated into German. A choir and an organ were introduced. Strict decorum replaced the informal and easygoing club atmosphere of the traditional *shul* (synagogue).

In the early phase, the object was simply to modify the service from within. But by the middle of the century, Reform had evolved into a new and separate movement in Judaism. It also became known as Liberal or Progressive Judaism, and spread to other Western countries, particularly the United States, Britain, France and Hungary. The break with Orthodox practices became more marked – for instance, in synagogue men and women were no longer seated separately, nor did men keep their heads covered.

With the innovation in observance went a deeper doctrinal spirit. The Reform movement rejected the concept that the Jews were still a national entity, and insisted that they were no more than Germans of the Jewish faith, or the equivalent in other lands. All reference to the hope of a Return to Zion was deleted from the prayer books. Instead, Reform acclaimed the belief of the time that an era of universal progress and brotherhood was dawning for Jew and Gentile alike.

(continued on page 244)

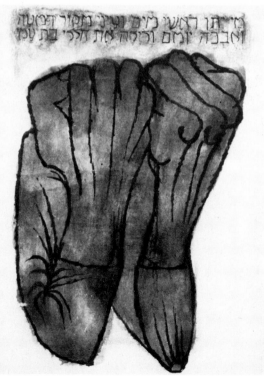

Jews in American Intellectual and Cultural Life

Top left *Jonas Salk (b.1914), microbiologist.*
Top right *Saul Bellow (b.1915), novelist, receiving the Nobel Prize for Literature from King Carl Gustav of Sweden, 10 December 1976.*
Bottom left *Leonard Bernstein (b.1918), conductor and composer.*
Bottom right *Jeremiah, 1968, a watercolour and gouache by Ben Shahn (1898–1969).*
Below *The Marx Brothers.*

Jews have been prominent in every field of American intellectual, scientific and cultural life, as indicated by these examples:

Nuclear Science: J. Robert Oppenheimer, Isidor Rabi, Edward Teller.
Medical Research: Jonas Salk and Albert Sabin (anti-polio vaccine), Selman Waksman (antibiotics)
The Novel: Saul Bellow, Edna Ferber, Norman Mailer, Bernard Malamud, Herman Wouk, Leon Uris
Playwrights: Arthur Miller, Clifford Odets, Lillian Hellman, Moss Hart, Ben Hecht
Music: Leonard Bernstein, Isaac Stern, Aaron Copland, George Gershwin, Irving Berlin

Art and Architecture: Ben Shahn, Mark Rothko, Louis Kahn
Theatre: Shubert Brothers, Flo Ziegfield, George S. Kaufman, Jerome Robbins
Press and Advertising: Adolph Ochs, Joseph Pulitzer, Albert Lasker
Radio and Television: David Sarnoff (RCA and NBC), William Paley (CBS), Leonard Goldenson (ABC)

Jews have had a dominant role in the general entertainment industry:

Motion Pictures

Motion Pictures may well have been the most important technological advance in the spread of culture since the invention of the printing press. In its infancy, the Hollywood industry was a new field, open to the talents and enterprise of Jewish immigrants. For the most part, the leading studios were founded and built up by Jews. That was the case with Metro-Goldwyn-Mayer (Sam Goldwyn and Louis B. Mayer), Warner Brothers (the four sons of an immigrant family from Poland), Paramount Pictures (Adolph Zukor), Universal Studios (Carl Laemmle), and 20th Century-Fox (William Fox and Sol Brill). (Several European film-makers have also been Jews. They include Sir Alexander Korda in Britain, Fritz Lang in Germany, Sergei Eisenstein in Russia, and Jan Kadar and Milos Forman in Czechoslovakia.)

Most of the well-known Hollywood producers and directors have been Jewish, as has been a galaxy of famous stars. Against the background of Jewish suffering, it may seem strange that so many of the great comic talents should be Jews – such as the Marx Brothers, Eddie Cantor, Danny Kaye, Zero Mostel and Woody Allen. Yet by tradition the jester is a licensed critic of society, and the clown's fooling is rooted in pathos.

The Musical

The musical has been a distinctive American contribution to the history of the theatre. It has been created mainly by gifted Jewish writers of songs and lyrics. The most successful has been the partnership of Richard Rodgers and Oscar Hammerstein II (*Oklahoma*, *South Pacific*, *The King and I*, *The Sound of Music*). Others have been George Gershwin (*Porgy & Bess*); Alan J. Lerner and Frederick Loewe (*My Fair Lady*); Frank Loesser (*Guys and Dolls*); Leonard Bernstein and Stephen Sondheim (*West Side Story*); and Gerry Bock and Sheldon Harnick (*Fiddler on the Roof*). Through film versions and foreign language stage productions, this form of American mass culture has reached a global audience.

The *Reform Movement* found fertile ground in the 19th-century United States, where the community was still dominated by affluent German-Jewish merchants and bankers. Of almost 200 American synagogues that existed in 1880, before the great influx from Eastern Europe, all but a dozen were Reform.

The ideology of the movement in the United States was formulated in the Pittsburgh Platform of 1885. It declared flatly that 'we consider ourselves no longer a nation but a religious community.' The Bible, the document continued, was not sacred revelation, but a record of the Jewish spiritual mission, and an instrument of moral instruction. In the Mosaic Code, only those laws that had moral value were binding, and only such ceremonies as were adapted to the views and habits of modern civilization. The prevailing trend towards universal culture and intellect would lead to the fulfilment of Israel's Messianic hope for a kingdom of truth, justice and peace among all men.

This optimistic view of the Jewish future was to be shattered by the realities of the 20th century. A revised platform adopted at Columbus, Ohio, in 1937 showed a far-reaching change in the outlook of American Reform during little more than a half-century from the Pittsburgh document. There was a shift back to more traditional Jewish tenets, a sympathetic attitude to the Zionist aim of a Jewish homeland in Palestine, and a call for the revival of the Hebrew language.

Reform congregations in twenty-six countries have a common framework in the World Union of Progressive Judaism. American Reform rabbis are trained at the Hebrew Union College that has its main campus in Cincinnati, Ohio, and European Reform rabbis at the Leo Baeck College in London.

The *Conservative Movement* in the United States sprang up in the second half of the 19th century as a kind of half-way house between Orthodoxy and Reform. It followed such basic elements of tradition as the Hebrew prayer book, the dietary laws and strict Sabbath observance. At the same time, the attitude to change was more open and revolutionary than that of Orthodoxy.

The Conservative philosophy derived from the Jewish historical school in 19th-century Europe. The Jewish people was depicted as a living organism, adapting itself to the challenges of each period without losing its special character. In keeping with its theme of historical continuity, the Conservative movement was, from its inception, pro-Zionist.

With the mass influx of Eastern European Jews into the United States from 1880 onwards, Conservative Judaism filled an important role. It helped the children of the immigrants to integrate into American life without jettisoning the strong Jewish traditions their parents had brought from the Old Country. The Conservative movement is today the largest of the three major Jewish trends in the United States.

The dominant figure in Conservative Judaism in the early years of

Abba Hillel Silver addressing a mass rally in Madison Square Garden, New York, in a salute to the new State of Israel, 16 May 1948.

The Israel Commitment

An overwhelming commitment to the survival and progress of Israel unites all sections of American Jewry, and has swept away earlier sensitivity to the charge of dual loyalty. This commitment finds an outlet in massive financial support; in the united front presented on political issues affecting Israel, through the Conference of Presidents of Major American Jewish Organizations, popularly known as the 'Presidents' Club'; and in the wave of excitement and anguish that sweeps through the community when Israel is in danger, as it was before the Six-Day War of 1967 and in the Yom Kippur War of 1973.

the 20th century was the renowned European scholar, Solomon Schechter, who headed the movement's teaching centre, the Jewish Theological Seminary of America. Schechter developed the institutions of the movement and shaped its ideas in his published works.

One off-shoot of Conservative Judaism was the Reconstructionist movement founded by Mordecai M. Kaplan, for many years the dean of the Teachers Institute of the Jewish Theological Seminary. In Kaplan's view, Judaism was an 'evolving religious civilization' and its perception of God changed as the scope of human knowledge expanded.

The major divisions of contemporary Judaism are by no means clearcut. Each has in its own way tried to hold a balance between Jewish tradition and the needs of modern societies. All of them face the same factors that threaten to erode present-day Jewish identity in the Diaspora: religious apathy, assimilation and intermarriage. Moreover, the distinctions between different trends have been overshadowed by the shared Jewish experiences of our time – the horror of the Holocaust, the birth of Israel and its battle for survival, and concern for Soviet Jewry and for threatened communities elsewhere. It has become accepted that Diaspora Judaism is and will remain a pluralistic faith, and that there is today peaceful co-existence between different trends. In 1926 the Orthodox, Reform and Conservative

245

movements in the United States jointly set up the Synagogue Council of America to represent the whole community in inter-faith activities and other fields of common interest.

The conflict is developing inside the State of Israel, where organized religion is firmly controlled by the Orthodox establishment. Reform and Conservative congregations, as yet small, are striving for equal status.

The period of mass immigration into the United States had produced the concept of the 'melting-pot'. The immigrant groups were expected to shed their foreign tongues and ways and become Americanized. In effect, that meant assimilation into the dominant WASP (White Anglo-Saxon Protestant) culture. However, that idea has been replaced by a concept more flexible and more suited to a predominantly immigrant nation – that of Cultural Pluralism.

American Jewry today is six million strong – half the world's Jews in the post-Holocaust era. It is a highly-organized community, with an elaborate network of institutions: synagogues and temples, welfare federations, community centres, Hebrew schools, recreation clubs and a spectrum of national organizations. At first glance it seems to be the traditional Jewish community writ large, but its relationship with its non-Jewish environment is quite different. The challenge it faces is whether it can maintain a strong Jewish identity in conditions of equality and assimilation.

The pessimists point to certain negative factors. For all but a small minority, the religious commitment is much weaker than the Judaism that sustained their ancestors in previous centuries. This is not an Age of Faith, for either Jew or Gentile. The intensely Jewish way of life and the Yiddish culture brought with them by the Eastern European immigrants have all but disappeared. Three-quarters of American Jewish youth go to college, where they share campus life with non-Jews; intermarriage among them is at a rate of 30-40 per cent. Large-scale Jewish immigration was stopped more than fifty years ago, and by the Second World War the majority of American Jews were native-born. The basic fact is that the immigrants found in America an open society, free of the mediaeval and feudal past that bedevilled even post-emancipation Europe. Assimilation would seem to be an inevitable process.

Yet in spite of the successful integration of the Jews in American life, there is less talk today of the Vanishing American Jew than there was a generation ago. The community has gained a marked self-confidence, and asserts its Jewish identity without feeling defensive or inhibited about it. It has been profoundly influenced by the Holocaust and the rise of Israel. Inside the community there is a revival of interest in its roots, in rediscovering its Jewish heritage. It has been said: 'What the son wished to forget the grandson wishes to remember.'

Moreover, though the American Jew feels secure, he has long lost the illusion that anti-semitism was something he left behind when he sailed from the shores of Europe. It has flared up from time to time on the American scene, even in the 20th century. The Jews have not forgotten the isolationist and xenophobic years after the First World War, when the Ku Klux Klan was riding high and Henry Ford was spending millions of dollars on attacking the 'Jewish menace' through his newspaper, *The Dearborn Independent*, and on propagating the *Protocols of the Elders of Zion*. The immigration quota act of 1924 was largely inspired by race theories – by the demand to preserve the Anglo-Saxon character of the American nation and prevent it from becoming 'a mongrel race'. In the Thirties there was the anti-semitism of the Depression years, and the rash of Nazi 'shirt-movements' brandishing swastikas. Today, the community is concerned about the potential backlash of the energy crisis with American dependence on Arab oil, and of a possible economic recession. In brief, while the American Jews are not seriously threatened by anti-semitism, they recognize the need to remain vigilant. They feel secure – but not totally so.

Over the years, the majority of American Jews have evolved a balanced attitude towards their own identity. They are not 'Americans of the Jewish persuasion', taking at best a philanthropic interest in less fortunate Jews elsewhere. They have come to accept that as Jews they belong to an historical community that is held together by profound ties of faith, emotion, and mutual responsibility, that cut across national frontiers and that have their centre in Israel. On the other hand, the United States is their country; they feel firmly rooted in it.

Canada

Jewish settlement in Canada started after the British conquest of New France (French Canada) in 1759. The community grew very slowly; in 1881, on the eve of the transatlantic migration from Eastern Europe, it numbered just over 2,000 with the largest congregation in Montreal. After that it expanded rapidly. Today the community numbers 280,000, a little more than one per cent of the total Canadian population.

Canadian Jewry is a cohesive community. It is predominantly Orthodox in synagogue affiliation and has always been strongly Zionist in sentiment. One representative national body, the Canadian Jewish Congress, is responsible for Jewish concerns in Canada and elsewhere in the Diaspora. All Zionist groups are included in the Canadian Zionist Organization. These two major bodies are closely co-ordinated and make joint representations to the government on political issues affecting the State of Israel.

Canadian Jewry has developed an outstanding network of Jewish day schools. There is a special reason for this in Montreal, Quebec Province – one of the two major Jewish communities in the country (the other is Toronto). There are two separate public school systems in that province, one Catholic and the other Protestant. The Jewish community belongs to the Protestant system, a situation that has given

rise to certain difficulties. This factor has encouraged the development of separate Jewish schools in Montreal.

Canadian Jews are fully integrated into the general life of the country. In the business world, they are concentrated in commerce and light industry, though there is still little Jewish representation in heavy industry or in the leading banking and insurance institutions. A number of Jews have held top positions in public service and the judiciary. Jewish poets and novelists have been prominent in Canadian literature.

The main area of concern for Canadian Jewry relates to the growth of French-Canadian nationalism in Quebec Province. In the past this separatist movement has had anti-semitic overtones, notably under the leadership of Adrian Arcand in the 1930s. The central question in Canadian political life – whether Quebec Province will secede from the Dominion – may have disturbing implications for the future of the Montreal community.

Jewish
Occupations
in
Spain

The Jews played an important role in all spheres of government, economics and public administration. The diversity of their occupations indicates their deep involvement in the economic life of the country. Although comprising only 4 per cent of the population, they paid 20 per cent of the taxes. The Jews had many varied professions in Spain; they worked as scribes, translators, ambassadors, wine merchants, pharmacists, physicians, surveyors, astronomers and money-lenders.

Above *The French Revolution. A collage depicting the main events and protagonists.*

Below *The House of Rothschild. The famous zebras of Lord Lionel Walter Rothschild (the second baron) of England, based on a photograph.*

The title page of part of Conciliador, *1651, a biblical commentary by the Amsterdam scholar Manasseh ben-Israel. It is dedicated to four leading Jewish residents of Recife, capital of the province of Pernambuco.*

Latin America

None of the Jews who had been expelled from Spain and Portugal was allowed to settle in the new World colonies of these two powers. (These former colonies are now known as Latin America.) A number of Marranos, however, migrated across the Atlantic and some of them became prominent in the colonial administration, trade and the professions. The Inquisition followed them overseas and started operating in the New World from 1570. During the next century Marranos condemned of secret Jewish practices were periodically burnt at the stake.

In the first two decades of the 19th century, in the wake of the American War of Independence, the Spanish colonies in Latin America and the Portuguese colony of Brazil rebelled against the mother countries and gained their freedom. They abolished the Inquisition, partly because it was one of the institutions associated with the colonial regimes, partly under the influence of the American and French Revolutions. Jewish communities were established from the 1860s onwards and benefitted from the tolerance that had been gained for the Protestant minorities in these Catholic countries.

Substantial Jewish immigration into Latin America began only after 1880. Of the 670,000 Jews living in the region today, at least ninety per cent have an Ashkenazi background, mainly Eastern European. The Russian Jews introduced their Yiddish culture, schools and 'landsmanschaften', as in the United States. The Sephardi immigrants – Ladino-speaking Jews from the Balkans, and Arabic-speaking Jews from Syria and North Africa – tended to form their own separate congregations.

The main country of immigration was the Argentine. It was the most European in population, had the most advanced economy and highest literacy rate, and actively encouraged newcomers. The Jewish community of the Argentine today numbers about 300,000, almost fifty per cent of the total for Latin America.

Since the Jews are predominantly occupied in commerce and industry, they naturally concentrated in the biggest and busiest Latin American cities: Buenos Aires in the Argentine (*c*.250,000); Rio de Janeiro (55,000), and Sao Paulo (75,000) in Brazil; Montevideo (48,000) in Uruguay; Mexico City (32,000) ; Santiago, in Chile (25,000); Caracas in Venezuela (9,000). The majority of the twenty-four states in the Latin American-Carribean region have fewer than 2,000 Jews each.

While many Latin American Jews have prospered and some have achieved positions of distinction, the overall situation of the Jewish communities has been more insecure and vulnerable than in the case of Western democratic countries. With few exceptions, the Latin American lands have been politically unstable, with one-man dictator-ships or government by military juntas more the rule than the exception. The Jews belong to a middle class which is relatively small by Western norms and is sandwiched between a landowning oligarchy and a depressed mass of workers and peons (farm labourers). The resultant economic and social tensions have produced an endemic anti-semitism, that flares up in different times and places. It was exploited and inflamed by the Nazi movements in the years preceding the Second World War. Today the Jewish leadership has to be vigilant concerning the influence of Arab oil, petro-dollars and propaganda drives. There is a steady, though not massive, re-emigration to the United States and to Israel, where an estimated 8,000 Latin American families have settled.

The Jewish communities were very active in the crucial period of 1947–9 in helping to secure Latin American backing for the establishment of Israel. At the United Nations, Latin American support was decisive in securing the adoption of the Partition Resolution of 1947, and in Israel's admission to the Organization in 1949.

South Africa

After England had acquired the Cape of Good Hope from the Dutch at the beginning of the 19th century, Jewish settlers came in from Britain, and a smaller number from Germany. In time, prosperous Jewish businesses grew up in the larger towns, and Jews played a leading part in the export of agricultural products such as wool, mohair, hides and skins, and wine.

South Africa entered a new economic era with the dramatic discoveries of the Kimberley diamond mines (1879) and the Rand goldfields (1886). Among the newcomers attracted to the country were several young London Jews who became leading mining magnates. The most prominent and colourful of them was Barney Barnato. He contended with Cecil Rhodes for control of the diamond fields and then went into partnership with Rhodes in setting up the De Beers Consolidated Mines, which has dominated the world diamond market ever since. It was later headed by a German Jew, Sir Ernest Oppenheimer, followed by his son Harry.

In 1880 there were 4,000 Jews in South Africa. In the next thirty years 40,000 Jewish immigrants came in, nearly all from Eastern Europe. More than seventy per cent were 'Litvaks' (Lithuanian Jews). That fact gave the South African community its distinctive character. It has been unusually close-knit, and imbued with the Litvak pragmatism, reverence for scholarship and wholehearted devotion to Zionism. South African Jewry has proportionally a higher level of Zionist fund-raising and a larger number of settlers in Israel than any other Free World community, while the South African Zionist Federation is regarded as a model of its kind.

A considerable number of the newcomers made their way into the rural districts, first as itinerant peddlers and then as village and small-town shopkeepers. On the whole they were well received by the

Recife, Brazil, in the 17th Century

Pernambuco had been a Dutch colony from 1630, and was the only place in Latin America where Jews could practise their religion openly. Recife had an organized congregation with a synagogue, two religious schools and a cemetery. As the effusive tone of his dedication implies, Manasseh Ben-Israel was interested in being appointed the rabbi of that community.

From 1652 the colony reverted to Portuguese rule, and its Jews and Marranos were again persecuted. Nearly all of them left, and the congregation disintegrated. One small group of twenty-three souls

(continued on page 256)

Jewish gauchos pose with Argentine colleagues, Mauricio, Buenos Aires Province, Argentina.

reached New Amsterdam and were the first Jews to settle in what became the United States of America.

Jewish Agricultural Colonies in Argentina

In 1891, the Jewish banker and philanthropist Baron Maurice de Hirsch, who had been born in Bavaria and settled in Paris, established the Jewish Colonization Association (ICA). Its main objective was to promote the settling of Russian Jews on the land in the New World. With the assent of the Czar's government a network of committees was set up throughout Russia and a number of farm and vocational schools operated for training the prospective emigrants. The main area of settlement was in Argentina, where a Jewish farm colony, Moisésville, had been founded two years earlier. Three small colonies were also started in Brazil but failed to develop. The colonization in Argentina reached its peak by about 1930, when 20,000 Jews were living from grain farming and cattle ranching on a million and a half acres. The Jewish gaucho on horseback was a familiar figure in certain districts of the Argentinian pampas. The Jewish colonies pioneered agrarian co-operatives, diversified farming methods and the cultivation of new crops.

As time passed there was a steady drift to the cities and the Jewish farming community dwindled to a few thousand. To a large extent this was part of the general process of urbanization, and the impact of the depression years on rural life. Other reasons were friction between the settlers and ICA overseers, losses from periodic droughts and locust swarms in marginal semi-arid areas, fluctuation in the market prices of beef and grain, and the chronic land shortage from which some of the Jewish colonies suffered.

Afrikaner (Boer) farmers – stern Calvinists who lived by the Old Testament. But the next Jewish generation tended to move to the big towns, where there were more opportunities and a better chance to bring up children in a Jewish environment. In the urban centres Jews pioneered modern methods of retailing and dominated certain fields of light industry, especially clothing and textiles. A considerable number of the sons of the Jewish immigrant merchants entered the free professions of law and medicine.

One interesting field in Jewish hands was the ostrich feather industry before the First World War, with its world centre in the Cape town of Oudtshoorn.

Jewish immigration into South Africa met with strong public resistance at certain times, and provoked a backlash of anti-semitism. The Eastern European immigration was virtually halted by the Quota Act of 1930. That Act, based on geographical quotas, did not block the entry of German-Jewish refugees after Hitler came to power, so in 1937 it was replaced by a new Aliens Act. Under its terms a selection board was given power to reject any individual immigrant, and few Jews satisfied its criteria. At that time Nazi propaganda was fomenting anti-Jewish feeling among the Afrikaners, and 'shirt movements' were sprouting in the country. With the curtailment of immigration, the low birth-rate and some younger Jews leaving the country, the size of the community has remained static, at a figure of about 120,000, and its percentage of the population has declined.

The South African Jews are part of a complex multi-racial society. They are half of one per cent of the population, but the significant statistic is that they are three per cent of the white ('European') minority that alone enjoys full political, economic and residential rights. Within the white community most of the Jews are identified with the English-speaking group in language, culture and urban life-style. The Nationalist Party, that represents the Afrikaner majority among the whites, has been in power since 1948. Initial Jewish fears have been allayed, since the government has shown itself well-disposed to the Jewish community, and has staunchly supported the State of Israel. South African Jews are not under any political or economic pressure, and overt anti-semitism died down after the fall of Hitler. But it is difficult for them to feel completely secure in a country where the racial problems remain unresolved and the future is unpredictable.

Smuts and Zionism. Field Marshal Jan Smuts, Prime Minister until 1948, on Table Mountain. Smuts was an eloquent supporter of the Zionist cause from the time he became a personal friend of Dr Chaim Weizmann while he was a member of the Imperial War Cabinet in London during the First World War. He had a hand in formulating the Balfour Declaration of 1917 and was one of the authors of the Palestine Mandate after the war.

Top *Sir Isaac Isaacs as Governor-General of Australia. From a painting by Sir John Longstaff, 1936.*

Above *Sir John Monash, general, commander of the Australian army corps in France during the First World War.*

Australia and New Zealand

European settlement in Australia started in 1788 with a British penal colony, where Sydney now stands. The first Jews were six convicts, who remained as settlers. With characteristic Jewish resilience, one of them became a policeman!

By the mid-19th century there were established congregations in Sydney, Melbourne and several smaller towns, with about one-quarter of the Jewish citizens scattered in the rural areas. The Jewish community had no problems of integration, and encountered no restrictions.

In the first half of the 20th century the small and semi-assimilated community was greatly expanded and revitalized by an influx of European Jews. In the years before and after the First World War they came from Eastern Europe. In the late 1930s Australia took in about 8,000 refugees from Nazi Germany. After the Second World War thousands of Holocaust survivors were admitted from the DP camps. Today there is an active and well-organized Jewish community numbering approximately 70,000, represented by the Executive Council of Australian Jewry. Although only five per cent of the total population, the Jews have a respected place in Australian life, and a number of them have been prominent in politics, business and the professions. Eminent Australian Jews have included Sir Isaac Isaacs, Chief Justice of Australia and its first native-born Governor-General; General Sir John Monash, who commanded the Australian and New Zealand forces on the Western Front in the First World War, and who was the highest-ranking Jew in any modern army; and Sir Zelman Cowen was appointed Governor-General in 1977.

The 4,000 Jews in New Zealand (two per cent of the population) are nearly all from families who originated in England. (New Zealand immigration laws have been designed to preserve the British character of the Dominion.) They have enjoyed complete freedom since the community started in 1829, and are well established in farming, business and the professions. The three main congregations are in Auckland, Wellington and Christchurch. The public offices held by Jews have included a Premier, Sir Julius Vogel; a Chief Justice, Sir Michael Myers; and a number of MPs and mayors of the main cities.

Important Events

United States

1492	Columbus discovers America.
1654	Marrano group reaches New Amsterdam.
1776	Outbreak of American Revolution.
1835	Beginning of German-Jewish immigration.
1861–5	7,000 Jews fight in Civil War.
1873	Union of American Congregations (Reform) founded.
1881	Beginning of mass immigration from Eastern Europe.
1890	Ellis Island immigration centre opened.
1898	Union of Orthodox Jewish Congregations founded.
1913	United Synagogue of America (Conservative) founded.
1917–18	Quarter-million American Jews serve in the First World War.
1919	American Jewish Delegation to Paris Peace Treaty.
1924	Immigration quota Act restricts Jewish immigration.
1948	United States recognizes Israel (14 May).

Latin America

1570	Inquisition introduced to New World.
1881	Beginning of substantial Eastern European immigration.
1891	ICA colonies launched in Argentina.

British Commonwealth

1759	First Jewish settlers in Canada.
1788	First Jews arrive in Australia (as convicts).
1820	British Jews settle in South Africa.
1820	Start of New Zealand community.
c.1882	Beginning of Eastern European Jewish immigration to Canada, South Africa, Australia and New Zealand.

Chapter Seventeen

The Return

One of the most powerful factors that held the Jewish people together in the Diaspora, and sustained them under stress, was the hope of a Messianic Return to the ancestral homeland.

The term 'Messiah' comes from the Hebrew word *mashiach*, meaning 'the anointed one'. In biblical times it was used for the Hebrew kings and high priests who, on taking office, were consecrated to God by the formal anointing of their heads with holy oil.

The Hebrew prophets foretold that the Jewish kingdom would be restored under a descendant of King David. This belief was further developed in the post-biblical period. There would be a time of convulsion in human affairs, 'the end of days'. A divinely-appointed Messiah would bring the Jews back to the Land of Israel. A kingdom of God would arise there, ushering in for all mankind a new era of peace, justice and national harmony. The Messiah was pictured as riding into Jerusalem on a donkey, in accordance with the prophecy in the *Book of Zechariah*:

Lo, your king comes to you;
triumphant and victorious is he,
humble and riding on an ass.

(Zech. 9:9)

Messianic expectations arose sharply in periods of general upheaval and Jewish persecution. Such a period was the 1st century BC and the 1st century AD. It saw the emergence of Rome as the imperial master of the Middle East, the birth of Christianity and the crushing of the Jewish State. The time produced a flood of apocalyptic literature – mystic revelations of the future – and a number of preachers who claimed that the redemption was approaching. The Gospels present Jesus as the awaited Messiah, a descendant of David, proclaiming that the kingdom of God was at hand. (The appellation 'Christ' is from the Greek word meaning 'the anointed one' – that is, the Messiah.) Jesus is described as entering Jerusalem on a donkey.

The Messianic theme runs throughout Diaspora history, but was most marked during the centuries of Jewish suffering in mediaeval Europe and in Moslem lands. The bloody massacres that attended the First Crusade (1096), the Black Death (1348), the Spanish pogroms

Jerusalem
See colour page 269

If I forget you, O Jerusalem,
* let my right hand wither!*
Let my tongue cleave to the roof of
* my mouth,*
* if I do not remember you,*
if I do not set Jerusalem
* above my highest joy!*
(Psalm 137:5, 6)

For out of Zion shall go forth
* law,*
* and the word of the Lord from*
* Jerusalem.*
(Isaiah 2:3)

One cannot enter Jerusalem for the first time without feeling the impact of forty centuries of continuous history. The very name 'Jerusalem' has a profoundly emotional sound to hundreds of millions of Christians, Jews and Moslems throughout the world. This is the city the kings David and Solomon, of the prophets Isaiah and Jeremiah, of Ezra and Nehemiah in the Return, of Judah the Maccabee

 (continued on page 264)

The Wailing Wall. An engraving by W.H. Bartlett, 1842.

and his brothers. This is the city of Jesus's Ministry and the Crucifixion. And Moslems hold this city to be the place from which Mohammed ascended to heaven; for them it is next after Mecca and Medina in holiness.

Many different breeds of men have sat in the seat of power in Jerusalem – Jebusites, Hebrews, Babylonians and Persians; Greeks and Romans; Arabs, Crusaders, Ottoman Turks and British. But throughout the flux of these thousands of years there runs one constant thread – the unique attachment of the Jewish people to Jerusalem. Only for that people has the city been the national centre. The attachment has remained unbroken from the time when King David made Jerusalem the capital of the Hebrew State to the time when David Ben-Gurion did likewise, 3,000 years later.

Through all the centuries of dispersion, from the farthest corners of the earth, Jews have prayed for the Return to Zion, and built the sacred Ark on the synagogue wall facing the direction of Jerusalem. History has no parallel to this mystic bond.

The Temple

Down the ages imaginative visions of the Temple of Jerusalem have been a frequent theme of Jewish and Christian art. King Solomon's Temple was completed in the 11th year of his reign, that is about 950 BC. The site was the threshing-floor that Solomon's father David had bought from Araunah the Jebusite for fifty shekels of silver. The fame and splendour of Solomon's Temple would suggest an imposing structure, but actually it was small. Scholars have calculated that the outside dimensions were about fifty metres long, twenty-five metres wide and fifteen metres high. It must be borne in mind that the interior was not a place of assembly; the congregation gathered in the great courtyard outside. The shrine itself was 'God's house', a dwelling for the Divine Presence.

The First Temple lasted nearly four centuries, until it was destroyed and Jerusalem sacked by a Babylonian army in 586 BC.

The Second Temple was constructed on the foundations of the previous one by a group of Jews that returned from the Babylonian Exile. It was completed around 515 BC. This must have been a more modest building, with none of the sumptuous adornments Solomon had lavished on the original one. The new Temple was no longer the shrine of an independent kingdom, but the house of worship of a small and struggling sect in an obscure corner of the Persian empire. However, it was of profound importance for the survival of the Jewish people that they should once more possess a focus of faith in their ancestral homeland and their holy city.

Herod the Great (37–4 BC) was the finest royal builder in Jewish history after King Solomon, a thousand years earlier. In 22 BC he convened a

261

national assembly and announced a sweeping plan to reconstruct the Second Temple that had served for five centuries. Herod gathered together a great labour force for the project, and hundreds of wagons to transport the materials. The building itself was put up in eighteen months. The ground plan and location remained the same, but Herod's Temple was higher and far more luxurious than the one it replaced. Herod's major change was to construct a huge platform on the Temple Mount, surrounded by massive retaining walls of enormous limestone blocks. The completion of the whole complex of buildings and courtyards on the enlarged platform took forty-six years in all – in fact, a generation beyond Herod's death. It was to be destroyed a few decades after it was finished.

After the destruction by the Romans in AD 70, Judaism survived and continued to develop, but the loss of the Temple remained a searing memory. For centuries the Jewish farmers had brought their first fruits to the sanctuary. On the great pilgrimage festivals thousands of worshippers had gathered in the courtyards from all over the Jewish world. They had been emotionally uplifted by the splendour of the Temple and by its time-hallowed rituals. Now the focus of their religious experience had been removed. The transition to a life without the Temple was painful.

For the next nineteen centuries Jews would come to pray and mourn at the Western (Wailing) Wall, an exposed section of Herod's great retaining wall. This was the closest they could get to the site of the demolished Temple, where, according to the rabbis, the Divine Presence still lingered. The Western Wall served as the holiest shrine of Judaism, and the tangible symbol of the First and Second Temples. Their destruction is commemorated by the annual fast day of Tisha b'Av (the ninth day of the month of Av, in July or August). On that day, the approximate date of both these national calamities, the biblical *Book of Lamentations* is recited in synagogues.

262

Jews cling to the mystical 3,000-year memory of the sanctuary that once stood on Mount Moriah. They believe with the biblical Prophets that in God's good time the Temple will rise again at the centre of a Messianic kingdom.

False Messiahs
See colour page 269

The most remarkable of the false messiahs in the mediaeval period were David Alroy in the 12th century, David Reuveni and Shlomo Molcho early in the 16th century, and Shabbetai Zevi in the 17th century.

David Alroy
David Alroy was the leader of a Messianic movement that sprang up in Kurdistan about twenty-five years after the Crusader capture of Jerusalem in 1099. The background to the movement was the struggle between Christianity and Islam for possession of the Holy Land. Alroy, whose real first name was Menachem, took the name of David when he claimed to be the king of the Jews. He was an exceptionally handsome young man who excelled in religious and mystical studies and was credited with possessing magic powers. His pretensions were promoted by his father Solomon, who himself claimed to be the prophet Elijah.

Alroy established his headquarters in the fortified town of Amadiya, astride the road leading to the Crusader kingdom of Edessa in Mesopotamia. Letters were sent to the Jewish communities throughout the region, calling upon them to prepare themselves by fasting and prayer for his return to Jerusalem. According to one tradition, the Jews of Baghdad spent a night waiting on their rooftops because of a story that they would be transported to Jerusalem by winged angels.

Alroy's expectations came to an abrupt end when he was murdered. A number of his followers, known as Menachemites, continued to believe he would reappear. Benjamin Disraeli's novel, *The Wondrous Tale of Alroy* (1839) is a largely fictional account of the episode.

David Reuveni
David Reuveni first appeared in Western Europe in 1522. He claimed that his brother was the ruler of a Jewish kingdom in the desert, inhabited by the descendants of the Lost Israelite tribes of Reuven – hence his name – Gad and part of Manasseh. (These were the tribes that had settled east of the Jordan River at the time of Joshua's Conquest.) Reuveni stated that he had come to offer an alliance to the Christian leaders against the Moslem Turks, who had recently conquered the Holy Land in 1516. With Christian support and weapons, an army from the Jewish kingdom under Reuveni's command would regain the Holy Land. That would be followed by the Return of the Jews to their homeland and the inception of the Messianic age.

Reuveni was at first regarded with scepticism by the Jewish leaders, but to their surprise he was taken seriously by the Church hierarchy. The influential Cardinal da Viterbo welcomed him and arranged an audience for him with the Pope. Armed with a letter from the Pope, Reuveni arrived in Lisbon in 1525 and was given ambassadorial treatment by the King of Portugal. His advent caused great excitement among the Portuguese Marranos (crypto-Jews), and speculation was rife among them concerning the Messianic redemption. For that reason Reuveni provoked the hostility of the powerful Inquisition and had to leave the country. It is likely that he spent the next few years in Spanish and North African prisons.

Shlomo Molcho
One of Reuveni's Portuguese disciples was an intellectual young Marrano called Diogo Pires (1500–32), who as a boy had secretly learnt Hebrew and studied Jewish religious books. With Reuveni's advent in Lisbon, Pires was swept by Messianic fervour. He publicly announced himself a Jew, circumcised himself and took the name of *Shlomo Molcho* (Molcho is from the Hebrew word for a king). He fled from the Inquisition and settled in Salonika,

Turkey. Having become convinced of his divine mission, he went to Rome, dressed in rags and lived for a month among the beggars gathered on a bridge over the River Tiber – acting out a Talmudic legend that the Messiah would emerge from these conditions. After that he started preaching in public and gained renown by predicting a flood in Rome and an earthquake in Lisbon. Arrested by the Inquisition, he was saved from death at the instance of the Pope.

Molcho renewed contact with Reuveni, who had emerged again in Venice. In 1532 the two of them set off on a visit to Emperor Charles V in Regensburg, Germany, for some unspecified purpose. But the Emperor had been turned against them by Church circles. He sent them back in chains to Mantua in Italy. Here Molcho was burnt at the stake by the Inquisition. Reuveni lingered on in prison, and died in about 1538.

The main source of information about Reuveni is a diary he kept in Hebrew. His real name and origin remain a mystery. Some scholars believe he was a Falasha, one of a black Jewish community in Ethiopia.

Shabbetai Zevi

Shabbetai Zevi (1626–76) caused a far greater upheaval in Jewish life than any other false messiah in Diaspora history. The son of a prosperous Jewish merchant of Smyrna, in Turkish Asia Minor, he was subject to strange moods of euphoria and melancholy, and would probably be diagnosed today as a manic-depressive. From his boyhood he was intensely religious, and absorbed himself in Kabbalistic studies. At the age of twenty-two he publicly declared himself the Messiah, purported to utter the forbidden name of God and announced that the redemption was imminent. He was not taken seriously, but some years later his recurrent Messianic claims and his eccentric behaviour during ecstatic spells, led to his being banned by the rabbis. After years of wandering he settled in Jerusalem. In 1665 he was proclaimed as the true Messiah by a well-known mystic and faith-healer,

Shabbetai Zevi in prison in Adrianople. From Ketzer Geschichte, *1701.*

Nathan of Gaza. That launched the Shabbatean movement, with Nathan of Gaza acting as Shabbetai's prophet and ideologue.

Increasing persecution, and especially the Chmielnicki massacres in the Ukraine, had left a mood of gloom and despair in the Jewish communities of Europe. Many believed that the darkest hour had been reached, which would be followed by the redemption. The expectations were strengthened by the mystical doctrines, with messianic overtones, that had been enunciated in Safad by the Kabbalist Isaac Luria (*ha-Ari*) in the 16th century and had permeated Jewish scholarship everywhere. These factors accounted for the extraordinary spread and joyful acceptance of the news about Shabbetai's advent. It was confidently expected, even in some Christian circles, that he would soon be crowned in Jerusalem as king of the Jews. A circular was sent to all Jewish communities in the name of 'the first-begotten Son of God, Shabbetai Zevi, messenger and redeemer of the people of Israel'.

Alarmed by the ferment he had stirred up, the Turkish authorities arrested and imprisoned him. In 1666 he was brought before the Sultan in Adrianople and given the choice between conversion to Islam and death. He chose Islam and was converted together with a group of his disciples. Gratified at gaining so famous a convert, the Sultan granted Shabbetai an honorary title and a pension.

The apostasy stunned the Jewish communities everywhere. Some of his followers interpreted it as part of the divine plan, a mystical 'descent' to redeem lost souls among the infidels. Even after Shabbetai died in a small Albanian town, small groups of adherents continued to believe that he would return as a redeemer. That belief persisted for a century, after which it faded.

One Shabbetean legacy was a strong rabbinical distrust of any movement that appealed to the mystical and emotional elements in Judaism. That helps to explain the force of the opposition aroused in the Orthodox establishment by the revivalist movement of Chassidism in the 18th century.

(1391) and the Chmielnicki uprising in the Ukraine (1648), as also the Expulsions (especially that from Spain in 1492), were regarded as 'the birthpangs of the Messiah', the darkest hour before the dawn. False messiahs arose, then disappeared or were discredited, leaving their followers forlorn. But the recurrent experience with imposters and religious cranks did not extinguish the messianic yearning.

However, the modern Return came about in the form of a secular national movement, and not through the miraculous instrument of a Messiah. This fact caused deep perplexity to the Orthodox Jews. Most of them were opposed to Zionism, thinking it an impious and impatient attempt to pre-empt the advent of the Messiah. There were some 19th-century religious Jews who thought otherwise. Among them were Judah Alkalai, a rabbi from Sarajevo in Bosnia-Herzegovina; the German Talmudic scholar Zvi Hirsch Kalischer; and the Lithuanian rabbi Samuel Mohilever. These men contended that God expected human effort to pave the way for the Return, and they sought support for practical programmes. They were the fore-runners of the Mizrachi (religious Zionist) movement.

Another road to Zionism in the 19th century was through the revolutionary socialist movement of the period. Moses Hess, a German socialist who worked for some years with Marx and Engels, became sceptical of the facile belief that socialism would eliminate anti-semitism. In 1862 he published a booklet, *Rome and Jerusalem*, advocating the revival of an independent Jewish State in Palestine on a basis of social justice.

In the mood of despair that followed the 1881 pogroms in the Pale of Settlement and the anti-Jewish May Laws, Leon Pinsker, a doctor in Odessa, published a pamphlet in 1882 called *Auto-Emancipation*. Attributing anti-semitism mainly to Jewish homelessness, he called on the Russian Jews to emigrate to a land where they could recreate their own independent nation. 'Help yourselves and God will help you!' Pinsker soon accepted that such a project was possible only in the ancestral homeland. He became a leader of the Lovers of Zion (Chovevei Zion) movement that sprang up in Russia and elsewhere. Its scattered societies joined into a single organization in 1884, at a conference at Kattowitz in Silesia. The same approach was developed by the Russian Hebrew writer, Moses Leib Lilienblum. His analysis of the Jewish problem in Europe concluded with the assertion that 'aliens we are and aliens we shall remain. . . . We need a corner of our own. We need Palestine.'

In the 1880s small groups of Jewish students started migrating to Palestine in order to live there on the land. They called themselves BILU, from the Hebrew initial letters of the phrase in *Isaiah*: 'O House of Jacob, come ye and let us go.' They were the vanguard of the first *Aliyah* (wave of immigration). The farm villages they set up could hardly have survived the grim local conditions without help from Baron Edmond de Rothschild.

The stirrings of Zionism among the Eastern European Jews was

Herzl

Dr Theodor Herzl (1860–1904) was the founder of the modern Zionist Movement. Born in Budapest, Hungary, of a well-to-do Jewish family, he became a doctor of law at the University of Vienna, and settled in Vienna as a journalist and playwright. Herzl was a striking-looking man, above average height, with a black beard and magnetic brown eyes. He was assimilated into the social and cultural life of the time, and uninvolved in Jewish affairs. But, while serving as the Paris correspondent of a leading Austrian newspaper, he became increasingly conscious of the anti-semitism that had persisted after the emancipation of the Jews in Western Europe.

The problem became an obsession with him as a result of the Dreyfus Affair, which he covered for his paper. In 1896 he published an epoch-making booklet, *The Jewish State*. Its sub-title read: *An Attempt at a Modern Solution of the Jewish Question*. In the preface he stated: 'We are a people – one people. We are strong enough to form a state...' The booklet set out a blueprint for such a State.

In 1897 Herzl convened the First Zionist Congress in Basle, Switzerland – the first international Jewish assembly for nearly 2,000 years. The Congress established the World Zionist Organization, with Herzl as its President. The programme adopted by Congress laid down that 'the aim of Zionism is to create for the Jewish people a home in Palestine secured by public law.' Herzl noted in his diary: 'In Basle I founded the Jewish State.'

Palestine at that time was under Ottoman rule. Herzl first sought German diplomatic support. In 1898 he was informed that the German Kaiser, Wilhelm II, was sympathetic to Zionist aims and would be willing to grant Herzl an audience in Jerusalem, which the Kaiser was about to visit. A preliminary meeting took place in Constantinople. Herzl requested the Kaiser's influence in favour of a colonization charter from

Theodor Herzl, who was the founder of modern Zionism.

dramatically converted into an international movement by the Viennese journalist, Dr Theodor Herzl, who established the World Zionist Organization in 1897. Herzl died in 1904, worn out by his unsuccessful attempts to obtain a political charter for large-scale settlement in Palestine. For the next decade, practical colonization continued quietly in Palestine. A new type of *chalutz* (pioneer) appeared – the young, idealistic men and women of the Second Aliyah, bent on self-help and manual labour. David Ben-Gurion was one of that generation. The first kibbutzim (collective farm villages) were born, and Tel Aviv, an all-Jewish city, was founded. By the outbreak of the First World War the Yishuv (Jewish community of Palestine) numbered 80,000.

The war radically changed the prospects for Zionism. Partly through the efforts of Dr Chaim Weizmann, a Russian-born chemist teaching at Manchester University in England, the British Government on 2 November 1917 issued the historic Balfour Declaration, that pledged support for the establishment in Palestine of a National Home for the Jewish people. After the war, in which Turkey was defeated, the Declaration was written into the Mandate for Palestine accepted by Britain under the auspices of the League of Nations. The Mandate was the international framework for the return of the Jews to

the Sultan of Turkey. The response was non-committal. The following morning Herzl and his delegation sailed for Palestine. He found it a poor and largely barren country, after centuries of Turkish misrule. The meeting with the Kaiser was an anti-climax, as the erratic monarch had lost interest in the matter.

In 1901 and 1902 Herzl carried on negotiations directly with the Sultan Abdul Hamid II and his ministers in Constantinople. Herzl promised to raise a large loan for the bankrupt Ottoman regime, but his efforts to enlist the help of rich Jewish bankers was unsuccessful.

With the direct road to Palestine through Constantinople blocked, a promising detour seemed to open up through Britain, the mightiest imperial power of the time. Herzl was received in London by the powerful Colonial Secretary, Joseph Chamberlain. They discussed the possibility of a temporary Jewish settlement in the El Arish district of Sinai, but the project proved impossible because of the water problem.

On returning from a visit to East Africa in 1903, Chamberlain proposed that a commission be sent out to establish whether a suitable territory along the new Uganda Railway could be made available for an autonomous 'Jewish colony of settlement'. Herzl placed the proposal before the Zionist Congress, urging that it might provide a home at least for the time being, for the refugees from the bloody pogroms in Russia earlier that year. To his dismay, most of the Russian delegates were fiercely against the proposal, refusing to consider any diversion from settlement in Palestine. The Uganda Project, as it was called, split the Zionist Movement into two bitterly opposed camps before it was abandoned. Herzl, who had suffered from a heart ailment for some years, emerged from the controversy exhausted, ill and burdened by a sense of failure. But for millions of Jews, especially in the Russian Pale of Settlement, he had already become a Messianic figure, the personal embodiment of the age-old hope of a Return. His death in July 1904, at the age of forty-four sent a wave of shock and bereavement through the Jewish world.

In 1949, when the State of Israel was a year old, Herzl's coffin was brought to Jerusalem and interred on a hilltop named Mount Herzl, looking out upon the Holy City from the west. Herzl's most fitting epitaph could be the words he wrote in his diary: '...it was, after all, no mean achievement for a Jewish journalist without resources...to turn a rag into a flag and a downtrodden rabble into a people rallying erect around that flag.'

The Pioneers

From the 1880s onward small groups of young Zionist pioneers (*chalutzim*) migrated from Eastern Europe to Palestine, filled with zeal to redeem the soil of the homeland. For centuries the Jews in the Diaspora had been cut off from agriculture. The chalutzim believed that the new society they wanted would develop on healthy lines only through a return to manual work, especially on the land.

Dedicated to this ideal, they went through great hardship and danger – draining malarial swamps, clearing stony hillsides, building roads, enduring heat, poor food and primitive living conditions, and protecting themselves against attack by armed Arab bands. Gradually the obstacles were overcome. They established farming communities centred on collective and co-operative villages (kibbutzim and moshavim); a progressive labour federation (the Histadrut); and a country-wide self-defence organization.

In the pre-State era of Zionist colonization, these chalutzim formed an elite serving in the forefront of the national effort, and viewed by the whole Zionist movement with admiration and pride. Their voluntary leadership role waned in the State of Israel, with its mass immigration, professional civil service and regular army.

Two of the tens of thousands of Jews from the European ghettoes who formed farming communities in Israel.

redeem their homeland – the equivalent of the Charter for which Herzl had so vainly struggled.

In the next two decades steady progress was made in developing the National Home. But the mass aliyah that Herzl had visualized did not take place at that time. The Russian Jews had been cut off by the Bolshevik Revolution of 1917. Economic conditions in Palestine were difficult. The Zionist concept was rejected by the Arabs, who plunged the country into disturbances in 1920–1, 1929, and 1936–8. In the Thirties, Britain started to retreat from the Mandatory obligation to promote the Jewish National Home. In May 1939, the British Government issued a White Paper (policy statement) that aimed at turning Palestine into an Arab State, with a Jewish minority that would not exceed one-third of the population. The Zionist leadership determined to fight the White Paper by every available means, as it spelt the doom of hopes for an independent Jewish homeland.

The crux of the conflict was aliyah, Jewish immigration. In the early years of the Mandate there had been a small-scale aliyah, with the number of immigrant certificates restricted to what the British authorities fixed as the 'economic absorptive capacity' of the country. The rate of aliyah increased somewhat in the Thirties, and included 70,000 refugees from Hitler Germany. Further immigration was drastically reduced when the Arab rebellion broke out in Palestine in 1936. When nothing came of the partition plan proposed by the Royal (Peel) Commission of 1936, an organized effort started to bring Jewish

refugees from Europe to Palestine without official immigration certificates. For the British Mandatory government this was an illegal and politically embarrassing movement that had to be blocked by any means. For the Jewish world it was a rescue operation of Nazi victims who had the right to come to their homeland; they called it Aliyah Bet (Immigration 'B'). Until the outbreak of the War, 41 'illegal' boats had sailed with a total of 15,500 refugees. Some of them succeeded in slipping through. Their passengers were disembarked at night and promptly mixed with the local Jewish population. Those who were intercepted were detained in the country.

During the early war years, a number of ships sailed from Rumania through the Black Sea and the Dardenelles. Several of them sank. Of the refugees who reached Palestine, 1,580 were rounded up and transported to detention camps on the island of Mauritius.

At the end of the war great numbers of the Jewish survivors gathered in the Displaced Persons (DP) camps, most of them in the American and British zones in Germany and Austria. The Jewish camps, with a population that rose to a quarter-million, were run as self-governing communities, with their own internal network of services. They taught Hebrew in improvised schools and adult classes, and a number of the young people went to agricultural training (hachshara) farms. The overwhelming urge of these DPs was to leave the bloodstained soil of Europe and start again in the National Home.

The renewed post-war Aliyah Bet was run by the Mossad, a clandestine body set up by the representative Jewish institutions in Palestine. It had its headquarters in Paris and a network of agents and

The 'Bericha'

A group of Holocaust survivors passing through Graz, Austria, in 1946, as part of the movement known in Hebrew as *Bericha* (flight). It was a large-scale underground migration of Jews at the end of the War, crossing borders at dead of night, moving westward to the DP camps in Germany and Austria and southward to the Mediterranean coast. Graz in southern Austria was one of the main assembly-points for crossing into Italy, where the refugees could be put onto the 'illegal' ships of the Aliyah Bet.

The Return from Arab Lands

Right *A mass meeting in front of the immigration offices, Tripoli, 1949.*

In the 20th century the situation of the Jews in the Arab countries became more difficult and insecure, owing to the growth of Arab nationalism and the conflict over Palestine. In 1947–8 the pressure on the Jews became intense in most of the Arab lands, and ugly anti-Jewish riots occurred in a number of places. After the birth of Israel two whole communities, in Yemen and Iraq, were evacuated by air to Israel. After the return of the Iraqi troops in 1949 from their inglorious Palestine campaign, resentment turned against the local Jews and repressive measures were imposed on them. The Iraqi government was willing to let them depart, while confiscating their homes, businesses and assets. In a matter of months in 1950–1, 120,000 Iraqi Jews were brought to Israel via Cyprus, by what was called 'Operation Ezra and Nehemiah'.

The immigration from other Arab countries was spread over a number of years, and was less dramatic. In Egypt and Libya the Jewish communities declined from 1948 but were finally evicted only in the aftermath of the Arab defeat by Israel in the Six-Day War of 1967. The Algerian Jews were French nationals and eighty per cent of them were absorbed in France when Algeria became independent in 1962.

In 1948, there were an estimated 870,000 Jews in the Arab world. Two-thirds of them were re-settled in Israel, and the rest absorbed elsewhere. The largest surviving number is in Morocco – 20,000 left out of nearly 300,000 in 1948. In Syria 4,000 Jews are held virtually as political hostages.

In Israel the influx of Jews from the Arab lands accounts for about half of the Jewish population. When one adds the aliyah from the non-Arab Moslem countries, Iran and Turkey, it is evident that the Sephardi dispersion in the world of Islam has come round full circle to its beginnings in the Land of Israel.

contacts throughout Europe. The personnel and ships' officers were drawn from the Haganah, the self-defence organization of the Palestinian Jews. The 'Scarlet Pimpernels' of the Mossad operated with an incredible daring and resourcefulness. They smuggled refugee groups across frontiers, turned out thousands of forged travel documents, purchased and outfitted scores of old vessels, and carried on a battle of wits with British intelligence in Europe. Influenced by their recent experience of Nazi occupation, and by the ghastly facts of the Holocaust, many Europeans were sympathetic to Aliyah Bet. But their governments were under heavy diplomatic pressure from Britain to prevent Jews moving through their countries towards Palestine, or embarking from their ports.

Once the crowded boats had sailed, some of them evaded the Royal Navy blockade and succeeded in making secret landings along the coast of Palestine. The estimated numbers that had entered the country in this way were debited against the meagre quota of legal immigration certificates (1,500 per month). Most of the ships, however, were intercepted and boarded, sometimes after stiff resistance. They were escorted into Haifa harbour, often in a damaged state. The refugees were transferred to 'prison ships' with caged-in

Left *Jerusalem from a 15th-century French manuscript.*

Below *False Messiahs. The Messiah on a white ass at the gate of Jerusalem, from the Ashkenazi Haggadah, Germany, 15th century.*

The Gateway. Immigrants on board ship approaching New York.

Overleaf *The Menorah. 'Wherever I go, I am going to Eretz Israel' Rabbi Nachman of Bratslav (1722–1811).*

Lower East Side, New York. Tenement housing on Lower East Side, New York.

decks, and deported to detention camps in Cyprus. World attention became focussed on the plight of boatloads of Holocaust survivors trying to reach the forbidden shores of the Promised Land.

In the three years from the end of the war in 1945 to the birth of Israel in 1948, the Mossad was responsible for the despatch of 64 ships, carrying nearly 70,000 refugees. Of these, 56,000 were interned in Cyprus, and brought to Israel after it became independent. The total number of 'illegals' arriving by sea and land from 1934 to 1948 was 120,000.

When Israel became independent in May 1948, all immigration restrictions on Jews were scrapped and the gates flung open for the Return. In the first year of independence over 200,000 immigrants flooded in from forty-two countries. The Law of the Return passed by the Knesset (Israel Parliament) in 1950 formally reaffirmed that 'every Jew has the right to immigrate to Israel'. Furthermore, a Jewish immigrant automatically became a citizen of Israel on his arrival, unless he chose to opt out. In the first four years the number of Jewish inhabitants more than doubled. After thirty years the original 650,000 had become over 3,000,000.

The two main sources for the Ingathering were the Holocaust survivors in Europe and the Jewish communities in the Arab lands.

The first European Jews to arrive after independence were the detainees in the Cyprus camps; this time they sailed into Haifa harbour not as 'illegals' but as free citizens of the Jewish State. About 70,000 were brought in from the DP camps in Europe. 300,000 immigrants reached Israel from the Iron Curtain countries other than the Soviet Union – Poland, Hungary, Rumania, Czechoslovakia and Bulgaria. While emigration was barred from the Soviet Union itself at that time, Moscow did not intervene when other Soviet Bloc states let their own Jews leave, for their own policy reasons. Jewish emigration from the Soviet Union started in 1970, and in the next decade about 150,000 came to Israel. By 1980 nearly 800,000 Jews had been taken in from Europe. From 1948 onward nearly all the Jews left the Arab World, and nearly 600,000 were resettled in Israel.

There has been a steady but small-scale aliyah from Western Europe, the English-speaking world and Latin America. The importance of these immigrants does not lie in their numbers. They have brought with them energy and ideas; professional, industrial and technical skills; investment capital; and a political and social background that have strengthened democracy and the quality of life in Israel. Their presence in the country also provides an essential living link with the Jewish communities in the Western world.

Absorbing this mass of human beings and moulding them into a vigorous new nation has been the dominant purpose of the State since its inception. In the process of immigration and absorption, the age-old dream of the Return has become a reality, and the central place of the Land of Israel in Jewish life has been restored.

הגנה Ship EXODUS 1947

יציאת אירופה ת

The Exodus 1947 *arriving in Haifa after being intercepted and boarded at sea by the Royal Navy.*

The 'Exodus 1947'

The *Exodus 1947* provided the most spectacular episode in the story of *Aliyah Bet*, the 'illegal' immigration from Europe to Palestine.

The ship was actually an old American river-boat of 1,800 tons that had been called the *President Warfield*. It was very high, with four decks and a flat bottom, and had served as a ferryboat across Chesapeake Bay before being bought by the Mossad and sailed across the Atlantic by a Haganah crew of forty, under the command of Captain 'Ike' Aranne, early in 1947. At a port in Italy she was fitted with stacks of bunks to take 4,500 people. That number of refugees were brought from DP camps in Germany to Marseilles, all of them equipped with travel papers for Colombia in South America. The embar-

shadowed by British destroyers. Twenty miles from the Palestine coast, at three a.m., the naval vessels launched a surprise boarding operation. It was fiercely repelled, with a running radio commentary from the Exodus on the battle reaching Palestine and from there going out to the world's press. After two hours, the specially-trained boarding parties had still failed to gain control. At this point it was decided to hand over the ship. It had been battered by the destroyers and was holed on both sides. Of the crew and passengers, three were dead or dying and 200 more were injured.

The ship was escorted into Haifa and the stretcher cases taken to hospital. The rest of the refugees were moved onto three caged vessels, that headed out to sea under the control of British troops. On opening his sealed orders, the Commander discovered that he was not to head for Cyprus as usual but to bring the refugees back to Port-de-Bouc, their port of embarkation.

Furious at the escape of the *Exodus* from Sète, Bevin had obtained the reluctant consent of the French government to dump its passengers back on French soil. The British ambassador in Paris, Duff Cooper, warned against the 'unedifying spectacle' of dragging the refugees off British boats at a French port. The French, he noted, were not concerned with the complexities of the Palestine problem but saw only 'survivors of a persecuted race seeking refuge in their national home'. Bevin was adamant. He would make an example of the *Exodus* and thereby discourage further illegal attempts.

The magnitude of this political blunder became clear at Port-de-Bouc when the refugees refused to land and the French authorities refused to compel them to do so. A French official who came aboard read out a statement that 'those who wish to land of their own free will, will be given asylum on the national soil, where they will enjoy all the liberties which France traditionally bestows on those who fight for human freedom'. Only thirty sick people and

pregnant women went ashore.

For the next three weeks of stalemate the refugees sweltered in the heat of the crowded holds, with their plight getting world coverage. Then orders were received from London that they were to be taken all the way back to Germany. After another month at sea the floating cages reached Hamburg, where their human contents were landed by force and taken to the camps in the British zone of Germany. Within the next few months, most of them had sailed again on other 'illegal' ships and had reached Palestine or the Cyprus detention camps.

The Exodus story dramatized the fact that Britain's Palestine policy was bankrupt. Earlier in 1947, the British government had referred the whole problem to the United Nations, that had appointed the eleven-nation UN Special Committee on Palestine (UNSCOP) to study it. UNSCOP was in Palestine during the *Exodus* affair, and members of the Committee were eye-witnesses to the boat's arrival. The United Nations endorsed UNSCOP's recommendation that the country should be partitioned into independent Jewish and Arab states. Britain terminated the Mandate and withdrew from Palestine by midnight on 14 May 1948. On the same day, the State of Israel was born, and threw open the gates to Jewish immigrants. Amongst the first to come in were those refugees from the *Exodus* who had ended up in Cyprus.

kation took place at nearby Port-de-Bouc. The vessel then moved to the small harbour of Sète, sixty-five miles to the west. Under pressure from the British Foreign Secretary, Ernest Bevin, the French authorities detained the ship at Sète, under armed guard; but it managed to slip away at dawn and manoeuvre itself through the narrow exit channel without a pilot.

At sea the *Exodus* was closely

A reunion in 1971 between an immigrant arriving from the Soviet Union and his sister living in Israel. In the decade from 1969, over 200,000 Jews succeeded in leaving the Soviet Union, and about 150,000 of them went to Israel.

The Renewed Russian Aliyah

While the Jews are officially recognized as a 'nationality' in the Soviet Union, the basic thrust of Soviet policy has been to bring about their assimilation and their ultimate disappearance as a separate community. Their religion, language and culture have been suppressed, and their ties with Jews elsewhere discouraged. Yet the reaction to the emergence of Israel, thirty years after the Russian Revolution, showed that Jewish sentiment remained strong. When Mrs Golda Meir arrived as Israel's first Minister to Moscow in 1948 and went on the Sabbath to the synagogue (usually attended only by a handful of old people), thousands of Jews gathered outside in an emotional mass demonstration of support for the Jewish State, to the dismay of the Russian authorities.

From the Sixties, Soviet Jews in increasing numbers took part in an open struggle for the right to leave. A few were let out to rejoin relatives in Israel. As a rule the applications for

exit permits were rejected, and the applicants penalized by being deprived of their jobs, expelled from universities and other punitive measures. At the same time the Soviet state press, media and publishing-houses carried on a venomous propaganda campaign against Israel and Zionism, with strong anti-semitic overtones.

For the regime, these deterrent efforts proved counter-productive. They increased among many Soviet Jews their sense of alienation from Soviet society, and intensified their urge to identify with Israel and the Jewish people. These sentiments came more strongly to the surface at the time of the Six-Day War of 1967. The plight of Soviet Jewry was dramatized in 1970 by the trial in Leningrad of a group of Jews from Riga, Latvia, accused of planning to escape by hijacking a small plane. The harsh sentences imposed on them provoked an outcry in the world press. From that year larger numbers of Jews were allowed to emigrate to Israel, in the hope that this would dispose of internal and external pres-

sures. That expectation has not been fulfilled. The number of 'refuseniks' (those whose applications were rejected) grew steadily, and included a list of 'prisoners of Zion' – Jews active in the emigration movement who were jailed, put in psychiatric wards or sent to labour camps in Siberia.

The solidarity in Israel and the Western communities with their Russian brethren became more active, vocal and organized. An international Jewish conference in Brussels at the end of 1970 adopted a programme of co-ordinated efforts on behalf of Soviet Jewry. Generally speaking, these efforts have met with the sympathy of Western governments and public opinion, and has thereby had some impact on Soviet policy. Next to support for Israel, no cause has aroused and united the Jewish people to such an extent in recent decades. But the primary factor has been the tenacity and courage of the Russian Jews themselves. The Soviet Union has tried in vain to stifle the revived cry of the biblical Exodus: 'Let my people go!'

Important Events

The Messianic Hope

*c.*132	Bar-Kochba Revolt with messianic overtones.
*c.*1124	David Alroy appears in Kurdistan.
1522	David Reuveni reaches Western Europe.
1525	Shlomo Molcho declares himself a Jew.
1532	Arrest of Reuveni and Molcho.
1648	Shabbetai Zevi proclaims himself the Messiah.
1666	Shabbetai Zevi converts to Islam.

The Zionist Movement

1882	Pinsker's 'Auto-Emancipation'.
	Beginning of BILU settlement in Palestine.
1884	Kattowitz Conference of Chovevei Zion.
1897	First Zionist Congress convened by Herzl.
1917	Balfour Declaration pledges support for Jewish National Home in Palestine.

The Palestine Mandate

1920	British Mandate over Palestine.
1936	Start of Arab Rebellion in Palestine.
	Palestine Commission proposes partition.
1937	Start of 'illegal' Jewish immigration.
1939	Palestine White Paper restricts immigration.
	Start of the Second World War.
1946	Renewal of 'illegal' immigration.
1947	Palestine Question referred to United Nations.
	The 'Exodus 1947'.
	UN partition plan adopted (29 November).

The Ingathering

1948	State of Israel proclaimed.
	Start of mass immigration into Israel.
1970	Immigration started from Soviet Union.

## Chapter Eighteen

The Making of the Museum

Is it possible to portray in a single three-storey building, twenty-five centuries of Jewish wanderings in a hundred lands? That is the challenge successfully met by the Nahum Goldmann Museum of the Jewish Diaspora (in Hebrew Beth Hatefutsoth) opened in May 1978 on the campus of the Tel Aviv University. Using colour, light, sound, movement and bold innovations in museum technology, it presents a rich and profoundly moving panorama of Jewish life in the Dispersion.

The Museum emerged from years of discussion and discarded plans. Two decades ago Dr Nahum Goldmann, then President of both the World Jewish Congress and the World Zionist Organization, proposed the setting-up in Israel of a museum to commemorate the ancient Jewish communities that were destroyed on the European continent in the Nazi Holocaust. It was originally intended to do this on a geographical basis. Each major community wiped out in the Holocaust, such as Poland, Lithuania, Hungary or Germany, would have its own exhibition, recalling its distinctive life and culture. Approaches were made to the *Landsmannschaften* in the United States – associations of Jews based on a common origin in Eastern Europe, from the same city, province or country. They agreed to collect from their members and to participate fully in the enterprise.

It was then pointed out that many other historic Jewish communities had ceased to exist in recent years as a result of the mass exodus from the Arab lands to Israel. For instance, the world's oldest Diaspora in Iraq, going back to biblical Babylonia, was no more; it too had to be commemorated, as did communities like those of Egypt, Libya and Yemen. The scope was widened to cover the entire Jewish Diaspora. Later, however, the regional framework was dropped, as being too restrictive and uneven.

It was next proposed to create an academic research centre that would contain all available documents – written or pictorial, originals or copies – with a bearing on Diaspora life and history. But this concept was also rejected. It would serve the needs of researchers and students but would lack wide popular appeal, and would cut across existing libraries.

Another plan put forward and discarded involved a series of life-

The photographing of the wall frieze in the 14th-century synagogue in Toledo, Spain. The synagogue was turned into a church and is now used as a Jewish historical museum.

size 'environments', each representing a home, a synagogue, the court of a Chassidic rabbi or some other focus of Jewish life.

The protracted debate among the Museum's planners did serve to clarify certain broad principles:

a The Museum should project the Diaspora story in a dramatic and popular form, and thereby serve an educational purpose.

b While martyrdom and persecution were a central theme of Jewish history, the Museum should also bring out the positive and creative aspects of Diaspora experience.

c The Museum should stress the pluralism of Jewish culture, and give due weight to the cultural background of Jews from Moslem lands.

d The presentation should be thematic rather than chronological. The wide dispersion of the Jews made it impossible to tell their story in a strictly 'linear' order.

On the basis of these principles, the Museum's permanent exhibition was divided into six sections:

The Family, based on the life-cycle from birth to death and the annual succession of festive occasions;

The Community showing the infra-structure of Jewish communal life and the extensive self-rule enjoyed by Jews.

Faith, paying particular attention to the synagogue and to religious learning;

Culture, covering a whole variety of sub-themes – the Hebrew and Yiddish languages, education, literature and the arts, the press, and the role of Jews in world civilization;

Among the Nations, reflecting the interaction between Jews and their non-Jewish environment in certain outstanding communities from different periods;

The Return to Zion.

These sections would hold a balance between elements special to individual communities and the basic features common to them all.

The general themes had to be translated into tangible exhibits, and that created a dilemma. An historical museum is normally based on collections of authentic artifacts surviving from the past. For a number of reasons, that basis was not feasible for the Diaspora Museum. Existing buildings and architectural remains could hardly be acquired or transported. Objects of ritual art and of Jewish ethnological interest were scarce and costly, and anyway were represented in the Israel Museum in Jerusalem and Jewish museums elsewhere. Moreover, such objects reflected Jewish life not in its totality but in a fragmentary way; indeed, there were entire regions and periods which could not be represented at all by material remains. The idea of gathering authentic objects was abandoned altogether. Instead, the exhibits would be specially designed and constructed, since the aim was to communicate, not to collect.

The reconstruction approach had its own problems, owing to the paucity of visual clues. For instance, the daily occupations of Jews in 1st-century AD Egypt are depicted in the form of a mural in the contemporary art-style of the period. To paint the mural, the general Egyptian civilization of the period had to be studied to learn how people dressed, what sort of houses they inhabited and what tools they used. Similarly, in making the striking bas-relief of a 5th-century AD Babylonian Talmudic academy, the artist relied on the Persian culture of the time. In reproducing the relief on the Arch of Titus, missing heads and limbs were added without any certainty that they resembled the original ones.

The Museum's concern for accuracy of detail is admirably illustrated in its exhibition of synagogue models. Thousands of photographs and measurements were taken of the synagogues concerned that were still extant in various countries, while documentary research and personal interviews with local Jewish families helped to reconstruct models of some that had been destroyed. Roof-top photographs were obtained in Amsterdam from a chartered helicop-

ter, and in Florence from a fully extended, swaying fire-brigade ladder. In Toledo, Spain, the interior frieze high up around the four walls of a former synagogue was photographed from scaffolding set up each night and removed each morning, as the building is now a museum open to the public. The massive key of the Danan synagogue in Morocco was found under the bed of a ninety-year-old Jewish lady, to whose family the building belonged. The vanished synagogue of Kai Feng-Fu in China had to be reconstructed on the basis of drawings made by an Italian Jesuit missionary in the 18th century.

The materials used in the synagogue models include gold, silver and zinc, plexiglass, chemical fibres, resins, dental cement and special alloys developed for the US space programme.

The Museum's academic research team collected reference materials from all over the world and prepared briefs for the workshops in Israel, Britain and the United States, where the paintings, models, dioramas and sculptured figures were produced. The making of the permanent exhibition took eight years and engaged the talents of hundreds of specialists: Jewish, general and art historians, architects and designers, painters, sculptors and model-makers, audio-visual, electronics, lighting and sound experts, photographers and documentary film producers. The craftsmen included a woman who designed figures for Madame Tussaud's wax museum in London, and technicians from the US space programme.

The complexity of translating abstract concepts into tangible form is shown by the Museum's largest exhibit, the Memorial Column. It symbolizes the theme of Jewish survival and continuing life in the midst of persecution and death. After many experiments, the design accepted was a thirty-foot structure suspended from the ceiling and stretching down for three floors in the interior well of the building. It consists of concentric black cages constructed of aluminium, enclosing a central core made up of 2,400 small light-bulbs, so arranged that the light gleams through the spaces in the grid from all angles. At first the cages were covered with light-refracting paint, but the effect was too bright, and the aspect of darkness too diminished. The dramatic balance between light and dark was achieved when the cages were covered with light-absorbent paint.

A number of sophisticated audio-visual techniques and special features enable the Museum to treat its subject-matter in far greater depth than would otherwise be possible in the limited floor space. Thus:

The Museum collects short documentary films from many countries and has others specially made from its own stills. Each of the three floors has one or two study areas equipped with mini-screens for the projection of selected documentary films on request.

There are 11,500 slides in daily use in the Museum's 'carousels'.

Recorded music, conversation and sound effects accompany a number of the visual exhibits.

An electronic computer is programmed to furnish 'print-outs' on over 3,000 Jewish communities. Eventually a comprehensive Jewish data bank will be computerized.

The Chronosphere is an imaginative feature of the Museum. It is a small circular hall resembling a planetarium, with a seating capacity of fifty. In a half-hour programme the ebb and flow of Jewish migration down the ages is presented in maps and pictures screened onto the curved walls and domed ceiling by thirty-five projectors, with a sound-track commentary.

The Permanent Exhibition is supplemented by temporary exhibitions on specific communities or topics. Among those already held have been:

'Beyond the Golden Door' – a picture history of New York Jewry;
'Image before my Eyes' – Jewish life in Poland, 1864–1939;
'The Ghettoes of Venice and Rome';
'Judaism in Mediaeval Art';
'Kafka and his Prague';

'Moses Mendelssohn and his times';
'The Jews of Manchester, 1780–1945.'

The Museum's photo archive will in due course cover Jewish life everywhere in modern times.

The Museum is wholly bilingual, operating in English and Hebrew. Such texts as exhibit captions, Chronosphere and film commentaries and computer data are in both languages.

The special character of this 'museum that is not a museum' is reflected in the make-up of its staff. A traditional museum relies on curators who are experts in their artistic or scientific fields, and are responsible for acquiring objects and selecting exhibits from those in storage. The Diaspora Museum does not acquire or store objects – hence, it has no curators. Its departments are functional and technical, and their main concern is the maintenance of the Museum's exhibits and equipment. Slides, for instance, become worn and need to be replaced four to five times a year, making a total of some 50,000 slides produced annually.

The Museum's network of educational activities extends through the school system (with the Youth Wing as its focus), the universities, the armed forces, adult education courses, and groups from abroad attending seminars conducted in English, French, Spanish and other languages.

Through the Museum, a new generation of Israelis is absorbing a more positive and knowledgable attitude to Diaspora life, past and present. Tens of thousands of Jews from abroad are gaining a renewed sense of identity with their Jewish roots. Jewish and non-Jewish visitors alike begin to understand how this small, gifted, embattled people was able to outlive its persecutors and retain the creative energies that have enriched the civilization of the world.

Acknowledgments

The author and publisher would like to thank the following museums, collections and private individuals by whose kind permission the illustrations are reproduced. The page numbers of those pictures reproduced in colour are italicized.

The Art Gallery, York 140
Avila Municipal Archives 135
Micha Bar-Am, Tel Aviv 61
Clive Barda, London 222 below right
Bayerische Staatsbibliothek, Munich 72–3
Beth Hatefutsoth 12, *17, 18, 19*, 22–3, 26, 31, *40 below* (David Harris), 62–3, 63, 103, *105 above, 108–9*, 113, 143, 146, *178–9, 183 above*, 194–5, 204, 206–7, 223 above, left and middle, 229, 241, *249–51*, 252, 253, 258 above, 267, *270–1*
Beth Hatefutsoth (Edgar Asher) 8, 15, 16, 28, 28–9, 30, 44–5, 48, 49, 50–1, 51, 53 above and below, 54, 56, 57, 59, 60 left, 66–7, 70, 79, 80, 84, 86, 104, 120–1, 124 above, 124 below, 127, 129, 138–9, 139, 186, 175, 206 right, 231, 235
Beth Hatefutsoth (David Harris) 27, 33, 35, 41, 74–5, 106, 117, 118–19, 131, 132–3, 134, 136–7, 160–1, 177 above, 190–1, 198, 205, 220–1
Bibliothèque Nationale, Paris 132, 151
Bibliothèque Royale, Brussels 142–3, 150
Bildarchiv d'Osterrische Nationalbibliothek, Vienna 222 middle
British Library, London 163
British Museum, London 225 top right
Brooklyn Museum, New York 115
Central Zionist Archives, Jerusalem 268, 274–5

Church of San Ambrogio, Florence 153, 158–9
Collection Viollet, Paris 222 above right
Einhorn Collection, Tel Aviv 206 left
M. H. Gano Collection, Amsterdam 162–3
Government Press Office, Tel Aviv 90, 200–1
Philip Halsman, New York 223 below right
Hermitage Museum, Leningrad 122
Israel Museum, Jerusalem *40 above,* 98 top left, 169, 261 (Teddy Kollek Collection), 263
Israel State Archives, Jerusalem 95
Jack Resnick Collection, New York 83
Jacob Shulman Collection, New York 242 bottom right
Jewish Agency Photo Service, Jerusalem 96, 228
Jewish Chronicle, London 89
Jewish National and University Library, Jerusalem *20 above,* 64, 91, 94, 98 below, 145, 158, 192, 193 left and right, 196–7, 218, 222 top left, middle left and bottom left, 225 top left, 225 below, 226, 240 left, 258 below
John Rylands Library, Manchester *269 below*
Dmitri Kessel *20 below, 39 above and below,* 100, *105 below, 110–11, 112, 177 below, 180–1, 182 above and below, 183 below, 184,* 208, *272*
Kupferstich Kabinet, Munich 148
Leo Baeck Institute, New York 168
Paolo Lombrozo, Venice 156–7
London Library 223 above right
Municipal Archives, Koblenz 154
Municipal Archives, Rome 157
Municipal Museum, Rseszow 209
National Film Board of Canada 248
National Historical Museum, New York 245

National Theatre Habimah Archive 92 below
New York Historical Society 92 above, 234–5, 237, 238–9, 239
Photo Mas, Barcelona 129
Popperfoto, London 240 right, 242 bottom left, 243, 256–7, 265
Public Records Office, London 98 top right
Repartagebild, Stockholm 96–7, 242 above right
Rijksmuseum, Amsterdam 164, 166, 166–7
Royal College of Art, London 223 below left
Sachsische Landesbibliothek, Dresden 141
The Salk Institute (D. K. Miller) 242 top left
Sarajevo National Museum 60 right
Stadtarchiv, Worms 34
Sherry Suris, New York 276
Tel Aviv University Theatre Archives 93
University Library, Bologna *38*
University Library, Wroclaw 152
The Vatican, Bibliotheca Apostolica, Rome *37 above and below*
Weidenfeld and Nicolson Archives 254–5
Winchester Cathedral 149
Yad Vashem Archives, Jerusalem 82–3
Yivo, Institute for Jewish Diaspora, New York 88–9, 212–13, 266

The author and publisher have taken all possible care to trace and acknowledge the source of illustrations. If any errors have accidentally occurred, the publishers will be happy to correct them in future editions, provided that they receive notification.

Index

Page numbers in *italic* refer to the captions to illustrations

B2B Application Integration

Addison-Wesley Information Technology Series
Capers Jones and David S. Linthicum, Consulting Editors

The information technology (IT) industry is in the public eye now more than ever before because of a number of major issues in which software technology and national policies are closely related. As the use of software expands, there is a continuing need for business and software professionals to stay current with the state of the art in software methodologies and technologies. The goal of the Addison-Wesley Information Technology Series is to cover any and all topics that affect the IT community: These books illustrate and explore how information technology can be aligned with business practices to achieve business goals and support business imperatives. Addison-Wesley has created this innovative series to empower you with the benefits of the industry experts' experience.

For more information point your browser to
http://www.awl.com/cseng/series/it/

Sid Adelman, Larissa Terpeluk Moss, *Data Warehouse Project Management*. ISBN: 0-201-61635-1

Wayne Applehans, Alden Globe, and Greg Laugero, *Managing Knowledge: A Practical Web-Based Approach*. ISBN: 0-201-43315-X

Michael H. Brackett, *Data Resource Quality: Turning Bad Habits into Good Practices*. ISBN: 0-201-71306-3

James Craig and Dawn Jutla, *e-Business Readiness: A Customer-Focused Framework* ISBN: 0-201-71006-4

Gregory C. Dennis and James R. Rubin, *Mission-Critical Java™ Project Management: Business Strategies, Applications, and Development*. ISBN: 0-201-32573-X

Kevin Dick, *XML: A Manager's Guide*. ISBN: 0-201-43335-4

Jill Dyché, *e-Data: Turning Data into Information with Data Warehousing*. ISBN: 0-201-65780-5

Dr. Nick V. Flor, *Web Business Engineering: Using Offline Activites to Drive Internet Strategies*. ISBN: 0-201-60468-X

David Garmus and David Herron, *Function Point Analysis: Measurement Practices for Successful Software Projects*. ISBN: 0-201-69944-3

Capers Jones, *Software Assessments, Benchmarks, and Best Practices*. ISBN: 0-201-48542-7

Capers Jones, *The Year 2000 Software Problem: Quantifying the Costs and Assessing the Consequences*. ISBN: 0-201-30964-5

Ravi Kalakota and Marcia Robinson, *e-Business 2.0: Roadmap for Success* ISBN: 0-201-72165-1

David S. Linthicum, *B2B Application Integration: e-Business-Enable Your Enterprise* ISBN: 0-201-70936-8

Sergio Lozinsky, *Enterprise-Wide Software Solutions: Integration Strategies and Practices*. ISBN: 0-201-30971-8

Patrick O'Beirne, *Managing the Euro in Information Systems: Strategies for Successful Changeover*. ISBN: 0-201-60482-5

Mai-lan Tomsen, *Killer Content: Strategies for Web Content and E-Commerce*. ISBN: 0-201-65786-4

Bill Wiley, *Essential System Requirements: A Practical Guide to Event-Driven Methods*. ISBN: 0-201-61606-8

Ralph R. Young, *Effective Requirements Practices*. ISBN: 0-201-70912-0

Bill Zoellick, *Web Engagement: Connecting to Customers in e-Business*. ISBN: 0-201-65766-X

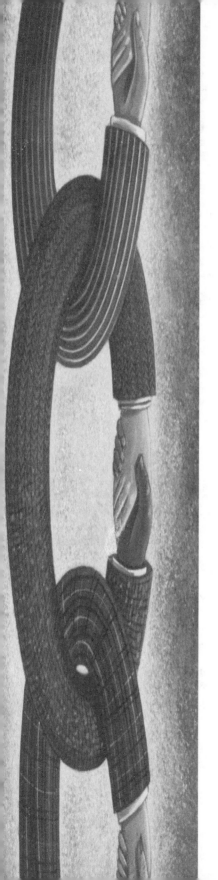

B2B Application Integration

e-Business–Enable Your Enterprise

David S. Linthicum

Addison-Wesley

Boston • San Francisco • New York • Toronto • Montreal
London • Munich • Paris • Madrid
Capetown • Sydney • Tokyo • Singapore • Mexico City

The publisher offers discounts on this book when ordered in quantity for special sales. For more information, please contact:

Pearson Education Corporate Sales Division
One Lake Street
Upper Saddle River, NJ 07458
(800) 382-3419
corpsales@pearsontechgroup.com

Visit AW on the Web: www.awl.com/cseng/

Library of Congress Cataloging-in-Publication Data
Linthicum, David S.
    B2B application integration : e-business–enable your enterprise /
    David S. Linthicum.
        p.   cm.—(Addison-Wesley information technology series)
    Includes bibliographical references and index.
    ISBN 0-201-70936-8
    1. Application software—Development.   2. Business enterprise—Data
processing.   3. Electronic commerce.   I. Title: Business to business application
integration.   II. Title.   III. Series.
    QA76.76.A65 L53 2000
    658'.05—dc21   00-048517

ISBN 0-201-70936-8
Text printed on recycled paper
1 2 3 4 5 6 7 8 9 10 — CRS — 0403020100
First printing, December 2000

For my mom and dad, Ronald and Joan Linthicum

Contents

PART II Types of B2B Application Integration

CHAPTER 5   PORTAL-ORIENTED B2B APPLICATION INTEGRATION   91

CHAPTER 6   PROCESS INTEGRATION–ORIENTED B2B APPLICATION INTEGRATION   105

PART III e-Business Integration Technology

PART IV   B2B Application Integration Standards

Preface

Business as usual? Does anyone remember what that phrase even means anymore? About the only thing certain about "business as usual" is that it is inadequate to survive in the new, technology-driven business environment. It just doesn't get the job done anymore. If IT organizations fail to transform and enable themselves to compete in the new Internet economy, they will find themselves among the "left-behinds," wondering what in the world hit them. Gartner Group has proclaimed that "e-commerce applications and technology have been elevated to 'core competency' status, and their success or failure will determine an enterprise's viability."

It is a whole new business world out there. It is dynamic and fluid. It is relentless. And it is dangerous. The thing that makes this new world so challenging to IT organizations is that the Internet e-Business model no longer exists solely in a technology domain. The new e-Business model is now being shaped and driven by the business units; technology has been reduced to an enabling role.

The importance of the Internet is mushrooming before our eyes. Forrester Research forecasts that the e-Business market will reach $1.3 trillion in only three more years. According to the IDC, businesses will spend $10 billion over the next five years to create the infrastructure that will support this e-Business market. In its research, Forrester found that almost half of the Fortune 500 executives surveyed had already opened up three or more corporate data systems to their business partners—and that 60 percent expected that number to grow threefold or more by 2001. Gartner predicts that by year-end 2002, more than 50 percent of large enterprises will have implemented at least one large-scale, extended-enterprise

application to support multiple trading partners or Web-based external access to applications.

Woe be to the executive who tarries!

Determined to add competitive advantages to their businesses, savvy IT executives are enlarging their roles to provide customized business information applications and e-Business systems. All other aspects of their businesses, including traditional development for the enterprise, will be outsourced, purchased via packaged applications, or managed in the most efficient, cost- and time-balanced manner. This coming business reality requires a new type of integration technology—a technology that is dependent on intelligent, flexible middleware layers that "glue" all of these disparate applications and processes together.

The purpose of this book is to describe to you just how those middleware layers will function to hold everything together—and allow your business to succeed in the new e-Business world.

Extending Enterprise Application Integration

The extended enterprise consists of automatic, electronic interfaces that link the computer systems of the ultimate selling business, the partners that finance or manage the transaction, external suppliers, carriers, and support operations. In turn, these external partners connect with a multitude of internal enterprise systems that support customer service, sales, manufacturing, procurement, logistics, accounting, human resources, and corporate finance.

The technology process of the extended enterprise is sometimes described in terms of "long transactions"—traditional purchases that are electronically and automatically linked across the supply, order, and financing chain in one continuous set of connected transactions. When an order is placed, all affected systems (supply replenishment, credit checks, financial accounting, sales reporting, feedback from marketing campaigns, and so on) are provided with real-time or near real-time updates so that the implications of the sale are recognized and acted upon.

e-Business depends on many of the same concepts and approaches that I outlined in my last book, *Enterprise Application Integration*. B2B application integration is a direct outgrowth of Enterprise Application Integration (EAI), reusing many of the same approaches and technologies. However, e-Business challenges all the existing rules, since both approaches and technology must morph around this new, and more complex, problem domain.

Many of the lessons we learned in solving EAI problems will aid us in finding a solution set for B2B application integration. However, some of the approaches to application integration that occur within a firewall will be nontransferable to B2B application integration. Moreover, we need to create new concepts and technologies that are unique to moving information between partner organizations. As we saw with EAI, current technologies are limited, and users must learn to pick and choose wisely, bypassing the hype in order to determine which technology is best for their needs.

Why This Book?

Although many books on the market address the high-level issues of e-Business, currently no other book details how to create B2B application integration solutions to move information and processes between organizations in real time. It doesn't take a genius to declare that applications should share information between organizations. Such declarations amount to little more than words. Accomplishing the task is something else again—action.

This book covers all aspects of B2B application integration, from concepts to technology. When you read it, you will understand the next level of e-Business technology. In addition to gaining the ability to apply this technology appropriately, you will clearly understand the enabling technology and standards, such as message brokers, application servers, XML, RosettaNet, BizTalk, and EDI. Whenever possible, I have taken advantage of case studies to make these concepts more accessible to you, and you'll also find case studies in the appendixes.

Ultimately, our task is to create the right e-Business strategy while keeping in mind the business drivers. After that, we must consider the architecture. Finally, we must consider the availability of various tactical solutions utilizing technology and techniques.

As we approach a real-time economy, the necessity of B2B application integration becomes more and more obvious. Even so, bridging the gap from "business as usual" to the benefits of the new e-Business is absolutely daunting for most organizations. The solutions will not come about overnight. It will take years of planning, analyzing, developing, and testing before we are able to take that first substantial step closer to e-Business nirvana.

Reading this book is the best way to begin mapping out your organization's path to B2B application integration success.

Acknowledgments

First and foremost, I want to thank Sherry Matincheck, my executive assistant. Sherry took on most of the heavy lifting in creating this book, including editing, gathering, and sending chapters and graphics, and learning how to deal with a new type-A boss.

Also, I can't forget Ursula Kappert, my last executive assistant, who retired early in 2000 but began this process for me. We wish her all the best in retirement.

I would also like to thank Steve Johnson, my graphics guy, who was able to take my abstract, modern art–like chicken scratches and turn them into understandable and enjoyable images. Thanks goes to David Woolfe, who did some of the editing work. Credit also needs to go to Mary O'Brien and Mariann Kourafas of Addison-Wesley, who had faith in this book and allowed me to bring it to market.

Others who inspired the B2B thought process include David Smiley, Director of Product Strategy at SAGA, who did some of the research for the process integration content. Thanks also goes to Gary Waymire and Aaron Press, who provided some of the B2B technology research.

I can't leave out the SAGA Software executive team, including Dan Gillis, the CEO, for the encouragement to take on and complete this project.

PART I

Introduction

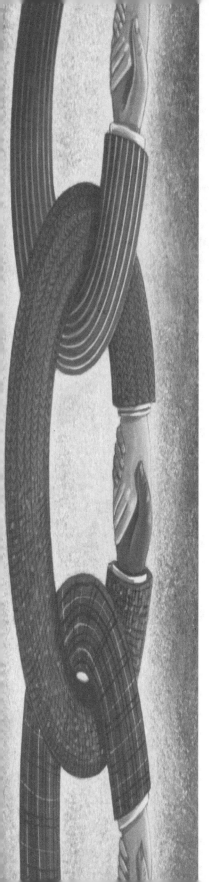

Defining B2B
Application Integration

We are moving inexorably toward an event-driven economy, an economy where demand realized translates into demand satisfied—in a matter of nanoseconds. Demand realized is accomplished by extending the capabilities and reach of an existing IT infrastructure so that enterprise applications, both inter- and intra-enterprise, are bound by a business event–driven paradigm. In the process, expectations about business methods must be redefined. Either businesses are getting on board and automating their common business events, inter- and intra-organization, or they are preparing to exit their market. There is no in-between. This is the fundamental reality of e-Business.

This new event-driven economy has several defining characteristics.

First and foremost, it is almost instantaneous. All supplying systems are instantly aware of demand, and they are able to react to that demand instantaneously. Likewise, all demanding systems are instantaneously aware of supply capability and are able to respond accordingly.

Second, all participating systems are able to communicate in any direction, with any system, automatically, and in real time. For example, when we create an order, which in turn creates an order event, a supplier's system may respond to that event with a "delay status" because of a material shortage. The order system would learn about the delay instantaneously and

just as instantly adjust the expected delivery time. As a result, customers (or more likely the customers' systems) are able to react to dynamic business realities in real time, perhaps even changing their order to work around the shortage automatically.

The benefit of this real-time, event-driven economy is obvious to anyone who has ever been frustrated when attempting to order an item from a retailer, either on the phone or online, only to discover that the retailer is incapable of determining when that item can ship. Few things are as discouraging as ordering a new car and being given a delivery date—plus or minus a month! Such a situation would be inconceivable in e-Business.

In an event-driven economy, every system affects every other system in real time. The business advantages of this are obvious: no missed delivery dates because of last-minute inventory shortages, shortages that result in valuable merchandise sitting idly on very expensive shelves. No scheduling conflicts on the plant floor because of under- or over-estimated demand. No human error or having to deal with reams and reams of paper.

Third, systems are bound at both the data and process levels. Exchanging information is not enough. Business rules, processes, and sequences need to be shared as well, ensuring that the data is processed properly and that common integrity constraints are enforced. A common business model needs to determine the path and order of each business event. For instance, the process of building, selling, and shipping a product may span as many as ten different systems housed in three different companies. A common process model needs to span the business systems, defining the properties of a business event, including the order, behavior, and characteristics of information moving from application to application, and it has to deal with concepts such as common agreements as well as private and public processes.

Finally, all relevant information existing in any participating system is accessible by any other participating system. Any information supporting any event or transaction is always available to anyone anywhere in the participating systems.

Sounds good, doesn't it? Now, all that remains is the simple question, How does your organization participate in this event-driven economy? As with most things of genuine value, the foundation must be understanding, planning, and integrating—the very things this book will explain in detail. Now is the time to begin your journey toward real-time business, something that will revolutionize your organization and every other organization that is prepared to commit to the new, challenging, exciting, and profitable economic realities that await us all.

e-Business Means Something (Different) to Everybody

The term e-Business means different things to different people and companies. To some it means Web-enabled selling. To others it means middleware. Most hold that e-Business is the next generation of Internet-enabled supply chain integration that picks up where EDI left off.

So, who's right?

No one. Everyone. The fact is, there is no clear, agreed-upon definition of e-Business. You only need to watch the IBM TV commercials to recognize this lack of consensus. "e-Business" has joined the ranks of those other popular buzzwords, such as "object-oriented," "client/server," and "Web-enablement." Everyone wants a piece of whatever it is that these terms suggest, even if few have any idea what they might actually mean. As always, there are those who crave the pure joy that comes along with buying into the current hype.

For those more determined to keep their feet firmly rooted on *terra firma,* we can say with certainty that whatever else e-Business means, it means using innovative technology to build global relationships and commerce. As such, it is the greatest opportunity and/or threat to existing business models since the industrial revolution. e-Business, that amorphous, ambiguously defined concept, is the force that is driving the fundamental reconfiguration of every existing industry.

We can also say with certainty that e-Business means more than simply doing business on the Internet. It is more than a more efficient variant of business as usual. e-Business affects nearly every aspect of business. Thanks to e-Business, customers demand more choice and convenience, brands play a bigger role, costs are dramatically lowered, and competition is bursting forth from every direction.

The finance community affords a clear example of these trends and benefits. Financial institutions are now clearing checks, trades, and loans in just minutes, not days. Manufacturing organizations are automating their supply chains in order to become more competitive and profitable.

As compelling as e-Business is as a business term, the reality is that it also refers to a cultural revolution that is taking place before our very

continued

---

e-Business Means Something (Different) to Everybody (*continued*)

eyes. A pleasant revolution for the most part. The explosive growth of the Internet, the proliferation of electronic commerce, sales force automation, call centers, and mobile computing, have all conspired to change the very fabric of business forever. Rather than *caveat emptor*, let the customer beware, we live at a time when the customer is becoming the single most powerful force in commerce. Relationships are changing, competition is increasing, distribution channels are exploding, and start-ups are bringing established giants to their knees.

At the risk of being redundant, we'll state it again: The value of e-Business is clear. How to make it all happen in the real world is much less clear. Bringing businesses together demands a very different technology than the one in place today. The current technology is developer-oriented. We need to advance to a business-oriented focus. We need to understand the wide range of design patterns that exist at the points of integration, and we need to understand the many scenarios for information exchange between systems, most of which may not even be under our direct control. Building e-Business systems is the biggest challenge we've faced since the first-generation mainframe systems were brought online.

Moving to e-Business

The event-driven economy is the next destination for e-Business, providing us with the ability to react instantaneously to internal or external events in order to meet consumer demand. It is also a mechanism to do business, dare we say it, "at the speed of thought."

Few examples illuminate the difference between the conventional method of doing business and e-Business more clearly than the purchase of a new car. Currently, a customer walks into an automobile dealership and orders a car. That order is then placed with the automobile manufacturer. The manufacturer in turn orders the parts and creates the car, while the suppliers order raw materials to create the parts. Paper purchase orders are sent to the suppliers, who ship the materials and send paper invoices to request payment. Only then, when all the

parts are received from the suppliers, can the car be manufactured and sent to the dealer—resulting in even more paper.

This process typically takes months, not weeks. It should only take days.

Of course, most "supply chains," such as the one described in our car procurement example, are at least partially automated these days. Many owners of supply chains already use enabling technologies such as Electronic Data Interchange (EDI) to share information, such as order and payment data.

Being partially automated is not enough. We need to think more comprehensively about how we capture and react to events. We need to recognize that all components of the supply chain affect the supply chain itself. For example, when that customer walks into our car dealership and orders a car, or when that customer orders a car via the Internet, that action is a business event that is captured. Our system must react to this event by performing several tasks instantaneously: logging the event, processing the rules bound to such an event, and moving information to other interested systems or humans.

The event must be logged so that it won't be forgotten should there be a failure as it is being processed. We need to process rules bound to the event, such as price limits and credit requirements. The internal (e.g., inventory) systems and external (supplier) systems must be informed of the event. Finally, the information created by this event, in this example customer and car configuration information, must move forward to the appropriate systems. Typically, this should be a second process, or subprocess.

What is of note here is that all relevant systems are notified of the event and are supplied with all appropriate information, in real time, so that they can in turn instantly react to the event (see Figure 1.1). In our car purchase example, the sales event captured by our manufacturer's system generates an instant requirement for parts to create the car. In turn, this information triggers a cascading series of additional events within systems owned by the suppliers, events such as notifying a supplier of the raw materials required to build the parts. A single, primary event could thus trigger as many as several hundred other events, which in turn could trigger several thousand more events. It is exactly this chain reaction of events, events that serve a business need, that we are hoping to create.

Remember, this event-driven supply chain scenario is an instantaneous process. Within seconds of the initial order, the suppliers are processing requests for the raw materials, the factory floor is scheduling workers, and the logistics group is assigning resources in order to ship a car to a particular dealer. There may be hundreds of systems involved with the sale, creation, and movement of

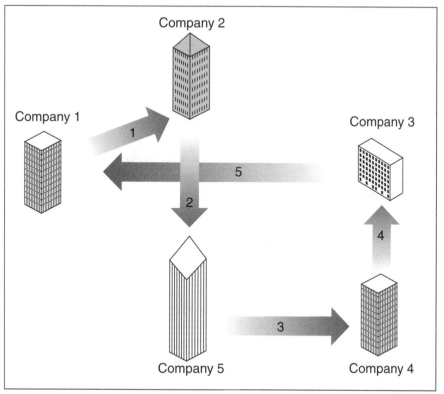

Figure 1.1   Example of an event-driven supply chain

this car, all exchanging event information simultaneously. Of equal relevance is that all systems participating in the event will be notified instantly should there be any change along the supply chain—that is, if demand changes (e.g., car sales go down) or if there is a parts shortage. Instantaneous notification is a two-way street, from orders to suppliers, from suppliers to orders.

As we learn more about integrating applications, the event-driven economy will become more of a reality. Today, systems are bound together by primitive connections, where batch and file transfers serve as the primary integration mechanisms. However, with the marriage of the Internet and more advanced middleware solutions, it won't be long before small versions of the event-driven economy are running, typically around supply chains.

This will only be the beginning. When businesses realize that this method of "speed of light" business processes means reduced costs and a huge competitive advantage, we will see the explosive growth of the event-driven economy and B2B

application integration. The value of B2B application integration, or the binding of systems in support of the event-driven economy, is the topic of this book.

Using B2B Application Integration

If it is fair to assume that at some point we would like to proceed to an event-driven economy, then we need to embrace the concepts, approaches, and technology of B2B application integration. In doing so, we will once again find ourselves having to define e-Business.

As corporate dependence on technology has grown more complex and far reaching, the need for a method of integrating disparate applications between enterprises into a unified set of business processes in support of B2B e-Business has emerged as a priority. After years of creating islands of automation within each company, users and business managers are demanding that seamless bridges now be built to join these islands together, thereby allowing commerce to proceed in real time. In short, they are demanding that ways be found to bind these applications into unified cross-enterprise e-Business applications. The development of B2B application integration allows many of the enterprise applications that exist today to share both processes and data. Thus, it allows us to finally answer the demand for real-time, inter-company application integration in support of e-Business.

Interest in B2B application integration is driven by a number of factors. As the pressures of the competitive business environment move IT management to shorter application life cycles, financial prudence demands that IT managers learn to leverage existing databases and application services rather than re-create the same business processes and data repositories over and over. Ultimately, it is this financial prudence, along with the opportunity for profit, that fuels the interest in B2B application integration. The integration of applications saves precious development dollars while creating a competitive edge for those corporations that share application information either internally or with external trading partners (B2B).

Currently, the vast majority of corporations use several generations of systems that rely on a broad range of enabling technologies, technologies that have been developed over many years. Mainframes, UNIX servers, NT servers, and even proprietary platforms whose names have long been forgotten, constitute the technological base for most enterprises. These technologies, new and old, all provide some value to the enterprise, but their value diminishes if they are unable to leverage other enterprise systems that exist within other trading partners.

The case for B2B application integration is clear and easy to define. Accomplishing B2B application integration, however, is not.

What's B2B Application Integration?

So, if B2B application integration is the solution, what exactly is it? Unlike so many other buzzwords, B2B application integration is not hype dreamed up by the press and analyst community. It is, at its foundation, the mechanisms and approaches to allow partner organizations, such as suppliers and consumers, to share information in support of common business events. In short, B2B application integration is the controlled sharing of data and business processes among any connected applications and data sources, intra- or inter-company.

The challenge of B2B application integration is to be able to share data and processes without requiring sweeping changes to the applications or data structures. Unless we are able to create a method of accomplishing this integration, B2B application integration will fail to be either functional or cost-effective.

When we consider the requirements of e-Business, we must look to leverage all existing systems and bind them, within or between enterprises, to support any and all business requirements. If Company A has a sales order entry system that provides a system for recording sales, then Company B, a parts supplier, must have a parts system that is instantly integrated with Company A's sales system. Otherwise, in order to receive the parts required to produce the product sold, information about the sales must be rekeyed into the manufacturing system, which in turn produces several paper purchase orders to obtain the proper parts for the parts supplier.

Currently, Company A and Company B operate with a combination of manual and automated processes that may require days before the pieces are in place to allow the product to be manufactured. This excessive time results directly from a lack of real-time integration between all of the information systems that participate in the business event.

In order to address this problem, organizations generally move to integrate systems within their enterprise, such as the sales order entry system or the manufacturing system, as in our earlier example. However, such a "solution" only addresses a piece of the puzzle. Unless the parts-supplier systems (Company B) are tightly integrated with the sales order entry systems (Company A), the time between the order and the delivery of the product will continue to be excessive.

A business transaction takes at least as long as the slowest system in the loop. It is easy to imagine a well-integrated set of systems within an organization,

systems that are able to share information in real time. However, unless that organization's trading partners also participate in the real-time exchange of information (B2B integration), the trading partner's latency will limit the efficiency of the organization. As a result, competitiveness and profitability will suffer.

B2B application integration extends EAI to include access to perfect information on demand to outside trading partners, enabling them to react instantly to a business event. To play off our previous scenario, integrating all information services means that an entry in the sales order entry system would automatically and instantaneously trigger events in the manufacturing systems, events that would in turn trigger events at all relevant trading partners, including the parts supplier (see Figure 1.2).

Leveraging Your Assets

Fundamentally, B2B application integration is about leveraging existing systems and databases (yours or your trading partners') by allowing them to communicate seamlessly in support of a business purpose. We want to integrate your current systems and avoid having to create new applications. As we will see, however, integrating systems that were typically built without integration in mind can be something of challenge.

Even as the technology supporting your applications has aged, the value of the applications to your enterprise likely remains fresh. Indeed, your "ancient" technology has probably remained critical to the workings of your enterprise. Therefore, access to those systems remains valuable to you and to your trading partners as well.

Unfortunately, many of these business-critical systems are nearly impossible to adapt so that they are able to communicate and share information with other systems. There is, of course, the option of simply replacing these older systems. However, the cost of doing so is generally prohibitive. In any case, the decision to do so may very well be beyond your direct control.

Packaged applications such as SAP, Oracle Financials, and PeopleSoft—which are natural stovepipes themselves—have only compounded the problem. Sharing information among these systems is particularly difficult because many of them were designed not to access anything outside their proprietary technology.

Applying Technology

If B2B application integration lays bare the problem, then traditional middleware seeks to reveal the solution—sort of. Unfortunately, traditional middleware only

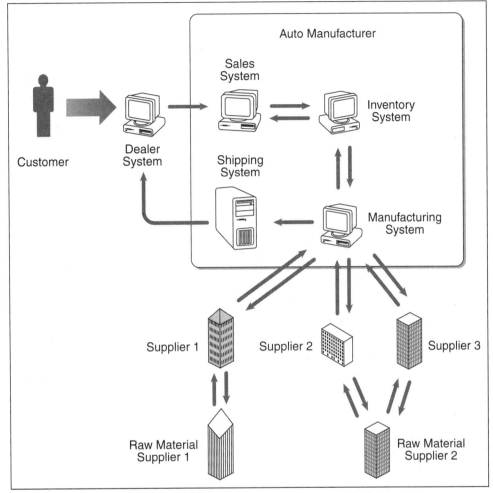

Figure 1.2   Using B2B application integration to leverage the value of all systems in a trading community

addresses the B2B application integration problem in a limited manner, primarily because traditional middleware was built to integrate applications within an enterprise and does not take into account the special needs of B2B integration.

The primary limitation is that the middleware that uses message queuing or remote procedure calls (RPCs) only provides point-to-point solutions—that is, a link between system A and system B. Unfortunately, any attempt to link additional systems rapidly deteriorates into a complex tangle of middleware

links, both intra- and inter-company (see Figure 1.3). Even more troubling is that traditional middleware requires significant alterations to both the source and target systems, embedding the middleware layer into the application or data store. Changing the source and target systems to support e-Business may be out of the question, because an organization rarely controls the systems of its trading partners.

For example, in attempting to integrate a custom accounting system running on Windows 2000 with a custom inventory control system running on a mainframe within another company, you may select a message-queuing middleware product. Such a middleware product will allow both systems to share information—over the Internet, for example. However, because a point-to-point middleware layer only provides a program interface, you generally have to alter the source system to make it understandable to the target system. This is costly and sometimes risky. Unfortunately, it is also sometimes impossible.

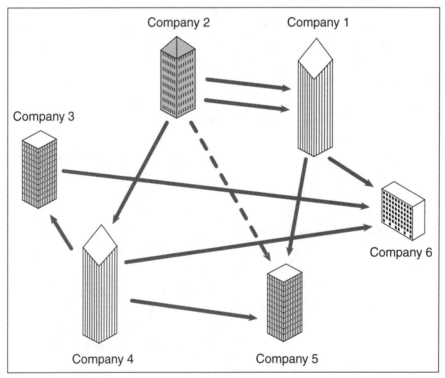

Figure 1.3   Point-to-point integration solutions are common but dysfunctional for B2B application integration.

As we use the same, or similar, technology to integrate other applications inside or between companies, the number of point-to-point solutions must grow to accommodate the increased information flow between various systems. The end result is a complex and confusing maze of software pipes running in and out of existing enterprise systems without any central control or management. As a consequence, this scenario results in a limited ability to react to change and a strategic value that is minimal at best.

This scenario is complicated by the demand on IT managers to perform integration projects inside fluid environments, using rapidly advancing technology.

As if these structural and strategic limitations weren't enough, the economics of traditional middleware have placed B2B application integration beyond the reach of most organizations. According to the Aberdeen Group, even a simple, dual-application linking is financially daunting, running as high as $10 million. Given these significant limitations, it follows that B2B application integration demands a very different method of application integration from one that relies on traditional middleware solutions.

The requirement of B2B application integration creates its own set of integration-level application semantics. Stated another way, B2B application integration creates a common way for both business processes and data to speak to one another across applications and between linked organizations. Although the problem of inter-process and inter-data communication is an old one, we approach it with a new set of technologies, technologies designed specifically for B2B application integration.

Keeping all this in mind, we can focus on the following differences between traditional approaches and the vision of B2B application integration:

- B2B application integration focuses on the integration of both business-level processes and data between organizations. The traditional middleware approach was data-oriented and was typically a simple, intra-company application-to-application solution.
- B2B application integration includes the notion of reuse in addition to distribution of business processes and data between several linked enterprises.
- B2B application integration is an application-to-application concept, always functioning in near real time and typically at the back-end with limited end-user influence.
- B2B application integration allows users who understand very little about the details of the applications to integrate the applications.

- B2B application integration works on the notion of common agreements between trading organizations and supports those agreements as information is exchanged between them.
- B2B application integration assumes that most source and target systems cannot be altered to support B2B application integration, thus the points of integration must be nonintrusive.
- B2B application integration takes into account the differences between integrating applications within and between enterprises, and supports a single process model that spans both.
- B2B application integration must take advantage of advanced security standards to ensure that information moving between companies is not visible to others on the public networks.

Making the Business Case for B2B Application Integration

We have already noted that the business environment no longer supports using technology for technology's sake alone. To justify its expense, a technology must demonstrate its usefulness. The technology supporting B2B application integration is no exception. Although the case for B2B application integration is clear to most people familiar with the technical aspects of this discussion, it might not be as clear to others who also need to understand its value. For example, will implementing B2B application integration between several enterprises provide a return worthy of the investment? If it will, how long will it be before the return is realized? Is B2B application integration a short-term or long-term proposition? Perhaps most important, what are the methods that best measure success?

In establishing an argument for B2B application integration, we should understand a number of things. First, implementing B2B application integration requires that at least one person in the organization thoroughly understand the business processes in the enterprise and in the enterprises of partner organizations. This knowledge determines the degree of integration necessary to optimize those business processes. Although methodologies and procedures exist that can be applied to the task, most competent managers understand the degree of value when applying B2B application integration without over-analyzing this information.

Not all organizations are equal. Some organizations will benefit more than others from B2B application integration. Some organizations clearly require a B2B application integration initiative, while others might find little value in implementing B2B application integration within their enterprises. Although it may be

possible to develop a common-sense method to evaluate the potential success of B2B application integration, the reality is that "success" must be defined on a case-by-case basis to account for the many factors that exist in any given e-Business problem domain. Unfortunately, there is no broad-based definition of B2B application integration success. Success must be measured "one enterprise at a time."

To evaluate the potential value of B2B application integration to your enterprise, you must establish a set of measures that define success for your organization. You can accomplish this by examining and measuring the current state of the enterprise. With this baseline, consider your goals and the effort that will be required for you to realize those goals. For example, if increasing sales is one of your goals, sharing inventory information with the sales order-processing system and the parts-supplier systems of your trading partners may help you realize your goal. Even so, this integration effort will have minimal value without

---

EAI Meets e-Business

At this point, you may be confused as you try to understand the differences between EAI and B2B application integration. At first glance, these differences *are* confusing. In a real sense, they share many of the same approaches and technologies. This book bears that out.

EAI typically deals with the integration of applications and data sources within an enterprise to solve a local problem. In contrast, B2B application integration is the integration of systems between organizations to support any business requirement, such as sharing information with trading partners (see Figure 1.4). Although EAI and e-Business exist in different problem domains, the technology and approaches applied to both EAI and e-Business solutions are similar. For example, both may employ middleware solutions, such as message brokers, to exchange information between various systems. Additionally, approaches to integrating systems can be very much the same. Within most e-Business problem domains, EAI solutions should come before B2B application integration. Logic suggests that you must be able to integrate your internal information systems before they can be externalized to foreign systems residing within your trading partners. EAI and e-Business are clearly integrated concepts that leverage much for each other.

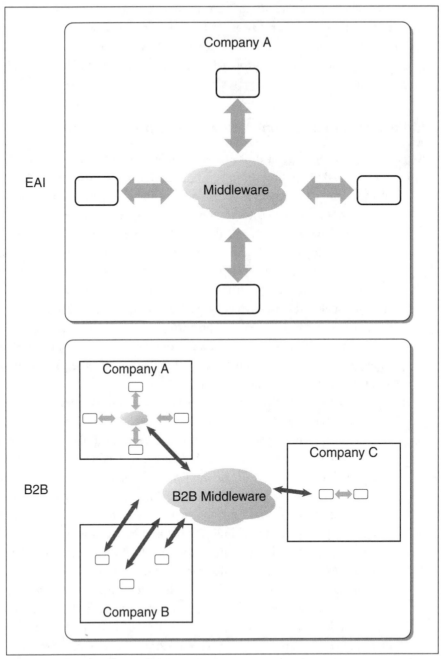

Figure 1.4 EAI and B2B application integration differ in both problem domains and approaches.

a concurrent and significant gain in user productivity or a reduction in error rate. In order to accurately assess the potential benefits of B2B application integration to your organization, you must assess both user productivity and error reduction. Only then can you determine the potential impact of B2B application integration on your enterprise's bottom line.

Middleware and B2B Application Integration

We will devote a great deal of our attention to middleware technology. In the context of B2B application integration, middleware is used as a simple mechanism to move information and shared business logic between applications. In short, it is the underlying technology of B2B application integration.

As we have previously noted, application integration, using a broad range of connection technology, has existed for years. In the past, application integration was low-level play, with developers working at the network protocol layer or just above, before advancing to true middleware solutions, such as RPCs, MOM, and transactional middleware (see Figure 1.5). Now, the next generation of middleware has arrived, with new categories such as message brokers, B2Bi servers, application servers, distributed objects, and intelligent agents. It is reasonable to expect more middleware and middleware categories to emerge as interest in B2B application integration grows.

Middleware is essential in that it hides the complexities of the underlying operating system and network in order to facilitate the integration of various systems in the enterprise. In most cases, developers deal with an API on each system. The middleware is responsible for passing information through the different systems on behalf of the application. These APIs are general-purpose, data-movement or process-invocation mechanisms. In most cases, they do not know the applications and databases they are tying together. Traditionally, developers have had to create the links for the middleware. However, we are moving rapidly to a "plug-and-play" solution set in which the middleware will integrate applications intelligently, with little or no programming.

Middleware provides developers with an accessible way to integrate external resources using a common set of application services. These external resources may include a database server, a queue, a 3270 terminal, Enterprise Resource Planning (ERP) applications, a custom API, or access to real-time information. In the world of distributed computing, middleware provides a means to connect clients to servers, clients to clients, and servers to servers without the need to navigate through many operating systems, networks, or resource server layers.

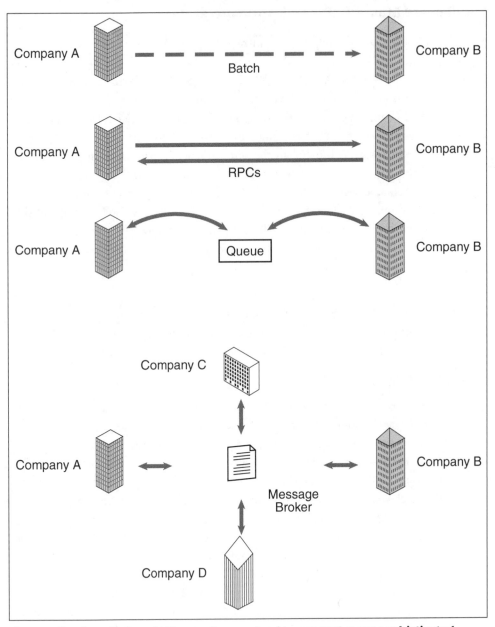

Figure 1.5 Over time, middleware has evolved to support more sophisticated solutions.

Middleware Makes B2B Application Integration

Middleware, once only for use intra-enterprise, has now become an enabling method for B2B application integration. Most major middleware vendors, including BEA, SAGA Software, IBM, NEON, Tibco, and even Sun, are reworking their products to address B2B application integration. It seems as if every vendor that can connect application A to application B is positioning itself to be able to claim dominance in the emerging e-Business marketplace.

Middleware is moving in the direction of e-Business. In many cases, this amounts to little more than "teaching an old dog a new trick." We are learning that the same technology that binds applications within enterprises can bind applications between enterprises as well. However, we are also learning that simply redirecting traditional middleware toward the new B2B problem domain is not going to be sufficient by itself to do the trick. Indeed, middleware is retooling for B2B, adding new features such as:

- Support for inter- and intra-process integration
- Support for B2B standards, including RosettaNet, ebXML, and EDI
- Support for Internet-enabled information exchange
- Support for advanced security models

Approaching e-Business

There is a certain bemusement that accompanies watching traditional and new middleware vendors approach e-Business. Each clearly believes that its technology represents the best approach to providing customers with the "most" of something—whether that something is flexibility, scalability, reliability, usability, and so on. Although "the best approach" is not always easy to assess, it is clear that each vendor attacks the e-Business problem in its own special way.

Although it's difficult to pigeonhole the e-Business approaches that middleware vendors are taking, we can create some general categories. These categories include business rules integration, information integration, process integration, and collaboration (see Figure 1.6).

Business rules integration refers to the binding of application logic between two or more e-Business partners. This means that the composite applications that exist are accessible to all interested parties. As a result, the exchange of both information and business rules is fully automated.

Although all vendors seem to claim that they provide the infrastructure for sharing rules and data, the application server and distributed object vendors

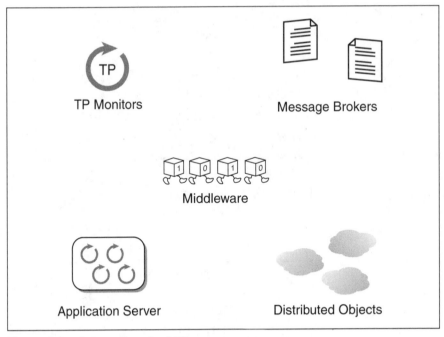

Figure 1.6   Categories of middleware

actually provide clear business rules integration approaches. They allow developers to rehost, or expose, existing rules or methods to other applications that may need them to support a virtual e-Business system. For example, many banks have established the Common Object Request Broker Architecture (CORBA) as a standard mechanism to share application services both within and between banks.

The **information integration** approach to e-Business enablement operates at a slightly lower level than business rules integration. It provides a platform for exchanging relevant business data in order to support e-Business initiatives—for example, the exchange of order and invoice data with a customer and vendor (see Figure 1.7).

Information integration is relatively inexpensive and generally does not require many changes to the participating systems. As such, it is often the first step with most e-Business projects. Message brokers, data replication engines, and data migration engines all take the information integration approach. The Extensible Markup Language (XML), which provides a common information exchange format for many incompatible applications and data sources, has been providing the most value in this context.

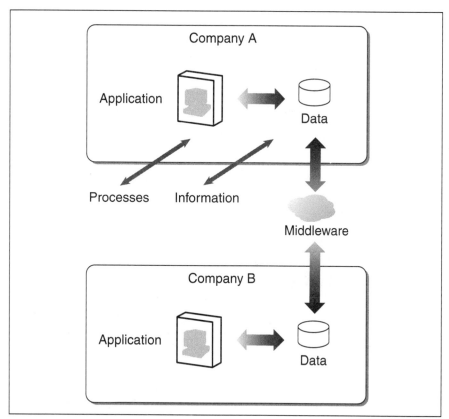

Figure 1.7   Information integration approach to B2B application integration

Process integration to e-Business enablement provides a set of processes that function above both business rules and information integration. Process integration is unlike traditional middleware. It is in actuality a process model that resides on top of middleware and provides both logical and physical information flows over existing business systems (see Figure 1.8).

Process integration is important to e-Business because it provides an abstract business layer that exists over the physical plumbing, a layer that allows process integration tool users to map out the logical flow of information between systems within the same enterprise.

Collaboration middleware provides a "soft touch" approach to information movement. Collaboration typically means providing a geographically dispersed

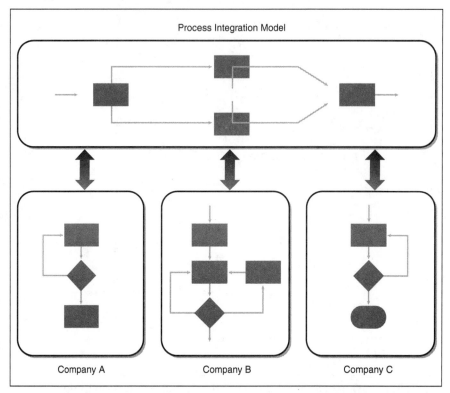

Figure 1.8   Process integration approach to B2B application integration

workgroup with the opportunity to share messages and other information in real time to support a business need (see Figure 1.9). Applications include customer relationship management, online customer service, and virtual product development.

Collaboration's great strength is its ability to support virtual communities of participating humans and computers. As a result, the middleware must be "human-aware" and capable of providing an interface to other humans and systems. It must also be data- and information-aware and capable of providing information to anyone from anywhere. Collaboration uses a centralized set of middleware to manage the movement of information. Collaboration and process integration approaches share many of the same design patterns. Throughout this book, we'll typically bind them into one concept—collaboration. (See the section Types of B2B Application Integration later in this chapter.)

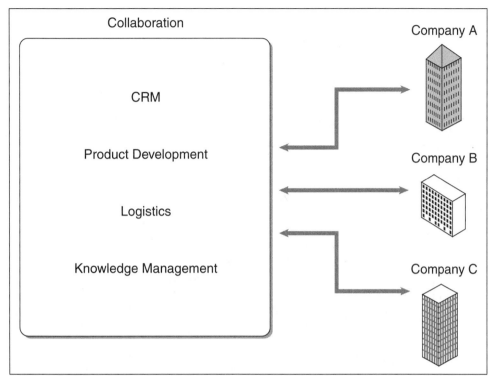

Figure 1.9   Using collaboration to approach B2B application integration

New e-Tricks for Old Dogs?

Is it reasonable to suggest that traditional middleware will provide the proper services for the new e-Business problem domains? Perhaps . . . in some cases. Traditional middleware still needs to add many more features if it is going to learn to do everything it needs to do.

In order to move forward, existing middleware vendors need to understand the various design patterns of the machine and the human entities they are interacting with. For the most part, traditional information movement applications utilized an API and employed synchronous and asynchronous mechanisms to communicate with systems. Unfortunately, APIs may have little value in the new world of e-Business. In most cases, changing the systems that exist within other enterprises in order to solve an e-Business problem is not an option. Instead, e-Business systems must interface with source and target systems through

innocuous points of integration. This might require extracting data from a database or dynamically reading Web pages. More to the point, e-Business–enabled middleware must understand how to use the Internet as its primary mechanism of communication. It must also learn to deal with such pesky realities as firewalls and bursty performance.

Additionally, middleware vendors must consider the type of interface to be employed. Traditional synchronous request-reply interfaces are much too primitive for a typical e-Business problem domain. B2B-enabled middleware must take a more event-driven approach. B2B interactions are bound to challenge the capabilities of today's static interfaces. New, more dynamic and intelligent mechanisms need to be devised to deal with systems that may not be under the control of the e-Business system owner.

We may have to interact with systems whose only interface exposes data through a set of Web pages. If the pages change, which they always do, the interface must be able to react to the change without requiring redevelopment. When XML becomes more of the standard, these types of interfaces will present less of a challenge. However, XML itself will inevitably bring its own set of complexities and level of sophistication.

Finally, information movement mechanisms, which include brokering and transaction processing, have been the traditional choice to provide middle-tier processing capabilities. Within the e-Business problem domain, we may have to mix and match the two, providing brokering capabilities (e.g., translation, routing, and rules) along with application and user interface processing. Therefore, transactional middleware needs to incorporate the basic features of a message broker, and message brokers must incorporate the basic features of transactional middleware, in order to provide the maximum amount of value to e-Business systems (see Figure 1.10).

To illustrate this point, let's consider that an application server might do a good job of externalizing information from many different systems through a Web interface. However, the application server's strict use of transactional semantics limits its ability to operate independently of the remote resources (e.g., queue, database, packaged application) it is interacting with. Message brokers are very good at moving information from place to place and do so independently of the source and target systems, but they are not particularly good at externalizing back office information through a user interface.

e-Business development demands the best of both worlds.

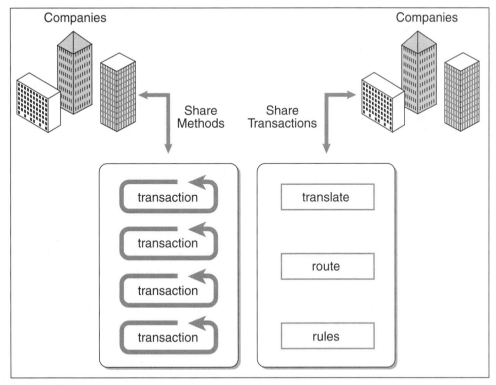

Figure 1.10   **In the world of B2B application integration, message brokers and transactional middleware must learn to work together.**

Types of B2B Application Integration

When contemplating B2B application integration for your organization, you must first understand the sum and content of the business processes and data in your organization. IT also needs to understand how these business processes are automated (or not automated, as the case may be) and the importance of all business processes. Depending on your enterprise, this effort may demand a significant amount of time and energy. Many organizations seek new methodologies to assist them in this process and use the opportunity to examine the best practices.

In brief, organizations must understand both business processes and data. They must then use this understanding to determine which processes and data elements require integration. This process can take on several dimensions (see Figure 1.11), including:

- Data-oriented
- Application interface–oriented
- Method-oriented
- Portal-oriented
- Process integration–oriented

Although this book includes chapters devoted to each type of B2B application integration, a brief overview of the various types is provided here.

Data-Oriented

Data-oriented B2B application integration is the process—and the techniques and technology—of extracting information from one database, perhaps processing that information as needed, and updating it in another database within another organization. Although this process may sound simple and straightforward, in a typical B2B application integration–enabled enterprise it might mean drawing from as many as 100 databases and several thousands of tables. It may also include the transformation and application of business logic to the data that is being extracted and loaded.

Cost is the primary advantage of data-oriented B2B application integration. Because we are mostly leaving the application alone and not changing code, we don't need to incur the expense of changing, testing, and deploying the application.

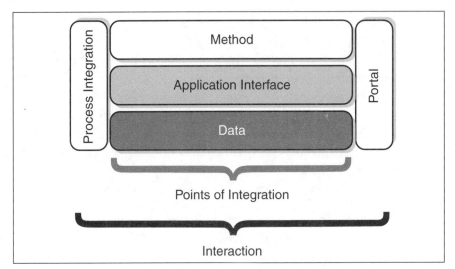

Figure 1.11   Dimensions of B2B application integration

What's more, the technology that provides mechanisms to move data between databases and reformats that information is relatively inexpensive when compared to other B2B application integration levels and their applicable enabling technology.

Application Interface–Oriented

Application interface–oriented B2B application integration refers to the leveraging of interfaces exposed by custom or packaged applications. Developers leverage these interfaces to access both business processes and simple information. Using these interfaces, developers are able to bundle any number of applications, allowing them to share business logic and information. The only limitations to this strategy rest with the specific features and functions of the application interfaces.

Application interface–oriented B2B application integration is most applicable to packaged applications, such as SAP, PeopleSoft, and Baan. These applications expose interfaces into their processes and data but do so in very different ways. In order to integrate those systems with others in the enterprise, we must use these interfaces to access both processes and data, extract the information, place it in a format understandable by the target application, and transmit the information. Although a number of different technologies can do this, message brokers seem to be the preferred solution.

Method-Oriented

Method-oriented B2B application integration is the sharing of the business logic that exists within the enterprise. For example, the method for updating a customer record may be accessed from any number of applications, within or between organizations. These applications may access each other's methods without having to rewrite each method within the respective application.

There are numerous mechanisms for sharing methods among applications. These include distributed objects, application servers, Transaction Processing (TP) monitors, frameworks, and even creating a new application that combines two or more applications.

There are two basic approaches to combining applications.

1. Create a shared set of application servers that exist on a shared physical server, such as an application server.
2. Share methods already existing inside of applications using distributed method-sharing technology, such as distributed objects.

Method-oriented B2B application integration is something we've been practicing for years as we sought to reuse application development efforts within the enterprises. We've not been largely successful because of both human and technological issues. Perhaps with B2B application integration, we may get it right.

Portal-Oriented

Portal-oriented B2B application integration is very popular today thanks to the mushrooming use of the Internet. Using this approach, application architects can integrate applications by presenting information from several local or partner applications within the same user interface.

Those of us who use Web portals such as www.excite.com, www.yahoo.com, or www.snap.com daily are already familiar with this concept. Information from many places, such as other sites or applications, is presented within the same user interface, typically a Web browser. Enterprises are avoiding the complexity and expense of traditional back-end integration by leveraging this integration approach as a means of integrating enterprise systems (such as inventory, SAP, and sales automation systems from the earlier example) at the user interfaces.

Process Integration–Oriented

Process integration–oriented B2B application integration, at its core, is a sophisticated management system that places an abstract business-oriented layer on top of more traditional B2B information movement mechanisms. Process integration–oriented e-Business provides those who are supporting B2B application integration with a business-oriented and process automation–like view of how business information flows between trading partners. Collaboration-level B2B application integration does not typically deal with physical integration flows and physical systems but with abstract and shared processes such as people, invoices, orders, companies, and merchandise. An example of process integration–oriented B2B application integration is integration that provides a common abstract process between trading partners to support the development, construction, and delivery of durable goods, such as an automobile.

Process integration–oriented B2B application integration is at the top of the food chain in the world of B2B application integration, leveraging other types of B2B application integration, including data-oriented, method-oriented, and application interface–oriented. This is an emerging concept but one that will

ultimately drive most B2B application integration activity going forward, once the physical integration problems are solved.

In Chapters 2 through 6, we'll take a closer look at these types of B2B application integration as well as the enabling technology that supports these concepts.

Types of B2B
Application Integration

Understanding Data-Oriented B2B Application Integration

Data-oriented B2B application integration represents the "entry point" for most enterprises that are considering B2B application integration. Which makes perfect sense. Data-oriented B2B application integration allows for data to be moved between data stores. Relevant business information can be shared among these data stores and ultimately with trading partners. The data level as an entry point for B2B application integration has the added benefit of numerous tools and techniques that enable the integration of information from database to database, tools and techniques that adapt information on the fly so it is represented correctly by both the source and target applications.

Accessing databases at the data level is a relatively easy task, accomplished with few—if any—significant changes to the application logic or database structure. This is a tremendous asset, because altering applications is not possible in many problem domains, where you are likely dealing with systems that are beyond your direct control.

However, the straightforward appearance of data-oriented B2B application integration should not create the impression that it is simple. It is not. Migrating data from one database to another sounds straightforward and reasonable enough, but in order for data-oriented B2B application integration to actually work, architects and developers need to understand both the complex world of database technology

and the way in which information flows throughout an enterprise. Moreover, it's dangerous to update databases without understanding any integrity issues that may exist at the application level. Therefore, those employing data-oriented B2B application integration need to make it their job to understand how the application handles data integrity, making sure that any integrity rules are not violated.

In most trading communities, databases not only number in the thousands but represent a complex and complicated mosaic of various database technologies and models that provide data storage for applications (see Figure 2.1). This reality makes integrating databases a difficult task, one that would have been nearly impossible before the introduction of powerful many-to-many, B2B application integration data-movement and transformation tools and technologies.

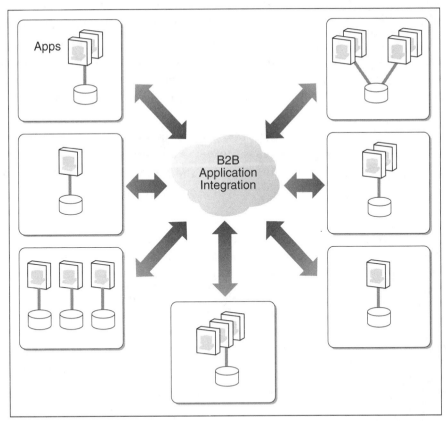

Figure 2.1   Typical trading communities that require integration may have thousands of databases.

However, this problem is even more complex. Data from one system may not be compatible with a different system—the semantics are so different that the two systems just can't understand each other; for example, sales accounting practices might be different. Data-oriented B2B application integration is not just about moving information between data stores but also about managing the differences in metadata and applications semantics.

Going for the Data

Data access in B2B application integration demands an "end run" around application logic and user interfaces to extract or load data directly into the database (see Figure 2.2). Fortunately, most applications built in the recent past decouple the database from the application and interface, but many do not. As a result, this once-daunting task is transformed into something relatively simple. Relatively simple *if* you are dealing with a recently created application. Unfortunately, many databases are still tightly coupled with the application logic. In these scenarios, it

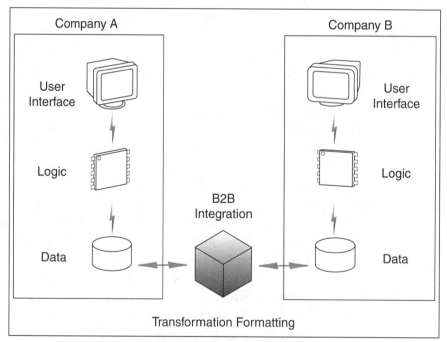

Figure 2.2   **Within the context of B2B application integration we sneak behind the application to extract or update data directly.**

Coupling versus Cohesion

In looking at the applications and databases that make up the B2B problem domain, you should always consider an integration alternative that generally comes down to one of two choices—coupling or cohesion. Coupling, in the context of B2B application integration, is the binding of applications together in such a way that they are dependent on each other, sharing the same methods, interfaces, and perhaps data.

At first glance, coupling may seem like the perfect idea. However, you should not lose sight of what it really requires—the tight binding of one application domain to the next. As a consequence of this requirement, all coupled applications and databases will have to be extensively changed to couple them. Further, as events and circumstances evolve over time, any change to any source or target system demands a corresponding change to the coupled systems as well. Coupling creates one application and database out of many, with each tightly dependent on the other.

Since coupling requires changes to source and target systems, it may not fit with most B2B application integration problem domains where the participating systems are not under central control.

In contrast to coupling, cohesion is "the act or state of sticking together," or "the logical agreement." Applications and databases cohesively integrated are independent from one another. Changes to any source or target system should not directly affect the others. In this scenario, information can be shared between databases and applications without worrying about changes to applications or databases, leveraging some type of loosely coupled middleware layer to move information between applications and make adjustments for differences in application semantics.

It should be clear then that the optimal B2B application integration solution is cohesion rather than coupling. We are always better off when changes to a source or target system do not require changes to the other systems in the B2B application integration problem domain.

Having made that statement, we should be quick to add that when we consider cohesion versus coupling, few things are straightforward, and there are pros and cons to either approach.

Cohesion provides the greatest flexibility as the B2B application integration solution moves into the future. Systems can be added to, changed, or removed from a cohesive B2B application integration solution without typically requiring changes to any of the other systems in the problem domain. Message brokers provide the technology infrastructure of most cohesive B2B application integration solutions, and so do some B2B integration servers. They are able to "broker" the differences between systems, accommodating differences in application semantics within a middle-tier process.

Despite cohesion's flexibility, if common business processes are to be reused, then a coupled approach provides more value. Distributed objects, transaction-processing monitors, and application servers provide a good technology solution for a coupled B2B application integration solution.

is impossible to deal with the database without dealing with the application logic as well. As we have suggested, this is a much more difficult proposition, so difficult that it may be reason enough to employ method- or application interface–oriented B2B application integration along with data-oriented B2B application integration or even to consider using another type of B2B application integration exclusively.

Data-oriented B2B application integration's simplicity and speed-to-market advantages are the consequences of a business logic that rarely has to be altered (a cohesive rather than coupled approach). It frees the enterprise from having to endure seemingly endless testing cycles or the risk and expense of implementing newer versions of applications. Indeed, most users and applications will remain blissfully ignorant of the fact that data is being shared at the back-end.

Numerous database-oriented middleware products allow architects and developers to access and move information between databases, thereby simplifying data-oriented B2B application integration. These products can integrate various database brands, including Oracle and Sybase. They also allow for the integration of different database models.

The advent of B2B application integration–specific technology, such as message brokers, B2B application integration management layers, and simple

data-movement engines, enables the enterprise to move data from one place to another—from anywhere to anywhere—without altering the target application source. What's more, this can now be done in real time, within online transaction-processing environments.

Although the technology for moving data between two or more data stores is familiar and well tested in real applications, this familiarity does not exempt the

---

Will XML Bring Standards to Data-Movement Metadata?

Even as several standards bodies seek to define data-movement and repository standards in support of B2B application integration, the best option may already be available to us. XML, borrowed from the Web, may be just what trading partners need for a unified look at data. As subsequent chapters will make clear, XML and B2B application integration are joined at the hip.

Like Hypertext Markup Language (HTML), XML is a subset of the Standard Generalized Markup Language (SGML), a venerable standard for defining descriptions of structure and content in documents (see Figure 2.3). However, although HTML is limited to providing only a universal method to display information on a page (without context or dynamic behavior), XML provides both context and meaning to data.

XML redefines some of SGML's internal values and parameters while simultaneously removing large numbers of the little-used features that make it so complex. It maintains SGML's structural capabilities, letting middleware users define their own document types. Indeed, one of XML's greatest benefits is to introduce and define a new type of document, one in which it is unnecessary to define a document type at all.

Any attribute that can be assigned to a piece of data can be XML metadata. This metadata can represent abstract concepts such as the industry associated with a particular document. XML can also be used to encode any number of existing metadata standards.

Because XML doesn't depend on any particular type of metadata format, there is little risk that a particular technology vendor will define its own set of metadata tags. In other words, XML cannot be made proprietary to a particular type of data. The Resource Description

Framework (RDF) brings all the metadata initiatives together so that the data can then be shared.

XML is so important to B2B application integration that we've included a chapter dedicated solely to leveraging XML for B2B application integration (see Chapter 14). We'll also refer to XML from time to time during the rest of the book as well as XML-enabled standards and how each applies to B2B application integration.

```
<customer>
<name>Joe Blow</name>
<customer_no>1</customer_no>
<address>1111 Main Street</address>
<city>Someplace</city>
<zip>11111</zip>
</customer>
```

Figure 2.3   Example of an XML document

architect or developer from understanding the data that is being moved or from understanding the flow and business rules that must be applied to that data.

Data-Oriented B2B Application Integration by Example

Just as a picture is worth a thousand words, understanding data-oriented B2B application integration is sometimes made easier by "painting a picture"—that is, examining a particular B2B application integration problem. For example, let us say that a copper wiring manufacturing company would like to hook up to the inventory control system that exists at its raw material goods producer, a client/server system using PowerBuilder and Oracle, and the ERP system (using an Informix relational database). Because the data-movement requirements are light to moderate and because changing the proprietary ERP application to bind its logic with the inventory control system is not an option (the supplier won't allow it), the company would like to solve this B2B application integration problem using data-oriented B2B application integration and the Internet.

First, in order to move data from the Oracle database to Informix, the B2B application integration architect and developer need to understand the metadata for each database so that they can select the data that will move from one database to the next. In our example, let us assume that only sales data must move from one database to the other. So, when a sale is recorded in the inventory system, creating an event, the new information is copied over to the supplier's ERP system to ensure that the correct amount of raw materials will be available to create the sold copper wire.

Second, the architect and developer must determine the frequency of the data movement. In our example, let us determine that real time is a requirement for this problem domain. The event to be captured must also be defined in order to signal when the data needs to be copied, such as a specific increment of time (e.g., every five seconds) or when a state changes (e.g., an update to a table occurs).

Once these two determinations are made, the architect and developer must choose the method for moving the data. Many technologies and techniques exist for moving the data from one database to the next, including database replication software, message brokers, and custom-built utilities. There are advantages and disadvantages to each, which will become apparent later in this book. In our example, we'll choose a database replication and integration solution—a piece of software that runs between the databases that can extract information from one database (say, the Informix database) reformat it (changing content and schema) if needed, and update the Oracle database (see Figure 2.4).

Although ours is a one-to-one scenario, one-to-many works in the same way, as does many-to-many, although with more splitting, combining, and reformatting.

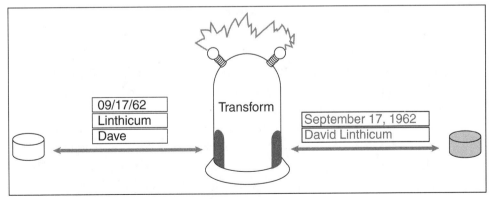

Figure 2.4   Moving information between databases may require changing both the content and the schema on the fly.

With the middle-tier database replication software in place, the information is extracted, reformatted, and updated from the Oracle database to the Informix database and then back again. The information is replicated between the two databases when an update occurs at either end of the corresponding sales table.

Using this simple approach, the data moves between the databases at the data level. The application logic is completely bypassed. There are no changes to the application logic at the source or, as in this case,' the target systems. This approach provides an effective B2B application integration solution whenever an application cannot be changed, which, as we've noted many times, is generally the case with B2B application integration problem domains.

Data-oriented B2B application integration makes sense for more complex problem domains as well, domains such as moving data between traditional mainframe, file-oriented databases and more modern, relational databases; relational databases to object databases; multidimensional databases to mainframe databases; or any combination of these. As in other domains, database replication and translation software and message brokers provide the best solutions. They are able to tie all source and target databases together cohesively, without requiring changes to the connected databases or application logic.

There are two basic approaches to data-oriented B2B application integration and its accompanying enabling technology: database-to-database B2B application integration, and federated database B2B application integration.

Database-to-Database B2B Application Integration

Just as with the point-to-point approach, we've been doing database-to-database B2B application integration well for years (see Figure 2.5). Database-to-database B2B application integration allows us to share information at the database level and, by doing so, integrate applications. Database-to-database B2B application integration can exist in a number of configurations—one-to-one, one-to-many, or many-to-many. Regardless of the configuration, our approach to database-to-database B2B application integration is essentially the same—utilizing traditional database middleware and database replication software (replication features are built into many databases; e.g., Sybase) or through database integration software. Message brokers also work with database-to-database B2B application integration.

Database-to-database B2B application integration problem domains can be addressed with two types of solutions—the basic replication solution, which moves information between databases that maintain the same basic schema

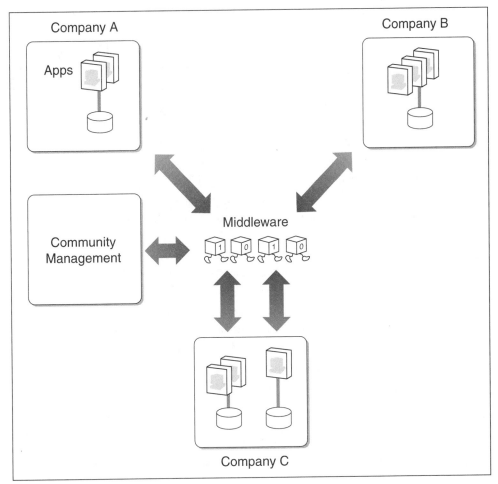

Figure 2.5　Database-to-database B2B application integration

information on all source and target databases, and the replication and transformation solution. Either of these solutions makes it possible to move information between many different types of databases, including various brands (e.g., Sybase, Oracle, and Informix) and models (relational, object-oriented, and multidimensional), by transforming the data on the fly so it is represented correctly to the target database or databases receiving the data. This is exactly what happened in our earlier inventory control system example.

The advantage of this B2B application integration approach is its simplicity. Generally, when dealing with application information at the data level, we don't

need to change the source or target applications enabling us to reduce the risk and cost of implementing B2B application integration. The downside to this approach, where it exists, is that there are still too many applications that bind the application logic to the data. These applications make it difficult to manipulate the database without going through the application or at least the application interface. This is the case with SAP R/3. In order to avoid integrity problems, updating the database generally demands using the SAP R/3 interface.

Federated Database B2B Application Integration

Like database-to-database B2B application integration, federated database B2B application integration works at the database level (see Figure 2.6). However, rather than simply replicate data across various databases, federated database software creates a single "virtual" database model that allows developers to use various brands, models, and schemas to access any number of databases. This

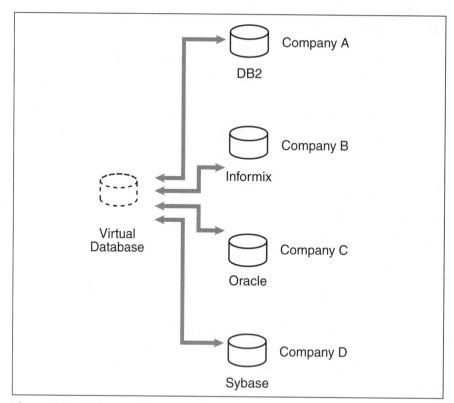

Figure 2.6   Federated database B2B application integration

virtual database model exists only in the software and is mapped to any number of connected, physical databases. This virtual database functions as a single point of application integration, accessing data from any number of systems through the same single database interface.

The advantage of the federated database approach is its reliance on middleware to share information between applications rather than a custom solution. An additional benefit is that the middleware hides the differences in the integrated databases from the other applications that are using the integrated view of the databases. The downside is that this approach is not a true integration approach. Although it provides a common view of many databases—a "unified model"—there is still the need to create the logic for integrating the applications with the databases. In addition, this approach does not work well for B2B problem domains, because it is difficult to create a common schema among systems that are not under central control.

Consider the Data Source

In considering the sources of the data, and the database technology that houses your data order, you will find both good and bad news. The good news is that most databases today use the homogeneous, relational database model, making "mixing and matching" from various databases relatively simple. The bad news is that there are still way too many heterogeneous models out there.

Relational databases represent a significant portion of the new application development that has occurred during the past 10 to 15 years. This portends well for the future. Unfortunately, traditional databases, such as those found on legacy systems, continue to command the lion's share of enterprise data. Implementing B2B application integration will force you to confront such old "friends" as IDMS, IMS, VSAM, ISAM, and even COBOL-driven flat files. Most of these "dear old friends" will be defined later in the chapter.

When dealing with databases, we must understand

- The model that the database uses to store information
- The nature of the database itself and how the differences between the databases existing within enterprises also provide an opportunity for integration

Relational

Relational databases are the reigning monarchs of a stable database kingdom. What's more, there is precious little sign of any palace coups occurring anytime

soon. Although some have questioned the enduring strength of relational databases, the simplicity of the model stands as the most compelling argument for its continued popularity.

We seem to think in the relational model, and we continue to use databases primarily as storage mechanisms for data versus as a location for application processing. In these regards, relational databases meet our needs nicely.

Other factors that contribute to the popularity of relational databases include the availability of the technology, their understandability, and the minimal risk they pose to systems. Nonrelational products (e.g., object-oriented and multidimensional databases) add risk to enterprise application development projects because they lack support from the mainstream development market. Even so, nonrelational databases serve niches and, depending upon the application, make sense.

This safe and stable kingdom could change in the near future as relational database vendors such as Oracle, Sybase, and Informix provide universal databases that can pretend to be object-oriented, multidimensional, Web-ready (intranet as well), and capable of storing binary information such as video.

Relational databases organize data in dimensional tables—and nothing but tables—that are tied together using common attributes (keys). Each table has rows and columns (see Figure 2.7).

Rows contain an instance of the data. For example, an address would be a row in a customer table in the database of a local power company (see Figure 2.7). Therefore, each row represents a record.

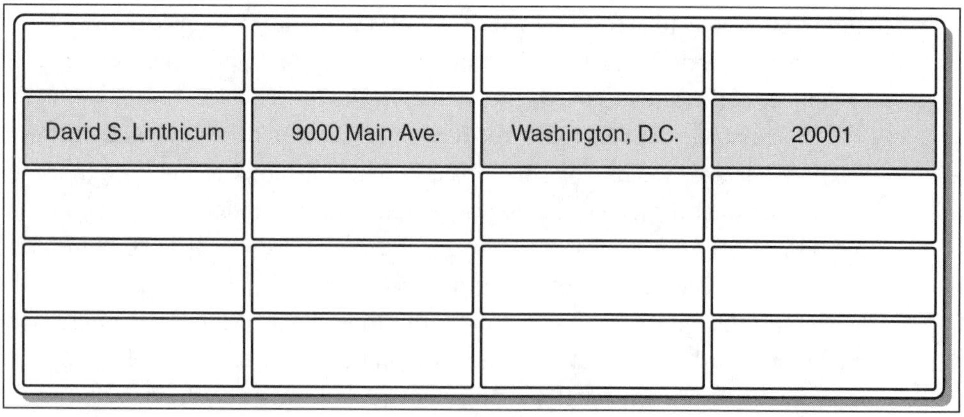

David S. Linthicum	9000 Main Ave.	Washington, D.C.	20001

Figure 2.7   Relational table

Columns are named placeholders for data, defining the type of data the column is set up to contain. As suggested previously, *keys* are columns common to two or more tables. Keys link rows to form groupings of data.

Object-Oriented

Not long after it was articulated, the object-oriented model was considered to be a fundamental threat to the dominance of the relational model. That threat never became a reality. Although object-oriented databases are more prevalent than they were, they are a long way from toppling Sybase, Oracle, Informix, or IBM. They do, however, exert tremendous influence. Most relational vendors now include object-oriented capabilities within their existing relational database technology—"universal databases." More important, the growing interest in the Web has renewed interest in the object-oriented model for content and Web-aware data storage.

So, for now we can state that the world remains very much a "relational" one. But the future is mixed. Many OODBMSs are making inroads into organizations that find the object-oriented database model is a better fit for certain applications, including persistent XML. OODBMSs meet the information storage requirements for mission-critical systems having complex information storage needs, such as applications requiring storage of complex data (repositories) or applications using binary data (audio, video, and images).

The good news for all of us is that the choice needn't be an "either-or" one. Universal servers, along with necessary middleware, exist to make relational databases appear object-oriented.

Those of you with experience in object-oriented programming languages (such as C++ or Smalltalk) already understand how objects contain both data and the methods to access that data. OODBMSs are nothing more than systems that use this model as the basis for storing information. In this way, they support the object-oriented concepts of encapsulation and inheritance.

Data management embodies the fundamental differences between traditional relational database technology and object-oriented database technology. In traditional relational databases, developers separate the methods (programs that act upon the data) from the data. By contrast, object-oriented databases combine data and methods. The synergy of object-oriented databases poses a significant challenge for B2B application integration. At this time, data-oriented B2B application integration works best by making the presumption that data and applications are separate. Only time will tell if that presumption will remain a valid one.

For now, the solution to addressing this challenge within object-oriented databases and both data-oriented and method-oriented B2B application integration must be a combined one.

Multidimensional

Multidimensional databases have evolved over the years to be repackaged as databases that support online analytical processing (OLAP), or data mining. All this is presented in a concept called "data warehousing." Currently, data warehousing is the focus of many MIS directors whose goal is to transform thousands of gigabytes of company operational data into meaningful information for those who need it. Multidimensional databases are the tools that will allow this goal to be realized.

Multidimensional databases manipulate data as if it resides in a giant cube. Each surface of the cube represents a dimension of the multidimensional database (see Figure 2.8). One side may represent sales, while another may represent

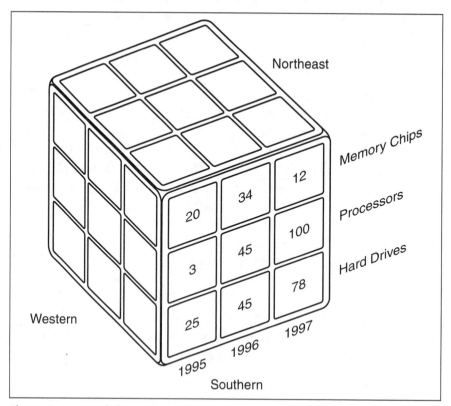

Figure 2.8   Multidimensional database

customers, and another, sales districts. The interior of the cube contains all the possible intersections of these dimensions, allowing end users to examine every possible combination of the data by "slicing and dicing" their way through the cube with an OLAP tool that, for our purposes, is joined "at the hip" with the multidimensional database.

OLAP products store data in one of two basic ways. One is a true multidimensional database server, where the data is actually stored as a multidimensional array—a "real cube." The other, more convenient way to employ OLAP is to maintain the data in relational databases while mapping that data so that it appears as multidimensional data. In other words, to present it as a "virtual cube," where the illusion of a "real cube" exists at the metadata layer.

The technology of multidimensional databases and OLAP provides a multidimensional view of the database that closely resembles the way the end user understands the organization. In other words, OLAP offers a natural, "drilldown" interface that lets users move through layer after layer of data abstraction until they come to the information they require. Once located, the data is easily graphed, printed, or imported into documents and spreadsheets.

Other Data Storage Models

We have described the primary models and methods of data storage. They are not, however, the only models. Many other technologies and models are available. Within the problem domain of B2B application integration, we may encounter older, but certainly workable, methods such as the hierarchical indexed sequential access method (ISAM), the virtual sequential access method (VSAM), Conference on Data Systems Languages (CODASYL), and Adabas. There may also be simple flat files and proprietary data storage techniques devised within the confines of the enterprise or by a now-defunct vendor.

If all this seems surprising, you should bear in mind that the only surprise in B2B application integration is no surprise at all.

Hierarchical

Databases subscribing to the hierarchical database model allow data representation in a set of one-to-many relationships. Each record in a hierarchy may have several offspring. IMS is an example of a hierarchical database.

ISAM and VSAM

ISAM stands for indexed sequential access method—the records are stored in a sequence determined by the indexed value—and it supports access either

sequentially or by index. ISAM is a simple file organization that provides sequential and direct access to records that exist in a large file. ISAM is hardware dependent.

VSAM is an updated version of ISAM. It is also hardware dependent. VSAM supports ISAM-type functions (keyed sequenced, or KSDS), but it also supports nonindexed processing (entry sequence, or ESDS) and direct record access (RRDS).

CODASYL

CODASYL is a standard created by an organization of database vendors to specify a method of data access for COBOL.

Adabas

Adabas, or the Adaptable Database, is able to support a variety of database models within a single database. It provides a high-performance database environment primarily for mainframes. Adabas provides a nested relational structure. In addition to document storage and retrieval, it supports a limited relational database model.

Working with Data-Oriented B2B Application Integration

The difficulty with data-oriented B2B application integration is the large scope of integrating various databases within the enterprise. Your initial goal might be to solve all the integration woes of your trading community at the same time by integrating all databases that need to communicate. However, given the complexity of the task, it is often better to move forward in a clear, paced manner. Attempting to accomplish the entire process at once is a massive undertaking and, for most trading communities, too much change to accommodate at one time.

You and your trading community should consider taking "baby steps" toward the goal of data-oriented B2B application integration—and B2B application integration in general. A smart strategy is to integrate two or three databases at first, allow them to become successful, and then move forward to bigger problem domains. This strategy eases the burden on the B2B application integration architects, who are shouldering a huge workload by pushing forward a new concept of B2B application integration. It also eases the burden on the users who have to test the systems and work through problems as they become apparent.

CHAPTER THREE

Application Interface–Oriented B2B Application Integration

Our discussion of the various types of B2B application integration has thus far centered on data-oriented interfaces. However, in addition to these categories, we must also examine those interfaces that exist solely to provide access to existing applications. In other words, we must examine application interface–oriented B2B application integration, or, stated another way, we must examine our ability to bind systems together by using standard or proprietary interfaces.

Our examination presents us with a technology in flux. Application interfaces are evolving rapidly. Once almost exclusively proprietary, APIs now use such standard mechanisms as Java's Remote Method Invocation (RMI), CORBA, Internet Inter-ORB Protocol (IIOP), and Microsoft's Component Object Model (COM+). This rapid evolution presents today's developers with a tremendous advantage over their predecessors. Rather than devote long hours to learning and implementing interfaces that are not portable to other applications, today's developers can familiarize themselves with standard interfaces and language bindings that exist from tool to tool.

Once standard interfaces become universal, inter- or intra-company application integration will no longer present such a difficult challenge for developers and architects. Development tools, which rarely communicate with applications that use a proprietary interface, will be able to communicate with those applications using a standard interface.

Once-monolithic applications will become "linkable" to other applications through these standard interfaces.

Application Interfaces

Application interfaces are interfaces that developers expose from packaged, or custom, applications to gain access to various levels, or services, of those applications. Some interfaces are limited in scope, while others are "feature rich." Some interfaces allow access to business processes only; some allow access directly to the data. Some allow access to both.

Developers expose these interfaces for two reasons. The first is to provide access to the business processes and data encapsulated within their applications without requiring other developers to invoke the user interface or to go directly to the database (as we discussed in Chapter 2). The use of such interfaces creates a benefit for B2B application integration by allowing external applications to access the services of these applications without making any changes to the packages or to applications themselves.

Exposing these interfaces also provides a mechanism for allowing encapsulated information to be shared. For example, if SAP data is required from Excel, SAP exposes the interfaces that allow you to invoke a business process and/or gather common data.

Such application oriented–interface B2B application integration is distinct from either method-oriented B2B application integration or user interface–oriented B2B application integration. (We will discuss method-oriented B2B application integration as a mechanism for allowing the sharing of business logic among various applications between trading partners in the next chapter.)

It is possible to distribute the methods that exist within enterprises among various applications. However, more often they are shared by using an application server, a distributed object, or some other common business logic–processing mechanism. Most popular applications provide traditional application interfaces, which are true data- and method-sharing mechanisms.

In addition to the potential complexities of application interfaces and their dynamic nature, this difference in approach distinguishes application interface–oriented B2B application integration from other types of B2B application integration. The range in the number and quality of the features that different application interfaces provide makes it nearly impossible to know what to anticipate when invoking a particular application interface. This is certainly true of packaged applications, which are "all over the board," as later chapters will make clear.

Implementing Application Interface–Oriented B2B Application Integration over the Internet

Lots of problems are associated with tightly bound integration across the Internet. First, the companies will have to open ports in the firewall; second, they will need to implement very complex authentication/authorization schemes to prevent misuse of the APIs; and third, tightly bound connections are very fragile—any changes to the application service (new release of the interface) will break the integration.

Therefore, those looking to implement application interface–oriented B2B application integration solutions need to take these issues into account when exposing APIs to other systems on the Internet. This is also an issue with data-, method-, and process-oriented B2B application integration.

What's an API?

In order to understand application interfaces, we must first understand application programming interfaces (APIs). APIs are well-defined mechanisms that are built to connect to a resource, such as an application server, middleware layer, or database (see Figure 3.1). APIs allow developers to invoke the services of these entities in order to obtain some value from them. Or in other words, an API is just a set of procedures that can be called from outside the application to get it to do something.

Programmers write APIs. Therefore, it should come as no surprise that APIs are as unique (and sometimes quirky) as the people who write them. The best APIs can access real-time data, such as information gathered from the floor of an industrial plant, or draw information residing on mainframes.

Interface by Example

Let us say we are attempting to integrate an ERP system that was just configured and installed at the site of our supplier and our long-running custom COBOL system. Both systems exist on their own processor at their respective sites, connected by the Internet. To further complicate our task, let us assume that a data-oriented B2B application integration solution won't work in this problem domain because of the complexity of the databases and the binding of logic to the data. As a result, any attempt to integrate the old and new applications should take place at the application interface.

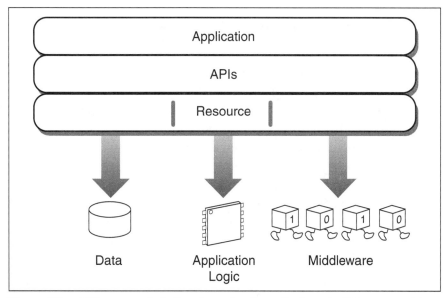

Figure 3.1   **APIs are well-defined mechanisms that are built to connect to some sort of resource.**

In our example, we are fortunate that the ERP vendor understood and anticipated the need to integrate business processes and data with the outside world. The vendor provided an API that works within C++, C, and Java environments, with the libraries that drive the API downloadable from the company's Web site.

For example, from a C application with the appropriate API libraries existing, the function:

```
GetInvoiceInformation("12345")
```

would produce:

```
<BOM>
John Smith
222 Main Street
Smalltown, VA 88888
Invoice Number: 12345
001        Red Bricks    1000      .50       500.00
<EOM>
```

The information returning from the API call is generated by invoking an API and passing in an invoice number as an argument. For processing, this

information would have to be placed within the application program in an array or another memory location. From this point, the information may be placed within a middleware layer—such as a message broker—or within XML, for transmission to other systems. Note that the database itself was never accessed. Further, the data is already bound to a business entity—namely an invoice.

Using this same interface, we can also get at customer information:

```
GetCustomerInformation("cust_no")
```

or inventory information:

```
QuantityAvailable("product_no")
```

Our example might not be so straightforward in COBOL. The developer and application architect who built the application failed to build in an API to access encapsulated business processes. Therefore, the application must be redesigned and rebuilt to expose an API so that the processes of the application can be bound with the processes of the remote ERP application.

The generally high cost of development and testing makes building interfaces into existing applications an unattractive option. However, let's assume in our current example that application interface–oriented B2B application integration is the best solution. Once we've built an interface into the COBOL application, our next move is simple—select the right middleware to bind to the ERP API within the supplier and to the lcoal custom application API. The middleware then allows the B2B application integration developer to extract business information (e.g., credit information) from one and place it in another. Middleware that will work in this scenario might include message brokers, message-queuing middleware, and application servers.

Unlike data-oriented B2B application integration, the interfaces in this example are able to provide access to both data and business processes. This is the reason we employ an application interface–oriented API. Unfortunately, the type of business information that we will be able to access is limited by the features and functions of the interface. That's the tradeoff with application interface–oriented B2B application integration.

Approaching Application Interfaces

Packaged applications (most often present in a typical B2B application integration problem domain) are only now beginning to open their interfaces to grant outside access and, consequently, integration. Although each application

determines exactly what these interfaces should be and what services they will provide, there is an evolving "consensus" to provide access at the business model, data, and object levels.

In accessing the business model, or the innate business processes, a set of services is typically invoked through user interfaces. For example, credit information for a particular individual can be accessed through the user interface by driving the screens, menus, and/or windows. (This same information can be accessed by invoking an API, if it is provided by the packaged application vendor.)

In the world of custom applications, anything is possible. Access to the source code allows us to define a particular interface or to open the application with standard interfaces such as CORBA, COM, or Java. For example, rather than accessing the user interface (scraping screens) to get to an existing COBOL application residing on a mainframe, we can build an application programming interface for that application by simply exposing its services through an API. In most cases, this will require mapping the business processes, once accessible only through screens and menus, directly to the API.

The Interface Tradeoff

If the world were a perfect place, all the features and functions provided by packaged applications would also be accessible through their "well-defined" application programming interfaces. However, the world is not a perfect place, and the reality is a bit more sobering. (See our discussion of interface service levels in the section Types of Services, later in this chapter.) Nearly every packaged application provides some interfaces, but, as we have emphasized previously, they are uneven in their scope and quality. Although some provide open interfaces based on open interface standards such as Java APIs (e.g., JavaBeans) or Object Request Brokers (ORBs), many others provide more proprietary APIs that are useful only in a limited set of programming languages (e.g., COBOL and C). Most disturbing is that too many packaged applications fail to offer any interface. These applications offer no opportunity for an application or middleware layer to access services cleanly. As a result, the business processes and data contained within the application remain "off limits." In these situations, half the anticipated expense of moving forward must be dedicated to more traditional mechanisms, such as leveraging scraping screens or data-oriented B2B application integration.

Packaged Applications

As we discussed in Chapter 1, packaged applications are natural stovepipes. This reality not only places them squarely within the problem domain of most B2B application integration projects, but it makes them the most challenging applications to integrate. You may need to access the information in these stovepipes and share the business logic locked within them with others in your trading community.

SAP, PeopleSoft, Oracle, and Baan dominate the many packaged applications on the market today because they recognized and responded to the need to share information. This is a tremendous advantage over their competitors. However, before making use of this advantage, remember that over the years, hundreds of packaged applications have likely entered your enterprise. Many of these packaged applications no longer enjoy the support of their vendors, or perhaps more likely, their vendors have gone out of business. Since there could be hundreds of these older packaged applications in your B2B application integration problem domain, you will face special challenges for B2B application integration. Most of these applications will provide some points of integration, others will not.

Packaged applications come in all shapes and sizes. Most large packaged applications in the enterprise are "business critical." SAP, for example, provides modules for accounting, inventory, human resources, manufacturing, and other vital functions. PeopleSoft and Baan provide many of the same types of services and modules.

Vendors such as Lawson Software, J.D. Edwards, and others—some with less than a dozen installations—offer packaged applications. For example, Scopus, a call-center management application, is limited to highly selected and specialized applications. Siebel, a sales-force automation package, is designed to allow sales organizations to function more effectively.

Packaged Application Technology Architecture

Packaged applications found in enterprises today tend to use one of three distinct architectures: centralized, two-tier, and three-tier.

Centralized architecture is the most traditional and easiest-to-follow approach. Centralized architecture places both data application logic and user interfaces within the same machine, generally a mainframe or large minicomputer, that houses a packaged application accessible by dumb terminals (see Figure 3.2).

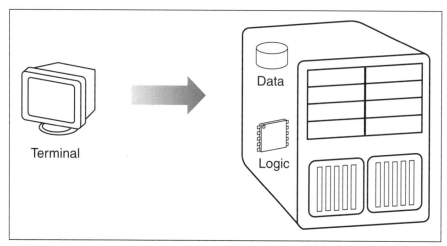

Figure 3.2   Using centralized architecture

Because the data, process logic, and user interface all exist together on the same processor, maintenance is much easier in centralized architecture than in traditional distributed environments. In addition, integration is more easily accomplished within one machine than among several. In a B2B application integration scenario, encapsulated services and data that reside on a central computer can be accessed by a single gateway.

Even as we acknowledge these advantages, the industry is moving away from the centralized structure and toward the distributed model. Although the distributed model lacks some of the advantages of centralized architecture, it does bring some real strengths to the table. It has the ability to tailor equipment, databases, and operating systems to the specifications of the enterprise. Perhaps more to the point, the graphical user interface, now a staple in the world of computing, is innate to traditional distributed-type architectures.

The evolution toward the distributed model parallels the evolution of SAP. The previous generation of SAP, SAP R/2, leveraged this centralized architecture and was found in traditional mainframe-type environments. The latest SAP generation, SAP R/3, uses a three-tier distributed model.

Two-tier architecture (see Figure 3.3) is drawn from the traditional, two-tier client/server model, where the application is separated into three distinct "pieces," or layers: the user interface layer, the business logic layer, and the data layer. (The difference between two-tier and three-tier architecture lies in the distribution of the layers). Although two-tier architecture is divided into three logical pieces, it is

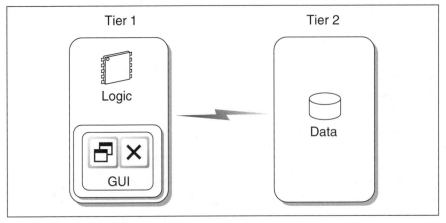

Figure 3.3   Using the two-tier architecture

physically and logically separated on just two layers (tiers)—the client and the server, which are connected by a network. The client always contains the user interface, but it may or may not also contain the business logic. Conversely, the database always contains the data, but it may or may not contain business logic.

When the business logic is placed on the client, you create a "fat" client. When it is placed on the database (or a middle tier, as in the three-tier architecture), you create a "thin" client. Most client/server systems opt for the "fat" approach. Note that with the two-tier approach, the difference is not simply the physical distribution of the application, between the client and the server, but the fact that the logic is bound to the user interface.

The significant difference between the two-tier and three-tier architectures is the placement of an application server between the client and the database to provide a location for the business logic (see Figure 3.4). As a result, the client in a three-tier system only interacts with the user, while the database only deals with the processing of the data. The middle tier, or application server, provides almost all application logic–processing services. The client, while interacting with the user, is able to invoke application services on the application server; the application server in turn is able to access information residing on a database on behalf of the client.

The three-tier architecture is the most popular architecture among packaged applications, with good reason. It provides a clean separation between the user interface, the business logic, and the data. It also enhances scalability. We know that the number of database connections increases in direct proportion to the

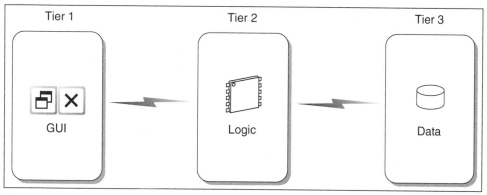

Figure 3.4   Using the three-tier architecture

number of clients. With a finite number of connections available to the database, two-tier architecture is self-limiting in relation to scalability because of a one-client/one-database connection limitation. With an application server that can multiplex connections in a process known as database funneling, or connection pooling, three-tier architecture circumvents this limitation. As a result, instead of the direct proportionality of the two-tier architecture, the three-tier architecture might require only ten connections to the back-end database for 100 clients.

Most major packaged applications use the three-tier architecture. However, the enabling technology they use to implement the architecture varies considerably from vendor to vendor. While SAP uses a proprietary application server to process its business logic, PeopleSoft leverages the Tuxedo TP monitor from BEA.

You might ask, What does architecture have to do with interfaces? The long and short answer is, everything. When invoking application interfaces, you must understand which portions of the packaged applications are being accessed. Interfaces allow access to the user interface and application as well as to the data (many allow access only to one or two tiers). Many packaged applications allow direct access to the database with the caveat, based on the fact that the business logic controls database integrity, that you do so only by using a business logic or application layer. To do otherwise could damage database integrity, thus producing erroneous results.

Perhaps the most important reason for understanding the architecture and enabling technology is that it presents you with opportunities for integration. Many packaged applications use open technologies, such as message-oriented middleware, application servers, or TP monitors. At times it may make sense to go directly to those layers, bypassing the interfaces provided by the packaged

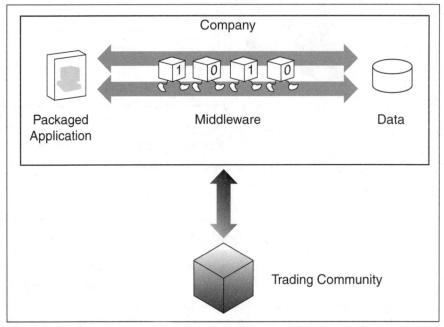

Figure 3.5   Using middleware as a point of integration

application vendors (see Figure 3.5). For example, invoking the Tuxedo inter-face allows access to the business logic in PeopleSoft. Just as Tuxedo is a major middleware technology, other third-party tools may be available that achieve the same result.

Packaged Application APIs

Some, but not all, packaged applications expose interfaces, or APIs, that allow other applications access to encapsulated services and data. Although these inter-faces vary widely in features and function, categorizing some types may clarify what is available. Three types of services are available to these interfaces—busi-ness services, data services, and objects.

Types of Services

Business services, as the name implies, include interfaces to any piece of business logic that exists within the packaged application (see Figure 3.6). For example, if you want to use the packaged application interface to update the customer database with a new customer from another application, business services would enable you to invoke the customer update business service from the API and pass

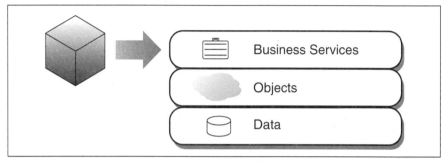

Figure 3.6   Invoking the business services layer

Packaged Applications Becoming Shared Services

Vendors are moving quickly toward allowing packaged applications to share services with other applications within or between companies. In one sense, these packaged applications are becoming elaborate distributed objects with preprogrammed functions that provide thousands of methods and database tables that are accessible to anyone within an enterprise who understands the interface.

Imagine the day when SAP information can be accessed directly from any tool that communicates using Java. When that day arrives, every packaged application will reside squarely on "Main Street," simplifying both the mechanism and the process for accessing the encapsulated methods and data. Whatever difficulty exists in moving all packaged applications to "Main Street" exists in architecture, not in concept.

Packaged application vendors are eager for their products to function like distributed object solutions, even though they are not truly distributed objects. In order to accomplish this, the vendors are forced to wrap their packaged application logic and data using some type of standard interface–CORBA, COM, or Java. When vendors are able to solve this shortcoming, the packaged application will appear as a true distributed object to other applications that exist within the B2B application integration problem domain–a clear benefit to those who seek to integrate other applications with these packaged applications at any B2B application integration level (see Figure 3.7).

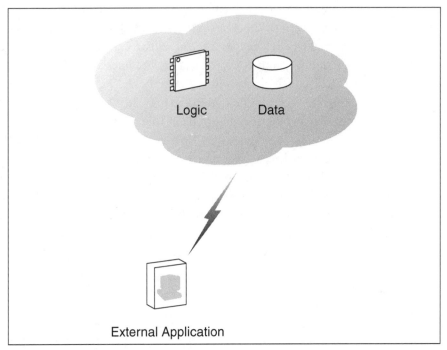

Logic   Data

External Application

Figure 3.7   Using packaged applications as distributed objects

along the new information. The interface would invoke that particular business service as if you were invoking the same business service through the user interface of the packaged application.

Tens of thousands of business services may be available within a single packaged application. Each business service, when invoked by the application interface or user interface, carries out preprogrammed functions. The B2B application integration architect must understand what each of these business services does, what the required information for each service is, and what the expected outcome is.

In addition to providing access to business logic, business services provide a virtual gateway to the data residing within packaged applications. As such, they function as sentries to the data by providing integrity controls. Directly adding a sales transaction to the database could circumvent integrity controls set up by the developers. Going through the business logic to access the data preserves the integrity of the application.

Data services, accessible by application interfaces, are direct routes to the logical or physical database, sometimes both (see Figure 3.8). These interfaces are

much like traditional, data-oriented access tools; however, the ERP vendor provides them as a verified mechanism to access the ERP data. (Of course, the features each vendor provides span a broad range.) Use of this interface is generally for extraction only. However, some data service interfaces offer database update services as well, either with or without integrity checks.

Although most application interfaces provide data services, the B2B application integration architect has the option of going directly to the database by utilizing database-oriented middleware. (However, doing so bypasses all the integrity controls that the packaged application may have put in place.) In the case of Oracle, doing this requires accessing the Oracle database by using its native middleware or other solutions such as Java Database Connectivity (JDBC), Open Database Connectivity (ODBC), or Object Linking and Embedding Database (OLE DB). We will discuss the details of database-oriented middleware later in the book.

Objects are simply data and business services bound as objects. Just as in the world of object-oriented development, the object inside packaged applications is the encapsulation of both data and methods that act upon the data (see Figure 3.9).

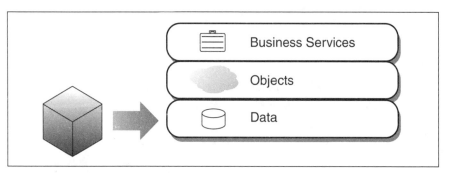

Figure 3.8　Accessing the data services layer

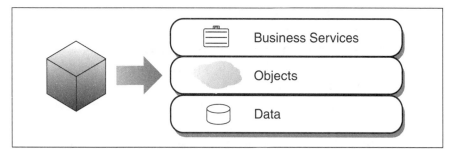

Figure 3.9　Leveraging the object layer

Because data cannot be accessed without invoking the method, objects have the advantage of never threatening the integrity checks set up by the packaged applications. However, as with most things we encounter enroute to B2B application integration, sometimes the very qualities that signify an advantage also suggest a disadvantage. Because we are discussing proprietary objects defined by the packaged application (rather than distributed objects), they might not fit directly into every development or reporting environment.

Many packaged application vendors are recognizing the need to expose these objects by using a standard interface such as CORBA or Java. SAP, PeopleSoft, Oracle, and Baan all have initiatives to provide standard object interfaces to their existing packaged applications. Obstacles may exist because packaged applications were never designed to be distributed objects.

Types of Interfaces

Having established that there are advantages to understanding the types of services available through an interface, we now need to turn our attention to the types of interfaces within packaged applications. As in other contexts, there is a broad spectrum of possible interfaces. Fortunately, these can be grouped in three convenient categories: full-service, limited-service, and controlled.

Full-service interfaces, as the name implies, afford the broadest range of benefits. These interfaces provide access to the business services level, the data services level, and the object level (see Figure 3.10). While most packaged applications, attuned to the marketing advantage of exaggeration, promote their interfaces as being "full-service," the reality is generally less promising. Packaged application interfaces are mostly little more than the "runt of the litter," added as mere afterthoughts. As a result, they are somewhat limited. For example, within the SAP interface infrastructure, many types of interfaces need to be

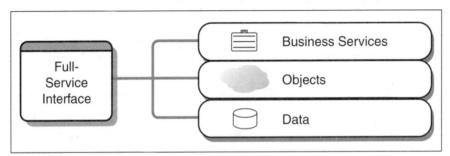

Figure 3.10   Using a full-service interface

invoked in order to access information and services. The same is true for PeopleSoft and Oracle.

Limited-service interfaces not only prove truer to the vendors' claims, they are also the most common. They generally allow access to only one level (e.g., business services level, data services level, or object level—see Figure 3.11). Not only are these interfaces limited when it comes to access, they generally provide only a limited set of services at whatever level they access.

As application interfaces gain in popularity, becoming the "next, greatest" thing for packaged applications, they will expand to include more levels as well as more features and functions within those levels. Perhaps, in an effort to live up to their promotional billing, they will eventually provide genuine full-service interfaces.

Controlled interfaces provide only the minimum number of features and functions (see Figure 3.12). These limitations are not the result of technology but of the marketing and/or economic decisions of the vendor. Controlled interfaces are *very* proprietary and closed, providing controlled access to business logic and data.

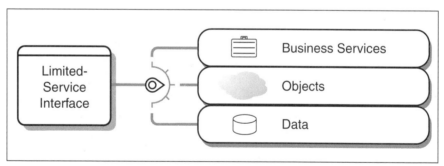

Figure 3.11   Using a limited-service interface

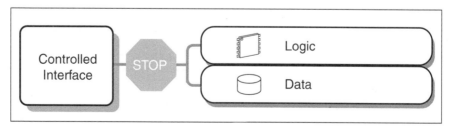

Figure 3.12   Leveraging the controlled interface

Other Interfaces

Although packaged application APIs represent the vast majority of application interfaces that you will confront, there are thousands of other standard application interfaces that you should also recognize. These all exist for the same purpose—to provide access to information that may be required from other remote applications.

We cannot discuss thousands of application interface types here. However, by confining our discussion to a review of the major categories of standard interfaces, including vertical market application interfaces and application interfaces built into custom applications, we can give you a better understanding of the available technologies and options.

Vertical Market Application Interfaces

Vertical market application interfaces provide access to industry-specific applications, such as industrial, health care, or finance. Vertical market application interfaces address the specific needs of a particular type of vertical market, needs that may include the manner in which the information is formatted, processed, or moved from application to application. For example, where security is paramount, as in the banking industry, interfaces place security high on their priority list.

(Note: We will discuss e-Business standard, or trading community, interfaces—including EDI, RosettaNet, XML, BizTalk, and cXML—later in this book.)

SWIFT

The Society for Worldwide Interbank Financial Telecommunications (SWIFT) is a messaging standard and a cooperative organized under Belgian law. Owned by member banks, including the central banks of most countries, it began operations in 1977. SWIFT provides communication services to the international banking industry, including payment and common administrative tasks. It also supports security settlements. Most message brokers that support the financial community, including NEON, SAGA Software, and Active Software, also support SWIFT. An integral part of the international financial community, SWIFT provides a rapid, cost-effective, *secure,* and reliable transmission service. In addition to providing message processing, a worldwide network, and the availability of an increasing number of message standards to support new financial instruments, SWIFT also provides a variety of specialized financial services and software network–compatible interfaces.

When it began in 1977, SWIFT was used by over 6,153 institutions to communicate with one another in a 7x24 environment. Today, SWIFT operates in 174 countries and processes more than 800 million messages each year. A typical SWIFT message load is 1.6 million messages per day.

FIX

As seemingly omnipresent as SWIFT is, it is not the only application interface supporting the world of finance. The Financial Information Exchange (FIX) protocol is a messaging standard developed specifically for the real-time electronic exchange of securities transactions. FIX is a public-domain specification maintained by the FIX organization, a cooperative effort of principal asset management and brokerage firms in the United States and Europe.

FIX offers shorter settlement dates, providing a straight-through processing package for the financial community. The FIX protocol specifications are maintained by the FIX Technical Committee. You can obtain information about FIX by visiting its Web site at www.fixprotocol.org.

The technical aspect of FIX is straightforward. FIX uses a flexible tag value message format, which imposes no structural constraints on a message. As a result, all validation must occur at the application level. This poses a problem that FIX has addressed by evolving FIX into FIXML—a structured, validated XML-derived grammar that is encapsulated within the standard FIX message. FIX, along with many other interfaces, is discovering that XML has the potential to provide a "least common denominator" approach that has proven successful for metadata.

HL7

HL7, or Health Level 7, is a standard for electronic data exchange in a health care environment. HL7 is designed for inpatient, acute-care facilities such as hospitals. HL7 was created by a committee of health care providers, vendors, and consultants established in March 1987.

Although HL7's primary environment is limited to hospitals and clinics (it is most useful when moving information in and out of MUMPs environments), it also exists within the pharmaceutical and biomedical industries.

Custom Applications

Standard application interfaces have many uses and benefits, as do the committees and vendors who are responsible for establishing standards. But what about

interfaces for your custom applications? Although interfaces may exist for many packaged applications and technologies, creating interfaces for custom applications poses a more interesting challenge.

Rolling Your Own API

Let's be honest. Our own short-sightedness created this problem. Creating an interface for a custom application is a nightmare, because the concept of custom applications is, by definition, built for exclusivity. It is the ultimate expression of "I'm not sharing!" Who could have anticipated the need, or the benefit, of sharing the information locked away in a custom application?

Custom applications were designed to be monoliths, proprietary stovepipes to serve a single purpose within the enterprise, not to share information within systems—or beyond the system in a far-flung B2B application integration scenario. What has become painfully apparent is that the premise of custom applications—that anything in an enterprise could, or should, exist in such a proprietary manner—was terribly short-sighted.

Okay, so the premise was incorrect and short-sighted. Beating ourselves up over our mistake won't solve anything. The question is, What do we do now? You might presume that building application interfaces for custom applications would be a gargantuan proposition. However, if thought through correctly, the task need not be nearly as difficult as it might first appear. There is no need to reinvent the wheel. Building an application interface to a custom application basically means exposing business processes that already exist within the application through another mechanism, namely an API (see Figure 3.13). Access to those business processes is already being exposed through the user interface. This is simply another mechanism to obtain the same service.

Although some organizations consider building application interfaces to be such an expensive proposition that they view it as a luxury beyond their reach, the fact is that applications are going to be changed in order to provide an application interface, and any change can range from very minor to very major. It might not be a luxury so much as a necessity. More to the point, applications that are not designed from the ground up to utilize an application interface may need a new architecture. In these situations, it may make more sense to rebuild the application from the first line of code. The prospect of rebuilding from the first line of code up is a daunting one that most organizations resist. It is the reason they integrate applications using other, less sophisticated approaches, such as leveraging the user interface as a point of integration and data-oriented B2B application integration mechanisms. Still, it may be the wisest choice.

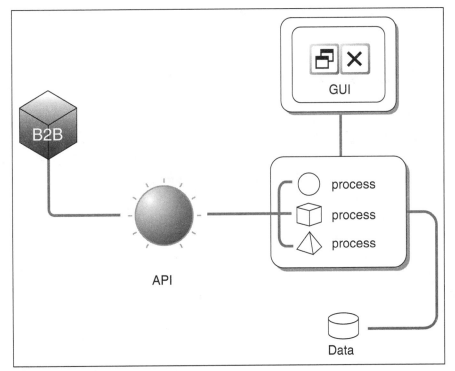

Figure 3.13   Exposing an API

Application Wrapping

A more sophisticated option to consider is application wrapping, the process of changing an existing application so that it appears as a distributed object to other applications inside or outside the company (see Figure 3.14). Application wrapping requires going through the entire application and exposing its business processes as methods within a distributed object standard, such as CORBA or COM.

Application wrapping has many advantages. Because it requires leveraging a standard, distributed object infrastructure, the application can be exposed to many more types of applications than if a proprietary application interface was built. Consequently, this makes sense for B2B application integration scenarios where applications of all types need to communicate without having to modify themselves to do so. Because they are wrapped using an available distributed object standard, many of these applications don't need to change in order to use

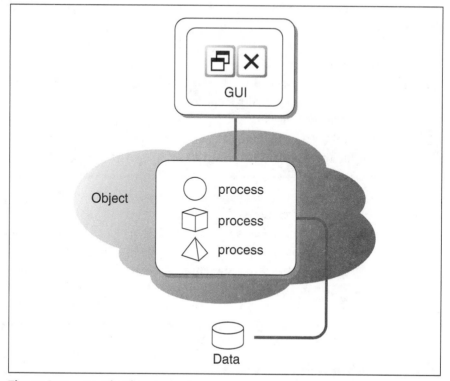

Figure 3.14   Application wrapping

the remote application services. In addition, the process for taking an existing application and rebuilding it as a distributed object is well defined. Many tools, techniques, and technologies support application wrapping.

The downside to application wrapping is time. It takes many man-months to wrap an existing application, and man-months inevitably translate into money, money that an organization might be unwilling or unable to spend on an existing solution. In addition, many applications have to be rebuilt from the ground up and may need a new application architecture. For these reasons, application wrapping should not be considered as a stopgap measure but as a mechanism that significantly extends the life of existing applications and supports the integration of those applications within the infrastructure of the enterprise.

COM and CORBA are the most popular of the many ways to wrap existing applications. Arguing the viability of either of these distributed object standards

is beyond our scope here. However, the following are some general guidelines to consider.

CORBA is the better fit for applications that have to exchange information with heterogeneous environments. Because CORBA solutions exist on a wide variety of platforms, CORBA is probably the best choice if the B2B application integration problem domain supports UNIX, NT, mainframes, and a number of other platforms. What's more, there are many proven CORBA applications in existence, along with the tools and technology that support them.

Of the two standards, COM (now COM+) is the more Windows platform–centric, which is not to suggest that it is not a powerful ORB. It is. COM is supported by most of the Microsoft line of tools, development environments, and office automation solutions. Therefore, for organizations looking to expose an application interface to most popular applications, it presents the path of least resistance. Wrapping an existing application and exposing its business processes in a COM ORB infrastructure allows those business processes to be invoked by any number of common office automation products, such as Word for Windows, PowerPoint, and Excel. COM is even making strides in becoming more heterogeneous, with support for most UNIX platforms as well as the mainframe platforms.

Using Application Interfaces

Given this chapter's discussion, the question begging to be asked is, What's the future of application interfaces when considering B2B application integration? The answer is not simple or straightforward. There are many different answers. Each depends on the way change will be wrought in any particular enterprise— by evolution or by revolution. As we've discussed, interfaces to both methods and data have been little more than an afterthought for most packaged or custom applications. As a result, supporting interfaces requires retrofitting existing applications.

This is a step in the right direction. But it is just one step—the first in that proverbial "journey of a thousand miles." Do not be fooled. It is going to be a long, slow journey. These applications generally support business-critical functions within or between companies. Making significant changes to these applications to support interfaces for B2B application integration may not excite the sensibilities in the boardroom. However, the B2B application integration problem has raised the profile of application interfaces, making them a priority for those who sell and maintain both packaged and custom applications.

And what of the future? Considering the content of this chapter, we see two possibilities looming. One, application interfaces will be standard equipment for most packaged applications. (Even more to the point, many custom applications will obtain application interfaces in future enhancements and upgrades.) Two, more applications will use standard interfaces such as CORBA and COM to enable remote applications to access both the data and services of these applications as standard object request brokers. Either of these two possibilities will add value to a B2B application integration scenario.

Method-Oriented B2B Application Integration

Method-oriented B2B application integration allows trading partners to share common business logic or methods. This sharing is accomplished either by defining methods that can be shared and therefore integrated or by providing the infrastructure for such method sharing. Methods can be shared either by hosting them on a central server or by accessing them interapplication (e.g., through distributed objects).

Attempts to share common processes have a long history, one that began more than ten years ago with multitier client/server—a set of shared services on a common server that provided the enterprise with the infrastructure for reuse and now for integration—and the distributed object movement. "Reusability" is a valuable objective. A common set of methods among enterprise applications invites reusability and, as a result, significantly reduces the need for redundant methods and/or applications.

Although most methods exist for single-organization use, we are learning that at times it makes sense to share between organizations. In a new twist on the long-standing practice of reusability, we now hope to expand this sharing beyond intra-enterprise to trading partners as well—for example, sharing common logic to process credit requests from customers or to calculate shipping costs.

Unfortunately, we have yet to achieve absolute reuse on the enterprise level. It is an even more distant goal between

trading partners. The reasons for this failure are primarily "political." They range from internal politics to the inability to select a consistent technology set. In most cases, the actual limit on reuse results directly from a lack of enterprise architecture and central control.

Utilizing the tools and techniques of B2B application integration gives us the opportunity to learn how to share common methods. More than that, these tools and techniques create the infrastructure that can make such sharing a reality. By taking advantage of this opportunity, we are integrating applications so that information can be shared, even as we provide the infrastructure for the reuse of business logic.

Sounds great, doesn't it? The downside might give you pause, however. This great-sounding B2B application integration solution also confronts us with the most invasive level of B2B application integration.

Although data-oriented and application interface–oriented B2B application integration generally do not require changes to either source or target applications, method-oriented B2B application integration requires that most, if not all, enterprise applications be changed in order to take advantage of the paradigm. This downside makes the method-oriented approach a tough sell between trading partners.

As noted in Chapter 1, changing applications is a very expensive proposition. In addition to changing application logic, we need to test, integrate, and redeploy the application within the enterprise—a process that often causes costs to spiral upward (see Figure 4.1).

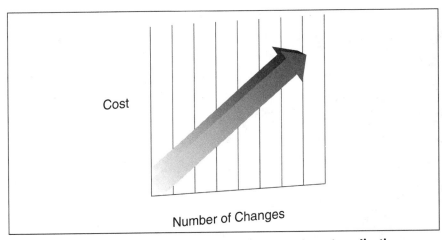

Cost

Number of Changes

**Figure 4.1   As the number of changes to source or target applications
increases, so do the costs.**

When to Leverage Method-Oriented B2B Application Integration

By now, some of you may be a bit confused about method-oriented B2B application integration and its use when establishing B2B connections between two or more organizations. Although many businesses are looking to exchange information with trading partners and even to participate in shared processes, few are looking to create applications that share methods with systems not under their control.

However, in some instances method-oriented B2B application integration is a good fit, such as the following:

- When two or more companies need to share common program logic, such as the calculation of shipping costs from a common supplier, which change constantly
- When two or more companies want to share the development costs and the value of a common application
- When the trading community is small and specialized and is able to collaborate on a common application that all companies share

---

Before embracing the invasiveness and expense of method-oriented B2B application integration, enterprises must clearly understand both its opportunities and its risks. Only then can they objectively evaluate its value. The opportunity to share business logic that is common to many applications—therefore making it possible to integrate those applications—represents a tremendous benefit. However, that benefit comes with the very real risk that the expense of implementing method-oriented B2B application integration will outpace its value.

Method-Oriented Example

A clear example of the potential benefit of method-oriented B2B application integration is the simple binding of two or more applications in order to integrate both business processes and data. Let us assume that two applications exist within a given enterprise. One application is C++-based and runs on a Linux machine. The other is an NT-based client/server application written in Java on the front-end, with Sybase serving as the back-end database.

Confronted with these independent applications, the B2B application integration architect seeks to create a composite application using method-oriented B2B application integration techniques and technology. To accomplish this, the applications need to be tightly coupled so that common business logic can be shared and the business logic of both applications can be exposed to other applications for future use.

Unlike at other B2B application integration levels, at the method level the architect has no option but to rebuild the applications so that they support method-oriented B2B application integration. The architect has only two choices in determining how to accomplish this. One, he can move much of the business logic to a shared server, such as an application server. Two, he can rebuild each application using a method-sharing mechanism, such as distributed object technology, to create a tightly coupled application that allows easy cross-accessing of methods.

If the architect decides that the second choice is the most attractive, he will have to "wrap" the application logic encapsulated inside both applications. To accomplish this, he will use a distributed object technology, such as CORBA or COM+, so that there is a common mechanism to share methods remotely. This will require rewriting the applications and then testing them. Fortunately, this is not as daunting a task as it might appear. Tools exist for each environment to wrap each application, re-creating the applications as truly distributed systems able to share both methods and data.

Even with such tools, the process is laborious. For example, if both applications need to add a common customer to their systems, they may invoke different methods—for example:

```
Add_Cust();
```

on the Linux/C++ system and:

```
AddNewCustomer();
```

on the NT/Java system.

By using a distributed object standard or a custom programming solution, the architect could expose each method. As a result, he or she could bind the methods or invoke one or the other. Once the methods are bound, the applications move to a coupled state where methods and data are shared easily within both domains, thus solving the B2B application integration problem.

Scenarios

Before implementing method-oriented B2B application integration, we must understand all the processes, methods, and programs that exist within the enterprise. Confronted with such a monumental task, we must initially ask, How best to proceed?

The first step is to break the processes down to their scenarios, or types. For B2B application integration, these types are rules, logic, data, and objects.

A **rule** is an agreed-upon set of conditions. For example, a rule may state that employees may not fly first class on flights of less than 5,000 miles or that all transactions over $1 million must be reported to the government. The rules that exist within a given enterprise are built into the applications in order to control the flow of information. Rules can also be placed in trading communities to control the flow of information between trading partners.

Normally, rules exist in stovepipes—in a single application and accessible by a single department. The challenge of B2B application integration is to provide the infrastructure that will allow the sharing of these rules between organizations. Thus, these rules will become accessible to many applications either from their current location or by moving them to a central location.

Rules need to be understood because they affect every aspect of moving data between trading partners, including identifying, processing, and transforming it. In fact, rules processing at the middleware level—through message brokers or process integration tools—will become the first generation of B2B application integration.

Logic differs from rules in that it is simply a sequence of instructions in a program. For example, if this button is pushed, then the screen pops up. The real difficulty in dealing with logic is the consequence of a very basic reality—any ten programmers, given the same set of specifications, may come up with ten slightly different versions of program logic that *all function perfectly well*. In many ways, logic is as much an art form as a science.

There are three classes of logic: sequential processing, selection, and iteration. **Sequential processing** is the series of steps in the actual data processing. *Input, output, calculation,* and *move (copy)* are examples of the instructions used in sequential processing. **Selection** is the decision-making dynamic within the program. It is performed by comparing two sets of data and, depending on the results, branching to different parts of the program. **Iteration** is the repetition of a series of steps. It is accomplished with DO-loops and FOR-loops in high-level languages.

In this context, **data** is nothing more than sharing information between trading partner applications, computers, or humans. Reporting systems, enterprise accounting systems, and human resource systems all share data. Because methods act on data, you need to understand the way in which information is shared at the method level in order for method-oriented B2B application integration to be successful.

As defined in Chapter 3, "**Objects** are simply data and business services bound as objects." They are bundles of data encapsulated inside an object and surrounded by methods that act upon that data. Objects are so important to method-oriented B2B application integration that we will devote much of this chapter to the discussion of the object model and its use within the B2B application integration problem domain.

Objects in systems generally use object-oriented technology, such as C++ or Java. Despite the fact that most objects are service-oriented objects (that is, objects that do something when an interface is invoked; more on these later in the book), the object "mix" may also include distributed objects.

Identifying objects within the trading community is more complex than identifying business processes. It requires an understanding of the object models used to construct the applications—whether they exist or, if not, whether they have ever been created. In the absence of the object model, the applications must be re-engineered from the existing code base. (Fortunately, a good set of tools and technologies exists to aid in this re-engineering. Without such tools, the task

Method Warehousing

Method warehousing identifies the methods that exist within many applications and moves them to a centralized entity, much as data warehousing does with data. Method warehousing, the process of aggregating all business processes within an organization and then hosting them on a centralized server (the method warehouse), comes directly from the concept of method-oriented B2B application integration (see Figure 4.2). The value of such warehousing should be clear—if all methods existing within the enterprise or between enterprises are located on a centralized server, then the method-oriented B2B application integration, or integration of all these processes, becomes simply a matter of remotely invoking these processes, or methods, for any application.

The advantages of method warehousing rest with its power to integrate all enterprise applications between trading partners through the sharing of methods (e.g., composite applications) and with its ability to maintain and reuse application logic from a centralized server. For example, should tax law change, method warehousing would make it unnecessary to locate all applications within the enterprise that use tax law in order to incorporate the changes. The changes would automatically propagate to all linked applications simply as a result of a change in the logic, or rules, within the method warehouse.

The disadvantage of method warehousing is as profound as its advantages. We can express this disadvantage in a single word—expense. As noted previously, method warehousing requires the conversion of the significant methods of every source and target application into a common enabling technology, one that all enterprise applications can access. For example, if you decide to implement a method warehouse project using an application server or a distributed object technology infrastructure, then in addition to creating the method warehouse itself, you must rewrite all applications in order to invoke these methods remotely. This is a pricey proposition.

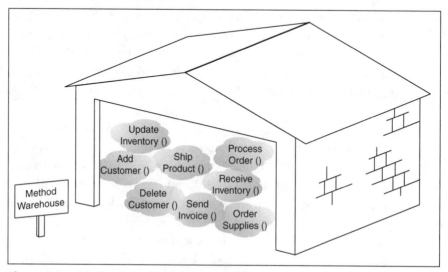

Figure 4.2   Method warehousing in support of B2B application integration

would demand reading each line of code and creating the object models from scratch.)

Creating object-oriented integration within a trading community is more than difficult, it may well be impossible. Although its value cannot be disputed, object-oriented integration is a highly invasive process. It demands tight coordination between IT departments within many different companies that exist in a trading community.

Leveraging Frameworks for B2B Application Integration

Frameworks can be helpful in integrating an enterprise at the method level. A fundamental difficulty with frameworks has been the many divergent definitions of the term itself. In the context of B2B application integration, the most useful definition appears in the *Computer Glossary, Sixth Edition* (Alan Freedman, American Management Association, 1993): "[Frameworks] consist of abstract classes and their object collaboration as well as concrete classes. While object-oriented programming supports software reuse, frameworks support design reuse."

Frameworks are debugged and tested software subsystems, centrally located and accessible by many applications (see Figure 4.3). They work well with method-oriented B2B application integration, where in many instances shared objects, processes, and/or methods are being identified for integration. Although frameworks may work at the application or enterprise level, at the method level frameworks are an enterprise approach or perhaps one between trading partners. They provide the infrastructure for sharing methods—providing objects that are accessible by a number of applications. As such, they allow the construction of a "library" of enterprise objects available to many applications. Although this concept is the basis of frameworks in general, it is particularly valuable when applied to B2B application integration.

The process of decoupling frameworks from the object-oriented development model is a reaction to the success of using component-enabled and procedural frameworks. Although the object-oriented, component-based, and procedural approaches hold very different views of frameworks, the goal of reuse is consistent among them and provides a commonality that is beneficial from all perspectives. Our focus is on object frameworks because they dominate the frameworks in use today and because many method-oriented B2B application integration projects will leverage object-oriented frameworks if they leverage frameworks at all.

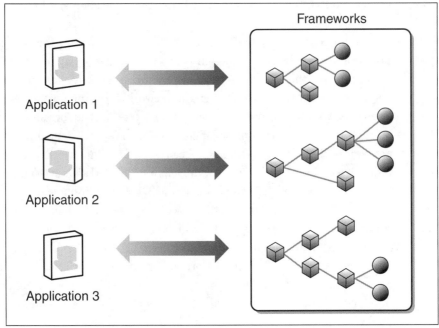

Figure 4.3   Applying frameworks to method-oriented B2B application integration

The Value of Frameworks

Although the concept of object frameworks is familiar, many development organizations remain confused about their value to B2B application integration. And though there are many benefits to object frameworks, nearly every one of them is accompanied by a note of caution. The most obvious benefit of frameworks is the ability to reuse existing code. Because frameworks contain prebuilt objects, those objects can be shared among many applications. As such, they represent a natural point of integration. Frameworks provide more than reuse within an organization; they provide reuse throughout an industry—such as shipping or the logistics business—where many of the processes are the same, and reusable frameworks make sense. Well-designed frameworks represent a billion-dollar third-party industry.

Frameworks also provide a standard set of predesigned and pretested application architectures and therefore a common infrastructure for all enterprise applications. Frameworks hide all the "dirty little details" from developers, allowing

them to concentrate on the functionality of the application and to remain architecture independent.

Although the benefits of frameworks are readily apparent, the downsides are not always so evident. First, design is an essential part of application development. It allows the B2B application integration and the application architect to derive the most benefit from using a framework. Knowing how the application and framework fit together is essential for success. Second, because of the difficulty in determining a common language or binary object standard, frameworks are typically bound to a technology. As a result, C++ frameworks are incompatible with a PowerBuilder application, Delphi frameworks are incompatible with Smalltalk, and so on. To be successful in the B2B application integration problem domain, you need a commitment to a common set of enabling technologies—something next to impossible to achieve in many organizations. Finally, the frameworks themselves must undergo a very costly process of design, architecture, development, and testing. Poorly designed frameworks lead to bad applications—no matter how well the applications themselves were designed and developed. In the final analysis, the cost of quality assurance in building frameworks is too high for many organizations.

Framework Functionality

Frameworks work by allowing B2B application integration architects to take advantage of prebuilt subsystems, application architecture, and code that already exist in the enterprise. Because frameworks largely define the architecture for an application, developers and application architects must build and leverage only those frameworks that are extensible and flexible. For example, when using object frameworks, developers can change as much of the existing functionality as required to meet the needs of the application—inheriting what is useful and overriding what isn't. Interface frameworks provide the best example of this. Developers can leverage the custom buttons in a data window while overriding the default fonts. Frameworks can be customized by adding sets of classes, or they may change themselves to take advantage of changes in hardware and software as revisions are released.

Components don't provide the same degree of customization as object-oriented frameworks (see Figure 4.4). For example, most components do not come with the source code. However, they generally provide mechanisms (or interfaces) that allow developers to change their look, feel, and behavior by altering their properties. ActiveX controls are a prime example of this capability.

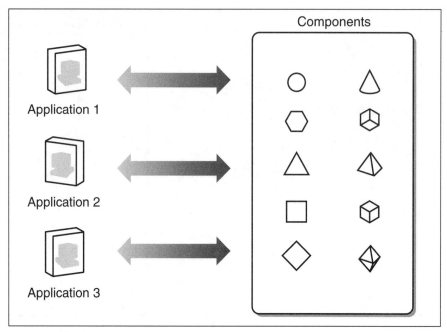

Figure 4.4   Using component frameworks

Object frameworks work with other frameworks, allowing developers to mix and match features from each (see Figure 4.5). For example, C++ applications leverage GUI frameworks for interface development, database access frameworks for communicating with databases, and system-level frameworks for interacting with native operating systems. Many of these "combined" frameworks are now bundled with object-oriented development tools.

Object frameworks generally provide access to their services through APIs, which are simply abstractions of the framework services. A framework approach to APIs differs from the traditional procedural approach in that most of the code runs inside the frameworks, and the code is invoked only when a particular state is reached. Although applications rarely invoke frameworks, developers may choose to leverage APIs to access the services of other frameworks.

The critical factor in successfully building frameworks is providing a complete framework that supports the features required by the client and his application. For example, providing concrete derivation for the abstract classes and implementing member function makes the functions easier to understand. Frameworks must allow a client to add and modify the functionality of the

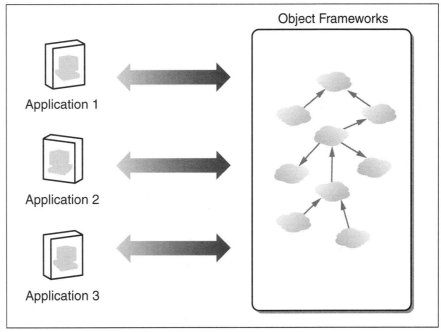

Figure 4.5   Using object frameworks

framework. Finally, frameworks should be well documented and understandable to all users.

Framework Types

The prominence of component service and procedural frameworks is gaining quickly on the dominance of object frameworks. As near parity is reached, it becomes useful to distinguish between these different types of frameworks and to delineate their use within a B2B application integration context.

Object frameworks are made up of both abstract and concrete classes. They provide application services through the inheritance mechanisms that most object-oriented languages and tools provide. This means that developers get a copy of the framework source code and have an opportunity to customize the framework. With the open source approach and the object-oriented mechanism of inheritance, developers have the ability to make changes to meet the requirements of the application. They make these changes using features of the object-oriented programming language such as encapsulation, polymorphism, inheritance, and

abstraction. The resulting object frameworks, or "white box" frameworks, allow developers to look inside and modify them where needed.

Object frameworks are language and tool dependent. Most are created using C++, although some are created for PowerBuilder, Delphi, and most Smalltalk tools. Most client/server and intranet-enabled development tools come bundled with some type of framework in order to provide common interface development and database access services.

Service frameworks, in contrast to object frameworks, lack inheritance. Although they provide services, they generally don't provide access to the source code for the distributed objects, making it difficult—though not impossible (depending on the tool or language)—to modify or extend the behavior of distributed objects and service frameworks for an application. As such, service frameworks are the best fit for most B2B application integration problem domains. Distributed object frameworks provide the best example of service frameworks in that they allow applications to invoke methods that are encapsulated in a centrally located distributed object.

Distributed objects, such as those created around CORBA and COM, offer a common approach to being created and deployed. CORBA-compliant distributed objects are sold through a number of third-party vendors. The Distributed Component Object Model (DCOM) comes with the infrastructure of the Windows operating systems. The goal in addressing an integration problem domain is to create a set of distributed objects, using either technology, and then to access those objects either locally or remotely through a well-defined interface from the application that needs a service. For example, distributed objects are built into service frameworks to provide access to accounting functions, financial trading functions, database access functions, and so on. Distributed objects also provide the "plumbing" for easy access to objects residing on network-connected computers.

As we have noted, object frameworks tend to be tool and language dependent. Distributed objects represent one of the best hopes for frameworks because they offer tool- and language-independent frameworks for applications. C++, PowerBuilder, Delphi, and Smalltalk applications can all access distributed object services.

Procedural frameworks provide a good approach to method-oriented B2B application integration. They also represent a "black box" perspective on frameworks in that they restrict developers from extending or modifying their basic set of services. Consequently, if functionality required for a particular application in a procedural language is missing . . . tough luck. The procedural framework itself

will have to be modified to add the functionality, or the function will have to be coded directly into the application without the use of a framework.

The ability to mix and match components allows B2B application integration architects to purchase expertise they may not already possess. For example, vertical market component vendors from the petroleum, financial, and retail industries offer developers specialized functionality that requires little or no custom coding.

In contrast to object frameworks, component frameworks usually contain fewer features and functions than applications, but they provide more services than a simple program function or object. In a number of respects, components are "retro." They adhere more to the modular program model of the past than to object-oriented development.

Framework Categories

Putting aside for now the different types of frameworks that exist, we can examine the three feature categories of frameworks: application service, domain, and support. These categories are consistent among the three framework types.

Application service frameworks encapsulate enterprise application functionality. They provide horizontal functionality across many B2B application integration problem domains. Most frameworks today are examples of application service frameworks. These include the GUI interface frameworks that come with C++ development tools such as Microsoft Foundation Classes (MFC).

Domain frameworks encapsulate expertise for certain problem domains and provide vertical functionality for certain areas of the enterprise (e.g., accounting, marketing, or logistics). These frameworks build common application architectures into a common framework shared across applications.

Support frameworks offer native, system-oriented services such as network support, device access, or file access. These frameworks are typically platform dependent.

Enabling Technology

Armed with a knowledge of the various approaches to method-oriented B2B application integration, we can turn our attention to the enabling technology that makes method-oriented B2B application integration possible. The best technology for this is represented by those software services that allow remote

applications to invoke a set of application services or methods maintained at a central server. With this criterion in mind, we can determine that the enabling technologies for method-oriented B2B application integration include application or transaction servers, distributed objects, and message brokers.

Application or Transaction Servers

TP monitors are industrial-strength middleware products that provide many features that make large-scale distributed transaction-oriented development possible. TP monitors provide the only option for high-volume, high-use distributed systems. They are a holdover from the world of the mainframe, allowing developers to make distributed systems scale to an enterprise-level system (1,000 client/server users or more) through a sound architectural solution.

In addition to such well-known TP monitors as BEA's Tuxedo, Microsoft Transaction Server (MTS), and IBM's CICS, there is a "new kid on the block"—a new breed of middleware known as application servers. Like TP monitors, application servers support the concept of a transactional system. Products like WebLogic, Kiva (now Netscape Application Server), and Net Dynamics are the best of these application servers. Recognizing the benefit of these new servers over TP monitors, many traditional development tool vendors and object database vendors are moving toward application servers as well.

Distributed Objects

When it comes to distributed objects, there are only two choices: COM+ and CORBA. Although it may be a stretch to refer to distributed objects as middleware, as they become more functional they will be able to provide many of the same features as MOM, message brokers, and TP monitors—including the ability to share data and application logic and provide a central clearinghouse for enterprise information.

Sharing Methods within Your Trading Community

The road to method-oriented B2B application integration is not an easy one, but it may yet be the best route to a solution or to the integration of all applications through the reuse of common methods. Most trading communities requiring B2B application integration will likely opt for data-oriented, application interface–oriented, or portal-oriented B2B application integration before attempting

method-oriented B2B application integration. The former types are easier to deploy and carry less risk. However, "no guts, no glory." Depending on the requirements of the problem domain, the method-oriented approach, for all its difficulties, could very well turn out to be the "best" solution for the B2B application integration problem.

Portal-Oriented B2B Application Integration

Portal-oriented B2B application integration allows us to view a multitude of systems—both internal enterprise systems and external, trading community systems—through a single user interface or application. Portal-oriented B2B application integration benefits us through avoiding the back-end integration problem altogether by extending the user interface of each system to a common user interface (aggregated user interface)— most often a Web browser (see Figure 5.1). As a result, it integrates all participating systems through the browser, although the applications are not directly integrated within or between the enterprises.

Portals have become so common and so much has been written about them that we will cover just the basic concepts here. The important point to remember in the context of B2B application integration is that portals have become the primary mechanism by which B2B application integration is being accomplished. Whether that is good, bad, or indifferent doesn't really matter. It is simply the way it is. The reach of internal enterprise systems has been extended to trading partners by utilizing the familiar Web browser interface.

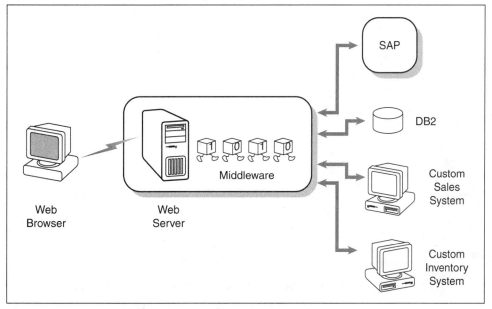

Figure 5.1   Portal-oriented B2B application integration

Why Portal-Oriented B2B Application Integration Deserves Its Own Chapter

Although the other types of B2B application integration focus on the real-time exchange of information or adherence to a common process model between systems and companies, portal-oriented B2B application integration is concerned with externalizing information from a multitude of enterprise systems to a single application and interface in support of B2B. That approach goes against the notions of the other types of B2B application integration, which are more real-time and event-driven oriented, so the inclusion in this book of portal-oriented B2B application integration was somewhat of a judgment call.

However, application integration—although typically referring to the automated movement of information or the binding of processes between two or more applications without the assistance of an end user—can also occur at the user interface for B2B. Indeed, most examples of

> B2B information exchange today are also examples of portal-oriented B2B application integration, with digital exchanges leading the way (see the explanation of digital exchanges later in this chapter). Therefore, it's different, but it still belongs within the discussion of B2B application integration.

Portals by Example

An example of portal-oriented B2B application integration is an automobile parts supplier who would like to begin selling parts to retail stores (B2B) using a portal. This portal would allow the retail stores to access catalog information, place orders, and track orders over the Web. Currently, the parts supplier leverages SAP as its preferred inventory control system, and a custom-built mainframe application written in COBOL/DB2 serves as its sales order system. Information from each system is required for the B2B portal, and the portal users need to update those back-end systems as well.

In order to create a portal, the parts supplier must first design the portal application, including the user interface and application behavior, as well as determine which information contained within the back-end systems (SAP and the mainframe) needs to be shared with the portal application. The portal application requires a traditional analysis-and-design life cycle and a local database. This portal application must be able to control user interaction, capturing and processing errors and controlling the transaction from the user interface all the way to the back-end systems.

Although you can employ many types of enabling technologies when creating portals, most portals are built using application servers (discussed in detail later in this book). Application servers provide the integrated development environments (IDEs) for designing the user interface, a programming environment to define application behavior, and back-end connectors to move information in and out of back-end systems, including SAP and mainframe systems. Although not integrating the application directly, the portal externalizes the information to the trading partner—in this case the owner of a retail auto parts store—and also updates the back-end systems—in this case with orders placed by the store owner or perhaps with the status of existing orders.

Other examples of portals include entire trading communities that are integrated with a single portal application. As many as a dozen companies may provide real-time information for a portal, and hundreds of companies may use that portal, B2B, to purchase goods and services from many companies at the same time. The same type of architecture and enabling technology applies in this case; however, the number of systems integrated with the portal application greatly increases.

Portal Power

The use of portals to integrate trading communities has many advantages. The primary one is that with no need to integrate back-end systems directly between companies or within trading communities, there is none of the cost or risk of doing so. What's more, you typically don't have to worry about circumventing firewalls or application-to-application security, since portals typically do nothing more than Web-enabling existing systems from a single enterprise. With portals, you simply connect to each back-end system through a point of integration (user interface, database, application server, etc.) and externalize the information into a common user interface (Web browser). Of course, portals themselves are applications and must be designed, built, and tested like any other enterprise application.

Portal-oriented B2B application integration also provides a good facility for Web-enabling existing enterprise systems for any purpose, including B2B and Business to Consumer (B2C) selling over the Web. If you need to move information to a user interface for any reason, this is the best approach.

In many B2B application integration problem domains, the users prefer to interact with the back-end systems through a user interface rather than have the systems automatically exchange information behind the scenes (as in data-oriented B2B application integration). Today more B2B information flows through user interfaces (portal-oriented B2B application integration) than automatically through back-end integration. However, the trend is moving from portals to real-time information exchange, which is the topic of this book. We will eventually remove from the equation the end user, who is the most obvious point of latency when considering portal-oriented B2B application integration.

The advantages of portal-oriented integration are clear.

- It supports a true noninvasive approach, allowing other organizations to interact with a company's internal systems through a controlled interface accessible over the Web.

- It is typically much faster to implement than real-time information exchange with back-end systems, such as the data-, method-, and application interface–oriented approaches.
- Its enabling technology is mature, and many examples of portal-oriented B2B application integration exist to learn from.

However, there are also disadvantages to portal-oriented B2B application integration.

- Information does not flow in real time and so requires human interaction. As a result, systems do not automatically react to business events within a trading community (such as the depletion of inventory).
- Information must be abstracted, most typically through another application logic layer (e.g., an application server). As a result, some portal-oriented solutions actually add complexity to the solution.
- Security is a significant concern when enterprise and trading community data is being extended to users over the Web.

Web-Enabled World

The interest in portal-oriented B2B application integration is driven by the widespread acceptance of the Web as a common platform for e-Business. Today we purchase products over the Web, update our bank accounts over the Web, even find romance over the Web. Why not exchange information between trading partners over the Web as well?

The notion of portal-oriented B2B application integration has gone through many generations, including single-system portals, multiple enterprise system portals, and now trading community portals (also known as digital exchanges).

Single-System Portals

Single-system portals, as you might expect, are single enterprise systems that have their user interfaces extended to the Web (see Figure 5.2).

A number of approaches exist for creating a portal for a single enterprise system, including application servers, page servers, and technology for translating simple screens to HTML.

Multiple Enterprise System Portals

When single-system portal architecture is extended to multiple enterprise systems, the result is a multiple enterprise system portal (see Figure 5.3).

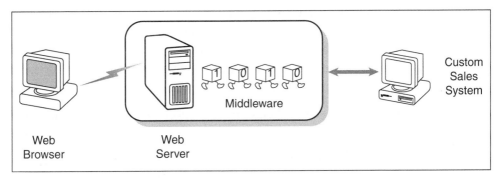

Figure 5.2   Single-system portal

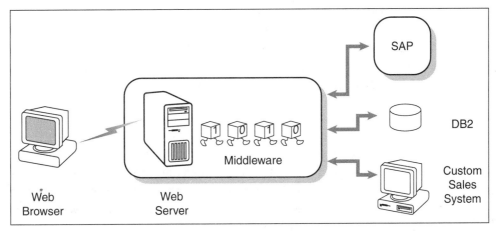

Figure 5.3   Multiple enterprise system portal

This type of portal represents a classic application server architecture, where information is funneled from several enterprise systems—such as SAP R/3, mainframes, PeopleSoft, and inventory systems—through a single Web-enabled application. Users are able to extract information from these systems and update them through a single Web browser interface accessed over an extranet or over the Web.

Trading Community Portals

When the multiple enterprise system portal is extended to include systems that exist within many companies, the result is a trading community portal (see Figure 5.4).

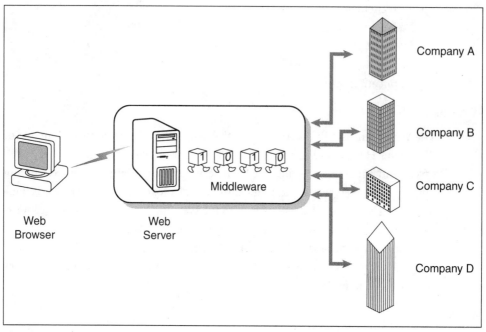

Figure 5.4   Trading community portal

Application servers are a good choice for trading communities, funneling information from the connected back-end enterprise systems. However, because hundreds of systems could be connected to this type of portal, it sometimes makes sense to leverage application servers within each enterprise to manage the externalization of information flowing out of the enterprise, then funnel that information through a single master application server and Web server. The end result of this structure is the information found in hundreds of systems spread across a trading community available to anyone who uses the portal. This is an extremely attractive proposition.

Portal Architecture

It should be apparent that portals are really Web-enabled applications. Given that reality, it might be a good idea to discuss the architecture and components of portals. Portal architecture is made up of the following components (see Figure 5.5):

- Web clients
- Web servers
- Database servers
- Back-end applications
- Application servers

Web Clients

The Web client is a PC or any device that runs a Web browser and is capable of displaying HTML and graphics. The Web browser makes requests to the Web server and processes the files the Web server returns. Rather than exchanging messages, the Web client exchanges entire files. Unfortunately, the process is inefficient and resource intensive. Still, with the Web our preferred common application platform, these drawbacks are also inevitable.

Today, Web browsers need not be PC-running Web browsers. They can also be wireless devices such as personal digital assistants (PDAs) and cellular phones running a Web interface.

Web Servers

Web servers at their core are file servers. Like traditional file servers, they respond to requests from Web clients, then send the requested file. Web servers are

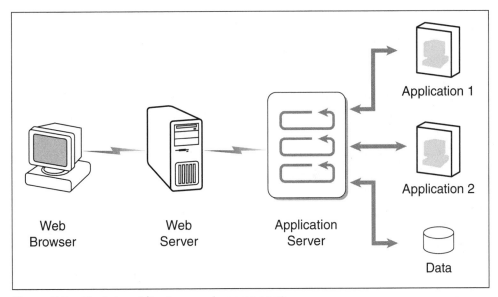

Figure 5.5   Portal architecture and components

required with portals because the information coming from the application server must be converted into HTML and pumped down to the Web browser using HTTP. HTML, graphics, and multimedia files (audio, video, and animation) have been traditionally stored on Web servers.

XHTML Bridges the XML/HTML Gap

Although HTML remains a vital site-development tool, XML (which we will discuss in Chapter 14) is becoming more and more important. Even so, the path from HTML to XML will require baby steps, given HTML's investment in the current Web infrastructure.

Extensible HTML (XHTML), a World Wide Web Consortium (W3C) standard, offers a "middle ground" between traditional HTML and XML. XHTML, considered the ultimate replacement for HTML by its creators, leverages XML for structure and extensibility, providing authors with the ability to use language subsets. More important, it brings structure to HTML, which has been drifting in too many directions for some time. These developments are very important for portal builders. Understanding this new technology and its impact on your site is vital.

With XML out there, along with DHTML, SSL, XSL, and other cryptic acronyms, why would we possibly need another Web-born standard? For two reasons. First, XHTML is built from the ground up as an extensible language. Its extensibility depends on the XML requirement that XHTML-compliant Web documents be well formed (that they conform to the standard, basically). This capability greatly eases the development and integration of new elements within documents. Second, XHTML is likewise built from the ground up for portability. XHTML can run within a number of containers, including devices such as PDAs and WebTV.

Those who resist the change to XHTML have to face facts. HTML is a mess. Portability across browsers is difficult enough without considering portability across static devices.

From a practical point of view, site builders who already understand HTML won't need to learn a great deal more to understand XHTML. In addition, a base of supporting authoring tools exists that simplifies the creation of XHTML documents.

continued

XHTML Bridges the XML/HTML Gap (*continued*)

One of XHTML's strongest features is that it "raises the bar high." It requires well-formed documents and won't accept sloppy coding. For example, there are no exceptions to the requirement to use lowercase-only coding and end tags. None. XHTML also requires that codes be validated against three document type definitions (DTDs) as specified by the W3C. (DTDs are collections of XML declarations that define a legal structure.) Like errant schoolchildren, we've been able to get away with sloppy coding for years thanks to browsers that have been too forgiving. In the long run, this has hurt us. To support portability, these constraints, these higher standards, have to exist.

The specification defines a strictly conforming XHTML document using the XHTML 1.0 namespace found at www.w3.org. This definition identifies a document supporting only the facilities described in the XHTML specification. This means meeting certain criteria: that the XHTML document must validate against the XHTML DTD, as mentioned earlier; that the root elements of the document must be <html>; and that the root elements of the document must designate the XHTML 1.0 namespace. Finally, a DOCTYPE declaration must be included in the document before the root elements. The public identifier included in the DOCTYPE declaration must refer to the XHTML DTDs.

When you use XHTML, all elements must either have closing tags or be written in a special form. And all elements must nest. Although overlapping is illegal with traditional SGML, it works with most SGML-based browsers that have chosen to ignore the rules.

Despite the benefits of XHTML's demands, it is by no means certain that XHTML will be the standard that weds traditional HTML and XML. However, the momentum behind XML and the desire to marry HTML and XML seem to make XHTML the likely bride. In other words, you'll have to support it simply because everyone else does.

The benefit of using XHTML is that you can create content that may be viewed by any number of browsers and devices, and devices seem to be the future of the Web. However, before buying into XHTML, you should consider a number of things, including the cost of changing your site over to XHTML and the risk that the standard will change faster than you're comfortable with when updating your site.

Today's Web servers pull double duty. Not only do they serve up file content to hordes of Web clients, but they perform rudimentary application processing as well. With enabling technologies such as Common Gateway Interface (CGI), Netscape Application Programming Interface (NSAPI), and Internet Server Application Programming Interface (ISAPI), Web servers can query the Web client for information, and then, using Web server APIs, they can pass that information to an external process that runs on the Web server (see Figure 5.6). In many cases, this means users can access information on a database server or on application servers.

Database Servers

Database servers, when leveraged with portals, work just as they do in more traditional client/server architectures—they respond to requests and return information. Sometimes the requests come from Web servers that communicate with the database server through a process existing on the Web server. Sometimes they come directly from Web client communication with the database server via a call level interface (CLI), such as JDBC for Java or ODBC for ActiveX.

Back-End Applications

Back-end applications are enterprise applications existing either within a single enterprise or across many enterprises. These are typically a mix of ERP systems, such as SAP R/3 or PeopleSoft, custom applications existing on mainframes, or newer client/server systems. Portals gather the appropriate information from these back-end systems and externalize this information through the user interface.

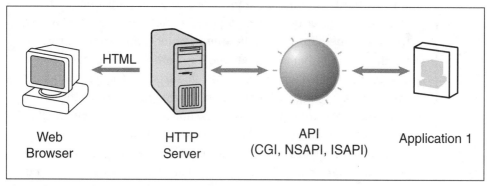

Figure 5.6   Using the Web server API to customize information sent to the client level

Although the mechanism employed to gather back-end information varies from technology to technology, typically portal development environments provide connectors or adapters to link to various back-end systems, or they provide APIs to allow developers to bind the back-end systems to the portal technology.

Application Servers

Application servers work with portal applications by providing a middle layer between the back-end applications, databases, and the Web server. Application servers communicate with both the Web server and the resource server using transaction-oriented application development. As with three-tier client/server, applications bring load-balancing recovery services and fail-over capabilities to the portal. (Application servers are covered in detail in the context of transactional middleware in Chapter 8.)

What Are Digital Exchanges?

Digital exchanges (also known as trading exchanges) are the latest trend in B2B application integration. They support the notion of a portal and are loosely defined by a few new vendors. Most digital exchanges are just portal sites set up by a particular industry to support trade within that industry (see Figure 5.7). Anyone can access information through the portal and execute trades, such as the transfer of inventory from one company to another.

Let us say, for example, that a digital exchange is established to create a trading community for the automotive parts industry. The digital exchange would be able to publish catalogs from various parts suppliers and allow parts-consuming organizations to order parts online. Digital exchanges would also be able to provide information on availability, current price (perhaps bidding between vendors), and logistics, such as when the part will ship and what time it will arrive. This scenario generally accounts for million-dollar trades in support of larger industries. However, smaller digital exchanges are cropping up, such as those that sell day-old bread to retailers. These exchanges, as you might imagine, deal with transactions of less than a thousand dollars.

There are two types of digital exchanges: active and passive. **Passive digital exchanges** publish catalogs for a particular industry, such as our

---

automotive industry example. They do so with information extracted from a static database and do not support direct interaction with a supplier's information system. At some point, the information is transferred from the operational systems to the digital exchanges and updated as needed. The disadvantage of this method should be obvious. Information published by the digital exchange is not current. Inventory that shows availability could in fact be out of stock—an eventuality that might not be discovered until the supplier organization processes the order.

For this reason, **active digital exchanges** provide a better solution. Active digital exchanges publish information extracted in real time from the supplier's information systems. The advantage of this approach is up-to-the-minute information presented to the digital exchange user, including up-to-the-second inventory levels. The drawback of this scenario is the investment of time and money required to get an active digital exchange up and running, and integrated with all of the supplier's systems.

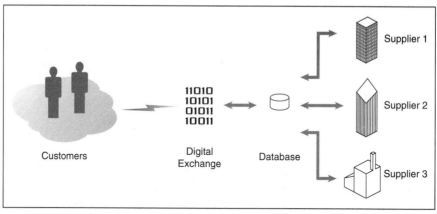

Figure 5.7   Digital exchanges provide portals for particular vertical industries.

Portals and B2B Application Integration

Portals are nothing new. We've been building them since the Web took off and we first understood the value of externalizing existing enterprise data through Web interfaces. That was the birth of B2C e-Business, which led the way to B2B

e-Business—which is, after all, what portal-oriented B2B application integration is all about. What *is* new is the reliance on portal-oriented B2B application integration to support huge transactions and to support trading communities that no longer have to pick up the phone or send a fax to buy, sell, or trade. Portal-oriented B2B application integration removes the need for human interaction to support a business transaction. All that is needed is an interaction with a Web browser.

Unfortunately, although they are a necessity today, portals do not support the ultimate goal of B2B application integration—the exchange of business information in real time in support of business events that do not require human interaction. The goals of B2B application integration are to design the user out of the process, thus removing the greatest source of latency in the exchange of information, and to support the new event-driven economy. However, portals will support most B2B information exchange activity for the next few years.

Process Integration– Oriented B2B Application Integration

Data- and application interface–oriented B2B application integration is the science of integrating numerous applications and data stores so that they benefit one another within a trading community. This application integration is more traditional and typically occurs at the information level by simply exchanging data between systems housed in different trading partners or perhaps by allowing systems to share common methods. Typically, this means defining information flows at the physical level, not taking into account abstract business concepts such as shared agreements and processes, which are becoming critical for B2B application integration.

Until now, what was missing from the application integration mix was the notion of process integration. Process integration is the ability to define a common business process model that defines the sequence, hierarchy, events, execution logic, and information movement between systems residing in the same organization (EAI) and systems residing in multiple organizations (B2B). We'll focus on the B2B discussion here.

Process integration is a strategy, as much as a technology, that strengthens your organization's ability to interact with trading partners, by integrating entire business processes both within and between enterprises. Indeed, process integration delivers B2B application integration by dealing with several organizations using various metadata, platforms,

and processes. Thus, process integration technology must be flexible, providing a translation layer between the source and target systems and the process integration engine. Moreover, process integration technology needs to work with several types of technologies, including message-oriented and transaction-oriented middleware.

Process integration is the science and mechanism of managing the movement of data and the invocation of processes in *the correct and proper order* to support the management and execution of common processes that exist in and between organizations (see Figure 6.1). Process integration–oriented B2B application integration provides another layer of easily defined and centrally managed processes that exist on top of an existing set of processes and data within a set of trading partner applications.

The goal of our discussion is to define a mechanism to bind relevant community processes that exist between trading partners in order to support the flow of information and logic between them, thus maximizing their mutual value.

Traditional Application Integration versus Process Integration

The following is a short description of the differences between traditional application integration and process integration.

- A single instance of process integration typically spans many instances of traditional application integration (information-level integration, including data-, application interface–, and method-oriented B2B application integration).
- Application integration typically means the exchange of information between two or more systems without visibility into internal process.
- Process integration leads with a process model and moves information between applications in support of that model.
- Application integration is typically a tactical solution, motivated by the requirement for two or more applications to communicate.
- Process integration is strategic, leveraging business rules to determine how systems should interact and better leverage the business value from each system through a common abstract business model.

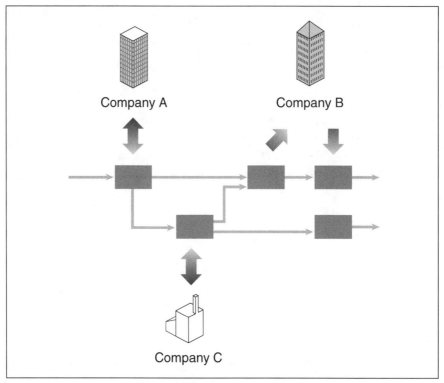

Figure 6.1 **Process integration–oriented B2B application integration manages the movement of information and the sharing of common process models between trading partners, using business-oriented semantics.**

Moreover, we're looking to define a common, agreed-upon process that exists between many organizations and that has visibility into any number of integrated systems as well as being visible to any system that needs to leverage the common process model.

Process integration–oriented B2B application integration views middleware, or the "plumbing," as a commodity with the ability to leverage both message-oriented and transactional middleware as points of integration into any number of source or target systems. In fact, most message brokers and application servers are beginning to offer process integration tools that support their middleware technology. Indeed, process integration generally provides easy-to-use visual interfaces for binding these processes together and along the way creating visual process integration–oriented B2B application integration.

Although some may question the relevance of process integration–oriented B2B application integration and even B2B application integration, we would argue that process integration–oriented B2B application integration is the ultimate destination of B2B application integration. (Acknowledging that, we still have a long way to go to perfect the middleware.) Despite current shortcomings, many B2B application integration vendors are aggressively promoting process integration–oriented B2B application integration as a vital component of their B2B application integration technology package. In doing so, their strategy is clear—they are eager to join the world of high-end process integration–oriented B2B application integration–modeling tools. They hope that their B2B application integration–enabled

---

Understanding the Semantics

As we move into the world of process integration, we are finding that the names for particular types of technologies and approaches can be somewhat confusing. As we mentioned earlier in this chapter, no standard definitions exist for these concepts, so perhaps it's time we created them.

Business process modeling (BPM) provides tools and approaches for the graphical design and simulation of business processes. Typically, these tools are not hooked up to existing enterprise processes but work as pure modeling tools.

Business process automation (BPA) tools and approaches provide mechanisms for the automation of business processes without end-user interaction at execution time. Most EAI tools provide this type of subsystem.

Workflow tools allow for the automation of business processes with end-user interaction at execution time. These categories of technology and approaches are typically document-oriented, moving document information between human decision makers.

Process integration is an aggregation of business process modeling, business process automation, and workflow. This approach implements and manages transactions and real-time business processes that span multiple applications, providing a layer for creating common processes that span many processes in integrated systems.

middleware, such as message brokers and application servers, will accomplish just that.

What Is Process Integration–Oriented B2B Application Integration?

Process integration–oriented B2B application integration is best defined as applying appropriate rules in an agreed-upon logical sequence in order to pass information between participating systems and to visualize and share application-level processes, including the creation of a common abstract process that spans both internal and external systems. This definition holds true regardless of whether or not the business processes are automated. For example, processing an insurance claim or delivering a car to a customer are business events that can be automated with process integration–oriented B2B application integration.

For example, three companies participate in a trading community: companies A, B, and C. Company A produces parts for skateboards, while Company B assembles and tests the skateboards, and finally, Company C sells the skateboards. Each has its own native set of processes and its own internal systems: a production system, an assembly system, and a sales system. Until now, automated integration has been nonexistent, and mail and fax serve as communications between companies.

In order to integrate these applications, the trading community has decided to implement process integration–oriented B2B application integration by defining a common process model that spans all companies and internal systems. This process model defines a sequence and logical order of events based on consumer demand, the purchase of raw materials, creation of the parts, assembly of parts into a product, product testing, and finally, the sale of the product to the ultimate consumer. This common model integrates with local systems by having visibility into their internal application processes, if possible, or perhaps through more primitive layers, such as the database or application interface. What's important is that the common process model is able to produce events that are understood by the systems participating in the process as well as react to events that the applications communicate back to the process integration engine.

The use of a common process model that spans multiple companies for B2B application integration provides many advantages, including:

- The ability to create a common agreed-upon process between companies automating the integration of all information systems to react in real time to

business events such as increased consumer demand, material shortages, and quality problems
- The ability to monitor all aspects of the business and trading community to determine the current state of the process in real time
- The ability to redefine the process at any given time in support of the business and thus make the process more efficient
- The ability to hide the complexities of the local applications from the business users and have the business users work with a common set of business semantics

To this end, B2B process integration provides three main services: the visualization of processes within all trading partner systems, interface abstraction, and the real-time measurement of business process performance.

By **visualizing enterprise and cross-enterprise processes** within trading partners, business managers are able to become involved in enterprise integration. The use of graphics and diagrams provides a powerful tool for communications and consensus building. Moreover, this approach provides a business-oriented view of the integration scenarios, with real-time integration with the enabling middleware or points of integration. This visualization provides business analysts with the ability to make changes to the process model, implement it within the trading community, and typically not involve the respective IT departments.

There are three types of processes to visualize: internal, community-wide, and specialized processes.

- Internal processes exist at the intra-company level, providing the business user with the ability to define common EAI processes that span only systems that are within the enterprise and not visible to the trading partners or to community-wide processes. For example, the process of hiring an employee may span several systems within the enterprise but should not be visible to processes that span a trading community or other organizations.
- Community-wide processes exist between companies and consist of a set of agreed-upon procedures for exchanging information and automating business processes within a community. This is the topic of this chapter.
- Specialized processes are created for a special requirement, such as collaboration on a common product development effort that only exists between two companies and has a limited life span.

Interface abstraction refers to the mapping of the process integration model to physical system interfaces and the abstraction of both connectivity and system

integration solutions from the business analyst. Process integration exists at the uppermost level in the B2B middleware stack. Those who use process integration tools are able to view the world at a logical business level and are not limited by physical integration flows, interfaces, or adapters. What's more, the middleware mechanisms employed are also abstracted and are not a concern of the business process analyst, as long as the common process model is interacting correctly with all source and target systems that exist within all companies.

Although each process integration tool and project may take a slightly different approach, the internal process of interacting with the physical systems typically consists of the following set of events.

1. The source system that exists inside a company posts an event to the process integration engine—for instance, a skateboard is sold.
2. The event is transformed, if required, so it adheres to a standard set of business semantics and information processing mechanisms (synchronous versus asynchronous). This adherence will be engine dependent, but a common set of process semantics and information processing mechanisms must always be defined at the engine level so the analyst can make sense of a business process that spans many types of applications, platforms, and databases.
3. The process integration engine reacts to the event, once transformed, invoking other processes in other systems to support the execution of the common B2B process model. For instance, if a skateboard is sold, the process then sends an order to the skateboard assembler, posting an event from the process engine to the assembler's target system, typically over the Internet.
4. Based on receiving that event, the local system reacts in accordance with its internal processes and posts an event back to the process engine (say, when the skateboard is assembled).
5. The common process model sequences the master process, sending and receiving other events in support of the common B2B process model. This is an ongoing activity, with information moving up to the process engine from the local systems, transformed if required, and moving down from the process engine to the local systems in support of the execution of the process model.

Another way to view the process of creating a process integration model is by defining the hierarchy of processes within the trading community. This means that smaller subprocesses can be linked at the lower tier of integration or are native to the source or target systems. Building up from the lower-level processes to the higher-level processes, you may link the subprocesses into higher-level processes within the domain of the trading community.

The **measurement of business process performance** provides B2B process integration with the ability to analyze a business in real time. By leveraging tight integration with the process model and the middleware, business analysts are able to gather business statistics in real time from the trading community—for instance, the performance of a supplier in shipping goods to the plant and the plant's ability to turn those raw materials into products.

Moreover, process integration provides the technology user with the ability to track and direct each instance of a business process—for example, processing individual orders or medical insurance claims through a life cycle that may consume seconds, minutes, hours, days, or weeks. Finally, we need to measure and maintain contextual information for the duration of a process instance that spans many individual activities.

The good news is that most business processes are already automated within trading communities. The bad news is that they tend to be loosely coupled and to exist on different systems. For example, adding a customer to a packaged accounting application may establish the customer in that system, but it may still be necessary to use another system (a *different* system that may exist within a trading partner) to perform a credit check on that customer and *still another* system to process an invoice (see Figure 6.2). You needn't possess exceptional insight

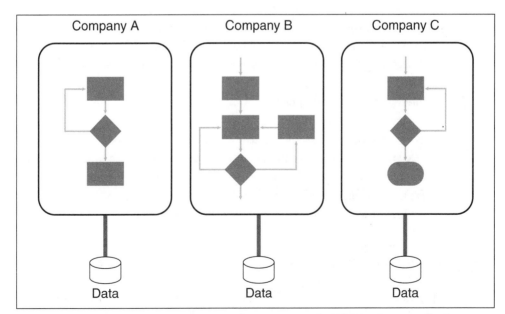

Figure 6.2   Although many automated processes exist within most trading communities, they tend to be loosely coupled or not coupled at all.

to recognize the potential for disaster that exists in this scenario. Not only do these disparate systems need to share information, but they need to share that information in an orderly and efficient manner.

Indeed, the goal of process integration–oriented B2B application integration, and of B2B application integration generally, is to automate the data movement and process flow so that another layer of process integration–oriented B2B application integration will exist over and above the processes encapsulated in existing systems (see Figure 6.3). In other words, process integration–oriented B2B application integration completes B2B application integration, allowing the integration of systems not only by sharing information readily, but also by managing the sharing of that information with easy-to-use tools.

In general, process integration logic addresses only process flow and integration. It is not traditional programming logic, such as user interface processing, database updates, or the execution of transactions. Indeed, in most process

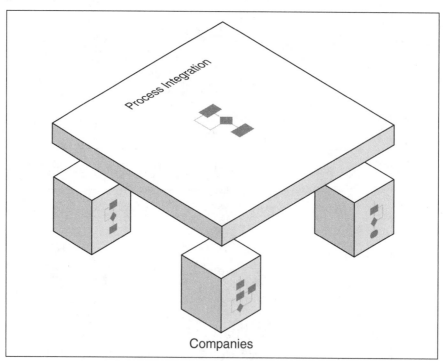

Figure 6.3   **Process integration–oriented B2B application integration is another layer of process and data-movement management that exists on top of the existing trading partner processes.**

integration–oriented B2B application integration scenarios, the process logic is separated from the application logic. It functions solely to coordinate, or manage, the information flow between many source and target applications that exist within organizations (see Figure 6.4).

Such a system operates on three levels of technology (see Figure 6.5). At the uppermost layer is the process integration–oriented B2B application integration level. Here, the process integration–oriented B2B application integration–modeling tools and engines exist, and the method of information movement is defined.

At the next level—the transformation, routing, and rules-processing layer—information movement and formatting occur. Usually, this layer is a message broker or perhaps a B2B exchange server, but it could also be transaction-oriented

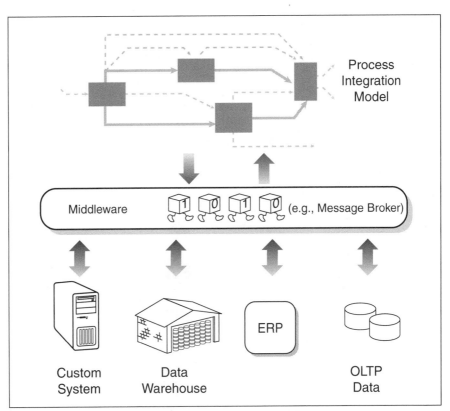

Figure 6.4   **The process logic coordinates the movement of information between many connected applications or data stores.**

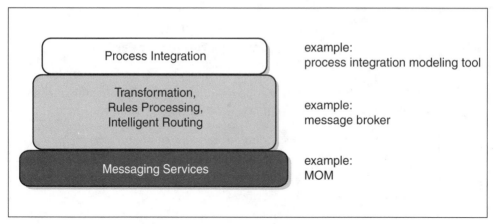

Figure 6.5   The three layers of process integration–oriented B2B application integration

middleware and even distributed objects. (Message brokers, transactional middleware, and distributed objects will be discussed in detail in Chapters 8, 10, and 13.) The only requirement here is that all trading partners support middleware technology or interfaces that can work with the process integration engine. Typically, the process integration engine interfaces with these various sets of enabling technology through adapters or APIs. The adapters or APIs abstract the native interfaces and/or middleware for the process integration engine, allowing the process integration analysis to deal with all systems using a common set of process and business semantics. Thus, the analyst is removed from the metadata and application-level processes that will always vary greatly from company to company and are typically not in our direct control when considering most B2B problem domains.

The application of rules to information moving from one system to the next—reformatting as required, reading and writing from the source or target system interfaces either through direct calls or through adapters—may be accomplished on this layer by B2B application integration standards, including XML, BizTalk, and EDI.

The bottom layer is occupied by the messaging system, which is responsible for moving information between all connected applications. Although application servers and other enterprise middleware function here, this layer is generally dominated by message-oriented middleware or servers that use standards-based messaging such as XML or EDI.

**Process Integration–Oriented
B2B Application Integration Standards**

Although they are covered later in Chapters 14, 15, and 16, it's helpful to take a quick look at some standards that are providing common mechanisms and semantics for B2B process integration.

- RosettaNet—A process-oriented standard created for the technology industry that defines a set of high-level business process flows called Partner Interface Processes (PIPs), which are exchanged and managed between trading partners.
- BizTalk—An industry initiative begun by Microsoft to drive rapid adoption of XML to enabled B2B application integration. BizTalk leverages the BizTalk framework, a set of guidelines for how to publish schemas in XML and how to exchange information between applications using XML.
- EbXML—A joint venture between the United Nations Body for Trade Facilitation and Electronic Business, and the Organization for the Advancement of Structured Information Standards (OASIS), developing a framework for using XML to exchange business data with visibility into common processes.

This schema graphically demonstrates that the most primitive layers reside at the bottom, while the more sophisticated layers reside at the top. Information ascends through the layers from the source system, where it is processed, and descends to the target system, where it is delivered.

Over the years, many existing business processes have been automated, with fair success. But as we have seen with the B2B application integration problem, the problem of how these systems will share information between companies has not received the same attention.

> ## B2B Process Integration and B2B Application Integration Levels
>
> If process integration–oriented B2B application integration is defined as a mechanism to coordinate the movement of information among various connected systems as well as the application of business logic, how does process integration–oriented B2B application integration relate to already established types of B2B application integration? In short, it encapsulates all types, providing process management at the data, interface, method, and portal levels (see Figure 6.6).
>
> Process integration–oriented B2B application integration is application independent. It should also be independent of the various types of application interfaces.
>
> Access to applications is gained in a number of ways. At times access will depend on the data-oriented method, when access is gained using the database as a point of integration, thus employing data-oriented B2B application integration. At other times, access will depend on the application interface–oriented approach, when application interfaces or user interfaces provide the point of integration. Typically, the middleware layer, employed by the process integration layer, determines the points of integration.

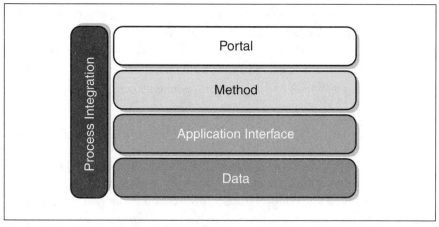

Figure 6.6 **Process integration–oriented B2B application integration encapsulates all levels of B2B application integration.**

Implementing Process Integration–Oriented B2B Application Integration

Integrating business applications into a process integration–oriented B2B application integration solution requires removing flow dependency from the application. The routing feature found in most process integration–oriented B2B application integration solutions allows relevant information to be extracted from any source application, target application, or data store. The advantage of this solution is that only the model itself needs to be altered when a change in process flow or logic is required. There is no need to change the applications that are part of the process model. In addition, this approach allows you to reuse any source or target system from model to model.

Here, as in almost every other context, appearances are sometimes deceiving. Implementing process integration–oriented B2B application integration solutions may very well appear to be relatively straightforward. It isn't. In many respects, it is similar in function to traditional business process re-engineering (BPR) solutions. The primary difference is a layer of automation underneath the model.

You should consider the following things when implementing a process integration–oriented B2B application integration solution.

- Business processes that exist within the trading partner must be *documented*. You must understand all processes and data within the source and target enterprise systems of each trading partner. This is a requirement of *every* type of B2B application integration solution.
- The missing processes required to tie existing processes together must be *defined*. You must understand not only how each process works, but also how each must leverage the other in order to create a more efficient set of processes.
- The processes using process integration–oriented B2B application integration technology to tie these processes together must be *executed*.

Documenting Processes

Wouldn't it be nice if there were a unified approach for properly documenting the processes found in source and target systems? Of course it would be. But for now, we are without such an approach. Approaches vary, depending on a number of technical and political issues. However, some commonalties include

- Reading application documentation, including system and application design graphics and text

- Reading application interface documentation
- Reviewing database schemas for applications
- Reading source code

Defining Processes

Most process integration–oriented B2B application integration solutions provide a way to graphically represent processes, clearly depict business activities, define how information flows between them, and show the logic that controls that flow.

Executing Processes

Very few approaches to executing processes exist. They include logical, physical read-only, and physical read-write (see Figure 6.7).

The **logical approach** executes the process integration–oriented B2B application integration model without actually changing states (e.g., invoking processes or changing the databases within the trading community) at the source or target applications. The logical approach is recommended for testing the process integration–oriented B2B application integration model without absorbing the risk of making real changes inside critical enterprise systems. (Of course, this approach does not solve the problem at hand, but it does provide simple modeling of some future, desired state.)

The **physical read-only approach** allows the process integration–oriented B2B application integration tool to *only* read information from the source systems. This approach protects the systems from a process layer "gone bad." It allows you to read and move information, not update target systems. This approach has the advantage of representing a low risk to you. However, it is underpowered. Reading and processing information generally provides minimal benefit, unless you're able to affect a target system. However, given the sensitive nature of most trading communities, this may be the consensus approach. It is at least a step in the right direction.

Trust could be the first casualty of an event that damages the system's integrity.

The **physical read-write approach** grants the process integration–oriented B2B application integration software *full access* to the source and target systems—the ultimate goal of full integration. However, this approach also carries the greatest risk. Any flaw in the process model could result in a source or target system left in an unstable or incorrect state. You might be able to minimize this risk by leveraging test systems independent of the mission-critical enterprise systems.

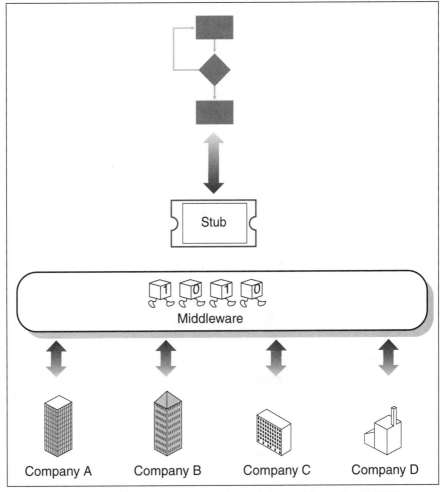

Figure 6.7 **Logical versus physical process integration–oriented B2B application integration**

The cost of such a precaution may be significant, but the ability to mitigate risks—and provide even greater savings in the long run—may very well justify the expense.

Tools and Approaches

As with every type of B2B application integration, a particular set of technologies and tools is available to approach the problem. A process integration–oriented

B2B application integration–modeling tool provides the user with the technology to depict the integration graphically (see Figure 6.8).

The four components of a process integration–oriented B2B application integration model are

1. The common process model
2. Real entities, such as companies, organizations, or people
3. The source and target systems
4. The trading partners

Although it should be self-evident that every process-modeling tool takes a slightly different approach, each generally models the preceding components. The process-modeling tool binds the components together in order to create the final solution by modeling

- The processes, either automated or manual
- The sequence of the processes and applicable logic

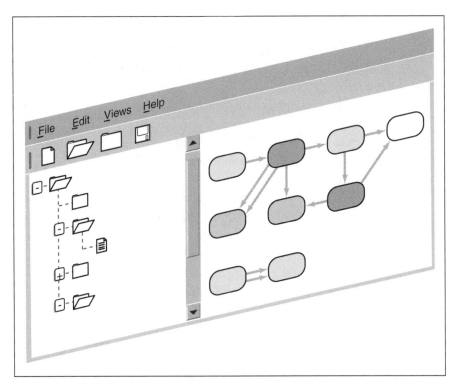

**Figure 6.8   Process integration–oriented B2B application
          integration–modeling tool**

- The human resources involved in the processes, if any of the activities can take place at the same time
- Visibility into all local processes through events
- Visibility into all data stores through events

Process Modeling

Creating the model using the process integration–oriented B2B application integration–modeling tool generally means drawing a diagram that depicts the processes, resources (systems and people), logic, and movement of information between the systems. If the process becomes too complex, subprocesses might have to be defined and even reused from model to model. For example, a credit check may be a complex subprocess that is included within many separate processes.

Drawing a process using a process integration–oriented B2B application integration–modeling tool is simply a matter of selecting items (e.g., resource, process, and data) from a palette and pasting them on a diagram. Once the diagram is in place, all that remains to be done is to define the processes' connections and sequence.

Using this model, we can further define the process integration–oriented B2B application integration logic, or the process logic, that is being layered on top of the existing process logic.

Each process integration–oriented B2B application integration tool approaches this generic description of activities in very different ways. As time goes on, de facto approaches will emerge, and each tool will function in a consistent manner according to a commonly accepted approach.

Middleware Interfaces

A process integration–oriented B2B application integration tool is just that—a tool. Without the proper connections to the source or target systems within the trading community, the process model that is created using such tools cannot execute a new model. In order to make those connections, we need to employ traditional B2B application integration–enabled middleware, such as message brokers, application servers, and other middleware solutions.

Unfortunately, there tends to be a disconnect between high-end process-modeling tools and middleware. Currently, for example, some message brokers may support an advanced process integration–oriented B2B application integration tool. However, they generally support the more rudimentary tools that come with the message broker product. Advanced process integration–oriented B2B

application integration tools *do* support middleware, but they require a fair amount of custom development work on the back-end before applications can be successfully integrated. This is the tradeoff that many B2B application integration architects and developers are confronting.

Things are changing, slowly. Middleware vendors are seeking ways to incorporate sophisticated process integration–oriented B2B application integration within their products, either by building their own product or by licensing a tool from a process integration–oriented B2B application integration tool vendor. At the same time, process integration–oriented B2B application integration tool vendors are building or licensing the middleware.

Process Integration and B2B Application Integration

Middleware still has a long way to go in order to enable process integration–oriented B2B application integration to work. Even so, process integration–oriented B2B application integration will soon be part of most B2B application integration solutions. Once we understand how to connect any data and process point to any other data and process point, workflow will be the way the movement, or flow, of information is managed intra- or inter-enterprise.

Most B2B application integration middleware vendors have begun to create process integration–oriented B2B application integration–modeling tools to augment their existing middleware solutions. This is a step in the right direction. Still, most client organizations will want to pick and choose from the best-of-the-breed solutions. In other words, they will want to mix and match middleware, adapters, and process integration–oriented B2B application integration–modeling tools. This is not possible today. However, once the industry responds with standard interfaces, definitions, and workflow engines, mixing and matching will be easily accomplished, and the ultimate solution to any particular problem domain will be well within reach.

The customization of process integration–oriented B2B application integration models for particular vertical industries is another direction that development is taking. For example, we can create models that define best practices in process integration–oriented B2B application integration and integration within any set of banking systems, because information moves in very similar ways within all banks (see Figure 6.9). Although shareable vertical-market process models are still a few years away, the potential benefit is plain.

The question remains, How will the next-generation process integration–oriented B2B application integration tools and technology add value to a typical

trading community? As businesses rapidly change over time, the need for a flexible information-movement and integration infrastructure increases, moving from the information to the process level. Although state-of-the-art B2B application integration solutions such as message brokers provide flexible solutions today, a tremendous amount of work still remains to be done to bind systems together at the back-end. Every time things change, similar "plumbing" work must be repeated. Process integration–oriented B2B application integration will provide the ultimate in flexibility, because you, the user, will no longer have to address these issues of "plumbing" with most of the complexity abstracted from you. This notion will define B2B application integration moving forward.

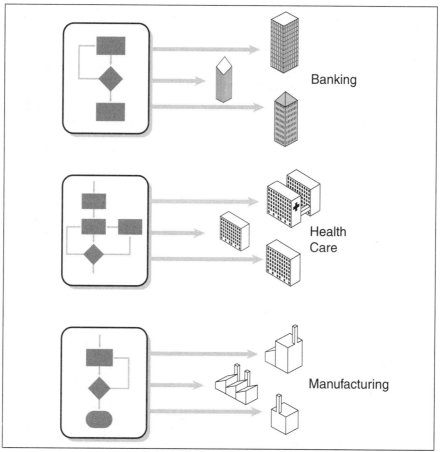

Figure 6.9   **Process integration–oriented B2B application integration models will eventually be shared across verticals.**

e-Business
Integration Technology

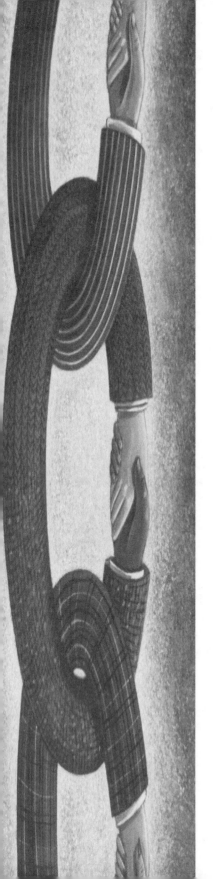

An Introduction to Middleware

We have devoted the first six chapters to B2B application integration approaches and implementation. In the following chapters, we will concentrate on the technology that makes B2B application integration possible: middleware and standards. This chapter provides an overview of middleware, setting the stage for the following chapters to describe several types of middleware technologies that may assist us in solving the B2B application integration problem.

First, middleware is not a magic bullet. What it offers is, quite simply, a mechanism that allows one entity (application or database) to communicate with another entity or entities. That's it. The idea that a middleware product can be installed within an enterprise or a trading community and information can suddenly—magically—be shared is simply not so. Even a good middleware product requires a great deal of work to get from A to B, work that includes the effort already outlined in Chapters 1 through 6.

So if middleware is nothing more than just another tool, why use it? The answer is as simple as middleware itself: It is the only solution that allows applications to communicate with one another. Middleware is able to hide the complexities of the source and target systems, freeing developers from focusing on low-level APIs and network protocols, allowing them to concentrate on sharing information. For example, a single middleware API can be used across many different

types of application development products and many different platforms. This use of a common API hides the complexities of both the entities being connected and the platforms they reside on. And *that's* the beauty of middleware.

Middleware is our best hope for moving information between applications and databases within trading communities. Unfortunately, middleware as it exists today does very little to solve the classic B2B application integration problem. Point-to-point middleware, such as RPCs and message-oriented middleware (MOM), provides connections between applications. But we must change the source and target applications in order to facilitate the use of the middleware. Further, creating many point-to-point connections between many source and target systems quickly becomes unmanageable and inflexible. New types of middleware must be brought into play to address these shortcomings, new middleware that includes application servers and message brokers.

What's Middleware?

There are many definitions of middleware. Ultimately, the definition that works best is the one that defines middleware in terms of its function. As we noted earlier, middleware is a mechanism that allows one entity (application or database) to communicate with another entity or entities. In other words, middleware is any type of software that facilitates communications between two or more software systems.

Such a broad definition is necessary when you consider that middleware can be as simple as a raw communications pipe running between applications, such as Java's RMI, or as sophisticated as information-sharing and logic-execution mechanisms, such as TP monitors.

Because of middleware's importance in the sharing of information, its importance to the B2B application integration solution is growing more and more evident. Although it once was just a tool for moving information between systems within a single enterprise, we now look to middleware to allow us to move information between multiple enterprises. This new demand on middleware presents vendors with a significant challenge, since middleware products were conceived and built exclusively for intra-enterprise integration.

It is a challenge vendors are eager to meet. They are aware of the market benefit they will reap by supporting B2B application integration. Of course, in their efforts to claim the marketplace, they are quicker to change their marketing message than their technology.

Middleware Models

Two types of middleware models exist: logical and physical.

The **logical** middleware model depicts how the information moves conceptually throughout the trading community. In contrast, the **physical** middleware model depicts both the actual method of information movement and the technology employed.

In order to discuss the logical middleware model, we must first discuss one-to-one and many-to-many configurations and synchronous versus asynchronous communications. Any examination of the physical middleware model requires a discussion of several messaging models.

Middleware can work in point-to-point configurations and in many-to-many (including one-to-many) configurations. Each type has its advantages and disadvantages.

Point-to-Point Middleware

Point-to-point middleware utilizes a simple pipe to allow one application to link to one other application—application A links to application B. When application A seeks to communicate with application B, it simply "shouts down the pipe" by using a procedure call or message (see Figure 7.1).

When compared to other types of middleware, point-to-point middleware is limited by its inability to properly bind more than two applications. It also lacks any facility for middle-tier processing, such as the ability to house application logic or to change messages as they flow through the pipe.

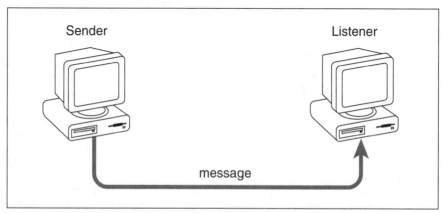

Figure 7.1   Point-to-point middleware

Many examples of point-to-point middleware exist, including MOM products (such as MQSeries) and RPCs (such as DCE). Although it is not impossible to link together more than two applications by using traditional point-to-point middleware, doing so is generally not a good idea. The purpose of these products is to provide point-to-point solutions primarily involving only a source and a target application. Dealing with more than two applications invites too many complexities. Effectively linking more than two applications using point-to-point middleware requires running point-to-point links between all the applications involved (see Figure 7.2).

The idea behind the point-to-point model should make it clear that it does not represent an effective B2B application integration solution, because most problem domains require linking many applications. Perhaps more to the point, in order to share information in this scenario, applications must be linked and information must be brokered through a shared, centralized server. In other words, sharing information requires a message broker or transactional middleware.

However, as with all things, these disadvantages are somewhat offset by advantages. The great advantage of point-to-point middleware is its simplicity.

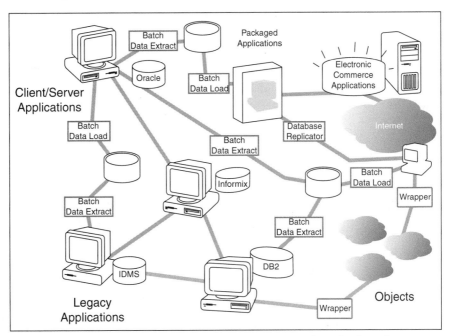

Figure 7.2   Point-to-point middleware does not work well when there are many applications.

Linking only one application to another frees the B2B application integration architect and developer from dealing with the complexities of adapting to the differences between many source and target applications.

Many-to-Many Middleware

As its name implies, many-to-many middleware links many applications to many other applications. This capability makes it the best option for B2B application integration. Being the best option makes it the obvious trend in middleware. In addition to this capacity to link many to many, it is the most powerful logical middleware model because it provides both flexibility and applicability to the B2B application integration problem domain.

Many examples of many-to-many middleware exist, including message brokers, transactional middleware (application servers and TP monitors), and even distributed objects. Basically, any type of middleware that can deal with more than two source or target applications at the same time is able to support this model (see Figure 7.3).

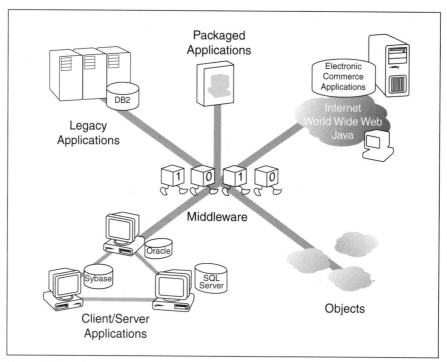

Figure 7.3   The many-to-many middleware model

Although the advantage of the point-to-point model is its simplicity, the disadvantage of the model is its complexity. The current generation of middleware products is becoming better at addressing the complexity of linking together so many systems, but much work remains. Struggling with this complexity falls primarily on the shoulders of the developer.

Synchronous versus Asynchronous

As noted previously, middleware employs two types of communications mechanisms: asynchronous and synchronous.

Asynchronous middleware moves information between one or many applications in an asynchronous mode—that is, the middleware software is able to decouple itself from the source or target applications. The applications are not dependent on other connected applications for processing. The process that allows this to occur has the application (or applications) placing a message in a queue and then going about its business, waiting for the response at some later time from the other application (or applications).

The primary advantage of the asynchronous model is that the middleware does not block the application for processing. Moreover, because the middleware is decoupled from the application, the application can always continue processing, regardless of the state of the other applications.

In contrast, **synchronous** middleware is tightly coupled to applications. In turn, the applications are dependent on the middleware to process one or more function calls at a remote application. As a result, the calling application must halt processing in order to wait for the remote application to respond. We call this a "blocking" type of middleware.

The disadvantage of the synchronous model is the coupling of the application to the middleware and the remote application. Because the application is dependent on the middleware, problems with middleware—such as network or remote server problems—stop the application from processing. In addition, synchronous middleware eats up bandwidth, because several calls must be made across the network in order to support a synchronous function call. This disadvantage, and its implications, makes it clear that the asynchronous model is the better B2B application integration solution.

Connection-Oriented and Connectionless

Connection-oriented communications means that two parties connect, exchange messages, and then disconnect. Typically, this process is synchronous, but it can also be asynchronous. Connectionless communications means that the calling program does not enter into a connection with the target process. The receiving application simply acts on the request, responding if required.

Direct Communications

In direct communications, the middleware layer accepts the message from the calling program and passes it directly to the remote program. Although either direct or queued communications is used with synchronous processing, direct is usually synchronous, and queued is usually asynchronous. Most RPC-enabled middleware uses the direct communications model.

Queued Communications

Queued communications generally require a queue manager to place a message in a queue. The remote application then retrieves the message—either shortly after it has been sent or at any time in the future (barring time-out restrictions). If the calling application requires a response (such as a verification message or data), the information flows back through the queuing mechanism (see Figure 7.4). Most MOM products use queued communications.

The advantage of the queuing communications model over direct communications is that the remote program does not need to be active for the calling program to send a message to it. What's more, queuing communications middleware typically does not block either the calling program or the remote program from proceeding with processing.

Publish/Subscribe

Publish/subscribe (pub/sub) frees an application from the need to understand anything about the target application. All it has to do is send the information it wants to share to a destination within the pub/sub engine or broker. The broker then redistributes the information to any interested applications. For example, if a financial application wants to make all accounts receivable information available to other applications that want to see it, it informs the pub/sub engine. The engine then makes it known that this information is available, and any application can subscribe to that topic in order to begin receiving accounts receivable information.

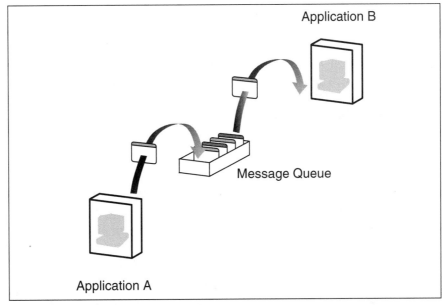

Figure 7.4   Queued communications

In this scenario, the publisher is the provider of the information. Publishers supply information about a topic without needing to understand anything about the applications that are interested in the information (see Figure 7.5). The subscriber is the recipient, or consumer, of the information. The publisher specifies a topic when it publishes the information. The subscriber specifies a topic that it's interested in. In this scenario, the subscriber receives only the information it's interested in.

Request/Response

The request/response model is exactly what its name implies. A request is made to an application using request/response middleware, and it responds to the request (see Figure 7.6). Examples of request/response middleware include any middleware that can facilitate a response from a request between applications, such as message brokers or application servers.

Fire-and-Forget

The fire-and-forget model allows the middleware user to "fire off" a message and then "forget" about it, without worrying about who receives it or even if the message is ever received. This is another example of an asynchronous approach.

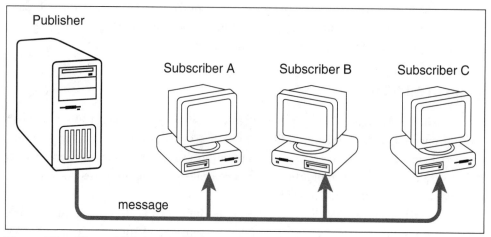

Figure 7.5   The publish/subscribe model

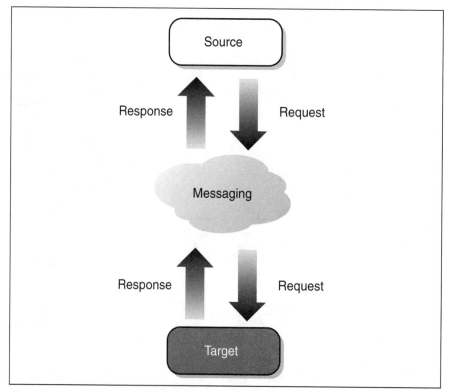

Figure 7.6   The request/response model

The purpose of fire-and-forget is to allow a source or target application to broadcast specific types of messages to multiple recipients, bypassing auditing and response features. It also allows central servers to fire off messages.

Types of Middleware

The evolution of middleware is changing many of the identifying features that had once made categorizing middleware such a straightforward task. For example, many MOM products now perform publish/subscribe tasks, provide transactional features, and host application logic. The challenge of appropriately categorizing such a product should be evident.

However, even as we acknowledge the difficulty in categorizing middleware, we note that several types of middleware continue to solve particular types of problems. For the purposes of our B2B application integration discussion, we will describe RPCs, MOM, distributed objects, database-oriented middleware, transactional middleware (including TP monitors and application servers), and message brokers (see Figure 7.7).

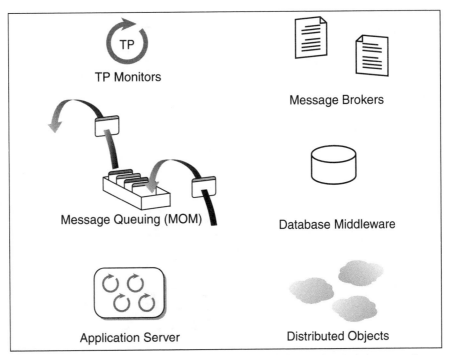

Figure 7.7   **Many types of middleware exist, each solving its own set of problems.**

RPCs

RPCs are the oldest type of middleware. They are also the easiest to understand and use. They provide developers with the ability to invoke a function within one program and have that function execute within another program on a remote machine (see Figure 7.8). To the developer, the function is executing locally. The fact that it is actually being carried out on a remote computer is hidden.

RPCs are synchronous (see the discussion of synchronous function in the section Synchronous versus Asynchronous earlier in this chapter). In order to carry out a remote procedure call, they stop the execution of the program. This quality is what defines RPCs as "blocking middleware." They also require more bandwidth than other types of middleware products, because carrying out a remote procedure call requires so much "overhead."

Over the years, RPCs have become a commodity product. For example, most UNIX systems ship RPC development libraries and tools as part of the base operating system. The best-known type of RPC is the Distributed Computing Environment (DCE) from the Open Software Foundation (OSF), now the Open Group.

DCE provides a very sophisticated distributed RPC mechanism with many layers of services (such as security, a directory, and the ability to maintain integrity between applications). Performance has been a problem with DCE. The DCE RPC performs as fast as any other RPC. Until quite recently, it worked faster than most implementations of IIOP. The problems are that the DCE directory (Cell Directory Service, or CDS) is not scalable, and the administration of a DCE environment is ugly. And for DCE to be effective, it must be deployed everywhere. Very few firms have been willing to make a total commitment to DCE.

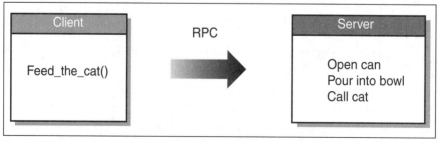

Figure 7.8   RPCs allow local function calls to execute on remote computers.

Despite their simplicity, most RPCs are not well-performing middleware products. To function well, RPCs demand a tremendous level of processing power. In addition, many exchanges must take place across a network to carry out a request. As a result, they "suck the life" from a network or a computer system. A typical RPC call may require 24 distinct steps in completing requests—in addition to several calls across the network. This level of performance limits the benefits of making RPC calls across slower networks, such as the Internet.

RPCs require 10,000 to 15,000 instructions in order to process a remote request. That's several hundred times the cost of a local procedure call (a simple function call). As is the case with DCE, the RPC software also has to make requests to security services in order to control access to remote applications. Calls to naming services and translation services may be required as well. All of this inevitably adds to the already bloated overhead of RPCs.

As we've noted, the advantage of RPCs is simplicity—of the mechanism and the programming. However, when this simplicity is weighed against the huge performance cost of RPCs and their inability to scale well (unless combined with other middleware mechanisms, such as a TP monitor or message-queuing middleware), it doesn't seem to be such a tremendous benefit.

RPCs are bundled into so many products and technologies, it is difficult to know when they are in use. For example, CORBA-compliant distributed objects are nothing more than an additional layer on top of an RPC. As a result, they rely on synchronous connections to communicate object to object (although they are now deploying messaging and transaction services as part of the standard). This additional layer translates directly to additional overhead when processing a request between two or more distributed objects.

This structure is the reason that distributed objects, although architecturally elegant, generally don't scale or provide good performance. The Object Management Group (OMG), the consortium of vendors that created CORBA, is working with CORBA vendors to solve the performance problem.

Message-Oriented

MOM was created to address some of the shortcomings of RPCs by the use of messaging. Traditional MOM is queuing software, using messages—byte-sized units of information that move between applications—as a mechanism to move information from point to point.

Because MOM uses the notion of messages to communicate between applications, direct coupling with the middleware mechanism and the application is not required. MOM products rely on an asynchronous paradigm.

The asynchronous model allows the application to function independently—that is, to continue processing after making a middleware service request. The message is dispatched to a queue manager, which ascertains that the message is delivered to its final destination. Messages returning to the calling application are handled when the calling application finds the time (see Figure 7.9).

Unlike the synchronous paradigm, the asynchronous paradigm does not block the application from processing. Although this model is more complex than the synchronous model, it is more convenient for developers and users. In addition, MOM can ensure delivery of a message from one application to the next for several sophisticated mechanisms, such as message persistence.

Developers find that MOM's use of messages is relatively easy to manage. Messages have a structure (a schema) and content (data). It is possible to think of them as little one-record databases that move between applications through message-passing mechanisms.

MOM supports two models: point-to-point and message queuing (MQ)—the second is our primary focus here.

MQ has a number of performance advantages over standard RPCs. MQ lets each participating program proceed at its own pace, without interruption from the middleware layer. As a result, the calling program can post a message to the

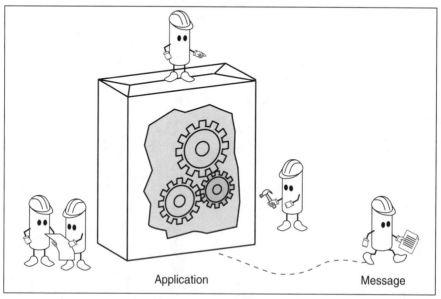

Application   Message

Figure 7.9   Message-oriented middleware does not stop the application from processing.

queue and then "get on with its life." If a response is required, the calling program can get it from the queue later. MQ allows programs to broadcast the same message to many remote programs without having to wait for the remote programs to be up and running.

Because MQ software (e.g., IBM's MQSeries or Microsoft MSMQ) manages the distribution of messages from one program to the next (although the program is responsible for putting messages into the queue and pulling messages from it), the queue manager can optimize performance by utilizing such methods as prioritization, load balancing, and thread pooling.

There is little danger of messages being lost during a network or system failure. Most MQ software allows messages to be declared as persistent or stored to disk during a commit at certain intervals. This ensures recovery from such situations.

Distributed Objects

Distributed objects are classified as middleware because they facilitate interapplication communications. However, they are also mechanisms for application development (in an example of the "middleware paradox"), providing enabling technology for enterprise- or trading community–wide method sharing. In fact, distributed objects are really small application programs that utilize standard interfaces and protocols to communicate with one another (see Figure 7.10). For

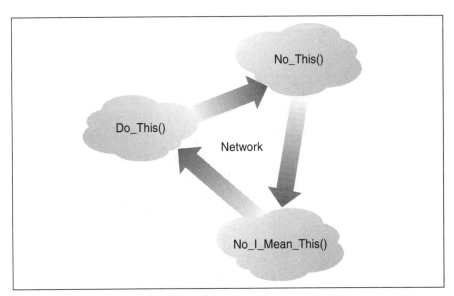

Figure 7.10   Using distributed objects

example, developers may create a CORBA-compliant distributed object that runs on a UNIX server and another CORBA-compliant distributed object that runs on an NT server. Because both objects are created using a standard (in this case, CORBA) and both objects use a standard communications protocol (in this case, IIOP), the objects should be able to exchange information and carry out application functions by invoking each other's methods.

Two types of distributed objects are on the market today: CORBA and COM. CORBA, created by the OMG in 1991, is more a standard than a technology. It provides specifications that outline the rules that developers should follow when creating a CORBA-compliant distributed object. CORBA is heterogeneous, with CORBA-compliant distributed objects available on most platforms.

COM is a Microsoft-promoted distributed object standard. Like CORBA, COM provides "the rules of the road" for developers who create COM-enabled distributed objects. These rules include interface standards and communications protocols. Although COM-enabled objects exist on non-Windows platforms, COM must be considered native to the Windows operating environments and therefore homogeneous.

Database-Oriented

Database-oriented middleware is any middleware that facilitates communications with a database, whether from an application or between databases. Developers typically use database-oriented middleware as a mechanism to extract information from either local or remote databases. For example, in order to extract information from an Oracle database, the developer may invoke database-oriented middleware to log on to the database, request information, and process the information that has been extracted from the database (see Figure 7.11).

Database-oriented middleware works with two basic database types: CLIs and native database middleware.

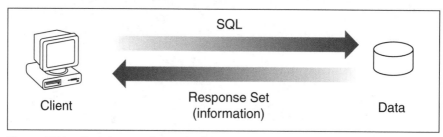

Figure 7.11　Database-oriented middleware

Although CLIs are common APIs that span several types of databases, providing access to any number of databases through a well-defined common interface, they are most often found working with relational databases. Such is the case with Microsoft ODBC. ODBC exposes a single interface in order to facilitate access to a database. It then uses drivers to accommodate differences between databases. ODBC also provides simultaneous multiple-database access to the same interface—in the ODBC architecture, a driver manager can load and unload drivers to facilitate communications between the different databases (e.g., Oracle, Informix, and DB2).

JavaSoft's Java Database Connectivity (JDBC) is another example of a CLI. JDBC is an interface standard that uses a single set of Java methods to facilitate access to multiple databases. JDBC is very much like ODBC, providing access to any number of databases from any Java application: applet, servlet, Java Server Pages (JSP), Enterprise JavaBeans (EJB), or standalone application.

The future of Microsoft database middleware is represented by its OLE DB. OLE DB (see Figure 7.12) provides a standard mechanism to access any number

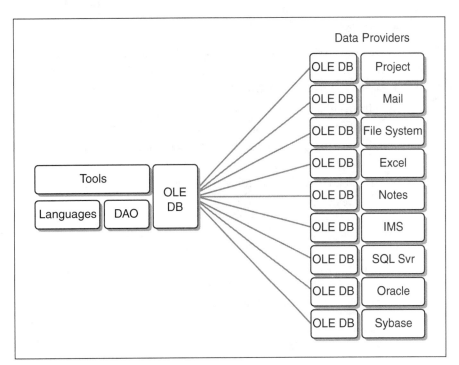

Figure 7.12   Microsoft OLE DB

of resources—including databases, Excel spreadsheets, and flat files—as standard objects (e.g., COM objects). OLE DB provides an object framework to retrieve a result set and then navigate and manipulate the result set in memory. OLE DB relies on the OLE Transactions transaction management framework to ensure the ACID properties (Atomicity, Consistency, Isolation, and Durability).

Rather than use a single multidatabase API, native database middleware accesses the features and functions of a particular database, using only native mechanisms. This limitation—communicating with only one type of database—is the primary disadvantage of native database middleware. Its advantages include improved performance and access to all the features of a particular type of database.

Transaction-Oriented

Transactional middleware, such as TP monitors and application servers, does a commendable job of coordinating information movement and method sharing between many different resources. However, although the transactional paradigm this middleware employs provides an excellent mechanism for method sharing, it is not as effective at simple information sharing—the primary goal of B2B application integration. For example, transactional middleware tends to create a tightly coupled B2B application integration solution, while messaging solutions tend to be more cohesive. In addition, in order to take advantage of transactional middleware, the source code in target applications has to be changed.

TP Monitors

In truth, TP monitors are first-generation application servers as well as a transactional middleware product. They provide a mechanism to facilitate the communications between two or more applications (see Figure 7.13) and a location for application logic. Examples of TP monitors include Tuxedo from BEA Systems, MTS from Microsoft, and CICS from IBM. These products have a long, successful history and continue to process billions of transactions a day.

TP monitors (and application servers) are based on the concept of a transaction—a unit of work with a beginning and an end. The reasoning is that if the application logic is encapsulated within a transaction, then the transaction either completes or is rolled back completely. If the transaction has been updating remote resources, such as databases and queues, then they too will be rolled back if a problem occurs.

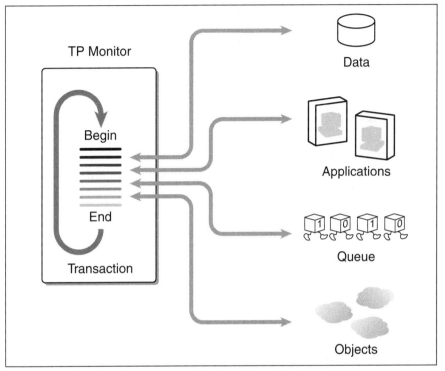

Figure 7.13   TP monitors

Transactions have the advantage of being able to break an application into smaller portions and then invoke those transactions to carry out the bidding of the user or another connected system. Because transactions are small units of work, they are easily managed and processed within the TP monitor environment. By sharing the processing of these transactions among other connected TP monitors, TP monitors provide enhanced scalability. They can also perform scalability "tricks," such as threading and database connection pooling.

The TP monitor performs two major services. On one side, a TP monitor provides services that guarantee the integrity of transactions (a transaction service). On the other side, a TP monitor provides resource management and runtime management services (an application server). The two services are orthogonal.

TP monitors provide connectors to resources such as databases, other applications, and queues. These connectors are typically low-level connectors that

require some sophisticated application development in order to communicate with these various resources. Once connected, these resources are integrated into the transaction and leveraged as part of the transaction. As a result, they are also able to recover if a failure occurs.

TP monitors are unequaled when it comes to supporting a high transaction-processing load and many clients. They take advantage of queued input buffers to protect against peaks in the workload. If the load increases, the engine is able to press on without a loss in response time. TP monitors can also use priority scheduling to prioritize messages and support server threads, thus saving on the overhead of heavyweight processes. Finally, the load-balancing mechanisms of TP monitors guarantee that no single process takes on an excessive load.

By taking advantage of these features, an application can provide performance as well as availability and scalability.

TP monitors provide queuing, routing, and messaging features, all of which enable distributed application developers to bypass the TP monitor's transactional features. As a result, priorities can be assigned to classes of messages, letting the higher-priority messages receive server resources first.

The greatest performance value of TP monitors is in their load-balancing feature, which allows them to respond gracefully to a barrage of transactions. A perfect example of this advantage is end-of-the-month processing. As demand increases, the transaction manager launches more server processes to handle the load, even as it kills processes that are no longer required. In addition, the manager can spread the processing load among the processes as the transaction requests occur.

Application Servers

The fastest-growing segment of the middleware marketplace is defined by the many new products touting themselves as application servers. What's interesting about this is that application servers are nothing new (and TP monitors should be considered application servers because of their many common features). Most application servers are employed as Web-enabled middleware, processing transactions from Web-enabled applications. What's more, they employ modern languages such as Java instead of traditional procedural languages such as C and COBOL (common with TP monitors).

To put it simply, application servers provide not only for the sharing and processing of application logic, but also for connecting to back-end resources (see Figure 7.14). These resources include databases, ERP applications, and even

traditional mainframe applications. Application servers also provide user interface development mechanisms. Additionally, they usually provide mechanisms to deploy the application to the platform of the Web.

Application server vendors are repositioning their products as a technology that solves B2B application integration problems (some without the benefit of a technology that works!). Since this is the case, application servers and TP monitors are sure to play a major role in the B2B application integration domain. Many of these vendors are going so far as to incorporate features such as messaging, transformation, and intelligent routing, services that are currently native to message brokers. This area of middleware is in the throes of something more than an evolution. It is in the throes of a genuine revolution.

Message Brokers

Message brokers represent the nirvana of B2B application integration–enabled middleware. At least, the *potential* of message brokers represents that nirvana. Message brokers can facilitate information movement between two or more resources (source or target applications) and can account for differences in application

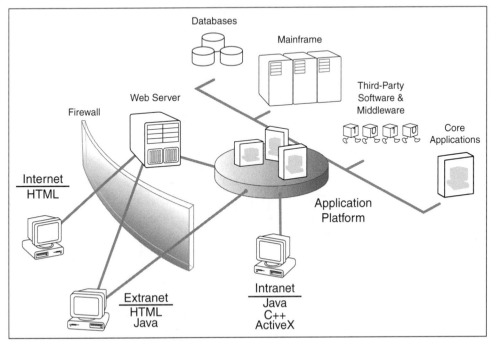

Figure 7.14   The architecture of a typical application server

semantics and platforms. As such, they are a perfect match for B2B application integration (see Figure 7.15).

Message brokers can also join many applications by using common rules and routing engines. They can transform the schema and content of the information as it flows between various applications and databases.

Message brokers, as we have already discussed in previous chapters, are servers that broker messages between two or more source or target applications.

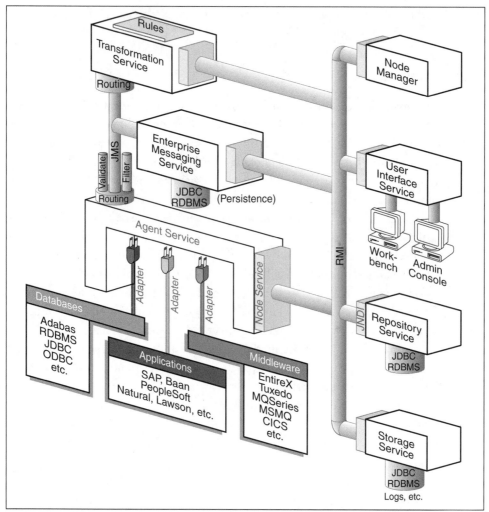

Figure 7.15   Message brokers are able to share information with a multitude of systems by using an asynchronous, event-driven mechanism.

In addition to brokering messages, they transform message schemas and alter the content of the messages.

The importance of message brokers is a function of their place within the trading community. In general, message brokers are not an application development–enabling technology. Instead, they are a technology that allows many applications to communicate with one another—without any application necessarily understanding anything about the other applications it is sharing information with. In short, message brokers "broker" information between applications and databases. By doing so, they broker information between the various members of trading communities.

Tough Choices

Ah, wouldn't life be wonderful if there were only one perfect middleware layer choice, one that provided all the features we needed, coupled with unexcelled performance? Well, wake up and smell the coffee. Life may be wonderful, but it's almost never that easy. Before hooking your application to any middleware technology, you need to examine all the technologies and carefully weigh their advantages and disadvantages as they apply to your particular situation.

RPCs are slow, but their blocking nature provides the best data integrity control. For example, although an asynchronous layer to access data may seem to be the best solution, there is no way to guarantee that an update will occur in a timely manner. It is not difficult (especially for us paranoid types) to envision a scenario in which an update to a customer database is sitting in a queue, waiting for the database to free up while a data entry clerk is creating a sales transaction using the older data. RPCs may be slow, but they would never allow that kind of situation to occur. When you use RPCs, updates are always applied in the correct order. In other words, if data integrity is more important than performance, RPCs may still be your best bet.

Still, as we move forward with B2B application integration, we are finding that within most trading communities, RPCs are not the best choice. This is a direct consequence of the need for instantaneous processing. We never want to hold up an application while it waits for a trading partner application to respond. As a result, asynchronous middleware is almost always the preferred solution within most trading communities, because it does not block an application while it awaits a response from another system. Thus, it supports the notion of long transactions, which are critical to the world of B2B application integration.

MOM vendors contend that synchronous middleware cannot support the needs of today's event-driven applications. Programs simply cannot wait for other programs to complete their work before proceeding. Yet RPCs could provide better performance than traditional store-and-forward messaging layers in some instances. Then again, messaging could provide better performance, because the queue manager offers sophisticated performance-enhancing features such as load balancing.

Middleware remains a great mystery to most people. It is difficult to use and even more difficult to explain. Most users typically never see middleware plumbing, as they do application development and database products. However, as we go forward, we are going to see more user interfaces and business layers included with middleware products. The days of "application program interfaces only" are almost over. Such is the case with newer middleware technologies such as application servers and message brokers that have been created from the ground up for B2B application integration. The presence of easy-to-use interfaces will take the power of middleware—at one time the exclusive domain of the developer—and place it in the hands of the business user.

This is where middleware is headed. It is also how we will ultimately solve the B2B application integration problem.

Transactional Middleware and B2B Application Integration

In this chapter, we will examine transactional middleware from a developer's point of view and from a functional perspective. We will establish those situations in which transactional middleware is a good match for B2B application integration, and we will discuss how to develop B2B application integration around transactional middleware. The first half of the chapter will be devoted to basic transactional middleware features. The remainder will be devoted to the integration of those features with "traditional" transactional middleware—TP monitors. We will conclude by exploring the new breed of transactional middleware—application servers.

Transactional middleware, including TP monitors and application servers, provides scalability, fault tolerance, and an architecture that centralizes application processing—benefits to distributed computing and B2B application integration that cannot be found in traditional development tools or even other types of middleware. Transactional middleware also provides virtual systems and single log-on capabilities. Its strengths often reduce the overall cost of a system.

Transactional middleware can be a good match for B2B application integration, because it provides a centralized server able to process information from many different resources, such as databases and applications. It ensures delivery of information from one application to the next and supports a distributed architecture (see Figure 8.1). However,

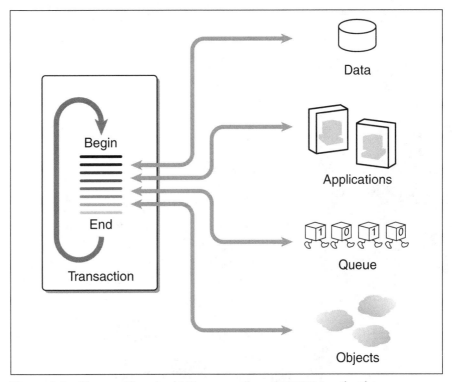

Figure 8.1   Transactional middleware solves the B2B application integration problem by coordinating the connection of many different resources.

despite transactional middleware's many advantages, the cost of implementing it, as well as its intrusiveness, may preclude its use in many B2B application integration problem domains. For transactional middleware to be most effective, applications must be altered to use it, an option that is generally forbidden within trading communities.

Despite its invasiveness, transactional middleware is still worth discussing, since application servers are a good match for many types of B2B application integration problem domains. For example, portal-oriented B2B application integration, which we discussed in Chapter 5, typically leverages application servers as a mechanism to externalize many applications and data sources through the Web.

Transactional middleware has clear limitations within most B2B application integration problem domains. Although transactional middleware excels at

method-oriented B2B application integration or at least the sharing of common business logic to promote B2B application integration, none of the current crop of TP monitors or application servers support "out-of-the-box" content transformation or message transformation services—at least not without a lot of programming. Nor do they generally support event-driven information processing. As a result, transactional middleware does not fit well into data-oriented or application interface–oriented B2B application integration. And if method-oriented integration proves to be transactional middleware's only benefit, then much better options may be available to the B2B application integration architect or developer.

Message brokers or traditional message-oriented middleware are better tools for the simple sharing of information at the data level or the application interface level between companies. This is not to suggest that transactional middleware is not worthwhile for some B2B application integration projects, only that it is of less benefit anywhere but at the method level. As in all aspects of B2B application integration, architects and developers need to understand the relative advantages and disadvantages of their options so that they can make the best choices.

Notion of a Transaction

Transactional middleware is not a new concept. It originated back in the days of the mainframe, at a time when most mainframe databases came with transactional middleware. These were in fact TP monitors that managed processes and coordinated access to the database.

To work, transactional middleware requires that complex applications be divided into bite-sized units called transactions. Transactional middleware controls transactions from their beginning to their end, from the client to the resource server and then back again.

In these scenarios, transactions are either all or nothing. Either they work or they do not. A transaction is never left incomplete. As a result, transactional middleware always leaves the system in a stable state. This provides the developer with a consistent and reliable programming model. This stability also makes transactional middleware a natural choice for distributed applications, which must deal with many different databases, queues, and batch interfaces running on heterogeneous platforms (see Figure 8.2).

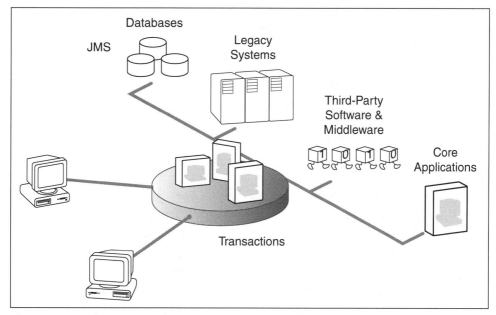

Figure 8.2   Using transactions to tie together back-end resources

The ACID Test

Before delving too deeply into transactional middleware, we must clearly understand the concept of transactions. An easy way to remember the properties of a transaction is to put it to the "ACID" test. That is, a transaction has **ACID properties**—it is Atomic, Consistent, Isolated, and Durable.

Atomic refers to the all-or-nothing quality of transactions. Either the transaction completes, or it does not. There is no available middle ground. **Consistent** refers to the fact that the system is always in a consistent state, regardless of whether or not it completes the transaction. **Isolated** refers to the transaction's ability to work independently of other transactions that may be running in the same TP monitor environment. **Durable** means that the transaction, once committed and complete, can survive system failures.

Although the ACID test might oversimplify the concept of a transaction, it is useful as an easy acronym for remembering the features and functions of transactional middleware.

Developers can count on a high degree of application integrity with transactional middleware—even in heterogeneous environments of very different

operating systems and databases. The most important benefit of transactional middleware is that a transaction is always secure. Even when other things go wrong, transactional middleware won't allow those problems to affect any other transaction, application, or data.

Scalable Development

Transactional middleware processes transactions on behalf of the client or node. It can route transactions through many diversified systems, depending on the requirements of the B2B application integration problem domain. For example, it is not unusual for a TP monitor to tie together a mainframe, an NT server, a multiprocessing UNIX server, and a file server. Transactional middleware also provides load balancing, thread pooling, object recycling, and the ability to automatically recover from typical system problems.

Although transactional middleware is correctly—though only technically—referred to as middleware, it is much more than a simple middleware connection layer. It provides a location for the application code to run and, as a result, a location for business processing and application objects to run. It is also a location where methods can be shared among applications. Transactional middleware can be used to enforce business rules and maintain data integrity or to create entire applications by building many transaction services and invoking them from the client.

Database Multiplexing

One of transactional middleware's great benefits is its ability to multiplex and manage transactions, thereby reducing the number of connections and processing loads that larger systems place on a database. With transactional middleware in the architecture, you can increase the number of clients without increasing the size of a database server. For example, by using a TP monitor requiring approximately 50 connections, more than a thousand clients can access the database server.

By "funneling" client requests, transactional middleware removes the "process-per-client" requirement (see Figure 8.3). In such a scenario (also known as database connection pooling), a client simply invokes the transaction services that reside on the TP monitor, and those services can share the same database server connections (threads and processes). If a connection overloads, the TP monitor simply starts a new connection to the database server. This is the foundation of three-tier architecture and the explanation for how three-tier architecture can scale to high user loads.

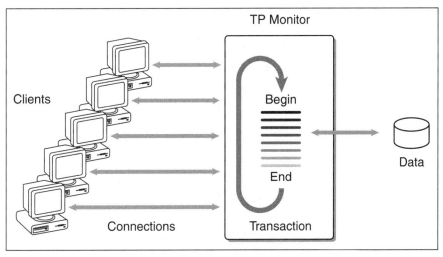

Figure 8.3   Database multiplexing

Load Balancing

When the number of incoming client requests surpasses the number of shared processes the system is able to handle, other processes start automatically. This is what is meant by load balancing. Some transactional middleware can dynamically distribute the process load over several servers at the same time or distribute the processing over several processors in multiprocessing environments.

The load-balancing features of transactional middleware enable it to define "classes" of tasks and therefore to prioritize tasks. This capability assures VIP clients of top-notch service. High-priority classes kick up the process priorities. As a rule, developers use high-priority server classes to encapsulate short-running, high-priority functions. Low-priority processes (such as batch processes) run inside low-priority server classes. Developers can also assign priorities by application type, the resource managers required by a transaction, high and low response times, or the fault tolerance of a transaction. By defining any number of parameters, developers can control the number of processes, or threads, available for each transaction.

Fault Tolerance

Transactional middleware was built from the ground up to provide a robust application deployment environment with the ability to recover from any number of

system-related problems. Redundant systems guarantee high availability. For example, transactional middleware uses dynamic switching to reroute transactions around server and network problems. The transactions work through a two-phase-commit process that ensures that the transactions complete and guards against transactions becoming lost electrons when hardware, operating systems, or networks

---

Building Transactions

With some understanding of how transactional middleware supports B2B application integration, we can now examine how to build transactions. Building transaction services simply requires that you define the functions that the service will perform programmatically when accessed by the required TP monitor APIs. For example, in Tuxedo, the `tpconnect()` function call sets up the conversation with the participating service. The function `tpsend()` returns a response, and `tpalloc()` allocates buffer space.

A problem that many developers experience is that these functions are decoupled from the database, and as a result, they can't work with the schema. This is a problem for developers of specialized development tools (e.g., Visual Basic, Delphi, and PowerBuilder) because they usually work with the schema to construct an application. By the same token, this is less of a problem for C++ developers, who usually work with Dynamic Link Libraries (DLLs) and APIs rather than directly with the schema from the development environment.

In a transaction, the client application generally communicates directly with the TP monitor through a TRPC. (Sometimes, however, another mechanism, such as RMI or IIOP, is invoked.) Once it has received the communication, the TP monitor "talks" to the resource manager (native database API, ODBC, or a proprietary database-dependent network protocol, such as Oracle's SQL*Net), using a native protocol or XA (which defines how transaction managers and resource managers, such as a database, communicate). When transaction services are handled through a 3GL interface, sufficient power exists to integrate many API services into a single transaction. This process can be very successful, but it is highly complex and laborious.

fail. Two-phase commit also makes sure that reliable transactions can be performed on two or more heterogeneous resources.

If the power fails, transactional middleware alerts all participants of a particular transaction (server, queues, clients, etc.) of the problem. All work accomplished up to that point in the transaction is rolled back, and the system returns to its "pretransaction" state, cleaning up any mess it may have left. Developers sometimes build transactions that automatically resubmit after a failure. The ability to create an automatic-resubmit feature is highly desirable in the context of a B2B application integration problem domain, because transactional middleware ensures delivery of the information being shared by the source and target applications. This is a desirable feature, one that has not escaped the notice of message broker vendors. Many vendors are moving to provide transactional integrity in their products.

Communications

Transactional middleware is a good example of middleware that uses middleware, including message brokers. Transactional middleware communicates in a variety of ways—including RPCs (specialized for transactional middleware and called transactional RPCs, or TRPCs), distributed dynamic program links (DPLs), inter-process communications, and MOM. Because transactional middleware is simply an API within an application, developers have the flexibility to mix and match a variety of middleware layers and resource servers to meet the requirements of an application or B2B application integration problem domain.

Application Servers

To this point, we've devoted our discussion of transactional middleware to general terms, highlighting the features and functions of TP monitors as prime examples of transactional middleware. We should never underestimate the importance of TP monitors. Even so, we must also consider a different breed of transactional middleware. (Although the press uses the terms "application server" and "TP monitor" interchangeably—and in reality they *are* morphing into the same feature function set—application servers are different enough and important enough for us to devote the remainder of the chapter to them.)

Application servers not only provide a location for application logic and interface processing, they also coordinate many resource connections (see Figure

8.4). They are typically Web-enabled and bring transaction processing to the Web through any number of mechanisms (see "Considering Object State Management and Application Servers").

The new application servers tend to support Java as both the native language and the development model (although in different ways) as they progress toward the new world of Enterprise JavaBeans, or EJB (described in the section Enterprise JavaBeans later in this chapter).

Application servers take many existing enterprise systems and expose them through a single user interface, typically a Web browser. For example, application servers can easily externalize information contained in mainframes, ERP applications, and even middleware without a user interface. As a result, developers can gain all the application development capabilities they require, including a programming language and an integrated development environment. This makes application servers ideal for portal-oriented B2B application integration.

As always, technology gives and technology takes. Where there are strengths, there are also weaknesses. Application servers are not strong in providing back-end

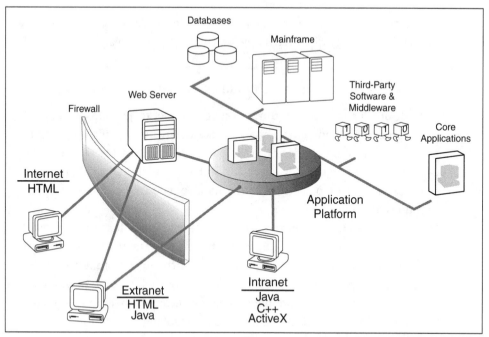

Figure 8.4   **Application servers provide both a location for application logic and a mechanism to coordinate connections to remote resources.**

integration or application-to-application integration, when the information is rarely externalized through a user interface. This weakness is a direct result of the need to code all parts of the information extraction, transformation, and update process, typically through traditional transaction semantics.

Because application servers were created for Web-based transactions and application development, their benefit to B2B application integration is obvious. The ability to perform back-end integration (to bind together several source and target applications through a series of connectors provided by the application server vendors—for example, SAP, PeopleSoft, Baan, relational databases, and middleware) makes them invaluable in this context.

In addition to being a mechanism for integration, application servers provide an up-to-date approach to sharing methods. Unfortunately, each application server has its own approach to how this happens. Because of this "individuality," making sound decisions about the selection of an application server—or application servers—for a B2B application integration project requires an understanding of both the category of features and the problem at hand.

Evolving Transactions

Application servers have been used extensively over the years, as have enabling mechanisms such as distributed objects. However, new demands have forced us

---

Considering Object State Management and Application Servers

Most application servers use a stateless model to provide component processing environments, enhancing scalability through the recycling of an object in the memory of the application server. Rather than destroy and re-create objects for every connected node, the application server keeps a pool of objects ready to hand out to any external process-requesting service.

The stateless component model has the advantage of improved scalability. Unfortunately, it also has two major disadvantages. The first is that it does not support multiple references to the properties of an object. As a result, it does very little to support object reuse through the object-oriented programming model. The second is that it has to create a new object for each database request, resulting in a performance hit when object data is loaded from a back-end database.

to re-examine this paradigm, adding up-to-date products such as those built around the notion of processing components with transactionality. This re-examination and development provides us with a dynamic window into the evolution of the technology. And what we see is that the progress is uneven. Despite the development of application servers, TP monitors remain far ahead in performance and reliability. By the same token, application servers have surpassed TP monitors in certain respects, such as having more advanced features (an integrated development environment, for example).

Taking the strengths and weaknesses of application servers into account, we can clearly see their benefit. By placing some or most of the application logic on a middle tier, developers can exert increased control over the application logic through centralization. Such placement increases the ability to scale the application through a set of tricks, such as database multiplexing and load balancing, described previously. The end result is a traditional three-tier client/server computing model (see Figure 8.5), consisting of a presentation layer (the part that presents the information to the user), an application layer (the middle-tier application logic) and a data layer (where the data resides).

The two dominating standards are Java, with its Enterprise JavaBeans initiative (also closely tied to CORBA), and COM+, integrating with products such as Microsoft Transaction Server and Microsoft AppCenter.

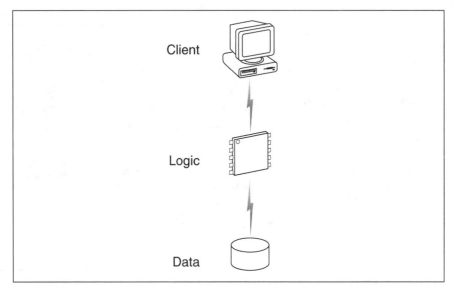

Figure 8.5   Application architecture, using an application server

Enterprise JavaBeans

The primary difference between application servers and traditional transactional middleware (such as TP monitors) is that that application servers are able to function around the notion of transactional components. Nearly every application server using this transactional component–type architecture is looking to employ EJB as the enabling standard. However, each application server is accomplishing this in its own special way.

This awkward reality is partially the result of standards that are still in a state of flux. Sun is working hard to address the issue of a standard and build a certification process.

Although EJBs are really Java-enabled middleware (and therefore a topic to be covered later, in Chapter 12), their discussion is appropriate in the context of application servers, because they add the most value to transactional middleware.

The EJB specifications (see www.javasoft.com) define a server-side component model for JavaBeans (see Figure 8.6). EJBs represent specialized JavaBeans that run on a remote server (known as the EJB container). From the point of view of architecture, EJBs look very similar to distributed objects, such as COM and CORBA.

Utilizing the same architecture as traditional JavaBeans, EJBs can be clustered together to create a distributed application with a mechanism to coordinate

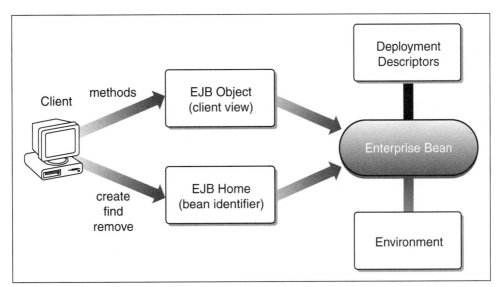

Figure 8.6   EJBs define a server-side component model.

the processing that occurs within the JavaBeans. As such, they reside on application servers, which are able to process the beans as transactional components.

The EJB model supports the notion of implicit transactions. EJBs do not need to specify the transactional demarcation point in order to participate in distributed transactions. This feature represents an essential benefit to the model. The EJB execution environment automatically manages the transaction on behalf of the EJBs, using transaction policies that can be defined with standard procedures during the deployment process. Of even greater benefit, transactions may be controlled by the client-side applications.

Although, the EJB model defines the relationship between an EJB component and an EJB container system, EJBs do not require the use of a specific container system. Any application execution system, such as an application server, can be adapted to support EJBs by adding support for services defined in the EJB specification, services that define the specified relationships between EJBs and a container. The application execution system also provides a portability layer. As a result, EJBs can run in any execution system (EJB container) that supports the EJB standard.

An EJB execution system is called an EJB Server. It provides a standard set of services to support EJB components. EJBs and the EJB Server are analogous to traditional transactional systems. Thus, an EJB Server must provide access to a standard distributed transaction-management mechanism.

An EJB container brings into play the management and control services for a class of EJB objects. In addition, this system provides life-cycle management, transaction control, persistence management, and security services. The larger concept and benefit here is allowing a single vendor to provide both the EJB Server and the associated EJB container.

Transactional COM+ (Using AppCenter)

In a strategy similar to the one employed with EJBs, Microsoft is seeking to support transactionality through COM+ and AppCenter, with AppCenter providing an environment to process transactional COM+ components along with traditional TP monitor features, such as support for ACID, database access, and recoverability.

You have likely discovered that the sophisticated application server architecture of Windows 2000 is a notable plus, as are the hundreds of application development tools available for the Windows 2000 platform. (This may very well be a comment more about what runs on what than how well something runs.)

Component-Dynamic Load Balancing within Windows 2000 supports up to eight connected application servers (nodes), providing application developers with the ability to process one or many COM+ components across a cluster using AppCenter Server. In reality, an AppCenter Server is a Microsoft Transaction Server for transaction support and a Microsoft Message Queue (MSMQ) server for message queuing support all rolled into a single distributed COM+ processing environment. AppCenter acts as a router, using server response time to find the least busy server to create COM+ components for processing. As a result, it balances the load

The market for AppCenter consists of those organizations seeking to support both Web- and enterprise-based application processing loads that exceed a single server or symmetric multiprocessing (SMP)-based server.

Component-Dynamic Load Balancing is built to compete with the high-end application servers. These products work primarily with the Enterprise JavaBeans standard from Sun, providing a similar component-processing model on both Microsoft and non-Microsoft platforms. Unfortunately for Microsoft, MTS never got the traction it had hoped. AppCenter is its attempt to roll over the existing leaders.

Future of Transactional Middleware

The future of transactional middleware and B2B application integration is both straightforward and open to change. Despite the lack of hype on their behalf, TP monitors will remain the dominant transactional middleware. They provide the best mix of standards, scaling features, and reputations. They are proven workhorses. (IBM's CICS has been around for decades, and Tuxedo continues to process billions of transactions a day.) However, even acknowledging those strengths, we have no intrinsic reason to cling to "traditional" technology. The new line of application servers holds great promise, with easy-to-use development features and the ability to leverage hype-driven standards such as EJB and COM+. More than TP monitors, application servers are well suited for creating portals. This feature will make them popular for creating portals in support of B2B application integration.

TP monitor vendors are hardly "sitting out" the application server revolution. Both IBM and BEA have enhanced their TP monitors with transactional servers that can function in a distributed computing environment. Still, the current state of TP monitors only brings up more questions. In the future, are application servers going to look more like TP monitors, or are TP monitors going to

look more like application servers? (Application servers have yet to match the robust transactional model and integrity controls provided by TP monitors.)

EJBs are a step in the right direction—but only a step. The specification does not give detailed definitions of the exact nature of the technology, such as thread pooling, concurrency control, and resource management. Although this ambiguity provides vendors with an excuse to differentiate their products, it also allows them to stray in different directions and to use different proprietary mechanisms. Fortunately, Sun understands the danger and is moving quickly to establish a certification program to ensure that all products promoted as being EJB-compliant actually are. Sun is also accelerating the progress of EJBs, providing vendors with the ability to adopt this standard sooner rather than later. Before long, we will be able to create a set of EJBs within any compliant tool and run those within any compliant container.

The benefit of coupling transactional middleware with B2B application integration is clear. B2B application integration problem domains that need to support transactions between applications, share logic and data, and are willing to incur the cost of changing all connected applications, are perfect for transactional middleware–type solutions. B2B application integration architects and developers, however, have to carefully consider the integration requirements (both technical and business) before committing to transactional middleware. In fact, most B2B application integration problem domains will need a suite of middleware, transactional and nontransactional, to meet their ultimate business requirements. Unfortunately, the problems are too complex to apply one generic solution, as we'll discover in the following chapters.

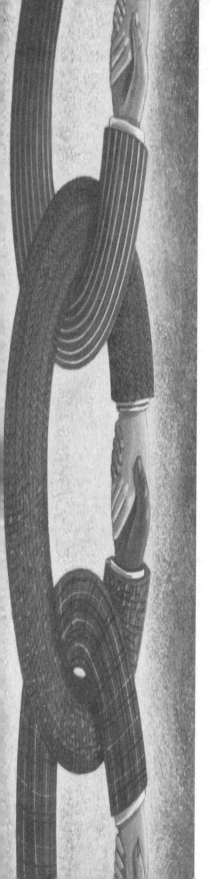

RPCs, Messaging, and B2B Application Integration

A couple of considerations make our discussion of MOM and RPC-based middleware both brief and possibly irrelevant. The first is that message-oriented middleware and RPC-based middleware tend to be traditional, point-to-point middleware and therefore ineffective solutions for most B2B application integration projects. The second is that there isn't a great deal we can add to what has already been published on the subject.

Because of these considerations, we are confronted with the question, Why devote time and energy to a discussion of this technology if it isn't an effective component of the solution set? The answer is simple and straightforward. We need to understand point-to-point middleware in order to integrate it within the enterprise. Our discussion will therefore center on the application of this technology to the new B2B application integration space and on the evolution of this technology in support of B2B application integration.

Middleware itself is a common point of integration for source and target systems. Despite the limitations of MOM and RPC-based middleware for B2B application integration solutions, the necessary tradeoffs in both technology and product decisions may make the inclusion of this middleware important to a particular B2B application integration problem domain.

RPCs

As we noted in Chapter 7, RPCs are nothing more than a method of communicating with a remote computer, a method in which the developer invokes a procedure on the server by making a simple function call on the client (see Figure 9.1). By functioning in this way, RPCs hide the intricacies of the network and operating system. (Recall that the client process that calls the remote function must suspend itself until the procedure completes.)

RPCs are easy to understand and just as easy to use. Even so, they can be problematic when incorporated into a B2B application integration problem domain. The need to stop an application from processing during a remote call could limit the performance of the application. In addition, because RPCs demand a high level

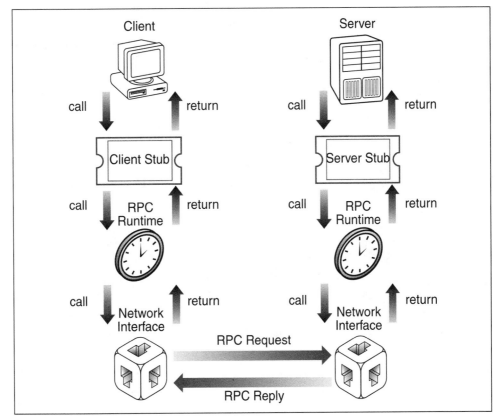

Figure 9.1   Using RPCs

of network communication between the client and the server, RPC architecture requires a high-speed network. Most B2B application integration solutions run across the Internet, which is anything but high-speed.

RPCs formed the base middleware layers in early client/server systems. Then, as now, they functioned as database-oriented middleware layers. In addition, they are capable of running network operating systems, such as Sun's Network File System (NFS) and Open Software Foundation's DCE. Distributed object technology, such as COM and CORBA, leverage RPCs effectively in order to provide object-to-object communications.

Understanding DCE

DCE is a complex, but effective, middleware solution. Developed by Open Software Foundation, DCE allows many diverse computers to function as a single virtual system—the ultimate goal of distributed computing (see Figure 9.2). Who could argue the relevance of this ability to B2B application integration? DCE can make it happen. But what causes the heart of DCE to beat? A classic RPC mechanism! As a result, every inherent limitation of RPCs—including blocking and the need for a high-speed network—exists in DCE as well. As they say, a chain is only as strong as its weakest link.

Despite these limitations, DCE is a key infrastructure component in many larger organizations. Developers can use DCE as a middleware layer to span every system in the company, tying together many systems, applications, and users. Despite DCE's ability to deliver a comprehensive, multivendor network operating system solution, many enterprises are moving away from it, opting instead for messaging technology, such as message brokers or other MOM.

As we noted earlier, at the heart of DCE beats an RPC. It lets developers reach across platforms to access many types of application services, including database, distributed objects, and TP monitors. DCE also provides a sophisticated naming service, a synchronization service, a distributed file system, and built-in network security. DCE is available on most platforms.

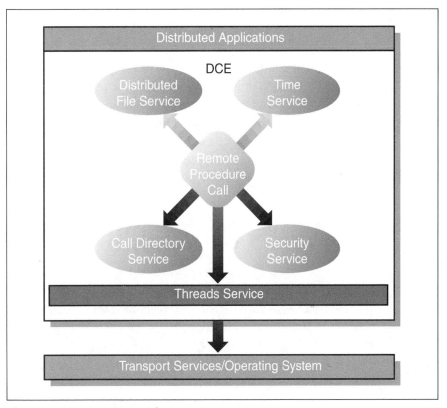

Figure 9.2   The DCE architecture

Message-Oriented Middleware

When bandwidth that can support RPCs is absent or in a situation where a server cannot be depended upon to always be up and running, message-oriented middleware may be the better choice for a B2B application integration project. Like RPCs, MOM provides a standard API across hardware, operating system platforms, and networks (see Figure 9.3). MOM has the additional benefit of being able to guarantee that messages will reach their destination—even when the destination is not available at the time the messages are sent.

MOM utilizes one of two "macro-messaging" models: process-to-process or message queuing. In the process-to-process model, to exchange messages, both the sending and receiving processes must be active. In the queuing model, only one process must be active, because messages can be stored in a queue. The queuing

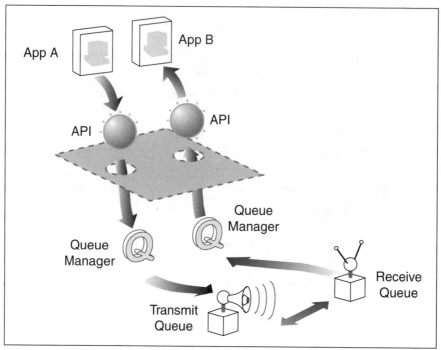

Figure 9.3 MOM provides an API to allow programmers to access its services.

model is best when communication is taking place between computers that are not always up and running, over networks that are not always dependable, or when there is a limitation on bandwidth. When taking into account MOM usage, we should not be surprised that there is a movement from process-to-process to queuing.

Unlike RPCs, which block processing until the procedure call returns, MOM is asynchronous and consequently allows the application to process when the middleware API is invoked. MOM message functions can return immediately, even though the request has not been completed. This allows the application to continue processing, assured that it will know when the request is completed.

The queuing model works best with transaction-oriented B2B application integration applications that must traverse many platforms. Unlike DCE, the queuing model does not require that the platform be up and running for an application to request services. If the server is down, the request remains in a queue. As soon as the server comes back online, the request is processed. In addition to these

---

Aren't Message Brokers MOM?

Of course they are. After all, they use messaging as the primary form of communications, don't they? Technically, that makes them MOM. However, for the purposes of this chapter's discussion, when we refer to MOM, we are referring to more traditional MOM, or message-queuing software. In fact, recently many people have begun to call message brokers integration brokers because of their complexity and specialized purpose of many-to-many application integration.

Queuing software requires that you use an API to change both source and target systems, adapting them to the middleware. They almost always function point-to-point (one application to one application). In contrast, message brokers are able to connect many applications to many applications. They can provide message transformation, routing, and rules-processing services. They can also leverage adapters that minimize the impact on the integrated applications.

Message brokers seem to provide a good fit for B2B application integration. Traditional messaging middleware generally does not. Message brokers are so important to application integration that they deserve their own middleware category, a category we will deal with more completely later, in Chapter 13.

---

queuing features, MOM provides concurrent execution features, allowing the processing of more than one request at a time.

With all these beneficial features, when should MOM be applied? It is a good choice for store-and-forward communications or when dealing with applications that are not expected to be reachable at the same time. MOM is a good choice for "defensive communication"—communication between applications when networks frequently fail. MOM is also a good choice for journaled communications—when communications between processes need to be logged.

MOM and messaging tend to be better application integration choices than RPC-based middleware. However, if we've learned anything during our examination of B2B application integration solutions, it is that there is no objective "best" choice. Most solutions require a certain amount of thoughtful mixing and matching. MOM is no different in this respect. By itself, it does not pro-

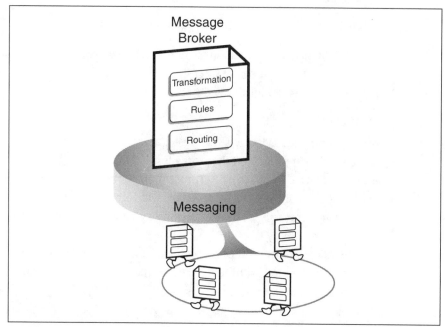

Figure 9.4   Message brokers may use MOM to transport messages.

vide the complete infrastructure necessary for B2B application integration. Message brokers add value to traditional MOM products by providing data and schema transformation functions, along with intelligent routing and event-driven processing to move information throughout an enterprise. Such a scenario relies on MOM products as little more than functional transport layers (see Figure 9.4).

All MOM products have some B2B application integration strategy. MSMQ, for example, is seeking to leverage Microsoft's SQL Server as both a message broker and a BizTalk Server. The goal is to be able to transform and route messages using MSMQ as the underlying transport layer. MQSeries uses its MQ Integrator product to add message broker services to MQSeries. SAGA Software's Sagavista is also able to leverage MQSeries for transport (in addition to using the Java Message Service, or JMS).

MQSeries is looking to build many of the features found in traditional message brokers into the base messaging layer. It's conceivable that MQSeries will become queuing software as well as a message broker in the years to come. In the meantime, other MOM, including MSMQ, will likely evolve along much the same path.

Examples of MOM

Each MOM product delivers messaging in its own way. Two of the most popular MOM products—MSMQ from Microsoft and MQSeries from IBM—give us insight into how different products approach their tasks.

MSMQ

MSMQ server is a Windows NT–based and COM-enabled MOM product. It is also a key product in Microsoft's foray into the enterprise computing arena. MSMQ joins Microsoft Transaction Server, Internet Information Server (IIS), SQL Server, and Active Platform in complementing an impressive array of products, technology, and tools that finally give Microsoft the ability to scale.

MSMQ provides a set of ActiveX components that implement an API to all MSMQ features. Although ActiveX allows the other Microsoft products to access MSMQ, you can also access MSMQ from such traditional Windows applications as Excel and Word or through any ActiveX-enabled development tool.

MSMQ can guarantee the delivery of messages by utilizing disk-based intermediary storage and log-based recovery techniques (an optional feature that, although beneficial, diminishes performance).

MSMQ leverages most popular network protocols, including IPX/SPX and TCP/IP. Using MSMQ as a common translation mechanism allows protocols to be mixed and matched.

Like MQSeries (discussed shortly), MSMQ supports transactions. In the MSMQ environment, transactions either work or fail. If they fail, they recover completely. The participating system is never left in an unstable state. For example, in a database update operation, any abort condition causes the database updates to roll back by stopping the send operation. As with transactional middleware, operations are never completed until the transaction is committed.

MSMQ is tightly integrated with MTS. When MTS is present, its services automatically participate in the MSMQ transaction.

MSMQ administrators work through the MSMQ Explorer, which manages all machines in the MSMQ environment from a single administration workstation. It uses shared and replicated directory services to

handle the configuration information. MSMQ is able to layer into the Windows NT security subsystem, leveraging the NT Access Control List facility.

Features of MSMQ include

- One-time, in-order delivery, which assures developers that messages are delivered to their destinations only once and in the order they were sent. (This feature addresses a common complaint about primitive MOM products, in which messages are out of order when they hit another application or resource server.)
- Message-routing services, which give the B2B application integration applications the ability to send messages to their destination using least-cost routing. (An administrator defines the cost of each route, and MSMQ automatically calculates the most economical path for the message.)
- Notification services, which inform the sender that the message was received and processed. They also handle messages that time out, giving developers the opportunity to take corrective action.
- Message priorities, which allow developers to assign priorities to messages. High-priority messages are placed before low-priority messages in the queue (allowing, for example, larger orders or orders from preferred customers to be processed before other orders).
- Journaling. The journaling subsystem maintains copies of messages moving through the system. Developers can select messages and queues for the journal. This capability allows developers to recover from failures by bringing the messages into synch with the journals.

Building a B2B application integration application using MSMQ is not particularly complicated. When an application needs to place a message in the queue, it uses the MSMQ Open API, which has an ActiveX control wrapped around it. Passing in the name and destination queue creates a queue handle, allowing MSMQ to identify the destination queues to the MSMQ server sending the message. Once a queue handle has been created, a message is created by allocating local memory and adding information to the message. Parameters (such as time-out values, names of response queues, and priorities) can be added at

continued

Examples of MOM (*continued*)

this point. The message is then sent through the MSMQ Send API (`MQSendMessage`). Finally, the application closes the queue handle by using the MSMQ Close API (`MQCloseQueue`). The queue handle can be left open if additional messages are slated to go out later—opening and closing queues too often degrades application performance.

The receiver application requires the Open API, along with queue identification information, to create the queue handle. When the application calls the MSMQ Receiver API, MSMQ passes back a pointer with control information to the message (such as the name of the response queue). After receiving the information, the application closes the connection to the queue. Figure 9.5 shows the architecture of MSMQ and the foundation for this process. (MSMQ supports both blocking and nonblocking receives.)

MSMQ is capable of Internet/intranet application integration. An MSMQ queue can be accessed directly from IIS using Active Server Pages (ASP) scripts. MSMQ is also able to use CGI and more traditional APIs for C and C++.

IBM MQSeries

In the world of MOM, IBM's MQSeries is the proverbial 800-pound gorilla. With a queuing middleware market share of over 65 percent, it can do just about anything it pleases. And although it may not be the most feature-rich messaging middleware product, MQSeries sits atop the B2B application integration world as the preferred messaging layer for moving information throughout an enterprise.

The most notable benefit of MQSeries is the number of platforms it supports. MQSeries works with IBM OS/390, Pyramid, Open VMS, IBM AIX, NCR UNIX, HP-UX, Solaris, OS/2, Windows NT, SCO UNIX, MacOS, and many others. MQSeries supports all the features of MSMQ, including support for transactions, journaling, message routing, and priorities. MQSeries also provides a common API for use across a variety of development environments. (These interfaces are sold by third-party vendors.)

MQSeries products provide a single multiplatform API. As a result, messages can be sent from a Windows 2000 workstation and routed

through UNIX, VMS, or even a mainframe before reaching their final destination. Platforms running MQSeries work in concert, ensuring that messages are delivered to their destination (see Figure 9.6). They can also route around network and system failures. MQSeries can be used as a transactional recovery method and a mail transport mechanism, ensuring the delivery of messages.

MQSeries supports what IBM refers to as an "advanced message framework." This framework consists of three layers: customer application options, a trusted messaging backbone, and comprehensive communications choices (see Figure 9.7). The customer application options provide services such as basic messaging, transactional messaging, workflow computing, mail messaging, option messaging, cooperative processing, data replication, and mobile messaging. Transactional messaging allows developers to coordinate message flow with updates to other resource managers. (For example, several databases on different platforms can be updated at the same time.) The mail-messaging feature allows any Vendor Independent Messaging (VIM) or Mail API (MAPI) application to transmit e-mail securely and reliably by leveraging the power of MQSeries' messaging infrastructure. MQSeries supports messaging between distributed objects and facilitates cooperative processing between two or more processes.

MQSeries' messaging backbone guarantees that messages are delivered to their destinations and that the information encapsulated in those messages is secure. Its comprehensive communications choices allow it to leverage any number of protocols and networks for message traffic.

The latest version of MQSeries offers a peek at "things to come" in messaging middleware. Traditional MOM focused on simple A-to-B asynchronous message passing. In an attempt to be competitive with other MOM vendors and other middleware products, MOM now provides many value-added services, services never envisioned in the original concept of MOM.

That original concept never included, for example, the encapsulation of transactions. Today, nearly every MOM package takes advantage of the notion of a transaction (a "unit of work"), with the ability to maintain

continued

Examples of MOM (*continued*)

states. MOM can now maintain message persistence and logging, enabling it to provide enhanced manageability and fail-over capabilities.

The best of the queuing products available (like MQSeries) are in the process of reinventing themselves by adding a publish/subscribe engine. It is a smart move. This positive development is intended to gain entry for queuing products into the exploding world of middleware products for information dissemination. Once the playing field is leveled, they will be competitive with existing publish/subscribe middleware from vendors such as TIBCO.

The current MQSeries has taken the leap directly from Version 2 to Version 5, stepping up the IBM installation procedures so that it will be "up to speed" with other IBM products. In the past, MQSeries was notoriously difficult to install. This upgrade should successfully address this frustration. IBM also claims that this new version of MQSeries works better with its DB2, Transaction Server, and other Software Server components. Other new features include Database-Message Resource Coordination (DMRC) and smart message distribution. Long available on a large number of server platforms, MQSeries now supports Windows NT and OS/2 as well.

Before this latest version, MQSeries required a transaction manager or a sophisticated application program in order to combine database updates and messaging activity into a single unit of work. With Version 5.1 and the introduction of DMRC, MQSeries includes MQ and SQL activity support through the new MZBEGIN verb to register a unit of work. Thus subsequent work can be committed or backed out, depending on whether the procedure succeeds. MQSeries supports the notion of a transaction, without having to employ a TP monitor or application server.

Smart message distribution minimizes the amount of network traffic required to distribute a copy of a single message to multiple users whose queues reside on a single node. MQSeries 5.1 is able to send a single copy of the message to each target MQ system, using a list of recipients at the target systems. From there, the receiving MQ system produces and queues the copies locally.

In addition, the package includes performance enhancements, such as fast messages (changes to MQSeries' message channel agents to reduce the time and resources required to move nonpersistent messages) and enhancements to internal channel architecture and trusted bindings.

Another significant improvement in this upgrade is MQSeries' ability to support large messages. The previous limit of 4MB per message has been extended to 100MB per message. Additionally, messages may now be built or retrieved in segments and passed by reference.

The publish/subscribe feature in the newest version of MQSeries automates the distribution of relevant information to people and applications desiring it. Using the new pub/sub engine, MQSeries developers can ensure that clients subscribing to a particular topic receive exactly what they want. Meanwhile, behind the scenes, MQSeries is using the MQ messaging infrastructure to move the messages throughout the enterprise.

Pub/sub frees an MQ-enabled application from the need to understand anything about the target application. Now, it only needs to send the information to be shared to a destination within the pub/sub engine, or broker. The broker can redistribute the information to any interested application.

The real advantage to offering pub/sub is the degree of reliability that MQSeries delivers. The most significant downside is not within the MQSeries environment but with those pub/sub vendors that now find themselves competing against Big Blue—IBM. TIBCO, which has long dominated pub/sub, might find that MQSeries' new features will finally threaten its "king of the hill" status in the world of finance. In addition, the pub/sub features of MQSeries are the same as many features offered by traditional message brokers, although without schema and content transformation facilities. IBM has adopted NEON's message-brokering features and placed them on top of MQSeries—the MQ Integrator.

IBM's ultimate goal is to become the information bus for the enterprise. With this latest release of MQSeries, it is taking a giant step toward achieving that lofty goal.

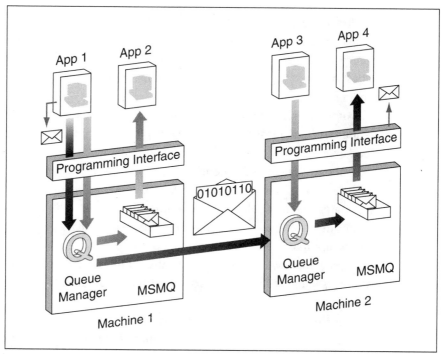

Figure 9.5   The architecture of MSMQ

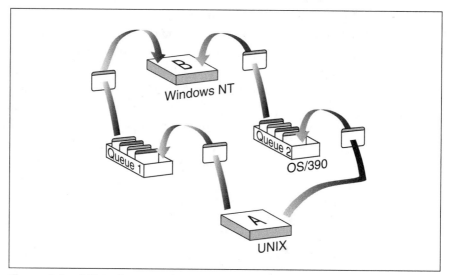

Figure 9.6   MQSeries MOM is a heterogeneous solution.

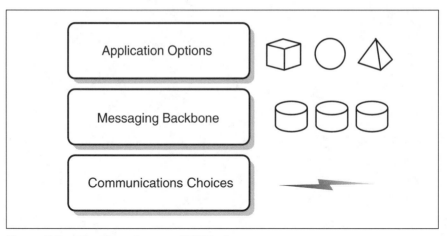

Figure 9.7   The three layers of MQSeries

Future of MOM

Despite its shortcomings, MOM still has its place within the enterprise and within some B2B application integration projects. Connecting applications to applications, it is more applicable to EAI than to B2B application integration. This is because MOM requires major changes to source and target applications, generally frowned upon in most B2B application integration problem domains. Still, our discussion of MOM has been worthwhile in the context of middleware, since messaging is the basis for many B2B application integration solutions, including message brokers.

RPCs have an even longer shot at becoming the basis of B2B application integration. Their synchronous nature and heavy overhead as well as deep impact on source and target applications will keep RPCs intra-enterprise. However, as with MOM, it's worth discussing RPC, since many B2B application integration solutions leverage RPCs, such as when using Java's RMI as a mechanism to enable application-to-application communications.

It is worth remembering: Good technology is always built on the foundation of good technology. Both RPCs and MOM are good technology. They will continue to be the basis of many technology advances.

Distributed Objects and B2B Application Integration

Distributed object technology has been around for nearly a decade. It creates an infrastructure for sharing methods by providing an additional location for application processing and for interoperability among processes. In addition, it provides a standard mechanism to access shared objects, objects that run on any number of servers. As a result, its usefulness to method-oriented B2B application integration should be clear.

As part of the B2B application integration solution set, distributed objects give architects the ability to create both applications that share common methods and composite applications that support method-oriented B2B application integration. The integration of applications by sharing a common business logic—"B2B application integration nirvana"—lies along this path. But it is hardly a smooth garden path. As we have already suggested in any number of contexts, the path is always risky and studded with expensive obstacles.

What Works?

Distributed objects work best in B2B application integration problem domains where a distributed computing model is being used and a large number of common methods need to be shared. For example, a trading community may have the following four major applications:

- Customer tracking system (Company A)
- Logistics system (Company A)
- Sales database application (Company B and Company C)
- Inventory planning system (Company C)

Although each of these applications functions independently, they have a number of methods in common, methods that may include

```
Add_Customer()
Edit_Customer()
Delete_Customer()
```

For these methods to be shared, an additional shared application layer must be created (physical or virtual). This layer must possess the enabling technology that allows applications to share methods over the Internet. Application servers, TP monitors, or distributed objects are the best options for such a layer. As we suggested earlier, each has advantages and disadvantages that need to be evaluated.

If method-oriented B2B application integration is the chosen approach, then the B2B application integration architect and developer may seek to create a set of distributed objects that house these common methods. Using a common structure, interface, and communications mechanism (e.g., IIOP or RPCs, which are discussed later in this chapter), distributed objects provide the enabling technology for sharing these methods (see Figure 10.1).

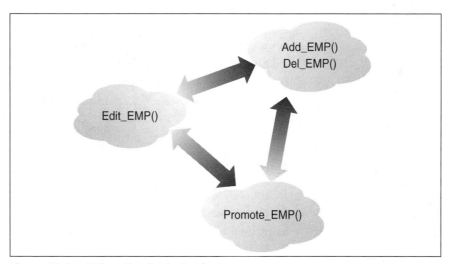

Figure 10.1   Using distributed objects

What's So Difficult?

Because we have become familiar with the workings of the marketplace, it should come as no surprise that distributed object vendors are quick to suggest that using distributed objects is easy—simply a matter of changing several applications and exposing application methods using distributed object technology for access by other applications or, more commonly, among the distributed objects themselves. What could be simpler? Plenty. For this method to be successful in an application similar to the previous example, the common methods would have to be stripped from all the trading community applications and be redeployed within some sort of distributed object technology. Code would have to be changed everywhere. Each application would need to be tested and then redeployed.

This is a monumental task. It may be worth the effort if it ultimately achieves the business objectives, but it is hardly simple. And it is not a good fit for most B2B application integration problem domains. Distributed object–based B2B application integration is an invasive integration approach. A lot has to change in order to accommodate this technology. As a rule of thumb, invasive middleware doesn't cut it when it comes to B2B application integration. But as in all things, there are no absolute rules, and in some cases such a solution is the right solution.

Before moving forward, however, consider this truism: A solid business case must be made to justify leveraging method-oriented B2B application integration and enabling technology such as distributed objects. Distributed object technology might or might not be simple or worthwhile. The only "objective" way to be sure is to utilize this calculus—assess what is to be gained from the B2B application integration project against the resources necessary to complete the project. If the resources required far exceed the gain, then other B2B application integration types are likely to be better approaches. However, if it appears that the return on investment is there, then method-oriented B2B application integration is the most elegant of B2B application integration solutions.

The failing in too many organizations is an absence of strict candor and realism in making such an assessment. Organizations that talk themselves into B2B application integration projects using distributed objects based on exaggerated claims by the media or by vendors are very often in for a rude awakening. Failed distributed object projects outnumber the successes. *That's* the reality. No hype.

What's So Easy?

Once we understand and appreciate the disadvantages of distributed objects, we should focus on the many advantages. The greatest advantage of distributed objects is their adherence to an application development and interoperability standard. CORBA and COM+ are specifications, not technologies. Vendors adhere to the established standard and therefore provide a set of technologies that can interoperate. Because the standard is open and the interfaces well defined, vendors discover that interacting with distributed objects is not difficult.

As distributed object technology continues to mature, vendors are adding new features that address previously acknowledged shortcomings, such as scalability, interoperability, and communications mechanisms. Distributed objects now provide better scalability through the ability to support transactions. As a result, they offer the same scaling tricks as application servers and TP monitors. OMG now endorses CORBA's Object Transaction Services (OTS). Microsoft expects AppCenter to bring transactionality to COM+. Interoperability continues to improve as common protocols are defined, including CORBA's IIOP and Microsoft's COM+ RPC (loosely based on the DCE RPC). Objects created by different vendors can share information by using a common object-to-object protocol as the least common denominator. Finally, where traditional distributed objects leverage simple, synchronous communications mechanisms based on the RPC (as is the case with both CORBA and Microsoft), they now provide asynchronous messaging mechanisms as well. (CORBA provides its own message service as part of the standard, while Microsoft is learning to leverage MSMQ as a way to bring messaging to COM.)

Thus, distributed objects, which were once difficult to deploy and provided few advantages over more traditional alternatives, are now easier to use and provide many more features that benefit an enterprise development technology. In short, distributed objects have become a key enabling technology (in addition to transactional middleware) for method-oriented B2B application integration.

What's a Distributed Object?

Several things contribute to the potential benefit of distributed objects for B2B application integration.

- We are moving toward multitier application development. Developers are beginning to realize that the enabling technology of distributed objects "gets

them there." Distributed objects give B2B application integration architects and developers the ability to create portable objects that can run on a variety of servers, objects that can communicate using a predefined and standard messaging interface over the Internet. This aspect of distributed objects has remarkable potential for B2B application integration.

- In the recent past, CORBA was the only real standard available (see the CORBA section later in this chapter). Microsoft eventually entered the distributed object marketplace with COM+, which promised to provide a distributed object infrastructure and the ability to tie applications created with traditional tools with a Windows-based operating system. (The Object Request Broker is part of the operating system and therefore a giveaway.)

- We learned to bring ORBs to the desktop through the use of application components, such as ActiveX. By mixing and matching components, developers can piece together an application like a jigsaw puzzle. This is the nirvana of application development, the ability to assemble applications the way the Ford Motor Company assembles Mustangs—from prebuilt component parts.

- The rise of the Web has renewed interest in distributed objects. Technologies and standards, such as CORBA's IIOP, promise to provide both an enabling technology for dynamic application development and a better application-to-application, object-to-object transport layer. Now that powerhouse Web companies such as Netscape have put their weight behind ORBs, Web developers will continue their rush to ORBs.

The General Idea of ORBs

With so much depending on ORBs, it seems particularly appropriate to address the question, What exactly is an ORB?

ORBs provide developers with standard objects to communicate with other standard objects, using a standard interface and line protocol. Like traditional objects (such as those found with C++, Java, or Smalltalk), ORBs can access the methods of other ORBs either locally or over a network (see Figure 10.2). ORBs can also exchange data and are platform independent.

A CORBA ORB can pass requests from object to object. One invocation method is for the client to invoke ORB services through the ORB core and the Interface Definition Language (IDL) stub. Another method is through a Dynamic Invocation Interface (DII) stub. (IDL and DII are described more completely in the next section, CORBA.) A stub provides mapping between the language binding

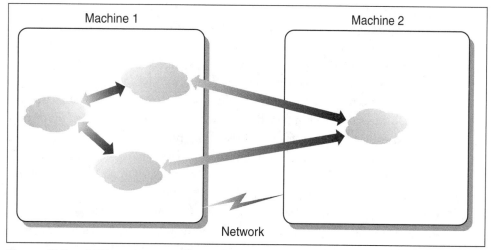

Figure 10.2   ORBs can access methods of other ORBs locally or over a network.

(e.g., C++ and Java) and the ORB services. Specific instructions are given to the ORBs through this process.

At this point, the ORB core moves the request to the object implementation, which receives the message through an up-call, using an IDL skeleton or a dynamic skeleton.

CORBA

In 1989, OMG began working with such vendor powerhouses as IBM, Apple, Sun, and many others to establish the first cross-compatible distributed object standard. In tackling this endeavor, OMG promised object reuse regardless of platform, tool, or programming language. In other words, OMG promised a common binary object that would work anywhere for any application. Such an object would allow developers to mix and match objects for distributed computing application development. The result of this effort—CORBA—was first released around 1991. This was just the start, however promising. A long, bumpy road remained ahead before B2B application integration and distributed objects could work together.

The first CORBA specification freed developers from their C++ compilers. With a standard finally in place, they were able to purchase objects to create applications. Unfortunately, there was a catch. The first CORBA specification came in two parts: the IDL and the DII. Both of these components exist within

every CORBA ORB, and each provides a communications service between ORBs—either locally (intra-computer) or over a network (inter-computer).

The IDL, at its core, defines an object's structure and provides developers with an API to access the object services during runtime. The IDL is the tool CORBA ORB developers must grapple with in order to build application-dependent features into an ORB. The DII is an API as well, one that provides developers with dynamic construction of object invocations. In contrast to the IDL, DII allows developers to do things while the objects run, such as allowing the client to establish the objects and operations, including any parameters.

Shortfalls

CORBA looked promising, without question. But CORBA's first release, CORBA 1.1, had many limitations. For example, as mentioned earlier, it did not provide enough detail to allow ORB vendors to create CORBA-compliant ORBs that were able to work together. Although CORBA 1.1 did define an object standard, it had no real value because of the lack of interoperability. In short, Version 1.1 was an important first step, but only a first step. OMG's 1994 release of CORBA 2.0 made great strides toward solving the interoperability problem. CORBA 2.0 contained specific syntax for a network protocol, allowing ORBs to communicate with one another. Version 2.0 also defined a TCP/IP-based inter-ORB protocol backbone, along with an inter-ORB communications service that allowed components to generate IDs for any of the interfaces they supported.

Essentially, CORBA ORBs remained the same in the 2.0 update. They still supported IDLs and DIIs. However, although CORBA 1.1 only included mapping to C, a nonobject language, Version 2.0 included mapping to C++, Smalltalk, and, later, Java.

CORBA 3.0 promises to get us "the rest of the way there." It solves most of the remaining shortcomings of CORBA 2.0. OMG is finally getting CORBA "right." Version 3.0 provides a robust specification to define transactionality, asynchronous communications, and a better development environment. Along with OMG, the vendors who dominate the CORBA-compliant ORB marketplace—such as Iona, IBM, and Inprise—are also making good on CORBA's longtime promise.

CORBA Internals

Our goal is not to add to the already voluminous information available about CORBA. Instead, we hope to provide an overview of distributed objects and their application to B2B application integration. If you are considering CORBA (or

COM) as the enabling technology for a B2B application integration project, this information should help you.

A CORBA ORB has the following four main parts (see Figure 10.3):

- ORB
- Object services
- Common facilities
- Application objects

These same features exist in other ORBs, such as Microsoft's COM+ and proprietary ORBs.

ORB

The ORB is an engine that shares information with other ORBs. Together, these "engaged" ORBs create a distributed object. ORBs exist as background objects, functioning behind the application. Applications are also layered on top of ORBs, providing the distributed infrastructure. This is the reason ORBs make such effective middleware layers—many communications services already exist

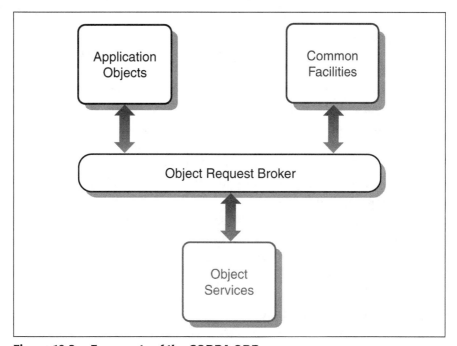

Figure 10.3   Four parts of the CORBA ORB

in ORB services (such as CORBA-compliant ORBs). Layering also provides heterogeneous application portability and interoperability, the feature that makes ORBs most valuable to B2B application integration.

Object Services

CORBA mandates object services, groups of services that leverage object interfaces for communications between services. The basic services that developers expect in an ORB are security, transaction management, and data exchange. Developers use object services as a base class upon which to build applications.

Common Facilities

Common facilities, optional for CORBA, are a collection of services that link with the client. Common facilities allow developers to build component characteristics in CORBA-compliant ORBs. Developers consider common facilities whenever they need to implement CORBA-compliant component-based objects.

Application Objects

Application objects support the application development features of a CORBA ORB, as defined by the ORB developer or application developer. Here "the rubber meets the road" in ORB development—ORBs can be turned into something useful. These features are built into ORB with the IDL, which ensures interoperability with other CORBA-compliant ORBs.

COM+

The dynamic that currently drives the distributed object world—and complicates it—is the emergence of Microsoft's COM, along with the further development of Microsoft's ORB into COM+. And Microsoft being Microsoft, emotion and power plays are in full view. Although a great ORB debate is raging with high emotion on either side, the bottom line is that COM is as much an ORB as CORBA. Microsoft very effectively devised COM, using its existing Object Linking and Embedding (OLE) model as its basis of design.

ORB provides an object standard that isn't really object oriented (e.g., that has the ability to support inheritance), but then, neither is CORBA. It also provides a common mechanism for inter-ORB communications. COM is based on automation (using the COM model), a standard on most Windows desktops and a feature of most Windows-based development tools. For example, Visual Basic, Visual C++, Visual J++, Delphi, and PowerBuilder all support the creation of

COM-enabled automation servers—servers an application can share through DCOM.

OLE Automation

OLE automation (also known simply as "automation") lets B2B application integration architects and developers take advantage of the services of other OLE/COM-enabled applications that, for example, allow access to the services of a PowerBuilder application from Visual Basic or that run a Visual Basic object from Word for Windows. OLE provides a standard interface to expose methods for access by other automation servers or containers.

There are two types of automation: the automation controller and the automation server. The automation controller is, in actuality, the COM client. The controller invokes the services of an automation server through the common COM interface (see Figure 10.4). Automation servers are ORBs that expose method functions available for use by other automation servers.

There are two types of automation servers: in-process and out-of-process. In-process servers are typically DLLs, which run in the same process and memory space as their clients (see Figure 10.5). ActiveX components offer the best examples of in-process OLE automation servers with some component features built in.

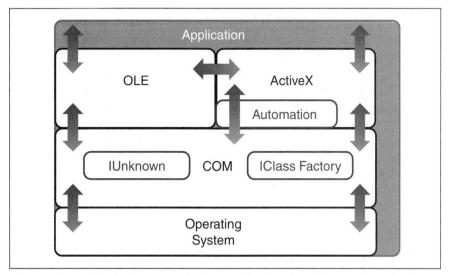

Figure 10.4   **The OLE automation controller invokes the services of an OLE automation server through a COM interface.**

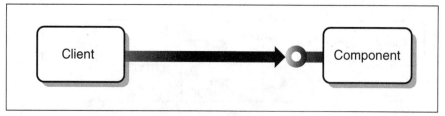

Figure 10.5   In-process automation server

By contrast, out-of-process servers run in separate memory and process space from their clients (see Figure 10.6). Out-of-process servers are typically .EXEs that communicate with other COM applications through a "lightweight" RPC mechanism (intra-computer). As with any ORB, out-of-process OLE automation servers can invoke the services of other COM ORBs, either locally or remotely through DCOM (see the next section, Moving to DCOM).

Moving to DCOM

The power of COM is lost without the ability to distribute COM-enabled ORBs. DCOM allows developers to create automation servers and make them available for other COM-enabled B2B application integration applications on a network (see Figure 10.7). DCOM is *not* a commercial ORB. Instead, it is part of the operating system. DCOM was first released with Windows NT 4.0 and is part of Windows 98 and Windows 2000.

Although CORBA-enabled ORBs demand a great deal of integration and coordination to work, DCOM is simple. With DCOM, the COM-enabled application checks the registry of the Windows operating system to locate and use remote COM-enabled ORBs, finding and invoking the service it requires.

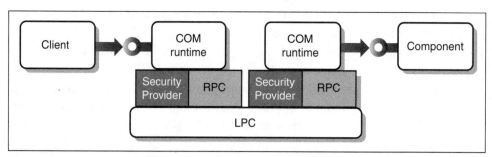

Figure 10.6   Out-of-process automation server

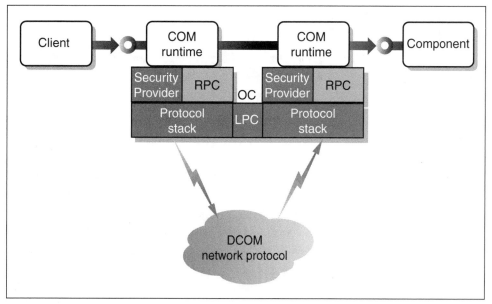

Figure 10.7   DCOM makes automation servers remotely accessible.

DCOM differs from the CORBA architecture in that it is built into the infrastructure of the operating system rather than as a product of an ORB vendor. DCOM is backward compatible with existing COM-enabled development tools as well as with tools that were not created specifically for the development of distributed objects. Although not so by design, these tools are now in the distributed object business simply because DCOM can distribute the automation servers they create.

With the exception of Inprise, CORBA has had trouble attracting mainstream tool vendors. The lack of tools translates into a lack of CORBA interest from the development community. In sharp contrast, COM is already part of most Windows-based development tools.

Still, DCOM has drawbacks. Despite the existence of DCOM implementations on UNIX, VMS, and even OS/390 from Software AG, DCOM will always be a Windows-bound ORB. This limitation alone makes CORBA the better choice for most B2B application integration applications that exist in a heterogeneous computing environment. In addition, DCOM is still immature and does not provide the performance of CORBA (not that CORBA is so much to write home about in this regard). However, as soon as one or the other develops to the point

of incorporating mature transactionality, it is sure to become the darling of the enterprise.

DCOM's strength, simply, is Microsoft. Microsoft's strategy has been straightforward—to make complex, high-end software (such as ORBs) a widely available commodity. The availability of tools, coupled with the popularity of Microsoft operating systems, guarantees a place for DCOM in any solution set.

The Realities

As in most things, there is both good news and bad news when considering a role for distributed objects in B2B application integration. Distributed objects *do* provide B2B application integration developers with an advanced distributed architecture to develop and deploy distributed applications. At the same time, issues remain that make them unsuitable for mission-critical B2B application integration computing. Not least of these is the simple fact that most commercial ORBs don't perform well, even with the transaction and messaging extensions.

When thinking about distributed objects, we must also consider middleware. Most ORBs, both COM and CORBA, use the synchronous communications model. They continue to lack support for asynchronous messaging (although CORBA and COM+ now provide some asynchronous capabilities). And the ORB code is still not completely portable from platform to platform, especially COM+. (As with other shortcomings, vendors and standards bodies plan to address these problems in new releases of specifications and products.)

So, what can we conclude about distributed objects and B2B application integration? Can they work together? Absolutely. However, as with all things, careful consideration must be employed in making a decision. The marriage of technology and B2B application integration is like any other marriage—partners have to mesh well to prosper over the long haul. After all, this *is* a marriage we're talking about, not an infatuation or an affair. A marriage is a long-term commitment. In B2B application integration, the ability to mesh well over the long haul may well be intrinsic to the architecture.

Database-Oriented Middleware and B2B Application Integration

To a large extent, B2B application integration depends on database access. This is particularly true for data-oriented B2B application integration. Databases once were proprietary and therefore difficult to access. Now, so many solutions for accessing data exist that we rarely have a problem when we seek to retrieve information from or place it in any database. The solutions that have been developed not only make B2B application integration a much easier proposition, but they speak directly to the idea that the capability of modern middleware drives the interest in B2B application integration.

However, even with many simplified database access solutions, databases and database-oriented middleware quickly grow complicated. Although database-oriented middleware was once simply a mechanism to "get at" data, it has matured into a layer for placing data in the context of a virtual database—a particular, common database model or format. For example, if we want to view data in a relational database as objects, the database-oriented middleware can map the data so it appears as objects to a source or target application. The same thing can be done "the other way around"—mixing and matching such models as hierarchical, flat files, multidimensional, relational, and object-oriented (see Figure 11.1).

Database-oriented middleware also provides access to any number of databases, regardless of the model employed or the platform upon which they exist. This access is generally

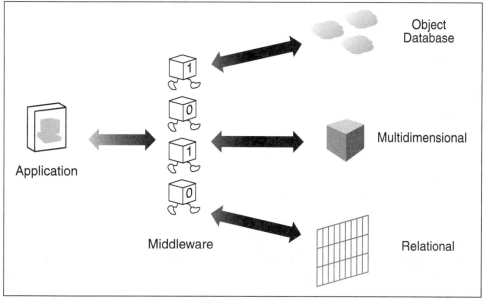

Figure 11.1   Database-oriented middleware allows the viewing of data using any model, no matter how the data is stored.

accomplished through a single common interface such as ODBC or JDBC, which we will discuss in detail later in this chapter. Thus, information stored in Adabas, DB2, Oracle, or Sybase databases can be accessed *at the same time* through a single interface (see Figure 11.2). By taking advantage of these mechanisms, we can map any difference in the source and target databases to a common model. As a consequence, they are much easier to integrate. (This process also supports the idea of a common enterprise metadata model, presented earlier in this book.)

These examples should make it clear that database-oriented middleware is a major player in the world of B2B application integration. It allows a large number of enabling technologies to process information coming and going from source and target systems. This ability makes database-oriented middleware the logical choice if a message broker or an application server requires information in a database. Vendors have recognized the advantage of database-oriented middleware. As a result, many B2B application integration products, such as message brokers and application servers, already contain the necessary database-oriented middleware to access the most popular databases. In fact, most message brokers and application servers come prepackaged with the appropriate adapters to

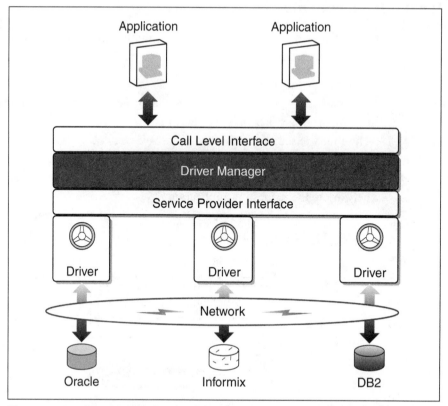

Figure 11.2 Database-oriented middleware provides access to a number of databases at the same time.

access most relational databases, such as Oracle, Sybase, and Informix. To a large degree, database access is now a problem solved, with many inexpensive and proven solutions available.

Nevertheless, we can benefit from understanding the role of database-oriented middleware in the context of B2B application integration in order to get the larger picture. Databases are going to serve as the primary point of integration for most B2B application integration solutions over the next few years. The bottom line—your choice of mechanism to move information in and out of databases can make or break your B2B application integration project. That alone makes our examination of database-oriented middleware worthwhile. More than that, integration with more modern middleware solutions is essential and carries with it its own complexities and opportunities.

What Is Database-Oriented Middleware?

Database-oriented middleware provides a number of important benefits (see Figure 11.3), including:

- An interface to an application
- The ability to convert the application language into something understandable by the target database (e.g., SQL)
- The ability to send a query to a database over a network
- The ability to process a query on the target database
- The ability to move a response set (the results of the query) back over the network to the requesting application
- The ability to convert a response set into a format understandable by the requesting application

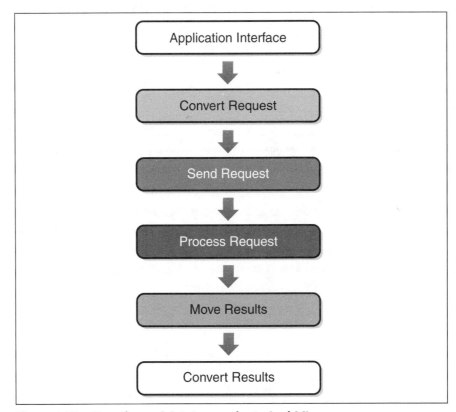

Figure 11.3   Functions of database-oriented middleware

In addition to these processes, database-oriented middleware must provide the ability to process many simultaneous requests, along with scaling features such as thread pooling and load balancing. These features must be packaged with management capabilities and security features. As in other contexts, the approaches to providing these benefits vary greatly from vendor to vendor and technology to technology.

Types of Database-Oriented Middleware

Again, we have no desire to repeat information that is easily available from other sources. Our goal is to provide you with an overview of information that applies to your B2B application integration problem domain. We will deal with JDBC in detail in this chapter and devote Chapter 12 to Java middleware (recognizing all the while that JDBC *is* Java middleware).

So, where do we begin? Ultimately, database-oriented middleware is "all the software that connects an application to a database." Any application. Any database. Anytime. Like primitive middleware layers, database-oriented middleware allows developers to access the resources of another computer—in this case, a database server that uses a single well-defined API. Database-oriented middleware appears straightforward in its architecture, yet each of the many products and standards that make up this market accomplishes the basic task in very different ways.

Although several types of database middleware exist, they are all basically native middleware—CLIs and database gateways. For our purposes, native middleware is simply middleware created for a specific database. For example, middleware provided by Sybase to access the Sybase databases from C++ is native database–oriented middleware. Native database–oriented middleware provides the best performance and access to native database features (such as stored procedures and triggers), because the middleware has been created specifically for that particular database. The downside to native database middleware is that once the links to a database have been created using native middleware, major renovations are required in order to change databases.

CLIs, such as ODBC and JDBC (both discussed later in this chapter), provide a single interface to several databases. CLIs translate common interface calls into any number of database dialects. They also translate the response sets into a common response set representation (see Figure 11.4) that is understandable to the application making the request to the database.

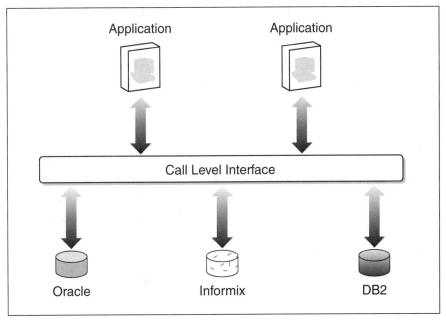

Figure 11.4   CLIs use a single common interface to access several different databases.

Database gateways provide access to data that was once locked inside larger systems, such as mainframes. They integrate several databases for access from a single application interface. They remap archaic database models (flat files, ISAM, VSAM, and so on) so they appear more traditional, and they translate queries and information as they move in and out of the database gateway software (more on this in the section Database Gateways later in this chapter).

ODBC

ODBC is not really a product. It began as a standard that Microsoft created in the aftermath of the Windows revolution. ODBC is a CLI that simplifies database access from Windows (as well as from a few other operating systems) by allowing a developer to make a single API call that works with most relational databases (along with a few that don't follow the relational model). In addition to establishing a Microsoft standard, ODBC is a translation layer (as is JDBC). Like all middleware layers, ODBC provides a well-defined and database-independent API. When an application uses the API, ODBC utilizes a driver manager to determine

which database the application would like to communicate with; then it loads or unloads the appropriate ODBC driver (see Figure 11.5). As a result, an application using ODBC is database independent. However, if an application has any database-specific calls (such as passing SQL directly through to the database or invoking a number of stored procedures and triggers), it is no longer database independent, because it becomes bound to a particular database brand. In such a case, a better option may be to avoid ODBC and take advantage of a native database middleware layer.

ODBC is currently available in a 32-bit version. Most relational databases have ODBC drivers available and although ODBC is free, the drivers are not. You can purchase these drivers from the database vendors or through third-party ODBC driver vendors. Most popular application development tool vendors provide database access features using ODBC. They do so for one simple reason: The market demands that they do. Vendors would be hard-pressed to ignore ODBC, when it is the only way Microsoft Visual Basic and other Microsoft tools can talk to a database.

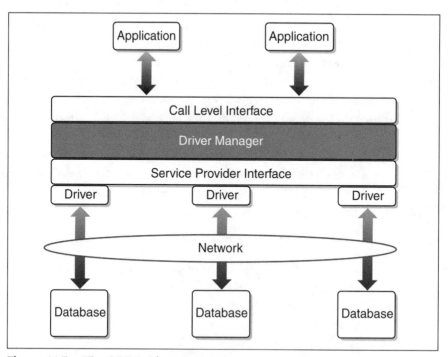

Figure 11.5   The ODBC driver manager

Does ODBC Hinder Performance?

There is some contention, to say the least, about ODBC's ability to provide performance, access database features, and provide a stable application deployment platform. Although it is true that ODBC had something of a rough start—falling short of the performance that developers were looking for—the ODBC of today (remembering that performance is driver dependent) provides high-performance database access. In some situations, ODBC has outperformed the native middleware layer. What's more, ODBC can access most native database features, such as accessing stored procedures and triggers, tracking transactions, and recovering from errors—although without the same degree of control as middleware that's native to a particular database.

The bottom line? ODBC is sufficient for most B2B application integration projects. It is particularly appropriate for those projects using Microsoft platforms. You should consider ODBC when you are operating in a multidatabase environment that requires access to several different databases from the same application or integration server (message broker or application sever). You should also consider ODBC if you envision a possible change to the database during the life cycle of the application (such as scaling to a larger user load).

ODBC enables a B2B application integration solution to move from database to database quickly. It is a good choice for most B2B application integration solution sets. However, you should avoid ODBC if you are wedded to a particular database or if your B2B application integration solution requires a large number of proprietary database functions.

JDBC

JDBC, from JavaSoft, was the first standard Java-enabled database API. Functionally equivalent to ODBC, JDBC provides Java developers with a uniform interface to most popular relational databases from most Java-enabled development or application-processing environments.

The JDBC API defines a set of Java classes that allow an applet, servlet, JavaBean, or Java application to connect to a database. In most cases, such an

applet links back through the network to remote relational database servers, such as Sybase, Oracle, or Informix. The native Java JDBC classes, sold or given away by the database vendors, exist with the custom application classes. They provide "pure Java," along with a portable mechanism for database access. With them, you can link to any database from any platform that supports Java. At least, that's the ideal. JDBC also provides uniform database access for many B2B application integration–enabled middleware products, such as message brokers, application servers, and even traditional MOM (e.g., message-queuing software).

JDBC Java classes allow the developer to use native Java to issue common SQL statements to request information from a remote database and then to process the result set. Because JDBC, like ODBC, is another translation layer, Java applications that employ JDBC are database independent. They can access any number of databases through a single JDBC interface. For example, you can gather data from a remotely running Oracle database, update a local Sybase database, and delete a record from a DB2 database running on a mainframe—all from the same Java applications, using one common interface, JDBC.

JDBC consists of two primary layers: the JDBC API and the JDBC Driver API (see Figure 11.6). The JDBC API provides application-to–JDBC Manager communications. Developers use this API to access database services that use standard Java mechanisms. (It is up to the database vendor to provide the JDBC

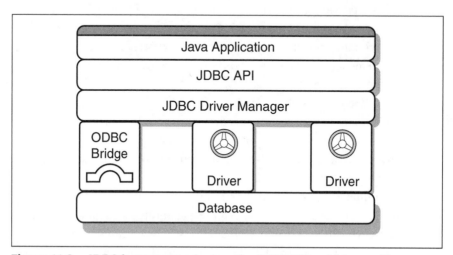

Figure 11.6   **JDBC features two layers: the JDBC API, which provides application-to–JDBC Manager connections, and the JDBC Driver API.**

driver interface. Vendors may also use a traditional ODBC connection through a JDBC-to-ODBC bridge.)

As suggested earlier, JDBC drivers are really a group of Java classes (including `java.sql.Connection`, `java.sql.Statement`, `java.sql.Prepared Statement`, `java.sql.CallableStatement`, and `java.sql.ResultSet`). These classes from the native Java applications can link to a database, send a request, and process the returning result set. They are available when developers want to access a database with JDBC.

The `java.sql.DriverManager` interface handles the loading and unloading of the proper DBMS driver. The `java.sql.Connection` interface exposes the database to the developer, representing the connection as a set of objects. The `java.sql.Statement` interface provides the developer with a container for executing SQL statements by using a connection to the database. The `java.sql.ResultSet` interface exposes the requested data as native Java for processing by the Java applet or application.

Like the ODBC driver manager, the JDBC Manager loads and unloads database drivers as required by the Java applet or application. JDBC supports a single or multiple database server connection. This means, for example, that an applet can connect to the inventory database in the warehouse and a public database on the Internet—at the same time.

The DBMS supports JDBC through the JDBC driver interface, with each driver providing an implementation of the `java.sql.Connection`, `java.sql.Statement`, `java.sql.PreparedStatement`, `java.sql.Callable Statement`, and `java.sql.ResultSet` classes. In addition, the driver must implement the `java.sql.Driver` interface for use by the `java.sql.DriverManager` interface.

When accessing a database from Java, a developer obtains the `java.sql.Connection` object directly from the JDBC management layer and the `java.sql.DriverManager`. The driver managers leverage the URL string as an argument, allowing the JDBC management layer to locate and load the proper driver for the target database. The driver manager performs this "magic" by examining each driver and determining the only one that can connect to the URL. At times the URL may require a subprotocol supported by the driver (see the next section, Types of JDBC Drivers). Once all this has been completed, the driver connects to the DBMS and returns the proper `java.sql.Connection` object for accessing the database.

In order for the driver manager to locate the correct driver, each driver has to register using the `DriverManager.registerDrive` method, invoked from the applet. JDBC, using Java's rather limited security, can only use drivers coming from the local file system or from the same class loader. Vendors are seeking to overcome this limitation through their own custom JDBC implementations.

Types of JDBC Drivers

JDBC drivers fit into one of four categories: a JDBC-ODBC bridge driver; a native-API, part-Java driver; a net-protocol, all-Java driver; and a native-protocol, all-Java driver. JDBC works with ODBC by providing a JDBC-ODBC bridge that translates JDBC calls to functions understandable by the ODBC API. (Although JDBC and ODBC are similar in many ways, they take slightly different approaches to connecting to databases.) When using this architecture, developers have no choice but to endure the overhead of a translation layer communicating with another translation layer.

The JDBC-ODBC bridge driver provides Java developers with JDBC access using most ODBC drivers. This method allows the greatest flexibility while providing the greatest degree of homogeneity. In most scenarios, the ODBC binaries must be loaded on each client machine using the driver. That said, it is likely that the Java application will be locked into a Windows platform, where ODBC is more native. Although it might be easier to access a shared set of ODBC binaries existing on an application server using JDBC, the architecture involved is much more complex and adds time to a development project.

The ODBC bridge is a requirement of JDBC if the standard is expected to support the vast majority of relational databases (and sometimes nonrelational databases) available. This situation exists because some database vendors and gateways of larger systems fail to offer JDBC drivers. There is no doubt that eventually middleware vendors will offer JDBC drivers and eliminate the need to communicate through multiple translation layers. However, even when this happens, the performance hit will not be as significant as we might like or expect.

A reasonable middle-of-the-road approach is the use of a native-API, part-Java driver. Such a driver converts JDBC calls into calls on the client API for any number of target databases (including Oracle, Sybase, Informix, and DB2). The downside is that for this option to be successful, some binary code must be loaded on the clients. Consequently, this option has many of the same limitations as the JDBC-ODBC bridge driver. It does have the advantage of not requiring access to ODBC, however.

The net-protocol, all-Java driver translates JDBC calls into a DBMS-independent net protocol, which a server subsequently translates into a native DBMS protocol. This driver can connect its pure Java clients to any number of databases, with the database vendor specifying the native protocol employed. This approach represents one of the most flexible JDBC solutions. We generally see this solution on intranets. Before it can become a good solution for Internet access, this architecture must support additional security requirements. Database vendors are working to ensure that they support net-protocol, all-Java drivers.

Finally, a native-protocol, all-Java driver directly converts JDBC calls into the network-native DBMS network protocol. This driver architecture provides direct calls from the client to the database server. It is most popular for intranet access, because it not only uses pure, portable Java, but, by taking a direct route to the data, also provides the best performance.

Database vendors recognize the need to provide this solution. Most have, or are working on, drivers to support this architecture.

Other JDBC Features

The beauty of JDBC exceeds its ability to link to and retrieve data from remote DBMSs. JDBC's beauty can be found in its robust array of database features. JDBC is able to access binary large objects (BLOBs)—handy for moving large amounts of binary information to and from the database. It can convert data, allowing JDBC to map the data back into Java by converting some SQL types into Java types. In addition, JDBC can support threading for pooling database connections, thus providing the source or target application (or integration server) with the ability to operate asynchronously against the database.

Utilizing JDBC's native feature that supports transactions, developers can define a starting point and an end point in a set of homogeneous or heterogeneous database operations. This creates a number of useful options. Developers can set the JDBC transaction manager to "auto-commit," allowing each database command to be carried out as the applet invokes it. Developers may decide to turn auto-commit off, allowing them to define several database commands as individual transactions, a capability that will complete all operations successfully or put everything back the way it was. This option has the advantage of allowing complete recovery should any of the commands in the transaction fail. An operation that records a sale in three separate databases (e.g., inventory, sales, and customer list) is a good candidate for a JDBC transaction, because if any of the updates failed, none of them would complete. This option maintains database

integrity. Most popular DBMSs (such as Oracle) provide native transaction features. JDBC simply extends those features to the Java applets or applications.

JDBC supports database cursors as well, using the `ResultSet.getCursor Name()` method of JDBC. A database cursor allows the developer to return a cursor name that points to the result set that still resides, as a cursor, on the database server. This feature relieves the network from having to send the entire result set to the requesting application. Using this feature, the Java applets or applications can move through the data and retrieve only what is required across the network. This feature also allows the invocation of positioned updates and deletes. (The target DBMS must support this feature in order for JDBC cursors to work. Fortunately, most do.)

There are even more benefits to JDBC, such as the use of SQL escape syntax. This feature allows developers to map escape syntax to DBMS-specific syntax. Developers can also invoke stored procedures from JDBC and pass in the proper arguments. Finally, scalar functions are available, such as `ABS()`, `DEGREES()`, `WEEK()`, and `DAYNAME()`.

Java, JDBC, and B2B Application Integration

The use of Java as a development language and architecture for B2B application integration is widespread. Currently, JDBC is filling the enterprise space even more than it is filling the Web space. This trend will likely continue as the future brings a Web-enabled existing corporate database. So, while JDBC will continue to exist on the Web, its real value will be on the inside of the firewall.

In many respects, JDBC is bringing the traditional, complex, multitier world of Web enablement back to the B2B application integration problem domain. With the advent of server-side Java (e.g., EJB and application servers), JBDC does not have to be client-only anymore. Many tool vendors are employing both RMI and JDBC to provide a flexible and complex architecture to solve a number of application problems—problems that include B2B application integration. The tradeoff (and there is always a tradeoff) is complexity and proprietary approaches. When a standard is used in a way that makes its architecture proprietary, then the value of that standard diminishes. Unfortunately, there is reason to fear that JDBC is heading toward such an unhappy ending.

OLE DB

OLE DB, referred to by many as ODBC's "big brother," is a specification that defines a set of data access servers capable of facilitating links to any number of

data sources. This capability enables developers to manage different data sources as a single virtual database. OLE DB uses a standard COM interface to grant access to data.

With OLE DB, developers have the means to access data that resides in relational databases, documents, spreadsheets, files, and electronic mail. Through COM, developers can easily integrate object-oriented and multidimensional (real cube) databases with OLE DB. The database simply becomes a component known as a data provider. Any component that uses a native data format and exposes methods through an OLE DB interface is considered a data provider, including a relational database (using ODBC), an ISAM file, a text file, e-mail, a Microsoft Word file, or a data stream (see Figure 11.7).

The goal is to create an individual OLE DB component object to deploy additional features that are layered on top of the data providers. These individual OLE DB components are called service providers. These service providers are similar to query processors in that they allow applications to take advantage of

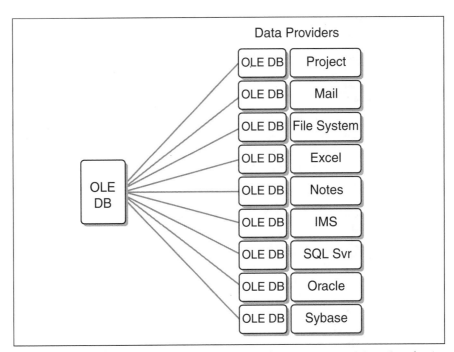

**Figure 11.7   OLE DB provides access to multiple resources through a single
           interface.**

providers that interconnect different combinations of data (homogeneous or heterogeneous). The data, regardless of model (object-oriented, relational, multidimensional, etc.), exists as a single view. In this way, the relational-bond limitations of ODBC are easily solved.

The flip side of data providers is occupied by OLE DB data consumers—applications written to a single data provider or generic consumer that work with any number of data providers. For example, Microsoft Excel, Word, and Project can become data consumers.

In this world, ODBC remains a player, but one whose role is diminished to a mechanism that communicates with relational databases from OLE DB. Microsoft has an updated ODBC driver manager with an OLE DB provider, making OLE DB compatible with any ODBC-accessible database.

Given all this, how is OLE DB programmed? It provides 55 new interfaces that are grouped into 7 object types: `DataSource`, `DBSession`, `Command`, `Rowset`, `Index`, `ErrorObject`, and `Transaction`. (An object type is a set of methods, or interfaces, that an object must expose. For example, developers can define the `Transaction Objects` using a group of methods that any data consumer can request from a transaction service.)

It is unlikely that many B2B application integration developers will have to deal directly with the OLE DB interface. Microsoft is perfecting a new set of products and development environments that allow developers to build applications with OLE DB hidden behind many easy-to-use layers. This OLE DB interface is analogous to the relationship between ODBC and development tools.

Going Native

In addition to ODBC, JDBC, OLE DB, and other database translation interfaces, many other native database–oriented middleware products exist. These are APIs provided by a database vendor or some third party with access to a particular database. In the past, these APIs tended to be older C and C++ libraries. Now, most B2B application integration development tools ship native database–oriented middleware with their products.

Native database–oriented middleware has an advantage over ODBC, JDBC, or OLE DB in its ability to provide high-performance database access along with the ability to access features native to a specific database. That's the upside. The downside is that native database–oriented middleware binds the user to that particular middleware vendor, because the B2B application integration application uses calls specific to that particular database.

Database Gateways

Database gateways (also known as SQL gateways) are APIs that use a single interface to provide access to most databases that reside on many different types of platforms (see Figure 11.8). They are like virtual database middleware products, providing developers with access to any number of databases residing in environments typically difficult to access, such as a mainframe. For example, using an ODBC interface and a database gateway, developers can access data residing in a DB2 database on a mainframe, in an Oracle database running on a minicomputer, and in a Sybase database running on a UNIX server. The developer simply makes an API call, and the database gateway does all the work.

Database gateways translate the SQL calls into a standard format known as the Format and Protocol (FAP), the common connection between the client and the server. FAP is also the common link between very different databases and platforms. The gateway can translate the API call directly into FAP, moving the request to the target database and translating the request so that the target database and platform can react.

A number of gateways are on the market. These include Information Builders' Enterprise Data Access/SQL (EDA/SQL) and standards such as IBM's Distributed Relational Data Access (DRDA) and ISO/SAG's Remote Data Access (RDA).

EDA/SQL

EDA/SQL is a wonderful general-purpose database gateway for several reasons. Among them is its ability to work with most database servers and platforms, bridging many enterprises where dozens of servers might be running on dozens

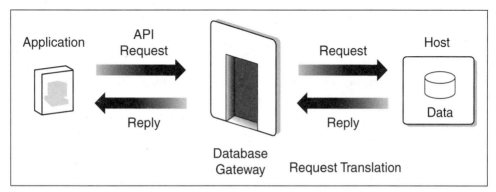

Figure 11.8   **Database gateways provide access to databases housed within difficult-to-access systems, such as mainframes.**

of different platforms, all needing to be accessed from a single application—a perfect fit for B2B application integration. EDA/SQL also has the advantage of using ODBC as the interface rather than a proprietary API. By using ODBC, it can access more than 50 relational and nonrelational database servers.

There are several EDA/SQL components, including the API/SQL, EDA/Extenders, EDA/Link, EDA/Server, and EDA/Data Drivers. API/SQL provides the CLI (ODBC), allowing the developer to access the EDA/SQL resources. EDA/Extenders are redirectors of SQL calls, which route the request across a network. EDA/Link provides the network connections by supporting more than 12 communications protocols. EDA/Server resides on the target database, processing the requests on behalf of the requesting application or integration server. Finally, the EDA/Data Drivers, like ODBC drivers, provide access to more than 50 different target databases.

RDA

RDA is not a product. It is a standard for developers to access data. RDA uses OSI and supports dynamic SQL. RDA also allows the client to be connected to more than one database server at the same time. However, it does not support typical transaction-related services. Because of a lack of vendor support and an inability to snap into popular B2B application integration development environments, it is no longer relevant for B2B application integration.

DRDA

DRDA is an IBM database connectivity standard that has the support of many database heavyweights such as Sybase, Oracle, IBI, and Informix. Like other database gateways, DRDA attempts to provide easy database connectivity between any number of databases operating in multiplatform environments.

DRDA defines database transactions as remote requests, remote units of work, distributed units of work, and distributed requests. A remote request means that one SQL request is sent to one database. A remote unit of work means that many SQL commands are sent to one database. A distributed unit of work means that many SQL commands are sent to many databases. However, each command is sent to a single database. Finally, a distributed request means that many SQL commands are sent to many databases, and each command can execute on several databases.

Although DRDA is a well-defined standard, the fact that DRDA requires that databases comply with standard SQL syntax diminishes its benefit to organizations

where many different systems run many different databases at different stages of maturity.

Ready for Prime Time

The strongest point in support of database-oriented middleware is that the technology is very mature, well tested, and ready for most B2B application integration applications. In other words, database access should not be a major concern for most B2B application integration projects.

Among the problems that remain to be solved for database-oriented middleware is the ability to make it more scalable. Currently, a TP monitor or application server must be employed to multiplex the database connections on behalf of the application or B2B application integration solution. Multiplexing (or connection pooling)—the ability to remove the one-connection-per-request restriction from database-oriented middleware—is becoming part of many database-oriented middleware layers, including JDBC and ODBC.

As interest renews in nonrelational database models, such as multidimensional, hierarchical, and object-oriented, middleware is learning how to emulate and translate data from model to model. Today we can view a relational database using the object-oriented model and a hierarchical database as a relational database. These emulation and translation services make B2B application integration a much easier proposition, because they make it possible to map very heterogeneous environments to a common database model, thus providing an easier starting point for integration (see our discussion of federated database middleware in Chapter 19). This capability adds the most value to data-oriented B2B application integration.

The world of database-oriented middleware isn't about to change much—even as B2B application integration grows in popularity. The simple fact is that solutions to most database access problems already exist.

Isn't it nice to come upon an area of technology where few problems are left to solve?

Java Middleware Standards and B2B Application Integration

Java, the once-revolutionary method for building Web-born applications, has now matured enough to benefit the enterprise and B2B application integration. Today's Java is driving an already growing middleware marketplace. Once inseparable from the browser, Java has become the mechanism of choice for application servers, component-based development, and now B2B application integration.

Recognizing this reality and recognizing that applets, servlets, and beans were of little use standing alone, JavaSoft promoted middleware standards for Java even before the release of the Java Development Kit (JDK) 1.0. As a result, JavaSoft can claim many successful standards, including JDBC, JMS, RMI, and the Java IDL for CORBA—all described in this chapter except JDBC, which is described in Chapter 11. These standards are all applicable to B2B application integration in that they provide a Java-enabled infrastructure.

It is useful to note that JavaSoft does not create products. Instead, it becomes partners with vendors that wrap their products in JavaSoft standards, writing their products to JavaSoft specifications and thus ensuring that their products will grow as Java grows. Our discussion in this chapter centers on specifications and the products that use those specifications.

We spoke earlier of the "re-revolution" in application servers—another form of middleware. Currently, most servers

exploit Java's hype, language, and platform. You can be sure that just as Java has ignited the world of middleware, it will ignite B2B application integration. Many, if not most, B2B application integration solutions will leverage Java as the middleware platform. This is not an idle prediction or a question of "reading the tea leaves." It is a certainty. The hard work of thousands of Java developers guarantees it.

Categories of Java Middleware Standards

If the idea of Java-based middleware sounds complex, don't be dismayed. It *is* complex. In order to simplify the complexity of Java's hype-driven standards and products, we have structured the following six major categories of Java middleware:

- Database-oriented
- Inter-process
- Message-oriented
- Application-hosting
- Transaction-processing
- Distributed object technology

Database-Oriented

Database-oriented Java-enabled middleware is the oldest and best supported of these categories. That makes perfect sense—for Java to be successful, it had to access most relational databases. The JDBC specifications have become the ODBC for the world of Java. They are now found in most tools and application servers that support Java.

Inter-Process

JavaSoft not only connects to databases, it also provides RMI, a simple synchronous mechanism that allows applets to communicate with one another and invoke one another's methods as needed. For example, you can download an applet that can connect to an Enterprise JavaBean that is running on a remote Web server and use it to invoke a method that updates a database with customer information. This communication can take place in the same machine or over a network. In effect, this creates "a poor man's distributed object." RMI benefits B2B application integration projects by sharing information with other applets and servlets scattered throughout an enterprise.

With RMI as an intra-machine and inter-machine IPC mechanism for Java applets and applications, we can reasonably suggest that RMI and CORBA provide the same value. This suggestion is supported by JavaSoft and OMG's exploration of the integration of RMI standards with CORBA standards. Although the ultimate corporate strategy (and a significant catharsis) might be to "gang up" on the Microsoft COM middleware revolution—all the while adding value to each set of standards—the benefit to a B2B application integration solution is less certain. B2B application integration benefits depend on the specific requirements of the particular project. In other words, don't buy into the message being spouted by that guy on the soapbox—at least, not yet.

A number of considerations arise when we compare RMI to CORBA. First, RMI-enabled applets and applications are limited by their ability to communicate only with other RMI-enabled objects. As a result, invoking methods written in other languages, such as C++, is about as useful as invoking them in Sanskrit. In addition, RMI fails to provide a language-neutral messaging service. Unlike Java, RMI does not support a wire protocol for security. It does not support the notion of transactions either. Nor can it support self-describing objects or dynamic invocations.

These limitations should give pause to any B2B application integration architect and developer who is feeling the seduction of the hype. *The name of the game always depends on the project at hand*. The perfect solution to one project could be a terrible waste of time on another. The focus must be on the specific problem, *not* the hyped solution. If the B2B application integration project is "Java and nothing but Java" and there is no requirement to link external resources or wire-level security—in short, if the B2B application integration project skirts wide of the shortcomings of RMI—then RMI might be a perfectly acceptable solution. However, the architect and developer should remember that the decision to use RMI means relinquishing features that may be required as the application matures.

The bottom line: RMI technology is lightweight and bound to Java, while CORBA is robust and language neutral. RMI lacks the basic features of IIOP, and Java does not provide features that are found in most ORBs. Got it?

Message-Oriented

Although some traditional message-oriented middleware products like IBM's MQSeries support Java, the real story is a new standard from JavaSoft called Java Message Service. JMS is attracting a critical mass of messaging vendors seeking to

bind their products tightly with Java. Some of the larger vendors riding this bandwagon include BEA, IBM, SAGA Software, Active Software, and Oracle.

JMS adds a common API and provider framework to Java, enabling the Java developer to dispatch and receive messages with other Java-enabled applications or applets existing anywhere on the network (see Figure 12.1). JMS defines a common set of messaging concepts and programming strategies. It provides a good mix of the messaging features common to most messaging products— important, yes, but hardly revolutionary. The difficulty is to support these concepts and strategies from JMS-compliant vendor to JMS-compliant vendor. If this obstacle is successfully overcome, the resulting products not only will share common characteristics, but will have the ability to share messages as well— something more traditional message-oriented middleware products have yet to perfect.

JMS consists of three major entities: the JMS provider, JMS messages, and JMS domains. The provider implements JMS for a particular product (for example, a Java applet, servlet, bean, or application supporting JMS). JMS messages are sets of messaging interfaces that define a common mechanism and format for moving information between providers.

JMS messages consist of several parts, including the header, properties, and body (see Figure 12.2). The header supports the same set of header fields as traditional messaging products. Both the JMS client and provider use the header to identify and route messages. The JMS message properties allow developers to add information to the standard header, such as application-specific properties,

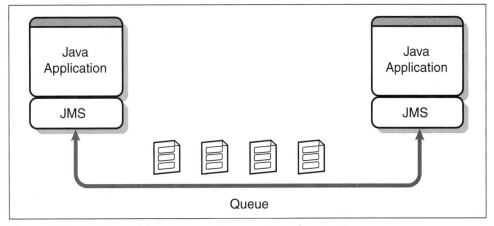

Figure 12.1   **JMS provides message transport services for Java.**

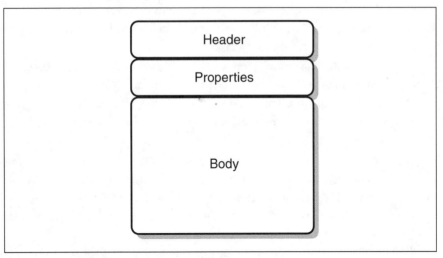

Figure 12.2   JMS message structure

standard properties, and provider-specific properties. The body contains the data that is being transported.

Messaging Models

JMS domains provide for the classification of messaging paradigms, including point-to-point and publish/subscribe. Point-to-point messaging generally relies upon queues to transport messages. Publish/subscribe, as we discussed in Chapter 7, addresses messages to some node in a content hierarchy. Pub/sub is particularly useful to B2B application integration projects because it does not require an understanding about the resource that is being subscribed to. JMS provides client interfaces created for each type of domain.

With these two paradigms available, the question that confronts the architect and developer is, Which one to use and when? The answer may be found in a closer examination of the two options. JMS point-to-point messaging defines how a client works with queues. For example, it defines how a JMS-enabled application finds queues, sends a message to them, and/or receives messages from them. JMS can send a message to a specific queue. Asynchronously, the receiving applet or application need not be engaged in order for the message to be placed in the queue; it picks up the message from the queue when it has time.

Point-to-point messaging is best applied when applications need to communicate with one another but in doing so do not need to delay the target or source application from processing tasks.

As with traditional queues, JMS queues may contain a mixture of messages. Unfortunately, JMS suffers from the shortcoming of not defining facilities to administer queues. The upside is that this shortcoming is not as significant as it might first appear, because JMS implementations leverage static, not dynamic, queues.

Developers should keep several Java concepts in mind when working with JMS queues. Among them are the `Queue` object, the `TemporaryQueue`, the `Queue ConnectionFactory`, a `QueueConnection`, a `QueueReceiver`, a `QueueSender`, and a `QueueSession`. Together, these represent a set of classes that developers can leverage within a JMS-enabled application.

The `Queue` object, the heart of this beast, encapsulates a provider-specific queue name. This object identifies a queue to a JMS method from the client. A `QueueConnection` is an active connection to a JMS point-to-point provider. The JMS client leverages the `QueueConnection` to create instances of `QueueSessions`, which produce and consume messages.

The `TemporaryQueue` is created for the duration of the `QueueConnection`. True to its name, it is a system-defined queue, available only to the `QueueConnection` object that created it as a temporary storage location. The `QueueConnectionFactory` creates an instance of a `QueueConnection` object within a JMS provider. The client uses a `QueueReceiver` to receive messages that exist in a queue, while a `QueueSender`, in contrast, places messages in a queue.

If the point-to-point model doesn't meet the needs of the project, the JMS pub/sub model probably will. This model uses a content-based hierarchy structure to describe how JMS clients publish messages and subscribe to them from a well-defined node. This model, as we noted in our earlier discussion of middleware models, is superior to simple point-to-point models. It is most practical when considering JMS for use with traditional B2B application integration projects (although either model can be used with B2B application integration implementations).

JMS refers to these nodes as "topics." A topic is in fact a small message broker that gathers and distributes messages from other entities (see Figure 12.3). JMS uses topics as quasi intermediaries. They create messages that are separated logically from subscribers. Topics are adaptive; they adjust as subscribers and publishers appear and disappear.

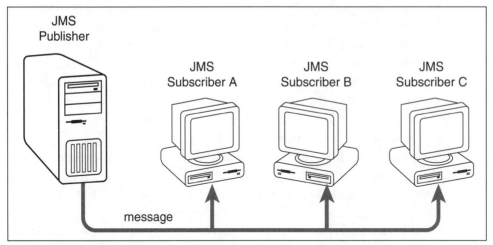

Figure 12.3   JMS is able to gather and distribute messages throughout an enterprise.

By drilling down to the next "topic level," we can discern that a topic is nothing more than a Java object that encapsulates a provider-specific topic name. Unlike most pub/sub vendors that group topics into hierarchies, allowing subscribers to subscribe to any part of the hierarchy, JMS places no such restrictions on its users. Instead, it organizes topics and the granularity of subscriptions in a completely open manner. There are no set policies for how developers should do this. This "openness" is a positive development. Strict pub/sub policies are, by definition, limiting.

JMS and Application Development

Because JMS is just another Java-enabled API, application development comes down to simply linking to and leveraging the proper JMS objects within an application. A JMS application can be created and deployed as a single unit, or JMS clients can be added to an existing JMS-enabled application or applet. Generally, JMS plays an important role in creating distributed Java applications and linking non-JMS messages into the world of Java. For example, IBM is in the process of ensuring that its MQSeries is able to exchange messages with JMS. And where Big Blue leads, other MOM vendors are sure to follow.

A typical JMS client application must go through a standard procedure to get up and running. This procedure includes using the Java Naming and Directory Information (JNDI) to find a ConnectionFactory object and then

finding one or more destination objects. To create a number of instances of a JMS session, the `ConnectionFactory` object is used to create an instance of a JMS connection and the `Connections` method. Finally, the JMS client must use the Session and the Destinations to create the `MessageProducers` and `MessageConsumers` required for the application. From this point, the connection to the queue or the pub/sub engine is set, and the application may use JMS as a mechanism to transport data into and out of an application.

A number of key issues remain that JMS must address. These include load balancing, fault tolerance, and error notification. We can probably anticipate that JMS-compliant software vendors will build such features into their products. Wouldn't it be nice if they all chose to use a consistent paradigm and mechanism? Sure it would. But don't count on it. As we mentioned earlier in this chapter, no notion of administration is built into the JMS specifications. IBM discovered that a weak administration initially hurt MQSeries, so they responded by fixing the problem. At this point, Java seems to have no such inclination to fix JMS. In addition, security seems to be an afterthought in JMS. Unfortunately, this is hardly unusual in the world of middleware.

Beyond JMS, Java integration with the big MOM products, such as MQSeries, is having a significant impact. With over 65 percent of the point-to-point message-oriented middleware marketplace, MQSeries is the "500-pound gorilla" that will always get its way. Providing Java links will only add value to that domination. IBM is "Java-tizing" just about everything these days. Java is going to be the least common denominator between CICS, Component Broker, and MQSeries—representing the largest enterprise growth area for Java. Although JMS will support smaller systems at first, it is only a matter of time before it supports larger systems as well.

Application-Hosting

Calling application servers "middleware" is a bit ingenuous, to say the least. However, because that is the way they are generally classified, it would be confusing for us to buck the trend. As we discussed in Chapter 7, an application server is any product that provides a host for application logic and processes all (or part) of an application. For example, interface logic can be defined by using client-side development tools, with all server-side business-logic processes using a remote application server. The benefit of this scenario is that both application logic and access to resources can be shared through a centralized entity.

The new generation of Java-enabled application server vendors (WebLogic, NetDynamics, and Netscape Application Server) provide hosting environments for server-side Java. These environments do a number of things; they access remote resources such as database servers, mainframes, ERP applications, and even other Java applications (see Figure 12.4).

Application servers control access to these environments by using "units of work," or transactions. A transactional paradigm enables them to recover from system- and resource-level problems and to scale to high user and processing loads. To accomplish this, application servers use mechanisms such as multiplexing database requests. However, every product implements these features in unique ways and so should be explored carefully before being used.

These environments include IDEs, which assist the developer in creating the logic for the application server, using an easy-on-the-eyes graphical user interface. They may also provide client-side tools or client-side development features through a partner.

From an architectural or features point of view, these application servers don't differ much from Java-enabled TP monitors. However, TP monitors generally

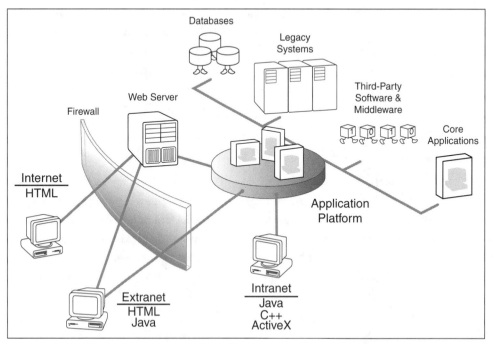

Figure 12.4   Typical Java-enabled application server architecture

support Java only at the interface level and then only as an afterthought. Java-enabled application servers are built from the ground up to support transactional, server-side Java.

TP monitors, such as BEA's Tuxedo and IBM's CICS, are best known for providing transaction-processing capabilities. With several traditional TP players entering the market by using Java as a programming mechanism (as well as a way to draw more attention to themselves), these well-known TP monitors have been forced to make adjustments. And to those who say that you can't teach an old dog new tricks . . . well, these old dogs are definitely learning new tricks.

Both Tuxedo and CICS are providing Java links to their TP monitor environments. This enhancement makes it possible to build applications using a Java client and invoke transactions housed within a TP monitor environment. These transactions may be built in any of the languages that the TP monitor supports.

The benefits of this capability should be clear. With the two largest TP monitor vendors moving in this direction—adding Java language capabilities within their environments—everyone should feel the discernable shift in the ground beneath them. "Traditional" programming languages such as C or COBOL will no longer have to be used to create transactions. It will be possible simply to use Java.

This development blurs the once-clear boundary between TP monitors and the new application servers. The vendors of these new products are moving aggressively to make sure that they don't lose their market share to the less mature Java-enabled application server. Although these products have yet to provide the scalability and the fail-safe environments traditional TP monitors provide, it is generally much easier to build applications around them.

Distributed Objects

Although there has been a great deal of talk about linking Java, CORBA, and other distributed object technologies, the software development projects using this type of technology are few and far between. Until now, the talk has been little more than just talk. However, with application servers looking to merge with distributed objects, the talk has grown more serious and more urgent.

CORBA extends the distributed features of Java using the CORBA infrastructure. Even with the integration of RMI (RMI-IIOP), Java applets were not designed to communicate across application address spaces. RMI provides an easy-to-use approach to distributed computing but does not support the advanced architectural features of CORBA-compliant ORBs.

CORBA allows Java applets to communicate with other objects written in different languages across different address spaces by using the common pipe of IIOP (see Figure 12.5). This capability allows developers to create truly distributed applications using any number of languages. CORBA provides a rich set of distributed object services that are built on top of the Java language. For example, the developer may create the client-side ORBs using Java, and the business logic at the middle tier using C++.

Java lends little to the world of distributed computing save for a very nice object-oriented programming language and a very nice binary application distribution mechanism. Still, Java is a good match for CORBA. Java's infrastructure seems to pick up where CORBA's leaves off. All the while, it allows CORBA to do what CORBA does, which is to provide a distributed object infrastructure that allows applications to extend their reach across networks, component boundaries, operating systems, and programming languages.

The integration of Java and CORBA lets developers do such things as move intelligent behavior from one ORB to another, using the common infrastructure and interfaces of CORBA. As a result, both clients and servers are able to dynamically gain behavior as required for the application development effort. CORBA

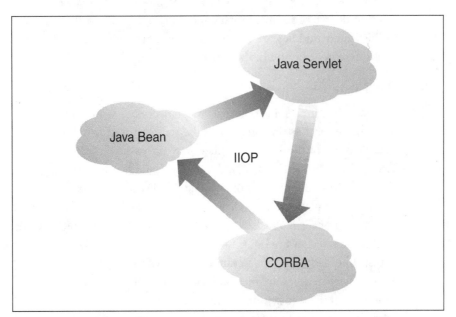

Figure 12.5   Using IIOP to allow Java applets, servlets, beans, and applications to communicate

also provides a language-independent partitioning technology and the technology to allow applications to run on a client or server without having to recompile (although adaptations must be made for each platform).

A Java ORB supports Java language mapping of the IDL. In most cases, Java ORBs are implemented in Java itself. The language mapping, or language binding, allows CORBA-compliant ORBs to be implemented using Java. Unfortunately, not all Java ORBs available today support the complete CORBA functionality.

In the simplest form of the Java-enabled CORBA ORB architecture, the client and the server are both implemented in Java. Using this architecture, the Java virtual machines on each platform allow each applet or application to execute. The applet or application shares a common ORB, which provides interprocess communication services. The client communicates with the ORB in order to transmit a request for an operation invocation to the server. The server in turn sends the results of the ORBs back to the client.

J2EE

Released in December 1999, Java 2.0 Enterprise Edition (J2EE) is the latest instance of the Java platform. Unlike past Java technology, which was simply a mixture of bytecode interrupters and APIs, J2EE fills in the blanks, providing sophisticated middleware mechanisms that are tightly coupled with a robust application development infrastructure.

Built-in Middleware

A striking feature of J2EE is that Sun has done a wonderful job in providing middleware services that are part of the standard platform, but at the same time leaving room for third-party middleware vendors to add value. These middleware services include transactional and messaging middleware services and distributed object services, all in support of Java-enabled distributed application development.

The J2EE platform is made up of the J2EE deployment specification, a set of Internet Engineering Task Force (IETF) standards, and a set of CORBA standards. The middleware built into J2EE includes EJB, Java IDL, JDBC, JMS, Java Transaction API (JTA), Java Transaction Service (JTS), and RMI-IIOP. Although each of these middleware mechanisms is important, the most critical features are contained in the transactional component middleware, where EJB adds the most value; in JMS, which provides asynchronous messaging capabilities; and in RMI-IIOP, which provides synchronous object-to-object method sharing.

Transactional J2EE

We've already discussed EJB in detail, and there is extensive literature about it, so we will not belabor its value. J2EE provides EJB as a component translation layer existing inside a container, providing most middle-tier services such as a transaction management layer, security, remote-client connectivity, and database connection pooling.

Fundamentally, EJB is a rudimentary transactional middleware environment that supports two types of components, or beans: session beans and entity beans. In short, session beans are nonpersistent, or transient, and can only link to one client for one session. An entity bean, by contrast, provides persistence.

If you are interested in mixing transactions and Java, you have JTA at your disposal as well. JTA defines a high-level transaction management specification for distributed transaction processing. In addition, there is JTS, which is an API providing links with other transactional resources, such as TP monitors (e.g., BEA's Tuxedo or IBM's CICS). Although both JTA and JTS are important, they have not gotten the "traction" of EJB, despite doing very different things.

Messaging J2EE

JMS is not as well known as EJB, and it provides a very different set of services. Still, it is quickly becoming the messaging middleware standard of choice for many organizations. Moreover, JMS is attracting existing middleware vendors, including IBM, BEA, and Progress Software, which have JMS-enabled their product lines.

Distributed App J2EE

RMI provides a very simple mechanism to allow both applets and servlets to communicate with one another and invoke one another's methods. RMI is a "poor man's" distributed object, providing Java developers with the ability to create distributed applications around a simple object-to-object synchronous communications infrastructure. RMI's power is its simplicity. Its weakness has been its difficulty in communicating with other distributed objects, including CORBA ORBs. Although both RMI and IIOP are based on TCP/IP (most of IIOP and RMI, actually), they still don't speak the same language.

With the advent of RMI-IIOP, this weakness has been overcome. RMI-IIOP provides developers with an implementation of the Java RMI API over IIOP, allowing them to write remote interfaces between clients and servers and implement them just using Java technology and Java RMI APIs.

RMI over IIOP is an exciting development, because it allows developers to combine the best features of RMI with the best features of CORBA. Until now, we have had to "fudge" such connections or depend on proprietary solutions. RMI over IIOP allows us to work entirely within the Java programming language, with no separate IDL or mapping to learn. This approach is much more flexible, allowing us to pass any serializable Java object between application components, including C++ and Smalltalk CORBA ORBs.

This marriage of RMI with IIOP provides more choices for developers who are looking to mix and match environments. It provides product developers with a better common object-to-object communication mechanism.

Middleware Platforms Emerging

Middleware is becoming part of platforms. J2EE is simply taking the lead. J2EE is significant in that it is a platform layer that runs within almost all platforms, including Windows 2000, Linux, and OS/390. Developers can write an application for J2EE and run it on any operating system that supports J2EE. J2EE applications can communicate with other J2EE applications using the J2EE middleware as described earlier in this chapter.

Windows 2000 is another platform that provides native middleware support. Although much more closed and proprietary than J2EE, Windows 2000 ships with a COM+ ORB, a component transaction layer (based on MTS), a messaging middleware layer (based on MSMQ), and even rudimentary middleware management services. Microsoft dominates the desktop and much of the server marketplace. It knows how to make using middleware easy. J2EE and Windows 2000 will battle it out once the marketplace figures out that they are going after the same e-Business applications.

Middleware is moving from a product-oriented technology to something becoming embedded in platforms, like other operating system services (e.g., disk I/O). This is a move in the right direction, considering that popular middleware is retooling for higher-level activities such as process automation, collaboration, and B2B information management. What was unique and innovative technology only a few short years ago is now just another commodity. So goes computing.

The Future of Java and Middleware

The future of Java-enabled middleware is as difficult to read as tea leaves at a picnic on a breezy day. (Okay, weird image, but you get the idea.) Depending on

who is doing the reading, the future can look very different. If database vendors are doing the reading, then Java will become an integral part of most core database technology, providing a common mechanism to build and deploy applications as well as program the database itself. If ORB people are doing the reading, they will say that Java is a good language and platform to further promote their ORB religion. They'll say that Java brings some much needed hype to a dying market. All the while, the messaging people will say that Java will become the preferred access method for most popular MOM products.

Basically, everyone is looking to "Java-tize" his or her middleware of choice, and the product vendors are only too happy to oblige.

The real advantage of Java is more than the sum of these parts. Java has finally brought about a general consensus on language and platform. Middleware is only adding power to that reality. With the help of such heavy hitters as IBM, Java is morphing into a full-blown, enterprise-class application development and processing environment. Middleware support is simply a natural progression of that reality.

So, the future? Count on message brokers written entirely in Java—transactional component environments and even Java-enabled intelligent agent technology. This is the next generation of Java-enabled middleware, representing another set of explosive growth opportunities that will add significant value to the B2B application integration space.

Message Brokers and B2B Application Integration

This latest category of middleware can broker information (messages) between two or more target entities (networks, middleware, applications, and/or systems) with significantly greater ease than traditional methods. What's more, they can accomplish this regardless of how the information is represented or accessed. However, message brokers, although working well for intra-company problem domains (EAI), have clear limitations when applied to B2B, even though these limitations are falling by the wayside as message broker vendors recreate this EAI technology for B2B and combine this technology with B2B integration technology.

Message brokers can be positioned between any number of source or target systems that exist within any number of organizations and broker the information exchange between them. They can account for differences in application semantics and database schemas, and process information by transforming the structure or format of the information so it makes sense to the target application receiving it.

Message brokers also provide a mechanism to integrate multiple business processes that to this point have remained more isolated than open—regardless of whether the business processes are new, old, legacy, centralized, or distributed. Message brokers bridge many different platforms and application development solutions. They are able to connect to each application and route information between them by

using any number of middleware and API mechanisms. More to the point, they are capable of a good deal more than simply routing information. They can provide enhancements such as hosting business functions that build on the existing business functions of the entities they connect.

Message Broker Services

The services provided by message brokers can be put into the following distinct categories:

- Message transformation
- Intelligent routing
- Rules processing
- Message warehousing
- Flow control
- Repository services
- Directory services
- Management
- APIs and adapters

The ability of message brokers to leave systems "where they are"—minimizing change while allowing data to be shared—lends tremendous value to B2B application integration. As we've noted time and again, such a capability is critical to B2B application integration, since you typically don't have control over the systems owned by your trading partners. Thus, you need to obtain information housed inside these systems through a nonintrusive point of integration. Message brokers fit the bill nicely.

Message brokers more closely resemble the way B2B activities "actually work"—providing greater efficiency and flexibility by automating functions currently performed manually, functions such as sending sales reports through inter-office mail or walking data down the hall on disk. Since message brokers mirror "the way business works," their success suggests that the B2B application integration solution in fact addresses a business flow problem. Technology such as message brokers serves as the necessary B2B infrastructure.

Why a New Layer?

Traditional middleware such as MOM (message-queuing software and pub/sub engines) solves only part of the B2B application integration problem. Message

brokers, by building on top of existing middleware technology, address the other part. This makes message brokers the "middleware of middleware" (see Figure 13.1).

An effective B2B application integration solution contains a number of components that are neither middleware nor applications but are in fact routing, reformatting, and flow components. Although these components may be placed in an application or middleware, they are a better architectural fit when they are placed in message brokers, providing a central point of integration.

Given all this, exactly what do message brokers offer? As with any new technology, vendors, seeking the greatest market share, have taken individual approaches to define their products while addressing the message-brokering problem. Despite this lack of standardization, message brokers share some common components—a message transformation layer, a rules engine, and an intelligent routing mechanism (see Figure 13.2)—as well as a number of features we will discuss later in this chapter.

A message broker is a software system based on asynchronous, store-and-forward messaging. It works simply to manage interactions between applications and other information resources, utilizing abstraction techniques—an application puts (publishes) a message to the message broker. Another application, or applications, consumes (subscribes to) the message.

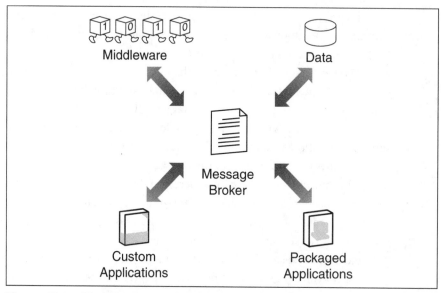

Figure 13.1 **Message brokers are able to integrate many different types of middleware as well as applications and databases.**

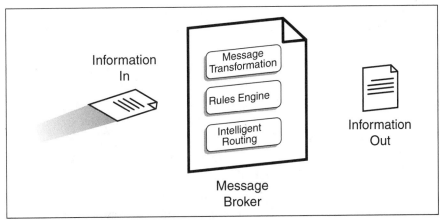

Figure 13.2   Message brokers have three primary components: the message transformation layer, the rules engine, and the intelligent routing mechanism.

The application does not need to be session-connected in order to work successfully. This eliminates, from the outset, the primary scalability problem associated with most integration technologies. Target systems need not be active. They can receive the information at some future time when they become active. (Again, this dynamic makes message brokers a natural fit for most B2B application integration problem domains, since systems participating within a trading community may not all be up and running at any given time. Asynchronous trading communities need asynchronous middleware.)

Message brokers do much more than simply function asynchronously. They extend the basic messaging paradigm by mediating the interaction between the applications, allowing the source and target systems to remain truly anonymous. They also translate and convert data, reformat and reconstitute messages, and route information to any number of targets (determined by centrally defined business rules that are applied to the message content).

To be the solid foundation for a successful B2B application integration strategy, message brokers must offer genuine any-to-any and many-to-many capabilities.

As you might expect, when vendors take individual approaches to solving the message-brokering problem, not all message brokers are alike. A complete message-brokering solution demands an underlying messaging system, a brokering layer (or rules engine), a connectivity (adapter) framework, design and development tools, and system management and administration tools. A handful of

products currently on the market provide many pieces to the puzzle, but none provide the entire puzzle. A systems integrator is often needed to combine those pieces with the other pieces necessary to complete the puzzle.

The success of the finished "picture" depends on the design and architecture of the solution—on how well the pieces integrate. This is what determines their scalability. IS organizations need to be thorough about "kicking the tires" in order to select the right solution for their B2B application integration initiative.

Message brokers are different from traditional middleware because of the services they offer above and beyond such products. They certainly use messages. Still, it's difficult to fit them into the MOM category. In addition to relying on the concept of a message, they provide value-added services from the uppermost layer in the ISO model, the application layer.

Considering the Source (and Target)

Too often, when we consider the details of message brokers, we put the cart ahead of the horse. The first step in evaluating a message broker must include an evaluation of the types of systems to be integrated.

The source and target systems may consist of any number of entities—database servers, Web servers, host applications, user screens, distributed objects, ERP applications, and custom, or proprietary, applications. The benefit of message brokers rests with their ability to link different types of systems, adjusting to the variations between all source and target systems. They are able to do this by exposing an API (and sometimes an adapter, which will be discussed later in this chapter).

It is also noteworthy that message brokers adhere to a noninvasive B2B application integration model, where the source and target applications don't require many changes in order for information to be moved among them. Because message brokers are able to leverage many points of integration (including database access, screen scraping, defined APIs, and middleware), in many cases no changes are required at all.

An API is nothing more than the mechanism that allows an application to access the services of a message broker (see Figure 13.3). When using APIs, the developer can create a link between the source or target application interface and the message broker API. This requires creating a program that binds the application's point of integration to the API of the message brokers or changing the application to communicate with the message broker using its API.

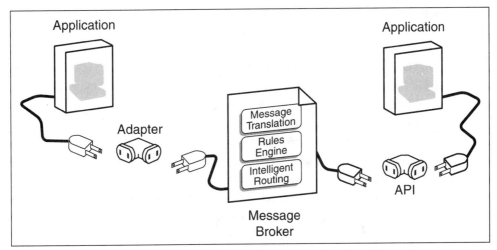

Figure 13.3 **Message brokers provide services to applications through an application programming interface or an adapter.**

Doing this has a huge downside. Binding an application to the message broker requires creating code to accomplish the task or changing the application to accommodate the message broker API—costly propositions, in terms of both time and money. The inevitable need for testing only adds to the costs.

By contrast, adapters are able to link deeply into an application or database. They move information to and from source or target applications without having to create new code (or any code, for that matter). Adapters, as we'll discuss later, hide the complexities of the integrated applications by managing the movement of information into and out of the application on behalf of the message broker. Adapters leverage points of integration, such as a native interface (e.g., SAP's BAPI). They manage the consumption of information from the source application, converting it into a form that the message broker can understand. On the other end, adapters publish the information to the target application in a form that the target application can understand.

Message Transformation Layer

The message transformation layer is the "Rosetta stone" of the system. It understands the format of all messages being transmitted among the applications and translates those messages on the fly, restructuring data from one message so that

it makes sense to the receiving application or applications. It provides a common dictionary that contains information on how each application communicates outside itself (application externalization) as well as which bits of information have meaning to which applications (see Figure 13.4).

Message transformation layers generally contain parsing and pattern-matching methods that describe the structure of any message format. Message formats are then constructed from pieces that represent each field encapsulated within a message. Once the message has been broken down to its component parts, the fields may be recombined to create a new message.

Most message brokers can handle most types of messages, including fixed, delimited, and variable. Messages are reformatted using an interface the message broker provides, which may be as primitive as an API or as easy to use as a GUI.

Message transformation layers generally store application information in a repository (see the section Repository Services later in this chapter) that keeps track of the source system, the format of the message, the target system, and the desired format of the target system. Transformation layers are vital because different systems deal with information in such different ways. For example, a SAP system tracks customer information in a manner very different from a Baan system. In order to exchange customer information between the two systems, the information must be reformatted. This reformatting, or transformation, may include a schema conversion and a data conversion. Reformatting ensures

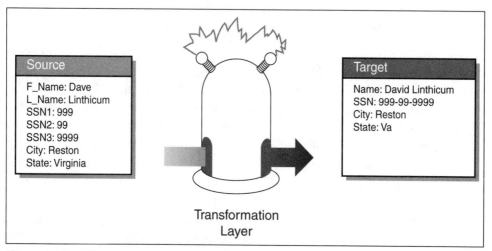

Figure 13.4   The message transformation layer

consistent application semantics between all integrated source and target applications.

Schema Conversion

A schema conversion is the process of changing the structure of a message and thus remapping the schema so that it is acceptable to the target system. Though it is not difficult, B2B application integration architects need to understand that this process must occur dynamically within the message broker. For example, if a message containing accounts receivable information arrives from a DB2 system on a mainframe, it may look something like this:

```
Cust_No                 Alphanumeric 10
Amt_Due                 Numeric      10
Date_of_Last_Bill       Date
```

With the following information:

```
AB99999999
560.50
09/17/98
```

The client/server system created to produce the annual report receives the information and must store it according to the following schema:

```
Customer_Number          Numeric          20
Money_Due                Numeric           8
Last_Billed              Alphanumeric     10
```

Clearly, the schema in the client/server system is different from the schema in the DB2 system. Moving information from the DB2 system (the source system) to the client/server system (the target system) without a schema conversion would most likely result in a system error because of the incompatibility of the formats. For the systems to communicate successfully, the information in Cust_No (which is alphanumeric and holds 10 positions) needs to be converted to all numeric information capable of holding 20 digits or positions. All data that is not numeric (that is, letters) must be translated into numeric data. This can be accomplished either by deleting all characters when translating Cust_No to Customer_Number or by converting characters into numeric representations (A=1, B=2, and so on). This process can be defined within the rules-processing layer of the message broker by creating a rule to translate data dynamically, depending on its content and schema. Moving information from one system to

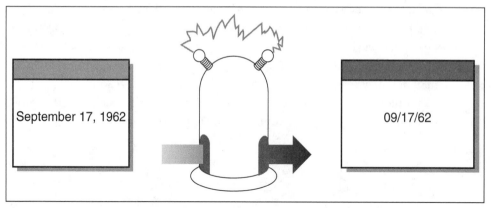

Figure 13.5   Translating message schemas/formats dynamically

another demands that the schema/format of the message be altered as the information is transferred from one system to the next (see Figure 13.5).

Although most message brokers can map any schema to any other schema, it is prudent to try to anticipate extraordinary circumstances. For example, when converting information extracted from an object-oriented database and placing it in a relational database, the message broker must convert the object schema into a relational representation before it can convert the data within the message. The same holds true when moving information from a relational database to an object-oriented database. Most message brokers break the message moving into their environment into a common format and then translate it into the appropriate message format for the target system. (As we already noted, the rules-processing engine within the message broker allows appropriate programming to take place.)

Data Conversion

In the previous transformation example, information in Cust_No (alphanumeric and holding 10 positions) needs to be converted to all numeric with a capability of 20 positions. The alpha component of Cust_No must be dealt with in another manner. It is possible to change the nature of the target application to accept letters, or the alpha component can be either deleted or converted. Deleting characters or converting them into numeric representations are examples of data conversion. The key to successful data conversion is to determine the data formats of the source and target applications, assess the differences between them (for example, which data elements need to be extracted and converted, and where they ultimately need to be placed), and adjust to them. Most message brokers

are able to understand most message schemas through message identifications. Therefore, they automatically convert data to a workable format. Sometimes, however, it will be necessary to program a rule to address a specific data-type conversion problem. The conversion of numeric information to alphanumeric information (and vice versa) generally requires such a programmed rule.

Although many formats exist within most B2B application integration problem domains, we will confine our attention to the following:

- Alphanumeric
- Binary integers
- Floating point values
- Bit fields
- IBM mainframe floating points
- COBOL and PL/I picture data
- BLOBs

In addition to these formats, there are a number of formatting issues to address, including the ability to convert logical operators (bits) between systems and the ability to handle data types that are not supported in the target system. These issues often require significant customization in order to facilitate successful communication between systems.

In data conversion, values are managed in two ways: carrying over the value from the source to the target system without change, or modifying the data value dynamically. Either an algorithm or a look-up table can be used to modify the data value. One or more of the source application attributes may use an algorithm to change the data or create new data. For example, attributes in the source application may represent "Amount Sold" and hold the value 8. Another attribute, "Cost of Goods Sold," may contain the value 4. However, in the target application, these attributes may have to populate a new attribute, "Gross Margin," which is the amount sold less the cost of the goods sold. In order to make this communication successful, the algorithm "Amount Sold minus Cost of Goods Sold" must be applied.

Algorithms of this type are nothing more than the type of data conversions we have done for years when populating data warehouses and data marts. Now, in addition to using these simple algorithms, it is possible to aggregate, combine, and summarize the data in order to meet the specific requirements of the target application.

When using the look-up table scenario, it might be necessary to convert to an arbitrary value. "ARA" in the source system might refer to a value in the accounts receivable system. However this can be determined, it must be checked

against the look-up table. Message brokers may use a currency conversion table to convert dollars to yen, which may be embedded in a simple procedure or, more likely, in a database connected to the message broker. The message broker may also invoke a remote application server function to convert the amount.

The B2B application integration architect or developer may encounter special circumstances that have to be finessed. The length of a message attribute may be unknown, or the value may be in an unknown order. In such situations, it is necessary to use the rules-processing capability of the message broker to convert the problem values into the proper representation for the target system.

Intelligent Routing

Intelligent routing, sometimes referred to as flow control or content-based routing, builds on the capabilities of both the rules layer and the message transformation layer. A message broker can "intelligently route" a message by first identifying it as coming from the source application and then routing it to the proper target application, translating it if required. For example, when a message arrives at the message broker, it is analyzed and identified as coming from a particular system and/or subsystem. Once the message is identified and the message schema is understood, the applicable rules and services are applied to the processing of the message, including message transformation. Once the message is processed, the message broker, based on how it is programmed, routes the message to the correct target system (see Figure 13.6). Virtually instantaneous, this all takes place at the same time, with as many as a thousand of these operations occurring.

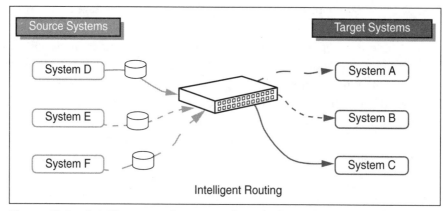

Figure 13.6 Intelligent routing means identifying the message and sending it to the proper destination.

Rules Processing

The rules-processing engine, found within most message brokers, provides the B2B application integration architect and developer with the ability to create rules that control the processing and distribution of messages. Rules processing is an application development environment supported by the message broker to address the special requirements of integrating applications. By using rules engines, message brokers can implement intelligent message routing and transformation. For example, at times a message will be required by a second target application. At other times a message will have to be routed to two or more applications. In both these cases, messages must be routed to any number of target applications that extract and translate data from any number of source applications. A truly flexible solution requires a rules engine to make these formatting and routing decisions dynamically. Combining a rules engine with a message transformation layer allows such a solution to be realized.

Essentially, a rules engine is an application that resides between applications, one that does nothing more than provide the logic for sharing information. Each rules engine solves an intelligent routing and transformation problem differently. Most have the capability of testing a message to determine its fields and values. Most often, rules engines use traditional Boolean logic (IF, ELSE, and OR) and high-level languages to create rules and associate actions with each rule according to its algorithm.

The rules-processing capabilities of message brokers should not be confused with the capabilities of traditional application servers. Application servers provide a full spectrum of element environments and tools. Most rules-processing engines only provide features sufficient to move a message from any number of source systems to any number of target systems. However, as message brokers have matured, they have begun to provide rules-processing services that rival those of traditional application servers. Pushing the envelope in this direction, some vendors have gone so far as to integrate application servers with message brokers. This strategy combines the best of both worlds while also addressing method-oriented B2B application integration.

Rules processing generally relies on scripting languages rather than on more complex programming languages (such as Java and C++) and on interpreters rather than compilers. However, as in almost all things about message brokers, the way in which each message broker processes rules varies from vendor to vendor and from message broker to message broker.

Rules are created through either the rules editor (which functions like a program editor) or a wizard. The rules editor creates rules by allowing commands to be entered into the message broker. These commands may be stored as a simple text file, or in more sophisticated message brokers, they may be stored within the repository. The rules wizard guides the user through the selection of each rule that is being applied to a particular message, group of messages, or events. For example, the wizard may ask if the message should be processed as soon as it comes into the message broker or at a specific time of day. Options such as these are particularly useful for things like updating customer information in a database, when such updates might be better made during off-peak hours. The wizard may also inquire about the transformation of information between the source and target systems, including the logic that may be required. It may create the opportunity to take many variables into account at the same time, such as checking for states and events that other systems may provide. For example, it may not be advisable to update the SAP database if the last update to the database produced an error message or an unstable state. Or certain users might have to be logged on before proceeding with a certain type of message processing. Depending on the need, it may be beneficial to wait for a specific event before extracting information from a source system.

Because rules processing is truly programming, almost anything can be done. Messages can be generated based on sales events over a million dollars. Other applications based on the monitoring of events for states can be invoked. Anything that can be programmed can be made part of the rules processing. With rules engines becoming more powerful and vendors providing easier mechanisms to create rules, there is no limit to what is attainable.

Message Warehousing

A message warehouse is a database that, as an option, is able to store messages that flow through the message broker (see Figure 13.7). In general, message brokers provide this message persistence facility to meet several requirements: message mining, message integrity, message archiving, and auditing.

Message mining allows the extraction of business data to support decisions, creating the message warehouse as a quasi data warehouse. For example, it is possible to use the message warehouse to determine the characteristics and amount of new customer information that is being processed through the message broker. All new sales orders for a given period of time can be displayed. Off-the-shelf data-mining and reporting tools work wonderfully for such applications.

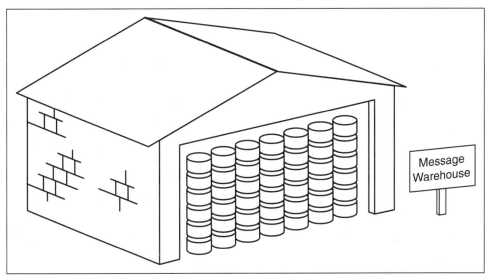

Figure 13.7   Message warehousing allows message brokers to remember all messages that they process over a given period of time.

Messages that are stored in the message warehouse are almost always stored without modification. However, in a few cases, the messages go through a data warehouse as they would an aggregation or transformation process. The data is combined and altered so that it will make sense to the average business user. In general, B2B application integration architects and application programmers accomplish this through the rules-processing mechanism of the message broker, or they may employ an outside application to alter the message for storage.

Message warehousing is able to provide services such as **message integrity** because the warehouse itself provides a natural, persistent state for message traffic. If the server goes down, the message warehouse may act as a persistent buffer, or queue, to store messages that would otherwise be lost. Messages may then be re-sent or compared with other message warehouses on the network to ensure message transfer integrity. The underlying principle is that of persistent message queuing supported by traditional message-oriented middleware. This also provides state-full messaging, or the ability to maintain states between two or more systems even when using asynchronous messaging, messaging that by definition is a cohesive, rather than coupled, mechanism.

Message archiving provides the message broker user with the ability to store months of message traffic in an archive for auditing or other purposes. It allows

information to be restored for analysis. Many B2B application integration administrators maintain message archives for just over a year, although no standard currently exists.

Auditing is the use of the message warehouse to determine the health of the B2B application integration solution and to provide the ability to solve any problems that are noted. For example, by using the auditing facilities of a message broker, it is possible to determine message traffic loads, message content variations, and the number of messages requiring transformation. Auditing also tracks messages that change, their state before the transformation, and their state following it.

Repository Services

Many message brokers embrace the concept of a repository—a database of information about source and target applications (which may include data elements, inputs, processes, outputs, and the interrelationships among applications). Although many experts view repositories primarily as part of the world of application development, they do not question their value to the world of B2B application integration.

B2B application integration–enabled repositories, in their simplest form, provide the message broker user with a database of information pertaining to the following:

- Owner of the system (company)
- Location of the system (directory)
- Security parameters
- Message schema information
- Metadata
- Enabling technology
- Transformation information
- Rules and logic for message processing
- Design and architecture information (e.g., UML)
- Object information

The goal is to provide a sophisticated repository that is capable of keeping track of a good deal more than simply the rudimentary information (such as directory data). It should track more sophisticated information about the source and target systems (such as metadata, message schemas, and even security and ownership). The repository should provide all the information required by the

B2B application integration architect and programmer to locate any piece of information within the enterprise and to link it to any other piece of information. The repository must be the master directory for the entire B2B application integration problem domain.

Many of the concepts about repositories have been taken from the application development world. Rules, logic, objects, and metadata are still tracked within a repository. The difference between the two is that by using the repository with a message broker, other, less sophisticated information—such as encrypted passwords, network addresses, protocol transformation services, and even error code transformations and maintenance information—can also be tracked.

In more sophisticated message brokers, the repository is becoming the "big brain," able to access both the source and target systems in order to discover necessary information (such as metadata and available business processes). Engaged in this "auto-discovery," the message broker will be able to populate the repository with this or any other information that may be required. Ultimately, the repository will become the enterprise metadata repository, able to track all systems and databases connected to the message broker.

The value of a repository should be clear. With the repository as a common reference point for all connected processes and databases, integrating data and methods is as straightforward as finding their equivalents and joining them together. The repository can also track the rules that the B2B application integration architect and developer apply within the B2B application integration problem domain. Moreover, because the repository knows the schema of both the source and the target systems, it also contains information for the proper transformation of messages flowing from source to target. In many cases, this transformation can be automatically defined, freeing the user from ever needing to be involved in the definition of the transformation procedure.

However, repositories remain only the storage mechanisms in this scenario. The message broker must read the information from the repository and carry out the appropriate process. In addition to the message broker engine, the graphical user interface that accompanies most message brokers provides B2B application integration architects and developers with a mechanism to alter the repository and so alter the behavior of the message broker.

Graphical User Interface

One of the wonderful realities of the message broker is that it is middleware "with a face"—or at least with a graphical user interface. This interface allows the

user to create rules, link applications, and define transformation logic (see Figure 13.8).

Although the features and functions of interfaces vary from vendor to vendor, all vendors claim that their product simplifies the B2B application integration process. For some, this claim is something of a stretch. These vendors provide only the most basic features (such as scripting and rudimentary administration) to justify their outlandish claim. However, the newest versions really do simplify the integration process and include such features as wizard systems to define rules and transformation, along with an interface that allows the user to drill down to any level of detail within any connected system. These interfaces can depict a B2B application integration solution, including connected systems, rules, and message routing, using diagrams that bring the entire solution to light. More than simply setting up the solution, these graphical user interfaces also provide administration features, such as the capability to monitor message traffic, the performance of the message brokers, the status of connected systems, and mechanisms to route around problems.

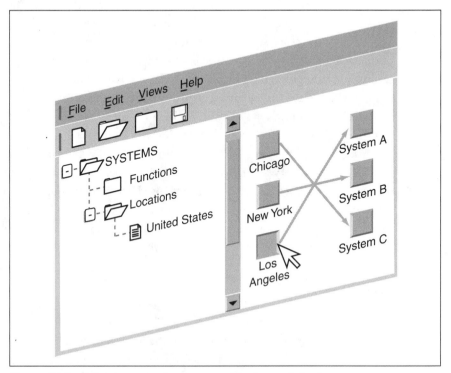

Figure 13.8   The message broker graphical user interface

Directory Services

Because message brokers deal with distributed systems, including systems that exist in other organizations, they require directory services to locate, identify, use, and authorize network resources for those systems. Directory services provide a single point of entry for applications and middleware (e.g., message brokers). In doing so, they lend a tremendous benefit to the system. They also support the use of a shared set of standards for directory and naming services. Directory services act as guides among the thousands of resources available to applications and middleware.

Using directory services, the message broker or B2B application integration developer can build applications that are able to intelligently locate resources anywhere on the network. Directories know where to find these resources on behalf of applications. They track them as they are reconfigured, moved, or deleted. For example, an e-mail application can locate a user group, a word processing application can find a printer, and a client/server application can find a database—no matter where these resources exist on the network.

Application objects exist on the network, not on certain servers. Therefore, it is essential that developers share a common infrastructure for locating objects.

At base, directory services are nothing more than a method of classifying resources on the network in a way consistent with every other method of classification. For example, in biology, biologists classify living things according to kingdom, phylum, class, order, family, genus, and species. Directory services identify and classify all computer systems by moving down a similar hierarchy and by using a naming system to determine the direction at the branches.

A number of directory services exist, including the Domain Name System (DNS), Novell's NetWare Directory System and Directory Services, Netscape Communications' Directory Server, Microsoft's Active Directory, and X.500. DNS gives all Internet users the ability to resolve server names. It has been a tremendous resource for years but is, unfortunately, limited to that one simple function.

Management

Administration and management of the B2B application integration problem domain is primarily the responsibility of the management layer of the message broker. Because of the level of the technology's maturity and the fact that several

enterprise management tools are on the market, too many message brokers are marketed with little or no management.

B2B application integration solutions require the ability to start and stop source and target applications as well as the ability to monitor important statistics, such as performance, message integrity, and the general functioning of the entire B2B application integration problem domain. Some message broker vendors are correctly anticipating the needs of B2B application integration management and are creating separate products to address these needs while enabling existing enterprise management tools to handle the special needs of B2B application integration. These vendors stand to win the lion's share of this growing market.

The management layers of message brokers need to support other features, including the ability to monitor message movement through the system. These features must include alerts to requeue throughput, alerts to requeue availability, and end-to-end performance tracking.

Although it is too early to predict with certainty, it appears that a new generation of management tools built specifically for the B2B application integration marketplace is on the horizon. However, until that generation arrives, users must either depend on what is bundled with the message broker or create their own management infrastructure.

Adapters

Adapters for message brokers have been considered for years; however, as with so many other things, each vendor has had its own concept of what an adapter should be. To date, there is no standard. (B2B application integration architects should note that regardless of the vendor, the capabilities of many adapters are *always* exaggerated.)

Adapters are layers between the message broker and the source or target application. For example, an adapter could be a set of "libraries" that map the differences between two distinct interfaces—the message broker interface and the native interface of the source or target application—and hide the complexities of those interfaces from the end user or even from the B2B application integration developer using the message broker. A message broker vendor may have adapters for several different source and target applications (such as SAP R/3, Baan, and PeopleSoft) or for certain types of databases (such as Oracle, Sybase, or DB2) or even for specific brands of middleware. Over time, adapters are becoming more sophisticated, trading a set of libraries that developers must manipulate for

binary interfaces that require little, if any, programming. Adapters are also getting smarter, with intelligence placed within the adapter and with adapters running at the source and target systems in order to better capture events.

Two types of adapters exist in the context of message brokers: thin adapters and thick adapters; and these adapters may have two types of behavior: dynamic and static.

Thin Adapters

Thin adapters are offered by the most popular message brokers today. In most cases, they are simply API wrappers, or binders, that map the interface of the source or target system to a common interface supported by the message broker (see Figure 13.9). In other words, they simply perform an API-binding trick, binding one API to another.

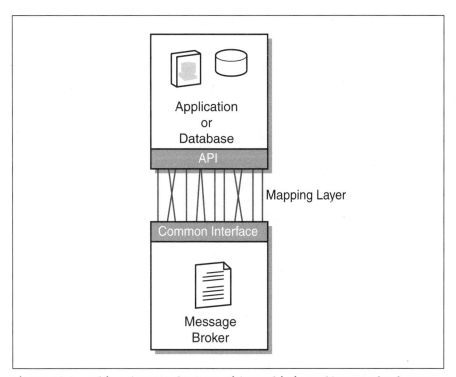

Figure 13.9   **Thin adapters don't provide sophisticated layers of software between the source or target systems and the message broker, and are just simple abstractions on top of existing APIs.**

Wrappers Are Also Thin Adapters

Other examples of thin adapters are wrapping application interfaces using open interface standards, such as CORBA or COM. Here again, one interface is being traded for another. However, in this case, providing a common, open interface is an advantage.

Most ERP vendors are seeking to create open interfaces to their applications, for both data- and process-oriented integration, making integration easier to implement with traditional tools while reducing the risk of proprietary interfaces. For example, SAP is seeking to provide interfaces based on CORBA and Java. Such moves represent progress.

Thin adapters have the advantage of being simple to implement. With no additional, "thick" layer of software between source and target applications, there is greater granular control. Thin adapters have a number of disadvantages, however. Since using them accomplishes nothing more than trading one interface software for another, thin adapters impact performance without increasing functionality. And a fair amount of programming is still required. Complicating matters is the fact that the common APIs that are being mapped are almost always proprietary.

Thick Adapters

Unlike thin adapters, thick adapters provide a significant amount of software and functionality between the message broker infrastructure and the source or target applications. The thick adapter's layer of abstraction makes managing the movement of information or invoking processes painless (see Figure 13.10). Because the abstraction layer and the manager negotiate the differences between all the applications requiring integration, almost no programming is needed.

The layer of sophisticated software that hides the complexities of the source and target application interfaces from the message broker user allows thick interfaces to accomplish this. The user sees only a businesslike representation of the process and the metadata information as managed by the abstraction layer and the adapter. In many cases, the user connects many systems through this abstraction layer and the graphical user interface, without ever having to resort to hand-coding.

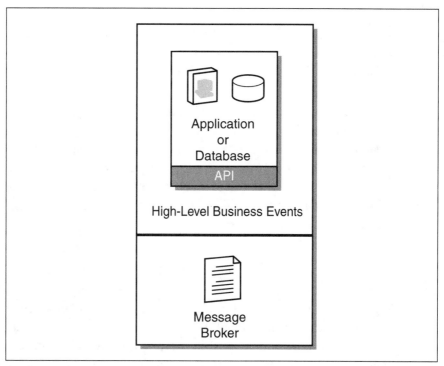

Figure 13.10   Thick adapters place an abstraction layer on top of the application interfaces.

Repositories are major players in the thick-adapter scenario. As we noted, the repository is able to understand much of the information about the source and target applications and is able to use that information as a mechanism to interact with those applications on behalf of the message broker.

In addition, several abstraction layers may be created around the types of applications to be integrated. For example, there may be an abstraction for common middleware services (such as distributed objects, message-oriented middleware, and transactional middleware). There may also be an abstraction layer for packaged applications and another layer that is able to address the integration of relational and nonrelational databases. This structure hides from the end user the complexities of the interfaces that each entity (middleware, packaged applications, and databases) employs.

With the many advantages and conveniences of thick adapters, it should come as no surprise that message broker vendors are moving toward them. Their

progress is slowed by the fact that thick adapters require a tremendous amount of time to develop, as much as six times that of a thin adapter. Right now, this time investment deters some vendors. However, as B2B application integration becomes more sophisticated, enterprises will continue to look for more sophisticated solutions, solutions that require no programming and provide an easy, businesslike method to view the integration of the enterprise. There is no question, thick adapters are the future.

Static and Dynamic Adapters

As noted earlier, in addition to being thick or thin, adapters are also defined by being either static or dynamic.

Static adapters, the most common adapters in play at this time, must be manually coded with the contents of the source and target systems. They have no mechanism for understanding anything about the schema of connected databases. As a result, they must be configured by hand to receive information from the source schema. If the connected database schema changes, static adapters have no mechanism for updating their configuration with the new schema.

In contrast, **dynamic adapters** are able to "learn" about the source or target systems connected to them through a discovery process that they go through when first connected to the application or data source. This discovery process

---

Centralized versus Distributed Adapters

Two distinct adapter architectures are emerging: distributed and centralized. As the name suggests, **centralized adapters** run with the message broker. Generally, these are thin adapters that only bind the message broker's API to the API of the source or target application.

Just as centralized adapters are thin adapters, **distributed adapters** are thick adapters that exist on the message broker *as well as on the source or target application*. Running an adapter on the application being integrated allows many processes of the source or target application to be better determined, such as capturing events, monitoring states, or even restarting the application as required. And because the adapter is in two parts, it is better able to coordinate the transfer of information between the message broker and the source or target application.

typically means reading the database schema information from the repository or perhaps the source code to determine the structure, content, and application semantics of the connected system. More important, dynamic adapters not only learn about the connected system, they are able to *relearn* information if something changes within the connected system over time. A dynamic adapter automatically understands when a customer-number attribute name changes.

Using an API

In addition to using adapters, message brokers leverage APIs as mechanisms to access the services of source and target applications. There is nothing particularly noteworthy or revolutionary about this approach. A message broker API is very much like the API of a traditional message-oriented middleware product. This construct has the advantage of allowing many applications to be integrated. Traditional message-oriented middleware, as we have noted, is best for linking a single application with one other application.

Other Features

Vendors are building other features into their message brokers all the time. These might include version control to track the changes made in integration models (including check in/check out), traditional configuration management capabilities, and impact analysis (the ability to examine how changing information flows will affect a trading community before making the actual changes to the physical flows).

Finally, all message brokers have some sort of integration, with a process integration tool that supports functions such as collaboration. Process integration tools place logical abstraction layers on top of existing physical integration flows, allowing users to view B2B application integration from a business-oriented perspective rather than from a technical perspective.

Topologies

Message brokers utilize a "hub-and-spoke" topology. The message broker, as the hub, rests between the source and target applications being integrated in a configuration that resembles a star (see Figure 13.11). Although this configuration is the most traditional one, new developments suggest the various

advantages of leveraging message brokers that use other topologies, such as multihub or federated.

In the **multihub** configuration, a number of message brokers are linked, with the source and target applications connected to any of the brokers in the configuration (see Figure 13.12). This configuration is able to scale, making it possible to integrate virtually unlimited numbers of source and target applications. As more applications than a single message broker can handle need to be integrated, more message brokers can be added to the network.

Like the multihub configuration, the **federated** configuration supports several message brokers working together to solve a B2B application integration problem. However, federated configurations typically mean that several different types of message brokers, independent of one another, are working in concert to integrate a trading community. This is a common configuration—which makes perfect sense, because most trading partners don't agree on the make and model of message brokers. Therefore, the various message brokers must learn to interoperate. What's important to understand about this configuration is the fact that the source and target applications are *statically bound* to a particular message broker (see Figure 13.13). The message processing is not shared among message

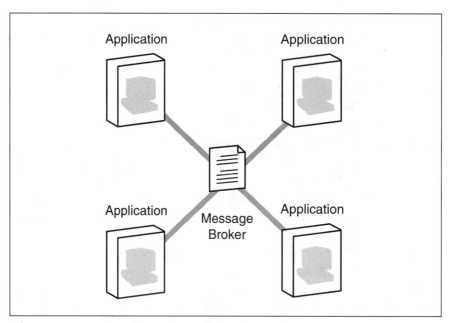

Figure 13.11   Hub-and-spoke configuration

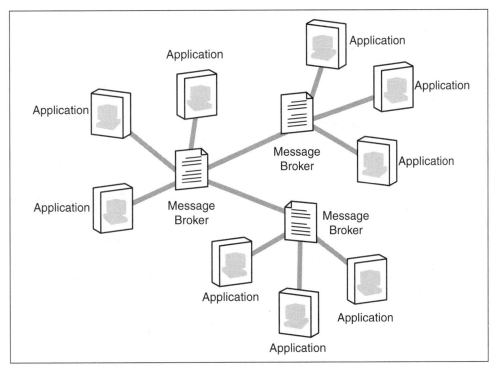

Figure 13.12   Multihub configuration

brokers. They typically hand off information one to another through a common interchange format, such as XML.

The evolution of message brokers is clear. As they become more sophisticated, there is a clear movement away from the simple hub-and-spoke configuration toward the multihub configuration. Unfortunately, this transition is not, and will not be, a smooth one. Some message brokers are able to support multihub configurations. Others are unable to intelligently share the message-processing load. Those message brokers able to exist in a multihub configuration are successful by learning to "share the load" with other message brokers on the network. Load-balancing mechanisms that are able to off-load message-processing work to message brokers with available capacity help make it possible to simply add message brokers to the network. They locate the broker, configure it, replicate the repository, and put the message broker to work.

In addition to the ability to scale—a definite requirement for B2B application integration—the multihub configuration provides a fail-safe service. With several

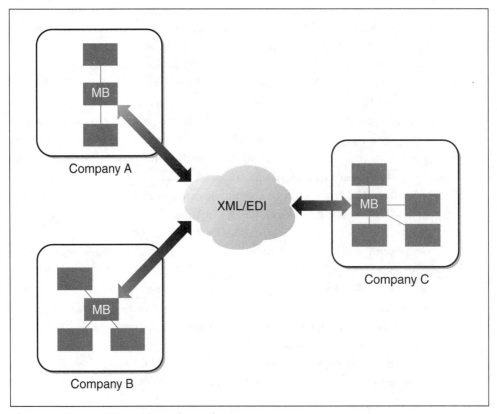

Figure 13.13   Federated configuration

message brokers sharing the network load, a single failure will not shut down the system. The others can continue processing the messages. To say that this is an advantage is a profound understatement. Unfortunately, it is an "uneven" advantage. Many of these fail-safe features vary from vendor to vendor, with some more effective than others. However, an uneven advantage remains an advantage. With the message broker as the beating heart of B2B application integration, it is only prudent to incorporate sound mechanisms to protect it from failure.

The Future of B2B Application Integration and Brokers

Are message brokers the next generation of middleware? They certainly fill a need in many larger trading communities, a need that traditional middleware cannot fill. However, as with any new technology that is introduced into a trading

community, there is a certain degree of initial confusion and a corresponding transition period while waiting for the dust to settle. In the end, message brokers may combine with pure B2B technology (e.g., B2B integration servers) or application servers to provide an even more powerful B2B solution (see Chapter 19).

Most message-brokering products on the market address the same problems with very different solutions. Wouldn't it be great if all the vendors would just "get on the same sheet of music" and offer a standardized product? Then we would have a symphony instead of a virtual cacophony. At this time, we still need to plug our virtual ears. It is easier to promote the concept of the message broker than it is to promote a particular product.

Message brokers, at least the core engine, are destined to become commodity products because many perform only rudimentary functions. In an effort to differentiate their products, many message broker vendors are putting layer upon layer of value-added software on top of the core message broker engine. Thin adapters are giving way to thick adapters. Vendors are learning that it is better to hide the complexities of enterprise systems behind abstraction layers and put a business face on all the "geeky" little details. These abstraction layers save the end user from having to deal with the complexities of the technology and put them in a better position to take care of the business at hand.

Given this reality, when all is said and done, message brokers may turn out to be more about business integration than middleware.

B2B Application Integration Standards

XML and B2B Application Integration

Extensible Markup Language, or XML, is gaining attention from the business-to-business community as it seeks more efficient ways to exchange business information between trading partners. Those interested in application integration are also looking to leverage the power of XML, making this new standard a common point of integration for source and target applications.

The strengths of XML make it extremely valuable in all types of application integration projects. Still, its real value resides in the world of B2B application integration as the infrastructure for information exchange and management.

XML provides a robust, human-readable information-exchange standard that is not just a consensus choice but a unanimous one. It can support the exchange of application semantics and information content, providing an application-level mechanism for producing business information that other applications can use without needing to understand anything about the transmitting applications (see Figure 14.1).

XML gets most of its "traction" from this common mechanism for information exchange. More specifically, it gets its traction primarily around two application integration problem domains: EAI and B2B application integration. (Although B2B application integration is our topic, the two share many common characteristics.)

Fundamentally, EAI is about binding applications and data stores together to solve business problems. Its strength

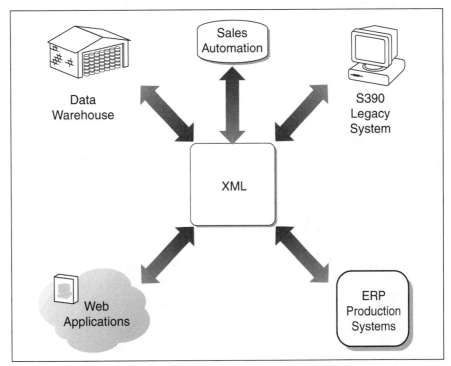

Figure 14.1   XML provides a common mechanism for data interchange that everyone can agree on.

A Strange Beginning

Ironically, XML was never intended for information exchange. It was derived from SGML for the publication of data within browsers. Shortly after XML's inception, organizations discovered that it also provided a tidy, self-describing message format, where both schema and data are bound together. It's curious that we're now leveraging XML for something it was not originally intended to do.

---

is facilitating the free flow of information from any system to any other system, with each of those systems gaining access to perfect external information in real time. EAI typically integrates ERP packages such as SAP, PeopleSoft, and Baan in addition to Customer Relationship Management (CRM) packages, databases,

> **XML Is Always Changing**
>
> XML is in a state of flux. To forget this basic dynamic is to do so at your peril. More detailed and current information (mostly about XML's application relative to the Web) can be found at www.w3c.org/xml. This site lists the current state of XML, along with the many proposals to evolve XML (most of these looking to expand its use into the enterprise). The site also lists the XML strategies (or lack thereof) employed by middleware vendors.

and older mainframe systems. EAI also allows organizations to externalize existing enterprise application information to interested parties through the Web, as evidenced in a portal-based solution.

Knowing, as we now do, that the essence of B2B application integration is the binding of applications and data stores together in order to share information with external organizations—typically trading partners—we can see that B2B application integration and EAI are intrinsically related. B2B application integration constructs the infrastructure that supports the free flow of information between companies. As such, it is functionally an extension of the EAI infrastructure that includes enterprise applications existing in other organizations. The design patterns of applications and data stores in the B2B application integration problem domain are similar to those in EAI problem domains. All that changes is the mechanisms employed to exchange the information, which in a B2B application integration environment are generally less intrusive and more data oriented than in the EAI environment.

In supporting these information interchange characteristics, XML has its greatest value to the B2B application integration solution.

The Value of XML

XML provides a common data-exchange format, encapsulating both data and metadata. This format allows various applications and databases to exchange information without having to understand anything about one other. In order to communicate, a source system simply reformats a message, a piece of information moving from an interface, or a data record as XML-compliant text and

moves that information to any other system that understands how to read XML (see Figure 14.2).

Although we can now appreciate XML's value to B2B application integration, it was originally created as a mechanism to publish data through the Web without the originator's having to understand anything about the system sending the data. As the application integration problem became more evident, B2B application integration architects and developers recognized the value of applying XML to the problem domain in order to move information between enterprises. The success of XML has led many people to refer to it as the next EDI.

Although XML's benefits sometimes appear revolutionary in scope, as a concept it falls short of being revolutionary. It also falls short of being the panacea for the application solution. We're not suggesting that it does not bring some real value to the B2B application integration solution set. That value simply requires stretching XML far from its original intent—which leads to a problem. Stretched too far, XML may be applied in areas where it stands little chance of success.

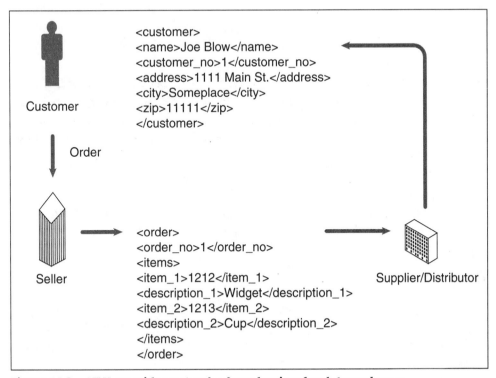

Figure 14.2   XML provides a standard mechanism for data exchange.

The *over-application* of XML in so many areas of technology diminishes its real value and results in a great deal of unnecessary confusion. Perhaps most damaging is the predictable behavior of many vendors that are looking to recast XML using their own set of proprietary extensions. Although some want to add value to XML, others are seeking only to lock in users.

What XML Is

XML's power resides in its simplicity. It can take large chunks of information and consolidate them into an XML document—meaningful pieces that provide structure and organization to the information (see Figure 14.3).

The basic building block of an XML document is the element defined by tags. An element has both a beginning and an ending tag. All elements in an XML document are contained in an outermost element known as the root element. XML can also support nested elements, or elements within elements. This ability allows XML to support hierarchical structures. Element names describe

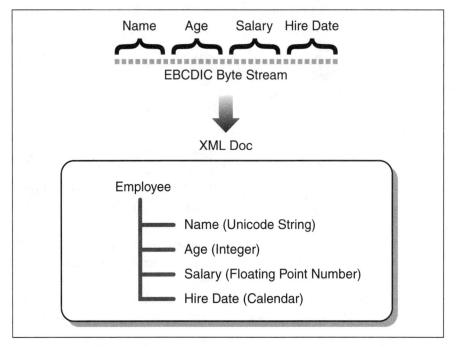

Figure 14.3   XML is a simple text representation of complex or simple data.

the content of the element, and the structure describes the relationship between the elements.

An XML document is considered to be "well formed" (that is, able to be read and understood by an XML parser) if its format complies with the XML specification, if it is properly marked up, and if elements are properly nested. XML also supports the ability to define attributes for elements and describe characteristics of the elements in the beginning tag of an element.

For example, XML documents can be very simple, such as the following:

```
<?xml version="1.0" standalone="yes"?>
<conversation>
<greeting>Hello, world!</greeting>
<response>Stop the planet, I want to get off!</response>
</conversation>
```

The **DTD** determines the structure and elements of an XML document. When a parser receives a document using a DTD, it verifies that the document is in the proper format.

Some XML documents may be DTD specified, contain an internal subset, and possess a more complex structure, such as the following:

```
<?xml version="1.0" standalone="no" encoding="UTF-8"?>
<!DOCTYPE titlepage SYSTEM "http://www.frisket.org/dtds/
        typo.dtd"
[<!ENTITY % active.links "INCLUDE">]>
<titlepage>
<white-space type="vertical" amount="36"/>
<title font="Baskerville" size="24/30"
        alignment="centered">Hello, world!</title>
<white-space type="vertical" amount="12"/>
<!- In some copies the following decoration is
        hand-colored, presumably by the author ->
<image location="http://www.foo.bar/fleuron.eps" type="URL"
        alignment="centered"/>
<white-space type="vertical" amount="24"/>
<author font="Baskerville" size="18/22" style="italic">
        Munde Salutem</author>
</titlepage>
```

[Source: W3C]

XML **parsers** read XML documents and extract the data for access by another program. Parsers are becoming part of the middleware layer (defined later), able to process XML documents into and out of the middleware infrastructure (see Figure 14.4).

XML **metadata** can be any attribute assignable to a piece of data, from something concrete to such abstract concepts as the industry associated with a particular document. XML can also be used to encode any number of existing metadata standards. The binding of data and metadata is a fundamental feature that maximizes XML's benefit to information-sharing scenarios. In fact, it is the feature most consistent with the concept of a common enterprise metadata repository supported throughout an organization or a common metadata layer shared within a trading community. Currently, XML is attempting to establish common metadata standards throughout the Internet in support of B2B and within the enterprise in support of EAI.

XML provides individual industries with the ability to define common metadata within their domain. For example, the pharmaceutical industry defines the structure of product data quite differently from the automobile industry. As a result, its metadata definitions must be different as well. XML provides mechanisms such as namespaces (see the description in the XML Namespaces box later in this chapter), XML-Schemas, and RDF (see the description in the RDF box) for defining localized metadata around particular industries or even between two or more trading partners. These metadata standards are just now emerging and have yet to find wide acceptance within trading communities.

Because XML is independent of any particular type of metadata format, there is little risk that a particular technology vendor will define its own set of metadata tags. In other words, XML cannot be made proprietary to any particular type of data. At least, that's the hope.

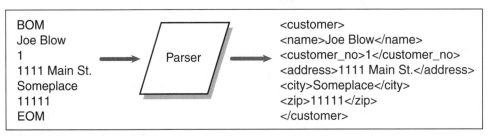

Figure 14.4   XML parsers extract information from XML.

RDF

RDF is an important part of the XML story. It provides interoperability between applications that exchange information. Like XML itself, RDF is a standard defined for the Web that is finding value in other, unanticipated places, including B2B application integration. RDF was developed by the W3C to provide a foundation for metadata interoperability across different resource description communities (trading communities).

RDF uses XML to define a foundation for processing metadata and for providing a standard metadata infrastructure for both the Web and the enterprise (see Figure 14.5). They differ in that XML transports data using a common format, while RDF layers on top of XML, defining a broad category of data. When the XML data is declared to be in RDF format, applications are able to understand the data without understanding who sent it.

RDF extends the XML model and syntax so that it is specific for describing either resources or a collection of information. (XML points to a resource in order to scope and uniquely identify a set of properties known as the schema.)

RDF metadata can be applied to many areas—including B2B application integration—searching for data and cataloging data and relationships. RDF is also able to support new technology, such as intelligent software agents and exchange of content rating.

RDF does not offer predefined vocabularies for authoring metadata. However, the W3C does expect standard vocabularies to emerge once the infrastructure for metadata interoperability is in place. Anyone or any industry can design and implement a new vocabulary. The only requirement is that all resources be included in the metadata instances using the new vocabulary.

RDF's benefit to B2B application integration should be clear. By supporting the concept of a common metadata layer that can be shared throughout an enterprise or between enterprises, it can be used as a common mechanism for describing data within the B2B application integration problem domain. However, before marching too enthusiastically in RDF's parade, we should remember that it is still in its infancy, and middleware vendors will have to adapt their products to it in order for it to be useful.

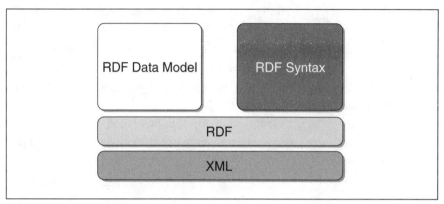

Figure 14.5   Using RDF to create a common metadata layer

What XML Adds

Ironically, XML's real power is not in the technology itself but the fact that everyone seems to agree that XML provides an acceptable common format for allowing applications, within or between enterprises, to exchange critical business information. XML is a momentum technology—almost all those concerned with storing or moving information, such as database and middleware vendors, have hyped their products as supporting XML. (Not surprisingly, they do so in very different ways.)

XML also adds a foundation that other standards can build upon. As we'll explore later in this chapter, XML-enabled standards now exist for transforming information between applications. These standards include Extensible Stylesheet Language Transformations (XSLT), BizTalk, XML for EDI (XEDI), and Commerce XML (cXML). They use XML as their base and expand in a specific direction to address a particular business issue. Some of these XML-enabled standards are so important that they warrant their own chapter in this book (see Chapters 15 through 17).

What XML Does Not Add

The hype around XML threatens to turn us all into wide-eyed kids at a carnival, ready to eat too much cotton candy and get drawn in to every attraction. We need to step back, take a deep breath, and consider not only what XML does but also what XML does not do. XML is no exception to the other momentum

technologies, which find end users of the technology tending to over-estimate their capabilities and thus incorrectly applying them within their problem domain.

One common and dangerous misconception about XML is that it is a substitute for B2B application integration technology such as middleware (including application servers and message brokers). Nothing could be further from the truth! In fact, the opposite is true.

As we already stated, XML is a simple, text-based document format that provides both metadata and information content. Nothing more. Nothing less. You or your vendor must provide the technology to move the XML documents from application to application. You or your vendor must make any necessary changes to your

---

XML Namespaces

A namespace is a collection of names that may be used in an XML document as elements or attribute names. These can associate names with a particular domain and thus avoid redundancy or allow the use of the same name with two different meanings. Namespaces in XML are identified by a Uniform Resource Indicator (URI), which allows each namespace to be unique. For instance, we may have three elements known as "account." The first refers to a frequent-flyer account, the second a bank account, and the third a customer account at a hotel. Using namespaces, we can identify these different classes with a different and appropriate URI. Each account name is associated with a particular domain—in our example, the airline URI, the bank URI, and the hotel URI, respectively. For example, we could place the following in the document to associate the element with a particular namespace:

```
http://www.airline.org.account
http://www.bank.org.account
http://www.hotel.org.account
```

The importance of XML namespaces in the context of B2B application integration is their ability to define common application semantics between trading partners within a vertical industry. In other words, we can come up with a common notion of a customer, a product attribute, and other property that's common within a particular vertical industry or trading community.

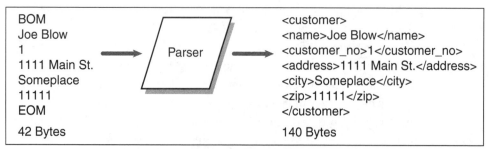

```
BOM                                          <customer>
Joe Blow                                     <name>Joe Blow</name>
1                    ┌────────┐              <customer_no>1</customer_no>
1111 Main St.   ──► │ Parser │ ──►           <address>1111 Main St.</address>
Someplace            └────────┘              <city>Someplace</city>
11111                                        <zip>11111</zip>
EOM                                          </customer>

42 Bytes                                     140 Bytes
```

Figure 14.6   **Text-based XML is huge and thus difficult to use as a format that's easily transportable from system to system.**

source and target applications so they can consume and produce XML. In other words, a lot has to occur before you can apply XML to B2B application integration.

In order for applications using XML to be integrated, the applications must externalize the information as XML. Currently, few applications are capable of doing so. In order to be most successful, either the existing applications must change so they produce and consume XML, or better yet, they must leverage XML-enabled middleware technology.

XML-enabled middleware technology manages the extraction of information from the source system (or systems) as well as the conversion of the information into XML (if required) and the placement of the information in the target system (or systems). All this occurs automatically and is transparent to the end user.

XML does not make a good message format for information exchange, either with EAI or B2B application integration. As we noted, XML is text based, and thus information that would normally exist in a binary message as "512 KB" could easily map to an XML document 20 times that size (see Figure 14.6).

Although XML provides a good point of integration when communicating with source or target applications within or between enterprises, moving information using native XML demands a huge overhead. As a result, most middleware and B2B vendors still use a binary message format, either proprietary or open, to move XML data and metadata from one system to another.

XML Meets Middleware

Now that we have established that XML is a simple, text-based standard and, as such, cannot provide everything needed to integrate disparate applications, it quickly becomes clear that in order to provide maximum value to the B2B

application integration solution set, XML needs middleware (and, conversely, middleware most likely needs XML).

XML's value to middleware is clear. Middleware simply "carries the load." It moves messages that encapsulate or abstract XML and ensures that those messages are understood by any source or target applications that need that information (see Figure 14.7). Middleware may also manage the interfaces with the source or target applications and move information into and out of the applications through an unobtrusive point of integration such as a database or an API.

Because of XML's value, every middleware vendor, new and old, has declared dominance in the XML space, applying its technology to B2B application integration problem domains. None of us should be surprised that there is a certain degree of "puffery" to these declarations. The truth is that it is not particularly difficult to XML-enable a product. Therefore, vendors were able to react quickly, for a change.

XML-enabling a product is simply a matter of embedding a parser within the middleware and teaching the product to read and write XML from and to the canonical message format. In addition, since many of these products already have native connectors to traditional enterprise systems and data stores, such as SAP, PeopleSoft, and DB2, they provide enterprises with the ability to produce and consume XML without impacting the applications.

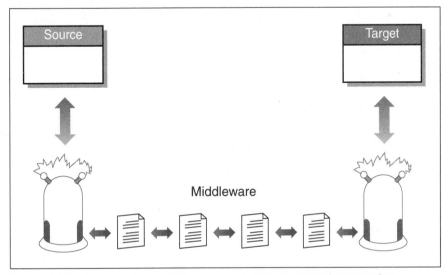

Figure 14.7   Leveraging middleware and XML to move information

Integration Solutions

Now that we understand what XML is, what its value is, and how middleware and XML coexist, we can turn our attention to XML-enabled solutions that include the available technology and approaches. In doing so, let's return once again to our macro problem domains: EAI and B2B application integration.

Within the domain of EAI, XML plays a lesser role, but its role is becoming more important. This somewhat convoluted observation is based on the fact that most systems within an enterprise come under central control. As a result, the integration solutions run deeper and may not benefit from converting information to XML for movement to other applications. Typically, standard information-exchange mechanisms, such as XML, take a backseat to native points of integration and binary messages as a simple matter of efficiency when we consider EAI. However, as information becomes less centrally controlled, XML will become more important.

Let us look, for example, at a situation in which an enterprise needs to exchange information between its PeopleSoft packaged application, its older COBOL/ISAM application running on the mainframe, and its new data warehouse. Although there are many ways to approach this problem, most enterprises would utilize some type of message broker to exchange information between the systems in real time, using whatever native interface the source or target applications provided. Although there is always the opportunity to convert the data moving between the applications into XML, binary messages typically provide better efficiency, as we noted earlier in this chapter.

Although native interfaces currently dominate application integration solutions, we are rapidly moving to a world where most applications and databases will be XML-aware. Therefore, XML will become a common point of integration rather than the hodgepodge of proprietary and complex native interfaces in use today. Taking this reality into account, we recognize that XML is becoming a more prominent player in application integration. Many packaged applications, including PeopleSoft and SAP, are going to leverage XML as the preferred native interface to their systems. Indeed, PeopleSoft has already defined its Open Integration Framework (OIF) and has outlined how information will move into and out of the PeopleSoft application using XML. SAP is not far behind.

Even as developers build interfaces to new and existing custom applications, XML is becoming the mechanism of choice for producing and consuming information within those systems. Moreover, most database vendors, including Oracle,

Sybase, and Informix, are providing mechanisms within their database engines to allow them to read and write XML directly from the database.

XML provides the most value within the domain of B2B application integration. Here we typically integrate applications that are not under centralized control and thus difficult to change. As we have explained, XML provides a reasonably good format for information exchange. Perhaps most important, the

---

Persistent XML

Although products that provide persistent XML storage exist, XML itself does not provide a good database format for medium to large data sets. To work, XML requires that portions of the XML document exist in memory. Otherwise, the document will be parsed and reparsed, resulting in significant performance problems. Although this approach may sound reasonable, it demands a large amount of memory over time, with typical organic database growth. Moreover, pre- and post-processing is required to take care of special characters (e.g., the ampersand) encapsulated within the XML document.

Database vendors are moving quickly to address this weakness. Virtually every major relational database vendor, such as IBM and Oracle, is pledging support for XML. Object-oriented database vendors, which have yet to see a significant market for their products, are looking to XML storage as their salvation. XML is so easy to incorporate into products, because of the simplicity of the technology, that most vendors can join the XML playing field with minimal effort. Which is a good thing—there probably won't be a lot of product dollars to be made here by technology vendors, but with XML on the checklists at most major corporations, they cannot afford to ignore it.

Data types represent another limitation of XML. An ASCII text–based format, XML does not provide facilities for complex data types or binary data (e.g., multimedia data). To address this weakness, many vendors are proposing new standards to the W3C to bind XML to binary information—while coming out with their own XML hybrids before the W3C is able to react. Unfortunately, the result is a smorgasbord of products without any notion of standardization.

majority of businesses can agree upon XML as the way information moves into and out of enterprises. XML standards provide additional value by including common metadata layers that may exist between one or more trading partners and even standard transformation mechanisms such as XSLT (see the discussion in the section XML-Enabled Standards and in Chapter 17).

A number of new companies, including OnDisplay, NetFish, and WebMethods, are focusing on the exchange of data between enterprises. These vendors generally don't focus on integrating applications within an enterprise but provide technology to exchange information between enterprises. These B2B solutions can consume and produce XML as well as other data interchange standards such as cXML, BizTalk, EDI, and Open Buying on the Internet (OBI).

As we look ahead, the ultimate application integration solution will be some hybrid of EAI and B2B application integration, providing integration within and between enterprises by using a similar, compatible infrastructure. Getting to this "glorious future" will be accomplished in stages. Enterprises will first learn to integrate their own applications, including understanding everything about the source and target systems that they own, and then will learn to integrate their applications with their trading partners' applications. XML belongs in this mix, but the majority of work in getting to the solution is associated with exploring both problem domains, understanding the requirements, and mapping the correct technology to the solution. In reality, most organizations have just begun the journey down this rather long and expensive road.

XML-Enabled Standards

The XML bandwagon is filling up, joined by many standards organizations. These entities are looking to standardize the way e-Business is conducted, using the common infrastructure they define and vendors provide.

The sad reality is that this bandwagon is overfull—there are more XML standards organizations than vendors and end users require. Fallout is bound to occur as one or two standards get traction and others do not. The few that appear to be most relevant in the world of XML and application integration include RosettaNet, XEDI, BizTalk, Extensible Financial Reporting Mark-Up Language (XFRML), XML-Schema, XML Query, and XSLT.

RosettaNet is a consortium of product vendors and end users that defines a framework for data and process interchange with e-Business. Primarily organized for the high-tech industry, RosettaNet outlines standard messaged data using XML

as well as standardized process flows, to react to standard business events. We feel RosettaNet is so important that we've dedicated a chapter to it (see Chapter 15).

XEDI is a published specification describing how to map traditional EDI to XML and back again.

BizTalk is an industry consortium founded by Microsoft to define a standard XML grammar for XML-based messaging and metadata. Microsoft is providing a BizTalk server to support this standard. This is another B2B application integration standard that warrants its own chapter in this book (see Chapter 16).

XFRML is a standards push led by the American Institute of Certified Public Accountants (AICPA) to define an XML standard for reporting financial information over the Internet to other interested parties.

XML-Schema is a working group of the W3C that's looking to describe a better mechanism for determining the structure of an XML document.

XML Query is another W3C working group looking to create a common set of operations and language syntax for accessing persisted (stored) XML data.

XSLT seeks to provide a standard XML document-transformation mechanism using a stylesheet as a common processing engine. XSLT is important to application integration because schema and information content often must be altered as information flows between applications. We will cover XSLT in Chapter 17.

XML and B2B Application Integration

XML and B2B application integration are joined at the hip. Application integration represents the larger problem of moving information between applications and data stores for any business purpose. XML provides a common mechanism for data exchange and integration with a variety of applications supporting a variety of design patterns.

Even with all the promise and "presence" of XML, we've also learned that it is not a panacea. Users must understand the limits, as well as the potential, of the technology before leveraging it for their B2B application integration solution. The real power of XML is the notion of the standard information interchange it brings between one or many applications existing within a single organization or within a trading community. It's just going to take some time before we're able to reinvent our existing middleware technology and applications around XML. But that day is coming—and it's going to be here sooner than we think.

In the next three chapters, we'll take a closer look at important B2B application integration standards based on XML and how they fit into your B2B application integration solution.

Using RosettaNet for B2B Application Integration

RosettaNet in its basic form is just another trading community standard. However, its innovative approach to managing trading communities at both the information and process levels makes it particularly important to B2B application integration.

The RosettaNet consortium was created to define standard processes and interfaces to manage supply chains within the high-technology industry. Building on the successes of RosettaNet, a movement now is underway to leverage the same standards or similar ones in other industries. The innovation within the RosettaNet community has been in defining how other trading community standards, typically structured around vertical industries, will operate.

For all its strengths and innovations, RosettaNet is still in its early stages of development. A proof-of-concept prototype, running in early 2000, is demonstrating that the concept will work. Indications are that there is enough interest from the partners to make production systems inevitable. At this point, things bode well for RosettaNet. But it is wise to be cautious. RosettaNet is a new, living standard. Only time will determine whether it has value in binding trading communities together.

RosettaNet History

RosettaNet was officially formed in 1998 to standardize e-Business activities in the high-technology industry (e.g.,

computer manufacturing and reselling). It defined open interfaces between manufacturers, distributors, resellers, and other participants in the supply chain. At
the time of this writing, close to 300 vendor members are participating in the
development of the RosettaNet standard. (More information about RosettaNet is
available at www.rosettanet.org.)

The high-technology industry provided a good test bed for the RosettaNet
concept. The industry uses many of the same component suppliers (semicon-
ductors, ICs, peripherals, etc.) and thus could quickly agree about information
formats. Catalyzing RosettaNet's development was the perception that EDI had
largely failed because of its expense, its proprietary nature, and its inability to
adapt to changes in B2B processes. In addition, EDI was weak at real-time information exchange and was unable to keep up with high-volume information
flows (although XML has not yet proved its viability here either).

What's RosettaNet?

Despite the common belief that RosettaNet is all about XML, it is not. RosettaNet
is a set of standard mechanisms, processes really, that allow companies to agree
on the processing of standard business transactions. XML was added to take the
place of EDI as a mere data interchange standard.

Since RosettaNet is about processes rather than data, the most important
aspect of RosettaNet is the development of common Partner Interface Processes
(PIPs) and common dictionaries. RosettaNet provides a master dictionary to
define properties for products, partners, and business transactions. This master
dictionary, coupled with an established implementation framework, can be used
to support the B2B application integration dialog. PIPs provide alignment within
the overall supply chain process, allowing businesses to interact at a number of
levels to support the processes of common trading communities.

For example, PIP2A2, Query Product Information, defines a common process
between companies. Since each company adheres to this common process, or PIP,
there is no confusion about what this particular process does. Common semantics
and common mechanisms automatically carry out the process.

The real value of RosettaNet is the common agreement on "which processes
do what and where." Although we long ago established processes for executing
common business activities, there has been little agreement about common
processes that exist between companies or a common set of application semantics (dictionaries). It should be apparent that, as we have suggested, RosettaNet is

less about technology and all about creating PIPs, which are really contracts or agreements.

Fundamentally, creating PIPs is a matter of understanding a process in detail, finding a way to make it more efficient, and defining it by using the standard PIP framework that RosettaNet offers. The process to create PIPs is depicted in Figure 15.1.

The stages to the process include

- Business process modeling
- Business process analysis
- PIP development
- Dictionaries

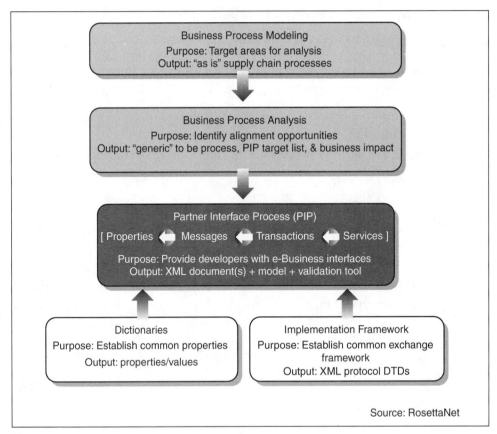

Figure 15.1   RosettaNet development process

Business Process Modeling

Those who want to leverage RosettaNet use business process modeling to identify and quantify the properties and behaviors of a particular business process. This is a laborious process of documenting what happens while selling a product, checking inventory, or shipping a product to a customer. Each stage is a process and each may have hundreds of steps. Each step must be inventoried, defined in detail, and completely understood, with the goal of automating the process based on an agreement between companies. The output of this effort is a model that reflects every detail of a particular process using a common framework.

Business Process Analysis

Once the business process model is understood, we must realign the process in the form of a PIP target list. This step determines how much value this process will have when automated by RosettaNet.

PIP Development

Each PIP provides a common business/data model and documents that enable system developers to leverage RosettaNet interfaces. Each PIP includes

- XML documents using a particular DTD, specifying PIP services, transactions, and messages, including dictionary properties
- Class and sequence diagrams in the Unified Modeling Language (UML)
- A validation tool
- An implementation guide

Dictionaries

During the development of RosettaNet, two data dictionaries were created to provide a common set of properties that exist within PIPs—a technical properties dictionary and a business properties dictionary. The **technical properties dictionary** provides the technical specifications for all product categories. The **business properties dictionary** describes attributes used to define supply chain partner companies and business transaction properties. These dictionaries, when bound to the RosettaNet Implementation Framework (exchange protocol), become the basis for each PIP.

It's the PIP

The real value of PIPs is the ability to allow manufacturers to *seamlessly* add new products to their partners' catalogs—for instance, adding a new part number using a common format and information interchange standard.

A PIP specification (see Appendix C for an example) comprises three views of the e-Business PIP model.

The **Business Operational View (BOV)** provides the semantics of the business data entities and their exchange flow between roles during normal operations. The content of the BOV section uses the PIP Blueprint document created for the RosettaNet business community.

The **Functional Service View (FSV)** defines the network component services, agents, and functions required to execute PIPs. These include all transaction dialogs in a PIP protocol. The FSVs are semantically derived from the BOV and include two major components: the network component design and the network component interactions.

Implementation Framework View (IFV) defines the network protocol message formats and communications requirements between protocols supported by network components. These messages are exchanged when software programs execute a PIP.

There are several categories, or clusters, of PIPs, such as the following (see the box RosettaNet PIP Clusters and Segments for a complete listing):

- Cluster 1: Partner, Product and Service Review
- Cluster 2: Product Introduction
- Cluster 3: Order Management
- Cluster 4: Inventory Management

As you might expect, there are several subcategories within each cluster (see the box RosettaNet PIP Clusters and Segments and the box Published RosettaNet PIPs within Clusters and Segments). Note that Clusters 1 through 3 are extensions, or a rehashing, of processes already specified in EDI during the past quarter century. Also, Cluster 4 PIPs are much like the VICS Collaborative Planning Forecasting and Replenishment standards administered by the Uniform Code Council.

RosettaNet PIP Clusters and Segments

Cluster 1: Partner, Product and Service Review
    Segment A: Partner Review
    Segment B: Product and Service Review
Cluster 2: Product Introduction
    Segment A: Preparation for Distribution
    Segment B: Product Change Notification
Cluster 3: Order Management
    Segment A: Quote and Order Entry
    Segment B: Transportation and Distribution
    Segment C: Returns and Finance
    Segment D: Product Configuration
Cluster 4: Inventory Management
    Segment A: Collaborative Forecasting
    Segment B: Inventory Allocation
    Segment C: Inventory Reporting
    Segment D: Inventory Replenishment
    Segment E: Sales Reporting
    Segment F: Price Protection
    Segment G: Ship from Stock and Debit/Credit (Electronic Components)
Cluster 5: Marketing Information Management
    Segment A: Lead/Opportunity Management
    Segment B: Marketing Campaign Management
    Segment C: Design Win Management (Electronic Components)
Cluster 6: Service and Support
    Segment A: Warranty Management
    Segment B: Asset Management
    Segment C: Technical Support and Service

Published RosettaNet PIPs within Clusters and Segments

Cluster 0: RosettaNet Support

Segment A: Administration
    PIP0A1, Notification of Failure

Cluster 1: Partner, Product and Service Review

Segment B: Product Review

    PIP1B1, Manage Product Information Subscription

Cluster 2: Product Introduction

Segment A: Preparation for Distribution

    PIP2A1, Distribute New Product Information

    PIP2A2, Query Product Information

    PIP2A5, Query Technical Information

    PIP2A8, Distribute Product Stock Keeping Unit

Cluster 3: Order Management

Segment A: Quote and Order Entry

    PIP3A3, Transfer Shopping Cart

    PIP3A4, Manage Purchase Order

    PIP3A5, Query Order Status

    PIP3A6, Distribute Order Status

The Technology

RosettaNet's technology is nothing new or revolutionary. Its implementation is based on CommerceNet's OBI specification, XML, X12 EDI, and PKCS#7 digital signatures.

The OBI specification was established to allow companies to use the Internet to purchase products that might not be part of their core business, such as coffee for the office coffee machine. OBI uses HTTP for communicating between companies, Secure Socket Layer (SSL) for security services, PKCS#7 for digital signatures, and X12 for purchase orders.

The RosettaNet communications model specifically defines the behavior that should occur within the OSI application and session layers, dividing the application layer into the action, transaction, process, service, agent, message handling, transfer, and security layers (see Figure 15.2).

The **action layer** provides business actions that act on or with accompanying information. The **transaction layer** provides transaction monitoring for sequences of message exchanges that support a unit of work. Either every party commits to the transaction or the transaction is rolled back completely. The **process layer**

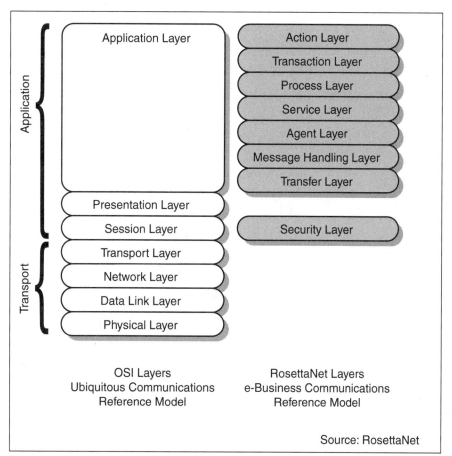

Figure 15.2   ISO/OSI and RosettaNet Communications Reference Model

encapsulates the conditional choreography of a transaction for executing a PIP. The **service layer** provides network resources that perform network and business-related functions. The **agent layer** provides a communications interface for other applications. The **message handling layer** provides asynchronous delivery of information. The **transfer layer** provides a mechanism for information transfer between uniquely named network resources. The **security layer** allows for a secure communications connection, which leverages digital signatures to implement authorization and authentication.

RosettaNet uses OBI as a subset of its enabling technology, adding more functionality within the data formatting area. It leverages XML rather than EDI (OBI

was created to use EDI) to move information from point to point. (Although many EDI-like semantics are maintained, XML was selected for its compact and simple nature and its acceptance in the market.)

PIP Communications

As we noted earlier in this chapter, the fundamental requirement of a PIP is to exchange business data between trading partners. RosettaNet-compliant networked applications receive data using a standard format that all systems and humans in the loop can understand.

Those who created RosettaNet PIPs created RosettaNet messages by using the set of elements and codes defined in the RosettaNet business and technical dictionaries. The set exists as a baseline from which PIP teams create message-exchange specifications and precisely define the values and codes that are assignable to each of the data elements—all of which are part of the PIP implementation guidelines.

These guidelines are sent from RosettaNet to trading partners and RosettaNet solution partners as a document. The guidelines define the vocabulary, structure, and allowable data element values and value types for each message exchange.

Moreover, PIP specifications enable the development of interoperable applications. Each message has three parts: the Preamble Header, the Service Header, and the Service Content. This information is typically packaged for exchanges as MIME messages.

PIP Message Structure

RosettaNet business messages consist of a message header and a message body, and both the header and body are a well-formed XML document. The header and body are encoded inside a multipart/related MIME message. The **message preamble** section of the MIME message contains elements that are global to the RosettaNet service and those that are common to the Service Header and Service Content. This information is specified as a DTD that is common across all messages. The **message header** is also specified using a DTD that is also common across all messages. There is a separate DTD or XML schema for each message, and that DTD or XML schema is used to validate the body of the messages. The idea behind a common message header DTD that is separate from the message content DTD is to support the logical segmentation of validation steps, which include validation of grammar, sequence, schema, and content. Grammar and sequence validations are performed against the message header DTD, and validation of message content is deferred

until the schema validation step. When this mechanism is used, the message header may be valid even when the content is not. RosettaNet has this structure in place so trading partners can send failure messages. The **message content** is specified in individual PIPs, and each PIP has one or more "actions" that are defined by the schemas or DTD contained in the message.

RosettaNet Networked Application Protocols

RosettaNet leverages most native Internet protocols, including HTTP and TCP/IP. The TCP/IP protocol provides the functionality defined for the transport layers. Sockets and SSL are OSI session layer protocols.

RosettaNet and B2B Application Integration

It is a safe bet that RosettaNet will shape the way we view inter-company process integration as it supports the goal of supply chain integration. To date, it is the most sophisticated standard available. This sophistication is due to the fact that it takes both process and data into account, defining common processes and points of integration within a vertical industry. Other trading community standards have yet to deliver both layers—and won't, unless they can get everyone on the same page for both application semantics and technology.

Sometimes we forget that even in the world of high technology we still have to deal with the psychology of people. The real strength of RosettaNet is not the technology but the fact that this organization was able get many in a larger vertical industry (high technology) to define and agree on a standard. What's more, it has succeeded at clearly defining the value of using such a standard as well as how new technology, including XML, fits into the framework. To its credit, it built upon past success, reusing what worked with EDI.

The future is clear in RosettaNet. As organizations seek to open automated trade, they have to agree on processes and semantics, an agreement that has thus far been frustratingly elusive.

BizTalk and B2B Application Integration

When it introduced the BizTalk Initiative in 1999, Microsoft made the leap into the world of B2B application integration. It built BizTalk in response to some of the more exciting topics of the day, including XML and e-Business. BizTalk now stands as Microsoft's platform for inter-company communications (and EAI).

What's important about BizTalk is *not* the standard itself—the BizTalk Framework—and *not* the enabling technology—the BizTalk Server (both covered in this chapter). Instead, the importance of BizTalk rests with the reality of its mere existence, with the fact that a major software vendor has thrown its hat into the B2B application integration ring. And not just any software vendor. Instead of there being a handful of vendors driving the standard together and equally, Microsoft stands alone as the driving force behind BizTalk. This makes BizTalk both unique and powerful.

Compared to similar standards, such as RosettaNet and ebXML, BizTalk is much more information oriented and not at all process aware. At its core, BizTalk seeks to solve several B2B application integration problems, including the following:

- Accounting for differences in application semantics between applications and companies
- Creating a common message format based on XML that many organizations can agree on
- Creating a common technology infrastructure that will become the standard for B2B application integration

The controversy that swirls around BizTalk is due in large part to its creator, Microsoft. Many argue that because Microsoft extends XML for its own purposes, BizTalk is more proprietary than a B2B application integration standard should be. But let's be fair. Even dominating software giants deserve a fair hearing. After reviewing the standard, we can see that Microsoft has done a good job in building something that is both understandable and obtainable for most companies seeking entree into B2B application integration.

With BizTalk, as with its other products, Microsoft has been able to render complex concepts and technologies easy to use and understand. BizTalk's accessibility (and the weight of Microsoft behind it) makes it a force in the industry and, not surprisingly, creates the justification for its own chapter.

BizTalk Framework

BizTalk has two parts: the BizTalk Framework and the BizTalk Server. The **BizTalk Framework** is a document that specifies a set of rules that allow many organizations to accept a common approach to XML. Within the framework is a specification for a core set of XML framework tags (BizTalk tags are known as BizTags), including a root tag and document body tag (both mandatory). Specifications also exist for optional routing and messaging mechanisms.

The BizTalk Framework does not provide any requirements for the structure or content of a BizTalk document, which is part of a BizTalk message. However, in order for BizTalk to know where a document is going, standard routing and identity tags must be provided.

BizTalk Documents

BizTalk moves everything—from application to application and company to company—as documents. In this context, a document is simply a grouping of data encapsulated in XML and the BizTalk Framework. Thus, a BizTalk document is nothing more than a collection of XML data. BizTalk Framework Documents are BizTalk-compliant, well formed, and valid.

The BizTalk Framework also contains a set of XML root and body tags for creating document structure. The structure tags are validated against the BizTalk Framework namespace and thus identify the document.

Document identification occurs before processing and must identify the document and define its behavior. In addition to authenticating the document,

BizTalk needs to determine the document's origin, purpose, and destination. Using this information, BizTalk is able to group documents based on their source.

BizTalk Message Structure

As noted previously, BizTalk messages are structured along with some additional information, such as routing information, which the BizTalk Server uses. A BizTalk message has several sections, including the following:

- Complete BizTalk Message
     Transport Specific Envelope
     BizTalk Document
     BizTalk Header
- Delivery Information
- Document Manifest
     Document Body
          Business Documents (Business Data)

See Listing 16.1 for an example of a BizTalk message.

Listing 16.1   An example of a BizTalk message, intermixing the schema and the data

```
<?xml version='1.0' ?>
<biztalk_1 xmlns="urn:biztalk-org:biztalk:biztalk_1">
    <header>
        <delivery>
            <message>
                <messageID>xyzzy:8</messageID>
                <sent>1999-01-02T19:00:01+02:00</sent>
                <subject>Purchase Order</subject>
            </message>
            <to>

<address>http://www.fabrikam.com/recv.asp</address>
                <state>
                    <referenceID/>
                    <handle/>
                    <process/>
                </state>
            </to>
```

```
        <from>
            <address>mailto:foo@contoso.com</address>
            <state>
                <referenceID>123</referenceID>
                <handle>7</handle>
                <process>myprocess</process>
            </state>
        </from>
    </delivery>
    <manifest>
        <document>
            <name>PO</name>
            <description>Purchase Order</description>
        </document>
    </manifest>
</header>
<body>
    <PO xmlns="x-
schema:http://schemas.biztalk.org/BizTalk/zi0124pf.xml">
            <POHeader>
                <poNumber>12345</poNumber>
                <custID>100200300</custID>
                <description>Order for 200 desktop
                PCs</description>
                <paymentType>Invoice</paymentType>
                <shipType>Express2d</shipType>
                <Contact>
                    <contactName>John Doe</contactName>

<contactEmail>jdoe@fabrikam.com</contactEmail>
                    <contactPhone>4250001212</contactPhone>
                </Contact>
                <POShipTo>
                    <attn>Fabrikam Receiving</attn>
                    <street>10 Main Street</street>
                    <city>Anytown</city>
                    <stateProvince>WA</stateProvince>
                    <postalCode>98000</postalCode>
```

```
                        <country>USA</country>
                </POShipTo>
                <POBillTo>
                        <attn>Fabrikam Payables</attn>
                        <street>101 Headquarters Road</street>
                        <city>Anytown</city>
                        <stateProvince>WA</stateProvince>
                        <postalCode>98000</postalCode>
                        <country>USA</country>
                </POBillTo>
        </POHeader>
        <POLines>
                <count>2</count>
                <totalAmount>192000.00</totalAmount>
                <Item>
                        <line>1</line>
                        <partno>pc1010</partno>
                        <qty>200</qty>
                        <uom>EACH</uom>
                        <unitPrice>800.00</unitPrice>
                        <discount>10</discount>
                        <totalAmount>144000.00</totalAmount>
                </Item>
                <Item>
                        <line>1</line>
                        <partno>monitor17</partno>
                        <qty>200</qty>
                        <uom>EACH</uom>
                        <unitPrice>300.00</unitPrice>
                        <discount>20</discount>
                        <totalAmount>48000.00</totalAmount>
                </Item>
        </POLines>
    </PO>
</body>
</biztalk_1>
```

[Source: Microsoft]

Document Routing

The BizTalk Framework contains a set of routing tags that support messaging. These tags provide the information required for rules-based messages using messaging systems—in particular, BizTalk Server. The tags are located in the routing block of a BizTalk Framework Document and work like an e-mail message in that the routing block contains information such as destination and origin.

BizTalk's goal is to define the delivery location independent of transport, destination, and routing mechanism. This goal enables BizTalk to abstract a message from the processes located at the source and target systems. However, in order for this message abstraction to be successful, the source or target application must "speak" BizTalk. Otherwise, it will be unable to consume and produce the BizTalk Framework Document. The document needs to be understood by the source and target applications as well as by the BizTalk Server. This is the same requirement we run into when we use other types of middleware. The source or target applications must adapt to the middleware. In this scenario, that means BizTalk.

There is no doubt that as time goes on, BizTalk will define adapters for certain types of source and target systems. As a result, end users will be liberated from having to change applications. This is no different from the need to define adapters for any other message brokers (see Chapter 13). Currently, however, BizTalk has resisted defining such adapters, and end users must make all appropriate adaptations.

BizTalk Architecture

When we take a step back, it becomes plain that the logical application model for the BizTalk Framework exists as the following three layers (see Figure 16.1):

- The application (sometimes adapters)
- The BizTalk Server
- Data communications

In the context of BizTalk, source and target applications share information by producing and consuming BizTalk documents. In doing so, they use a BizTalk Server as the message-exchange and transformation mechanism. Functioning like a scaled-down message broker, the BizTalk Server uses BizTalk-enabled XML as its common information-exchange format.

Data communications occur using many different types of transport mechanisms, including HTTP or MSMQ. These communication systems are logically "plugable," with BizTalk having no preference for one over another. BizTalk only requires that the application format the BizTalk document and submit it to the

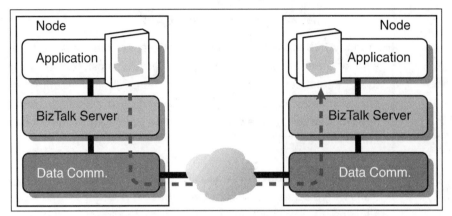

Figure 16.1   The BizTalk architecture provides three logical layers: the application, the BizTalk Server, and data communications.

BizTalk Server. Once the BizTalk Server consumes the message, the BizTags provide the routing information for the server. This information is then transmitted to the appropriate application (typically to a trading partner's application via the Internet) that is also responsible for consuming the message.

Schema Management

Like message brokers, BizTalk must manage differences in application semantics or schemas found in all source or target systems. Since XML brings schemas "along for the ride" with the data, this is just a matter of mapping one schema to another for information interchange. Although traditional message brokers use transformation to accomplish this task, BizTalk uses **schema mapping**, an old trick found within most EDI servers and even some message brokers. Like transformation, schema mapping defines how data coming into the BizTalk infrastructure in one format can make sense to another schema (see Figure 16.2).

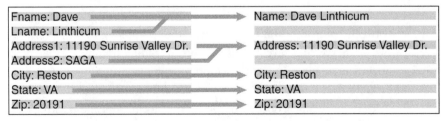

Figure 16.2   BizTalk provides a mechanism for schema mapping.

> ### Use SOAP
>
> In many B2B scenarios, trading partner applications must communicate with one another over the Internet. Because most companies protect their internal systems from outside systems, disallowing most types of data communications, a standard mechanism is needed to access systems hidden behind firewalls, using an allowable communications mechanism such as HTTP.
>
> Simple Object Access Protocol, or SOAP, is an XML-based protocol for invoking RPCs through firewalls. SOAP uses a method-invocation mechanism where return values are carried as HTTP requests and responses, allowing the protocol to operate through firewalls. Information about the methods being carried out is placed into the HTTP header and body and carried over the network. SOAP leverages an XML-based document for encoding the operational details.
>
> Since Microsoft is hyping both SOAP and BizTalk, how do they relate? Basically, they complement one another. SOAP is a tightly coupled RPC over HTTP. BizTalk is structured around loosely coupled messaging using any acceptable protocol. BizTalk provides translation mechanisms, while SOAP does not. SOAP is about simple communications. BizTalk is about complex document management and transport operations.

Framework Portal

The BizTalk **Framework portal** (www.biztalk.org) provides a collection of schemas from different organizations. It offers a place to locate BizTalk schemas submitted for both public and private review.

BizTalk Server

BizTalk, the standard, is based on the management and movement of documents between companies. BizTalk Server is the technology that makes it all happen. BizTalk Server has several components, including trading partner management, document mapping and translation, document routing and delivery, and data extraction and storage facilities. In addition, it provides a rules-enabled document-delivery mechanism, document format transformation, and tracking facility.

BizTalk Server provides a secure environment for sending messages and returning receipts using any number of communications mechanisms. It is possible to configure the number of attempts when sending a document as well as the maximum amount of time between retries. BizTalk is also able to switch to a secondary communications mechanism when the primary communications mechanism fails.

BizTalk Server, like message brokers, leverages queues. All documents are placed into a queue when they enter the BizTalk Server. Queues can be shared among many BizTalk Servers, with the first available BizTalk Server picking up the document from the queue for processing (see Figure 16.3). As long as the

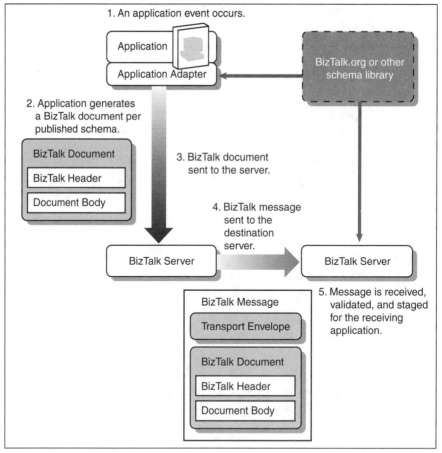

Figure 16.3   BizTalk Server leverages queues, and multiple BizTalk Servers can process documents from the same queue.

queue can handle the load, the BizTalk Server can scale to larger message rates. Documents that are not processed for some reason—because of errors in the document, for example—are sent to a "suspended queue" for manual processing.

BizTalk not only supports BizTalk documents, it can communicate with other types of formats as well, such as the following:

- EDI (ANSI X12 and EDIFACT)
- XML
- XML DTDs
- Structured document formats
- Flat files

BizTalk leverages XSLT (see Chapter 17) for transformation and formatting.

Routing Documents

Header information found on top of each BizTalk document determines how a particular document is routed. (Once again, documents that don't have proper routing information or are bounced back for any reason are placed in the suspended queue for manual processing.)

Documents are routed between two or more trading partners based on an agreement that defines their document exchange policies. This agreement represents the rules that govern the exchange of documents. Typically these rules exist as general expressions.

Delivering Documents

When we talk of managing a BizTalk Server, we're basically talking about managing a bunch of BizTalk documents that exist in a bunch of BizTalk queues. The BizTalk Server Shared Queue databases are graphically represented in the BizTalk Server administration console as a series of queues that show the progress of a document inside the BizTalk Server. This graphical representation allows you to monitor the status of each document, including its status in processing. Documents exist in one of the following queues:

- Schedule
- Work
- Retry
- Suspended

BizTalk Server provides fault-tolerant services through several facilities. First, BizTalk Server checkpoints, or logs to, the Shared Queue database all documents that progress through the state engine. This transactional control allows BizTalk Server to restart services in the event of disruption, returning to the last checkpoint.

In addition, you can remove BizTalk Server from production and move all documents currently being processed in the server to another available server. This is known as "freeing documents." BizTalk Server leverages existing Microsoft technology, including MSMQ and Microsoft SQL Server, allowing you to leverage their replication features to provide further redundancy.

BizTalk Server supports most poplar transport components, including the following:

- HTTP
- HTTP/S
- Simple Mail Transfer Protocol (SMTP)
- MSMQ
- DCOM
- FTP
- Fax

Security

BizTalk Server uses Microsoft Windows 2000 security features, including public-key infrastructure and Microsoft Component Services. Public-key certificate management includes requesting certificates, processing certificates in a certificate-request response, and exchanging certificates with trading partners.

Application Integration Components

In addition to using the BizTalk Server capabilities of transformation, digital signature and verification, encryption and decryption, parsing, and transport of documents, users can create their own application integration components (AICs) to extend BizTalk Server facilities. The two separate approaches for creating AICs are

- Pipeline application integration components
- The `IBTSAppIntegration` interface

Pipeline components are special types of COM objects borrowed from the Microsoft Site Server Commerce Edition products. BizTalk Server uses them to deliver data to an application. If an agreement is configured in a BizTalk Server

to include the use of pipeline components for application integration, the component is automatically given the appropriate data. From that point, the component determines how to handle communications back to the application. This is typically done using a method-, data-, or application interface–oriented call to an application.

Those who have programmed COM need to know that the `Execute` method of the `IPipelineComponent` interface is BizTalk Server's method to transfer control and pass the data to the component. Those looking for an easier model for application developers will find that the `IBTSAppIntegration` interface works well. However, this model does not support design-time UI or configuration properties, and it requests a single interface that is exposed, using a single entry point (the `ProcessMessage` method).

Using the `IBTSAppIntegration` interface is a simpler approach to application integration than pipeline components. BizTalk Server checks for this interface first, and only when it is not found does it check for the pipeline component interfaces.

BizTalk Management Desk

To enable users to perform functions such as trading-partner management, BizTalk Server provides the BizTalk Management Desk, which is a Web-based GUI for local or remote use. The BizTalk Management Desk supports the following features:

- Trading partner to internal application
- Internal application to trading partner
- Internal application to internal application
- Trading partner through value-added network (VAN) to trading partner
- Internal application to distribution list
- Internal application to open destination
- Open source to internal application

The BizTalk Management Desk has two subsystems: the Agreement Editor and the Pipeline Editor. There is also a BizTalk Mapper and a BizTalk Editor.

In terms of BizTalk Server, an agreement is just a functional rule that makes sense to all trading partners (how shipping costs are calculated, for example). The **Agreement Editor** allows BizTalk Server users to create new agreements between trading partners and internal applications.

When creating an agreement, users can specify a source or target system (trading partner) or declare it as an open agreement. They can also select document

definitions, which indicate the types of documents that the source system can send to the target system and define how these documents should be processed (formatted, secured, transported, and translated).

When data is processed, the outbound agreement provides document-processing and transport information to a pipeline that links one of its document definitions to an inbound agreement. The pipeline leverages the agreement information, along with the additional pipeline properties, directing the steps in document processing.

The **Pipeline Editor** creates pipelines for a complete outbound agreement of distribution lists. When a BizTalk Server receives a document, a pipeline directs it through the steps required for processing that document. You may create one or many pipelines for document definition supported by an outbound agreement. The pipelines link a document definition of an outbound agreement to a document definition of an inbound agreement.

The **BizTalk Editor** is a tool for creating and editing specifications (see Figure 16.4) or combining XML-Data with a document content description (DCD). DCDs specify the rules that pertain to the structure and content of XML files. The

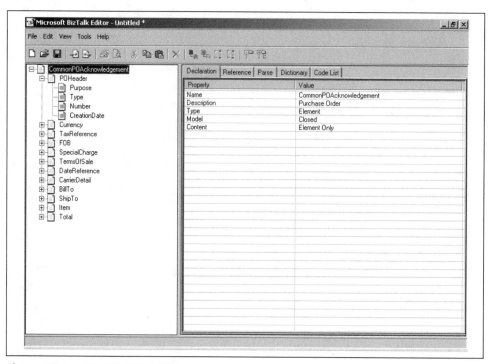

Figure 16.4   The BizTalk Editor

BizTalk Editor creates these specifications by understanding the properties of the records and fields existing within a file. These specifications include XML-Data Reduced (XDR) schemas, where XML represents structured data. This editor also provides common data descriptions used to transform data from one format to another so the information is understood by the target systems. Specifications can be based on EDI (ANSI X.12 and EDIFACT), flat files, XML, DTDs, or XML-based document templates.

The BizTalk Editor allows the creation of new specifications by using a blank specification or importing an existing schema (for example, importing a DTD, XDR, or well-formed XML document). When an instance of a document is imported, the structure is translated into a specification that is represented as XML. At this point, it is possible to add or throw away any document properties as required and then save the specification.

The **BizTalk Mapper** is BizTalk Server's data translation tool that allows users to map one schema into another schema (see Figure 16.5). The Mapper functions

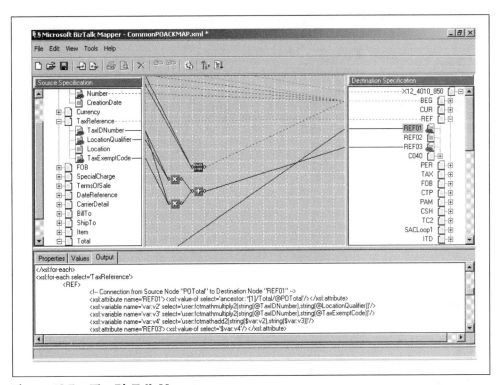

Figure 16.5   The BizTalk Mapper

in a way similar to message translation subsystems found inside most message brokers (see Chapter 13). The transformation is carried out through links and "functoids." As evidenced in Figure 16.5, the BizTalk Mapper graphically depicts the mapping and application of functions to ensure that the data is translated into the proper format. These formats, source and target, are defined by the BizTalk Editor as specifications.

BizTalking

A detailed examination of BizTalk, both its specifications and its technology, is an aid to understanding how B2B works. BizTalk, although not perfect, provides enough rudimentary functionality to allow trading partners to share information and common policies. BizTalk provides a well-defined mechanism for implementing XML-based data integration, including tools to create and design XML specifications, mapping of data from one specification to another, managing process flow, document verification, and data exchange between trading partners.

Still, as we've asserted, BizTalk is not perfect. It has been criticized for not supporting the W3C XML-Schema standards. Instead, BizTalk is based on order standards. What does stand out about BizTalk is that it is the first standard to define how information is structured—the BizTalk Framework—and the mechanisms to process the information—the BizTalk Server.

We must remember that a single company (although a powerful one), Microsoft, is driving this product. Other companies provide similar technology based on XML standards (cXML, ebXML, XML, and RosettaNet), including WebMethods, NetFish, and OnDisplay. Perhaps of equal importance, most message broker vendors have retooled, extending their EAI capabilities to provide similar value.

What is missing from BizTalk and other, similar solutions is the notion of end-to-end B2B application integration. There are no adapters for BizTalk Server. Therefore, it is necessary to create the links to the source and target systems. As we've discussed, this means programming to bind source and target systems to BizTalk Server. Otherwise, it will be necessary to modify the systems so they produce and consume information using formats that BizTalk can also produce and consume. Once again, it's desirable that you leverage a B2B application integration solution that's nonintrusive to the source and target systems found within the trading partners.

BizTalk takes us only part of the way there. In this regard, it is very much like other approaches.

Using XSLT for B2B Application Integration

Although a number of standards exist for information interchange and process definition, industry
standards have yet to emerge for defining common message broker and B2B integration server services such
as routing, rules processing, and transformation. In the
absence of such standards, individual vendors have created proprietary approaches to these basic information-
processing services. As a result, we are confronted with
features that are not interchangeable, require specialized training, and do not provide a common framework
of services.

Even as we begin to implement standards such as XML,
ebXML, RosettaNet, and BizTalk as mechanisms to manage
information interchange, we are also looking to create standards that support information processing within the middleware. These standards will define services common to most
message brokers and to B2B integration servers, including
rules and transformation.

XSLT seeks to fill the need for a standard approach to
both rules and transformation processing. Like XML, XSLT
is a standard written by the W3C, and it could become the
preferred standard mechanism for transforming content and
application semantics as information moves from application to application and business to business.

The power of XSLT resides in its simplicity, tight integration with XML, and completeness of the standard. Although

it does not provide every type of out-of-the-box transformation service currently found in most message brokers and B2B integration servers, XSLT provides the infrastructure to create such services through an extensible and declarative programming language. The operative word here is "currently." You can bet the farm that as this standard evolves, more EAI and B2B vendors will create their transformation and rules-processing technology to reflect XSLT.

What's XSLT?

XSLT is a language designed to transform one XML document into another, changing both its schema and content in the process. At its most primitive, XSLT is a text-processing system, enabling the programmer to transform XML documents or, if required, generate other standard markup languages such as HTML (or any text, for that matter).

In previous chapters, we have discussed the need for transformation as information moves between applications, so we will not devote our attention to it here. However, it is important to remember that XML documents are like messages. And since each application has its own unique set of application semantics, documents moving from application to application need to be transformed (see Figure 17.1).

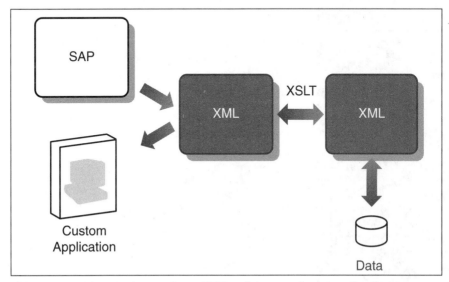

Figure 17.1 **You must transform XML as it moves from application to application.**

Both data structure and content must be semantically correct in order to load into the target application. If the data is not in the proper format, the update operation is likely to fail.

In addition to transforming the schema and content of XML documents, XSLT can perform other types of text-processing and transformation operations, including creating text-based standard data formats such as comma-delimited files, PDF, or other industry-standard formats that use text (see Figure 17.2).

Leveraging XSLT Inside Middleware: The Tradeoff

Although XSLT has tremendous promise, a huge disconnect remains between what XSLT provides and what middleware needs to offer in terms of transformation. Still, it is finding its way into more than a few middleware products, including B2B integration servers such as BizTalk Server.

The state of the technology of most message brokers—supporting complex but valuable information transport—is a better fit for binary messaging, which is more efficient than text-based messaging and is easier to manage and process. However, it does require that specialized systems, such as message-oriented middleware, manage it, and it is not as easily managed by external systems as text-based messaging (e.g., XML).

Since that is the case, for messages to be processed using XSLT, they must first be transformed into XML text (or any text) for XSLT transformation and then be transformed back into a binary message. Efficient? Clearly not. Even as a few message brokers look at XSLT as their standard mechanism for transformation, it is apparent that building text processing into existing binary messaging systems will be difficult.

B2B servers, such BizTalk Server, do not support such sophisticated message-processing operations. As a result, they are able to maintain their messages as XML or EDI text. Therefore, they have a better opportunity to leverage XSLT as their standard transformation mechanism, which they do.

XSLT will fit into some middleware products and not others. XSLT almost certainly will succeed as a standard transformation mechanism in products that already process information as raw text or XML. If XSLT continues to pick up speed, other middleware vendors will inevitably follow the crowd.

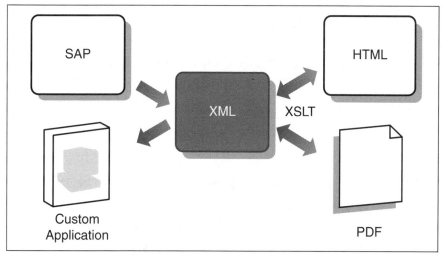

Figure 17.2   XSLT is also able to create other text-based formats, such as comma-delimited.

Before XSLT existed, most XML developers could process incoming XML documents only by creating custom applications that typically invoked one of two APIs: the Simple API for XML (SAX) and the Document Object Model (DOM).

The SAX API was an event-based interface that used a mechanism through which the parser notified the application of each piece of information in the document as it was read. In the DOM API, the parser interrogated the document and created an object tree structure that represented the structure of the XML document in memory. From that point, a traditional program (e.g., C++ or Java) transformed the tree.

The limitation of both approaches was the same—each time you wanted to transform a new XML document, you had to write a new program.

XSLT provides several advantages over SAX and DOM. XSLT's design is based on the fact that most transformation programs utilize the same design patterns and therefore can be automated using a higher-level, declarative language. (Stating that the XSLT language is declarative means that it describes the transformation behavior rather than a sequence of instructions necessary to perform the transformation. In other words, XSLT describes the transformation, then leverages the XSL processors to carry out the deed.) Moreover, when XSLT is used, the requirements of transformation can be expressed as a grouping of rules that define what output should be created when a particular pattern is encountered.

XSLT and XPath

As the development of XSLT progressed, its creators discovered that there was an overlap between the expression syntax in XSLT for selecting parts of a document and the XPointer language that was being developed for linking one document to another. Taking advantage of this, the creators of XSLT and XPointer decided to combine both efforts, defining a single language known as XPath.

In the world of XSLT, XPath provides a sublanguage encapsulated within the XSLT stylesheet. Most programming operations, including simple calculations or even testing for conditions, can be done using an XPath expression.

The Mechanisms

Transforming an XML document using XSLT requires two main steps. The first step consists of a structural transformation during which the data is transformed from the input structure to the output structure (see Figure 17.3). This step may involve selecting data, grouping it, sorting it, or aggregating it, depending on the needs of the transformation. For example, within an XML document, we can change U.S. dollar values to French francs. Such a transformation would be based on the current conversion rate, either found statically within the transformation program or read from a remote database.

The second step consists of formatting the text so it takes on the new characteristics. In this step, information is placed in a particular type of text structure: XML, HTML, PDF, and so on.

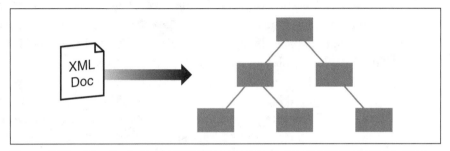

Figure 17.3   The first step in XSLT processing is structural transformation.

XSLT Processors and Processing

XSLT does not operate directly on the XML text. Instead, it relies on a parser (DOM or SAX compliant) to convert values to an object tree for processing. It uses this tree to manipulate the structure in memory. XSLT enables the user to take advantage of the native language to navigate around the node tree, select nodes, and alter the nodes as the transformation requires.

XSLT processors apply an XSLT stylesheet to an XML source document and thus create a results document—all the while remaining consistent with the way processors handle XML through trees. Thus, XSLT must process three trees: the input, stylesheet, and output trees, which we will discuss in more detail later in this chapter.

The XSLT processor applies a stylesheet to an input document and produces an output document (see Figure 17.4). Having the output document be the same kind of object as the input document enables XSLT to carry out a transformation. The stylesheet document defines the transformation to occur.

Again, text documents are not dealt with directly. They are dealt with in object trees that exist in memory. A tree is an abstract data type. There are no predefined ways for representing trees. A tree resembles the W3C's DOM but without the API, and the structure and processing models of trees are localized to the particular XSLT processor. For instance, MSXML3 uses a different structure than the Saxon XSLT processor.

Adhering to the rules of the XSLT specification, the processor must read a stylesheet tree and use it to transform the input document tree to the output document tree. However, no formal rules govern how source documents are read or how output documents are produced.

Where Do You Get an XSLT Processor?

Several XSLT processors are available, including Microsoft MSXML3 (which is also embedded within BizTalk Server). Generally, these XSLT processors can be downloaded free of charge or are bundled within products (often without the knowledge of the user).

In addition to MSXML3, other XSLT processors include Saxon, an open source XSLT processor developed by Michael Kay and written in Java, and xt, another open source XSLT processor. It was built by James Clark, the editor of the W3C XSLT Specification. Like Saxon, the xt processor is written in Java.

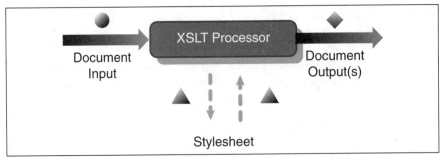

Figure 17.4 **The core purpose of a processor is to read an input document and produce an output document.**

Most real-world applications of B2B application integration are much more complex than this example, and many different types of problem domains will stretch the capabilities of the XSLT processing model (see Figure 17.5), including handling

- Multiple document inputs
- Multiple stylesheet inputs
- Multiple documents outputs

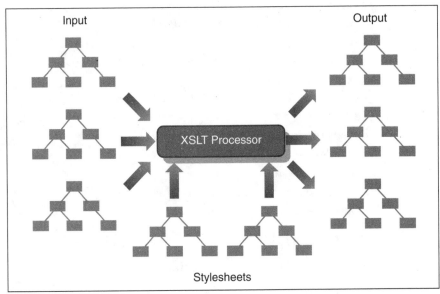

Figure 17.5 **XSLT, when leveraged for B2B application integration, will have to handle complex operations such as processing multiple input, output, and stylesheet documents at the same time.**

Transformation Process

In the domain of XSLT, the stylesheet contains a number of templates expressed as an <xsl:template> element with a match attribute. The value of the match attribute is a pattern, and the pattern determines which nodes in the source tree the template rule matches. For example:

```
<xsl:template match="/">
```

Several events occur during a typical transformation. When an XSLT transformation is executed, a stylesheet is applied to evaluate and process a source document. As we discussed earlier in this chapter, the first event to take place is the remapping of the document to a tree that is contained in memory. This prepares the schema and content for the transformation process.

The next step is to find a template rule that matches the root node of the source tree. Then the XSLT processor initiates the contents of the template rule, which, within the stylesheet, is a sequence of elements and text nodes.

For example:

```
<xsl:stylesheet
id = id
extension-element-prefixes = tokens
exclude-result-prefixes = tokens
version = number>
<!- Content: (*, top-level-elements) ->
</xsl:stylesheet>
<xsl:transform
id = id
extension-element-prefixes = tokens
exclude-result-prefixes = tokens
version = number>
<!- Content: (*, top-level-elements) ->
</xsl:transform>
```

[Source: W3C XSLT Specification]

A template rule has the following two parts:

• A pattern that is matched against nodes in the source tree and a template that can be initiated to form part of the result tree

- A template that is initiated for a particular source element to create part of the result tree

A template can contain elements that specify literal result-element structure. A template can also contain elements from the XSLT namespace that are instructions for creating result-tree fragments. When a template is initiated, each instruction is executed and replaced by the result-tree fragment that it creates. Instructions can select and process descendant source elements. Processing a descendant element creates a result-tree fragment by finding the applicable template rule and instantiating its template. Note that elements are processed only when they have been selected by the execution of an instruction. The result tree is constructed by finding the template rule for the root node and initiating its template.[1]

XSLT B2B Applications

In addition to XSLT's primary purpose in the context of B2B application integration, XSLT has a number of other applications.

Schema Conversions

The main application of XSLT, and the reason for its inclusion here, is for schema conversions as XML documents move between applications, accounting for the differences in the way applications manage data structures.

XSLT is the preferred method of converting data structured within XML. You can leverage XSLT for the following:

- Extracting data
- Validating data
- Persisting data
- Converting attributes to elements
- Converting elements to attributes
- Changing the metadata and content of an incoming XML document to create a new outgoing XML document

Converting XML to Something Else, and Vice Versa

In addition to converting XML document A to XML document B, typically changing its structure and content, XSLT can be a mechanism for reading most

---

1. W3C XSLT Specification

types of text files and creating XML, or for reading XML and creating most types of text files.

Within the B2B world, the best examples of this are

- Reading EDI from a source application that externalizes information as EDI and converting it to XML
- Converting XML to EDI so information is accepted in a particular target system
- Reading other data interchange text, such as comma-delimited data, and converting it to XML
- Converting XML to a data interchange text format, such as comma-delimited, so information is accepted into particular target systems
- Reading and writing information to and from nondata text sources, such as PDF documents
- Publishing information to standard text formats used by publishing systems

XSLT and B2B

XSLT is not the solution to every B2B application integration requirement. It is, however, an important piece in the puzzle. Its great potential is its ability to finally provide a standard transformation mechanism that everyone can agree on, one that does not require that B2B application integration architects relearn technology as they move from vendor to vendor.

There are several other advantages to using XSLT for transformation, including the following:

- A common language for transforming application semantics as text or XML moves between applications
- A common standard for representing transformation behaviors
- A common input and output message/document structure
- Backing from most major B2B and EAI technology vendors and consultants.

However, there are limitations to consider as well, including the following:

- The slow emergence of vendor support because of the limitations of existing technologies (e.g., moving from binary messaging to XML text)
- The technical limitations, including performance and security, of using text, and only text
- The fact that not all standards make it, and XSLT could lose momentum and thus wide support like so many other standards in the past

CHAPTER EIGHTEEN

Understanding Supply Chain Integration

Trying to succeed in today's business environment is like riding a wild roller coaster. Organizations face fluctuating demand, abbreviated product life cycles, and significant customer attrition every year. Those organizations able to align both their human and information resources to meet the demands of the supply chain are the ones best positioned to own their market. For these companies, success is a function of intelligence, creativity, and innovation. They understand the need to bind the members of their supply chain. They also understand that technology is the glue that will hold that chain fast. B2B application integration gives us the opportunity to take command of our supply chains and to expand their use.

The difference between supply chain integration and B2B application integration is in their relationship to one another. One is the rail, the other is the train. B2B application integration, as we've discussed, requires placing new approaches and technologies around the process of extending the reach of applications, enabling them to exchange information with other applications that exist in other organizations. Supply chain integration represents the enabling processes that run on top of the infrastructure that B2B application integration creates (see Figure 18.1). Whereas B2B application integration is about a tactical process that depends heavily on technology, supply chain integration is more about strategy.

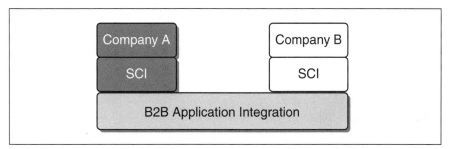

Figure 18.1   B2B application integration creates the infrastructure that allows supply chain integration to work.

The symbiosis of supply chain integration and B2B application integration is clear. The technology, the approaches, and even the benefits are much the same. A tightly coupled supply chain is dependent on the success of B2B application integration, along with such B2B application integration technology as message brokers, application servers, and standards such as XML and EDI.

Supply chain integration is a well-known and time-proven concept. There is significant literature dealing with it, so we will not cover it exhaustively here. Our purpose is to understand the basic notion of supply chain integration and its usefulness in the context of B2B application integration.

Value of the Chain

Supply chain integration may well represent the promised land. But as with most promised lands, the road leading to it is hardly smooth or straight. A substantial commitment to technological and organizational change must be made for supply chain integration to work. Companies with little corporate patience, companies with little corporate vision, and companies looking for short-term gains need not apply. There is risk a-plenty on the road to this promised land. This glory bus is only for organizations willing to confront the risk, willing to face new and changing technological approaches, willing to absorb significant short-term expenses, and willing to invite the need to layer into other organizations not under their direct control—other organizations that could even include a competitor or two.

No foolproof method for integrating a supply chain exists. However, organizations can take steps to ensure that they minimize the risks. The smart strategy is to plan for the long term, implement in the short term, and keep your eye on the "ball"—the business reasons for supply chain integration. The most difficult

trick may well be keeping the technology in perspective. It is there to be controlled, not to be worshipped. Ultimately, it is the tool, not the master. Finally, organizations must make decisions wisely. They must avoid the carnival barkers in the technology marketplace. They need to base their decision making on what adds the most value to the chain, not on what "glitters" or what is trendy.

It is a fool who does not respect the risks involved. Every organization should feel the weight of these risks. However, the remarkable opportunity that supply chain integration represents is beginning to outweigh the risks. We are fast approaching a point of critical mass where the greater risk might well be in failing to integrate.

Organizations can no longer afford the luxury of perceiving their operations as if they existed in a vacuum. No organization is an island, to quote a phrase. Every organization needs to collect comprehensive, accurate, and timely information throughout the supply chain.

Once this information is gathered, it must be analyzed in order to better comprehend the causes and effects of the business environment on the core business. Once such an analysis has been accomplished, the resulting knowledge will allow the organization to make informed business decisions and to utilize information as a mechanism to gain market share.

Defining Your Supply Chain

Supply chains support the flow of goods and services from their origin to their endpoint—the customer. The components of the supply chain may include the original suppliers, multiple production operations, logistics operations, retailing, the customer, and even the customer's customer. For example, an organization that builds birdhouses has a supply chain that includes the lumber company that processes trees into lumber, the plant that turns the lumber into birdhouses, the company that supplies the paint for the birdhouses, the logistics department that ensures the availability of supplies, the sales staff, the shipping department, the retailer, and the customer who ultimately purchases the birdhouse (see Figure 18.2). As we suggested earlier, not all of these organizational components may be under the direct control of the organization that heads the value chain.

Supply chains include many concepts, such as the following:

- Collaborative planning and forecasting
- Design collaboration
- Coordinated manufacturing
- Coordinated distribution management

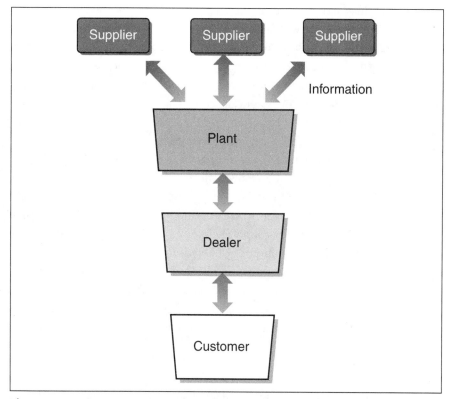

Figure 18.2   Example of a supply chain

These concepts represent such sophisticated processes that a number of large software companies, such as Manugistics and I2, have established a strong market in selling software that addresses them. Moreover, supply chain simulation software, such as that sold by Gymsym, provides users with the ability to model supply chains before they go into production. Even getting to this preliminary point depends on a sound B2B application integration infrastructure.

The supply chain determines the speed of operation and time-to-market as well as the inventory an organization must carry at any time. Supply chain management determines the overall cost-of-goods-sold as well as customer service and satisfaction. Supply chain management relies on the planning and the control of the flow of goods and services, information, and money back and forth throughout the supply chain.

Saturn Leverages a Supply Chain to Ensure Success

Saturn's successful ability to deliver a high-quality, low-cost vehicle depends on its supply chain management operations. Saturn employs a sophisticated information system to practice just-in-time inventory and keep inventory costs low. Unlike traditional, "dinosaur" companies, Saturn does not maintain inventory beyond the minimum required to complete a certain number of cars.

Saturn is successful because it manages not only its automobile-manufacturing facility and the logistics operations but also the operating systems that encompass its parts suppliers and dealers. This management strategy gives Saturn the ability to determine demand and *then to react* to that demand by ordering more parts and building more cars.

Saturn commands this high degree of supply chain integration by insisting that its suppliers tie into its information systems in one way, shape, or form. The purchase of a Saturn vehicle automatically triggers an order for the inventory and the plant time to build another car. *People are not part of this process.* The technology exchanges information and makes decisions based on criteria determined by management. The minimal presence of human, and therefore inefficient, intervention is the benchmark of a well-integrated and automated supply chain.

Extending Applications

To consider supply chain integration is, in reality, to consider extending the enterprise. Just as an extended family might include aunts, uncles, second cousins, and other distant relatives, the extended enterprise comprises all of the members in a company's supply chain, such as the various legal units within the company, suppliers, supplier vendors, and customer organizations.

Extending the enterprise demands leveraging technology, such as B2B application integration–enabled middleware and traditional application development technology. For example, common network infrastructures must be in place, such as those offered by VANs, proprietary wide area networks (WANs), or the Internet. A significant benefit of the Internet is its ability to level the playing field for

smaller organizations seeking to leverage the power of supply chain integration. By taking advantage of the common links of the Internet and the common platform of the Web, organizations can become part of a set of informally connected systems.

Although some organizations may be fighting against this evolution, they are fighting a battle that they have already lost. The Internet has, on a fundamental level, already accomplished the task by creating its own natural supply chain.

Consider a typical direct-order apparel company. Consumers access the company's Web site, where they are able to browse the available merchandise. The consumer is able to get an immediate price for an order, including tax and shipping charges, along with a ship date, the estimated time of arrival, and a confirmation number to track the order as it progresses through the chain. The value this capability provides to the consumer is the ability to shop without sales pressure and time constraints and an enormous amount of information about the costs, timing, and status of the order. These benefits are part of the reason that online storefronts are doubling their sales every year and in the process adding value to the concept of the supply chain.

Web-enabled commerce benefits the company as well as the consumer. With orders collected directly from the consumer, point-of-sale data is immediately available to the supply chain systems. This data provides real-time feedback to various points within the organization's business processes. For example, suppliers are made aware of the demand for a particular garment, enabling them to adjust production. Sales knows the success or failure of a product line before its effect reaches the bottom line. A company that not only has automated its own business processes but has integrated its systems with the systems of the supply chain partners becomes part of a team and can build a mechanism for dealing automatically with the volatility of the most aggressive markets.

Binding the Home System to a Stranger's

The integration of information and business functions is only the first step in effective supply chain management and B2B application integration. Those individuals responsible for automating the supply chain must analyze the information available to them to determine the required courses of action. The best systems automatically trigger a corresponding transaction by evaluating conditions and providing decision makers with sufficient data to make effective decisions.

The flow of information must be unimpeded among all members of the supply chain. All communication barriers must be removed. The degree of difficulty in creating links to members—and opening this flow of information—ranges from very low to very high. Most members have information systems in place. This is the upside. The downside is that the types of information retained and the standards they rely on vary greatly. For example, many information systems are proprietary and fail to provide points of integration. In addition to being difficult to integrate with the supply chain, such proprietary technology results in higher cost and diminished value.

The Internet provides the supply chain with an inexpensive network for sharing information between members. As we have seen, the Web provides the additional benefit of linking unknown users (e.g., customers) into the supply chain. Those responsible for integrating supply chains should look to the Web-enabled customer base as a mechanism to extend supply chain integration, not simply as a simple link to it.

The Process

Although the Big Four consulting firms promote a number of methodologies for creating an automated supply chain, the process is really just like traditional system development—with a twist.

The first step is to automate and optimize all of the major business processes within each member organization. Attempting to integrate a supply chain before the members have their core systems in place will be costly, frustrating, and futile. The second step is to extend the enterprise to incorporate all members in the supply chain. This is the most difficult and time-consuming part of the process. This step requires psychology as well as technology. Once your members' "hearts and souls" are in the right place, you will find that B2B application integration technology and techniques add the most value.

At the heart of this process is a system architecture-and-design effort that extends the enterprise systems to all the member organizations. Not only is the enterprise being automated (and the process flows, object models, database models, and so on being created), but the way in which all of this integrates with other systems in other organizations is being defined. (In a way, this integration method is analogous to the integration process outlined for the types of B2B application integration.) The end result is a common information infrastructure that integrates all member business systems with those of customers and suppliers.

Once such an infrastructure is in place, the new family of B2B application integration technology—message brokers and application servers—creates the best new opportunity to take command of the supply chain problem. Using message brokers, supply chain integrators can bind systems, even custom proprietary systems belonging to a trading partner, with their own enterprise systems. This is not significantly different from addressing any other integration problem in the enterprise. In this case, the problem domain is simply extended to include the relevant systems owned by the trading partners (see Figure 18.3). Here, you must rely on what we've learned in this book—first defining the infrastructure for integration, then defining the processes that control communications between the systems.

Throughout the process, organizations should look for opportunities to add value to the supply chain system, such as real-time decision support to increase responsiveness—for example, defining triggers to automatically perform business processes, such as reordering inventory, increasing the marketing budget for a best-selling product, or informing management of other issues that need to be addressed. Other examples include evaluating an organization's leveraging systems to automatically select suppliers based on price and availability, freeing the staff from performing a complete analysis of the business drivers.

This type of sophisticated processing lends itself well to the process integration or collaboration aspect of B2B application integration; that is, the ability to create a workflow/process integration layer on top of existing inter-enterprise processes. A real-time solution brings with it the greatest degree of flexibility, because changing a process or a flow is a simple matter of dragging icons around on a screen.

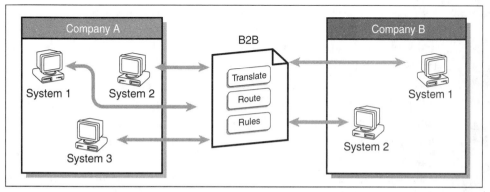

Figure 18.3   **Supply chain integration builds on B2B application integration techniques and technologies.**

Near-time decision support information is important as well. Almost all supply chain systems need to leverage the power of data warehousing technology to provide decision makers with the information they need to drop a product line, increase promotional activities, or normalize the number of participants in the supply chain.

As we've suggested, in addition to the technical issues these solutions raise, there is a human component to the process. Supply chain integration is not complete unless it is accompanied by an investment in re-educating and re-orienting employees, suppliers, and other interested parties. Too often "techies" forget about the "soft" aspects of supply chain integration only to discover, to their dismay, that these soft aspects are as vital to the process as the hard aspects are.

Absent from this process is the ability for all the players in the chain to make enterprise-wide commitments to creating and managing a complex organization and business system that's better able to fit the needs of the market. Organizations that are doing this today are going to own the market in the future.

Supply Chain Technology

Although some organizations are using new B2B application integration–enabled or traditional middleware to tie custom systems together with those of their supply chain members, many others are looking to ERP packages as points of integration. ERP provides members in the supply chain with a common application layer to exchange information through well-defined interfaces, business logic, and repositories. Unfortunately, getting all members of the chain to run the same ERP application, or any other application, for that matter, is an almost impossible task.

ERP systems are designed to provide their owners with a system for planning, controlling, and monitoring an organization's business process. What's more, ERP systems offer easy, system-to-system integration through standard mechanisms for communications. They also build a common understanding of what the data represents and a common set of rules (methods) for accessing the data. However, traditional ERP systems are not necessarily supply chain systems. Supply chain systems must deal with the complexity of integrating information from any number of disparate systems that span multiple organizations. Although some properties of ERP systems are appropriate for use with the supply chain, others are not. Typically, ERP systems exist within a single organization, using a single database as the point of integration with internal organizations. As a result, there is a single

database and network protocol standard; thus the enterprise system is able to work with other departmental systems without having to deal with complex integration problems.

When supply chains integrate external systems, it is nearly impossible to get all member organizations to agree on a set of standards (e.g., network protocol, database architecture, and process integration). Because of this difficulty in arriving at a unanimous agreement, the best solution is layers and layers of middleware, gateways, and adapter technology so that information can be moved from system to system. In most cases, very little processing can be shared among the members. As a result, the supply chain system architecture can grow exceedingly complex and confusing.

Because of this reality, two problems need to be solved. The first is getting all member organizations to agree on a single communications standard and a single set of application semantics. Although it might appear that communications would be an easy problem to solve, it rarely is. Some of the member organizations, especially the smaller manufacturing concerns, face significant costs to get their systems ready to link to others in the chain. Once everyone is ready, the second problem has to be addressed—all members need to agree on a common communications mechanism and middleware approach, allowing all member systems to seamlessly access processes and data in the extended enterprise.

As difficult as these two problems might appear, implementing the solutions is often even more difficult.

These difficulties will not be overcome anytime soon. The value that the new B2B application integration technology brings to this problem domain is the ability to integrate many of these systems without requiring that significant changes be made in the systems owned by any of the trading partners. Instead of an organization's having to change the database, application, and possibly even the network, B2B application integration–enabled middleware is able to adapt each system into the larger system by accounting for the differences in data and methods within a middle tier (see Figure 18.4).

The middleware best suited for supply chain systems is represented by message brokers and application servers. Because message brokers are message oriented and asynchronous, they're able to move information from system to system without requiring that all systems be up and running at the same time.

Application semantics is another issue that organizations must confront. Although most organizations can agree on relational databases, few can agree on a common schema and architecture that can be shared across the chain. Supply

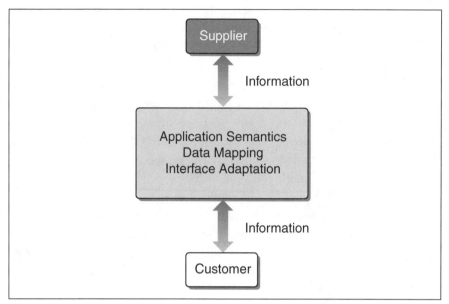

Figure 18.4   B2B application integration technology is able to link many different systems in the supply chain by not requiring that changes be made to the source or target systems.

chains solve this problem either by forcing a common data architecture among the members or by using message brokers or data translation middleware to adapt the data to various models and schemas. The latter is, as in other contexts, the path of least resistance.

Supply Chains Organize

A more objective set of standards is being developed by the National Initiative for Supply Chain Integration (NISCI), a nonprofit, private organization that receives backing from the Department of Commerce. NISCI's mission is to assist member businesses in understanding and building the most effective methods and technologies to optimize the performance of supply chains consisting of more than three members. NISCI provides thought leadership in supply chain optimization by making available a central repository of information on both problems and solutions. Thus far, organizations have been dependent on large consulting companies to provide both methodology and technology. NISCI is committed to functioning through a board of directors made up of producers, suppliers, and

intermediate processors. NISCI will work to improve its member organizations by following several objectives, including stimulating value creation, certifying education, and designing chain architecture supporting real-time, consensus decision making.

Supply chain integration is in its first stages in most organizations, and many organizations have wisely chosen to move forward with "baby steps." Although all have a supply chain, few have moved to optimize it through process re-engineering, training, and, most important, technology. However, the time for such small, cautious steps may well be behind us. The value of such cooperation is only now becoming apparent.

When it comes to supply chain integration, the future is easy to define but much harder to implement. We need to examine our information infrastructure to determine how we are doing business. Then we need to look at what it will take to modify the infrastructure to extend the enterprise to other members. Only then will it be possible to tackle the integration issues—which will be innumerable.

## CHAPTER NINETEEN

B2B Application Integration Moving Forward

It's appropriate that as we conclude, we take the long view of B2B application integration technology—how it exists now and, perhaps more important, the direction it is likely to take in the next few years. This information is important to those organizations considering B2B application integration approaches and who had best "lay their cards on the table" to solidify their considerations and decisions.

B2B application integration is a complex problem. Although we have seen some notable successes in addressing it, these successes have been narrow and limited. The simple reality is, most B2B projects exist just at the entry level. We have yet to see the real-time coupling of thousands of applications, which is the goal for many trading communities. This should not necessarily be discouraging. As with any complex problem, once it is broken down to its component parts, the solution becomes simply the aggregation of a number of solution sets. In this case, it's a combination of a variety of approaches and several types of technology.

The world of B2B application integration is no different from the larger world of technology—it is advancing and changing rapidly. And ironically, as the technology changes, so does the problem it is designed to solve. The B2B application integration problem is morphing from the very simple to the very complex, even as it moves from a departmental problem to an enterprise-wide problem and ultimately to a

trading community problem. Consequently, few companies have been able to get ahead of the "B2B application integration curve." Short of a complete solution, they have yet to discover the full potential and benefit of B2B application integration.

We are seeing that as the problem grows, so does the potential benefit of the solution. The technology continues to respond to the perceived need. In this context, our pursuit of B2B application integration is like chasing the tail of a growing beast. For now, that beast remains ahead of us. A great deal of work remains ahead of us. But rest assured, a solution will be found and the once unimaginable benefits of B2B application integration will become an everyday reality.

Problem Domains Change

As we suggested earlier, as the problem domains become more complex, the B2B application integration solution set evolves to address that growing complexity. No sooner is a "traditional" B2B application integration problem solved (such as application-to-application and database-to-database integration) than the developed B2B application integration expertise and technology is being applied to more complex, but more rewarding, business issues.

In fact, it is not unreasonable to see in the development of the solution the growth of the problem.

This is both natural and intelligent. As systems are integrated within the enterprise, it is just plain old good business sense to take that experience and technology and apply it to other opportunities that influence the bottom line.

B2B Applications Emerging

In Chapter 18, we discussed supply chain integration, or inter-enterprise application integration. Supply chain integration is an old issue, one well served by new B2B application integration techniques. By using familiar approaches and technologies, we can bring together very different systems that exist in different companies and allow these systems to easily share information.

Using automation to integrate the supply chain is nothing new. However, the application of new technology and standards, such as message brokers and XML, to the problem provides many additional opportunities to address this challenge effectively and efficiently (see Figure 19.1).

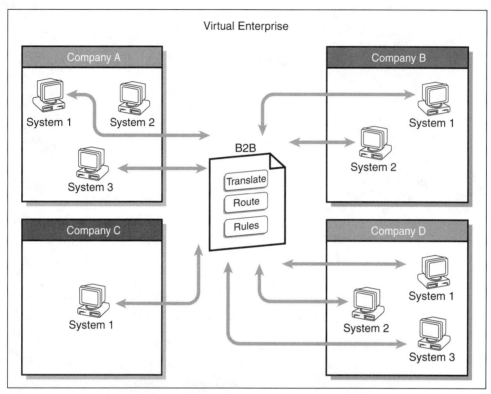

Figure 19.1 **B2B application integration technology provides the infrastructure for efficient and effective supply chain integration.**

Moving from EDI to XML

Although EDI represents a sound solution, its complexity and expense largely doom it—even though it will remain a point of integration for some time. Because EDI does not generally support real-time integration between applications, since it is traditionally batch oriented, XML provides a much more efficient approach and, as such, a much less expensive approach (see Figure 19.2).

Many organizations have opted for "none of the above." That is, they've chosen not to use either XML or EDI. Instead, they have adopted some other message standard (e.g., JMS) or a proprietary communications mechanism. The hodgepodge of technologies and standards that has resulted from these various in-house decisions will remain in place as we seek to address the supply chain integration problem.

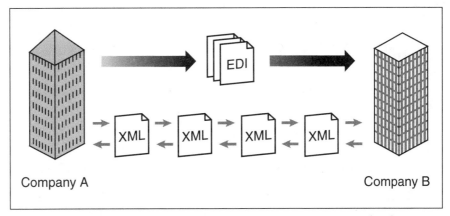

Company A   Company B

Figure 19.2   EDI and XML provide different values to B2B application integration.

Where's the Chapter on EDI?

Although EDI deserves kudos—EDI is where B2B application integration and, more accurately, supply chain integration got their start—its role in real-time B2B application integration is somewhat limited. Thus, we have not dealt with it directly in this book.

We're not suggesting that EDI will never have value for B2B application integration. But its limitations, which include proprietary technology, batch orientation, and lack of support for real-time information exchange, minimize its usefulness to most new B2B application integration projects. (Remember that EDI provides a great point-of-integration technology, and many B2B information-exchange applications will have to move through EDI and other legacy technologies to be successful.)

EDI continues to bring value to B2B application integration. But other technologies, such as XML, are becoming more acceptable and gaining better vendor support. Even so, most existing EDI-enabled trading communities are not likely to dump EDI anytime soon in favor of more up-to-date technology. It is just too expensive to make the change for the near future.

Moving from Data-Oriented to Application-Oriented Integration

Another clear trend is the movement away from data-oriented integration to application-oriented (application interface–oriented and method-oriented B2B application integration) integration. As we noted previously, data-oriented integration provides an inexpensive mechanism to integrate applications because in most instances there is no need to change the applications.

Although data-oriented integration provides a functional solution for many B2B application integration problem domains, the integration of both application services and application methods generally provides more value in the long run. The downside, at least with method-oriented integration, is that this approach makes it necessary to change the source and target applications or, worse in a number of instances, to create a new application (a composite application). As we have noted many times, data-oriented integration is a much more difficult sell within trading communities.

Still, the upside of this approach is that it is consistent with the "baby-step" approach most enterprises find comfortable when implementing solutions to integration problems. B2B application integration solutions tend to be created in a series of small, low-risk steps. This type of implementation can be successful from department to enterprise to trading community but never the other way around—from trading community to department.

Data-oriented B2B application integration provides most organizations with a low-risk option for getting B2B application integration under control. After that, as more time and money become available and the appetite for risk increases, they are able to plot a strategy to "step up" to application-oriented integration.

Loose Ends

Unfortunately, any discussion of B2B application integration tends to leave a number of loose ends—issues that don't fit neatly into any other discussion of the solution. Despite their awkwardness, we must discuss these issues before we can close the subject. Among these important loose-end issues are security, performance, and administration.

Security

To the detriment of many, security is too often an afterthought in the implementation of a new technology. To address security properly, you need to build it

from the ground up. Although a detailed discussion of security is beyond the scope of this book, remember that whenever information is sent or received from enterprise-wide systems, when interfaces to the systems are built, or when middleware is being implemented, security *must* be considered. The vulnerabilities of any enterprise are never more than a handful of mouse clicks away—a very sobering thought when your money and time are on the line.

With just a couple of mouse clicks, an enterprise's most valuable asset—its information—can be laid bare to the world. The importance of security should be a given in the world of B2B integration when sensitive information is being sent out from your organization, usually over the Internet, and outside users are given some degree of access to your internal systems.

In most cases, B2B application integration security will be built on top of an existing security structure within the source and target applications (e.g., Top Secret, RACF, or Windows NT security). Therefore, in addition to integrating applications, B2B application integration needs to integrate the security systems.

Performance and Scalability

As with security, performance and scalability issues must be part of the B2B application integration design from the ground up. This ensures that a set of integrated systems perform well. Many organizations consider security during the B2B application integration development process, but they fail to adequately address performance and scalability until it is too late.

Complex issues such as message rates, transactions per second, and interface performance must be taken into account when considering performance engineering and B2B application integration. The most reliable approach to performance in the design of an integration solution is to select the technology and then create a simulation model to make an educated assessment of how well it will perform. Using simulation tools, you can determine the time it will take for a message or a transaction to move between applications. This simulation must test the various entities of the system at the component (e.g., server) and system levels (e.g., integrated systems) to ensure the overall performance of the B2B application integration solution (see Figure 19.3). Just as a chain is no stronger than its weakest link, an integration solution is no more efficient than its slowest-performing component. Testing identifies problem components before the solution is implemented.

Scalability differs from performance in important ways. The scalability of the system refers to the B2B application integration solution's ability to support

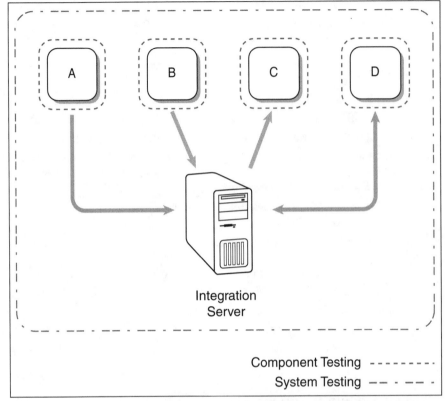

Figure 19.3 **In order to ensure that a B2B application integration solution performs well, the solution must be tested at the component and system levels.**

an increasing number of source and target systems and transaction rates. Unfortunately, scalability is rarely considered until very late in the game—often, too late. Like performance, scalability requires an architect's input from the ground up. Never, never assume the technology will get you there.

Making a B2B application integration solution scale requires selecting the correct approaches and enabling technology for the problem domain. For example, if the message rate is going to be a limiting factor, select a technology that can distribute message processing among any number of connected message brokers. If transaction load and database access integrity are the limiting factors, then transactional middleware may be a better fit. No hard-and-fast rule exists for designing a system to scale. The first step is to determine your requirements and then "back" the appropriate architecture and technology into those requirements.

Putting the technology first is a very costly example of putting the cart ahead of the horse. Again, simulation tools and performance models are your first stop in determining the requirements of your scalability issues.

Administration

With application servers, message brokers, TP monitors, and even new composite applications all finding a place in a typical B2B application integration solution, you must figure out how to administer and maintain these "unruly children." Such maintenance includes

- Performance management
- Disaster recovery (backup and restore)
- Security administration
- Configuration management

Over time, the administration of most problem domains will require more budgeted money than the creation of the original solution. For this reason alone, you should create a B2B application integration solution with an eye to administrative efficiency. Solutions that are easy to administer generally provide more uptime and a better user experience.

Middleware Vendor Approaches

Although we have devoted most of our attention to the various approaches organizations can take to B2B application integration, vendors themselves have some interesting views on the subject—which leads us to the inevitable question, Who is right and who is wrong? It quickly becomes apparent that our difficulty lies not in the answer but in the question. As with everything else in the B2B application integration domain, the answer is not black and white.

As we've realized, B2B application integration is a combination of problems. Each organization and trading community has its own set of integration issues that must be addressed. Therefore, it is next to impossible to find a single technological solution set that can be applied universally. Each B2B application integration solution generally requires products from several different vendors. Now and in the foreseeable future, one-stop shopping is simply not a B2B application integration reality.

Although vendor approaches to B2B application integration vary considerably, we can create some general categories. These include

- Data-oriented
- Application integration–oriented
- Process integration–oriented
- Transaction-oriented
- Distributed object–oriented

These vendor solutions are independent of the types of B2B application integration (data, method, application interface, and portal) and may apply to one, two, or three of the types of B2B application integration.

Data-Oriented

Vendors that promote the data-oriented approach to B2B application integration argue that integration should occur between the databases—that is, databases should be viewed as the primary points of integration. These vendors throw their hats in the data-oriented B2B application integration ring. However, even in data-oriented B2B application integration, many approaches exist. It is no surprise that each vendor is quick to promote its particular solution. Data-oriented solutions can be grouped into two categories: data replication and data federation.

Data Replication

Data replication is simply moving data between two or more databases. These databases can come from the same vendor or from many vendors. They can even be databases that employ different models. The fundamental requirement of database replication is that it accounts for the differences between database models and database schemas by providing the infrastructure to exchange data. Solutions that provide such infrastructures are plentiful and inexpensive. Most relational database vendors, including Sybase and Oracle, provide database replication services in their product offerings. These replication engines typically exist within the database engines, at either end (see Figure 19.4).

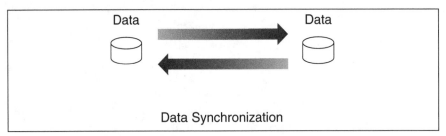

Figure 19.4   **Most major database vendors offer database replication solutions.**

Many database-oriented middleware solutions on the market provide database replication services as well. Replication services are accomplished by placing a layer of software between two or more databases. On one side, the data is extracted from the source database or databases, and on the other side, the data is placed in the target database or databases. Many of these solutions also provide transformation services—the ability to adjust the schemas and the content so they make sense to the target database (see Figure 19.5).

The advantages of database replication are simplicity and low cost. Database replication is easy to implement, and the technology is cheap to purchase and install. Unfortunately, these advantages are quickly lost if methods need to be bound to the data or if methods are shared along with the data. If these requirements exist, method-sharing solutions such as transaction-oriented or application integration–oriented B2B application integration must be considered (see the related sections later in this chapter).

Data Federation

Database federation is the integration of multiple databases and database models into a single unified view of the databases (see Figure 19.6). To put it another way, database federations are virtual enterprise databases that consist of many real physical databases. Although database federation has been around for some time, the solution set has been perfected only recently.

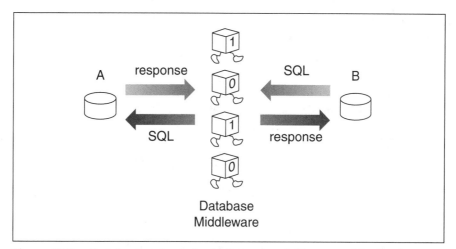

Figure 19.5   Database-oriented middleware solutions provide database replication solutions as well.

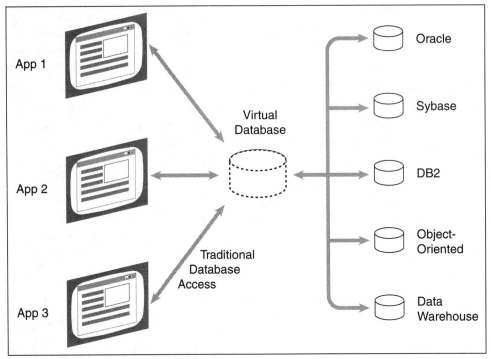

Figure 19.6 **Data federation software is middleware that allows an application to view a number of databases through a single view.**

Database federation software places a layer of software (middleware) between the physical distributed databases and the applications that view the data. This layer connects to the back-end databases by using available interfaces and maps the physical databases to a virtual database model that exists only in the software. The application uses this virtual database to access the required information. The database federation handles the collection and distribution of the data as needed to the physical databases. The advantage of using this software is its ability to bind many different data types into a unified model that supports B2B information exchange.

Database federation allows access to any connected database in the enterprise through a single well-defined interface. This is the most elegant solution to the data-oriented B2B application integration problem. Unlike replication, this solution does not require changes to the source or target applications. Still, changes do have to be made at the application level to support federated database software, because different interfaces are being used to access a different database model (the virtual database).

Application Integration–Oriented

Application integration–oriented product solutions use well-defined application interfaces to focus on the integration of both packaged and custom applications. This approach supports the data, method, application interface, and portal B2B application integration types. Interest in integrating popular ERP applications (e.g., SAP, PeopleSoft, and Baan) has made this the most exciting B2B application integration sector. (Although distributed object–oriented and transaction-oriented solutions may be applied to this space—because it is possible to program success here—message broker vendors are promoting their products as the preferred solution.)

Message brokers support application integration–oriented solutions by providing adapters to connect to as many custom or packaged applications as possible. They also connect to technology solutions that include middleware and screen scrapers as points of integration (see Figure 19.7).

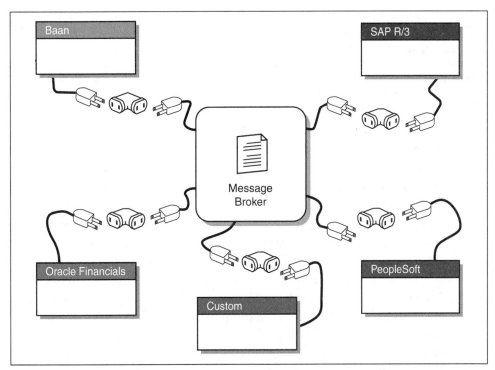

Figure 19.7   Application integration–oriented solutions link to packaged or custom applications or other points of integration to integrate applications.

The efficient integration of many different types of applications defines the primary advantage of using application integration–oriented products. In just days, you can connect a SAP R/3 application to a Baan application, with the application integration–oriented solution's accounting for differences between schema, content, and application semantics by translating the information moving between the systems on the fly. Moreover, this type of solution can be used as a database replication solution, able to connect to application interfaces.

The downside (there is always a downside) to using application interface–oriented products is that there is little regard for business logic and methods within the source or target systems, logic and methods that may be relevant to a particular integration effort. In such a case, transaction- or distributed object–oriented solutions (composite applications or a pure method-oriented approach) probably make the better choice. Ultimately, application interface–oriented technology will learn to share methods and information, perhaps by joining forces with transaction-oriented or distributed object–oriented solutions. However, for now you will have to make an either-or decision.

Process Integration–Oriented

Process integration–oriented products layer a set of easily defined and centrally managed processes on top of existing sets of processes within a set of enterprise applications (see Figure 19.8).

The goal is to bring together relevant processes found in a trading community to obtain the maximum amount of value while supporting the flow of information and logic between these processes. These products view the middleware, or the plumbing, as a commodity and provide easy-to-use visual interfaces for binding these processes together.

In reality, process integration is another layer of value resting upon existing B2B application integration solutions, which include message brokers, application servers, distributed objects, and other middleware layers. Process integration offers a mechanism to bind disparate processes together and to create process-to-process solutions that automate tasks once performed manually. However, by diminishing the importance of the plumbing, vendors can easily lose sight of the larger picture. In reality, no single B2B application integration vendor has solved the plumbing issues. Ultimately, the solution to these issues will be delivered by a combination of process integration and middleware vendors. Thus, the binding of middleware and process integration tools represents the future of B2B application integration.

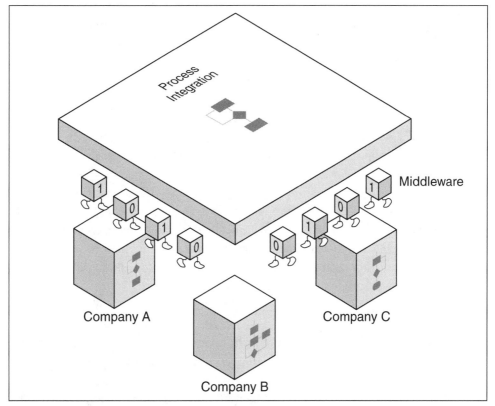

Figure 19.8   Process integration–oriented products layer a set of centrally managed processes on top of an existing set of enterprise processes.

Transaction-Oriented

Transaction-oriented middleware products use the notion of a transaction—with connectors to back-end systems—to integrate applications. This is a clear method-oriented B2B application integration approach. Examples include TP monitors and application servers. Although transaction-oriented products can be used for data integration, method-oriented integration is where these products shine. With these products, you can create common methods (transactions, really) and share those methods among many connected applications (see Figure 19.9).

Transaction-oriented products offer the advantages of scalability and reliability. However, these products are intrusive to applications exchanging information within a trading community, and success demands a significant amount of coding. As we go forward, we will see transaction-oriented middleware combining

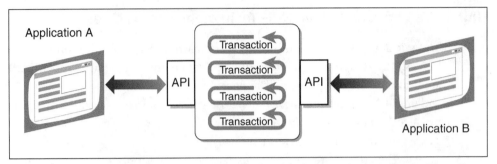

Figure 19.9   Transaction-oriented B2B application integration products allow the sharing of methods.

forces with messaging and message brokers, providing B2B application integration architects and developers with the best of method-oriented, data-oriented, and application interface–oriented B2B application integration.

Distributed Object–Oriented

Like transaction-oriented products that exist in method-oriented integration, distributed objects (such as those based on COM or CORBA standards) also provide B2B application integration architects and developers with an opportunity to share methods. The elegance of the distributed object architecture, the built-in communications, and the ability to support the distributed model have led to the suggestion that this is the ultimate B2B application integration technology. But as we have learned, nothing is precisely as it seems in the world of B2B application integration projects. Distributed objects still have a long way to go before they can support most large-scale integration projects. They continue to fall short in supporting transactionality, messaging, and easy-to-use tools for building and deploying distributed object B2B application integration solutions.

A great deal of custom coding is required to leverage the power of distributed objects within a B2B application integration solution. Perhaps more chilling, they are invasive to all participating applications.

Distributed object standards are moving in the right direction by including built-in support for transactions and integration with Web standards such as Java. Still, it will take some time and momentum before distributed objects and B2B application integration make a good match. Unfortunately, distributed objects don't have the luxury of either in the rapidly evolving world of B2B application integration.

United We Win, Divided We Fail—Technologies Join Forces

These technologies represent different approaches to B2B application integration. Most B2B application integration problem domains use most types of B2B application integration (method, application interface, data, process integration, and portal) when integrating an enterprise. Therefore, we must select the appropriate technology that works for each type. Wishing for a single technology and a single vendor for all types is just that—wishing.

Developers and architects may use any number of tools to pass information between databases, supporting data-oriented B2B application integration. These tools include newer message brokers as well as more traditional data replication software. In the application interface type, message brokers do a better job connecting to and moving information into and out of packaged applications. That's the upside. The downside is that all message brokers fall short in implementing method-oriented B2B application integration or creating composite applications.

Message brokers are not designed to house, or share, application logic. Instead, they provide rudimentary rules engines to support operations, such as the identification, transformation, and routing of messages to the appropriate systems. If this is the B2B application integration requirement, then application servers are the right choice, providing the ability to integrate many different systems by sharing common business logic and thus information.

At this point, it should be clear that message brokers and application servers are complementary and converging. Although message brokers do a more than adequate job in providing event-driven, asynchronous access to many different types of systems, application servers do a much better job in providing the infrastructure to share common logic. Both technologies integrate the enterprise—solve the B2B application integration problem—but do so in very different ways (e.g., application servers are good at supporting portal-oriented integration, while message brokers are not). Although both application servers and message brokers use the middle-tier integration approach, application servers are front-end and application development focused, while message brokers are back-end, operations, and process oriented.

Application server and message broker vendors alike believe the adage "If you can't beat 'em, join 'em." And that's precisely where they are going. Most message broker vendors are partnering with application server vendors to ensure that, at least in the short term, they'll have a solution for the method type. The end result of these partnerships is sure to be the creation of hybrid products that

support both application server and message-brokering features. The speed and approach will vary greatly from vendor to vendor, with larger message broker vendors purchasing smaller, more vulnerable application servers and larger application server companies consuming the smaller message broker players. At the same time, some application server vendors will incorporate message-brokering features into their products, and some message broker vendors will learn to provide products more like application servers.

The integration of application servers and message brokers will result in a hybrid "superproduct" that may be called an "application and integration server." This product will offer a location for shared application logic and the ability to build composite applications (see Figure 19.10) as well as the ability to access any system using a synchronous or asynchronous communications model. Moreover, this new product will be able to account for the difference in application semantics, schema, and content.

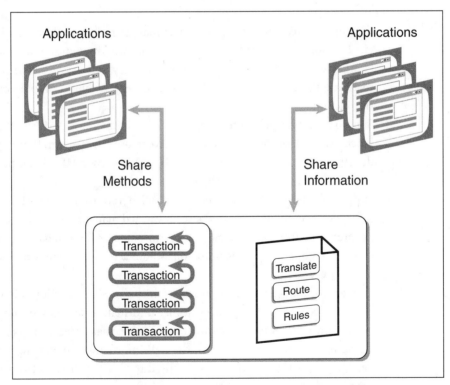

Figure 19.10　**Application and integration servers combine the best features of application servers with message brokers.**

Selecting B2B Technology

You are responsible for choosing your B2B middleware solution. You have the daunting task of evaluating the players, understanding the approaches, and backing the right solution into your B2B application integration problem domain. Although we examined some of the ins and outs of various types of enabling technology in the previous section of this chapter, most of those solutions are general-purpose middleware products sold for use in both EAI and B2B application integration problem domains. Each vendor has its own approach to the specific type of B2B application integration. It is helpful to observe where they are coming from. In other words, we need to drill down on new features and functions that are specific to the B2B problem domain.

Although B2B information interchange and the products that support it are not new concepts (e.g., traditional EDI and commerce servers), the current trend is to provide additional features in support of modern B2B integration notions.

- Support for real-time information exchange: In the traditional EDI and custom solutions world, we dealt with information movement between companies through large batch transfers. Today, businesses are demanding real-time information with as little latency as possible to support business transactions.
- Support for emerging interchange standards, including XML: EDI is very batch oriented, proprietary, and expensive to use. Thus, new B2B projects are demanding new interchange standards, particularly XML, as the preferred mechanism to exchange information.
- Support for B2B collaboration (e.g., e-Collaboration): Along with real-time information exchange, we need a sophisticated management layer (with lots of pretty pictures) to manage the movement of business information between companies. We need to collaborate across companies on complex business events.
- Support for long-term transactions: Many business transactions are instantaneous, such as sending new customer information to many trading partners. Many other transactions are long-term, such as ordering and installing a DSL line for your house. Thus, the B2B information interchange engines need to support long-term transactions, durable over an extended period of time—perhaps weeks, months, or even years.
- Support for digital exchanges aligned with vertical markets: Most vertical industries, including the automotive and high-tech industries, have established

digital exchanges to support information-and-process interchange between trading partners in their industry. B2B middleware solutions need to be aware of these digital exchanges and make wise use of them.

- Support for sophisticated security models: Since we typically exchange information with external organizations over a public network (the Internet), B2B middleware needs to provide security, including support for SSL- and RSA-based security.

To these ends, next-generation B2B technology needs to approach B2B differently. It should remove itself from the restrictions of the older models, providing better services and management layers to solve the ultimate business problem.

Approaches

The three vendor product-oriented approaches to B2B integration technology on the market today are

- EDI to B2B
- B2B to EAI
- EAI to B2B

EDI to B2B refers to products that exist primarily in the EDI space, providing batch and EDI-oriented information interchange technology. These vendors leverage EDI mapping servers and value-added networks to send and receive EDI documents to support supply chain integration. These vendors include GEIS, Sterling Commerce, and Harbinger.

These vendors are moving into the emerging B2B space through technology that is more XML-aware and is able to integrate with emerging trading communities, including RosettaNet, BizTalk, and new digital exchanges. Although these vendors have been doing B2B longer than anyone else, to their distress they are finding that customers new to this space prefer the newer players, including the pure B2B and EAI players. These vendors further damage their position with these new customers by failing to provide connectors into existing enterprise applications, relying on the customers to change their applications to accommodate the vendors' products.

These vendors typically try to leverage their existing EDI mapping servers and value-added networks to support more modern B2B mechanisms. What these vendors lack in "sexy" technology, they more than make up in experience. All of these vendors have already changed their strategy to support the next-generation B2B technology, including XML and digital exchanges.

B2B to EAI refers to new products that were built from the ground up to support emerging B2B standards, including XML, cXML, OBI, RosettaNet, and BizTalk. These products typically use the Internet as a point of transport and provide new, sophisticated management and process integration layers to manage the movement of information between companies. These vendors include WebMethods, OnDisplay, NetFish, and Cyclone Commerce.

Although providing modern mechanisms for consuming and producing business information in a variety of formats (e.g., XML, cXML, and EDI), these vendors typically do not provide integration down to the application interface level. Instead, these vendors rely on the customers to alter their systems to support the vendors' products, much like the traditional EDI players. Finding a justified resistance to having to do so, many vendors are looking to provide application connectors and thus provide the same capabilities as EAI vendors (discussed next), offering integration within and between enterprises. This is known as end-to-end B2B integration. It is also offered by the EAI-to-B2B vendors, although the pure B2B players don't do it nearly as well as the EAI players do it.

EAI to B2B refers to those EAI players, including NEON, Active Software, SAGA Software, and STC, that are adding B2B capabilities to their existing product offerings. This means deploying their general-purpose message-brokering technology and adapters to bind systems together within the enterprise and between enterprises, or extending their EAI solution to include systems outside the organization. Little notion of B2B process management, trading community management, or B2B-oriented security tends to exist here, although most EAI vendors are looking to add these capabilities shortly and are hyping these capabilities today. There is some overlap in what the pure B2B players and EAI players provide.

The advantage of using one of these vendors is their ability to provide end-to-end, application-to-application integration from any system to any system in a B2B problem domain. Thus, many don't require that you change your source or target systems, communicating with those applications by using nonintrusive adapters and points of integration. However, these products were typically designed with EAI in mind, not B2B. This means their movement into this space will at first be awkward until they provide rules, routing, and management layers that fit better with B2B solution sets.

Which One?

As you have no doubt figured out by now, selecting a B2B middleware solution isn't easy. Each vendor provides a unique approach and value. The important thing is

---

EAI and Pure B2B Vendors Begin to Merge

As we look to connect applications both within and between enterprises, vendors that specialize in EAI or B2B are beginning to join forces. The merger of these types of products and technologies is driven by both the differences in the products and how they complement each other.

Although EAI players are very good at integrating applications within an enterprise, they lack the pure B2B features—such as community management, profile management, sophisticated security mechanisms, and deep support for B2B standards such as OBI, cXML, EDI and XML—to provide good B2B solutions. However, although B2B integration software provides all of the features that are lacking in the EAI solutions, they don't provide deep, nonintrusive integration with enterprise applications that need to participate within a trading community.

Thus, the pure EAI players (even though they've been promoting B2B) and the pure B2B players are beginning to join forces. The first instance of this was the acquisition of Oberon Software by OnDisplay (now owned by Vignette), followed by the acquisition of Active Software by WebMethods. These mergers allow the vendors to offer a true end-to-end B2B application integration solution with all the features, functions, bells, and whistles to support application integration inside and between enterprises (they hope). These mergers represent a natural consolidation of the industry and one that will provide more powerful solutions.

---

not to allow the vendor to dictate the choice. You need to understand your requirements in detail and *then* back the appropriate technology into your solution. Following the hype and the crowd will likely lead you where you don't want to go.

The good news is that no matter where the vendor comes from—pure B2B, EDI, or EAI—they are all looking to provide the same feature function set. Unfortunately, it will still be a few years before they are able to refurbish their products—for example, pure B2B with end-to-end application connectors and the pure EAI with B2B management infrastructure. For now, the best approach is to understand the advantages and disadvantages of each approach—and do your homework.

B2B Application Integration—Clearly the Future

Enter B2B application integration—along with an opportunity to finally integrate all of these disparate systems with minimal impact on the applications and the way an enterprise does business. B2B application integration provides a clear competitive advantage for most industries, an advantage that includes the ability to do business at light speed, along with the ability to satisfy customer demand in record time (by using automated processes instead of paper, faxes, and humans). We are truly moving forward into a digital economy, where business runs within and between computers, where everything is automated and customers learn to expect no less than instantaneous access to information.

The future is clear. Unfortunately, the approaches and technology behind B2B application integration are still in their infancy. The knowledge necessary to fully integrate trading communities is lacking. The ultimate goal of B2B application integration is to bind all trading community systems together in such a way that any application can access any method or any piece of data without delay to support any business process.

PART V

Appendixes

Integrating SAP R/3

It is no surprise that SAP R/3, the most popular packaged ERP application for the enterprise, is the one that most B2B application integration architects and developers will encounter. Architects and developers tend to be pragmatic people. Knowing that most B2B application integration products are driven by the need to move information into and out of packaged applications like SAP R/3, they figure that since they are unable to break free from having to link into these beasts, they might as well learn to use them to their best advantage.

As with most things, connecting to SAP has an upside and a downside. The upside is that unlike many packaged applications, SAP has well-defined and well-tested built-in interfaces that adequately provide for the sharing of data and processes with the outside world. The downside is that these same interfaces are complex, their architecture is confusing, information is lacking about how best to leverage them, and various other technical issues still require resolution. SAP is working toward resolving these issues, but don't expect answers anytime soon.

In addition to these problems is the problem of what to do with the information once it's been wrenched out of SAP. In most cases B2B application integration architects and developers pass the information directly to a middleware layer (e.g., the application server or message broker), converting the information into something the target system understands. This transformation and transportation difficulty needs to be solved as well. At this point, finding the proper solution is more an art than a science.

Finally, there is the question of SAP's future. With the popularity of more open interfaces such as Java, CORBA, and COM, SAP is looking to provide uses for these interfaces that access their underlying system. Although this is an opportunity for SAP to open access to its system, it is important to consider just how the movement to these interfaces will impact a particular B2B application integration solution. In many instances, the more traditional interfaces can be used now, but an upgrade to the newer interfaces will be necessary when they're available. It doesn't require a genius to see that means having to do the integration work twice.

The Basic Problem

SAP, like most other packaged applications, was built as a monolithic solution never intended to communicate with the outside world. The later addition of interfaces changed that. They first allowed SAP systems to communicate with each other and then allowed SAP to interact with many different types of systems.

The original SAP R/3 architecture did not contain these interfaces. They were added over several years. As a result, they often seem ill conceived and poorly structured. For example, there are many ways to extract the same information from SAP. Deciding the exact method and manner is something of a crapshoot, with the correct choice not always obvious. A thorough knowledge of SAP, including data, process information, and business objects, is the only insurance that enables the successful use and manipulation of SAP.

The nirvana of SAP access rests in the hands of the B2B application integration vendors that are looking to place an abstraction layer on top of interfaces to SAP (see Figure A.1). The purpose of this abstraction layer is to hide the interface complexities from those who need to integrate SAP with other systems. As a result, SAP will appear as a set of business objects, sharable among applications. The result is a shift in burden from the B2B application integration architect and developer to the B2B application integration solution—where it belongs.

Although the use of abstraction layers remains the ultimate goal, users today must deal with intermediary realities—APIs and middleware layers. They may be ugly, but they're all that's going to be available for a while.

SAP Architecture

SAP uses a three-tier architecture consisting of a presentation layer, an application server layer, and a database layer (see Figure A.2). SAP runs on smaller

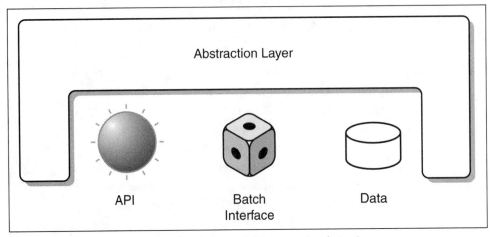

Figure A.1   Using an abstraction layer to hide complex interfaces

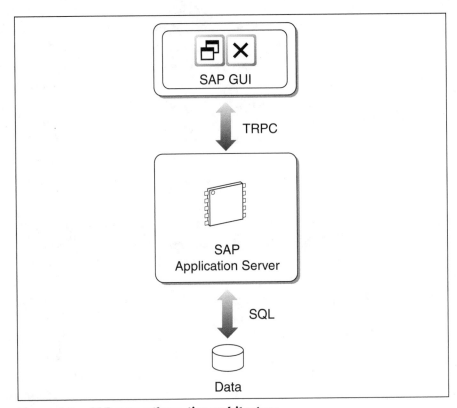

Figure A.2   SAP uses a three-tier architecture.

SAP Adapters and Connectors

Most advanced middleware layers, such as application servers and message brokers, provide adapters or connectors to SAP R/3. However, most of these, although promising easy connections to SAP, typically solve only portions of the problem.

Middleware vendors provide adapters or connectors to better position and sell their middleware. This is a wise marketing strategy. After all, most enterprises leverage packaged applications such as SAP. Many middleware products are purchased less for their inherent merits than for the availability of adapters or connectors. Unfortunately, such purchases are mistakes. Each middleware vendor has its own definition of an "adapter." These can range from the most primitive API layers and simple exits to easy-to-use connectors that hide the complexity of the SAP interface from the B2B application integration architect and developer. The latter is the best solution—as long as the underlying middleware transport layer meets the particular needs of the solution set as well.

The moral is the same moral of all purchases—*caveat emptor!* Buyer beware! Ask many questions when selecting an B2B application integration—enabled middleware product or vendor-provided SAP connectors or adapters. Which SAP interface (or interfaces) do they leverage? How do they move the information? Do they handle transformation? How much custom programming is involved? A pilot test wouldn't be a bad idea either.

---

platforms and operating systems, including most popular flavors of UNIX and Windows NT. You can mix and match operating systems at the client, the application server, and the database levels, making the SAP architecture both flexible and scalable. SAP uses the Advanced Business Application Programming (ABAP/4) language, along with the ABAP/4 development workbench and toolset, to configure and customize R/3.

The other basic services supporting R/3 include printing, security, and communications. In addition to these services, R/3 allows the interplay of applications, user interfaces, and data. The movement of this information is provided through the use of standard interfaces, application interfaces, and open data formats. These

services constitute the basis of SAP's ability to integrate applications. We will further explore these services later in this appendix.

SAP supports most major standards, including TCP/IP, SQL, OLE, X.400/500, and EDI. It also supports its own Remote Function Call (RFC), which enables remote calling to SAP functions from other systems. RFC was originally built by SAP for use by other linked SAP systems. However, over time RFC has become the primary interface for most B2B application integration efforts.

The SAP Repository

SAP provides an advanced repository that contains a description of all metadata, modules, and processes. This information includes screen forms, business rules, and the location of application servers. In the SAP scheme, all applications are extracted from the repository and sent to the connected application servers, providing automatic updates for system upgrades.

The SAP Presentation Layer

The SAP clients are very thin, very terminal-like. The client communicates with the application server and presentation server and simply provides the interface to the end user. One such SAP client is a GUI that supports Windows 98/2000, Windows NT, OS/2, OSF/Motif, and Apple Macintosh.

The SAP Application Server Layer

The application server is able to perform all of the application and interface processing in addition to providing such rudimentary transaction-processing features as load balancing and fail-over. The R/3 architecture allows the application tier to uncouple from the presentation and data tiers.

The SAP Database Layer

The database simply provides a location for data storage. It handles data access through the use of SAP SQL, which is at its heart a standard SQL called from within the ABAP/4 toolset. Because relational database systems offer different subsets of standard SQL functions, the ABAP/4 toolset supports SQL at two levels: SAP SQL and native SQL. The database interface translates SAP SQL into the native SQL dialect. It is possible to use either of these two levels (see Figure A.3). Note that most relational databases, such as Oracle, Informix, and SQL Server, work with SAP R/3.

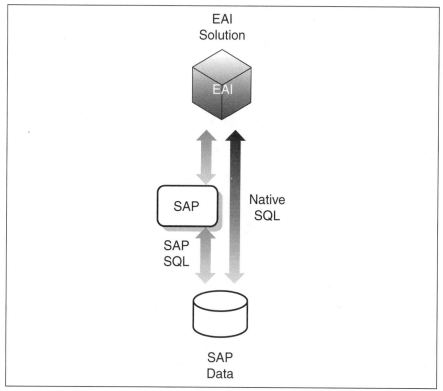

Figure A.3   **SAP provides two levels of database access, either of which can be leveraged for integration.**

SAP Middleware

SAP uses traditional and proprietary middleware layers. Program-to-program communications are implemented with the older Common Programming Interface for Communications (CPI-C). RFCs are the most prevalent mechanism to mine SAP processes and data. The other layers, such as Java and COM access, are nothing more than wraparound RFCs.

CPI-C

CPI-C, an older middleware layer left over from the days when traditional IBM mainframes roamed the earth, is part of IBM's System Application Architecture (SAA) of the late 1980s. CPI-C is included in ABAP/4, allowing an ABAP/4 program to link to a CPI-C session. The program-to-program communications are

always performed via an internal gateway that handles the conversion of CPI-C communications to external protocols, including TCP/IP and LU6.2.

If asynchronous communications are required, SAP supports the notion of queues, allowing a system to create a queue for transmission to another SAP system at a later time. The Queue Application Programming Interface (Q-API) handles this process. SAP is able to use this interface to accept information into the system through standard batch processing. Although some people judge this practice as inelegant and outdated, it's still in wide use.

RFC

Although CPI-C and Q-API provide mechanisms that allow SAP to communicate with the outside world, many people find these "traditional" middleware mechanisms limiting and unable to support SAP's more advanced features, including RFC, which is included in ABAP/4. RFCs remain the mechanism for accessing the SAP program interface. They provide a standard procedural approach for moving all sorts of information into and out of SAP.

RFCs are callable from a multitude of platforms, development environments, and applications. The R/3 Automation Software Development Kit provides RFC libraries and RFC DLLs, user dialogs, and an error-processing facility. Documentation and sample programs for RFCs are included in this software, allowing access to SAP processes and data from standard software such as Microsoft Excel, PowerBuilder, Visual Basic, C++, and Java. Even more beneficial is the ability to access RFCs using other, more "standard" Microsoft interfaces such as COM, COM+, and OLE DB.

RFC brings program-to-program communications to SAP, allowing B2B application integration architects and developers to incorporate business objects across several platforms, programs, and databases (see Figure A.4). RFCs hide the layer of CPI-C calls (the actual communications mechanism used by SAP) from those using RFCs.

Transactions and RFCs

The question remains, Why use RFCs when it is possible to go directly to the database? Although there are many reasons to do so, the most compelling is transactional integrity. It is simply too dangerous to read and write directly to the SAP database without using the application server, which controls access to the data and thus enforces database integrity. For example, simply updating customer information within SAP could mean invoking a single transaction that is

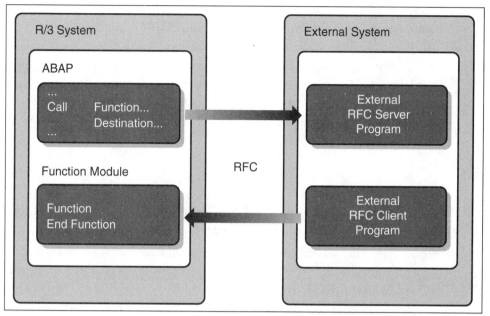

Figure A.4   RFC provides program-to-program communications for SAP.

linked to several hundred tables. Without using the transaction contained on the application server, it would be necessary to update each table in the same order, making sure that the data is in the proper format. Although it is certainly possible to do all this, why not take the easier and safer route of updating and accessing information using the application server layer, using RFC? Without question, doing so is the safest bet.

RFCs ensure transactional integrity by making sure calls are executed in the same order and within the same program context. In addition, RFCs guarantee that a single RFC is not invoked more than one time and that the status of an RFC call may be accessed at any time.

RFCs are synchronous calls (recall, they are really RPCs). However, you can use queues to place requests for RFCs for later processing or to process when the SAP server returns to life. You can also leverage other middleware to make RFCs asynchronous. Message-brokering technology is particularly valuable in this regard.

At base, RFC technology is a middleware technology meant to interface with other middleware. As a result, although you can use an RFC to access a SAP system directly, it is more common to bind RFCs to a more traditional middleware

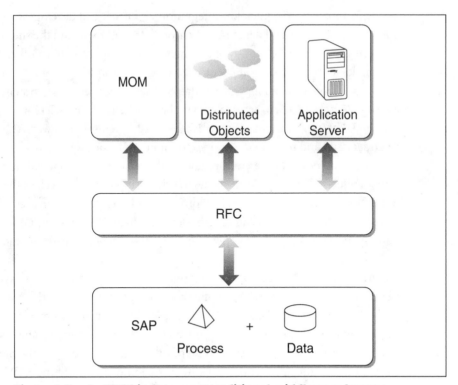

Figure A.5   An RFC binds to most traditional middleware layers.

layer, such as MOM, distributed objects, or application servers (see Figure A.5). Bear in mind that the links to RFCs don't magically occur. In most cases those links will have to be created from scratch—or leveraged from a SAP adapter that may come with the middleware.

ALE

Knowing what's going on behind the scenes, we can turn our attention to the heart of B2B application integration access to SAP. It lies within the Application Link Enabling (ALE) technology, which is able to combine business process with middleware. ALE provides a robust distributed architecture for SAP, providing transparent distributed access to SAP data and processes. The ALE architecture is also essential for moving information to non-SAP systems and ultimately supporting the entire B2B application integration effort.

ALE allows B2B application integration architects and developers to set up application modules and databases at various sites and then bind the sites in both a business process– and data-oriented method (see Figure A.6). In other words, they make several SAP sites appear to be a single monolithic system.

In addition to enabling simple data exchange between SAP systems, ALE allows external systems to access SAP. This benefit results from "tricking" ALE into thinking that it's communicating with other SAP systems. In this way, ALE is able to understand and route data required to support a business process.

ALE provides a competent mechanism that enables B2B application integration architects, developers, and clients to achieve integration as well as the distribution of applications and data. SAP provides ALE technology with a set of tools, programs, data definitions, and methodologies that B2B application integration developers or vendors may apply to unlock the information from traditional SAP systems.

ALE consists of three layers: the application layer, the distribution layer, and the communications layer. The application layer provides ALE with an interface to the R/3 application. This interface is needed in order to send or receive messages to and from the SAP system you're attempting to integrate. The distribution layer, applying a predetermined set of rules, filters and converts the messages containing the information that is being moved into and out of the SAP system. This capability is required because of the different releases of SAP (R/2 and R/3). (It is not a substitute for transformation engines, such as message brokers, which

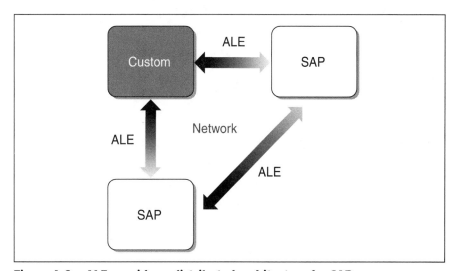

Figure A.6   ALE provides a distributed architecture for SAP.

make short work of B2B application integration.) The communications layer carries out the communications between systems, both asynchronously (for the transmission of data) and synchronously (for the transmission of control information). The transactional RFC (tRFC) mechanism allows the real-time exchange of information.

IDOC

An Intermediate Document (IDOC) is a structured information set providing a standard format for moving information into and out of a SAP system. In this regard, it represents a similar concept to EDI, but IDOC is not a standard. You can invoke an RFC at the SAP level and get an IDOC as a result. That IDOC becomes a basis to structure a message that's transported through a standard middleware layer. For example, most message brokers are able to convert an IDOC into another format so it may be understood and processed by a target system.

IDOCs contain a control record, a data record, and a status record (see Figure A.7). Each IDOC is a single SAP business object. The control record contains

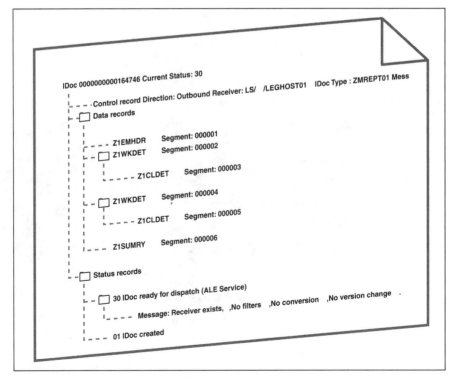

Figure A.7   Structure of an IDOC

several fields with information about the IDOC, such as its type, its sender, and its receiver. The data record contains the application data, and the status record contains information on the state of the document.

As a single business object, an IDOC may contain only one shipment document. This represents both an advantage and a limitation of IDOC; although it is easy to use (because of the simplicity of having only one business object per IDOC), a large number of IDOCs must be sent and received in order to handle real-time integration.

BAPI

Business Application Program Interfaces (BAPIs) provide an object-oriented mechanism to get at the underlying proprietary SAP middleware technology, such as RFCs (see Figure A.8). In addition to providing access to the data and

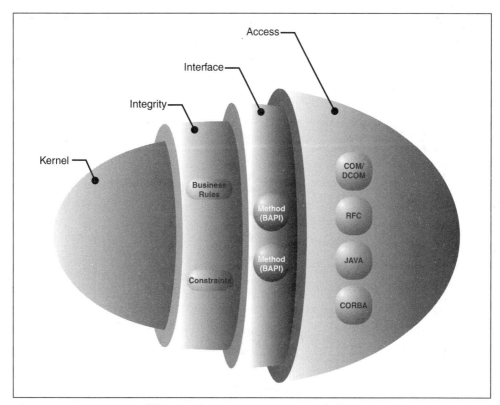

Figure A.8 **BAPIs provide an object-oriented layer existing above the SAP middleware (e.g., RFCs).**

processes, a benefit once only possible by means of specific methods, a BAPI allows access to the SAP business objects held in the Business Object Repository (BOR), encapsulated in their data and processes. In other words, a BAPI provides a layer of abstraction above the primitive interfaces that SAP provides.

To use a BAPI method, an application program simply needs to know how to call the method, such as knowing its structure and parameters. The BAPIs in the R/3 system are implemented as function modules, all of which are held in the Function Builder. Each function module underlying a BAPI supports the RFC protocol and has been assigned as a method to a SAP business object in the BOR.

The importance of BAPIs resides in the power they give developers to provide SAP access from many different tools and technologies. For example, using the BAPI interface makes it easy to build applications that are able to gather information from SAP without having to drop down to primitive function calls. However, a BAPI does not provide everything needed to access SAP as a true set of objects. For example, a BAPI provides access to only a limited number of functions. However, BAPIs are expanding their reach every day.

Using the Repository

The SAP repository, as mentioned previously, contains most of its business engineering information, including business models, programs, and objects. The R/3 repository is also the container for all of R/3's application information, including development and design information. The repository comprises the business- and application-related metadata and provides a means to explore the features and functions of a SAP system in order to provide better integration.

The advantage of using the SAP repository is the ability to discover as much as possible about the SAP system that is to be integrated. This knowledge enables the B2B application integration architect and developer to automatically link SAP with other systems in a business object–oriented (method-oriented) or data-oriented way, without having to create a common set of functions.

Although using the SAP repository requires a more sophisticated level of B2B application integration, the ability to react automatically to changes to the source or target SAP system makes a compelling argument for going to that next level. Many who are integrating SAP have leveraged the repository as a mechanism to intelligently integrate the system. The real value of this approach will come from vendors that are looking to create B2B application integration solutions that link deeply into SAP. Currently, the SAP adapters are more at the RFC level and do not take into account the content of the repository.

SAP and B2B Application Integration

SAP is a dynamic ERP and is constantly morphing into new, more marketable products. This evolution will only drive the need for additional integration and will certainly add to the already formidable challenge of integrating SAP. For example, SAP is going to sell Web-delivered application services for mid-market companies. Thus, you do not need to host your own copy of SAP. Although this capability does provide a low-cost alternative to hosting your own SAP R/3 system (which runs in the millions of dollars), the integration complexities of this approach have yet to be considered.

SAP will be a part of most B2B application integration efforts where an ERP is involved. Fortunately, many people have already been down this road and cleared a trail of approaches, interfaces, and technology that make it possible to move information into and out of SAP. The question is, How much is SAP going to change to accommodate the new interest in B2B application integration? As SAP matures, it must provide better interfaces than it currently has, if it is to successfully open up. At this time, most SAP systems accomplish integration in such a way that they reach a wider set of technologies. In the end, ERPs may all have standard connections, allowing ERP systems to appear as databases, Java objects, or distributed objects. If that occurs, ERP systems such as SAP will be able to be bound seamlessly with existing enterprise applications—which is exactly where they'll have the most value.

Integrating PeopleSoft

Of all the popular ERP packages, PeopleSoft is the most open—which is not to suggest that it is simple or easy to use. This beast is very difficult. It provides the least amount of information on how it can be integrated with the rest of the enterprise. In fact, obtaining information for this chapter was a bit of a challenge. Fortunately, there are enough projects, and vendors muddling through with them, to allow us to elucidate some basic approaches.

PeopleSoft is significantly less proprietary than SAP. As such, it provides greater opportunity for integration without forcing the B2B application integration architect and developer to rely on the vendor interface. PeopleSoft interfaces, however, are hardly cut-and-dried. In order to create an optimal B2B application integration solution, you need to understand the native and enabling technologies of PeopleSoft.

This world, however, could be changing for PeopleSoft. PeopleSoft has already announced and loosely defined its Open Integration Framework. Although OIF does not define its B2B application integration technology in detail, it does more clearly outline the options that are available to those looking to integrate with PeopleSoft, including up-to-date mechanisms such as XML and the latest Business Component API, appearing with PeopleTools 8.

PeopleSoft Architecture

Like SAP, PeopleSoft uses standard relational databases for information storage, allowing the possibility of mixing and matching databases between modules (see Figure B.1). The databases provide the best point of integration—as long as there is no need to access the business processes that are encapsulated within the application. There are ways to accomplish this as well but not as readily.

Unlike SAP, the PeopleSoft application server is based on open technology— BEA's Tuxedo. Because there are tools and techniques to access transactions on the Tuxedo platform, there is another point of integration. In spite of this additional benefit, PeopleSoft does not promote going directly to the application server (TP monitor).

PeopleSoft relies on a three-tier client/server architecture with a client, an application server, and a database (see Figure B.2). The client communicates with the application server, which in turn communicates with the database. This architecture provides PeopleSoft with good scaling capabilities and an extensible architecture.

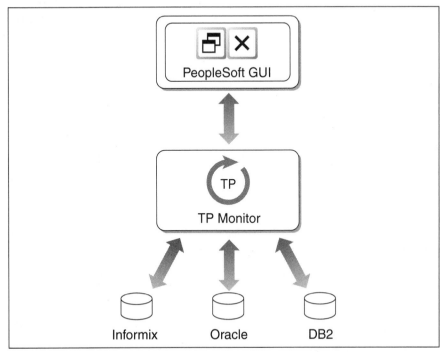

Figure B.1   **PeopleSoft is able to communicate with a number of relational databases.**

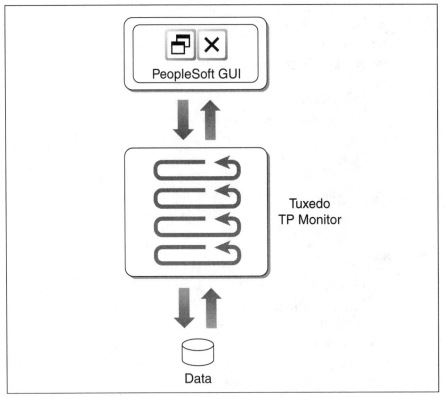

PeopleSoft GUI

Tuxedo
TP Monitor

Data

Figure B.2   PeopleSoft, like SAP, uses a three-tier client/server architecture.

The supplemental products offered with the PeopleSoft application solution include

- PeopleSoft Financials
- PeopleSoft Distribution
- PeopleSoft Manufacturing
- PeopleSoft HRMS
- PeopleTools

PeopleSoft Financials provides a general ledger system, payables, receivables, asset management, projects, budgets, treasury, and expenses. PeopleSoft Distribution provides purchasing, inventory, order management, billing, enterprise planning, demand planning, and product configuration. PeopleSoft Manufacturing provides bills and routings, production management, production planning, cost

management, engineering, and quality management. PeopleSoft HRMS (Human Resources Management System) provides payroll, time and labor, pension administration, Field Sales Automation (FSA) administration, benefits administration, and stock administration. PeopleTools is an application development environment that enables the PeopleSoft developer to customize, maintain, and implement PeopleSoft applications without changing the PeopleSoft source code.

PeopleTools provides facilities for modifying panels, records, and menus as well as importing information from other systems. PeopleTools also provides a facility for reporting.

Although the methods for moving information into and out of PeopleSoft are not well defined, we can define some approaches to PeopleSoft integration: data-oriented and application interface–oriented.

Data-Oriented

Fundamentally, data-oriented PeopleSoft application integration is data-oriented B2B application integration. This means that information can be moved into and out of PeopleSoft-supported relational databases (including Oracle, Informix, and SQL Server) in order to integrate PeopleSoft with other external applications in the data-oriented method. This is accomplished with any number of database-oriented middleware products, message brokers, data migration software packages, or even with the replication and data link features of most popular relational databases.

As in any other data-to-data integration effort, you must first understand the structure of the database or databases from which information is being extracted as well as the structure and integrity features of the database that is receiving the data.

PeopleSoft provides B2B application integration architects and developers with well-defined database schema information and a built-in database movement facility (although not real-time). This approach includes the Data Mover and SQRs and leveraging the PeopleSoft Workflow interfaces.

Data Mover

The PeopleSoft Data Mover is a platform-independent PeopleTools feature that enables the user to transfer data between PeopleSoft databases and to unload and reload data from other external, non-PeopleSoft databases. Data Mover may also be used for archiving data. Although this is a useful tool, more traditional database-to-database integration solutions may be the better choice.

SQRs and Moving Data

PeopleSoft provides a tool known as SQR, a reporting tool that's part of all PeopleSoft applications. This tool allows the exchange of data between two databases with different data structures. In order to use this tool for data movement, developers must first write two SQR procedures. The first procedure runs against the source database, selecting the appropriate data. This information is then placed into a sequential file. A second SQR procedure reads the sequential file and updates the target databases (see Figure B.3). PeopleSoft Process Scheduler allows the user to schedule regular transfers of this information. (This is not a real-time solution but more of a batch-oriented one.)

Workflow and Moving Data

Within the PeopleSoft environment, workflow activities and worklists can be triggered to established database agents. These database agents are able to monitor one or more tables in the databases, searching for conditions that should trigger an event. Features found in most relational databases, such as database links, enable workflow activities to also be triggered by events occurring within remote databases.

Workflow activities for multiple databases are set up by first creating the appropriate external tables as database links from the source database (if supported), then creating an agent to monitor the tables awaiting an event (such as a change in state, deletion of a row, or insertion of a row). This mechanism may be

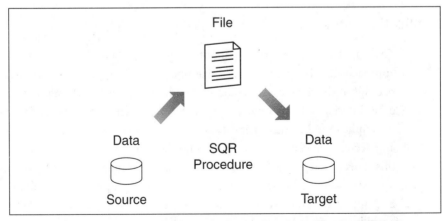

Figure B.3   Using SQR procedures to move data between PeopleSoft databases

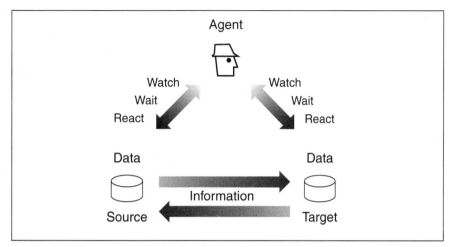

Figure B.4   Using a PeopleSoft database agent to move information between two databases

leveraged for B2B application integration by using the agent to watch for changes in the source database, such as a table update.

When such an event occurs, a stored procedure or replication process could be fired off to move the appropriate data from a source database to a target database (see Figure B.4). In this way, a "mini message broker using intelligent agent technology" is being created. However, note that this PeopleSoft mechanism was not designed exclusively for database movement.

Application Interface–Oriented

There is nothing remarkable about PeopleSoft's database-oriented integration approach. It is independent of the application, leaving the user to deal with the package at the database and database middleware levels. Leveraging some of the other interfaces that PeopleSoft provides for accessing not only the data stored in the application but the business information as well (e.g., invoices, work orders, and accounts receivable reports) requires a bit more sophistication. If we grade this aspect of PeopleSoft, it earns a C– (SAP isn't much better, earning only a C) for the quality of interfaces that it provides for this purpose. Fortunately, most B2B application integration middleware vendors (e.g., message broker vendors) provide interfaces to PeopleSoft. As a result, it may be possible to obtain appropriate technology and avoid having to understand the details of the interface.

Proper integration of PeopleSoft with the rest of the enterprise requires an understanding of other existing interfaces. As the PeopleSoft product matures, it's a good bet that PeopleSoft will enhance its business-oriented interfaces, opening up the PeopleSoft processes for other systems both inside and outside the enterprise.

Screen Scraping

Scraping screens to access application information has always been a viable option. In this regard, PeopleSoft is consistent with existing products. Using 3270, ASCII terminals, or even Windows user interface access mechanisms (e.g., COM automation), you can extract information from PeopleSoft. In fact, most of the interfaces that PeopleSoft provides for the application interface–oriented method already scrape screens.

EDI

Although there are many ways to move information into and out of PeopleSoft, most consider EDI, which exists to exchange business information with systems outside the enterprise, to be the best overall solution. Although the PeopleSoft EDI interface was not created for B2B application integration, it works effectively in the B2B application integration domain.

The PeopleSoft EDI is like any other EDI interface in that you need to map the information within it in order to transmit it outside PeopleSoft. Once outside the PeopleSoft environment, the information may move to any system that understands EDI or be reformatted by a middle-tier middleware layer, such as a message broker or an application server (see Figure B.5). Such reformatting ensures that the target system will understand the message.

In the context of B2B application integration, EDI is a simple method to access relevant business data. It represents a method of "tricking" the PeopleSoft system into believing that information is being moved to and from a system existing at a trading partner. In actuality the interface is being used to exchange information between systems within the company. The enabling technologies that will make short work of this include EDI-mapping software, message brokers that can read and write EDI (EDI adapters), application servers with EDI connectors, and traditional queuing middleware such as MQSeries.

If this technology is not beyond the budget of the corporation, it could well be the best bet for situations requiring the exchange of application information and not just simple data.

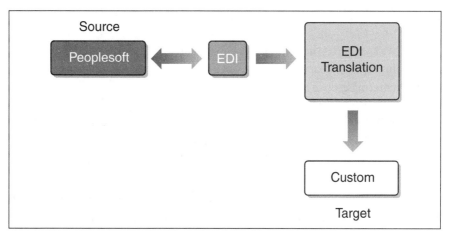

Figure B.5   EDI can be used to move information into and out of PeopleSoft.

Workflow

The PeopleSoft Workflow subsystem enables the user to integrate rules, roles, and routing associated with the localized processing of the enterprise. Clever B2B application integration architects and developers may incorporate this workflow mechanism as a method to integrate PeopleSoft with other applications. Although the database agent has been discussed previously, you can use similar techniques to send and receive electronic forms and messages.

Application Designer

The PeopleSoft Application Designer can be used as the graphical tool for creating visual business process maps to define workflow scenarios. Again, although this feature was not created for B2B application integration, moving information between PeopleSoft modules is particularly suited to the needs of B2B application integration in that it creates the opportunity to move information out of PeopleSoft.

Message Agent API

The PeopleSoft Workflow subsystem provides a Message Agent API that allows third-party applications to integrate with PeopleSoft Workflow. This interface processes electronic messages sent to and from PeopleSoft. These messages may be sent through COM automation, a C program, or Windows Dynamic Data Exchange (DDE) as well.

Business Component API

PeopleSoft's Business Component API, new with PeopleTools 8, allows internal and external applications to invoke business rules encapsulated within PeopleSoft. The Business Component API is also able to perform simple data access operations. This interface provides a high-level abstraction layer hiding the complexities of the PeopleSoft system from developers who invoke the Business Component API.

The Business Component API employs online business component logic running through a set of processing events. When creating the logic, business component–specific events provide the infrastructure for sharing components between external applications and transition logic. This API is accessible through C++ or COM and is analogous to SAP's BAPI.

Workstation

In addition to moving information between databases or using the workflow or EDI interfaces, you can integrate PeopleSoft with other applications that traditionally exist on the desktop. By using utilities that are provided within PeopleTools, you can invoke another workstation application. For example, the WinExec function can be run synchronously or asynchronously. This mechanism is used to launch such Windows applications as Microsoft Excel.

PeopleSoft also supports COM automation, allowing PeopleSoft to control a Windows application through this standard interface. PeopleTools includes a set of COM functions that allow PeopleSoft applications to appear as a COM automation client on a COM automation server existing on a Windows-based PC (see Figure B.6). These functions include creating an instance of a COM automation object, obtaining COM properties, setting properties, and invoking methods existing on the automation server. DCOM may also be used to extend COM automation over a network as a true distributed object.

In addition to supporting COM automation, PeopleSoft supports external DLLs using the PeopleCode scripting language. This feature allows PeopleSoft

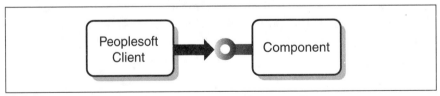

Figure B.6   PeopleSoft is able to be a COM automation client to another application existing on a PC.

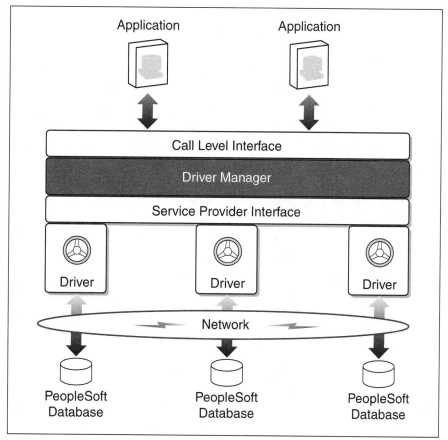

Figure B.7   Using ODBC to access PeopleSoft data

applications to call an external C function defined in a Windows DLL, giving the developer a low-level interface to hook PeopleSoft into desktop tools and applications.

You can also access PeopleSoft data by using ODBC and going directly to the databases. This method allows you to view PeopleSoft data within any Windows application that supports ODBC, such as Visual Basic and Excel (see Figure B.7).

What's Best?

Before integrating PeopleSoft with other enterprise applications, you need to understand the architecture, the modules, and the various interfaces available. In

addition, you should be familiar with the details of the database schema, along with the best mechanisms to access the data. For most B2B application integration projects, the best method to access PeopleSoft information is through the standard database interfaces. Standard technology—including database middleware, data replication and translation software, and message brokers—allows for access and movement of data as well as the translation of the schema and content.

As with every other data-oriented approach, you must consider both data integrity issues and how the data is bound to the application logic. PeopleSoft provides most of the necessary information, but testing and then retesting is still a smart move to ensure that a particular B2B application integration solution is the correct one.

The PeopleSoft application interfaces are adequate. The EDI interface is the best choice for moving business information into and out of PeopleSoft. It's designed to share information with external systems, making it a good mechanism to exchange business data with other applications both inside and outside the enterprise. Unfortunately, like most EDI-based B2B application integration solutions, the enabling technology is expensive. What's more, it is difficult to move information out of PeopleSoft on a real-time basis; near-time is the best to be hoped for.

Although the workflow interface shows real promise, it's still not much more than a mechanism that uses agents to monitor and react to events as it moves data between databases. If PeopleSoft can build on this interface and provide true message-brokering features, it may be better able to open its business information to the outside world.

The workstation integration tools are little more than methods to integrate PeopleSoft with a Windows-based PC, providing only rudimentary mechanisms to share information and methods. Not only is this handy for client-to-PeopleSoft integration, it may also be useful to B2B application integration architects and developers looking to integrate PeopleSoft as a set of COM objects. PeopleSoft, however, needs to do some more work to make complete integration through COM a reality.

PeopleSoft will continue to be a leading ERP in the packaged application marketplace, second only to SAP in the number of installations. As the PeopleSoft installations settle in for the long haul, integration will become the next big problem to solve. In an effort to solve this problem, look to PeopleSoft to shore up the interfaces into its software.

PIP™ Specification— PIP3A1: Request Quote

Cluster 3: Order Management
Segment A: Quote and Order Entry

Beta 01.00.00B
22 May 2000

RosettaNet

Contents

1 Document Management

1.1 Legal Disclaimer

RosettaNet™, its members, officers, directors, employees, or agents shall not be liable for any injury, loss, damages, financial or otherwise, arising from, related to, or caused by the use of this document or the specifications herein, as well as associated guidelines and schemas. The use of said specifications shall constitute your express consent to the foregoing exculpation.

1.2 Copyright

1.3 Trademarks

RosettaNet, Partner Interface Process, PIP and the RosettaNet logo are trademarks or registered trademarks of "RosettaNet," a non-profit organization. All other product names and company logos mentioned herein are the trademarks of their respective owners. In the best effort, all terms mentioned in this document that are known to be trademarks or registered trademarks have been appropriately recognized in the first occurrence of the term.

Trademark or Registered Trademark		*Company or Organization*
D-U-N-S	Data Universal Numbering System	Dun & Bradstreet

1.4 Acknowledgments

This document has been prepared by Edifecs Commerce (http://www.edifecs.com, http://www.CommerceDesk.com) from requirements in conformance with the RosettaNet methodology.

1.5 Prerequisites

The audience should be familiar with the RosettaNet User's Guide, "Understanding a PIP Blueprint." This document can be downloaded from the RosettaNet EConcert Document Library at the following web address.

http://www.rosettanet.org/usersguides/

1.6 Related Documents

- RosettaNet IT Technical Dictionary
  http://www.rosettanet.org/techdictionaries/
- RosettaNet Business Dictionary
  http://www.rosettanet.org/businessdictionary/

1.7 Supply Chain Requirements

This PIP includes design and technology requirements utilized in the supply chains listed below.

1. Information Technology

1.8 Document Version History

Version	Date	PIP Specification Development
Beta 01.00.00A	14 Apr 2000	RosettaNet: approved, untested, published Specification
Beta 01.00.00B	22 May 2000	Edifecs Commerce: Per DRT, Message Guidelines changes to line items 6 and 101 authorized by RosettaNet.

2 Introduction

A Partner Interface Process (PIP) Specification comprises the following three views of the ebusiness PIP model.

1. **Business Operational View (BOV).** Captures the semantics of business data entities and their flow of exchange between roles as they perform business activities. The content of the BOV section is based on the PIP Blueprint document created for RosettaNet's business community.

2. **Functional Service View (FSV).** Specifies the network component services and agents and the interactions necessary to execute PIPs. The FSV includes all of the transaction dialogs in a PIP Protocol. The purpose of the FSV is to specify a PIP Protocol that is systematically derived from the BOV. The two major components within the FSV are the network component design and network component interactions.

3. **Implementation Framework View (IFV).** Specifies the network protocol message formats and communications requirements between peer-protocols supported by network components in the RosettaNet Implementation

Framework. These messages are exchanged when software programs execute a PIP; RosettaNet distributes these as XML Message Guidelines.

3 Business Operational View

3.1 Business Process Definition

The Request Quote Partner Interface Process (PIP) allows a Buyer to request a product quote from a Seller. The Seller may return a quote, or a referral to another Seller. The Buyer then has the option of requesting a quote from the referral.

Quotes may involve:

- One or more items.
- Fixed price quotes or negotiated prices.
- Configurable or standalone product.

The PIP supports following two scenarios:

1. The first scenario is a simple one, involving only two entities; a Buyer, who requests a quote, and a Seller that provides the quote. For example, "Generic Reseller" might request a quote from "ABC Distributor" who will provide the quote back to "Generic Reseller."
2. The second scenario is similar to the first, except that the Seller returns a referral to a different Seller. For example, Buyer "Generic Reseller" might request a quote from Seller "ABC Distributor" who returns a referral to Seller "Acme Keyboards" in the Quote Response. The Buyer then has the option of sending a new Quote Request to the Seller "Acme Keyboards" referred in the Quote Response.

3.2 PIP Purpose

The purpose of the PIP is to support a process between trading partners that involves requesting and providing quotes.

3.3   PIP Business Process Flow Diagram

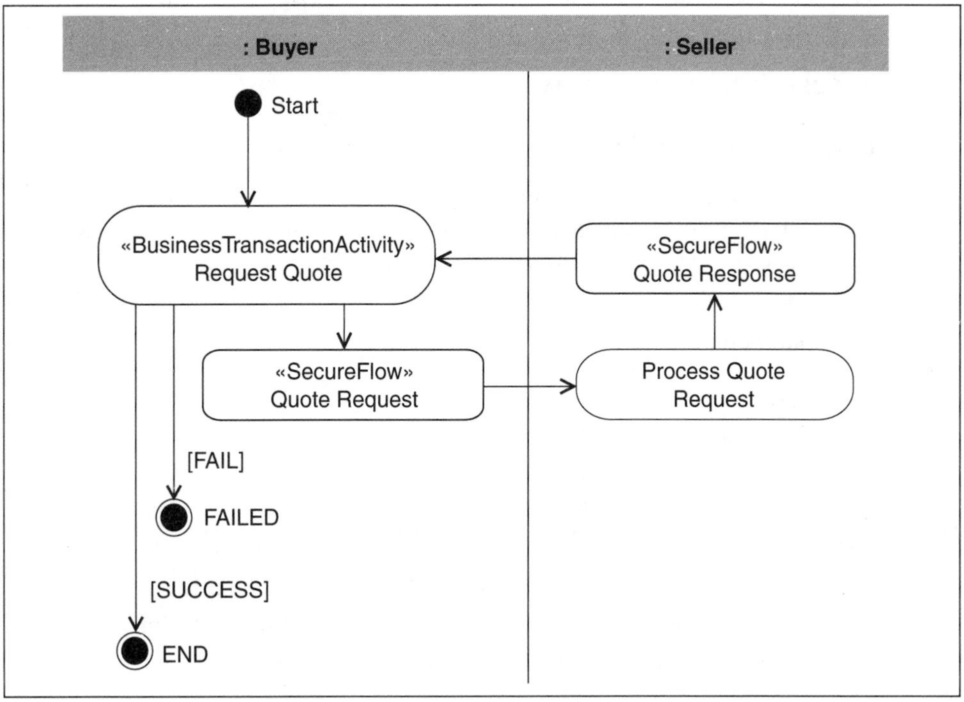

Figure 3.1   Request Quote

3.4   PIP Start State

The start state is comprised of the following condition:
- A valid Trading Partner Agreement must be in place between the Buyer and Seller.

3.5   PIP End States

End states are comprised of one or more conditions:

END

- Quote Response was received from Seller.

FAILED

- PIP0A1, "Notification of Failure," has been executed. (This is a RosettaNet convention.)
- Quote Response was not received from Seller.

3.6   Partner Role Descriptions

Table 3.1 describes the partner roles in this PIP.

Table 3.1   Partner Role Descriptions

Role Name	Role Description	Role Type
Buyer	An employee that buys products for a partner type in the supply chain.	Functional
Seller	The role is performed by any organization that provides initial quotes to a Buyer.	Organizational

3.7   Business Process Activity Controls

Table 3.2 describes the interaction contract between roles performing business activities in this PIP.

Table 3.2   Business Activity Descriptions

Role Name	Activity Name	Activity Description	Pre-Conditions	Post-Conditions
Buyer	Request Quote	Activity requests a quote from a Seller.	D&B D-U-N-S Number® of the Seller and GTIN are provided.	Quote Request sent.

Table 3.3 details the security, audit and process controls relating to activities performed in the PIP.

Table 3.3   Business Activity Performance Controls

Role Name	Activity Name	Acknowledgment of Receipt			Time to Perform	Retry Count	Is Authorization Required?	Non-Repudiation of Origin and Content?
		Non-Repudiation Required?	Time to Acknowledge	Time to Acknowledge Acceptance				
Buyer	Request Quote	Y	2 hr	N/A	24 hrs	3	Y	Y

3.8   PIP Blueprint Data

3.8.1   PIP Business Documents

Business Documents listed in Table 3.4 are exchanged by roles performing activities in this PIP. The Business Documents can be downloaded from the RosettaNet Business Document Repository using the Uniform Resource Locator (URL) specified Section 1.6, "Related Documents."

Table 3.4   PIP Business Documents

Business Document	Description
Quote Request	Request for a quote from a Seller.
Quote Response	The response to a Buyer for a product quote. Allows for an actual quote, or a referral to another Seller.

3.9   Business Data Entities

The business data entities, fundamental business data entities, and global identifying properties can be found in the RosettaNet Business Dictionary using the URL specified in Section 1.6, "Related Documents."

3.9.1   Business Data Entity Security

There are no security controls specified for this PIP.

4   Functional Service View

This Functional Service View (FSV) of the ebusiness partner interface process defines the business actions and their flow (exchange) between network components that support business activities. The purpose of the functional service view is to specify a PIP protocol that is systematically derived from the business operational view of the PIP model. There are two major components to the FSV:

1. A network component design comprising Agent components and Business Service components. These components enable roles to perform business activities in a networked environment.

2. A specification of the possible network component interactions that are necessary to execute the PIP using the specified Agent and Business Service components.

4.1   Network Component Design

A network component design specifies the network components necessary to execute the PIP and the network component collaboration. A network component design is comprised of Agent components and Business Service components that enable roles to perform business activities in a networked environment. Network components collaborate by exchanging business action messages and business signal messages.

4.1.1   Network Component Collaboration

Figure 4.1 specifies the network components and their message exchange.

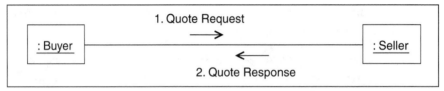

Figure 4.1   Request Quote Collaboration

4.1.2   Network Component Specification

Each network component maps onto a role in the BOV of the PIP model. Table 4.1 specifies the mapping between roles in the BOV and network components in the FSV.

Table 4.1   Network Component Specification

Network Component in FSV	Classification	Maps to Role in BOV
Seller Service	Business Service	Seller
Seller Agent	Agent	Seller
Buyer Service	Business Service	Buyer
Buyer Agent	Agent	Buyer

4.2 Business Action and Business Signal Specification

Each business action maps onto a Business Document in the BOV of the PIP model. Table 4.2 specifies the mapping between Business Documents in the BOV and business actions in the FSV.

Table 4.2 Business Action—Business Document Mapping

Business Action in FSV	Maps to Business Document in BOV
Quote Request Action	Quote Request
Quote Response Action	Quote Response

4.3 Business Transaction Dialog Specification

Each business activity between roles in the BOV is specified as a business transaction dialog between network components. There are two fundamental network components modeled in the Functional Service View.

1. **Service network component.** Implements protocols that include the service layer, transaction and action layer. A service has "network identity" as a business service. The service has an identity URI that can be registered in directories and used for component communication in a distributed computer system.
2. **Agent network component.** Implements protocols that include the action layer and the agent layer. There is no service layer or transaction layer.

The FSV allows the following network component interaction configurations.

1. **Agent-Service interaction configuration.** An agent can request service from a service component and a service can respond to the request. Agents cannot respond to requests for service.
2. **Service-Service interaction configuration.** There can be any number of services between end-point services, but no agents. Services both provide services to agents and other requesting services as well as request services for other services.
3. **Agent-Agent interaction configuration.** One agent can transfer an action to another agent.

From these three interaction configurations it is possible to derive three additional network-component configurations specific to a trading partner agreement.

1. **Service-Agent-Service interaction configuration.** Services interact using two or more agents as a bridge. This configuration is typical in configurations where the two services do not know each other's identity, or when an employee must include additional private information to an action that is sent to another service.
2. **Service-Service-Agent interaction configuration.** The second service acts as a mailbox for the agent.
3. **Agent-Service-Service interaction configuration.** A service-to-service transaction is a sub-transaction of a larger agent-service transaction.

The rest of section 4.3 specifies the network component configurations possible for this PIP. Each figure specifies the message exchange sequence as network components collaborate to execute this PIP. Each table shows the properties for each of the messages exchanged by the interactions in the corresponding figure.

4.3.1 Request Quote Dialog: Service-Service

The following figure specifies the message exchange sequence as network components collaboration to execute this PIP.

Table 4.3 shows the properties for each of the messages exchanged by the interactions in Figure 4.2.

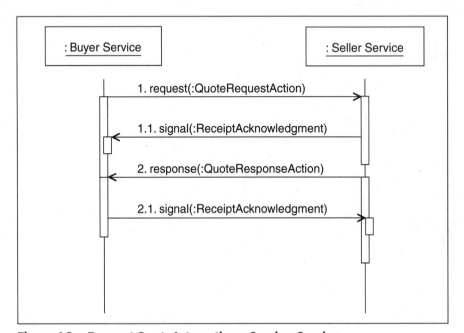

Figure 4.2   Request Quote Interactions: Service-Service

Table 4.3　Message Exchange Controls–Request Quote

#	Name	Time to Acknowledge Receipt	Time to Acknowledge Acceptance	Time to Respond	Included in Time to Perform	Is Authorization Required?	Is Non-Repudiation Required?	Is Secure Transport Required?
1.	Quote Request Action	2 hrs	N/A	24 hrs	Y	Y	Y	Y
1.1.	Receipt Acknowledgment	N/A	N/A	N/A	Y	Y	Y	Y
2.	Quote Response Action	2 hrs	N/A	N/A	Y	Y	Y	Y
2.1.	Receipt Acknowledgment	N/A	N/A	N/A	N	Y	N	Y

4.3.2　*Request Quote Dialog: Service-Agent-Service*

Figure 4.3 specifies the message exchange sequence as network components collaborate to execute this PIP.

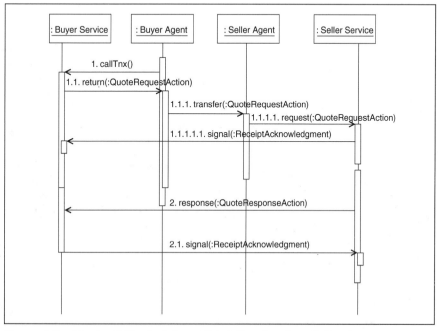

Figure 4.3　Request Quote Interactions: Service-Agent-Service

Table 4.4 shows the properties for each of the messages exchanged by the interactions in Figure 4.3.

Table 4.4   Message Exchange Controls–Request Quote

#	Name	Time to Acknowledge Receipt	Time to Acknowledge Acceptance	Time to Respond	Included in Time to Perform	Is Authorization Required?	Is Non-Repudiation Required?	Is Secure Transport Required?
1.1.	Quote Request Action	2 hrs	N/A	24 hrs	Y	Y	Y	Y
1.1.1.	Quote Request Action	N/A	N/A	N/A	Y	N/A	N/A	Y
1.1.1.1.	Quote Request Action	N/A	N/A	N/A	Y	N/A	N/A	Y
1.1.1.1.1	Receipt Acknowledgment	N/A	N/A	N/A	Y	Y	Y	Y
2.	Quote Response Action	2 hrs	N/A	N/A	Y	Y	Y	Y
2.1.	Receipt Acknowledgment	N/A	N/A	N/A	N	Y	N	Y

4.3.3   *Request Quote Dialog: Agent-Service-Service*

Figure 4.4 specifies the message exchange sequence as network components collaboration to execute this PIP.

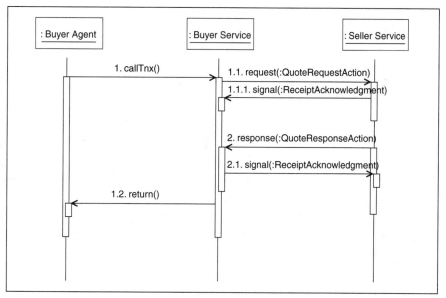

Figure 4.4   Request Quote Interactions: Agent-Service-Service

Table 4.5 shows the properties for each of the messages exchanged by the interactions in Figure 4.4.

Table 4.5   Message Exchange Controls–Request Quote

#	Name	Time to Acknowledge Receipt	Time to Acknowledge Acceptance	Time to Respond	Included in Time to Perform	Is Authorization Required?	Is Non-Repudiation Required?	Is Secure Transport Required?
1.1.	Quote Request Action	2 hrs	N/A	24 hrs	Y	Y	Y	Y
1.1.1	Receipt Acknowledgment	N/A	N/A	N/A	Y	Y	Y	Y
2.	Quote Response Action	2 hrs	N/A	N/A	Y	Y	Y	Y
2.1.	Receipt Acknowledgment	N/A	N/A	N/A	N	Y	N	Y

5 Implementation Framework View

The Implementation Framework View (IFV) of the PIP model specifies the message format and communications requirements between peer-protocols supported by network components in the RosettaNet Implementation Framework.

The following sections specify the business messages and their communications requirements for executing this PIP.

The Implementation Framework View (IFV) of the PIP model specifies the message format and communications requirements between peer-protocols supported by network components in the RosettaNet Implementation Framework.

The following sections specify the business messages and their communications requirements for executing this PIP.

5.1 Request Quote Dialog: Service-Service

Table 5.1 Business Message and Communications Specification

#	Business Message Guideline	Digital Signature Required?	SSL Required?
1.	Quote Request Guideline	Y	Y
1.1.	Receipt Acknowledgment Guideline	Y	Y
2.	Quote Response Guideline	Y	Y
2.1.	Receipt Acknowledgment Guideline	Y	Y

5.2 Request Quote Dialog: Agent-Service-Service

Table 5.2 Business Message and Communications Specification

#	Business Message Guideline	Digital Signature Required?	SSL Required?
1.1.1.	Quote Request Guideline	Y	Y
1.1.1.1.1.	Receipt Acknowledgment Guideline	Y	Y
2.	Quote Response Guideline	Y	Y
2.1.	Receipt Acknowledgment Guideline	Y	Y

5.3 Request Quote Dialog: Service-Agent-Service

Table 5.3 Business Message and Communications Specification

#	Business Message Guideline	Digital Signature Required?	SSL Required?
1.1.1.	Quote Request Guideline	Y	Y
1.1.1.1.	Receipt Acknowledgment Guideline	Y	Y
2.	Quote Response Guideline	Y	Y
2.1.	Receipt Acknowledgment Guideline	Y	Y

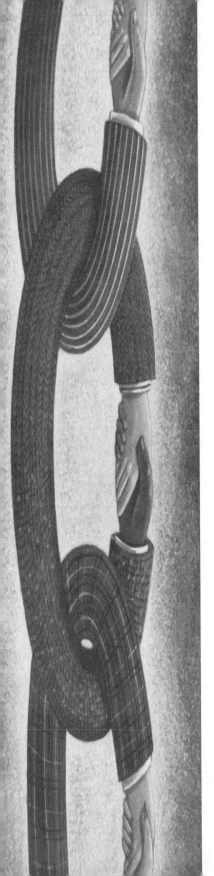

Bibliography

Aberdeen Group, "Advanced Technologies and a Sense of Process," *Aberdeen Group Report,* Boston, Mass., 1998.

Berson, A., *Client/Server Architecture,* New York: McGraw-Hill, 1992.

Black, U.D., *Data Communications and Distributed Networks,* 2d edition, Englewood Cliffs, N.J.: Yourdon Press, Prentice-Hall, 1987.

Boar, B.H., *Implementing Client/Server Computing, A Strategic Approach,* New York: McGraw-Hill, 1993.

Booch, G., *Object-Oriented Analysis and Design with Applications,* 2d edition, Redwood City, Calif.: Benjamin/Cummings, 1994.

———, *Unified Method for Object-Oriented Development,* Version 0.8, Rational Software Corporation, 1996.

Chorafas, D.N., *Systems Architecture & Systems Design,* New York: McGraw-Hill, 1989.

Claybrook, B., *OLTP, Online Transaction Processing Systems,* New York: John Wiley & Sons, 1992.

Coad, P., and E. Yourdon, *Object-Oriented Analysis,* 2d edition, Englewood Cliffs, N.J.: Prentice-Hall, 1991.

Date, C.J., *An Introduction to Database Systems,* vol. I, 4th edition, Reading, Mass.: Addison-Wesley, 1987.

———, *An Introduction to Database Systems,* vol. II, Reading, Mass.: Addison-Wesley, 1985.

Firesmith, D.G., *Object-Oriented Requirements Analysis and Logical Design, A Software Engineering Approach,* New York: John Wiley & Sons, 1993.

Freedman, A., *Computer Glossary,* 6th edition, New York: American Management Association, 1993.

Gartner Group, "Application Integration: Better Ways to Make Systems Work Together," *Gartner Group Conference Proceedings,* November 18–20, 1998.

Goldberg, A., *Object-Oriented Project Management,* Paris, France: Tutorial TOOLS, 1991.

Goldberg, A., and D. Robson, *Smalltalk-80: The Language,* Reading, Mass.: Addison-Wesley, 1989.

Gray, J., and A. Reuter, *Transaction Processing: Concepts and Techniques,* San Mateo, Calif.: Morgan Kaufmann Publishers, 1993.

Green, J.H., *Local Area Networks, A User's Guide for Business Professionals,* Glenview, Ill.: Scott, Foresman and Company, 1985.

Hackathorn, R.D., *Enterprise Database Connectivity,* New York: John Wiley & Sons, 1993.

Hutchison, D., *Local Area Network Architectures,* Reading, Mass.: Addison-Wesley, 1988.

Kerninghan, B.W., and D.M. Ritchie, *The C Programming Language,* 2d edition, Englewood Cliffs, N.J.: Prentice-Hall, 1988.

Krol, E., *The Whole Internet User's Guide and Catalog,* Cambridge, Mass.: O'Reilly & Associates, 1992.

Linthicum, D.S., *Enterprise Application Integration,* Reading, Mass.: Addison-Wesley, 2000.

———, *Guide to Client/Server and Intranet Development,* New York: John Wiley & Sons, 1997.

———, "Client/Server Protocols: Choosing the Right Connection," *DBMS Magazine* 7, no. 1 (1994): 60.

———, "Moving Away from the Network, Using Middleware," *DBMS Magazine* 7, no. 1 (1994): 66.

———, "Operating Systems for Database Servers," *DBMS Magazine* 7, no. 2 (1994): 62.

———, "Client/Server Strategy," *DBMS Magazine* 7, no. 4 (1994): 46.

———, "4GLs: Productivity at What Cost?" *DBMS Magazine* 7, no. 5 (1994): 22.

———, "A Better PC?" *DBMS Magazine* 7, no. 7 (1994): 24.

———, "Defending OOP with VisualAge," *DBMS Magazine* 7, no. 9 (1994): 22.

———, "CASE Does PowerBuilder," *DBMS Magazine* 7, no. 10 (1994): 24.

———, "Lockhead Succeeds with C/S," *DBMS Magazine* 7, no. 13 (1994): 26.

———, "A Multiplatform Power Tool," *DBMS Magazine* 8, no. 1 (1995): 20.

———, "System Architect 3.0," *DBMS Magazine* 8, no. 1 (1995): 62.

———, "Reconsidering Message Middleware," *DBMS Magazine* 8, no. 3 (1995): 24.

———, "EOF—a Next Step for C/S," *DBMS Magazine* 8, no. 4 (1995): 26.

———, "Rethinking C++," *DBMS Magazine* 8, no. 5 (1995): 23.

———, "Symantec Enterprise Developer 2.0," *DBMS Magazine* 8, no. 7 (1995): 22.

———, "Delphi 1.0," *DBMS Magazine* 8, no. 7 (1995): 28.

———, "Putting TP Monitors in Their Place," *DBMS Magazine* 8, no. 8 (1995): 22.

———, "Breaking Up Is Easy to Do," *DBMS Magazine* 8, no. 9 (1995): 22.

———, "One-Stop Shopping with Oracle," *DBMS Magazine* 8, no. 10 (1995): 28.

———, "Travel Like a Native," *DBMS Magazine* 8, no. 11 (1995): 24.

———, "Keeping an Eye on Your Database Server," *DBMS Magazine* 8, no. 12 (1995): 60.

———, "Banking on Delphi," *DBMS Magazine* 8, no. 13 (1995): 26.

———, "The Client/Server Internet," *DBMS Magazine* 9, no. 1 (1996): 26.

———, "Visual Basic 4.0: Ready for the Enterprise?" *DBMS Magazine* 9, no. 1 (1996): 44.

———, "ProtoGen+ Goes Virtual," *DBMS Magazine* 9, no. 2 (1996): 24.

———, "Moving Towards Remote Controlled OLE," *DBMS Magazine* 9, no. 3 (1996): 28.

———, "Cruising the Galaxy," *DBMS Magazine* 9, no. 4 (1996): 30.

———, "Battle of the Visual Masters," *DBMS Magazine* 9, no. 4 (1996): 91.

———, "Rise of the Intranet," *DBMS Magazine* 9, no. 5 (1996): 24.

———, "The Successes and Failures of Application Development Tools," *DBMS Magazine* 9, no. 5 (1996): 71.

———, "DCE Lightens Its Load," *DBMS Magazine* 9, no. 7 (1996): 24.

———, "Partitioning Power," *DBMS Magazine* 9, no. 8 (1996): 28.

———, "Selecting a Client/Server Application Development Tool," *DBMS Magazine* 9, no. 8 (1996): 41.

———, "Selecting a DBMS," *DBMS Magazine* 9, no. 8 (1996): 48.

———, "Here Comes the Java Tools," *DBMS Magazine* 9, no. 9 (1996): 24.

———, "C++ Tools for Client/Server Development," *DBMS Magazine* 9, no. 9 (1996): 89.

———, "The Staying Power of C++," *DBMS Magazine* 9, no. 10 (1996): 24.

———, "Objects Meet Data," *DBMS Magazine* 9, no. 10 (1996): 72.

———, "The ABCs of SAP R/3," *DBMS Magazine* 9, no. 11 (1996): 28.

———, "Tool Time," *DBMS Magazine* 9, no. 11 (1996): 15.

———, "The JDBC Connection," *DBMS Magazine* 9, no. 11 (1996): 21.

———, "Distributed Objects Get New Plumbing," *Internet Systems* 10, no. 1 (1997): 4.

———, "OLE-Enabled Middleware," *DBMS Magazine* 10, no. 1 (1997): 26.

———, "Reevaluating Distributed Objects," *DBMS Magazine* 10, no. 1 (1997): 44.

———, "The Good, the RAD, and the Ugly," *DBMS Magazine* 10, no. 2 (1997): 22.

———, "Moving to N-Tier RAD," *DBMS Magazine* 10, no. 3 (1997): 24.

———, "Complexity Revisited," *Internet Systems* 10, no. 4 (1997): 4.

———, "The Java APIs," *Internet Systems* 10, no. 4 (1997): 16.

———, "Driving Development," *DBMS Magazine* 10, no. 4 (1997): 36.

———, "Visual Basic 5.0," *DBMS Magazine* 10, no. 4 (1997): 50.

———, "Building in Java," *Internet Systems* 10, no. 5 (1997): 0.

———, "Another Tool, Another Repository," *DBMS Magazine* 10, no. 5 (1997): 26.

———, "Microsoft Repository 1.0," *DBMS Magazine* 10, no. 6 (1997): 27.

———, "Performance Anxiety," *DBMS Magazine* 10, no. 7 (1997): 26.

———, "The Midas Touch," *DBMS Magazine* 10, no. 8 (1997): 22.

———, "Fun with Partitioning," *DBMS Magazine* 10, no. 9 (1997): 24.

———, "Next-Generation Middleware," *DBMS Magazine* 10, no. 9 (1997): 69.

———, "Patterns Demystified," *DBMS Magazine* 10, no. 10 (1997): 26.

———, "Get the Message," *DBMS Magazine* 10, no. 11 (1997): 24.

———, "Finding Your Way," *DBMS Magazine* 10, no. 11 (1997): 55.

———, "Mixing Tuples and Objects," *DBMS Magazine* 10, no. 12 (1997): 22.

———, "The Magical Framework Myth," *DBMS Magazine* 11, no. 1 (1998): 22.

———, "Crossing the Streams," *DBMS Magazine* 11, no. 2 (1998): 24.

———, "Getting Along," *DBMS Magazine* 11, no. 3 (1998): 26.

———, "Integrating Enterprise Applications," *DBMS Magazine* 11, no. 3 (1998): 38.

———, "Java Realities," *DBMS Magazine* 11, no. 4 (1998): 24.

———, "Conducting Components," *DBMS Magazine* 11, no. 5 (1998): 26.

———, "Emerging Solutions," *DBMS Magazine* 11, no. 6 (1998): 32.

———, "Please Move to the Middle," *DBMS Magazine* 11, no. 7 (1998): 22.

———, "Middleware Performance," *DBMS Magazine* 11, no. 8 (1998): 22.

————, "Database-enabled Java Tools," *Software Development* (August 1998): 50.

————, "Site Building," *Computer Shopper* 18, no. 8 (1998): 476.

————, "Profiting from the Year 2000," *Computer Shopper* 18, no. 8 (1998): 0.

————, "Standards Smooth Software Development," *Network World* 15, no. 32 (1998): 31.

————, "Message Brokers Rising," *DBMS Magazine* 11, no. 9 (1998): 20.

————, "Site Building: Building Web Sites with SMIL," *Computer Shopper* 18, no. 9 (1998): 478.

————, "Site Building: Microsoft Provides New Interfaces for IIS," *Computer Shopper* 18, no. 10 (1998): 469.

————, "Site Building: Understanding Internet Application Servers," *Computer Shopper* 18, no. 11 (1998): 447.

————, "Drag and Drop Your Way to Scalability," *Enterprise Development* (Fall 1998).

————, "Site Building," *Computer Shopper* 18, no.12 (1998): 441.

————, "Site Building: Understanding Directory Services," *Computer Shopper* 19, no. 1 (1999): 453.

————, "Don't Hold Your Breath for Zero Latency Enterprises," *Enterprise Development* (January 1999).

————, "Intershop 3 Merchant Edition," *PC Magazine* 18, no. 1 (1999).

————, "AbleCommerce Developer 2.6," *PC Magazine* 18, no. 1 (1999).

————, "Site Building," *Computer Shopper* 19, no. 2 (1999): 423.

————, "Is JMS the Missing Link? Maybe," *Enterprise Development* (February 1999).

————, "Site Building," *Computer Shopper* 19, no. 3 (1999): 411.

————, "Java Reaches for the Middle," *Enterprise Development* (March 1999).

————, "Site Building," *Computer Shopper* 19, no. 4 (1999): 271.

————, "What's New in Java Middleware," *Enterprise Development* (April 1999).

————, "Enterprise Application Integration from the Ground Up", *Software Development* (April 1, 1999).

————, "Site Building: Getting Your Site Ready for the 5.0 Browsers," *Computer Shopper* 19. no. 5 (1999): 270.

————, "MOM Begins to Morph," *Enterprise Development* (May 1999).

————, "Site Building: Getting Yourself and Your Site Ready for P3P," *Computer Shopper* 19, no. 6 (1999): 216.

————, "When Do You Adopt XML?" *Enterprise Development* (June 1999).

————, "Mastering Message Brokers," *Software Development* (June 1, 1999).

————, "Integrating with PeopleSoft," *EAI Journal* 1, no. 2 (1999): 22.

————, "Site Building," *Computer Shopper* 19, no. 7 (1999): 266.

————, "EAI without the Hype," *Enterprise Development* (July 1999).

————, "What to Expect from EJB 1.1," *Enterprise Development* (July 1999).

————, "Tag Your Site for High Visibility," *Computer Shopper* 19, no. 8 (1999): 246.

————, "Externalize Your Apps," *Enterprise Development* (August 1999).

————, "12 Steps to EAI," *Enterprise Development* (September 1999).

————, "Sign On to Process Automation ... but Not Today," *Enterprise Development* (October 1999).

————, "Middleware Paves the Way to the Responsive Enterprise," *Enterprise Development* (November 1999).

————, "Mind Versus Muscle," *Enterprise Development* (December 1999).

————, "XML: It's EAI for the Rest of Us," *Enterprise Development* (December 1999).

————, "Reinventing Middleware for e-Business," *Enterprise Development* (January 2000).

————, "Creating Enterprise Metadata Repositories," *EAI Journal* (February 2000).

————, "Say Goodbye, EDI," *Enterprise Development* (February 2000).

————, "Process Automation and EAI," *EAI Journal* (March 2000).

————, "Ready for Distributed Message Process?" *Enterprise Development* (March 2000).

————, "Lessons Learned from J2EE," *Enterprise Development* (April 2000).

————, "Integrate Enterprise Applications with XML," *e-Business Advisor* (May 2000).

————, "Microsoft May Have App Server Winner," *Enterprise Development* (May 2000).

————, "Managing Mission-Critical Middleware," *Enterprise Development* (June 2000).

————, "Application Servers and EAI," *EAI Journal* (July 2000).

————, "Can ASPs Link to Your Existing Apps?" Enterprise Development (July 2000).

————, "Application Integration for Real-Time B2B," *e-Business Advisor* (September 2000).

Mann, J., "Workflow and Enterprise Application Integration," available online: *http://www.messageq.com/workflow/approaches_to_EAI_2.html*, 1998.

Object Management Group, *The Common Object Request Broker: Architecture and Specification*, OMG document no. 91.12.1, revision 1.1, 1992.

———, *CORBAservices: Common Object Services Specification*, OMG document no. 95-3-31, 1995.

Orfali, R., and D. Harkey, *Client/Server Programming with OS/2 Extended Edition*, New York: Van Nostrand Reinhold, 1991.

Orfali, R. et al., *The Essential Client/Server Survival Guide*, New York: Van Nostrand Reinhold, 1994.

Renaud, P.E., *Introduction to Client/Server Systems*, New York: John Wiley & Sons, 1993.

Rumbaugh, J. et al., *Object-Oriented Modeling and Design,* Englewood Cliffs, N.J.: Prentice-Hall, 1991.

Salemi, J., *PC Magazine Guide to Client/Server Databases*, Emeryville, Calif.: Ziff-Davis Press, 1993.

Shlaer, S., and S.J. Mellor, *Object-Oriented Systems Analysis—Modeling the World in Data,* Englewood Cliffs, N.J.: Prentice-Hall, 1988.

Smith, J.D., *Reusability & Software Construction: C and C++*, New York: John Wiley & Sons, 1990.

Smith, P., *Client/Server Computing*, Carmel, Ind.: Sams Publishing, 1992.

Tannenbaum, A.S., *Distributed Operating Systems*, Englewood Cliffs, N.J.: Prentice-Hall, 1995.

Webster's New World Dictionary of Computer Terms, New York: Prentice-Hall, 1988.

Wirfs-Brock, R. et al., *Designing Object-Oriented Software,* Englewood Cliffs, N.J.: Prentice-Hall, 1990.

Index